PRACTICAL LOGIC

PRACTICAL LOGIC

Third Edition

Vincent E. Barry

BAKERSFIELD COLLEGE

Douglas J. Soccio

SHASTA COLLEGE

Holt, Rinehart and Winston, Inc.

New York   Chicago   San Francisco   Dallas
Montreal   Toronto   London   Sydney

Library of Congress Cataloging-in-Publication Data

Barry, Vincent E.
    Practical logic / Vincent E. Barry, Douglas J. Soccio.—3rd ed.
        p.   cm.
    Bibliography: p.
    Includes index.
    ISBN 0-03-012693-2
    1. Logic.   I. Soccio, Douglas J.   II. Title.
  BC108.B27 1988
  160—dc19   ·87-23086
                                                                                   CIP

0-03-012693-2

Printed in the United States of America
8 9 0 1   118   9 8 7 6 5 4 3 2 1

Holt, Rinehart and Winston, Inc.
The Dryden Press
Saunders College Publishing

PREFACE

"There was a time when, to paraphrase Gertrude Stein, logic was logic was logic. If two students who had taken introductory logic courses at different institutions chanced to meet, they shared conversational ground. 'Undistributed middle,' 'existential import,' and 'truth table' were familiar landmarks on the landscape of logic. But things have changed."

So began the preface to the second edition of *Practical Logic*. Today, the soup of introductory logic courses may be even a bit thicker than it was in 1980. We still have the more traditional courses which emphasize "formal" logic—the *science* of logic as it were. But those courses shaped around the *art* of logic continue to increase in number, as evidenced by "critical thinking" courses, which extend the range of "informal" logic to cover a greater emphasis on language and problem-solving strategies, and less-structured analysis than many of us associate with "logic courses."

For all that, the challenge remains: to balance rigor (the science of logic) with accessibility and usefulness (the art of logic).

This third edition, an outgrowth of the direction set by the second, was crafted in light of the advice of happy past users, disgruntled former users, and even hostile antagonists. But it is more than just a response to helpful advice from other logicians; the new edition of *Practical Logic* is in effect the natural "evolution" of the seeds planted in 1976 with *Practical Logic*'s first incarnation. Like its two previous versions, this edition aims to give beleaguered instructors some middle ground between the extremes of a very traditional, formalistic approach and the exclusively informal approach.

The new edition of *Practical Logic* continues to start with *the student*. Based on the conviction that a text that retains scholarly respectability while being engaging and lively will be equally beneficial to both students and instructors, *Practical Logic* strives both to reach students "where they are" and to not cheat them by being so "accessible" as to be vague, overly simple, misleading, or demeaning. Thus, it breaks down the unnecessary barriers often found between content and style, logic and everyday life, student and instructor.

Stylistically, *Practical Logic* remains as informal and jargon free as possible. Although a relaxed, easygoing style sometimes signals superficiality, there is no reason that a solid introductory logic cannot also be interesting, often fun, and even on occasion exciting to read and teach from. That being so, the text is written in a style designed to respect, not to pander to, the interests, anxieties, and abilities of today's logic students—and implicitly recognizes that a well-prepared and interested class invigorates teaching.

The principal changes in the new edition, however, relate to content. Numerous alterations have been made to maximize clarity, accuracy, and thoroughness. The most striking changes are the addition of two new chapters.

The first new chapter, "The Logical vs. the Psychological" (Chapter 2), acknowledges the common and understandable beginning student lament that "We're not just rational creatures. We've got feelings, too." By identifying some of the common "extra-logical" impediments to clear thinking, Chapter 2 confronts the connection between the logical and the affective.

The other completely new chapter, "Bogus Knowledge Claims" (Chapter 8), is about "pseudoscience," and it is "serious fun." Using the arguments and implied knowledge claims of get-rich-quick systems, faith healers, psychics, astrologers, and the like, this chapter provides a fertile laboratory of actual pseudoscientific specimens. Although self-contained, this material can serve as a source for the analysis of both deductive and inductive arguments and claims, as well as a cache of fallacies and linguistic deceptions.

The remaining significant changes in content are as follows:

In Part One, "Argument and Language," Chapter 1, "Arguments," has an expanded treatment of soundness, a clearer distinction between truth and validity, a simple truth table illustrating the relationship of truth to validity, and an amplified discussion on recognizing arguments.

"Buzz words," "puffery," and "psychobabble" have been added to the discussion of obscure language use in Chapter 3, "Language and Logic."

Part Two, "Informal Fallacies," includes a chapter on "Fallacies of Ambiguity" (Chapter 4) and "Fallacies of Relevance" (Chapter 5). Here the examples and exercises have been expanded and updated, and the treatment of some of the fallacies (e.g., begging the question) has been fine tuned.

In Part Three, "Knowledge," Chapter 6, "The Meaning of Knowledge," has an expanded section on justification and a new discussion of objective and subjective claims. Chapter 7, "Sources of Knowledge," includes an added discussion of rationalism and empiricism.

In Part Four, "Induction," Chapter 9, "Inductive Reasoning," includes analogies and analogical reasoning. Chapter 10, "Scientific Method and Hypotheses," has new exercises, and Chapter 11, "Cause," incorporates "magical thinking" among causation fallacies and includes a new chart clarifying Mill's methods.

In Part Five, "Deduction," Chapter 13, "Categorical Syllogisms," and Chapter 14, "Testing Categorical Syllogisms for Validity," have various new study hints and graphic aids for comprehending the concept of "logical form" and a streamlined approach to Venn Diagrams, including the visually instructive "crescent" and "ellipse." Chapter 16, "Symbolic Logic: Disjunctive and Conditional Syllogisms," provides a rudimentary introduction to the statement calculus, including symbols for negation, conjunction, disjunction, and implication, and a few simple truth tables.

In Part Six, "Evaluation and Values," Chapter 17, "Evaluating Arguments: Normative and Nonnormative," reinforces the emphasis on the practical aspects of correct reasoning as it applies to value arguments and presents an eight-step procedure for evaluating arguments. Chapter 18, "The Extended Argument: A Strategy," extends logical principles to argumentative essays.

Finally, a word about the text's array of pedagogical features. Committed to making the book as "user friendly" as possible, we have included new graphics, cartoons, and boxed "Study Hints" to aid in the mastery of important concepts. At the end of each chapter are several open-ended Summary Questions which require the student to organize and apply concepts from the chapter. Most important, the exercises have been increased and updated, and solutions for approximately half of them have been provided at the back of the book. A concise glossary of key terms and concepts appears at the end of the text. For those instructors who so desire, an Instructor's Manual is available, which contains solutions to the remaining exercises, a Test Bank, additional Summary Questions, and suggested readings for each chapter.

Of course no text can be all things to all instructors, and no textual organization will suit every teaching style. A useable text, however, should be flexible enough to accommodate diverse approaches. *Practical Logic* is intended to meet this standard by permitting instructors to pick and choose, skip over, amplify, and even reorder. Thus, Chapter 2 will appeal to some instructors, but others probably will prefer to ignore it. The same is true for Chapter 8. Some users may prefer to treat deduction before induction; the text works well that way, too. The material on symbolic logic in Chapter 16 can be easily expanded with a few simple one- or two-page handouts covering DeMorgan's Theorems, for example, for those wishing to emphasize deductive logic. And for those who might be intimidated by the length of the text, it is not imperative to cover every chapter. Moreover, many of the chapters or parts of them (e.g., 2, 3, 4, 5, 8, 12) lend themselves to self-study.

An excellent traditional introductory logic course can be built around Chapters 1, 3, 4, 5, and 9–16. A "critical thinking" program might be arranged as follows: Chapters 1–9 and 17–18.

We are indebted to the countless logic students who over the years have resisted, cajoled, and coerced us so that we have had to learn from them about teaching logic. We would both like to thank the many reviewers of this revision. Of these, Tom Davis, Ulster County Community College; Robert Hollinger, Iowa State University; Pablo Iannone, Central Connecticut State University; Deborah Mayo, Virginia Polytechnical Institute; Hugh Moorhead, Northeastern Illinois University; Mel Peet, Montgomery College; Leslie Read, Sacramento City College; Paul Roth, University of Missouri-St. Louis; and Ronald Uritus, Barry University, were especially helpful, going well beyond the call of duty to offer incisive and thoughtful advice. Karen Dubno, Jon Blake, and Paula Cousin at Holt have been kind and encouraging, and most of all, patient. Margaret L. Malone has offered moral support while proofreading extensive passages of text.

Doug Soccio would like to acknowledge his friend J. Ronald Munson, who taught him so much about teaching logic; his collegues at Shasta College; Sandy Delehanty for recommending him for this project; and his family for providing him with an atmosphere of intellectual freedom, respect for reason, and a love of learning.

CONTENTS

PRACTICAL
LOGIC

part **O N E**

Argument and Language

chapter 1

Argument

. . . all our dignity lies in thought. Let us strive, then, to think well.

BLAISE PASCAL

Do you ever get the feeling that everyone's trying to sell you something?

"I realized my own potential by reading *Dianetics*," you hear an attractive young woman tell you in a television commercial. Then she adds, "Buy it. Read it. Use it."

Before you can digest that pitch, another voice exhorts, "Energize your love life!" It goes on to reassure you that "You can have as much love as you want once you discover how to tap the incredible energy of your inner sexuality!" And to discover how to do that, "You ought to know about a wonderfully helpful new book. . . ."

Bored with television, you open a magazine to find an ad that asks, "Can't find a pair of jeans to fit? Inseams too short? Rises too low?" If so, "Try a pair of Wranglers." Opposite that ad is one that swears, "You can bet your gas-guzzling dinosaur that the vehicle of the future is a Puch moped." And on the following pages. . . .

There's no point in going on. Everywhere somebody has something to sell, whether in politics, business, education, religion, sports, or entertainment; you name it, someone has it—a product, a belief, a candidate, a pastime, even a mate. It's little wonder that many today feel angry, confused, and frustrated.

So how do you handle it all? Which of the claims for your loyalty do you accept? Which do you reject as just more blooming, buzzing confusion?

Once asked what it takes to be a successful writer, Ernest Hemingway replied, "A good crap detector." Crude? Perhaps. What he meant was an ability to separate the authentic from the phoney, the real from the illusory, the significant from the trivial, the artistic from the artful.

Well, it's not only the writer who needs that capacity. Everyone does today. Lacking it, we can do little more than surrender, go along with our own exploitation—or, perhaps, withdraw from society altogether.

Neither choice is attractive. We need a middle position that allows us to receive the sensible and reject the nonsensical. We need to sift and filter the input that bombards us daily. We must so refine our powers of perception and judgment that we can distinguish the legitimate claim from the bogus, the appeal we should accept from the one we should ignore. In short, we need a good "crap detector."

One way to meet this need is through *logic, the study of the rules of correct argument*. In this opening chapter, we begin to refine our powers of perception and judgment. We take the first steps toward shoring up our intellectual defenses, toward arming ourselves against the onslaught of the inane. We move toward so improving our reasoning that we exercise a significant measure of control over our lives.

Specifically, this chapter focuses on argument. We'll find out what an argument is and how we recognize one. We'll also be introduced to two kinds of argument: inductive and deductive. By the time we've completed the chapter, we'll have taken the first step toward making sense of things, toward constructing our own "crap detector."

One other thing: In our eagerness to stress the function of logic in helping us gain control over our lives, we don't mean to imply that this is logic's sole function. Logic has, in fact, what we can term an aesthetic dimension. It's fun, and at times even elegant. Indeed, for the professional logician, even for the serious student of logic, this aesthetic dimension is logic's ultimate appeal. Although you may not be able to appreciate this now or in the early stages of your study, at some point you'll probably glimpse the "beauty" of doing logic. Then you can begin to sense the excitement, the sheer exhilaration the logician often feels.

ARGUMENT

Logic, as we noted, is the study of the rules of correct argument. This needs some explaining.

First, just what is an argument? In some circles an argument is a fight; in others it's a discussion. In logic an argument is neither. *An argument is any group of propositions* (true or false statements) *one of which is claimed to follow logically from the others*. The key phrase here is "follow logically from."

STUDY HINT: PAY ATTENTION TO KEY TERMS.

One of the best ways to get off to a good start in your study of logic is to think of learning logic as if you were learning a foreign language. When key terms are introduced they will be identified by *italics*. Sometimes, as you will see in this chapter, these key terms are familiar words but with more precise definitions. It is helpful to pay extra attention to these terms right away. Try to see how their new definitions are different from the ways in which we usually use these terms.

EXAMPLE: Logical arguments are not the same things as disagreements, disputes, or fights. How are they different?

For a group of propositions to be an argument, one of them must be claimed to *follow logically from* the others. Here's a simple example: "Mothers are females. Jane's a mother. Therefore, Jane's a female." Now the statement "Jane's a female" supposedly follows logically from the two preceding statements. In other words, the first two statements are said to entail, or logically guarantee, the third. This means that if the first two statements are taken as true, then, logically speaking, the third statement must also be taken as true. To accept the first two statements while rejecting the third would be self-contradictory. Taken as a group, then, these three statements comprise an argument. We could combine all these statements into a single sentence: "Since (1) mothers are females and (2) Jane's a mother, therefore (3) Jane's a female." We still have an argument. An argument, then, can be a group of statements that take the form of individual sentences or just a single sentence.

Now, often we simply assert things without claiming that one assertion follows logically from the others. Take, for example, these assertions: "Oaks are big trees." "Elms are trees found throughout the United States." "Cherry trees are trees that beautify Washington, D.C., in springtime." These statements are mere assertions. There is no internal connection between them. One is not intended to follow logically from the others. Taken as a group, then, they do not constitute an argument.

Similarly, there are times when we just offer explanatory information in a group of statements. Take these statements as examples: "The class on the history of music has been canceled for lack of enrollment." "The horse was frightened by a snake in the grass." "Marie looks better since her vacation." These are *explanatory statements*. They help explain some phenomenon: the cancellation of the class, the fright of the horse, the improved look in Marie.

The difference between nonarguments and arguments is essentially one of interest or purpose. If someone is interested in establishing the truth of a claim and offers evidence intended to do just that, the person is arguing. What the person offers is an argument. But if a person regards the truth of a claim as unproblematic, and he or she is just interested in explaining why it is the case (as opposed to demonstrating that it is, in fact, the case), the person is explaining. What the person offers is an explanation, not an argument. In short, if a person's intent is to establish the truth of a statement, the person formulates an argument. In contrast, if the person's purpose is to explain why something is the case, the person formulates an explanation.

Thus, when I say, "Marie looks better since her vacation," I'm not trying to establish that Marie, in fact, does look better. I'm taking that as a well-established truth, and I'm trying to *explain* why I think it's the case. In contrast, suppose I said, "Marie ought to be hired for the job since she has qualifications superior to all the other applicants." Here I'm attempting to establish my claim, "Marie ought to be hired for the job." I am not taking this statement as a well-established truth. Quite the opposite; I am trying to show how it follows logically from the other statement.

In speaking of arguments, logicians give special names to their ingredients—premises and conclusions. *The premises of arguments are those statements that are claimed to entail, or logically guarantee, the conclusion. The conclusion is the statement that supposedly is entailed, or logically guaranteed, by the premises.* Thus, in the argument "All mothers are females. Jane is a mother. Therefore Jane is a female," the first two propositions are the premises and the third is the conclusion. Similarly, in the argument "Marie ought to be hired for the job since she has qualifications superior to all the other applicants," "Marie ought to be hired" is the conclusion, and "she has qualifications superior to all the other job applicants" is the premise. Notice from these two examples that premises and conclusions can occur anywhere in the argument. Premises don't have to appear at the beginning; conclusions don't have to appear at the end.

We've intentionally made these examples simple. Recognizing arguments, let alone their premises and conclusions, isn't easy. It takes considerable experience and often intensive analysis of passages. Let's dwell for a moment on this point.

PARTS OF AN ARGUMENT

Logical arguments consist of two main ingredients: premises and conclusions. The premises of an argument constitute the evidence offered to prove the truth of the conclusion. Premises and conclusions must always be propositions. That

THE LOCKHORNS

"WE HAVEN'T BEEN TALKING FOR FIVE MINUTES AND YOU'RE ALREADY RESORTING TO LOGIC!"

Reprinted with special permission of King Features Syndicate, Inc.

is, the parts of an argument are propositions (statements with truth value) arranged in a certain relationship. One of these is the proposition whose truth value we are interested in supporting (the conclusion). The other propositions are statements that we hope will show that the conclusion is indeed true (the premises). Premises, then, are statements whose truth value is presumably already established.

In the argument "All mothers are females. Jane is a mother. Therefore Jane is a female," the first two propositions are the premises and the third is the conclusion. So arranged, the premises, which presumably are true, are intended to establish the truth of the conclusion.

In the argument "All mothers are females. Jane is a female. Therefore Jane is a mother," once again the first two propositions are premises and the third is the conclusion. Here again, the conclusion is claimed to be demonstrated by the presumably true premises.

Notice how we can have two completely different arguments using exactly the same propositions. The difference is in how the propositions are used: whether they are treated as evidence or as conclusions. Although both arguments contain the same information, the internal relationship of the parts of the arguments is different. The first example is logically acceptable whereas the second one is flawed. (We will discuss the qualities of good arguments as we proceed, but you might want to stop a moment and analyze these two examples to see how you think they differ logically.)

S T U D Y   H I N T :   **NOT ALL PROPOSITIONS ARE PREMISES OR CONCLUSIONS.**

The important thing to understand is that a premise is any proposition used as evidence in a logical argument. A conclusion is any proposition whose truth value we are attempting to establish by means of a logical argument.

Premise and *conclusion* are relative terms. The very same proposition may be a premise in one argument and the conclusion in another.

We might encounter another kind of argument: "Because all logic students are bright people, Marie must be bright, since Marie is a logic student." Here we notice that the middle proposition (Marie must be bright) is the conclusion whereas the first and third propositions are the premises. The stated order of propositions is not what determines how they function in an argument. *Whether a proposition is a premise or a conclusion is determined by how it is used, not by where it happens to occur in the passage.*

It is possible to express the very same argument in a number of ways:

1. Since Marie is a logic student, and since all logic students are bright, Marie must be bright.
2. Marie must be bright. After all, she is a logic student, and we know that all logic students are bright.
3. It follows logically that because Marie is a logic student she must be bright, since all logic students are bright.

Although each of these expressions of the same argument varies in stated order, the conclusion and premises remain the same.

What we should strive to develop at this point is an increased awareness of arguments, a change in sensitivity—which will occur for most of us as a natural consequence of studying this material. Others may have to work at it a bit, but it will happen. And when it does, logic becomes fun.

RECOGNIZING ARGUMENTS

The best way to recognize arguments is from context.

Context refers to the "environment" surrounding statements and claims. One element of this environment is "rhetorical context": elements leading up to and following a passage. These are such things as place, purpose, and certain key expressions. Place: Does the passage occur in an advertisement, in a court of law, over coffee? Purpose: Is someone trying to sell us something, a cause, a product, an idea? Phrases: Terms like *it follows that, since,* and *so we must conclude that* strongly suggest the presence of an argument. In other words, we must learn to recognize the surroundings in which arguments are most likely to occur.

The intention or purpose of the author of a passage is extremely important in recognizing arguments. (Don't let the term *passage* mislead you. Some passages are written, but many are spoken or thought.) Is the most likely purpose one of proving or showing that something is true by offering evidence in its support? If so, we count the passage as an argument. If the most likely purpose is simply to state a fact, convey information, explain something, elaborate on a theme, or express emotion, we probably do not have an argument.

In a complicated passage, many of these functions may be present. Indeed, in real life, we usually embellish our arguments with explanations, expressions of strong feelings, and other "nonlogical" matters. These are analogous to the color of paper or style of print used in a book or to the accent and vocal qualities of a speaker. They are often powerful influences on what and how we think— as they are meant to be. But strictly speaking they are not part of the argument; they are not evidence that can logically support a conclusion. We will study many of these factors as we look at the influences of language on logic, at bad arguments called *fallacies,* and the psychological elements that influence our reasoning. Our present task, however, is to be as clear as we can about exactly what logical arguments are and then to practice recognizing them.

Often, we will have to infer what we think someone else probably meant. Not only is that fair; it is unavoidable. When we are listening to the radio or reading something, for example, we cannot ask the author whether or not he or she is arguing. So we must make our own best assessment. If, upon careful reflection, a passage seems to be an argument, we evaluate it according to the standards of good reasoning that we are learning.

Developing contextual sensitivity is a skill. Some of us have a natural knack for it; others of us must develop it. In all cases, however, it is a skill that can be developed or refined with some practice. One of the smartest things you can do early in your logical studies is to start wondering about things you read and hear everyday. Ask yourself: Is this an argument or not? Why is it—or isn't it? Don't worry about being absolutely correct (that expectation isn't reasonable). Instead, concentrate on what clues you can uncover to support your own conclusion that this is or is not an argument.

You will probably discover that you spontaneously begin to notice that logical arguments are everywhere. One of the most exciting things about beginning logic is the common student reaction: "Wow! All of a sudden I see arguments all over the place." Even television commercials become entertaining as we see them in this context.

Imagine that you've had the experience of greatly wanting a new car. Perhaps you test-drive the new Guzzler XL. You read about it, drooling over the brochures the salespeople give you. And what happens? Suddenly, every other car on the highway is an XL. How is this possible? Obviously, the number of XLs has not changed; you have changed. Your sensitivity to XLs is heightened. That's what we hope will happen with arguments. The number of arguments will not change; our awareness of them will. And believe it or not, that new awareness is a very valuable skill. It helps us deal more effectively with life, and it makes life more interesting.

With persistence and proper guidance, most of us can become better thinkers than we are today. In the beginning, distinguishing arguments from nonarguments may seem frustrating. Don't despair. In fact, one of the most common frustrations students face occurs when suddenly it seems as if virtually everything is a potential argument. Stick with it. Things clear up with practice. Recognizing arguments is a skill, and like other skills, our initial efforts are often awkward.

But there are some guidelines that will help us. Among the most helpful are the so-called signal words. Let's look at these.

Signal Words

A signal word is a word that indicates the presence of a premise or conclusion. We have a vast array of such words in English. Among the conclusion signals are *so, thus, therefore, consequently, it follows that, as a result, hence, finally, in conclusion,* and similar words. Among the premise signals are *since, as, because, for, inasmuch as, for the reason that,* and the like. Although helpful in recognizing arguments— their premises and conclusions—signal words are no substitute for contextual analysis. In fact, these words can be downright misleading inasmuch as they don't always indicate the present of an argument.

To see how misleading these words can be, recall the earlier distinction we drew between arguments and explanations. Arguments attempt to establish the truth of a proposition; explanations take the truth of a proposition for granted and offer information to account for it. Thus, we saw that the statement "Marie looks better since her vacation" is an explanation. In contrast, "Marie ought to be hired for the job since she has qualifications superior to all the other applicants" is an argument. Yet, the word *since* appears in both statements. In the first, *since* serves as a temporal connective; that is, it merely shows a time connection between two events. In the second statement, *since* functions as a logical connective. It signals a reason, a premise, which is offered to justify the truth of a proposition, a conclusion. Thus, there are two different uses of *since*— one in an explanation, the other in an argument. The only way to differentiate between the two functions of *since* and other such words is from context.

The lesson is simple but important. Yes, signal words are useful in helping us recognize arguments, their premises and conclusions. But blindly relying on them can lead us astray. It can make us mistake an argument for a nonargument.

STUDY HINT: **USE SIGNAL WORDS, WORD ORDER, AND PUNCTUATION AS INITIAL CLUES TO THE STRUCTURE AND PRESENCE OF ARGUMENT.**

Although signal words often indicate the presence of an argument, they do not guarantee it. Therefore, it is important for us to pay close attention to their use in the particular passage we are analyzing.

The absence of signal words does not guarantee the absence of argument. We must also be sensitive to such things as overall context, speaker's intention, and such.

---

*EXERCISE 1-1 _____

Decide which of the following you think are arguments and which you think are non-arguments. The important point here is to understand *why* you think a passage is or is not an argument. Try to determine *the most likely context* for each passage, look for signal words and see how they are used, and distinguish premises from conclusions when you think you've spotted an argument.

1. She is upset today because of the terrible accident.
2. Jones cannot be the murderer because he was miles away when the crime occurred.
3. The flight has been delayed by bad weather.
4. We must begin to develop alternative energy sources, for our existence as an autonomous nation is at stake.
5. Most doctors want to set their own fees. So doctors are natural opponents of socialized medicine.
6. Nobody will take advice, but everybody will take money. Clearly, then, money is better than advice.
7. Political dissenters have no place in our society, for those who criticize and disrupt a nation are its enemies.
8. There's no good reason for a fence around a cemetery. After all, those inside can't get out, and those outside don't want to get in.
9. I've read enough of what you've written to know you'll understand what I'm going to say.
10. "It's possible that television viewing, with all its breaks and cuts, and the inattention, except for action and spinning the dial to find some action, is partly responsible for destruction of the narrative sense." (Pauline Kael, *I Lost It at the Movies*)
11. "In politics nothing happens by chance. If it happens, you can bet it was planned that way." (Franklin Delano Roosevelt)
12. "The Golden Rule obviously concerns itself with one of the very basic paradoxes of human existence. Each man calls his own a separate body, a self-conscious individuality, a personal awareness of the cosmos, and a certain death; and yet he shares this world as a *reality* also perceived and judged by others and as an actuality within which he must commit himself to ceaseless interaction." (Erik Erikson, *Insight and Responsibility*)
13. "It is no wonder. . .that we as often dislike others for their virtues as for their vices. We naturally hate whatever makes us despise ourselves." (William Hazlitt, *Characteristics*)
14. "Guadalajara, Mexico: Something is very much out of kilter here. . . . [The cars are] from New York, New Jersey, and Ohio. . . . Willy's, a bar-restaurant stuffed into

---

*Exercises with an asterisk are answered in an answer section at the back of the book.

an old converted house . . . sounds like a Sunset Strip joint on Saturday night. . . ." (Michael Seiler, "Second Chance Med School in Mexico," *Los Angeles Times,* May 12, 1974, Part IV, p. 1)

15. "The shad, perhaps, or any fish that runs upriver [would be ideal for sea ranching]. You simply raise the young in a pond and release them; they range out to sea, using their own energies, grow, and then come back." (Oceanographer John D. Isaacs, "Interview," *Omni,* August 1979, p. 122)

DEDUCTIVE AND INDUCTIVE ARGUMENTS

In speaking of argument, we ordinarily distinguish two kinds: deductive and inductive. We will consider them separately in order to isolate their unique and defining characteristics. But we shouldn't consider them as incompatible with one another. In fact, they're complementary modes of reasoning.

Deductive Argument

A deductive argument is one whose conclusion is claimed to follow from its premises with logical certainty. In other words, in a proper deductive argument, it's logically impossible for the argument's premises to be true and its conclusion false. A simple example: "Because all humans are vertebrates and Smith is a human, therefore Smith is a vertebrate." Given the truth of the premises, there is no way under the sun that the conclusion will not logically follow. The conclusion must follow; the premises logically entail, or guarantee, it. We can imagine no additional facts, events, or conditions that while being consistent with those premises, could deny that conclusion. Indeed, the very meaning of the premises makes the conclusion logically necessary. If we understand what it means to say that "All humans are vertebrates" and "Smith is a human," we will know that Smith must be a vertebrate.

Notice that in our definition of a deductive argument we said that it is one whose conclusion is *claimed* to follow with logical certainty from its premises. The word *claimed* implies that not all deductive arguments are correct ones. This is precisely one of the reasons we study logic: to discover when a deductive argument is correct, that is, when its premises logically entail its conclusion. *In logic, a deductive argument whose premises necessarily lead to its conclusion is termed a valid argument*. A deductive argument whose premises do not necessarily lead to its conclusion is termed an invalid argument.

STUDY HINT: IN MATTERS OF DEDUCTION, WE ARE CONCERNED WITH LOGICAL CERTAINTY, NOT WITH FACTUAL TRUTH.

A deductive argument is an attempt to establish a relationship of **logical certainty** between the premises of an argument and its conclusion. When this relationship exists, the argument is said to be valid.

Inductive Argument

An inductive argument is one whose conclusion is claimed to be more or less probable but not certain. In an inductive argument, the conclusion is likely or probable but never logically certain, for example, "Employee Brown has arrived on time for work the last thousand days. Therefore, he'll probably arrive on time today." There's nothing certain about this conclusion. We can easily imagine some event or condition that will disprove the conclusion. Brown may be ill or have had an accident or have overslept. The evidence stated in the premise of itself does not necessitate the conclusion. But it does make the conclusion probable or likely. Thus, the word *probable* must be used or understood before the conclusion of any inductive argument. So, when one argues, "Since many drug addicts who come through the courts admit that they started on pot, pot probably causes hard-core drug addiction," one argues inductively.

STUDY HINT: **INDUCTIVE REASONING IS CONCERNED WITH DEGREES OF LIKELIHOOD, NOT LOGICAL CERTAINTY.**

Inductive arguments can grow better or worse as new evidence comes in. They are **justified** when they have enough good evidence to support their conclusion.

As with deductive arguments, inductive arguments may be well constructed or poorly constructed. We shall term a well-constructed inductive argument *justified,* as opposed to *valid,* which characterizes correct deductive arguments. *An inductive argument that's justified is one whose premises lend its conclusion a high degree of probability.* What constitutes a high degree of probability is something we will discuss in detail later. But here it's enough to understand the basic difference between inductive arguments and deductive arguments. Also, you should realize that the primary purpose of our study is to learn how to detect and formulate valid deductive arguments and justified inductive arguments.

Summarizing, a deductive argument is one whose premises, it is claimed, lead to a logically certain conclusion. A correct deductive argument is termed valid; an incorrect one is termed invalid.

In contrast, an inductive argument is one whose premises, it is claimed, lead to a probable, but never certain, conclusion. A well-constructed inductive argument is said to be justified; a poorly constructed one is said to be unjustified. At this point, it's important for us to deepen our understanding of the concepts of justification and validity.

EXERCISE 1-2 _____

Think about the following arguments. Decide whether they are inductive or deductive. Look for contextual and linguistic clues. Absolute terms like *must* or a tone of certainty will almost always indicate deduction. A "softer" tone, indicated by terms like *often* or *usually,* reflects inductive reasoning.

   1. No triangle is a square because all triangles have three sides and squares have four sides.

evidence to support conclusions and decisions. But technically, logic does not evaluate the factual content of our arguments. As far as the logician is concerned, all premises in an argument are *considered to be* true. Assuming this, logicians determine whether those premises lead to probable (justified) or certain (valid) conclusions.

A helpful analogy here is to visualize logic as a kind of computer. Given a body of information, a computer will respond to our queries. But the computer, generally speaking, is in no position to evaluate the truth of the data we've fed it. The computer simply takes the information we've provided and draws conclusions from it. If the information is incorrect, the computer's conclusions are no less justified, or invalid. Based on the data we've given it, it makes logical judgments.

Nonetheless, the title of this book is *Practical Logic*. As a result, you could rightly ask, "How *practical* is a study of logic, which teaches me the rules of correct argument, if ultimately I may be left with patent falsehood and not know it?" For example, given that "All X are Y, and all Y are Z," it follows that "All X are Z." Practically speaking, what "good" is it to know that this argument is valid but not to know whether, in fact, all X *are* Y and all Y *are* Z?

Understandably, most studies of logic avoid this question. Logic is, after all, a study of correct reasoning, not the study of truth. So it really isn't within the province of logic to determine truth. That's primarily the job of the sciences. But this text differs from others in that it acknowledges the legitimacy of the objection, which in effect, claims that it is of little *practical* value to have justification and validity without truth.

So at the outset, let's be clear on one thing: We have no intention of turning logic into a mental gymnastic that while exercising our analytical powers, ultimately may leave us disengaged from ordinary living. Yes, we want to discover whether arguments such as those encountered in our daily affairs are justified or valid and, if not, why they aren't. But we also want to know whether the premises of these and the other arguments we formulate and encounter are true. In other words, we want to be able to recognize and construct *sound* arguments.

SOUNDNESS

"I, Joe Doe, being of sound mind. . . ." We're all familiar with the expression "a sound mind in a sound body," but what exactly does *sound* mean? A sound mind or body is one that is basically healthy. There is nothing significantly wrong with its performance of its essential functions. Similarly, a sound argument also has nothing wrong with it. There are two basic ways for an argument to "go bad." The first is whether or not the reasoning is logically correct. The second is whether or not the information being reasoned from is in fact true.

An argument is sound if (1) its logic is good and (2) the information in it is correct.
A deductive argument is sound when it is both valid and contains only true propositions.
An inductive argument is sound when it is both justified and contains only true propositions.

In both cases, note that we are concerned with the logic of the argument and also with the truth of the propositions. There are two possible general sources of errors in arguing: reasoning and fact. As we've just noted, strictly speaking, logic is only concerned with the study and analysis of correct reasoning, not with truth. However, we also want and need to know whether the arguments we encounter are sound. We want to know both if the reasoning behind them is good and if the information in them is correct.

Computer programmers use the expression GIGO (pronounced *gee-go*) to mean "Garbage in, garbage out." It is possible for a logically impeccable argument to contain premises that are flawed. When this happens, the conclusion will be flawed. And since we often make important choices based on the conclusions we believe to be true, it is obviously of utmost importance for us to consider both the logical quality of any argument before us *and* the truth of its premises. If we put "garbage" (false propositions) into a good "computer" (argument), we will still generate unacceptable conclusions.

Consider this example: "Since pornography causes increased sex crimes, we should ban all pornography." Or this example: "Evidence shows that access to pornographic materials decreases the rate of sex crimes. Therefore, we should not ban access to pornographic materials." Certainly such issues as free speech, the protection from crime, and so forth are crucial issues. But to decide which of these two conclusions to support, we need to do more than merely analyze the logic of these arguments. We need also to analyze the factual claims made in the premises. This is true of all significant issues facing us.

A good rule of thumb is first to analyze the logic of an argument for fallacies (which are errors in reasoning). We do this first because once we have learned the basic rules of correct reasoning, we can apply them to arguments even if we do not possess knowledge of the facts being cited. Then if the logic is good, we can take steps to determine whether or not the premises are true. In deduction, the division between logic and fact is clear-cut; in induction it is often less clear. But in both deductive and inductive arguments, we can take significant steps in analysis by first checking for errors of logic, even if we are unsure of the facts being discussed.

All this means that our study will cover more than just the rules of correct argument. It will also explore truth. This requires an investigation into some rather philosophical subjects such as the nature of knowledge and the difference between belief and truth. As a result, we will not only be learning the rules of correct argument, but also be grappling with some basic philosophical issues that undergird logic and that have an immediate and profound impact on how we think and act. We'll even consider such things as the influences of psychological factors on our beliefs and thinking. We'll look at logic applied to real life—at truly *Practical Logic*.

SUMMARY

In this chapter we learned that logic is the study of correct argument. An argument is a group of propositions (true or false statements), one of which is claimed to follow logically from the others. Arguments consist of premises and conclusions. The premises are those propositions that are claimed to entail logically the conclusion. The conclusion is the proposition that is claimed to be logically entailed by the premises.

The best way to recognize arguments is from context, although signal words are also helpful if used with care. In logic we speak of two sorts of argument: deductive and inductive. A deductive argument is one whose conclusion is claimed to follow from its premises with logical certainty. A valid deductive argument is one that makes good on this claim: Its premises logically entail its conclusion. This means that the truth of the premises logically guarantees the truth of the conclusion. *If* the premises are true, the conclusion must also be true. Deductive arguments are either valid or invalid; there is no middle ground. They either establish their conclusions with logical certainty, or they do not.

Inductive arguments are different. An inductive argument is one whose conclusion is claimed to be more or less probable, not certain. The very intention of inductive arguments, then, is different from that of deductive arguments. A well-constructed inductive argument is considered to be justified; that is, it has enough good evidence to establish its conclusion with a degree of probability sufficient to its claims.

Neither justification nor validity is defined in terms of the actual truth of the premises of an argument. It is possible for all the propositions in an invalid deductive argument to be true. And it is also possible for all the propositions in a valid deductive argument to be false. Validity is only concerned with the logical relationship that exists between the premises of an argument and its conclusion.

Similarly, the premises of an unjustified inductive argument may all be true, even though the conclusion does not follow from them.

In the end, we seek to formulate *sound* arguments. Sound arguments are ones that in the case of deduction are valid *and* that have true premises, and in the case of induction are justified with enough good evidence.

Summary Questions
Refer to the material in this chapter to decide whether the following are true or false. If a statement is false, explain why.

1. The statement "Jane is a student" is a premise.
2. If both the premises and the conclusion of a deductive argument are true, the argument is valid.
3. One false premise is enough to make a deductive argument invalid.
4. It is possible to have a valid deductive argument in which every proposition is false.
5. An inductive argument is valid when it is justified by having enough good evidence.

ADDITIONAL EXERCISES _____

*1. Study the following to see if they seem to be arguments. Concentrate on spotting premises and conclusions. (This is more difficult than it seems, so do not be discouraged. What is important is that you explain *why* you think a passage probably is or is not an argument.)

    a. Since we can know only our own experiences of things, we can't ever be sure that things really exist.
    b. It's unwise to exceed posted speed limits, for statistics indicate that speeders have a greater chance of having accidents than those who don't speed.

c. Whether we survive depends on whether we can solve internal problems. History indicates that nations divided against themselves don't last long.

d. "The coarsest type of humor is the *practical joke:* pulling away the chair from under the dignitary's lowered bottom. The victim is perceived, first as a person of consequence, then suddenly as an inert body subject to the laws of physics: authority is debunked by gravity, mind by matter; man is degraded to mechanism." (Arthur Koestler, *Janus: A Summing Up,* New York: Random House, 1978, pp. 122–23)

e. The ultimate motivation for hostility lies in the impulse to destroy. We don't destroy to live, then, but live to destroy.

f. "An arctic mirage is caused by a temperature inversion created when the air immediately above the earth's surface is cooler than air at higher elevations. Under these conditions, light rays are bent around the curvature of the earth. The stronger the inversion, the more bending. With a high degree of bending, the earth's surface looks like a saucer, and the landscape and ship normally out of sight below the horizon are raised into view on the saucer's rim. The effect can last for days and cover thousands of kilometers." (Barbara Ford, "Mirage," *OMNI,* August 1979, p. 38)

g. "The joints of our bodies are particularly susceptible to mechanical wear and tear. The ends of the long bones must rub against each other without destroying themselves and must bear the weight of the body. The joints are surrounded by tough connecting tissues, ligaments and muscles which bind the bones together in a tough but flexible unit while permitting movement often against great force. When any of the tissue in and around the joints fails, arthritis is said to be present." (Abram Hoffer, M.D., "Good Nutrition + Supplements + Minerals: Three-Way Attack on Arthritis," *The Health Quarterly,* 16th issue, vol. 4, no. 2, p. 30)

h. "The third group of values lies precisely in a man's attitude toward the limiting factors upon his life. His very response to the restraints upon his potentialities provides him with a new realm of values which surely belong among the highest values. Thus, an apparently impoverished existence—one which is poor in creative and experiential values—still offers a last, and in fact the greatest, opportunity for the realization of values. These values we will call attitudinal values." (Victor Frankl, *The Doctor and the Soul,* New York: Vintage Books, 1965, p. 44)

i. "Our mass culture—and a good deal of our high, or serious, culture as well—is dominated by an emphasis on data and a corresponding lack of interest in theory, by a frank admiration of the factual and an uneasy contempt for imagination, sensibility and speculation. We are obsessed with technique, hagridden by Facts, in love with information. Our popular novelists must tell us all about the historical and professional backgrounds of their puppets; our press lords make millions by giving us this day our daily Facts; our scholars—or, more accurately, our research administrators—erect pyramids of data to cover the corpse of a stillborn idea." (Dwight Macdonald, *Against the American Grain,* New York: Random House, 1962, p. 393)

j. "Like the American philosophers William James and John Dewey, the existential philosophers are appealing from the conclusions of 'Rationalistic' thinking which equates Reality with the object of thought, with relations or 'essences,' to Reality as men experience it immediately in their actual living. They consequently take their place with all those who have regarded man's immediate experience as revealing more completely the nature and traits of Reality than man's cognitive experience." (Paul Tillich, "Existential Philosophy," *Journal of the History of Ideals,* vol. 5, no. 1, 1944, p. 48)

k. "And the tragic history of human thought is simply the history of a struggle between reason and life—reason bent on rationalizing life and forcing it to submit to the inevitable, to mortality; life bent on vitalizing reason and forcing it to serve as a support for its own vital desires." (Miguel de Unamuno, *The Tragic Sense of Life*)

l. Jocasta (trying to console husband/son Oedipus, when she realizes that he knows that he is in fact her son):

> . . . But why should men be fearful,
> O'er whom Fortune is mistress, and foreknowledge

Of nothing sure? Best take life easily,
As a man may. For that maternal wedding,
Have no fear; for many men ere now
Have dreamed as much; but he who by such dreams
Sets nothing, has the easiest time of it.

(Sophocles, *Oedipus Rex*)

2. Each of the following passages contains more than one argument. Identify the arguments, indicating premises and conclusions.

a. DONNA: I'm all for capital punishment.
DICK: Why's that?
DONNA: Because it deters crime.
DICK: Oh, I don't know.
DONNA: What do you mean? I can give you a book full of statistics to prove it does.
b. PHIL: Women should be allowed to have an abortion on demand.
DIXIE: I don't think so. That could lead to some really bizarre events, such as aborting a fetus in the eighth month simply because the mother wants to take a vacation.
PHIL: But if the state doesn't allow women to have abortions when they want them, then it's violating their basic freedom to do with their bodies what they want.
c. JACK: There should be considerably more government control of advertising. Otherwise, consumers are going to be increasingly harmed and victimized.
JERYL: But don't you realize that such intervention is an insult to the whole concept of free enterprise? No, I say there should be far less government policing of advertising, inasmuch as every government intervention injures the free enterprise system.
d. ". . . You have been at your club all day, I perceive."
"My dear Holmes!"
"Am I right?"
"Certainly, but how—"
". . . A gentleman goes forth on a showery and miry day. He returns immaculate in the evening with the gloss still on his hat and his boots. He has been a fixture, therefore, all day. He is not a man with intimate friends. Where, then, could he have been? Is it not obvious?" (Arthur Conan Doyle, *The Hound of the Baskervilles*)
e. "A teacher who asks a question is tuned to the right answer, ready to hear it, eager to hear it, since it will tell him that his teaching is good and that he can go on to the next topic. He will assume that anything that sounds close to the right answer is meant to be the right answer. So, for a student who is not sure of the answer, a numble may be the best bet" (John Holt, *How Children Fail*)
f. "I was so impressed by those computers . . . that I thought about writing a constitutional amendment to allow a computer to become President. . . . I thought better of my constitutional amendment. . . . There is something about human decision makers, for all their mistakes and irrationality, that a computer simply cannot replace" (Senator Sam J. Ervin, Jr., in a speech at Miami University, Ohio, June 28, 1973)
g. "If a man or woman is found guilty of secret lust before marriage, the offender is severely punished and both are forbidden to marry forever, unless the President pardons them and forgives their offense. . . . The reason for the severe punishment of this crime is the realization that very few people would join in married love, in which they saw they had to spend all their lives with one person and endure all the consequent inconvenience, if they were not carefully restrained from random sexual relations." (Thomas More, *Utopia*)
h. "Love is necessary to righting the estate of woman in this world. Otherwise nature itself seems to be in conspiracy against her dignity and welfare; for the cultivated, high-thoughted, beauty-loving, saintly woman finds herself unconsciously desired for her sex, and even enhancing the appetite of her savage pursuers by these fine ornaments she has piously laid on herself." (Ralph Waldo Emerson, *Journal*)

chapter 2

The Logical vs. the Psychological

He who knows others is learned;
he who knows himself is wise.

CHUANG-TZU

"Whew!" Jimbo exclaimed, "this logic stuff is a waste of time. And for what? I mean, what's the point of learning all this stuff? People don't care if they're rational or not. Nobody in 'real life' worries about premises and conclusions and what's valid and what's not. Ms. DeMorgan, our logic instructor, thinks she can turn us all into Mr. Spocks. But what's the use? Everybody acts on how they feel anyway."

"Who's Mr. Spock?" Maryanne asked.

"Who's Mr. Spock? Gee, where've you been? Don't you ever watch *Star Trek* on TV or at the movies?"

"Not really. I'm not into science fiction. But who's this Spock?"

"Oh, he's just a character from that series. He's supposed to be half 'Vulcan'—the Vulcans are people from another planet who are purely rational; they're a lot like us except that they are not distracted by emotions."

"That doesn't sound so great to me," Maryanne said. "What fun would there be without feelings?"

"I didn't say it was great to be like Mr. Spock," Jimbo corrected. "I said that Ms. DeMorgan acts like we're supposed to be all logic and no heart. It seems like she's trying to tell us that emotions are irrelevant. Or else that they interfere with thinking clearly or something."

"Yeah," Maryanne mused, "I get the same feeling."

"Sure. Everybody in class does. And I can just hear her now: 'I'm not interested in your *feelings about this argument* but in what you know and can demonstrate with sound reasoning.' Geez!"

"I'm glad to hear somebody else feels like I do," confessed Maryanne. "I was beginning to wonder if I was the only frustrated person in class."

"That's just what I was getting at," an excited Jimbo continued; "we're not reasoning machines like Spock. We're flesh-and-blood people. Who wants to be too logical anyway? That's not human. It's . . . Vulcan?"

"Yeah!" Maryanne said. "It's downright Vulcan!"

Maryanne and Jimbo have raised an important issue concerning a commonly held misconception about logic courses, logic books, and logicians (not to mention scientists, engineers, mathematicians, and others). Is it possible to be "too logical"? What might that mean? Is it possible to be "too reasonable"? Is it reasonable to be logical all the time? And just where do emotions and other nonlogical influences on thinking fit into the study of logic?

It's a good idea at the beginning of our study of *practical logic* to look at some recurring nonlogical aspects of thinking that affect, and even impede, our capacity to reason soundly. In so doing, we acknowledge the fact that any practical study of logic must take into account the "contexts" in which people reason—and that must include at least a cursory look at what we will term the psychological dimension of reasoning.

Our goal as logic students is ultimately sound arguments—not just logically good arguments, but arguments that reach true conclusions. That being the case, we should alert ourselves to at least the most basic factors likely to interfere with our search for true conclusions. If the mind that is reasoning is subject to errors in judgment induced by diminished sensory acuity, by stereotyped values, or by rigid thinking, or it is overwhelmed by emotional needs that distort its best efforts, any conclusions it reaches are suspect.

THE LOGICAL VS. THE PSYCHOLOGICAL

Logic, as we've seen in Chapter 1, is the study of the rules of correct argument. An argument, recall, is any group of propositions, one of which is claimed to follow logically from the others. Thus, an argument is an attempt to demonstrate some claim to truth by offering *reasons* for its acceptance. Let's define *a reason as any proposition capable of providing support for the conclusion of a logical argument*. This is a refinement of our earlier definition of a premise as any proposition claimed to entail logically the conclusion of an argument.

We need to contrast reason-propositions with emotion-propositions in a way that distinguishes *logically relevant reason-propositions* from *logically irrelevant emotion-propositions*. We can define *an emotion as any feeling, mood, or state of consciousness,* and an *emotion-proposition as any proposition reporting any feeling, mood, or state of consciousness.*

Emotions are often important "extra-logical" factors bearing on critical thinking skills because, although they may be logically irrelevant to a particular claim, they tend to be *psychologically relevant.* In other words, we may believe that our emotions are logically relevant to a particular argument even though they are not. This is especially so in the case of intensely experienced emotions or emotions associated with deeply held beliefs.

Emotions themselves lack truth value; they are neither true nor false. Emotion-*propositions,* on the other hand, like all propositions, do have truth value: they are either true or false. For example, the claim "Smith is angry" is either true or false, whereas anger is an emotion Smith may or may not have experienced. If we fail to take adequate note of the distinction between an emotion and an emotion-proposition, we will inevitably confuse emotions with reasons.

When emotions are confused with reasons, the intensity of our feelings and the sincerity with which we hold our beliefs become substitutes for logical evidence. Thus, the sincere atheist offers as "evidence" to support her claim that there is no God the intensity with which she holds her conviction. She is in turn "rebutted" by the sincere theist who "simply knows with all my heart" that God exists.

STUDY HINT

Psychological conviction—of itself—is not proof of the truth of any belief. We must distinguish reasons from feelings, logical evidence from psychological sincerity.

The Shiite Muslims of the Middle East may be as sincere in their convictions as are the Israelis or Christians. Indeed, all around us we see deeply sincere Christians, Jews, agnostics, and atheists (to confine our list to a manageable few). Yet to the detached observer, the intensity of any other individual's beliefs is insufficient to justify its acceptance as true. In the end, sincerity and intensity always tell us more about the believer than about the belief.

It is important to our critical thinking skills that we do not confuse *psychological conviction* with *logical demonstration.* Where reasons are appropriate, good reasons should be demanded. Ironically, clear thinking may be most helpful where it is most difficult: when we face problems, especially personal problems, that involve strong, often conflicting, feelings, values, or obligations. And it is precisely during periods of intense feeling that we are likely to forget to think clearly—assuming that we even want to. It is in just such times of emotional intensity that we are most prone to rationalize the conclusions we most deeply desire; that is, we offer up "reasons" for preselected conclusions. When we engage in psychological rationalizing we, in effect, let the tail wag the dog— we let the truth we desire shape the evidence, or our perception of it, rather than letting the facts suggest the truth.

We can diminish the likelihood of confusing the logical with the psychological and also improve our critical thinking skills by learning some of the ways in which the nonlogical aspects of the human personality impede clear and critical thinking. Let's begin with basic human needs.

EXERCISE 2-1 _____

Discuss the following passage from Schopenhauer's *The World as Will and Representation:*

> How little absolute sincerity is to be expected, even from persons otherwise honest, whenever their interest in any way bears on a matter, can be judged from the fact that we so often deceive ourselves where hope bribes us, or fear befools us, or suspicion torments us, or vanity flatters us, or a hypothesis infatuates and blinds us, or a small purpose close at hand interferes with one greater but more distant.

1. What do you think Schopenhauer means by "absolute sincerity" here?
2. Give your own examples of "insincerity" generated when
   a. "hope bribes us"
   b. "fear befools us"
   c. "suspicion torments us"
   d. "vanity flatters us"
   e. "a hypothesis infatuates and blinds us"
   f. "a small purpose close at hand interferes with one greater but more distant"

NEEDS

All living organisms have needs that must be satisfied if the organism is to survive. On a biological level, life can be understood as a dynamic process, rather than as a constant, or static, state. By ongoing adaptation to changes both within the organism itself and to its environment, a fully functioning, healthy organism is able to maintain a basic equilibrium. Human beings function in varying degrees of well-being and satisfaction according to how well a complex set of needs—including physical, emotional, intellectual, aesthetic, and spiritual needs—are met and integrated with one another.

STUDY HINT

When one of the elements necessary for sustaining a state of balance is disturbed or altered, the organism instinctively acts to correct the imbalance. If this is not possible, the organism will attempt to compensate for the missing element by providing a substitute, or by altering itself to adapt to the new condition.

The late psychologist Abraham Maslow considered a need to be basic if, among other things, (1) its absence breeds illness, (2) its presence prevents illness, (3) its restoration cures illness.[1] By "illness" Maslow meant both physical diseases and psychological disorders. In more general terms, we can consider a need to be basic—or "genuine"—if its presence or absence significantly affects our ability to function as effective, happy human beings. Satisfaction of genuine needs bears directly on the ability to think with clarity sufficient to distinguish reality from illusion.

[1] Abraham Maslow, *Toward a Psychology of Being,* 2d ed. (New York: D. Van Nostrand, 1968), p. 22.

We attempt to achieve equilibrium not only within one area of needs but also among a hierarchy of needs. And none of our genuine needs will just disappear because we choose to ignore it or are incapable of satisfying it. When such a need is unfulfilled, we feel some sense of distress or diminution of happiness, sometimes to such a degree that our thinking and perceiving skills are seriously impaired.

Physical Needs

Clearly, our first order of needs are essentially physiological: We need food, water, air, physical activity, rest, and so forth to maintain our biochemical balance. Included in our list of physical needs are such things as a need for shelter, an instinct to avoid pain, and so forth. Unmet physical needs have immediate and often dramatic effects on our thinking ability, which in turn affects our ability to satisfy other needs.

We find it difficult to think, for example, if the air is thinner than we are used to. Perhaps you have suffered through a lecture in a classroom that was so hot or cold that you were virtually unable to concentrate on anything but your own discomfort. Then, too, there are all those afternoon logic students who erroneously conclude that they cannot think well logically, when the chief cause of poor comprehension is not too little gray matter but perhaps too much lunch too close to class time. In other words, blood that could be rushing oxygen to excited brain cells is, instead, aiding in the digestion of two burritos or an avocado and sprout delight.

Too much noise, too little sleep, poor nutrition, and other physical factors all contribute to a diminished ability to perceive clearly and to think well. When these needs are poorly satisfied, we suffer from various forms of discomfort or dysfunction that affect our abilities to concentrate, to identify, to remember, and to organize—all crucial analytic skills (which are discussed in detail throughout our text). As a general rule, we must satisfy physical needs before we can adequately address other needs.

Emotional Needs

We also require a certain emotional equilibrium. Maslow said, for example, that the need for love is as evident as the need for iodine or vitamin C.[2] Moore, McCann, and McCann suggest that our basic emotional needs include the following: affection, group acceptance, approval, autonomy, achievement, prestige, service to others, conformity to conscience, and self-growth.[3]

When any set of needs or any one need is satisfied at the expense of other needs, our critical judgment is impaired. Our ability to reason critically and clearly can diminish if a genuine need goes unmet long enough. And, clearly, we cannot satisfy a need if we misidentify it or are unable to understand how to meet it. Consider the following:

Lacking self-approval, Ron seeks the approval of others. This is, however, like trying to satisfy the need for a complex carbohydrate with a candy bar—no matter how tasty the candy, it is not what our bodies need. Similarly, on

---

[2]Ibid., p. 23.
[3]W. Edgar Moore, Hugh McCann, and Janet McCann, *Creative and Critical Thinking* (Boston: Houghton Mifflin, 1985), pp. 368–75.

the emotional level, the approval of others, although altogether delicious, is no substitute for self-approval.

There are many variations of this form of confusion. As long as we remain unaware of our actual needs, we are in danger of confusing them with pseudoneeds. *A pseudoneed is any condition that is used to substitute for a need, and which fails to compensate for the unmet original need.*

Actualizing Needs

Actualizing needs affect the quality of our lives in a special way. They include what Maslow referred to as "metaneeds."[4] These "higher-level needs" can be met only after our basic physical and emotional needs are adequately satisfied. Maslow considered metaneeds to be growth needs, including truth, justice, order, beauty, meaningfulness, and unity. Metaneeds are not hierarchical; they coexist. They involve our attempts to find increased and increasing satisfactions—for example, realizing one's potential, satisfying intellectual and spiritual hungers, building linkages with the outside world, "becoming a person," and the like. This process is sometimes called "self-actualization."[5] Among our actualizing needs we find the following:

Aesthetic Needs.   Philosophers of art and aesthetics sometimes talk of the aesthetic sense as being the experience of beauty—a way of appreciating something for a special intrinsic quality, unconnected to its utility. We shall consider aesthetic needs to include our hunger for and appreciation of beauty in any aspect of our lives.

Indeed, all about us we see evidence that we appreciate beauty: Our homes usually contain some ornamentation in the forms of pictures, contrasting trim, well-cared-for gardens. We buy automobiles for their "lines"; we spend hard-earned money for music, plays, novels. The poorest among us, the least educated, and the most deprived find some way to add beauty to our lives.

Meaning Needs.   Virtually every known culture has attempted to find the "meaning of life." Certain contemporary philosophers sometimes assert that the phrase "meaning of life" is itself meaningless. Rather than quarrel over this, we'll pay special attention to the virtual universality of attempts to provide *some meaning for life*. This suggests a basic human need for "meaning" in a very general sense.

Psychologist Irvin D. Yalom distinguishes between the general question "What is the meaning of life?" which he sees as "an inquiry about *cosmic meaning*, about whether life in general or at least human life fits into some overall coherent pattern," and the particular question "What is the meaning of *my* life?"[6] The latter he says is a basically different inquiry and refers to what some philosophers term "terrestrial meaning."[7] After our lower- and middle-order needs are met, most of us encounter meaning needs either implicitly or explicitly. When these

[4]Louis H. Janda and Karin E. Klenke-Hamel, *Psychology: Its Study and Uses* (New York: St. Martin's Press, 1982), p. 291.
[5]Ibid., p. 292.
[6]Irvin D. Yalom, *Existential Psychotherapy* (New York: Basic Books, 1980), p. 423.
[7]For a detailed overview of the meanings of *meaning*, see *The Encyclopedia of Philosophy*, vol. IV, ed. P. Edwards et al. (New York: Macmillan and Free Press, 1967), pp. 467–78.

needs are ignored or inadequately met, we may find ourselves ill at ease, confused, vaguely dissatisfied with life—no matter how well our basic needs are satisfied. Further, adequate satisfaction of intellectual needs often aids us in the adequate satisfaction of other needs, since clear thinking is our best way to determine which needs to satisfy in what order and in what way.

Unmet needs of any sort can result in adjustive demands, or more simply, stress. Let's take a brief look at the effects of stress and anxiety on critical thinking skills.

*EXERCISE 2-2 _____

Discuss each of the following cases in terms of our basic categories of needs: physical needs, emotional needs, and actualizing needs. For each case, decide what you think the most important unmet need is and why. Then consider such factors as whether or not more than one need is involved, what might be done to satisfy relevant needs, and whatever else seems pertinent to you.

Case 1: Bob is carrying eighteen semester units of solid academic classes, is working two jobs for a total of thirty-two hours per week, and is on the swim team. His grades are not as high as he would like.

Case 2: Louise is the office drudge. She's always complaining about the practical jokes other people play among themselves. Louise is always the first to arrive at work and the last to leave. She does volunteer work for Save the Whales Group, for Ban the Bomb Coalition, and for Mothers Against Child Abuse. Often too busy to eat lunch, Louise is surprisingly slim for someone who virtually lives on coffee and items from the office vending machine.

Case 3: Tom never goes to church. He reads only the sports and business sections of the newspaper—no novels, no poems. He sees no plays and only an occasional movie on TV. Mostly he watches sitcoms. In college, Tom avoided literature and humanities courses like the plague. His life is okay, he feels, but Tom's also a little bored. He can't quite figure out why.

Case 4: Jody's the life of any party: fun and funny. She's got a great sense of humor and an attractive style. She dresses well and her apartment is stylishly decorated and furnished. She is always ready to party and is willing to sacrifice to have either a good time or nice clothes or furnishings. She is not sure who the Contras are, thinks Herman Melville was the leader of the 1960s' rock group Herman's Hermits, and does not subscribe to a newspaper. She's fine as long as she's busy but vaguely uncomfortable if there's nothing exciting going on.

Case 5: Larry's been a lumberjack in Oregon and a follower of Guru BuBu, was married three times, has a B.S. in physics, worked as an insurance salesman, and is now going to night school to become a potter.

STRESS AND CLEAR THINKING

Unmet needs result in adjustive demands, which we experience as various forms of stress and anxiety. Most of us cannot avoid some stress in our lives, and indeed, there appears to be evidence that some stress is healthful. At the same time, prolonged, unrelieved chronic stress is physiologically, psychologically, and intellectually debilitating.

Stress refers to a state of tension caused by the body's reaction to both internal and external stimuli. Some scientists believe that stress is our natural way of preparing for "flight or fight." Stress symptoms include increased secretions from the adrenal glands, increased rates of respiration and circulation, contraction of certain muscle groups, and so on. Unrelieved stress is thought to produce ulcers, to increase rates of heart disease, and to cause some forms of asthma, allergies, high blood pressure, colitis, headaches, and more. These symptoms become themselves sources of stress, and a cycle of tension occurs. Physical, financial, romantic, academic, and other conditions may, in turn, all increase stress. Clearly, too much unrelieved stress is a major stumbling block to clear thinking and accurate acquisition of knowledge. Conversely, clear thinking can give us a handle on stress—help us distinguish between constructive and destructive stress, aid us in exploiting the former while reducing the latter.

Anxiety

We all experience periods of anxiousness: waiting for the dentist; moments before a speech, athletic contest, or test; the days before our wedding. Such specific, focused periods of fearfulness are not uncommon. Some psychologists even think that a certain amount of fear can sometimes increase our effectiveness, sensory acuity, and overall performance at certain tasks by increasing secretions from the adrenal glands and causing other physiological changes, which increase our sensory acuity, reaction time, attentiveness, and so forth.

There is, however, a vague, lingering, chronic state of fearfulness and tension called anxiety: *Anxiety is the name for a pervasive, all-consuming, often unfocused sense of fear or panic.* It's effects can be debilitating. It may—but need not—be accompanied by a dry mouth, rapid pulse, rapid, shallow breathing, excessive sweating, clamminess, and other physical symptoms. The intensity and duration of this kind of anxiety interfere with our ability to perceive accurately, to retain information, or to recall information. In its most extreme form (agoraphobia), anxiety often confines individuals to their homes or, in rare cases, to one room for years.

If we are extremely anxious, we misread questions on a test, fail to hear crucial directions to the freeway, forget where to find the distributor cap of the motor we're tuning up—in short, find ourselves so involved with our own fear and discomfort that we cannot concentrate on what's before us. Anxiety is considered extreme when it hinders clear, effective thinking or when it interferes with our ability to function effectively.

If we can identify the cause of intense fear, we can take steps to alleviate our discomfort and enhance our performance. Indeed, this is probably the natural function of anxiety: to prepare us for some stressful or threatening event. If we are unusually fearful during logic tests, we can take simple but effective steps to help ourselves: First—yes! you guessed it—be prepared; read and study in a timely fashion since having to cram and hurry only increases our reasons for worrying. Then arrive in plenty of time, dress comfortably, don't eat a heavy meal right before the test, get plenty of sleep, monitor your breathing, slow down, look at each question carefully, and so on. In other words: *think* about the stressful event before it occurs, and *plan* a strategy to minimize sources of anxiety.

If self-help seems ineffective or beyond us, perhaps professional advice is called for. It is difficult to think well when we are consumed by an uncomfortable psychological state.

Guilt

Maybe our problem is not anxiety over an upcoming logic test so much as it is guilt over not studying. *Psychological guilt is a feeling of discomfort that accom-*

panies a perception of failure to act in accord with our own values. Guilt feelings are unavoidable for most of us. They occur whenever we violate our own values. Consequently, appropriate feelings of guilt can help us make peace with ourselves, live closer to what we believe in, and thus enhance feelings of self-worth and self-respect. This in turn puts us in a much better position to use our critical thinking skills to the utmost.

If we feel too little guilt, we are likely to create social, if not legal, problems for ourselves. On the other hand, counselors have long recognized the fact that there is no correlation between feelings of guilt and actual guilt. If we assume guilt for things beyond our control and responsibility, we will be consumed trying to atone for the unatonable. We will probably commit various inductive causal fallacies as we erroneously conclude that our constant bickering as children caused our parents' divorce, that it's our fault the Christmas party bombed, or most draining and wasteful of all, that it's our fault someone else is not happy.

Without diminishing the complex genetic, environmental, and past causes of various emotional and behavioral traits, we notice that poor thinking is involved in many psychological problems. Intense, but misleading, emotional states both nurture and require confused, biased, rationalized, and self-serving thinking.

If we do not learn to deal effectively with our needs and anxieties, we are likely to use defense mechanisms, rationalizations, and evasions to help us cope with them. We'll turn to defense mechanisms next.

EXERCISE 2-3 _____
1. Discuss the differences between stress and anxiety. Do you think that stress can cause anxiety? Can anxiety cause stress? Explain by giving one or two hypothetical cases of your own.
2. "Psychological guilt is not the same as actual guilt." What's the difference?
3. Discuss some of your own experiences with guilt, stress, and anxiety that might cast further light on their effects on clear thinking.
4. Would a life without stress be more desirable than a life with some stress? Discuss.
5. What do you think are the likely practical consequences of being entirely without the capacity to experience guilt? Would that be a good thing? Explain.

DEFENSE MECHANISMS

A defense mechanism is a strategy designed to support a favored self-concept despite contradictory fact. A defense mechanism is actually a complex set of behavioral, emotional, and intellectual habits working together to "defend" a favored concept of ourselves.

Our self-concept consists of the impression we have of the kind of person we are. Our self-concept is created by the values we have been taught, by value judgments we make of ourselves, by how we view our various abilities and limitations. The self-concept is heavily imbued with data acquired in early childhood: Do we see ourselves as intrinsically lovable or must we barter for love? Are we able or inept? Our answers to these and other questions that bear directly on our self-concept reflect what we have been taught about ourselves by parents, teachers, friends, and strangers.

In this context, the term *favored* is value-neutral in the sense that it simply means "selected over others." The favored, defended self-concept need not be a healthful or accurate one; we might, for example, develop a mechanism for defending a view of ourselves as incompetent or inferior such that attempts by others to improve our self-concept are routinely and efficiently deflected. For example, individuals suffering from the psychological disorder anorexia nervosa view themselves as obese regardless of their actual weight. Their "favored" self-concept is that they are overweight. On the other hand, a favored self-concept might be one that insists on viewing the self as great or magnificient in spite of clear evidence of only modest ability.

The important point here is that defense mechanisms, by their very nature, are opposed to our search for true conclusions. Defense mechanisms function as psychological rationalizations: They are used to find and/or create evidence to support a preselected conclusion. Honest reasoning has as its goal the acceptance of *whatever* conclusion the evidence legitimately supports.

STUDY HINT

Rationalizing has as its goal the support of a desired conclusion *regardless of the actual evidence*. Reasoning has as its goal sound arguments.

When, for whatever reasons, we hang on to an inadequate, distorted, inaccurate self-concept, we have also developed defense mechanisms designed to support this particular vision of ourselves, others, and the world in a way that reinforces the distorted self-concept. Because our basic consideration in all decisions is how to protect the favored self-concept, the truth as such is evaluated in light of its potential to support or refute a particular point of view.

In such cases, we do not reason to satisfy legitimate needs; rather, we use reason to support illegitimate pseudoneeds or to justify too much or too little attention to a genuine need. Let's consider three of the more common techniques available that foster defensive rationalizations.

Scapegoating

Scapegoating is a pseudojustification that singles out an innocent individual or group to blame for some undesired condition. Rather than consider the possibility that his teaching methods are ineffective, Mr. Christopher blames his current troubles on the influx of single mothers into college classes. In fact, he indiscriminately blames high divorce rates (his own included) and increased drug use on single mothers—just the way Hitler and his Nazis blamed most of post–World War I troubles in Germany on Jews and other "inferior types."

Note how such scapegoating requires us to prejudge and stereotype others, to "leap to conclusions" based on skimpy or absent factual "evidence," and so on. In other words, in addition to whatever cultural and personal influences lead us to scapegoat, we cannot resort to scapegoating without falling into logical errors also. We'll study many of these in subsequent chapters.

Here are some examples of scapegoating: "Every time the Democrats begin to get things in pretty good shape, the Republicans mess it up." At some companies, low morale is conveniently blamed on the Boss, when it is in fact the product of more complex factors than any one person's frailties. A young, white male might be able to assuage any hint of self-doubts by blaming his failure to get a job on "affirmative action"—meaning minorities of all sorts. The price this person will pay for uncritically defending a concept of himself as highly capable and desirable, but cheated and abused by affirmative action laws, may make him feel good for the moment—but it will discourage him from honest introspection and assessment of his skills in light of the current job market. Without a clear, rational analysis of his actual circumstances, talents, and the like, he is apt to fail to identify a solution to his real problem: perhaps more schooling or retraining.

Projection

John hates hypocrites. And he finds them everywhere. The reason is that John is a hypocrite himself. *Projection refers to the process of attributing to others traits that we find undesirable in ourselves.* Projection acts as a barrier between our self-concept and some undesirable trait of ours that could threaten or destroy that self-concept. Projection is often accompanied by intolerance, judgmentalism, and hostility.

For example, Don Hopeso has a strong sexual drive. As a child, however, he was taught that sex is bad and nasty, and so all his life he has avoided any sexual activity. What he cannot avoid, though, are his own strong sexual desires—desires he believes are evil and unwholesome. Whether they are or not is not nearly as important as his belief that they are. Unable to confront his own sexual needs, and thus unable to satisfy them in a healthy way, Don projects his obsessive sexual desires onto all the women he encounters. Every day becomes a challenge: The clerk at the supermarket says "Hi," and Don hears "My place or yours?" A co-worker asks him what he's doing for lunch; he hears "My place or yours?" And so it goes: Don "sees" his own sexual obsessions in others—but not in himself.

(We should be wary of the defensive maneuver of dismissing all criticism of ourselves as projection on the part of others. Projection is commonly—but not always—accompanied by extreme, unwarranted hostility, resentment, or aggression.)

Introjection

Introjection is a process in which we internalize the values, beliefs, and experiences of others. We may introject the values of our parents, our political party, our church, our friends, anyone or anything for that matter. Introjection almost always inhibits our ability to perceive clearly for ourselves. When introjected beliefs overcome our own actual experience, the price we pay for identifying so strongly with the source of introjection is a decline in our own self-esteem, as well as a diminished ability to assess conditions accurately. This result is inevitable since we must repress, distort, or deny our own perceptions, experiences, and judgments in favor of someone else's.

Members of cults have been known to introject the values of the cult or its charismatic leader to such an extent that they no longer experience things as they are; intead they "see" whatever the official position dictates. Other examples of introjection are the child who introjects a parent's attitudes toward men or women so deeply that the child sees things only as the parent does. Introjection differs from influence in degree—introjected values interfere with perception, judgment, and reality testing. As in the case of Don, introjected values may be in turn projected onto others.

We've seen a few of the ways that defense mechanisms make life momentarily bearable at a price that can get pretty steep over the long run because they require a distortion of evidence, even a denial of our own experiences, judgments, and beliefs. They may create extreme hostility or aggression in us, as we become increasingly sensitive to even the slightest threat to our carefully balanced rationalizations, pseudoneeds, and self-deceptions. A good defense against defensive mechanisms includes clear, critical thinking skills. But to think as well as possible, we must also avoid the following psychological stumbling blocks, which function as methods of distortion.

*EXERCISE 2-4 _____

Discuss the following cases in terms of scapegoating, projection, and introjection. Explain.

Case 1: Bud hates what he sees as his Dad's bullying behavior of Dad's employees. Bud regularly pushes his little brother, Buster, around.

Case 2: The president of the Coalition for Clean Thoughts works very hard to remove *Playboy* and *Penthouse* magazines from local stores. He tries to have them replaced with *Clean Living* and *Wholesome Hobbies*. He is especially angry at the "liberal establishment" and "secular humanists" for wanting to "enforce their morals on the rest of us."

Case 3: After two weeks of law school, an excited Melvin begins to smoke a pipe—just like his favorite professor, Professor Kingfish. Over the semester, Melvin finds out what brand of tobacco Kingfish smokes, and he begins to read everything Kingfish ever wrote. By the end of the term, Melvin's a devout Libertarian, just like Kingfish.

Case 4: Kay is frustrated. She hasn't had a good job in over eighteen months, when automation made her old job obsolete. She's especially annoyed because of the large influx of Latino and Asian immigrants and the influx of Japanese imports. Kay is convinced that foreigners are taking jobs away from "loyal, real Americans."

Case 5: Frustrated by "Irangate," President Reagan accuses the press of being unfairly aggressive and hostile for dwelling on the issue. Embarrassed by a handful of U.S. Marines who allow a breach of security at the U.S. Embassy in Moscow in exchange for the sexual favors of some Soviet women, the President decries the failure of American educators to inculcate values in the young.

Case 6: The President's staff sees the press the same way the President does, and echoes his criticism of American educators.

METHODS OF DISTORTION

Perhaps you've been to a funhouse at a carnival or county fair. One of its more popular parts is the exhibit of what have come to be known as "funhouse mirrors." Rippled, convex, concave, and other unusual reflective surfaces produce bizarre and amusing visual effects: We look short and squat or long and lean; our heads look like peas or watermelons. We laugh at these deliberate, innocuous distortions of how we really look, but there is another class of distortions that is not innocuous and often not acknowledged. These occur either through ignorance or as a deliberate device to manage our impressions and the conclusions we draw from them. We'll consider some of the most common.

Denial

Psychological denial is an attitude that refuses to acknowledge the true existence or nature of some unpleasant circumstance. For example, most of us are aware that alcoholics and drug addicts often deny their addictions. What's not so commonly recognized is the extent to which the friends and families of addicts also deny the extent and power of the addiction. They assert that the addictive behavior is "not that big of a deal," that it is "caused by marital problems," that "everybody gets a little stoned now and then," and so forth. What such denials overlook, for example, is that many people who have marital or family problems do not abuse drugs, or that most people do not get cited for driving under the influence. Denial distorts the true nature of the addictive behaviors.

Followers of cult leaders like Bhagwan Shree Rajneesh or Jim Jones often "overlook" increasingly clear signs of danger: paranoiac isolation of the leader and the cult from nonbelievers; inconsistency between official cult doctrines of liberation, love, and openness and the actual behavior of cult members; and so on. Most of us have seen the sad consequences of failing to acknowledge the truth. In its most serious cases, denial is manifest in victims of spousal abuse who insist that their abuser is kind and loving in spite of clearly contradictory evidence. On a perhaps less serious scale, we see it in those individuals who insist on the efficacy of astrological predictions in spite of clear cases of failed and/or vague predictions (see also Chapter 8).

We see denial in the ever-faithful followers of political or religious figures who have openly lied or embezzled money or falsified credentials. We see powerful denial at work when drug addicts continue to share hypodermic needles or when individuals engage in sexual habits that place them at high risk for contracting AIDS or herpes. We might suspect denial when effective birth control measures are simply ignored, with the following rationalizations: "Not me; I won't get pregnant." "Not me; I won't get a lethal dose of diluted cocaine." "Not me; I won't get AIDS." Or "Somehow, I will be the one college student who gets good grades without effort. Not me; I won't get caught short for not studying tonight."

We hear echoes of denial in the lament of the freshly divorced person who says, "I can't understand it. We were a perfect couple. Everything was wonderful. We never argued at all." Of course, one way of denying trouble is to refuse to argue about it. The marriage that was so placid on the surface might have been deeply troubled for years. We see denial in the parents who don't notice fourteen-year-old Nancy's constantly dilated pupils; rapid, agitated behavior; falling grades; bizarre eating habits; and new, less desirable friends—or who notice them but chalk them up to typical teenage behavior. The list is endless.

Clearly, we cannot be effective thinkers if we deny and distort the actual nature or consequences of what's going on around us. If we are lucky, we are forced to face facts before we have suffered extensively from our denial. Sadly, however, we are sometimes unable to face reality until we actually flunk chemistry, see our unhappy spouse move out, find our troubled teenager unconscious from an overdose, and learn other tragic lessons.

Distraction

Okay, you've finally stopped denying your slipping World Lit grades and have decided to do something about them. You get out your textbook, sharpen some pencils, put on the coffee, and sit down at the kitchen table to study. It's then that you notice the cobwebs behind the stove. . . .

We all know what happens next: Consumed by an irresistible desire to clean house, you spend hours dusting, sweeping, wiping. After all, the mess around you is distracting you from your studies. *Distraction is a method of distortion by which we avoid a difficult or painful task, idea, or feeling by substituting a more palatable activity.*

Such distraction, as we've just seen, is especially potent and sneaky because it is often accompanied by the rationalization that the distracting activity is actually a vital part of the undesired one. We can even be clever enough to disguise the true nature of our distracting maneuver under the pretense of getting rid of a distraction! "I'm cleaning up now so that I can study without distraction later."

Instead of studying logic, you might, for another example, use the earlier material about stress as an excuse to unwind by sitting lazily in the yard, telling yourself, "I can't study effectively if I'm stressed out; my *Practical Logic* text says so. I'll just relax in the yard, like it suggests, as a way of preparing my mind to learn logic."

This argument would be fine if (1) you were truly suffering from stress that could be alleviated by relaxing in the yard and (2) you relaxed just long enough to get back to your logic studies. Distraction (and possible denial) is present, however, if your real, deep-seated purpose is simply to sit in the yard *instead* of studying. You may be denying the fact that your "stress" is really anxiety caused by getting behind in logic class. If so, the only truly relevant and lasting solution to your predicament is *more* studying, not relaxing.

We might distract ourselves from facing up to our own life's difficulties by becoming overly interested in international affairs or worrying about how to feed the hungry or stop the threat of nuclear war. Praiseworthy causes—just like house cleaning—can be used as distraction devices. That's the whole point here: Any activity, regardless of its particular merits, can be used in an evasive, distracting way if we engage in it to avoid dealing with an important, more immediate or basic issue. When the distraction is socially praiseworthy, it is especially dangerous, for then it functions as a form of denial as well, allowing us to deceive ourselves about the true nature of our cleaning, volunteering, or picketing.

This kind of ignorance about our own motives is truly invincible for not only are we unaware of its presence, many of our friends and acquaintances are likely to be gulled as well.

Rationalizing

Professor Cash is determined to use the university computer for his own private consulting practice. This use is against university policy. More significantly, Professor Cash himself thinks it might be unethical. After some reflection, he concludes that such use is all right since professors use university equipment to write journal articles and textbooks.

Professor Cash is rationalizing. *A psychological rationalization is a pseudo-justification in which "reasons" are constructed for the sole purpose of justifying a desired conclusion.* In this case, we cannot determine whether or not Professor Cash is rationalizing his use of the university computer just by considering his offered reasons. We can conclude that he is rationalizing only if we know that he has determined to use the computer *one way or the other,* and that his sole motive for "reasoning" at all in this case was to construct a defense for his behavior.

The essential difference between reasoning and rationalizing is one of intention. If our purpose is to see where the evidence leads, we are reasoning. If, rather, our real purpose is to find reasons to support a conclusion that we insist on holding, we are rationalizing.

Rationalizing is common enough so that most of us recognize its occurrence—in others. We are not so adept at recognizing its presence in our own case. Here is a handy list of some common species of rationalizing:[8]

1. *Sour grapes.* The name of this form of rationalization comes from Aesop's fable about a fox who was unable to reach some sweet grapes hanging overhead. Rather than admit his disappointment, the fox chose to call the sweet grapes sour. Betsy turns you down for a date? "Whew! What a relief. I only asked her to be kind. She's a real bore anyway," you rationalize.
2. *Sweet lemon.* Imagine that you've bought a pair of shoes at a sale. All sales are final, so you cannot return them later. It turns out that they pinch after an hour's wearing. "No problem," you rationalize. "They look great with my evening dress, and I hardly ever wear it. When I do I'm usually sitting at a table or in a theatre. I'm really glad I have these shoes even if they do hurt my feet."
3. *Excuse making.* "It's not my fault I failed home economics. The room was stuffy. The book was second-rate. I had the flu for four days, too." The problem with this rationalization is that most other students passed the course, so the room and the book could not have been insurmountable obstacles. And missing four days with the flu would have had a negligible effect on my grade if I had not also missed three days skiing. Thus, my excuse, though *perhaps* face-saving, is still only a rationalization of my own failure.

A desire to look good, to save face, or to appear competent often triggers a rationalization. It is helpful to realize that most rationalizations are spotted by others, and that rationalizations only provide public face-saving, at best, and they often fail to do even that. They rarely provide peace of mind because on some level we are usually aware of our true motives. Thus, rationalizations generate many of the uncomfortable feelings that accompany all forms of denial and distortion. This, in turn, provokes even more defense mechanisms, until the truth is deeply buried from our view. The best course, we know, is to do what we can to face facts as they are. In this way, we stand the best chance of changing unpleasant circumstances, of identifying harmful patterns, and of learning from our mistakes. This is virtually impossible if we distort our real motives or if we make excuses rather than diagnoses of our shortcomings.

Prejudging

A prejudice is a conclusion arrived at prior to pertinent experience. In other words, we make up our minds before we have sufficient evidence to draw our conclusion. Racial, sexual, and religious prejudices are unfortunately common. And

[8]*Creative and Critical Thinking,* p. 404.

yet, it is also common to discover that many highly prejudiced individuals have had virtually no personal experience with the objects of their prejudgments. Indeed, prejudice thrives on limited contact with its object.

Anti-Semitism flourishes even among people who have never knowingly met a Jew. Strong negative prejudices against Christian fundamentalists flourish in academic circles among seemingly well-educated intellectuals who know no fundamentalists. This list, too, could go on and on.

Prejudices seem to thrive because they are easy ways of mimicking genuine self-esteem. It is often easier to reduce your status in my eyes than it is to elevate my own. So it is that unhappy individuals find some group or groups over which they can feel superior without having actually to be superior.

Prejudging almost always involves faulty generalizations and oversimplification (subjects of Part Four). Prejudices centering around assertions concerning "all" blacks, Jews, logicians, homosexuals, humanists, Christians, and so on are guaranteed to be so sweepingly general as to be virtually meaningless. They often include elements of our next source of distortion.

Stereotyping

Stereotyping occurs when we overlook an individual's unique qualities by viewing him or her only according to a rigid preconception. When this happens, we tend to expect certain behavior patterns—and to convince ourselves of their occurrence regardless of their actual presence.

A white racial bigot, for example, might have a stereotyped picture of all blacks as being lazy. Thus, he notices every time his black neighbor's yard badly needs mowing (which in reality is infrequently) as this occurrence confirms his stereotype. He overlooks all those times his neighbor's yard is well cared for as well as ignoring the fact that his own yard is much more poorly cared for—acknowledging these facts weakens the stereotyped pictures he holds of blacks and of himself. Meanwhile, his black neighbor holds a stereotyped view of Chicanos. She notices every discourtesy her Mexican-American neighbor commits while overlooking the fact that her daughter's kindergarten teacher, Mr. Olivarez, has paid special attention to little Monica in order to help the child overcome a slight stuttering problem.

When exceptions to cherished stereotypes are pointed out, we tend to invoke various forms of bad arguments called fallacies to defend the stereotype and thus maintain our own pseudoesteem. Here, too, the price for such distortion is high: We must willingly distort the truth to save our oversimplified, stereotyped view of things.

EXERCISE 2-5 _____

Identify in the following passages any of the methods of distortion you find: denial, distraction, rationalizing (specify sour grapes, sweet lemon, excuse making), prejudging, and stereotyping.

1.. NEIGHBOR: Aren't you worried that Teddy's been arrested again? This is the fourth time, isn't it?
   MOM: Fifth. But, no, I'm not worried. He's just an exuberant kid. You know how it is with teenagers.
2. EBENEEZER: How'd you do in logic class?
   JACOB: I flunked. But it was a lousy class anyway.

EBENEEZER: I thought you said you really liked Ms. DeMorgan.

JACOB: That was before I realized what a lousy teacher she is. I'm actually glad I flunked—anybody who passed that class had to kiss up to old DeMorgan. Yeah! Now that I think about it, I'm real glad I flunked.

3. The story goes that upon being denied membership in an "exclusive" country club because he was Jewish, Groucho Marx said, "I wouldn't belong to any club that would have me as a member anyway!"

4. MAUREEN: I bet you're sorry you didn't wait a little longer to buy that stereo at Joe's, now that the same thing's on sale for 40 percent off.

KEN: Not at all. I've gotten to use it for an extra couple of weeks.

5. BUBBA: Geez, I wish we didn't have to hire women firefighters.

TAB: Who knows, they might be just fine. Why don't you give 'em a chance.

BUBBA: Hey, man, come off it. They're gonna be all muscles with short hair, and they're gonna hate men and stuff. That's the way these feminists are.

TAB: You ever meet a real live feminist, Bubba?

BUBBA: Don't haf'ta. I know what they're like before I meet 'em.

6. Yeah? Well I'm glad you don't like me 'cause I don't like you either. I only asked you out 'cause I felt sorry for you.

7. Look, for now I want to smoke. Do you mind? Smoking keeps me calm, helps keep my weight down. If I really wanted to quit I would.

8. Anorexic teenage girls see themselves as fat no matter what their real weight is.

9. I'm getting depressed just thinking about studying my logic. I know what I need: I'll go on a picnic to unwind. Let's see? Where's that picnic basket? Gotta go to the store, get the car lubed. . . .

10. I'm sorry my assignment's not ready, but I forgot the due date.

SUMMARY

In this chapter we've seen some of the "nonlogical" factors that bear on critical thinking in real life. We refined our understanding of "premise" by distinguishing between propositions that are never capable of being premises and reasons, propositions capable of providing support for the conclusion of an argument. We discussed the relationship between emotions and reasons, distinguishing *psychological conviction* from *logical justification*.

Among the major nonlogical factors that influence our thinking are basic needs.

Physical needs. These are the most basic needs of all, and they include physiological requirements for survival and health.

Emotional needs. The need to give and receive affection, and such things as autonomy, approval, achievement, prestige, service to others, and conformity to a group make up the complex set of emotional needs that must be adequately met if we are to achieve sufficient emotional equilibrium to function as effective thinkers.

Aesthetic needs. Often overlooked among our many needs is the need to experience beauty, which helps us maintain mental balance and relieves stresses and anxieties that may interfere with accurate critical thinking.

Actualizing needs. These address the meaning, purpose, and quality of life in a nonspecific way. Among our specific needs are intellectual needs, the need for play, and the need for meaning.

A *pseudoneed* is any condition used as a substitute for a genuine need.

Our self-concept consists of the impression we have of the kind of person we are. When our basic needs are not fully met, we resort to defense mechanisms: A defense mechanism is a strategy designed to support a favored self-concept despite contradictory facts.

Scapegoating is a pseudojustification that singles out an innocent individual or group to blame for some undesired condition.

Projection refers to the process of attributing to others traits that we find undesirable in ourselves.

Introjection is a process in which we internalize the values, beliefs, and experiences of others.

In addition to avoiding psychological defense mechanisms, clear thinking demands that we also avoid stumbling blocks to clear thinking:

Anxiety is the name for a pervasive, all-consuming, often unfocused sense of fear or panic.

Psychological guilt is a feeling of discomfort that accompanies a perception of failure to act in accord with our own values.

Stress refers to a state of tension caused by the body's reaction to both internal and external stimuli.

Psychological denial is an attitude that refuses to acknowledge the true existence or nature of some unpleasant circumstance.

Distraction involves the avoidance of a difficult or painful task, idea, or feeling by substituting a more palatable activity.

A *psychological rationalization* is a pseudojustification in which "reasons" are constructed for the sole purpose of justifying a desired conclusion. Some forms of rationalizing are sour grapes, sweet lemon, and excuse making.

Prejudging is a conclusion arrived at prior to pertinent experience.

Stereotyping occurs when we overlook an individual's unique qualities by viewing him or her only according to a rigid preconception.

Summary Questions

Note: In addition to learning a little more about ourselves, discussing the material in this chapter can be entertaining as we laugh at some of the common foibles that beset most of us. Without diminishing the serious side of defense mechanisms, distortions, and the like, you might find it helpful and enjoyable to discuss the following questions with other students of *Practical Logic*. If you do, it is probably best to keep personal examples on the light side.

1. Discuss some of the specific ways clear thinking is inhibited by emotional factors.
2. What plausible strategies can you suggest to avoid the need for defense mechanisms?
3. See if you can identify three or four ways in which you might improve your grades by taking better care of your physical needs. You might, for example, modify the place in which you usually study: Is it comfortable? Quiet? Too quiet? Too warm or cold? Are there other physical conditions (in yourself or your environment) that might be beneficially modified in a way that will enhance your critical thinking?

4. Being both imaginative and realistic, assess one or two of your classrooms in aesthetic terms. Are there any "aesthetic factors" that you see as either encouraging or inhibiting learning? Discuss.

5. Using your own (not too personal) experience, discuss a circumstance in which you tried to substitute a pseudoneed to a genuine need. What was the result?

ADDITIONAL EXERCISES _____

Scrutinize the following situations. Identify the likely presence of any of these aspects of the psychological dimension: physical needs, emotional needs, aesthetic needs, spiritual needs, scapegoating, projection, introjection, anxiety, psychological guilt, stress, psychological denial, distraction, sour grapes, sweet lemon, and excuse making. Your analyses will, necessarily, be speculative, so be prepared to explain your thinking.

1. Ken is always chiding Pete about Pete's physical condition. Pete is overweight and rarely exercises. Pete goads Ken about the fact that Ken has not read a whole book in the last year.

2. Sylvia notices a slight lump on the back of her neck. She decides it's probably a cyst and forgets about it.

3. Because his GPA is so important to him, Art buys a term paper for his literature class from a professional term paper service.

4. Pastor Richards hates the Ayatollah Khomeni of Iran. He says, "That Khomeni is a fanatic. He tries to force his religious beliefs on the rest of the world."

5. Hector's a little depressed this evening. His daughter, Laura, just came home from college on semester break. She's especially proud of her A in World Lit. This reminded Hector of Mr. Wilder, his old lit teacher when he was in high school. Mr. Wilder used to say that Hector had a fine natural talent for literature, but Hector never studied much. He barely got Cs.

6. Tim is trying to write a sociology essay while his roommate, Tad, is practicing the drums.

7. Joann's dad is an alcoholic. Joann knows that if it weren't for her dad, the rest of the family would be fine.

8. Bob's parents are worried when they visit him for the first time in his new apartment. His refrigerator is nearly empty. But Bob points out that he feels fine, hasn't lost any weight, and has been using most of his money to buy attractive prints to hang on his walls.

9. Sue has nearly gotten married three times. In each instance, the men she was involved with were fine persons, she got along with them well, and she even loved them. In each case, however, Sue insisted on maintaining her maiden name and keeping her finances separate from those of her future husband. This arrangement bothered Sue's fiancés; any other arrangement bothered Sue.

10. Les is a liberal. He despises the way conservatives are trying to censor pornography, rock and roll, and even textbooks. He's often heard to say, "Freedom of speech and expression, that's what this country is founded on. Lose that and you lose everything." Les was recently arrested for getting carried away while demonstrating against granting a permit for a rally to the local chapter of the American Nazi Party. He was quoted in the paper as saying, as he was led to jail, "Nobody should have to listen to that garbage. Freedom of speech doesn't include the right to be degenerate or immoral or to offend the values of the community!"

11. Asked how he felt about losing an unusually hard-fought and expensive campaign for the Senate, ex-Senator Fiskew replied, "Now I'll have time to be with my family. My family's always been the most important thing in my life. I've served the people of this great state for six terms; I could use a rest. I'm glad I lost, actually."

12. Natasha has a great job. It's more than she ever dreamed she'd have at this stage in her career. Her family life is fine, too. Yet she's restless, somehow. One day, she looks around her plush office, glances fondly at a picture of her husband and children she keeps at her desk, stares out and window, and asks herself, "Okay, Natasha. You've got everything you said you wanted, and you're still not happy. Why? Is this all there is to life?"

13. Hubbard was enjoying his new car quite a bit—until his brother said that he'd be afraid to travel on the freeway in such a small vehicle. Now Hubbard's uneasy, too.

14. Molina has lots of homework to do this weekend. It's also the last weekend before Hanukkah and Christmas and she wants to make fudge treats for the guys and gals she hangs around with. She decides to make the fudge.

15. Trish always takes over an hour to get ready for school. She tries to look attractive to the boys in her class and goes out of her way to flatter them. She is annoyed at the way Elvira is always flirting. She told her mom, "Oooo, I hate Elvira! Every time I'm talking to a cute guy she butts in. All she cares about are boys, boys, boys. And she's shameless. Always dressed up and flirting. I can't stand it when girls are like that!"

16. J. Birch hates the way the Russian Communists get involved in the internal affairs of other countries. He can't stand the way they won't stay out of other countries. That's why he enlisted in the Army. He's hoping he'll get to go fight in Central America.

17. Recalling the old Lionel model train set he had as a child, Chester ordered a train set from the Sunday supplement. It looked great in the picture. When he received his set, however, it was much smaller than he expected and made of low-grade plastic. When his wife expressed disappointment, Chester said, "Hey, this is better than the old sets. It's small enough to store easily, it's lightweight, and we don't have to worry about the grandkids busting it up. I'm glad I ordered it."

18. Nora's having trouble with her Spanish test—the most important test of the year. Nora's vision seems to be blurring, her palms are sweaty, and she can't concentrate, even though she's well prepared for the test.

19. Marsha's been upset ever since she learned that her new office mate was from Georgia. "How could they do that," she moaned, "put a bigot in my office. You know how prejudiced southern white males are."

20. Irving's a bit worried about how well he's doing in logic class, but he never stopped by Professor Oscar's office to pick up his graded tests.

chapter 3

Language and Logic

*The limits of my language mean the limits of
my world.*

LUDWIG WITTGENSTEIN

After a typical Fourth of July picnic of too much fried chicken and corn on the cob, you settle down to a good-sized hunk of watermelon under the shade of a large oak tree and listen to Senator Washington's annual Fourth of July speech. You figure it's just the thing you need to put you to sleep so that you can get a little rest before the fireworks; they're why you're there in the first place.

The platform is covered with red, white, and blue bunting; the Stars and Stripes are billowing along with your state flag; the P.A. system is blaring "America the Beautiful," and the Senator begins:

> My fellow Americans, I just want you to know how grateful I am to live in this wonderful country of ours. I believe in freedom! I believe in democracy! I believe in education! I believe in free enterprise! I believe in the rights of all Americans to the pursuit of life, liberty, and happiness.

I want to say that it is an honor to serve you. And if reelected, I promise to work for tax reform. I'm in favor of strong law and order. I will do the best I can if you just give me the chance. Now, would you all join me in a chorus of "The Star Spangled Banner"?

Instead of your anticipated nap, you find yourself vaguely uncomfortable. Instead of dozing off, you are agitated, without knowing precisely why. Something about the Senator's speech has bothered you, but you can't quite put it into words.

Since you have over an hour before the fireworks begin, you decide to take a relaxing drive. You find that a quiet drive often clears your head.

As you drive, it occurs to you that you have heard this speech hundreds of times. Not always from Senator Washington, of course, but from mayors and governors and presidential candidates and even folks running for dog catcher, it seems. It might be called the "Generic Political Speech."

Driving along, you are unexpectedly overwhelmed by road signs. It seems like billions and billions of road signs and bumper stickers have sprung up everywhere!

SLOW. ROAD CONSTRUCTION NEXT 17 MILES. FLY NOW, PAY LATER. 4 MILES TO FREDDIE'S FREAK FARM. STOP. DETOUR AHEAD. POST NO BILLS! DEER CROSSING. DO IT IN A DATSUN! FALLING ROCKS. LEFT LANE MERGE. I'VE FOUND IT! FLY NOW, PAY LATER. ROAD ENDS AHEAD. 3 MILES TO FREDDIE'S FREAK FARM. VOTE YES TO OUTLAW BILLBOARDS! HONK IF YOU LOVE JESUS. NO VACANCY. CHEAP TIRES! ADULT ENTERTAINMENT!!! FIGHT INFLATION. FIGHT CANCER! FIGHT VIOLENCE! QUESTION AUTHORITY. HAVE YOU HUGGED YOUR KID TODAY? DO YOU KNOW WHERE YOU KID IS RIGHT NOW? KIDS ARE PEOPLE TOO, YOU KNOW. STOP AT 2! 2 MILES TO FREDDIE'S FREAK FARM! I'M A NAVY WIFE. LOVE A NURSE. SUPPORT YOUR LOCAL POLICE. KING OF THE ROAD. COWBOYS MAKE BETTER LOVERS. IF YOU CAN READ THIS, YOU'RE TOO CLOSE. HAPPY WANDERER. RELAX—GOD HAS EVERYTHING UNDER CONTROL. 1 MILE TO FREDDIE'S FREAK FARM! FOR SAFETY OUR LIGHTS ARE ALWAYS ON. FLY MONA TO NEW YORK. THINK YOUNG—VOTE YOUNG IN NOVEMBER. IMPEACH THE PRESS! I GAVE THE UNITED WAY. STAMP OUT BUMPER STICKERS! STOP—TURN BACK—YOU JUST PASSED FREDDIE'S FREAK FARM!

Arriving back at the picnic grounds, you are still trying to sort things out. Political speeches. Road signs. Your agitation. What's going on? Ah, well, at least the fireworks ought to be enjoyable.

What's going on is language—the aspect of human behavior that involves sound and symbols to express thoughts and feelings. There's no escaping it or denying its significance and power.

What happened to you during the Senator's speech might be thought of as waking up. Without initially being aware of it, you began to sense that although the Senator could talk like this for a long time, he was actually saying very little. In fact, he is a master of using language to persuade and influence others. This is called the *rhetorical* use of language. There are many others.

This chapter is about logic and language. There are several reasons to include language in our study of logic. First, logic and language are closely connected both in history and in their functions. Etymologically, the word *logic* derives from the Greek *logos*, meaning "word" or "speech" or "reason." The logic and language connection is altogether understandable when you realize that every argument, every proposition, involves language. In fact, some would say that the critical process of thinking or reasoning itself requires language.

More specifically, language has certain features that can complicate our job of understanding the logical relations between propositions, of determining the soundness of arguments. So part of the task of the logician is to discover and describe these features.

But don't think that this is some abstract, academic enterprise with no practical value. Quite the opposite. By understanding how language works, we develop insights into its impact on our lives—on how we think and see things, on what we assume, on how we live. Such insights help us deal with a world that is very much shaped and influenced by language. They give us a measure of self-control we'd otherwise lack. And when we get bogged down in the morass of language, such insights buoy us up, give us some footing, provide us something to grab onto.

*EXERCISE 3-1 _____

Here are five questions to get you thinking about language.

1. Do you think peoples' names could affect the way they think of themselves and, subsequently, how they behave? Illustrate.
2. In correcting a small child, an English, Italian, or Greek speaker will often say, "Be good." A French speaker will say, "Be wise"; a Scandinavian, "Be friendly"; a German, "Be in line"; and a Hopi Indian, "That is not the Hopi way." Would these societies be encouraging a value in the child? What value? What are the long-range implications of associating behavior with this value?
3. The following words and phrases were prominent during the Vietnam War. What concept of reality do they foster? What, in fact, did they really mean?
   a. pacification program
   b. relocation
   c. strategic hamlet
   d. limited protective strikes
   e. defoliation
   Are you able to add to the list?
4. A U.S. attorney general once said about the administration he served in, "Watch what we do, not what we say." What would he think is the relationship between language and action? What would you say are the consequences of such a belief? Why?
5. A U.S. Vice-President once described himself politically as a "downfield blocker" and saw the President as the only quarterback on the team. The rhetoric of sports is pervasive in our language usage. Naturally it reflects our interest and affection for competition in general. But what would you say are the wider ramifications of seeing things in terms of sport? Can you point to examples to support your view?

LANGUAGE AND LOGIC

What we think can't be separated from language. This may seem like a pretty strong claim, and it is. Too often, we think of language skills as nothing more than "manners," the "proper" or "polite" or "socially accepted" way of speaking and writing. Certainly language skills affect us: They influence how others see us and think of us. If they are poor they may hinder us socially, may embarrass us, and may keep us from high-level jobs. Most of us are aware of these aspects of the power of language. But to say that our thinking is limited by our language is a bolder claim.

And yet, how we see things certainly affects how we think. And how we see things is strongly influenced by our language. We cannot divorce how we perceive the world from the language we use to express ourselves.

There are two noteworthy aspects of this language and thought connection. One is that language reflects what people or groups think about things, how they see their world. Language reveals how individuals and groups order their world, what assumptions they make, what perspectives they hold. The second noteworthy aspect of language is that it influences the individual's and the group's outlook on things. Language can help mold beliefs, assumptions, and viewpoints. It can get us thinking in predetermined ways. Sometimes, language is like a fine piece of optically pure glass through which we basically view the world "as it is" (with as little distortion as possible). But more often, it is like tinted glass or like a prism or a funhouse mirror—language shapes what we see through it.

Some years ago a small midwestern community made national news when a local resident noticed strange little chips and pits in the windshield of his car that had mysteriously appeared there overnight. He mentioned this to a neighbor, who discovered that his windshield also had such markings. Soon, the entire neighborhood noticed similar markings on their windshields. The local press got on the story. No one could track down the cause of this mysterious "overnight" pitting. No government agencies were doing any strange experiments or spraying powerful pesticides. Some residents suggested that perhaps "extraterrestrials" had done something. Whether this was a serious suggestion is highly doubtful, but the national press had some fun with this mysterious case of the damaged windshields.

Finally, the owner of an autoglass shop pointed out that most, if not all, windshields get pitted from use. There was nothing different about these windshields at all! What had apparently happened is simply that one morning an individual looked *at rather than through* his windshield. The pits had been there for some time, but he had looked past them—as well he should while driving.

Now what does this story have to do with language, much less with logic? If we think of language as a kind of windshield on our world, our beliefs, our thoughts, and even on our understanding of ourselves, we can try to look *at rather than through* this powerful part of the language and logic connection. At first, some claims made about the power of language may seem as strange to us as those pits did to people when they first noticed them. But the pits had probably been there for some time, and language has been shaping our perceptions and our thoughts whether we have been aware of the degree of its influence or not.

As we become more conscious of the presence of arguments in our lives and of the myriad factors that affect our thinking (for good or for ill), we will gain additional control over our lives. We will no longer be at the mercy of the smooth talkers, of all those people who know just how to package a pitch to tug at our heart strings, to touch our egos, to awaken a fantasy and so get us to buy this car, vote for that woman, send in our pledge of support. We will be better able to make choices that are good for us, that are responsible, and that are consistent with our most important beliefs and values.

Upon reflection, we discover that virtually every pitch made to us includes a linguistic component. And every argument we encounter is couched in some symbolic form, whether ordinary language or the abbreviated symbols of logic or mathematics. This chapter is devoted to heightening our sensitivity to the presence and influence of language in our daily lives. Let's take a closer look at some of the more important elements in the language and thought connection.

SAYING WHAT WE SEE (LANGUAGE AS REFLECTING THOUGHT)

If we study language closely, we can learn a lot about what individuals think, how they see things, what values they hold, even what kind of people they are. Consider, for example, the irascible character who for years entered our living rooms to bewitch and besmirch, humor and horrify, endear and enrage. We speak of Archie Bunker of television's "All in the Family" and "Archie's Place." Although both shows are no longer currently in production, Archie is widely recognized, his and Edith's chairs are in the Smithsonian Institution in Washington, D.C., and both TV shows are widely syndicated.

As everyone knows who has seen these programs even once, Archie is notorious for his slaughter of the English language. Recall just his use of malapropism, the misapplication of a word. "I come home and tell you one of the great antidotes of all time," Archie tells the family, "and you sit there like you're in a comma." On other occasions, Archie has been known to say, " 'Sorry' ain't gonna clench my thirst," "You gotta grab the bull by the corns and heave-ho," "We don't want people thinking we live in no pig's eye," "On the sperm of the moment, it's like making a sow's purse outta silk!" Funny, no doubt about it. But Archie's malapropisms do more than entertain. They tell us about Archie Bunker himself, that he is pretentious and vain, ignorant and arrogant, and in the unvarnished words of the show's creator Norman Lear, "a horse's ass."

When "All in the Family" premiered in the early 1970s it created quite a furor. Some social critics asserted that Archie made narrow-minded bigotry seem attractive, funny, or harmless. They argued that his humorous misuse of the language made him seem more like a buffoon than like the unpleasant characters real-life Archie Bunkers are. Other commentators agreed with Norman Lear that Archie's language revealed him for the "horse's ass" he was.

Regardless of our personal opinions in this matter, we have a remarkable example of the importance of language. Here was a full-blown media controversy brought on by the speech patterns of a television character. Scholars and armchair critics alike took note of what for the time was a daring breakthrough in "realism" and "candor" on television.

Remember the child's rhyme: "Sticks and stones may break my bones but words will never harm me"? In fact words can do enormous harm (and enormous good). By reflecting what we value and how we perceive life, our words act as reinforcers of those values. They announce to others what we think about blacks or gays or abortion or sex. And if we get into the habit of using words with powerfully negative, disparaging associations, we reveal certain attitudes. Words like *nigger* or *fatso* or *skinny* are not value-neutral. They are linguistic sticks and stones.

When Archie Bunker referred to Jews as "hebes," to Puerto Ricans as "spics," to homosexuals as "fruits," and to blacks as "jungle bunnies" on prime-time television, he was bound to attract a great deal of attention. To some people, he was appealing because his language reflected their values; to others, his poor grammar and many malapropisms revealed the "horse's ass" nature of his values. The point for us to take special notice of is the impact "mere words" have.

When some women first publicly complained that there was no honorific title for adult women that did not reveal their marital status, there being only *Miss* or *Mrs.,* they were identifying a strong cultural value reflected in our language. The language simply reflected the long-held belief that a woman's marital status was one of if not *the* most important thing about her, whereas a man's marital status was irrelevant (*Mr.* being the title for both married and unmarried men). Some people objected that the proposed *Ms.* was silly. They said that it was "hard to pronounce" or looked funny or that they didn't know whether to put a period after it. These were bogus objections. The real issue was over values and beliefs about the relative roles of men and women in our society. A similar discussion arose over the term *black* as a replacement for *Negro* and *colored.* It is now going on over *gay* as a replacement for *homosexual.*

In all these cases, we see that words can and do hurt us. Even though we may disagree radically over women's rights, civil rights, or gay rights, we can clearly see how words are not trivial at all. They reflect deeply held values, values we often would never question as long as our language reinforced them with ease. The next time someone says, "Well, it's only a word. I don't see what the _____ (blacks, women, gays, Hispanics, Native Americans, sanitation engineers, police officers, chairpeople, and so forth) are making such a fuss for," we will understand that words do not exist in a vacuum. Like arguments, language must be viewed in context. And language can tell us a great deal about how we and others think and believe.

Just as language can give us insight into individuals, so it can reveal information about groups. Has it ever occurred to you, for example, that we have only one word for snow and for camel? It probably hasn't. In fact, now that you have thought about it you might be inclined to ask, So what? How many words for snow and camel do you need? Lots, if you're an Eskimo or an Arab.

In fact, Eskimos have a separate word for each kind of snow: soft snow, hard-packed snow, slushy snow, wind-driven snow. And Arabic has over five thousand different names for camels, names that point up most minute differences of age, sex, and bodily structure. Similarly, although English precisely distinguishes among the multitude of flying things in our experience—birds, airplanes, kites, blimps, rockets, skydivers—Hopi, an American Indian language, has just one noun for everything airborne other than birds. Likewise, Zulus have words for white cow and red cow but none for plain old cow. And aborigines of Central Brazil have no word for parrot or palm but many names for the different varieties of parrots and palms in their experience.

The point is simple: The language of a people reflects how they see and think about things. It reveals their assumptions, biases, and interests; it discloses what's important and what's trivial in their lives.

So developing a sensitivity to language and its usage can help foster invaluable insights into ourselves and others. Such insights can be extremely helpful in understanding and analyzing arguments, in uncovering their hidden assumptions, in detecting their errors.

SEEING WHAT WE SAY (LANGUAGE AS INFLUENCING EXPERIENCE)

In recent years, the impact language has on a person's subsequent experience of things has attracted the attention of many philosophers, linguists, and semanticists (scholars primarily interested in the connection between language and one's experience of reality). The appropriate literature from these fields suggests that language can provide a kind of script or map for people to follow in how they think about and experience the world.

The simplest examples of this point can be seen in the impact of words with high emotive value. For example, words such as *politician, crisis, corpse, abortion, Communist, motherhood, liberation,* and *sex* deliver an emotional wallop to lots of people. Often our feelings are so identified with such words that their mere mention sets off an emotional reaction. The reaction may be positive or negative.

Thus, for many of us, *bureaucrat, radical,* and *pedagogue* carry a negative emotional impact. In contrast, *statesperson, moderate,* and *professor* may carry a positive one. Similarly, ethnic slang such as *spade, honky, Jap,* and *wetback* carry different emotional implications from *black, white, Japanese,* and *Mexican-American*. The importance of word choice in argument, therefore, cannot be overstated. Remember: Arguments attempt to persuade. When arguments carry emotionally "loaded" words, they can persuade, not for logical, but for psychological reasons. What's more, this effect can occur subtly.

Sometimes what purports to be strictly information carries with it an interpretation of the facts reported. If we're not careful, we may accept the interpretation along with the information. For example, suppose a journalist wished to report the presence of 50,000 illegal aliens living in Los Angeles. The journalist might write, "Fifty thousand illegal aliens are living in deserted buildings in Los Angeles." Or the journalist might write, "Fifty thousand illegal aliens are holed up in the warrens along the back alleys of lower Los Angeles." Although both statements report essentially the same fact, the second gives you a different impression from the first. Because *holed up* and *warrens* suggest rodentlike creatures, and *back alleys* reinforces the verminlike image, you might infer that these illegal aliens are unclean, perhaps a threat or a source of violence and upheaval. How the journalist chooses to report the fact can influence how we eventually interpret it.

The implications of language's impact on thought and subsequent experience are far-reaching. For example, once-polite words such as *Negro* and *colored* have rapidly vanished from contemporary American language usage. With these words have disappeared their mental associations of separatism and inferiority. Replacing *Negro* and *colored* is *black,* a descriptive term as neutral as *white* or *red*. But neutrality in this instance is a comparative victory in the black's struggle for equality. Hence, *black* represents semantic, if not social and economic, equality with *white*. And since it does not produce the mental images of separation and inferiority that *Negro* and *colored* did, it will affect our perceptions differently. The result will help create a new reality. This is already happening and is laying the basis for new assumptions about race relations—assumptions that, in turn, form the bases for thinking, reasoning, and arguing.

And so it seems with *People's Republic of China*. If we examine the periodicals of the early 1970s, we detect a change in our references to mainland

China. Whereas before this time, the news media and our leaders generally referred to mainland China as *Red China* or *Communist China,* in the early 1970s they began to speak of *the People's Republic of China.* Now, the emotional impact of *Red China* or *Communist China* is strikingly different from *the People's Republic of China.* The two former terms call up an oriental, communistic (and, therefore, in many minds atheistic) threat to the "free world." In contrast, *the People's Republic of China* simply denotes a nation. In fact, the word *republic* gives us a point of identity with China, since we are ourselves a republic. This identity is most important in fostering a new relationship with China. It helps us to start thinking about China in a way that is perceived as compatible with this new and friendlier relationship.

Consider, furthermore, the title *Ms.,* which offers mental associations distinctly different from *Mrs.* or *Miss.* The latter terms make a point of a woman's marital status. Moreover, *Mrs.* alters a woman's most intimate identification label, her name, by merging it with her husband's. Language here reveals long-standing cultural biases: The male, we seem to have assumed, has an identity; the female does not—she must borrow hers from him. The result? He receives more name recognition than she, and what receives recognition is usually what is thought important. *Ms.* balances this recognition somewhat by giving the woman a title that—like the man's—leaves marital status unannounced. Such changes are likely to affect the way we think and the way we experience the world. To those born into a society that uses exclusively *Ms.* to denote any female, such notions as the following might come more easily than if that society were using *Mrs.* or *Miss:* (1) that marriage does not mean the sacrifice of the woman's personality on the altar of male egotism; (2) that the husband-wife relationship is not one of employer employee; (3) that the marriage contract may be a commercial debasement of a unique psychophysical relationship that union between a man and a woman should foster; (4) that this psychophysical relationship might just as easily be pursued outside marriage as in; and (5) that the unmarried woman is not by definition a failure. Naturally, language alone will not bring about these new attitudes, but it can help create a soil in which such attitudes grow. And, to repeat, our attitudes usually form the assumptions from which we do much of our reasoning.

We can also observe a shift in the rhetoric of the "gay" movement. The terms *lesbian* and *homosexual* are rapidly falling into disrepute, even among those who are neither one. With the banishment of those terms go their mental associations: sexual deviance and perversion against whose threats society must be forever on guard. The term *gay* suggests mirth, liveliness, and fun. As an adjective, *gay* suggests a single quality, perhaps one among many possessed by the people it refers to, that is, those who are gay. This effect is important, since the gays wish to emphasize the *incidental* nature of their sexual preferences. What's incidental is minor; what's minor requires little attention; what requires little attention is harmless; and finally, what's harmless cannot threaten society. Therefore, this language choice advances the contention that society has no reason either legally or socially to ostracize gays. So, whether in the gay, women's, or black movements, language plays a vital role in advancing a cause. This is so because the cause identifies itself with the positive implications of the words it uses to describe itself; and through the persuasive language, the cause induces others to view reality from its viewpoint, winning sympathizers if not converts.

Language can be a most persuasive tool in advancing a position. Be wary of arguments that contain words of high emotional content. Such arguments invite a psychological, not a logical, response. This doesn't at all mean that emotive language has no place in communication. Some of our greatest literature glitters with emotive expression. It's just that in argument, we should minimize if not avoid its use altogether. Otherwise we're apt to throw reason to the winds. Also, we should be suspicious of any argument that tries to persuade us primarily on the basis of emotionally loaded words and phrases. If there are sound reasons for a position, we have a right to hear them. Indeed, we should demand them. In their absence, in the presence of emotive language, we should assume that someone is trying to manipulate our emotions to gain adherence to a position.

STUDY HINT

Emotive language is language used for the primary purpose of evoking emotions in order to influence thoughts, actions, or beliefs.

Even well-intentioned arguers can unwittingly use emotive language if they don't pay close attention to a word's meaning. And audiences can be suckered into accepting all sorts of shoddy claims if they lack sensitivity to the implications of certain words and phrases. In large part, then, we can avoid being either a victim or abuser of emotive language by learning some basics about meaning and definition.

DEFINITION AND MEANING

A *definition* is an explanation of the meaning of a term. *Meaning,* in turn, can refer to either denotation or connotation. Let's briefly consider each of these meanings of *meaning,* with an eye to their impact on argument.

Denotation

The denotation (or extension) of a term is the collection or class of objects to which the term may correctly be applied. For example, the denotation of *chair* would be any example of a chair. The denotative definition of *politician* would be an example of a politician: Ronald Reagan, Tip O'Neill, Geraldine Ferraro, and so forth. Defining denotatively is defining through example; a term is said to denote the objects it can be applied to.

Connotation

In a second sense, meaning refers to a term's connotation or intension, which can be either objective or subjective. *The objective connotation (or intension) of a term is the collection of properties shared by all and only those objects in a term's extension (denotation).* Thus, the connotation of *chair* is "a piece of furniture used to sit on." Another way of stating this is to say that in a connotative definition we ordinarily place the term being defined in a class of similar terms (pieces of furniture) and then show how it differs from them (used to sit on).

Depending on the term, we may need to specify a number of increasingly precise differences. For example, a couch is also a piece of furniture used to sit on, so we may need to specify dimensions or other factors to get an acceptable definition.

There is another kind of connotation that is of crucial importance to our study of language. *The subjective connotations of a term include the moods, images, attitudes, and values commonly or individually associated with it.* For example, we might objectively define the term *law students* as "all those individuals currently studying legal practices and procedures for the purposes of becoming licensed lawyers." But suppose that to you the term *law student* immediately calls to mind aggressive individuals willing to do anything to get into and graduate from law school. Strictly speaking, that's not part of the objective meaning of the term. On the other hand, it is the *associated meaning* you have somehow acquired for the term.

In addition to their objective connotations, then, many words acquire associated meanings. The number *1* has different subjective connotations for most of us than does *13*. *Blue* has come to be associated with emotional depression, *red* with anger or a "hot" temperament.

A young man may rankle at being called *Bobby* and insist on being called *Bob* because to him (and often to others) *Bob* has more adult associations than *Bobby*. We can all think of countless examples of various terms that actually denote the same object but in ways that reflect widely divergent values, moods, and images.

Recall Senator Washington's speech. Statements like "I believe in education" are often used to evoke favorable but deliberately vague associations. What does it really mean to "believe in education"? Does it mean that the Senator believes that education exists as in the parallel expression "I believe in God"? If so, it is a rather vacuous remark. We all know that education exists. Notice, that "believe in" is quite vague. In the Senator's speech, very little is denoted. And this is deliberate. The Senator is a master at the use of terms whose powerful subjective connotations obscure a lack of precise denotative or objective meaning.

In its place, powerfully subjective and emotive language is a wonderful way of expressing ourselves and of communicating emotions. It is part of great literature, a welcome embellishment to conversation and even to formal speeches. But we must not use empty phrases to substitute for thoughtful communication and reasonable discussion or in lieu of argument and assertion when significant matters are being decided.

It is easier to evoke feelings than it is to change someone's mind through reason. We should be on guard against the misuse of powerful phrases that create attractive or moving sentiments for the sole purpose of persuading us. The very same medical procedure can, for example, be "described" as "an abortion," "the termination of pregnancy," "medical intervention in gestation," or "murdering the baby." Obviously, the emotional impacts of the different descriptions vary markedly. That is why people with different beliefs speak differently. To one person, the procedure is "seen as" a murder, whereas to another the very same thing is "seen as" the simple termination of a pregnancy.

What we see here is just one example of the powerful effects of subjective connotations on perception and, often, behavior. The misuse of emotive language occurs when these associations are used to evoke emotions for the purposes of persuasion in a fashion that (1) makes it more difficult to think clearly because emotions are raised before an opportunity for reflection, (2) distorts events in a manner favorable to those attempting to influence us, and (3) deliberately avoids making clear assertions that can be rationally analyzed.

This misuse of the emotive power of language is deliberately vague in order to encourage us to supply the "meaning" we would like to hear. That's why Senator Washington said things like "I favor tax reform." "Tax reform" has a nice "feel" to it for most of us; we assume it means making our taxes fairer, perhaps even lowering them. But it might mean raising them or it might mean no more taxes for oil companies. We don't know because in the context of the Senator's speech, the term is denotatively imprecise—its power is in its shared positive subjective connotations.

Rules for Objective Connotation

To avoid the pitfalls of vague and ambiguous definitions, it's useful to keep in mind some basic rules. The following rules have not been chiseled in stone, although some people seem to think they have been. Frequently, exceptions should be and are made to these rules. Indeed, some authors take the view that uncritical reliance on them can obstruct the definitional process. Nonetheless, the rules, if viewed as guidelines and not commandments, do seem useful in helping us avoid vagueness and ambiguity in word usage and argument, and also for spotting what may be wrong with the word usage in arguments we encounter. For these reasons, we present them here.[1]

Rule 1: *A good connotative definition should state the essential characteristics of the term being defined.* "Essential characteristics" refers to those properties, the possession or lack of which constitutes the conventional criteria for deciding whether or not an object is denoted by a term. For example, people have agreed to use the property of being a closed plane curve all of whose points are equidistant from a point called the center as the conventional criterion for deciding whether a figure is to be called a circle. So, in defining a circle connotatively, we should list this essential characteristic. In contrast, although it is characteristic of a circle to enclose a greater area than any other plane closed figure of equal perimeter, this is not *the* property that people have agreed to mean by the term *circle*. So we shouldn't use this characteristic in defining *circle*.

Rule 2: *A good connotative definition shouldn't be circular.* A definition is circular if it defines a word in terms of itself. Thus, defining *entropic* as "of or pertaining to entropy" is a circular definition. Similarly, to say that "Poison means something that has a toxic effect" is to give a circular definition of *poison,* for *toxic* means "poisonous." In effect, we end up defining *poison* in terms of itself. In circular definitions, we usually offer definitions that are understandable only to those who already understand a term's meaning. But such definitions in no way illuminate a term's meaning for those ignorant of it.

Rule 3: *A good connotative definition should be neither too broad nor too narrow.* This rule means that definitions should not denote more or fewer things than are denoted by the term itself. Thus, to define *fragrance* as "any odor" is far too broad: Some odors are unpleasant, whereas *fragrance* means "*pleasant*

---

[1]For a thorough discussion of these rules, see Irving Copi, *Introduction to Logic* (New York: Macmillan, 1972), pp. 139–40.

odors." On the other hand, to define *coed* as "a young woman attending a high school or college that both sexes attend" is too narrow: Coeds needn't be "young."

Rule 4: *A good connotative definition shouldn't be expressed in obscure or figurative language.* Since the function of a definition is to clarify meaning, language not understandable to an audience—obscure language—does nothing to illuminate the term *meaning*. Of course, obscurity is relative: A medical definition may be "obscure" to laypersons but not to medical doctors. But in nontechnical matters, in defining for people with nontechnical backgrounds, using obscure language amounts to attempting to explain the unknown in terms of the unknown. Thus, to define *net* as "anything made with interstitial vacuities" would be obscure to all but the most technically minded technicians.

Using figurative language in definitions is just as unwise as using obscure language. Figurative language is language that's highly expressive or that contains what are called figures of speech, such as comparisons. Thus defining *architecture* as "frozen music" is quite picturesque but doesn't serve as a serious explanation. Similarly, defining *discretion* as "something that comes to a person after he's too old for it to do him any good" is amusing but unenlightening. In fact, to be amused by this figurative definition, you must have some idea of what *discretion* means.

Rule 5: *A good connotative definition should not be negative where it can be affirmative.* The rationale behind this rule is that a definition is supposed to explain what a term means, *not* what it doesn't mean. Just think of the countless things that a book or house or triangle *aren't*. Listing all those things doesn't at all indicate what *book, house,* or *triangle* means. Of course, some terms are essentially negative in meaning. *Orphan* means "a child whose parents aren't living"; *bald* means "the state of not having hair on one's head." Barring such cases, definitions should be stated affirmatively.

EXERCISE 3-2 _____
Criticize the following definitions in terms of the criteria for a good objective connotative definition.

1. A circle is a figure whose radii are equal.
2. A bad person is one who does bad things.
3. Hell is other people.
4. Heaven is where nobody goes.
5. Democracy is a government in which everybody may vote.
6. A cat is a domesticated animal having four legs.
7. Alimony means when two people make a mistake and one of them continues to pay for it. In contrast, palimony means when two people *knew* they would make a mistake and one of them continues to pay for it.
8. A star is a stellar body visible in the heavens at night.
9. A horse: "Quadruped. Graminivorous. Forty teeth, namely, twenty-four grinders, four eye teeth, and twelve incisive. Sheds coat in the spring; in marshy countries sheds hoofs, too. Hoofs hard, but requiring to be shod with iron. Age known by marks in mouth." (Charles Dickens, *Hard Times*)
10. "A cynic is one who knows the price of everything and the value of nothing." (Oscar Wilde)
11. Ornament means something not necessary for practical use.
12. "Faith is the substance of things hoped for, the evidence of things not seen." (Hebrews 11:1)

13. "Faith may be defined briefly as an illogical belief in the occurrence of the improbable." (H. L. Mencken)
14. "Economics is the science which treats of the phenomena arising out of the economic activities of men in society." (J. M. Keynes)
15. "Justice is doing one's own business, and not being a busybody." (Plato)

Additional Definitions

Although the preceding discussion addressed the spirit of most defining, it didn't by any means exhaust the various definitions that people construct. In fact, in addition to denotative and connotative definitions, we employ several others, two of which occur in arguments often enough to be mentioned here: the stipulative and persuasive definitions.

Stipulative Definitions.   Sometimes in our use of a term we depart from convention and employ it in a unique way. There's nothing wrong with such departures, as long as we explain precisely how we're using the term, that is, indicate the stipulative nature of our definition. *A stipulative definition is one that attaches unique, or at least unconventional, meaning to a term.* Thus, by *full employment* someone may mean that 4 percent or less of the work force is actively seeking employment. Similarly, by *a part-time student* someone may mean a student taking fewer than twelve semester units or its equivalent. As long as it's clear that the meanings are being stipulated and as long as the stipulative definitions aren't confused with conventional meaning, the stipulative definition is legitimate and can be valuable.

Persuasive Definitions.   We sometimes depart from conventional word usage in an attempt to pass off opinion as fact, to set down not what a term conventionally means but what the author or speaker would have it mean. Such a definition is termed persuasive. *A persuasive definition is one that departs from conventional word meaning in order to influence attitudes.*

When a word or phrase evokes certain attitudes or feelings, people sometimes want to use it to carry a connotative or intensional meaning different from its ordinary one. For example, consider a typical after-dinner discussion about just what it means to be "cultured." For the sake of argument, let's assume that a "cultured" person is one who is acquainted with the arts. What's more, since to be cultured is a mark of esteem in our society, *cultured* evokes positive attitudes or feelings. At one point in the discussion, the hostess said, "A truly cultured person isn't just acquainted with the arts but with science and technology as well." Now notice what she did. She attached a different connotative meaning to *cultured,* whereas the positive emotive meaning of the word remained the same. She, in effect, performed a kind of sleight-of-hand trick: She shifted or extended the connotation of *cultured* while its emotive meaning remained constant. What's more, she got away with it, for the others agreed: "Maybe you're right. Maybe a truly cultured person *is* acquainted with science and technology."

Many words, especially in controversial subjects such as politics, religion, the arts, and morality are subjected to this kind of manipulation, to persuasive definition. Persuasive definitions aren't necessarily objectionable, nor must we scrupulously avoid them. But we should be able to spot them. Otherwise we can be taken in by them; we can be led to unsound conclusions.[2]

A final word on the subject of persuasive definition: Any definition can serve the rhetorical purpose of influencing attitudes. For example, a person may express a stipulative definition, not only to show how a term is being used, but also to persuade. It then counts as a persuasive definition as well as a stipulative one. Indeed, any definition that serves the rhetorical purpose of influencing attitudes should count as a persuasive definition in addition to whatever other kind of definition it is.

*EXERCISE 3-3 _____
Which of the following definitions are persuasive? Which are stipulative?

1. The only true criminal is the one who commits crimes, not in the heat of passion, but calculatingly, cold-bloodedly.
2. Any real American would stand up and support the President's energy program.
3. Patriots stand by their country, right or wrong.
4. A trial by jury is the right that guarantees justice to every citizen by allowing them to be judged by their peers.
5. " 'The true,' to put it very briefly, is only the expedient in the way of our thinking, just as 'the right' is only the expedient in the way of our behaving." (William James)
6. "By good, I understand that which we certainly know is useful to us." (Baruch Spinoza)
7. "Political power, properly so called, is merely the organized power of one class for oppressing another." (Karl Marx and Friedrich Engels)
8. "Political power, then, I take to be a right of making laws with penalties of death, and consequently all less penalties, for the regulating and preserving of property, and of employing the force of the community in the execution of such laws, and in defense of the commonwealth from foreign injury, and all this only for the public good." (John Locke)

OBSCURE LANGUAGE USE

When language conceals more than it reveals, it is said to obscure. One meaning of *obscure* is "to cover up." Three particular language uses are especially likely to obscure the truth: euphemism, slang, and jargon. Let's see how they relate to clear thinking and logical arguments.

Euphemism

A euphemism is a polite way of saying the offensive, harsh, or blunt. Thus, instead of *lying*, we *fib*; rather than *fighting* a *war*, we *engage* in a *conflict*. We don't *cheat* on our spouses, we *have affairs*. When the Reagan administration wanted to weaken the support of Libyan dictator Moammar Kadafi, by implying that extensive military action against him was being planned—when in fact no such action was planned—it waged what administration spokespersons called a campaign of *disinformation*. Public figures caught in public lies now speak of *misspeaking*.

[2]See John Hospers, *An Introduction to Philosophical Analysis* (Englewood Cliffs, N.J.: Prentice-Hall, 1967), pp. 53–54.

Euphemisms gloss over unpleasant facts or add dignity to undignified circumstances, positions, events, or conditions. Reality gets buried under euphemism; it's hard to see. Thus, a couple can gloss over the reality of promiscuous and irresponsible sex by referring to the main event of a one-night encounter as *making love*. A coach can gloss over an athlete's brutality by calling it *aggressive*. Ideologies can minimize illegal, unconstitutional, and dangerous actions by attributing them to "overzealousness." Euphemisms affect their users as well as their audiences. As a result of their power to distort reality, euphemisms are widely used; they are not to be taken lightly.

To better understand how euphemism can persuade is to understand that euphemism reveals the assumptions of its users and their culture. In the realm of sexual behavior, for example, we have a long history of puritanism, which many think has left us with sexual inhibitions. The legion of sexual euphemisms we use to speak around the subject of sex reflects this attitude. People have *affairs* and *make love*. For some the *stork* still delivers *bundles of joy,* who grow up to have *steadies*—even *steady steadies*—with whom they *neck, pet,* and, well, *make love*. But euphemism in this area is not confined to sexual activity; it seems to enshroud most activity that involves sexual areas of the body.

We have created, accordingly, a whole list of terms to substitute for *toilet,* a term denoting a room or booth containing a disposal apparatus consisting of a hopper, fitted with a flushing device, used for urination and defecation. Outside the home this room is often referred to as the *men's* or *ladies' room*. At home *bathroom* is used most frequently, even to denote rooms containing neither bath nor shower. At different times in our lives and in various places, we encounter *lavatory, washroom, can, jake, john,* and *head. Toilet paper* masks as *toilet tissue, bathroom tissue,* or simply *tissue paper*. Ads for laxatives avoid the offensive *constipation* for the more polite *irregularity*. ("When irregularity strikes, reach for. . . .") Even sanitary napkin advertisements are scrupulous in avoiding their reason for existence: menstruation. Instead, their makers talk in hushed terms of "that time of the month"; their appeals rely more often on fear and embarrassment than on hygiene. Hence, the main problem with euphemism in argument is that when we feel that a word is offensive, we are inclined to talk around the word and what it represents. In doing this, we permit arguments to assume all kinds of erroneous appeals.

Consider this:

> Why not do something about your problem breath before you don't even have a best friend who wouldn't tell you about it? Use FRESH—the mouthwash for those who want to keep their best friends and *make* a lot more.

Can you spot the euphemism in this ad? It's *problem breath*. Precisely what does this phrase mean? Since it doesn't say "temporary bad breath," we can't assume that the ad refers to the scent that onions, garlic, and the like leave in our mouths. *Problem breath* seems to mean a chronic, persistent foulness of breath that resists normal hygienic practices such as tooth brushing. But is such a problem a breath problem? More likely the problem originates in the esophagus or stomach and signals a far more serious condition than the euphemism *problem breath* would indicate. We are led to make mistaken assumptions about the origin of the problem and thus to another mistaken assumption—that the advertised product can cure it.

> *STUDY HINT:* **THE *PRIMARY* PURPOSE OF EUPHEMISM IS TO GLOSS OVER SOMETHING THAT TROUBLES US BECAUSE WE VIEW IT AS UNPLEASANT OR THREATENING.**
>
> We should be wary of euphemisms in discussing important matters since their function is to conceal rather than to reveal.

In talking around this "delicate" problem, in being so vague, the ad relies on emotion, not correct reasoning, to make its appeal. The ad generates and preys on fear; it magnifies the social importance of the problem and simplifies its cure. Do people with bad breath necessarily lose their best friends, as the ad predicts? Do best friends *never* mention problem breath to us? Would they then be best friends? Is problem breath in fact the cause of broken friendships? Finally, in assuming that even a best friend wouldn't tell a person about problem breath, the ad plays on our fear of offending without knowing it. Such appeals breed in the soil of euphemism.

Let's look at another example to see how euphemism pollutes reasoning. Most of us are probably familiar with preneed burial plots, which are often pitched with claims like this: "When your time has come, will you be ready? Or will you only be ready to pass on a financial burden to the dear ones you leave behind?"

Consider what this ad would say stripped of its euphemism. Perhaps "When you die, will your family have enough money to bury you?" Of course, the chances of getting a "no" response with this question are far less than with "When your time has come, will you be ready?" The reason is that the ad capitalizes on the fear and anxiety that death holds for many of us. After all, no one is ever *ready* to die. True, some of us are eager enough to commit suicide or so ill that we wish we were dead. But this is being *desperate,* not *ready.* Undoubtedly, the ad is referring to *economic* readiness. But by first asking whether we'll be ready when our time comes, it predisposes us to the resounding "No!"; it seeks to make the pitch for preneed plots. Then, it places us in a dilemma of being "ready" or only "ready to pass on a financial burden."

The fact is that most of us probably lie (no pun intended) somewhere in between: We've salted away some money but not quite enough for the bash we think we'd want, need, or deserve or will have imposed on us, like it or not, *ready* or not.

"Dear ones"—how's that for a euphemism? *Dear ones* has more emotional appeal and is more guilt-laden than that straight *family.* And the term *pass on* allows a ghoulish play on the most common euphemism for death.

Now consider the ad without the euphemisms: "When you die, will your family have enough money to bury you?" There's nothing in that question that clouds our reasoning or obscures our deliberation. Nor is there anything in the question that appeals to fear, pity, or guilt. In short, such a question invites a *rational* assessment of our finances, not an *emotional* one. Indeed, it may even invite this most important question: "Just how much money does a person *really* need to be buried?" That, in turn, might encourage us to assess rationally the rather common practice of putting the living in hock to bury the dead.

What, then, can we say of euphemism? First, euphemism tends to reflect what we think about things such as sex and death. These viewpoints often serve as assumptions for arguments, particularly in the form of commercial pitches. Second, euphemism introduces emotion and obscurity into argument. By capitalizing on our fears and insecurities and other feelings, euphemism inevitably elicits an emotional, not a rational, response.

EXERCISE 3-4 _____
Give the noneuphemistic equivalent of the following expressions:

1. to pass away
2. to go to the bathroom
3. make love
4. in a family way
5. senior citizen
6. powder room
7. to terminate an employee
8. to terminate with extreme prejudice
9. the dearly departed
10. a woman's time of the month

*EXERCISE 3-5 _____
Provide your own examples of euphemisms for the following:

1. bad breath
2. sexual intercourse
3. being overweight
4. being underweight
5. being rich
6. a corpse
7. stealing
8. boring
9. lying
10. marital infidelity

EXERCISE 3-6 _____
Find five advertisements that capitalize on euphemisms in their appeals. Translate the euphemistic appeals into straightforward language. Do any of the ads lose their appeal? Why?

Slang

Most of us use slang. What can slang tell you about yourself? Where does slang come from?

We don't raise these questions only because slang is a fascinating topic. We raise them because slang reports how we see the world and ourselves. And what relates to the way we see, our perception, also relates to the way we reason. To find out precisely how slang relates to reasoning, we must learn a few things about slang itself.

Generally speaking, we can define _slang_ as _the language that a large portion of a group often uses and always understands but that most do not consider good, formal usage_. We Americans seem to like slang more than most people. At least we use it enough; about 25 percent of the words we use most frequently are slang words. Slang, in fact, has three characteristics that seem peculiarly American and may explain our use of it. Stuart Flexner, in the preface to his *Dictionary of American Slang,* lists them: (1) Slang is simple, quick, and forceful; (2) slang springs from subgroups; and (3) slang never intellectualizes or moralizes.[3] Let's focus our discussion on these three traits.

First, slang is a simple, quick, and forceful way of communicating. It is verbal quick justice: It's a no-nonsense approach that doesn't allow for "pussyfootin' " around and always "shoots from the hip." It is short, clipped, and pointed.

Spic, hebe, and *gook* in one word reveal more of the user's mental, psychological, and social background than most long autobiographical statements could. This ethnic slang can express where we stand and where our loyalties lie. By using such slang to refer to a person, the speaker attempts to extend the meanings of Puerto Rican, Jew, and Vietnamese to include the mental associations these words evoke. But not all slang is ethnic.

Less vicious but equally thoughtless are *dope, clown, freak, klutz, weirdo,* and the many others that come and go in language usage and allow us to draw quickly and pungently sharp social lines between ourselves and the targets of our slang. Thus, calling someone a *fag, queer, fruit,* or *flit*—slang for homosexual—probably does more to reinforce our own sexual identity than to identify another's behavior.

A second characteristic of slang is that it originates in the subgroup. A social subgroup, or subculture, is a separate and distinct division within a larger "dominate culture." Members of a subculture share certain clearly defined values, beliefs, and norms. Little wonder that we have such an abundance and variety of slang no other country contains such a diversity of subcultures. Slang, in fact, helps define them, helps give each a sense of identity. Where union and identity with the larger group is impossible or unwanted, slang helps the subgroup to identify itself, to unite itself. It can also keep a group separate and distinct.

Today it is not uncommon to be a member of many subgroups: student, veteran, single parent, taco maker, aerobicist. Our loyalties tend toward the group with which we most identify, the one most important to our self-image.[4] We will use the language of that subgroup to demonstrate group loyalty, and to help define who we are. The flappers did this in the Roaring Twenties, the beats in the 1950s, and the hippies in the late 1960s. Today, punkers do it; even Valley Girls had their own slang ("Gag us with a spoon!").

It's hard to resist the freshness, originality, and informality of slang. It's especially hard to resist slang when we are confused about who we are, when we feel threatened by absorption into or rejection by the dominant group (the "establishment," or the "man"). This is why so much slang is now associated with adolescence—that turbulent period of inconsistency: rebellion/insecurity, individuality/fear of individuality, identity/lack of a clear sense of identity. Because slang itself is so often dynamic, forceful, and vital, it has a special appeal for those who feel threatened and overlooked.

At least part of slang's vitality is due to its tendency to oversimplify things because, as Flexner reminds us, slang almost never intellectualizes or moralizes.

[3]Stuart Flexner and Harold Wentworth, eds., *Dictionary of American Slang,* 2d ed. (New York: Crowell, 1967), pp. ii–vii.
[4]Review the discussion in Chapter 2 on how self-concept affects logical thinking.

It concentrates instead almost entirely on social acceptance or rejection. In the value system of slang, it is much more important to be part of the group than it is to think carefully about ideas or values.

Just consider this not too unrealistic conversation between two real "hunks" about a couple of "foxy chicks": "Hey, look at those two pieces!" "Yeah! Boy would I like to get a little off that blonde. I bet she could do it all night." "An all-nighter! Wow! I bet I can get a little off that pig with her. Owwooooo!"

Of course the entire value system reflected here is one that not only dehumanizes the young women being described, but also degrades the young men as well. It reduces all of them to something nonhuman, perhaps even inanimate in some cases. It reduces them all to functions of the sexual appetite of the two males. And young men, even today, feel group pressure to be "macho," to be "studs," and to conform to this value system if they want to belong to the "men's club." It is relatively difficult—if it is not downright impossible— to have a truly enriching relationship on any level between a hunk and a chick, a fox and a stud. (Think about it.)

By failing to deal straightforwardly with ideas and with moral values, slang is inadequate for addressing value judgments. "Yeah, man, that Nicaragua deal— what a drag, y'know." "Abortion, wow, that's a real downer." "This child abuse stuff really bums me out." Such claims can mean almost anything from the reflection of personal tastes to significant, verifiable claims subject to rational analysis. We don't know, however, exactly what they mean.

The overuse or inappropriate use of slang diminishes our capacity for thoughtful discussion. Because of its breezy, informal nature, slang tends to trivialize whatever it touches. Sometimes this may be appropriate, or at least relatively innocuous. But at other times, slang interferes with a reasoned and responsible approach to an issue.

Slang reflects a particular subgroup's partisan and self-serving world view: It reinforces the belief that "we" are superior to "them." It distorts reality and muddles thinking. It is primarily a tool of identification, used primarily to aid group membership. Because group affiliation is of paramount importance, other factors like morals, accuracy, and thoroughness become of lesser importance, if they are viewed as important at all. Slang casts value judgments into the twilight zone of vagueness and imprecision. We encountered the same problem with euphemism. But nowhere is it more evident than with the third of our obscure language usages: jargon.

STUDY HINT: **TO SAY THAT SLANG NEVER INTELLECTUALIZES OR MORALIZES DOES NOT MEAN THAT IT DOES NOT REFLECT THE SUBGROUP'S VALUES.**

Many—if not most—slang expressions *suggest* moral or other values, but in a vague, sloppy way. Thus, dealing with such values is difficult until they are cast in clearer language.

---

*EXERCISE 3-7 _____

How many slang expressions can you think of for the following academic phenomena?

1. study diligently for an exam
2. study intensely for a short period of time

3. an easy college course
4. a difficult college course
5. a remedial college course
6. cheat during a test
7. fail
8. get an A
9. an unexpected test
10. a stupid student
11. curry favor with a professor
12. a serious student
13. an attempt to pad the length of a term paper
14. a college athlete
15. miss a class deliberately

EXERCISE 3-8 _____

What do the following slang expressions connote to you?

1. stag
2. drag
3. dork
4. nerd
5. wimp
6. hunk
7. fox
8. my old man
9. my old lady
10. snow job
11. kissy
12. rad
13. blast
14. weird
15. Stay cool, my man.

*EXERCISE 3-9 _____

1. List as many slang expressions as you can think of that describe an effeminate young man.
2. List as many slang expressions as you can think of that describe a masculine young woman.
3. Which list is longer? What do you think that tells us about our values in general?

EXERCISE 3-10 _____

1. How many slang expressions can you think of that describe a state of alcoholic intoxication?
2. How many slang expressions can you think of that deal with other kinds of drugs and their use?
3. What do you think the connection between drug use and this slang might be?

*EXERCISE 3-11 _____

Most new slang words result from new conditions in society. The automobile, for example, produced *gas buggy, jalopy, bent eight, straight six, Chevy,* and *convertible,* as well as encouraged *dusters, hitchhikers, road hogs, necking, chicken,* and *suburbia.* What slang can you attribute to the following sources:

1. music in general
2. rock music
3. jazz

4. classical music
5. country and western music
6. rhythm and blues
7. food and eating
8. science and technology

EXERCISE 3-12 _____

What other examples of slang do you know? Why do you think a student's slang vocabulary is large? Why do you think the seventeen-to-twenty-four-year-old group coins more slang expressions than any other in society?

Jargon

British essayist and historian Thomas Carlyle once wrote, "Wholly a blessed thing: when jargon might abate, and . . . genuine speech begin." Although, as Carlyle suggests, jargon is meaningless language, we will define *jargon* as *the technical language of a trade, profession, or membership*.

Although slang and jargon are found in subgroups, they are quite different. First, slang has a certain raciness about it not found in jargon. But even more important, whereas slang is always considered substandard, that is, inappropriate on formal writing and speaking occasions, jargon is acceptable discourse in many respectable circles. Indeed, jargon seems to be a universal characteristic of formal occasions! This social acceptance makes jargon particularly menacing to the logician. As an illustration, let's consider a staff memo recently typed for a college president:

> The need for communication between the echelons of education has never been as great as it is today. What with student unrest, faculty unionization, administrative accountability, and citizen involvement, it behooves any college president to set into motion machinery that will provide for a free and open dialogue among all parties committed to the goal of better education for all. Some think that the single most serious problem confronting schools today is to meet the needs of the community. But this is impossible unless we learn what those needs are, and we can only do this by relating to the community at large and allowing them to relate to us. Only through such a sensitive interchange can we hope to reach the nitty-gritty of this basically existential problem and so root out the paranoid distrust that all too often destroys communication on a relevant, meaningful level among all parties concerned. Today's whole educational thrust is toward greater awareness of individual needs, and it's with this in mind that I am creating a new administrative office, hereafter to be known as Director of Communication, whose job it will be to break down many of the barriers that have prevented real dialogue in the past among concerned parties. Any suggestions you may have to facilitate this critical responsibility would be greatly appreciated. (You will find forms in my office for your ideas—leave the white one with my secretary, send the pink one to the Director of Public Affairs, and give the blue one to your Department Chairperson. You may file the yellow one.)

It would be hard to find a better example of the unfortunate use to which we often put our precious forests. This is not to imply that the problems that urge such a memo are not real and pressing; they are. But how many of the president's sentences are intelligible, let alone precise enough to evaluate for truth? Surely, intelligibility is necessary if the staff is to understand, argue with, and act on the message.

If you examine the memo, you'll see that it contains catchwords from various professions—social science, psychology, philosophy. Also, despite the tedium it puts us through, the memo contains words and phrases probably familiar enough to us to woo our hearts, if not our minds.

STUDY HINT: **THE MISUSE OF JARGON OCCURS WHEN TECHNICAL TERMS ARE USED OUTSIDE OF THE FIELD TO WHICH THEY BELONG AND/OR FOR PURPOSES OF IMPRESSING WITHOUT CLARIFYING.**

There is a proper and valuable use of jargon. Indeed, most special fields require a precisely defined jargon for purposes of quick, accurate communication. However, terms that may be clear and precise in one context may be unclear and misleading in another.

EXAMPLE: We have already learned some helpful logical jargon: valid, sound, and the like.

No doubt the language here was once forceful, but indiscriminate use has weakened it, reduced it to gibberish. Yet this failing often goes unnoticed and unmentioned by those who read such a memo. Even though the president probably doesn't know what he's said, certainly he feels he's said the right thing. And some of his readers may feel the president has things "well in hand." That's the danger.

Consider that the president senses no need to define "citizen involvement," "free and open dialogue," "needs of the community," "relating to the community," "sensitive interchange," "nitty-gritty," "existential problem," "paranoid distrust," "relevant," or "meaningful level." The new post is supposed to satisfy all the needs the president has listed. But this is unlikely, for its charge is not clear and specific enough to give direction. If we had to evaluate performance a year later, what criteria would we use? Probably our criteria would be as vague as the duties of the "Director of Communication."

In fact, if we had to choose one word to characterize jargon, it would be *vague.* To be vague is to be imprecise. A word is vague when its meaning is obscure and blurred. This usually results when the connection between the word and what it's supposed to stand for is uncertain. Thus, *citizen involvement, sensitive interchange,* and *nitty-gritty* are vague. So is the rest of the jargon. The same

B.C. **BY JOHNNY HART**

By permission of Johnny Hart and Creators Syndicate, Inc.

applies to euphemism and slang. Each of these language uses is vague, though admittedly persuasive. They are persuasive primarily because they carry high emotive overtones; they win our minds by capturing our hearts.

Of course, when we use words imprecisely we risk not being understood. Maybe at times we'd rather not be understood; many persons in public life seem so predisposed. But most of us probably want to be understood most of the time. And we'd like to be *understood,* not misunderstood. When we use language in such a way that it can mean more than one thing, we court misunderstanding. When we use language with high emotive value, we invite emotion, not reason, into the argument. In fact, careless language leads to specific errors in argument. These we'll consider in the next chapters. However, it's fitting here to take a brief look at three forms of the misuse of jargon that can hinder clear thinking— indeed, that are often deliberately used for just that purpose.

Buzzwords.   The expression *buzzwords* has been attributed to Edmund G. "Jerry" Brown, Jr., a former governor of California. Brown was referring to the use of words that, although vague, ambiguous, and often devoid of content in a particular context, had a dynamic, exciting "feel" to them. They generated a kind of "buzz," but they meant nothing.

Buzzwords are vague words and phrases that create an impression of action, dynamism, and vitality without actually denoting anything. Examples include the *misuse* of expressions such as *exciting concept, meaningful interchange, new coalition,* and *moral majority.* The use of such terms does not necessarily imply the presence of buzzwords. We must always take context and intention into account. Both are important.

Terms that create a "buzz" one season may be dated the next. Buzzwords must be constantly changed: They need to be perceived as "fresh" and "exciting"—two still commonly overused buzzwords.

When a talk show host on a stale TV show says, "We have an exciting show for you folks tonight," *exciting* is probably a buzzword. In political circles, the vague expression *tax reform* has been used as a buzzword. Terms like *democracy, wonderful, marvelous, beautiful,* even *God,* are prime candidates for buzzwords. Buzzwords make us feel good; they make us feel alert, dynamic, part of something exciting and vibrant, without actually saying much at all. In other words, they substitute exciting feelings for meaningful communication.

And as is true in so many cases of the misuses of language, buzzwords are used to encourage us to feel that the speaker agrees with us in a vague way so that he or she can avoid making any specific commitment. The advantages of buzzwords for those who use them are that exciting language can substitute for sound reasoning, and the less specific a claim, the more difficult it is to criticize—not because it is well supported but because there is nothing there to analyze.

Puffery.   *Puffery* is an old term. One of the meanings of *puff* is "to inflate with air or pride." *Puffery is the use of obscure, technical, or complex words and grammar for the purpose of inflating the content of a claim.* In other words, puffery is a snow job.

For example, some academic administrators now refer to students as *ed-*

ucational consumers. This sounds more impressive than the common word *students*. It also tells us something about how these administrators view students, education, and their roles in it.

One tip-off to puffery is that two words are used when one will do, three are even better, and so on. Best of all, the words should be impressive: Technical jargon from the sciences and technology is especially prized. So are any expressions that are just out of the grasp of the ordinary person's vocabulary. (No, the correct use of jargon by your professors is not puffery—though professors have been known to succumb to the tendency to impress and dazzle their students with pretentious language. When the purpose is to impress rather than to communicate clearly, however, puffery is present—even among professors.)

In a brochure for a $29.95 "Limited Edition" pocket watch, we find this: "Designed in the traditional style of the finely crafted pocket watches carried by people of taste and distinction for centuries, each of these true collector's items is also a fine quartz-accurate chronometer. . . ." What does it mean to say "designed in the traditional style of finely crafted pocket watches"? Does it mean that these watches are themselves finely crafted? It *might*—but then again, it might not. This "might or might not" is the charm of vagueness (assuming your wish is to obscure, not to reveal). We are, it seems, meant to *assume* that this is a finely crafted watch.

Interestingly enough, however, in the three enclosures that accompany this colorful brochure, not one single word is mentioned about any warranty for this watch. Is that perhaps a hint? What exactly is it to "design" something "in the traditional style of finely crafted pocket watches"? Does "design" mean "thought out," crafted by watchmakers, manufactured? And what is "quartz-accurate"? Is it the same thing as highly accurate? It *might be* (there's that vagueness again)—but it might not be. Aren't many of those inexpensive watches given away with laundry detergent and magazine subscriptions built around a "quartz-accurate" microchip? And, of course, "chronometer" is just a pretentious word for watch in this case. In other words, the brochure never really says that this *is* a fine watch at all!

Sadly, this example is of a common sort. We find such advertising puffery everywhere. That is why we should always try to find out as much as we can about claims made to tout a product. Is the term "rack and pinion steering" used to designate a type of steering mechanism or is it used to imply that this particular car has superior handling characteristics? "Motoguzzle Buzzer 210—rack and pinion steering, disk brakes, 4-ply tires, all original equipment." When such technical terms are used out of context chiefly to impress a general audience that is unlikely to understand fully their meanings, they cease being technical jargon and become jargon misused as puffery.

Psychobabble. *Psychobabble* is a term coined by writer R. D. Rosen[5] in his book of the same name. It refers to the misuse of technical terms from various forms of psychotherapy, psychological and self-help systems, and the social sciences. We will define *psychobabble* as *the misuse of psychological terms and expressions referring to inner states and feelings*.

[5]R. D. Rosen, *Psychobabble* (New York: Atheneum, 1978).

Our definition is rather general, because, as Rosen points out, psychobabble is part of a particular cultural outlook. On the surface, it is the language of "real dialogue," of "meaningful interchanges," of "sharing our space." Upon reflection it proves to be ambiguous and misleading.

Certainly not every use of such expressions is troublesome. Rosen's basic point, however, is that psychobabble—like puffery, jargon, slang, and euphemism—both reflects and reinforces a particular value orientation and corresponding way of dealing with the world. Of special interest to our study of logic is Rosen's claim that "to the psychobabbling mentality all behavior is a matter of taste."[6] In the sense that Rosen means, psychobabble is devoid of objective, independent standards, since whatever feels right is right.

Psychobabble is the language of feelings carried to an extreme. Each individual becomes the sole arbiter of everything. Examples of psychobabble include such expressions as "it may not be valid to you, but reincarnation is valid to me." "It's not part of my reality, so it's not true for me." "You can be anything you want to be." "If I can tell you the truth, just lay it out there, then I have totally opened up a space for you to be who you are and that really opens up all the room in the world for us to do whatever we want to do in regard to each other."[7]

What does it mean to "really open up all the room in the world for us to do whatever we want to in regard to each other"? Does "whatever we want to" include *anything at all*? If it does, we have entered the realm of moral and legal danger. Psychobabble sounds and often feels warm, open, life affirming, even wholesome. But upon reflection, it turns out to be vague, ambiguous, evasive, and, Rosen claims, self-centered.

You may have noticed that psychobabble, puffery, and buzzwords often occur together. Indeed, sometimes there is no clear line separating them. What is important here is for us to develop a sensitivity to language used to obscure unpleasant facts; to puff up thin ideas or shoddy goods until they appear to be substantial; to disguise shallow self-centeredness under the mantle of openness, of heartfelt, loving criticism; or to elevate a refusal to make moral distinctions to the level of wisdom.

With a little effort, we can find countless examples of language uses that hinder our efforts to be clear thinkers. By identifying some of the more common ones, we have taken the first step toward avoiding the pitfalls they lay out for us.

EXERCISE 3-13 _____

1. Look at a recent issue of *Vital Speeches*. How much jargon do you find in some of the speeches?
2. During the next local, state, or national election campaign, pay close attention to the campaign ads and flyers. See how many examples of buzzwords, puffery, or jargon-type ambiguity you can find.
3. Watch some television interview shows. Keep a list of the jargon you hear. (Do the same thing for news conferences and speeches.)
4. Examine one of your textbooks for jargon. Distinguish between examples of useful jargon and vague or ambiguous jargon.

[6]Ibid.
[7]Ibid.

5. Students often "b.s." their way through exams. Is this a form of jargonizing? Examine one of your own essays that you think is a good example of "throwing the bull." Do you find any jargon in it? Do you think the instructor was "taken in" by your technique? If so, what does this say about your instructor? What, if anything, does it say about the human susceptibility to be gulled by jargon?

6. Examine advertisements in print form from magazines, newspapers, and brochures for the presence of puffery and jargon. List the copywriters' jargon and then provide your own straightforward translation.

7. New technologies often provide us with new jargon. For example, jargon now in common use includes such terms as *input, data, programming,* and the like. Make a short list of some of the most common jargon-type terms in use today.

8. Consult one or two "self-help" books for examples of psychobabble. Translate your examples into clear-cut, ordinary English.

SOCIETY AND TRUTH

In the 1950s social psychologist Solomon Asch conducted some ground-breaking experiments dealing with an individual's responses to group or peer pressure.[8] Among his surprising findings was the discovery of the extent to which individuals could be pressured into "seeing" what a group of strangers *said* was real even when that contradicted the immediate perceptions of the individual. The individuals in Asch's experiments often trusted the group's claims over their own perceptions.

This is a troubling discovery since it means that many of us are more highly susceptible to group pressure than we might expect. Most interesting of all, the experiment involved the most basic kind of evaluation: looking and seeing for ourselves. If people actually thought they "saw" something that was clearly not correct in a simple experiment involving something as basic as the lengths of various lines, what pressures might they be susceptible to in graver matters: moral pressures, political pressures, religious pressures?

Asch speculated that the need to belong—coupled with a tendency to simply assume that if we alone disagreed with the majority, we must be wrong—explained our willingness to distort the evidence of our own senses until we were in agreement with the false claims of the group. Imagine, then, what pressures we might feel in areas more significant, complex, and abstract than simply looking at two lines?

Twenty years later, Stanley Milgram conducted his now famous "electric shock" experiments.[9] You may have studied these elsewhere. Although no actual electric shocks were administered, Milgram found that significant numbers of "typical" college students could be coerced into administering what they believed to be painful, even dangerous, electric shocks to other students, selected, so they believed, at random as part of a psychology department experiment. The significance of Milgram's experiment also lies in the triviality of its conditions. If people were so susceptible in an experiment, what, he wondered, might they

---

[8]Solomon E. Asch, "Group Forces in the Modification and Distortion of Judgments," reprinted in *Conformity, Resistance, and Self-Determination: The Individual and Authority,* Richard Flacks, ed. (Boston: Little, Brown, 1973), pp. 39–49.

[9]Stanley Milgram, "Some Conditions of Obedience and Disobedience to Authority," ibid., pp. 25–38.

do if pressured by a totalitarian government or out of fear for their own safety or by a strong belief in a political or religious mandate?

Both experiments demonstrate something we all know and experience daily: We feel strong pressures to belong, to go along, not to rock the boat. Suppose, for example, that you are the lone holdout on a jury. Everyone else is certain that the defendant is guilty. You have been sequestered for days, and fatigue and a desire to go home are strong. The pressure to go along must be enormous. To what extent might such pressure affect your judgment?

The point is that as members of a democratic society, we have a general obligation to "tell it like we see it," to paraphrase the notorious Howard Cosell. A democracy rests on the principle that each citizen votes and speaks the truth as he or she can best determine it. Good friendships and family relationships are also best served by sensitive candor. So are our jobs. We saw the devastating effects of group pressure in the 1986 space shuttle tragedy that took seven lives. Although a few courageous individuals insisted on postponing that fatal launch, more were pressured by fear of losing face, fear of being fired or demoted, and the like. They "saw" what it was safe, polite, or popular to see or not see.

We should not overlook the power of such fears. On the personal front, it is risky to tell the truth about our spouse's new hairdo or Mom's new novel. Yet the benefits of truthfulness are clear. Avoiding what is unpleasant does not change it—there were serious design flaws in the space shuttle whether or not they were acknowledged. Ditto the so-called "Iran initiative."

We have gotten used to being lied to by public officials who, when caught in a deception, claim to have "mispoken." *Mispoken* is a euphemism for "lied." Imagine what would happen if Junior, caught in a lie about breaking Dad's favorite lamp said, "Gee, Dad, I mispoke myself." Or more in keeping with the times: "Gee, Dad, that was just disinformation."

Most of us feel betrayed when a friend says, "You know, I really didn't like that poem you wrote, but I didn't want to hurt your feelings." And what of the personal and social harm that follows from lying to ourselves when we use the euphemism *make love* to describe sexual intercourse. We imply that it is possible to "make love" to the attractive stranger we met two hours ago at a dance. Or perhaps we "sleep together" or "spend the night." Responsible sexual conduct is difficult if we cannot even talk about it candidly without having to resort either to euphemism or slang.

No matter how sound the justification offered for social lies, the ultimate price is high. We have, sadly, accepted political lies, lies from the news media, from our friends, from our doctors, even from ourselves as part of life. A doctor may rationalize not telling a patient of a fatal disease because "There's no point in depressing him; he's going to die anyway." Yet this deprives a dying man of making peace with family and friends, of making or altering a will, and so on. And yet, most of us feel angry and hurt whenever we discover that others have lied to us—even when they claim it was "for our own good."

It is clear that the quality of our lives and the world in which we live depends on the best clear assessment of reality possible. Social lies, group pressure, advertising and political exaggeration—all diminish that quality. To the extent that we distort the truth that we see—for any reason—we become less likely to make sound judgments. When this happens we are more at the mercy of chance and others than we need to be.

There are kind ways to tell the truth. And sometimes being honest is risky.

It may cost us a friendship or a job. But in the long run, there is more peace of mind and more chance of making sound judgments in direct proportion to our truthfulness as a culture and as individuals.

Euphemisms, slang, and jargon may have their places. But they are each language uses that should be carefully controlled and used in moderation. Clear thinking and clear speaking go together. And though we cannot always be "right," we can minimize the likelihood of being wrong by being honest with ourselves and others. Scientific progress, as one example, requires the honest reporting of experimental findings. Good marriages, to cite another example, thrive on honest communication. A good grade in logic might require you to ask honest questions of your instructor—even if your friends all appear to understand what's going on. In fact, if your class is typical, many of your classmates will probably silently thank you for having the wisdom and courage to speak out instead of pretending to understand.

The truth is the best source we have for living good lives. Anything that creates habits of distortion, denial, phony agreement, or exaggeration for the purpose of substituting emotions, vague hopes and promises, or prejudices for an honest assessment of issues interferes with good thinking.

We shall continue to see throughout our study of logic in the practical dimension that logical concerns are best understood in the context of real life. There are very practical reasons for demanding honesty from ourselves and others. We must begin with how we speak and write, and with careful analysis of what is spoken and written to us, for language is the heart of logic. To the extent that we accept vague, ambiguous language, we settle for unclear thinking. To the extent that our thinking is unclear, we lose control and influence over our own lives. And although perfect precision and absolute clarity are not always possible, improvement is. The study of logic is a valuable tool for life, not just something of academic interest.

Remember the acronym GIGO (garbage in, garbage out): The best logic in the world cannot overcome false information. There are very few reasons for avoiding the truth. There are, perhaps, no good reasons for avoiding it.

With that in mind, let's turn now to the study of some common errors in reasoning that are called informal fallacies.

SUMMARY

This chapter dealt with the connection between language and logic. We learned how closely what we think and what we perceive are connected to language: Language reflects thought and language influences experience. We learned about denotation and connotation, emphasizing the power of subjective connotations to persuade without argument. We also reviewed some of the more basic rules for connotative definitions as well as persuasive and stipulative definitions.

Next, we turned to the study of obscure language use, which conceals more than it reveals. Obscure language use is a widespread hindrance to clear thinking. We singled out three such uses to illustrate how language reveals what we think we see, how we feel, what we want to see, and what we want others to see: euphemism, slang, and jargon. Euphemism is a polite way of saying the blunt. Because it avoids reality and reinforces basic assumptions about reality, it hinders logical analysis. Slang is the language used and understood by a large portion of a group, but it is not considered good formal usage. Its primary function is social: group acceptance and loyalty. Of concern to us is slang's tendency to obscure intellectual and moral evaluations and to rank group allegiance over a clear view of reality. Jargon is the technical language of a trade group, profession, or academic discipline. Used outside of narrowly confined limits, jargon, like slang and euphemism, is inevitably vague. We also looked at three subcategories of jargon: buzzwords, puffery, and psychobabble. Buzzwords attempt to create an aura of dynamic vitality, puffery attempts to create an aura of precision and profundity, and psychobabble creates an aura of psychological insight. All three forms of jargon are fraudulent for they are used to manipulate, persuade, and impress—without regard for accuracy. We finished with a look at society's general obligation to the truth. We saw how social and emotional pressure to belong is so powerful that we sometimes do things we don't want to, and more frighteningly, *see* things that aren't there—just to belong. Throughout the chapter we saw the stunning power of emotive language to influence us. Words with high emotive impact can persuade for psychological, not logical, reasons. And excessively vague and obscure language is fertile ground for emotionally charged expressions.

Summary Questions

1. Read the list of ingredients on a product label. How helpful is the technical language used on such lists. Try to find the meaning of some of these technical terms.
2. What conclusions, if any, can you draw about our culture based on the fact that most of our euphemisms are about sex, death, and bodily functions?
3. Under what conditions might the use of euphemisms be acceptable? Why?

ADDITIONAL EXERCISES _____

1. In Nootka, a language of Vancouver Island, all words are what we'd call verbs. Thus, "a house occurs" or "it houses" is the way to say house. By adding a suffix to the verb, the Nootka designate the duration of the event: "long-lasting house"; "temporary house"; "future house." Would this usage encourage the speaker of such a language to see reality as fluid or static? Why?
2. Construct a short dialogue between an eleven-year-old and one of his or her parents. The parent is attempting to explain the "facts of life" to the child. Have you used much euphemism?
3. Construct a dialogue similar to that in question 2. This time, however, suppose that one eleven-year-old is explaining the facts of life to another. Which do you find predominating: euphemism, slang, or jargon; or are they used equally?
4. Would you recognize Robert Frost's line "Good fences make good neighbors" if it said, "We have observed that the barrier, for the purpose of discouraging and preventing intrusion, tends to enhance the amicability of those whose property it abuts"?
5. What maxims or proverbs do you see camouflaged in these jargon-laden sentences?
   a. The pursuit and capture of winged insects of the family *Muscidae* is more easily affected when, as opposed to sour, a dulcet substance is, for the purpose of beguilement, made use of. For example, the viscid fluid derived from the saccharine secretion

of a plant and produced by hymenopterous insects of the superfamily *Apoidea* has proved to be more successful in this endeavor than has dilute and impure acetic acid.

b. Bubbles of gas, rising from a liquid contained in a vessel, receptacle, or the like, to the surface of said liquid is a phenomenon not witnessed by those who subject such liquid to constant, searching scrutiny.

c. Seeking a suitable place for the purpose of courting a state of dormant quiescence during the first part of the crepuscular period and forsaking said suitable place during the first part of the matinal period results in myriad benefits to *Homo sapiens,* among which benefits may be noted a substantial increase in salubrity, prosperity, and sagacity.

d. A warm-blooded vertebrate of the class *avis* grasped in terminal prehensile of the portion of the upper limb of the human body is equal in value to two of the aforementioned vertebrates in a shrub.

e. A mineral matter of various composition when engaged in periodical revolutions exhibits no tendency to accumulate any of the cryptogamic plants of the class *musci.*

part **T W O**

Informal
Fallacies

chapter 4

Fallacies of Ambiguity

Arguments, like men, are often pretenders.

PLATO

Like most high school sophomores taking English, Andy Munson had to read Shakespeare's famous historical drama *Julius Caesar*. In studying the play, Andy became intrigued with one part in particular: Mark Antony's celebrated and oft-quoted funeral oration over Caesar's corpse (Act III, Sc. 2).

Recall that Antony has been asked to deliver the oration because Caesar's assassins think that he will sympathize with their cause. Just before Antony speaks, one of the conspirators in the murder, Brutus, addresses the crowd and convinces them that he slew Caesar for the good of Rome. In fact, so persuasive is Brutus that the crowd wants him to be the next Caesar.

With false modesty Brutus demurs, urging the crowd to hear Antony eulogize the fallen emperor. But instead of condoning the assassination, Antony in fact turns the mob against Brutus and the other conspirators. He does this so skillfully that by the time he's finished the crowd literally wants blood—Brutus's and that of the other conspirators.

At one dramatic point in the oration, Antony alludes to Caesar's will. The mob wants it read. Antony resists. He tells them,

> Have patience, gentle friends, I must not read it.
> It is not meet you know how Caesar loved you.
> You are not wood, you are not stones, but men;
> And being men, hearing the will of Caesar,
> It will inflame you, it will make you mad:
> 'Tis good you know not that you are his heirs,
> For if you should, O, what would come of it!

When Andy read this passage he felt mad. "Those creeps!" he thought, with Brutus, Cassius, Casca, and the other murderers in mind. "Knocking off a guy who thought enough of the people to remember them in his will. How bad could this Caesar have been?"

The mob thinks the same. They insist that Antony read the will. Of course, he knew they would. So Antony asks them to "make a ring about the corpse of Caesar" so they may see "him that made the will." The crowd does, Andy right there with them.

Like a good director who has effectively positioned his characters, Antony is now ready to allow the action to unfold. He shows the crowd Caesar's bloody cloak, each dagger hole made by the assassins. He reminds them when Caesar first wore it: " 'Twas on a summer's evening, in his tent, that day he overcame the Nervii." Already Brutus's arguments for the assassination, which only minutes before had won over the mob, have lost their appeal. Indeed, Andy, like the mob, can't even remember the arguments. The hearts and tears of all are now with the fallen leader, their will in the hands of Antony, who is about to deliver the coup de grâce that will set the mob on a bloody course of revenge. Using the mantle as his prop, Antony speaks:

> Look, in this place ran Cassius's dagger through.
> See what rent the envious Casca made.
> Through this the well-beloved Brutus stabb'd,
> And as he pluck'd his cussed steel away,
> Mark how the blood of Caesar follow'd it,
> As rushing out-of-doors, to be resolved
> If Brutus so unkindly knock'd, or no.
> For Brutus, as you know, was Caesar's angel:
> Judge, O you gods, how dearly Caesar loved him!
> This was the most unkindest cut of all,
> For when the noble Caesar saw him stab,
> Ingratitude, more strong than traitors' arms,
> Quite vanquish'd him. Then burst his mighty heart;
> And in his mantle muffling up his face,
> Even at the base of Pompey's statue,
> Which all the while ran blood great Caesar fell.
> O, what a fall was there, my countrymen!
> Then I, and you, and all of us fell down.
> Whilst bloody treason flourished over us.

"Treason!" thought Andy "That's what it is, treason!" And thus he went on to read the play with undiminished fervor, as the scoundrels got their just deserts, some at the hands of the angry mob.

If asked whether Antony had made a sound case against the conspirators, Andy undoubtedly would have said, "The best." So might we, if we were to come across such an argument against the assassins of our political leaders. In fact, Antony's argument is a classic illustration of mob appeal, an argument in which an appeal is made to emotions, especially to intense feelings that can sway people in crowds.

Mob appeal is only one of many ways that an argument can persuade psychologically or emotionally but not logically. This chapter and the next deal with some of those ways. In logic they are usually termed informal fallacies. In becoming familiar with informal fallacies, you will take a giant step toward being able to detect the unsound argument.

FALLACIES

Sometimes arguments appear to be correct. They look and sound good and we're prepared to accept them. Sometimes we do, as Andy did with Antony's argument. Later, on closer inspection, we discover that the argument is incorrect because it contains one or more fallacies.

Generally speaking, *a fallacy is a type of argument that may seem to be correct but is not.* Fallacies may be broadly divided into formal and informal. Formal fallacies are those usually discussed in connection with valid inference or deductive argument. So we'll leave our treatment of them for a later chapter. *Informal fallacies are commonplace errors in reasoning that we fall into because of careless language usage or inattention to subject matter.*

We won't be able to cover all the informal fallacies because they number well over a hundred. But in this and the next chapter we will discuss the most common. So that we are not guilty of a "fallacy overkill," we'll save some of the informal fallacy coverage for subsequent chapters, where the fallacies can be best understood in the light of the subject being discussed.

One word before beginning. There's no universally agreed-on classification of these fallacies. For simplicity, we'll break them down into fallacies of ambiguity and fallacies of relevance. Although one might quibble about these divisions, or even about the placement of specific fallacies within each group, the classifications are far less important than a working knowledge of the fallacies themselves.

The various fallacies of ambiguity are best understood in the context of our earlier discussion of language meaning. So let's first expand on those observations before considering ambiguous arguments.

MEANINGFULNESS, VAGUENESS, AND AMBIGUITY

In Chapter 3 we studied denotation and connotation. We discussed the powerful effects of subjective connotations and emotive language. Building on that, we can see that not all sentences are meaningful. In logic, we do not use the term *meaningful* to mean "important" or "significant," in the sense, say, that a particular song is "meaningful" to someone because it was played on his or her honeymoon. Logicians use the term *meaningful* to refer to a specific class of propositions.

We recall from Chapter 1 that propositions are statements with truth value: They make claims that are either true or false. In some cases, we may not yet know if a proposition is true or if it is false, but we can still recognize that it is a proposition. An example of this is the claim "The first draft of the Third Edition of *Practical Logic* was written on onionskin paper in July 1986." Most readers of this passage will not know for sure if the proposition is true. But they will still realize that the statement itself is a claim that does have truth value. Thus, it is a meaningful claim. (It is, as it were, "full of meaning.")

Vague Language

Now suppose we consider a claim such as this: "Lord Jones Cigarettes have uptown taste." Is this a proposition? Well, it *looks* like one. It has the basic grammatical structure of a declarative sentence, a sentence that provides information. But does it really provide any clear and specific information? Does it, in our terms, have truth value?

To test for the presence of truth value we must first determine the precise meaning of the claim. And to do that, we must consider the meanings of the words and phrases it contains. What about the expression "uptown taste?" Does it denote anything at all? And here we run into trouble. It is so vague as to be meaningless. *A term is vague when its meaning requires clarification in a given context. A term is meaningless when it is used in such a way that clarification in the ordinary sense is not possible.*

In this case, "uptown taste" may *feel* meaningful without being meaningful. Even its subjective connotations are likely to be relatively vague and imprecise. Consequently, the hypothetical Lord Jones Cigarette Company appears to be making a meaningful claim, but in fact it is not. (When a claim is "meaningless" it is empty of meaning, as it were.)

For our purposes, we will consider as meaningful only those claims that have truth value. To have truth value, a claim must be capable of a specific enough interpretation to be clearly understood in some context. What happens when we apply this requirement to the proposition "Lord Jones Cigarettes have uptown taste"?

We have no clear idea what the expression "uptown taste" means. How is it different, say, from "downtown taste" or from "out-of-town taste" or "up-the-river taste"? These examples are silly because such expressions are meaningless—they do not denote any object, idea, or experience that can be clearly expressed.

Ambiguous Language

If, then, an argument is a group of propositions, a sound argument must be a group of meaningful claims. Any argument or any attempt at persuasion that contains excessively vague, meaningless, or ambiguous claims will be flawed. *A term or proposition is ambiguous if it has more than one possible meaning in a given context.* Although terms or propositions may be both vague and ambiguous, we should not confuse ambiguity with vagueness. The "front of the room," for example, is vague but it is not ambiguous nor is it meaningless. It has only one meaning, even though the precise demarcation of the area denoted by "front of the room" may be unspecified. Let's consider a case of ambiguity for contrast.

"John and Mary dove into the pool where she kissed him on the bottom." The humor in this statement in part rests on its ambiguous nature. It has two possible meanings, and so it is not meaningless. But it is still far from clear. It may be telling us that John and Mary smooched under water—or it may have an "X-rated" meaning. That's why people usually laugh or groan on hearing it. Since two meanings are possible, this statement is ambiguous. In most cases, ambiguity is a result of either unclear reference or context or faulty grammatical construction (as in this case).

To sum up: Vagueness and ambiguity often occur together but are distinct concepts. Meaningfulness is a characteristic of all propositions occurring in sound arguments. The meaningfulness of propositions is a function of language usage and context. Since we are ultimately interested in accepting only sound arguments, it is necessary for us to study commonplace errors in reasoning caused by meaningless, vague, and ambiguous language usage. These are called fallacies of ambiguity, and are the subject of this chapter.

STUDY HINT: **ALTHOUGH VAGUENESS AND AMBIGUITY CAN OCCUR TOGETHER, THEY ARE DISTINCT CONCEPTS.**

When a term is vague, it has only one meaning, but that meaning is not specific. When a term is ambiguous, it is used in a way that gives it more than one possible meaning.

---

*EXERCISE 4-1 _____

Determine whether the following are meaningless, vague, or ambiguous. If they are vague or ambiguous, restate them in a clear fashion.

1. Al is bigger.
2. Save soap and waste paper.
3. Your term papers must be finished by Friday afternoon.
4. Clean Up brand soap gets you cleaner than you ever thought possible.
5. We stand behind every bathtub we install.
6. Come to the Main Street Health Center for unwanted pregnancies.
7. I have never read a student paper like yours.
8. Nothing is too good for my friends.
9. "Defendant Attacked by Dead Man with Knife" (newspaper headline)
10. Let's have lunch some time.
11. "The secretary is available for reproduction services." (from an *English* department memo!)
12. "Father of 10 Shot Dead—Mistaken for Rabbit" (headline)†
13. "Woman Hurt While Cooking Her Husband's Dinner in a Horrible Manner" (headline)†
14. "Jack's Laundry. Leave your clothes here, ladies, and spend the afternoon having a good time." (advertisement)†
15. "Soviet Bloc Heads Gather for Summit" (Plymouth, Indiana, *Pilot News,* quoted in "CT Flea Market," Fall 1986).

---

†These and many other examples of humor created by scrambled syntax can be found in Denys Parson's *Too Funny for Words* (London: Futura Publications, 1986).

FALLACIES OF AMBIGUITY

Considering what we have learned so far about the nature of arguments and the importance of careful language usage, we are now ready to begin looking at fallacies of ambiguity. *Fallacies of ambiguity, therefore, are those fallacies arising from careless language usage.* We'll consider eight such fallacies: equivocation, accent, amphiboly, composition, division, meaningless claim, cliché thinking, and hairsplitting.

Equivocation

When we confuse the separate meanings of a word, using it in different senses in the same context, we are using the word equivocally. For example, the word *laws* may refer to human-made laws, which prescribe how people should behave. It may also refer to scientific laws, which describe how things in the physical universe operate. When we confuse the separate meanings of *laws,* using it in both senses in the same context, we are using the word equivocally.

If we use a word equivocally in the context of an argument, we're guilty of the fallacy of equivocation. *The fallacy of equivocation refers to an argument or proposition that confuses the separate meanings of a word or phrase.* Suppose, for example, someone argues,

> All laws have a lawmaker.
> The laws of gravitation and motion are laws.
> ———————————————————————————————
> Therefore, the laws of gravitation and motion have a lawmaker.

The argument commits the fallacy of equivocation. For the first premise to be true, *laws* must be intended as human-made laws. But *laws* in the second premise refers to scientific laws. Human-made laws are prescriptive: They prescribe proper human behavior. Scientific laws are descriptive: They report or describe how things function, but they do not say how things *ought to* function. So *laws* is being used in two separate senses in the context of an argument. That's why we can say this argument commits the fallacy of equivocation.

Fallacies of equivocation often arise in the use of relative terms. A relative term is one whose meaning depends on some point of reference. Words such as *small, big, bright, tasty,* and *smooth* are relative terms. Their meanings can vary according to what they're describing. Here's a humorous argument that equivocates on the relative term small:

> Since a buffalo is an animal, a small buffalo must be a small animal.

Don't buy one for a house pet. What "small" means relative to an animal is hardly what it means relative to a buffalo.

Beware the fallacy of equivocation in advertisements. For example, a cigarette manufacturer tries to persuade you to smoke a brand because "It's only natural." What does "natural" mean here? That the cigarette contains "natural" ingredients? That everyone is smoking this cigarette? That smoking this cigarette is as "natural," say, as eating or sex?

Often such ambiguity is intentional. An ad for an MG sports car, for example, once showed a young couple tightly fitted into a two-seat sports car. The ad read, "MG. Big enough for two. Exciting enough to breed a generation of sports car enthusiasts." The appeal intentionally equivocates on the word

YOU HEARD ME... ARREST HOWDY DOODY AND PINOCCHIO, THEN STRING THEM UP.

PUPPET DICTATOR

breed, mixing sexual and nonsexual meanings. Clever and amusing, and probably harmless enough, if you take "safety measures."

But sometimes intentional equivocations can really mislead. Suppose you pass a newspaper vending machine and see a headline that reads PRESIDENT TALKS OF WAR. You insert your quarter and quickly start scanning the paper for news about some international conflict you inferred the nation was about to get embroiled in. It turns out that the "war" is on poverty or disease or slums. "Duped again," you think, discarding the paper, and with it what could be information on an important issue, though not as sensational as "blood and guts." The fallacy of equivocation has led you to an erroneous conclusion and also to a subsequent course of action.

Accent

The meaning of a word or phrase can shift with the emphasis we give it. Take, for example, the sentence "We should not speak ill of our friends." Now that statement seems clear enough. But watch the various meanings the sentence can carry when we emphasize different words, indicated in the following by italics:

1. "We should not *speak* ill of our friends." We might infer from this that it's all right to *do* ill to our friends.
2. "We should not speak ill of our *friends*." We might infer from this that it's all right to speak ill of our *enemies*.
3. "We should not speak ill of *our* friends." With this emphasis we might conclude that it's okay to speak ill of *someone else's* friends, perhaps our enemies' friends.
4. "*We* should not speak ill of *our* friends." Here the implication might be that it's fine if *others* speak ill of our or their friends but that *we* shouldn't speak ill of *our* friends.

Four points of emphasis, four different meanings.

The fallacy of accent is an argument or claim whose justification depends on a misleading shift in emphasis on a word or phrase. In the preceding example, the intended meaning of "We should not speak ill of our friends" is a legitimate moral injunction when its words don't receive undue emphasis. But if we infer, as we did in sentence 1, that it's all right to *do* our friends ill or, as in 2, to speak ill of our *enemies,* our conclusions are only justified if we fallaciously give undue emphasis to certain words. In sentence 1 we'd be stressing *speak,* in 2 *friends*. But when we do that, the statement no longer is acceptable as a moral principle. In fact, we have altered the premise.[1]

> **S T U D Y H I N T : IN CASES OF ACCENT, THE INTENDED MEANING OF THE ORIGINAL PASSAGE IS ALTERED.**
>
> In cases of equivocation or amphiboly, we don't know what the intended meaning is. In cases of accent, a specific meaning is distorted by lifting parts of a passage out of context or by laying undue and unexpected stress on parts of a statement.

Newspapers often rely on the accent fallacy to persuade us to buy a newspaper or read a story. The type size given to a headline can accomplish this by giving undue emphasis to words. Ads use the same device: "CHILDREN ADMITTED FREE" an announcement claims. Then in much smaller print: "with one paying adult." This appeal also equivocates on the word *free*. Be advised: Fallacies don't always travel alone.

Amphiboly

Sometimes a statement is ambiguous because its very structure is flawed. *An amphiboly is a statement with more than one meaning because of ambiguous grammatical construction.* "Leslie told her mother she was a fool." Who's the fool? Did Leslie tell her mother that her mother was a fool? Or did she tell her mother that she (Leslie) was a fool? Both meanings are possible because of the faulty structure of this sentence. To dissolve the ambiguity, we must do more than change a word or expression, as is the case with equivocation. We must actually restate the sentence.

In the mid-1970s, one of Jimmy Carter's campaign slogans was "Carter—a leader for a change." Here, the amphiboly was deliberate. Its purpose was to catch our attention, to make us chuckle, and ultimately, to encourage us to think about and vote for Carter. The possible desired meanings included these: "Carter—a leader who will bring about change" or "Carter—it's about time we elected a leader" or "Let's change leaders—elect Carter." An unexpected and humorous meaning, which no doubt disconcerted Carter's campaign advisors, was something to this effect: "Carter's finally acting like a leader." That's the problem with amphibolies; we can't always anticipate the ways others will interpret them.

It's tempting to confuse equivocation, accent, and amphiboly. In most cases, equivocation and accent do not involve the major grammatical confusion found in amphiboly. In an equivocation, the ambiguity is caused by an unexpected or unusual meaning being given to a particular word or phrase. In accent, one part of a passage is over- or underemphasized, but the basic grammar is sound. What can, and does, sometimes happen is that an amphibolous construction can confuse us so that we do not know which meaning to apply to a

---

[1]See Irving Copi, *Introduction to Logic*, 4th ed. (New York: Macmillan, 1972), p. 94.

term or which terms to stress. The rule of thumb is that if the only way to avoid the ambiguity is to restate the entire sentence, it is an amphiboly. That is, if we have to add punctuation, move entire phrases or clauses around, add words, or otherwise perform "major surgery" to clarify a passage's meaning, it is an amphiboly.

The differences between equivocation and amphiboly are easier to identify if we remember that although they are both ambiguous, we distinguish between them based on the *source of ambiguity*.

STUDY HINT: **IN CASES OF EQUIVOCATION, THE SUBSTITUTION OF A WORD OR PHRASE DISSOLVES THE AMBIGUITY.**

As a general rule, no modification of grammar or syntax is necessary for equivocation. If such modifications are necessary, the ambiguity is an amphiboly.

Composition

The fallacy of composition is an argument that erroneously attributes characteristics of the parts to a whole. "Since I can lift up each individual part of my car," I claim, "I can therefore lift up the whole car." Of course, I can't. The mistake is in assuming that a property of parts of a whole is also a property of the whole itself. Again, someone might argue. "Because each chapter of the book is an artistic masterpiece, the book itself must be a masterpiece." Not necessarily; taken as a whole, the book may be far less than an artistic masterpiece, even though each of its chapters is brilliant. Simply because each member of a choir sings well doesn't mean that the choir as a unit will sing well.

STUDY HINT: **IN COMPOSITION, THE CONCLUSION IS ABOUT THE WHOLE AND THE PREMISES ARE ABOUT ITS PARTS.**

Sometimes the composition fallacy can arise when we reason that what can be said of a term distributively can also be said of it collectively. Thus, it may be that there are more fatalities per year in air accidents than in any other kind of transportation accident—but only distributively, that is, when you consider *individual* air accidents, or air accidents as single, isolated occurrences. Thus, in the average commercial air accident more people are killed than, say, in the average car accident. But when air accidents are considered collectively, that is, taken as a group and not just individually, there are far fewer fatalities than in automobile accidents taken as a group, in any single year. Again, taken distributively, considered individually, students at a college may enroll in only five courses a term. Taken collectively, as a total body, students enroll in far more than five courses; indeed in hundreds of them.

Division

The fallacy of division is the reverse of the fallacy of composition. *The fallacy of division is an argument that erroneously attributes to the parts of a whole the characteristics of the whole itself.* Thus, "The United States is a rich nation. Therefore, every American is rich." Scratching around for movie money, you'd not likely swallow that argument. The mistake, of course, is in assuming that a property of the whole unit is also a property of any part of the unit. In fact, what is true of the whole is not necessarily true of its parts any more than what is true of the parts is true of the whole. Because a choir is ready for a performance doesn't mean that "Perfect Pitch" Petersen, a member of the choir, is also ready.

As with the composition fallacy, sometimes the fallacy of division occurs when we confuse the group taken collectively with the group taken individually. It's true that consumers consume thousands of pounds of meat per year, but only collectively. Taken distributively, consumers consume far less meat. Again, college students take many thousands of courses per year, but only collectively. Distributively, college students take only a handful of courses per year.

S T U D Y   H I N T :   IN DIVISION, THE CONCLUSION IS ABOUT THE PARTS (OR A PART) AND THE PREMISES ARE ABOUT THE WHOLE.

The quickest way to distinguish composition from division is by examining the conclusion. If it is about the *whole,* the fallacy is *composition.* If the conclusion is about a *part,* the fallacy is *division.*

EXERCISE 4-2 _____

Each of the following passages is guilty of some form of ambiguity. Identify the fallacy of ambiguity it commits.

1. Living within a budget is good for any individual. So it must be good for a nation, too.
2. This book is tough. So I bet the next chapter will be tough.
3. PHIL: Some kind of animal has just been here.
   FRAN: My dog has just been here.
   PHIL: Your dog must be some kind of animal.
4. Since advertising costs billions of dollars a year, any new business that advertises is just asking to be wiped out.
5. FRAN: Jones is weird.
   PHIL: Why's that?
   FRAN: He figures out math problems in a weird way.
6. The end of something is a thing's perfection. Death is the end of life. Thus, death is the perfection of life.
7. FRAN: Why do you dislike Frank so much, when the Bible says, "Love thy neighbor"?
   PHIL: But Frank's not my neighbor. He doesn't live anywhere near me.
8. PHIL: I have an obligation to picket any apartment house that discriminates against couples with children.
   FRAN: Why do you say that?

PHIL: Because I have a right to picket it, and I always have an obligation to do what's right.

9. CONTRIBUTOR: I'm not going to contribute any more to your charity.

SOLICITOR: Fine. I'll just put you down for the same amount as last year. 'Bye now.

10. FRAN: Isabelle must be a very influential woman.

PHIL: Why do you say that?

FRAN: Because she's a member of the most influential union in the country.

11. PHIL: There's no question about it: The universe must some day come to an end.

FRAN: Oh, I don't know.

PHIL: Think about it—all humans are mortal, aren't they? That's reason enough for me.

Meaningless Claim

The fallacy of meaningless claim is any argument consisting of assertions that are unverifiable because they contain words or phrases that are unclear in any ordinary context.

For example, the ad "Bob White Chevrolet has the best deal in town" is actually a meaningless claim. Bob White has said nothing specific about his business. Does he mean that he has the lowest prices? Does he mean that he can get financing cleared faster than other car dealers? Might he mean that although his prices are higher, his product is better than, say, that of Ford or Olds dealers? We don't know. And we can't begin to verify his claim until we know what exactly is being claimed. Bob White knows this. His hope is that we will *assume* that he means whatever we would like to hear. The word *best* is common in meaningless claims.

So is the word *perfect.* Consider this typical type of ad: "*Sounds of the Eighties!* Over 100 great pop tunes on 10 audiocassettes. Only $1.95. The perfect Christmas gift!" What on earth is "the perfect Christmas gift"? Is this the "perfect Christmas gift" for an infant? Is it "the perfect Christmas gift" for Granpa, who hates pop music? Is it the "perfect Christmas gift" for everybody? That seems to be what the word "perfect" is meant to suggest to us. Yet, obviously, there is no such thing as "the perfect Christmas" gift is any literal sense since *perfect* means that any change makes things worse. In other words, something is "perfect" when it cannot be improved in any way whatsoever.

What about *extra?* "Excedrin contains *extra strength.*" Does this mean that it contains more strength than it needs? Then why should we pay for something unnecessary? Perhaps it means that Excedrin contains more aspirin than we might expect it to? This is surely a strange claim. We should expect it to contain a reasonable and useful dosage. Might it mean that Excedrin contains more aspirin than it used to? It might. The point, of course, is that *any one of these claims might be true.* But since the claim—as stated—has no specific usage, we cannot verify it. Therefore, it is effectively meaningless. It sounds as if it tells us something informative, but in fact it is devoid of meaning.

Notice that in all three examples, the key terms, *best, perfect,* and *extra,* have generally positive subjective connotations for most of us. That is their charm for advertisers: The terms feel good to us. Yet at the same time, those using such terms commit themselves to no specific claim. Thus, they cannot be held accountable for failing to justify their claims: They have not actually made any claims at all. They only appear to make meaningful claims.

STUDY HINT

A good rule of thumb for testing for the presence of meaningless claims is to ask the following hypothetical question: "If I were going to sue someone for failing to live up to this claim, what—exactly—would I tell the judge had been claimed?" If no clear and specific answer is possible, the claim is most likely meaningless.

Cliché Thinking

The fallacy of cliché thinking occurs whenever a cliché is used uncritically as a premise in an argument or as a substitute for an argument. A cliché is an expression or statement that has become trite through overuse. Often, clichés become clichés because at one time they were fresh and insightful. But by definition, once they are clichés they are usually neither. Clichés tend to be pithy sayings, often couched in figurative language (review the material on figurative definitions in Chapter 3), which lack precise meanings.

Cliché thinking substitutes for clear thinking. Once more we have the appearance of good thinking substituting for the real thing. We must not overlook the emotional power of clichés, either. The problem with cliché thinking is that clichés tend to oversimplify, which in turn encourages us to draw shallow or hasty conclusions or to act on imprecise, unclear assumptions.

Suppose that you are trying to decide whether or not to take Physics 1A next term. You are not very strong in the physical sciences, but Physics 1A is required for the general education portion of your degree. You consult your academic advisor, pointing out that you work twenty hours a week, that Physics 1A is offered only in the fall, that you also need to take either Biology 6 or Anatomy 3 before you graduate. You wonder whether to take Physics 1A now as a junior rather than wait until the fall of your senior year. Your advisor says, "Well, the early bird catches the worm."

This *sounds* like well-thought-out advice to you. But is it? If your advisor fails to go on and "flesh out" this cliché with sound argumentation, he or she has fallen prey to cliché thinking. And if you accept this advice without careful analysis, so have you.

Cliché thinking is especially prevalent in areas of personal conduct, psychological advice, and religious counseling. This is unfortunate, for these are areas of great importance to most of us. They are prone to hackneyed thinking because of the complexities involved and because there are so many clichés about personal conduct, philosophical insight, and the like. Add to this the common desire to cut quickly to the heart of the matter, to simplify the complex, and we have fertile ground for the substitution of smooth-sounding clichés for good thinking.

You are now frustrated because, taking your advisor's advice, you have just flunked Physics 1A (you decided to "go for it"). Talking to your best friend, pointing out that you have only one more "shot" at it (the dreaded senior-year push), and that if you fail it you will not be allowed to graduate, you hear, "Well, don't worry about it. Everything works out for the best." Does it? What about your other friend, the one who flunked Physics 1A twice, lost his scholarship, and is now looking for work? Is that "for the best" you ask? "There's a reason for everything," your cliché-touting pal answers. You point out that you don't see it in this case. "Ours not to reason why," your literary friend reminds you.

This could go on endlessly—indeed, with some people it does, or at least seems to. But is it helpful? That, of course, depends on the particular circumstance. There are times when the judicious use of a cliché can be helpful. It might remind us of a strong religious or philosophical belief, and so help us make a clear decision in light of well-thought-out considerations.

Clichés become clichés, as we have noted, because they offer us popular "insights" and bits of "wisdom" in a simple, easily understood and remembered form; because they are powerfully expressed; or for other reasons. But typically they impede clear thinking. We must use clichés with caution; they must be scrutinized to determine exactly what it is they mean; then we must see if that is relevant and correct in the case at hand. As a general rule, clichés are inadequate guidelines for decisions. They must be supported by sound arguments showing both their relevance and their truthfulness.

Hairsplitting (Trivial Objection)

The fallacy of hairsplitting, also known as trivial objection, is a demand for more precision than is possible or necessary in a given case, either because of the nature of the case or its importance. Have you ever observed a discussion that seemed to get hung up in an obsessive concern for accuracy and precision to the point that the main issue was entirely obscured? A colleague refers to this as "an obsessive concern with minutiae." Minutiae are tiny, tiny details and unimportant distinctions.

To be sure, precision often is important, even crucial. Your logic instructor is not hairsplitting by demanding some degree of exactitude from you on tests and quizzes. That's a logic instructor's job. However, to demand the same precision in an informal conversation about an unimportant matter would be hairsplitting. Let's see what the difference is between a reasonable demand for precision and a fallacious one.

Meet Bob and Betty Quarrels, hairsplitters *par excellence*. We join them in mid-discussion. The evening had been going well. We've just had a nice supper with Bob and Betty and are now enjoying a relaxing cup of coffee on the patio. Bob starts it all when he says that the sunset reminded him of the first time they dated, back in May 1942. Betty points out that it was April. Bob says, "No, it was May. I remember as if it were yesterday. You had that carnation behind your left ear. You were so beautiful!" "Thanks," Betty replies, "but it was a rose, behind my right ear, and it was April." "May," Bob insists. "I can still hear Tommy Dorsey's band playing as we watched the sunset." "April, rose, right ear, Jimmy Dorsey!" Betty says sharply. It's going to be a long evening.

Given the subject under discussion, the circumstances of the evening, and the fact that neither Bob nor Betty has any records to check, both are guilty of hairsplitting. The fact is, the issue is not likely to be verifiable; and if it is verifiable, it is hardly worth the effort.

On the other hand, if in his job as a nurse, Bob is discovered to have confused grams with milligrams in preparing a medication and replies, "Grams, milligrams, what's the difference? Don't split hairs," he is guilty of misunderstanding this fallacy. In cases of hairsplitting, the issues being so carefully defined are of little or no importance to the main issue. Whether or not Bob and Betty first dated in April or May, to Jimmy or Tommy Dorsey's music, while Betty wore either a carnation or a rose behind one ear or the other, is not particularly relevant to Bob's sentimental remark that tonight's sunset reminded him of special feelings for Betty.

It is one thing for your literature instructor to correct your claim that Harry Melville wrote *Moby-Dick,* and quite another for you to point out to your geometry instructor that the rectangle she has sketched on the blackboard is "not really a rectangle since its corners are not precisely 90 degree angles."

Hairsplitting, then, is the insistence of precision to the detriment of the issue being considered. It involves applying rigorous standards out of context. The precise use of the term *valid* to signify only logically correct deductive arguments in a logic course is appropriate. Correcting Aunt Lina's use of *valid* to mean "true," accompanied by a mini-lecture on the relationship of validity to truth, is not only discourteous but also hairsplitting.

On a television talk show, for example, a "discussion" of pornography and free speech included the following claim: "In a recent issue of *Penthouse,* an editorial stated such and such," to which one of the guests, objected, "It was *Playboy,* not *Penthouse.*" The first speaker acknowledged his error, pointed out that the source of the article was not as important to his main point as was its content, and attempted to continue with his argument. He was once more interrupted and repeatedly criticized for "not getting his facts straight." This is an example of hairsplitting because although, in this case, the point was technically correct, it was also trivial. Here, the demand for precision actually obscured the main issue.

We see, then, that an inappropriate demand for precision can be a source of confusion, that it can actually obscure rather than clarify an issue. Objections are trivial when they are not pertinent to the main issue, when they substitute an overzealous concern for the accuracy of minor or irrelevant details for a deeper and clearer understanding of a more significant concern.

---

*EXERCISE 4-3 _____

Identify the fallacies or sources of ambiguity in the following. If possible, indicate ways to clear up any vagueness or ambiguity.

1. "Pesticides have no effect on corn crop" (newspaper headline)
2. "Iranians to try Americans as spies" (newspaper headline)
3. If I told you that you had a beautiful body would you hold it against me?
4. My learned opponent accuses me of being absent from Congress during the crucial session on Friday, May 12. Everybody knows that May 12 was a Thursday!
5. Being in love is no illness. And no illness is worse than cancer. So being in love is worse than cancer.
6. Every third child born in New York is Protestant, so Catholics should have only two children.
7. Every nine seconds someone somewhere drinks Burpo Cola.
8. The patient complained of a numb leg, but he walked it off.
9. JUDGE: Order! Order in the court!"
   PRISONER: I'll have a cheeseburger.
10. JUDGE: Quiet! Anything you say will be held against you!
    PRISONER: Joan Collins. Joan Collins.

SUMMARY

We've seen how careless use of language can pose serious problems of both communication and reasoning. As we continue our study of logic, we will also see how fallacies usually "travel in packs." That is, often, one ambiguity will accompany others, or one error in reasoning will accompany others. Sloppiness because of either haste or inattention can infect an entire argument, not just an isolated aspect of it; and in some cases, these fallacies are deliberately used to confuse us, to manipulate us, or to obscure something their user does not want us fully to understand.

Then, too, there are the common tendencies to be in a hurry, to see what we want to see, to react impulsively (and highly emotive language inappropriately used encourages such tendencies), or simply to confuse the parts of an entity with its overall characteristics. It is important to us as clear thinkers that we insist on sufficient clarity and precision to make sound judgments of the cases that present themselves to us for our consideration. The first place to start is by demanding clarity and precision in our language, without slipping into splitting hairs. With effort and experience, we become "fine tuned" to the fallacies and ambiguities covered so far. In the next chapter, we will look at more fallacies.

In this chapter we learned about

1. *Equivocation:* an argument that confuses the separate meanings of a word or phrase.
   Example: Good steaks are rare these days, so don't order yours well done.
2. *Amphiboly:* a statement with more than one meaning because of ambiguous grammatical construction.
   Example: I love candy more than you.
3. *Accent:* an argument whose justification depends on a shift in emphasis of a word or phrase.
   Example: We might infer from the moral injunction "We should not *speak* ill of our friends" that it is all right to *think* ill of them.
4. *Composition:* an argument that attributes to a whole characteristics of the parts.
   Example: Since I can lift up each individual part of my car, I can lift up the whole car.
5. *Division:* an argument that attributes to the parts of a whole the characteristics of the whole itself.
   Example: The United States is a rich nation. Therefore, every American is rich.
6. *Meaningless claim:* any argument or claim that is unverifiable because it contains a word or phrase that is unclear in any ordinary context.
   Example: Bob White Chevrolet has the best deal in town.
7. *Cliché thinking:* whenever a cliché is used uncritically as a premise in an argument or as a substitute for an argument.
   Example: Upon asking your college advisor whether or not it is wise to take Physics 1A this term or later, you are told only, "The early bird catches the worm."
8. *Hairsplitting (trivial objection):* a demand for more precision than is possi-

ble or necessary in a given case, either because of the nature of the case or its importance.

Example: Aunt Lina uses the term *valid* in ordinary conversation to mean "true." Her meaning is perfectly clear to you, and she has never studied logic. You correct her, insisting that she use the term *valid* in the precise fashion of this text.

Summary Questions

1. Meaningless claims are found in advertisements, political speeches, and everyday conversation. Compile a list of five examples and analyze them. What do you think most people believe them to be saying? What subjective connotations accompany them?
2. Comedians love "word play." Have some fun and learn some logic at the same time by identifying five or six jokes that rest on material covered in this chapter. Here's a shop worn starter: "Take my wife. Please."

ADDITIONAL EXERCISES _____

Identify any sources of ambiguity you find in the following. In some cases, there may be more than one.

1. Original sentence in movie review: "This film is about as exciting as watching grass grow and as interesting as oatmeal."
   Quote in ad for movie: "exciting . . . interesting"
2. Memo from Big Boss to Little Boss: "Your secretary has been submitting reports with too many typographical errors. You must monitor her work more carefully. Please stay on top of her."
3. AAA Refrigerator Repair Company has three employees, Ross, Dean, and Joe. Ross has worked as a refrigerator repair person for twenty-five years, Dean for fifteen, and young Joe for ten. They advertise on the radio: "AAA Refrigerator Repair—50 years of experience!"
4. Pete's been repairing cars for a living for over thirty years. He must be exhausted.
5. I love coffee more than you.
6. "Out of habit, nun repairs convent autos." (newspaper headline)
7. "Woman critical after being run over by bicycle"
8. In a northern California community some years ago, a young man was involved in a fatal automobile accident. His girlfriend, who was a passenger in his car, was killed when the vehicle swerved off the road and hit a power pole. The young man was accused of reckless driving, for driving at excessive speed on a road well known for its dangerous curves. An uproar ensued when his lawyer argued—and won a significantly reduced sentence for his client—that the young man was not "driving" since at the time of the accident he was talking to his girlfriend and not looking at the road, and since his hands were not on the wheel. (Believe it or not, this is a true case.)
9. Last year her husband left her in a cheerful frame of mind.
10. This is one of the world's finest watches: It contains only the finest material available.
11. Mary had a little lamb.
12. I just flew in from Chicago and my arms are killing me.
13. That is your dog. And that dog is a mother. Therefore, that dog is your mother.
14. He said that he would be here by noon, and it's already 12:03. I'm going home!
15. DAUGHTER: Mom, may I have an allowance?
    MOM: Not on your life! "Money's the root of all evil."
16. ASSERTIVE GIRL, after unexpectedly kissing her boyfriend on the right cheek: Now

you have to let me kiss you on the left cheek, too.

STARTLED SHY BOYFRIEND: I do? Why?

GIRL: Because the Bible says to turn the other cheek!

17. If you don't go to other people's funeral's, they won't go to yours.
18. We dispense with accuracy. (sign at pharmacy)
19. EXASPERATED MOTHER: Don't yell so loudly, I'm trying to rest.

    CLEVER CHILD: How else can I yell?
20. I just read that the big elephant ran away from the zoo and has gotten lost. They're wasting their time looking for him. Elephants aren't found in North America.
21. No man is wiser than Socrates.
22. PROUD PAPA: Bud, Jr., is practicing medicine now that he's passed his board exams.

    JEALOUS NEIGHBOR: Let me know when's he through practicing and I might make an appointment.
23. America is a wealthy country. You are an American. You must be wealthy.
24. Woman without her man would be lost.
25. So what if I lied to you? The Bible says, "Thou shalt not bear false witness against thy neighbor." You live on the other side of town.
26. Which is heavier, a pound of feathers or a pound of lead?
27. IRATE CUSTOMER to clerk: Hey! What's goin' on here? I unwrapped this shirt at home and found it's been cut in half.

    CLERK: Did you buy it on sale?

    CUSTOMER: Yeah. But what's that got to do with it?

    CLERK: Well, our ad clearly stated, "All sale items, 50% off."
28. You'll have to look long and hard to find a car with this quality.
29. Wearing a long white gown, he escorted his daughter to the altar.
30. The fetus is a human being because it's part of the mother, and the mother is a human being.
31. Since this is a great novel, every sentence in it must be great.
32. The government is inefficient. You work for the government. You are inefficient.
33. After the Barlowes watched the lions and tigers do tricks, they were lead back to their cages.
34. You've never tasted anything like it.
35. Eat at Casa de Nachos! Unexpected fine dining.
36. "*Eau de Milwaukee:* For that sophisticated scent."
37. "FREE GIFT: you pay only for postage and handling."
38. After the exhausting race, the winner stood wiping his brow on the winner's stand.
39. DOWAGER: And you, Mr. Costello, will sit on my right hand during dinner, and Mr. Abbot will sit on my left.

    COSTELLO: And how are ya' gonna eat? With a straw? (paraphrase of an old burlesque routine used by Abbot and Costello)
40. "Gets you cleaner than clean."

5

Fallacies of Relevance

Good, too. Logic, of course; in itself, but not in fine weather.

ARTHUR HUGH CLOUGH

Gloria Richards was tired. She'd had a bad day at work, it was hot, and traffic on the way home was worse than usual. Pulling into the driveway, she saw that Little Gloria had left her bike in the flowerbed again, and Wally, her husband, had forgotten to move the hose, so the evening paper was soaked through.

She turned off the motor of the car, and sat for a few minutes, trying to unwind. Closing her eyes, she practiced some relaxation exercises she had recently read about. Feeling better, she moved Little Gloria's bike, turned off the hose, and hung the newspaper on a lawn chair to dry out.

"I'm home," she called out, as she headed to the bedroom to shower and change. "Hi, honey," Wally answered. "Supper's just ready. I made your favorite—liver and onions!"

Ahhh! Liver and onions. Gloria felt better already. She congratulated herself on picking Wally for a husband. He was so thoughtful. But best of all, to Gloria, he was sensible. She hated irrational people.

After a pleasant dinner, Gloria and Wally took their evening walk. This was her favorite part of the day. In late summer, the evenings were great. Walking through the neighborhood and making small talk with her husband was just what Gloria needed. Then it happened.

"You know, Gloria," Wally said, "with us both working, we don't have much time for grocery shopping."

"Un huh," Gloria answered, lost in reverie.

"Well, I was just thinking. Why don't we buy a freezer and keep it in the garage? We could buy food cheaper in bulk, and we'd sure save time. There's a fantastic sale at Zeppo's Appliance Carnival. What do you think? Can we go look?"

Now Gloria was alert. "Here it comes," she thought, "another big purchase. If we don't cut back, we'll never be able to save any money for that speedboat we want."

"You know we don't need a freezer," Gloria said.

"Just consider it," Wally said. "That's all. I've got the figures all worked out. We'll look at them when we get home."

And they did. But Gloria's mind was made up, and so was Wally's. Somewhere in the middle of the discussion—Gloria was never sure where—Wally began to clam up. Then he got angry and said, "Okay, if we can't afford a freezer, we certainly can't afford a speedboat! And this discussion is making me angry. I think I'll sleep in the living room tonight."

"Aw, c'mon," Gloria pleaded. "Be reasonable. We'll talk about it tomorrow. You don't need to sleep in the living room."

"Well, I'm sorry," Wally said. "I can't help it. I'm disappointed and angry. I'd rather not be around you. You're right, I know. We just can't afford things like freezers and speedboats. . . ."

At this mention of speedboats, Gloria panicked.

". . . And," Wally continued, "maybe I am being childish, but that's just the way I feel. I can't be nice to anyone when I'm this mad!"

They bought the freezer. They didn't need it, hardly used it, and had trouble paying for it. Gloria gave in to Wally's use of two fallacious appeals to the emotions, pity and fear. When he withdrew, he upset her, subtly introducing emotions into the argument where they did not belong. Then when he threatened Gloria's precious dream of a speedboat he added another emotion, fear, to the already boiling pot of Gloria's emotions. Wally reinforced Gloria's feelings of fear by threatening to "sleep in the living room." Gloria knew from experience what this really meant: *days* of a grouchy, surly Wally. And Wally knew that Gloria would do anything to get her speedboat and to keep him from getting too upset.

But lest we erroneously conclude that Wally was alone in fallaciously appealing to emotions, we must not overlook Gloria's part in the whole scenario. Knowing good and well that they could not afford the freezer, Gloria went along with buying it in order to justify buying a speedboat—which cost even more than a freezer! She invoked her own emotional appeals to try to get her way. First, she bullied Wally into going along with her by pointing out that since he was able to buy his freezer, she was entitled to buy her speedboat. Since both purchases were foolish, Gloria invoked a version of two-wrongs-make-a-right and introduced feelings of guilt into Wally's consideration of the issue. She complemented all of this by invoking her own appeal to pity. She reminded Wally of how rough things had been at work lately, of how long it had been since she had been able to afford any "neat stuff" for herself, and she moped dreamily while ostentatiously reading boating magazines. As we are discovering, "fallacies travel in packs," and Gloria and Wally were both guilty of invoking and succumbing to irrelevant appeals.

This chapter is about *fallacies of relevance*. An argument that commits a fallacy of relevance has a premise that is *logically* irrelevant to its conclusions or to the purpose of demonstrating its conclusion. Irrelevant premises often arise when arguers rely on emotion, diversion, or assumption in order to try to establish the truth of conclusions. It's useful, therefore, to organize our coverage of fallacies of relevance around these three categories.

RELIANCE ON EMOTION

Both reasons and emotions are, of course, inescapable and valuable tools for making choices. But there are times when our emotions can interfere with our ability to think clearly, much to our detriment and even to our sorrow.

An emotional appeal is an attempt to persuade without reasons. In other words, an appeal to emotions is a deliberate attempt to invoke an emotional response to persuade someone to accept a conclusion, to adopt a belief, or to act in a certain way. It is often easier to influence another's feelings than it is to change his or her mind. Under certain conditions, we can change a person's thinking by first changing how he or she feels about something. We are often more susceptible to emotional appeals than we are to reasons.

It's worth especially noting that fallacies are difficult to spot when emotions cloud our thinking. Note, however, that as clear and critical thinkers we are concerned with the *logical* adequacy of arguments, not their *psychological* "relevance" or persuasiveness. In other words, arguments can be highly persuasive because of various emotions they stimulate—hostility, fear, enthusiasm, pity, lust, and so on—even though they are logically flawed. We may be overcome by the *feeling of logical justification*. An argument's logical adequacy, however, is not determined by how we feel about it.

Whenever others deliberately attempt to persuade us by using factors of which we are unaware, we are being manipulated, not reasoned with. And this is the *desired* effect of a fallacious appeal to emotions. Feelings are used *in place* of reasons—where reasons are appropriate. Used this way, feelings weaken our ability to think carefully and clearly. We'll begin our study of six of the more common fallacious appeals to emotions with one of the most common forms: arguments directed "at the person" rather than at the issue.

But first, meet Roscoe and Sweeney, two "characters" who will help remind us of the practical, everyday aspects of logic. Roscoe and Sweeney are the sorts of guys whose friendship consists of one feud after another. They would defend each other to the death, even if they had to kill one another to do it!

Along the way, we'll run into members of Sweeney's family. (Roscoe is a bachelor who over the years has drifted away from his own family.) Sweeney's wife is named Wilma. The Sweeneys have two children: Susan, a sophomore at a local college, and B.J., a high school junior. Susan's nickname is Slim, and

B.J. is short for Bartholomew Jason (B.J. prefers the connotations of B.J. to those of Bartholomew).

Throughout the rest of our study, we'll see Roscoe, Sweeney, Wilma, Slim, and B.J. express a variety of logical arguments of the sort we encounter daily. Some of them are good ones, but most are not.

One of their more common sources of fallacious reasoning is one that affects most of us: confusing persons with arguments.

Ad Hominem

Often, in argument, we attack the person with whom we're contesting and not the person's argument. The result is the ad hominem appeal. *Ad hominem* is Latin for "to the man." *The fallacy of ad hominem is an argument that attacks the person who makes an assertion rather than the person's argument.*

The ad hominem comes in many forms. In one version, the *abusive* ad hominem, we attack the person's character. Here's an example:

> SWEENEY: I just read this article by former President Nixon about U.S.–China relations. It made a lot of sense.
>
> ROSCOE: Are you kidding? I wouldn't believe a word Nixon said after Watergate

Roscoe's argument is fallacious because Nixon's personal character is logically irrelevant to the truth or falsehood of what he says about U.S.–Chinese relations. To argue that a proposal is bad or incorrect because of the personal character of the person who holds it is to be guilty of an ad hominem fallacy.

A particularly vicious example of this fallacy is found in the case of French film actress Jean Seberg. In the 1960s, the FBI wanted to discredit Seberg because of her expressed sympathy toward the cause of the Black Panthers, a black political group. So the FBI circulated the lie that the baby Seberg and her husband were expecting actually had been fathered by a member of the

Black Panthers. In so doing, the FBI believed that it would so damage Seberg's moral reputation that no one would take her views seriously. In effect, the FBI had manufactured an ad hominem through character assassination, thereby expecting to discredit any political view that Seberg would express. And, of course, the lie would also have an impact on the reputation of the Black Panthers and, presumably, would detract from their political credibility. Of course, even if the claim were true, it would be logically irrelevant to Black Panther and Jean Seberg politics.

As it turned out Jean Seberg was the biggest loser in the ugly skullduggery. According to her husband, she was thoroughly traumatized by the rumor, so much so that she attempted to take her life every year on the birthday of their child. In the fall of 1979 she succeeded. Shortly thereafter, the FBI admitted it was all a lie and said it didn't do that sort of thing any more.

Sometimes the ad hominem fallacy takes the form of attacking the circumstances of a person's life. Thus, someone might argue that Eric Hoffer can't know anything about philosophy because he's a longshoreman by trade. Of course, Eric Hoffer has made a lifelong study of philosophy and has authored several books on the subject. Somebody else might argue that Dr. Jonas Salk's view on national health insurance is invalid because he is, after all, a medical doctor and is bound to be prejudiced. Still another holds that William F. Buckley's political views are not to be taken seriously because he is a television personality. In each case, an argument is offered against the circumstances of a person's life rather than against the position that person represents. Such ad hominem appeals are termed *circumstantial* ad hominem.

Still another version of the ad hominem results when we insist that an argument is worthless because those proposing it fail to heed their own advice. This is sometimes termed the *tu quoque* ("you also") fallacy. The *tu quoque* fallacy is an argument that charges someone with acting in a manner inconsistent with the position he or she is advocating. For example, the most common retort to warnings about the danger of drug use is "How can you tell us not to use drugs when you smoke and drink and take all sorts of pills?" The argument may sound good; it certainly puts many of us on the defensive. But logically it's irrelevant, because whatever we may actually do has no bearing on whether or not taking drugs is wise or healthful.

Poisoning the Well[1]

The fallacy of poisoning the well occurs when, prior to deliberation, we place an opponent in a position that excludes an unwanted reply. This is not the same thing as logically refuting a certain position. Rather, in the case of poisoning the well, we assume, *prior to discussion,* a position that arbitrarily and without logical justification excludes a point of view by decree. By merely "decreeing" the unacceptability of our opponent's position, we in effect assume the truth of our own.

---

[1]According to S. Morris Engel, the historical origin of the name goes back to the Middle Ages when anti-Semitism was especially virulent. Whenever a plague struck a village, it was blamed on the Jews, whom the people accused of "poisoning the well." *With Good Reason,* 3d ed. (New York: St. Martin's Press, 1986), p. 199.

In the nineteenth century, John Henry Cardinal Newman engaged in frequent disagreements with clergyman and novelist Charles Kingsley. During the course of one of these disputes, Kingsley suggested that Newman could not place the highest value on truth because he was a Catholic priest. Newman rightly objected to this "poisoned well" on the grounds that it made it impossible for him (or any Catholic) to state his case: No matter what reasons Newman might offer to show that he did, indeed, highly value truth, Kingsley would automatically rule them out *because they came from Newman the Catholic priest!*

We poison the well whenever we summarily discount everything that comes from a certain source (the "well"). Examples include statements like this: "There's no point in listening to anything she says about this class; she teaches it." "I'd like to hear your so-called proofs for the existence of God—but don't waste my time quoting C. S. Lewis." "There's no point in asking the General what he thinks about Star Wars—he's a military man, so he has to think along official lines."

Or consider the psychologist who insists that you are repressing certain feelings. When you deny it, he points out, "Aha! See how deeply you repress them!" To this you might reply, "I'm not repressing anything." "There! See how afraid you are to face this." As you grow more agitated, your agitation becomes "proof" that your psychologist has hit a nerve. No matter what you do, you cannot refute the claim that you are repressing some feelings because this view is a poisoned well: If you deny it, you affirm it! If you affirm it, you affirm it!

STUDY HINT

As a general rule, circumstantial ad hominem arguments are directed at individuals. Poisoned wells are more sweeping in scope.

Mob Appeal

At the beginning of Chapter 4 we saw how Mark Antony's funeral oration over the corpse of Caesar stirred the passions of the Roman crowd—and of high school sophomore Andy Munson. As we noted then, Antony's speech is an example of mob appeal.

The fallacy of mob appeal is an argument that attempts to persuade by arousing a group's deepest emotions. In a mob appeal, one always tries to win support by arousing the feelings and enthusiasms of the crowd. This is exactly what Antony did so effectively.

Mob appeal is a particularly favorite device of any propagandist or demagogue. For example, the American patriot Thomas Paine used mob appeal in his opening paragraph to "The American Crisis," in which he tried to alert his compatriots to their peril and need to respond. As is true in most mob appeals, Paine uses highly emotive language: *patriot, crisis, shrink, service, country, love, tyranny, hell, conquered, conflict, glorious, bind, slavery,* and *impious.* Not a skimpy litany for one paragraph, if you're interested in arousing public opinion behind a war.

In fact, some of the greatest oratorical movements in American history resorted to mob appeal. Here's William Jennings Bryan opposing gold as a monetary standard in his famous "Cross of Gold" speech:

> We care not upon what lines the battle is fought. If they say bimetalism is good, but that we cannot have it until other nations help us, we reply that, instead of having a gold standard because England has, we will restore bimetalism, and then let England have bimetalism because the United States has it. If they dare to come out in the open field and defend the gold standard as a good thing, we will fight them to the uttermost. Having behind us the producing masses of this nation and the world, supported by the commercial interests, the laboring interests and the toiler everywhere, we will answer their demand for a gold standard by saying to them: You shall not press down upon the brow of labor this crown of thorns, you shall not crucify mankind upon a cross of gold.

Mob appeal, however, need not appear only in addresses. Beware of it in advertisements, where generally every attempt is made to associate a product with things that we can be expected to approve of strongly: patriotism, status, sexual gratification. Also, pictorial ads can be most effective in appealing to our deepest feelings. For example, there's no counting how often a picture of the White House or the Capitol has been used as a background for an ad. The daughter of a former U.S. President has even appeared in one such ad—for an automobile.

Also, mob appeals occur in everyday conversation. Thus, Sweeney says to Roscoe, "I know that you're going to understand what I'm about to say because, like me, *you're a working man.*" In every case, by appealing to our deepest feelings rather than to reason, the mob appeal introduces into the argument what is essentially irrelevant. This doesn't at all mean that emotion has no place in human debate and dialogue. Rather, emotion that *replaces* or *substitutes for* reason has no place.

Sex.   *A most common version of the mob appeal today is the argument that uses sexual feelings to advance its conclusion.* In the late 1960s and early 1970s, Noxema Shave Cream ran a clever television commercial featuring a very attractive blonde who spoke with a Swedish accent. This sexy Swedish woman (a doubly appealing combination, for Sweden was viewed as a sexually liberal country) would watch an equally sexy man shave with Noxema Shaving Cream. She would smile and stroke the clean-shaven part of his face while a popular tune entitled "The Stripper" played in the background. Looking provocatively into the camera, she would seductively blow a bit of shave cream off her open palm, and whisper, "Take it off. Take it off. Take it all off." Another example of a fallacious appeal to sex can be seen in the long-running theme used to sell English Leather Cologne. Attractive women purr, "All my men wear English Leather—or they wear nothing at all."

In our time, a preponderance of appeals to sex involve sexually attractive women. This is a consequence of the so-called "double standard," which holds that men are "just naturally" more interested in sex-as-sex than women, and which—inconsistently—views most women as sexual objects, reserving for a few the cherished status of wife/mother/sister. In fact, however, women and men are equally susceptible to such manipulative appeals.

When a man attempts to get special treatment at work by flirting with a co-worker, by being sexually suggestive in the hopes of advancing some cause or project, he is using *logically irrelevant* appeals. Today baseball player Jim Palmer poses for ads in Jockey Brand Briefs. Calvin Klein ads feature attractive young men and women barely covered by rumpled bedclothes. And of course we are invited to wonder what they've been doing to have so rumpled those sheets. Although such ads are sometimes humorous and "campy," they must also be classified as fallacious appeals to sex.

The problem with such blatant sex appeals is that they effectively, perhaps intentionally, interfere with our ability to make a thoughtful decision. The sexual instinct is so strong in us, and our culture is so sexually sensitive, that by associating something with a sexy fantasy, we often confuse a strong attraction with a good reason.

Pity

The fallacy of pity is an argument that uses compassion to advance a conclusion. A good example occurred just the other day when Roscoe was pulled over for speeding in his new sports car. When it became obvious he was getting a ticket, he said to the officer: "Oh, c'mon, will you? One more ticket and I'll lose my insurance." Recognizing the irrelevancy of Roscoe's appeal to pity, the officer replied, "You should have thought of that before you sped."

Appeals to pity frequently arise in the courtroom when defense attorneys are backed against a wall. Then there's often talk of the defendant's misspent youth, deprived childhood, neglectful parents, and so forth. Here's an example involving perhaps the most famous defense attorney of all time, Clarence Darrow. In this instance he's defending Thomas Kidd against the charge of criminal conspiracy. In addressing the jury, Darrow says,

> I appeal to you not for Thomas Kidd, but I appeal to you for the long line—the long, long line reaching back through the ages and forward to the years to come—the long line of despoiled and downtrodden people of the earth. I appeal to you for those men who rise in the morning before daylight comes and who go home at night when the light has faded from the sky and give their life, their strength, their toil to make others rich and great. I appeal to you in the name of those women who are offering up their lives to this modern god of gold, and I appeal to you in the name of those little children, the living and the unborn.[2]

Despite the effectiveness of such an appeal, the question is still whether the defendant is guilty of the crime. In that light, this appeal, though psychologically persuasive, is logically irrelevant to the question. We should quickly add, however, that the line between relevance and irrelevance is often blurred. Sometimes what appears to be an appeal to pity actually is an attempt to demonstrate that a defendant's will was so constrained that the person didn't freely choose to commit a crime.

Salespeople are fond of appeals to pity, particularly in selling life and health insurance. It's not surprising. After all, if a pitiful picture is painted of a provider's children scratching around for food and clothes in the absence of the provider, the person's likely to take out some life or health insurance. The beauty of such

[2]Quoted by Irving Copi in *Introduction to Logic,* 4th ed. (New York: Macmillan, 1972), p. 78.

an appeal is that it makes a person live with guilt *before the fact*. The pitches for purchasing a "preneed" burial plot work the same angle. It's tough for people to live with the guilt of making their loved ones scurry around making funeral arrangements for them, so why not arrange for all that "before the time comes"? In that way people can presumably just sit back and enjoy your funeral.

Fear or Force

The fallacy of fear or force is an argument that uses the threat of harm for the acceptance of a conclusion. Also known as "swinging the big stick," the appeal to fear or force is summed up in the addage "might makes right." Of course, might doesn't make right; that's the whole point.

Thus, the lobbyist who says to a politician "The best reason for supporting my proposal is that I represent 2 million people" is using fear or force to persuade. How many people the lobbyist represents is logically irrelevant to the merits of the proposal, although emotionally it's most relevant to the politician's future. That's precisely why the lobbyist makes and gets away with such appeals.

Appeals to fear are widely used by those who support mandatory testing of federal employees for drugs—and by those who oppose such testing. The former appeal to our fears regarding drug-impaired individuals in crucial jobs: air traffic controllers, military personnel, police officers and firefighters, and so forth. Their opponents appeal to our fears of a "1984"-type world in which a "Big Brother" government pries into our very bodies. Appeals to fear are widespread in discussions of AIDS or the purported dangers of rock and roll. Proponents of the Strategic Defense Initiative, the so-called "Star Wars" defense system, appeal to our fear of being defenseless against the Russian's technologically sophisticated missile system.

Such appeals are often used to exert pressure on average people in their everyday work lives. Thus, a male boss might expect sexual favors from a female employee as a condition for employment or promotion. A doctor might demand gratuities from a neighborhood pharmacist in exchange for sending patients to that pharmacy. A teacher might be pressured not to join a union under threat of tenure denial or getting unattractive assignments. New workers at a job might be told "to clam up" or "don't rock the boat" if they want to "get ahead." In all cases, the appeal is to fear, which although emotionally persuasive, is logically irrelevant to the positions being advanced.

---

*EXERCISE 5-1 _____

Identify the fallacies in the following passages from among ad hominem (specify which form), poisoning the well, mob appeal, sex, pity, and fear or force. If you think that some form of ambiguity is also present, identify it.

1. RAQUEL: How about joining me in my aerobics workout? I have Jane Fonda's new exercise tape.
   DEBBIE: Are you kidding? I won't watch anything she's in—even an exercise video.
   RAQUEL: Why not?
   DEBBIE: Because back in the 60s and 70s she was opposed to the Vietnam War, she's antibusiness in her support of migrant workers and secretaries. Hey, face it, she's anti-American.
2. Nibbling on the back of his wife's neck, Bob asks, "Don't you think it'd be fun to spend a week with my brother's family at the cabin?"

Squirming to get loose, Blanche replies, "But, Bob, you know that we promised the kids we'd all go to Disneyland this year. We've promised them for the last three years, and never go. Besides, this is the last year Bob, Jr., will be living at home."

Bob says (nibbling, patting, squeezing), "You know how romantic I get at my brother's cabin."

3. "You and I are about to reach a crossroads in county government. We can choose a path that will lead us into more of what we have experienced in the last few years, or we can choose a new direction, a new agenda, with new and creative solutions to the complex problems we face today. The choice is yours.

"It is difficult to find people willing to do their very best nowadays, people who will choose the right path, the honest path, even if it hurts. We need more people willing to help . . . people committed to giving their all . . . people willing to go the extra mile, just because it's right!" (political brochure)

4. JAN: I think it's only fair that members of oppressed minorities get special treatment for jobs and things.

   DEAN: Well, you're a woman; of course you can't be objective. After all, everything you think is biased according to your experiences as a woman.

5. A. U.S. Senator arguing for Senate ratification of the Strategic Defense Initiative: Any red-blooded American, who places his country's interest above all else, as he should, would vote for this. Why? Because it prevents the most powerful nation on earth, the United States of America, from becoming a second-rate power.

6. Mother to daughter: Oh, don't worry about me, dear. Go out on your date. I'll be all right. After all, I've got the TV to keep me company.

7. Father to daughter: Be home by eleven tonight, or you can forget about next weekend at the beach.

8. MEG: Driving as fast as you did on such slick pavement is really dumb.

   PEG: Oh yeah? I suppose you've never driven that way.

9. FRED: You know, I really have to laugh when the Congress asks the Pentagon how much money the military needs.

   JUDY: Why do you say that? Who would be in a better position to know than the Pentagon?

   FRED: Are you kidding? As representatives of the military, everybody in the Pentagon is naturally going to want as much money as they can get.

10. Commercial: "You're in a strange city. Suddenly someone snatches your wallet. Your traveler's checks are inside it. What will you do now? What will you do? . . . American Express—never leave home without it."

11. Review of the film *Jonathan Livingston Seagull:* It's strictly for the birds.

12. Union leader: Of course, you'll have to vote your consciences on whether to strike. But just let me say this. All loyal members would see their duty and not cower to the thought of what management might do to them. . . . Okay, let's pass out the ballots!

13. Student to teacher: I know I earned a C in the course. But if I don't get an A, my GPA isn't going to be high enough to get me into medical school. How about giving me the A?

EXERCISE 5-2 _____

1. Mob appeal is present in virtually every radio and television commercial. One currently widespread trend is the use of well-recognized music to enhance a product's appeal. This may be classical, country and western, rock, jazz, or blues, or whatever. The producers of such ads hope that we will identify their products with the lifestyle, values, or positive personal feelings we associate with the selected music. Thus, there is a built-in identification factor at work. Collect five or six examples of these "musical mob appeals." What special values do you think they are trying to sell? Do they work?

To what extent has the clever use of music influenced your own attitudes toward a product?

2. Political figures also use music to create an image. This, too, is a form of mob appeal. Can you think of some widely used songs that are of special appeal in the political arena? Can you identify three or four especially effective uses of music in a political campaign?

3. Under what circumstances, if any, are personal traits relevant to an individual's argument? Explain and justify your answer.

4. The appeal to pity can be persuasive because most of us believe that compassion is a virtue. Under what circumstances might "pity" be a legitimate consideration?

5. In the 1950s, household products such as bleaches, detergents, refrigerators, food stuffs, and the like were often sold on television by well-dressed women in evening gowns, with tightly permed hair, wearing jewelry and high heels—they looked like Mrs. Cleaver, Beaver's mom. After thirty years of the civil rights movement, the Vietnam War, Watergate, and a public debate over sex roles, such ads seem naive and silly. What kinds of people are now used in commercials? Discuss some of the ways in which advertisers keep up with lifestyle and value changes in order to make the most powerful mob appeals they can.

RELIANCE ON DIVERSION

As we've seen, fallacious emotional appeals can interfere with critical thinking skills. They can also distract us so that we become concerned with secondary or peripheral, logically irrelevant, issues before we've adequately analyzed logically prior and more significant considerations. In a sense, most fallacies of emotion involve some element of diversion from logically relevant concerns. There is also a class of fallacies that more directly involves diversion and distraction.

Let's first take a look at the most basic fallacy of diversion, the infamous red herring.

Red Herring

A form of psychological distraction, the fallacy of red herring is the introduction of a logically separate and irrelevant issue into a discussion. The story is told that dog trainers used to teach hunting hounds to follow a trail by dragging the fresh carcass of a rabbit, bird, squirrel, or other prey through a field. This track was allowed to grow cold overnight. The next morning, a smoked "red" herring, which had been allowed to "ripen," was dragged over the original trail. The young dog was then set off on the original trail. When he came to the scent of the red herring, he would be distracted by the fresher, stronger odor—and his trainer would put him back on the scent of his original prey.

We don't have such trainers, and so we often resort to and take off after all sorts of red herrings. Consider what happened when B.J.'s geography teacher asked him to remain after class to discuss his declining grades. B.J. was ready for her. "Ms. Roe," he said, "I'm glad you asked me to stay. I've been meaning to ask you about the San Andreas fault. I'm fascinated by this, but I'd like to know more about it. Can you recommend any good books on it?"

Of course, B.J. may or may not be telling the truth. The point is that he has deliberately attempted to distract Ms. Roe from the original issue (B.J.'s declining grades) with a red herring—and a flattering one at that, for it appeals to Ms. Roe's love of geography and geology. Most of us quickly recognize the concept of the red herring, for changing the subject is a nearly universal instinct when the subject is in some way difficult for us or threatens us in some way.

Appeals to flattery (which some logic texts treat as a specific fallacy) are also commonly used as red herrings. Let's see how they work.

Sweeney's just come in the door when he remembers that he forgot to buy milk—and Wilma was very emphatic about needing milk for breakfast. Just as she asks him about the milk, he rushes up to her, takes her in his arms, and says, "Gosh, you're pretty. Sometimes I forget how pretty." Sadly for Sweeney, Wilma knows most of his tricks, and answers, "I'll be even prettier when I know I have enough milk for breakfast. Did you buy it?"

When we are confronted by red herrings, the best thing to do is to refuse to be tempted by the new issue, no matter how appealing it may be, until we have resolved the initial one. Changing the subject is not a fallacy, but changing the subject to distract others from a weakness in our position is.

Here's a more subtle example of red herring. In charging a business executive with embezzlement, a prosecutor quotes harrowing statistics about white-collar crime. His statistical barrage may influence a jury, but it is irrelevant to establishing the guilt of the defendant. The alarming statistics only support the assertion that white-collar crime is a serious, widespread social problem. They divert attention from the real issue.

Humor and Ridicule

A common form of diversion is the appeal to *humor and ridicule, an argument that relies strictly on humor or abuse in attacking something.* Humor and ridicule often accompany ad hominem attacks and mob appeals. They are especially effective when strong prejudices or stereotypes can be invoked. But as British novelist Graham Greene's *Monsignor Quixote* reminds us, "Laughter is not an argument. It can be a stupid abuse." And yet, the substitution of the sarcastic rejoinder or the cruel retort are unfortunately both prevalent and effective—especially in front of an audience.

For example, a member of the British Parliament named Thomas Massey-Massey introduced a bill to change the name of Christmas to Christide. He reasoned that *mass* is a Catholic term. Since Britons are largely Protestant, they should avoid the suffix *mass* in *Christmas.* Thus, he proposed "Christ-tide," whereupon another member suggested that Christmas might not want its name changed. "How would you like it," the member asked Thomas Massey-Massey, "if we changed your name to Thotide Tidey-Tidey?" The bill died in the ensuing laughter.[3]

Here's another example. When, at the post–World War I Versailles conference, French leader Clemenceau heard Woodrow Wilson propose the so-called Fourteen Points, Clemenceau supposedly reacted, "Fourteen Points! God Almighty had only ten!" Clearly Clemenceau was being more than amusing. Like the member of Parliament, Clemenceau was being contemptuous. Neither one, of course, joins the issue. Instead he relies on humor and ridicule to demolish the opponent's proposal.

[3]See Engel, *With Good Reason,* p. 109.

Some years ago *Esquire* magazine asked a number of leaders in the women's liberation movement to identify the prime movers among "The Enemy." The women asked included Gloria Steinem, Caroline Bird, Florynce Kennedy, and Anita Hoffman. Notice the humor and ridicule they relied on to justify their responses:

> *Pope Paul VI:* Unyielding stand on birth control. Why should anyone be forced to dance to his rhythm?
>
> *Daniel Patrick Moynihan* [ex-Nixon aide, now U.S. senator from New York]: He's the administration's Nigger Expert; couldn't find Roxbury [a black ghetto] with a flashlight.
>
> *Eldridge Cleaver* [revolutionary]: Women are slaves to him, although unlike Algerians, he doesn't require a veil.
>
> *Richard Nixon and William Rogers* [former secretary of state]: For their dialogue after the Women's Political Caucus: "What did it look like?" Nixon asked. "Like a burlesque," Rogers said. "What's wrong with that?" Nixon asked.
>
> *The late Al Capp* [cartoonist, talk-show guest]: Because of his cartoon attacks, and because he said, "Unwed mothers should be capable of some other form of labor."
>
> *Hugh Hefner* [publisher of *Playboy*]: Are you kidding?[4]

We note, however, that no amount of ridicule can substitute for a logically cogent and relevant critique of an argument. Sarcasm and humor may or may not reflect wit; they do not, of themselves, substitute for reasoned analysis and argument.

Two Wrongs Make a Right

The fallacy of two wrongs make a right is an argument that attempts to justify what is considered wrong by appealing to other instances of the same or similar action. For example, Wilma scolds B.J. for ripping the funnies out of the paper before she's had a chance to read it. B.J. replies that Slim tears the sports section out of the paper before anybody gets a chance to read it. The fact is two wrongs *don't* make a right. When we argue to the contrary, we're introducing a premise that's irrelevant to the conclusion, either that we are innocent of wrongdoing or that our wrongdoing is justified.

Apologists for Vice-President Agnew came to his defense immediately before his resignation and even afterward by pointing out that he wasn't the first or only politician involved in nefarious activities. Likewise, defenders of the Nixon administration still point out that government scandals did not begin with that administration and that in fact almost every administration had its own version of Watergate. Certainly, political scandals did not begin with Nixon and Agnew. But such a defense blurs the central questions: Was either of these individuals guilty of wrongdoing?

Similarly, when Senator Edward Kennedy swam away from the bridge at Chappaquiddick, his defenders claimed that it wasn't the first time that a man's personal life had unfairly obscured his public life. True, but that objection was

---

[4]"Bad Dudes," *Esquire,* November 1972, pp. 132–35.

irrelevant to the question the courts had to decide: Was Kennedy party to a crime?

Again, defenders of the Carter administration were quick to point out in the wake of Bert Lance's forced resignation as manager of the budget because of banking improprieties (is that a euphemism?) that other Presidents had had their "Lances." For example, Lyndon Johnson had Bobby Baker and Dwight Eisenhower had Sherman Adams. So what? That's irrelevant to what Lance did or didn't do and to the aspersions his behavior cast on the Carter administration. The same applies to similar "wrongs" used to defend the bevy of Reagan appointees who have been forced to resign under nefarious circumstances. The "wrong" actions of past political administrations do not mitigate the misconduct of present ones.

A common variation on the two-wrongs theme is the fallacy of common practice. *The common practice fallacy is an argument that attempts to justify wrongdoing on the basis of some practice that has become commonly accepted.* For example, when Roscoe was new to the job, he was taken aback to see Sweeney take company tools home with him for his personal use. One day he asked him about it. Sweeney said, "Oh, that's one of the *perks* of the job." By "perks," of course, Sweeney meant perquisites, fringe benefits, as it were. Since it was a practice that most of the other workers followed, Sweeney didn't see anything wrong with it. Yet a short time afterward, management issued a memo forbidding the common practice.

One of the issues raised during Senate hearings to confirm Justice William Rehnquist's appointment to the position of Chief Justice of the United States Supreme Court centered on the fact that Rehnquist once owned property whose deed contained a clause forbidding sale or transfer to blacks and members of other minorities. This raised the question of whether or not Rehnquist was bigoted. Some of Rehnquist's defenders pointed out that at the time, over twenty years before, many parcels had such riders, and many decent people owned property with the same conditions. Thus, they argued, even though Justice Rehnquist was a lawyer, who could be expected to understand the legal language of this proviso, what he did should not be held against his appointment since it was "common practice for the time."

Have you ever had to fill out a form in triplicate, perhaps even in quadruplicate? Maybe you couldn't see the reason for it and asked somebody. If you were told, "That's just how we do things here," you were being given a common practice appeal. Possibly four separate offices or departments needed copies of what you'd signed. If so, that would be a logically relevant reason. But "That's just how we do things here" is logically irrelevant; it's a common practice appeal.

Years ago, Regimen, manufacturers of weight-reducing tablets, was charged by the Justice Department with deliberate misrepresentation and falsehood in advertising its product. In fact, the U.S. Attorney General charged that Regimen's was "one of the most brazen frauds ever perpetrated on the public, mostly women."[5] Regimen's reply: "Thousands of other advertisers and agencies are doing the same kind of thing."[6] No matter how common the practice, misrepresentation is misrepresentation—hence, the irrelevancy of Regimen's defense.

[5]Samm Sinclair Baker, *The Permissible Lie* (New York: World, 1968), p. 24.
[6]Ibid.

Straw Man

The straw man fallacy is an argument that so alters a position that the result is easier to attack than the original and yet claims that it has provided grounds for attacking the original. The name of this fallacy is particularly revealing of what it accomplishes. In effect, it sets up a "straw," which is easy to blow over. Of course, the "straw" is not the original argument at all. But that's the whole point. The original was much harder to assail than the straw. Having set up the straw, the arguer is then in a position to "blow it over." And if we're not careful, we may erroneously conclude that the original argument has been demolished.

For example, many critics of laws guaranteeing equal rights for women argue this way: "If these laws pass, we'll have to draft women into the army. This will weaken our military posture and jeopardize the security of our country. And I, for one, don't want a militarily weak nation." Notice what's going on here. The original issue was equal rights for women. The straw issue is military strength. It's probably a lot easier to get people to support a position in favor of military strength than against equal rights for women. Thus, the original issue—equal rights for women—has been cleverly altered into an issue about military strength. And thus, the straw man, or in this case—the straw woman?

In the 1964 presidential campaign, pro-Johnson people effectively used the straw man against Barry Goldwater. Rather than engaging Goldwater on the issues, they generally made a vote for Goldwater sound like a vote for a third world war. In the light of subsequent events, the irony here needs no comment. This was also an appeal to fear.

A particularly fine example of the successful use of the straw man fallacy can be seen in the so-called Princeton plan,[7] a plan adopted by Princeton University in the fall of 1970 whereby the university would schedule no classes for a short period before the congressional elections of 1970, thus enabling students to campaign for candidates if the students so wished. Princeton officials sponsored the plan in the aftermath of our invasion of Cambodia in June 1970. You may remember how that incident touched off considerable protest throughout the country, especially on college campuses. The Princeton administration thought that its plan would help defuse any further unrest, even violence, that might result during election time among students who believed they were being excluded from the electoral process. The immediate reaction to the plan among other colleges was quite favorable. For a time it appeared that many other institutions would adopt it.

At this point, Senator Strom Thurmond of South Carolina attacked the plan. In fact, he asked the Internal Revenue Service to investigate how this would affect the tax-exempt status of educational institutions that adopted it.

In the aftermath of Thurmond's warning, the American Council of Education cautioned member institutions to be careful about engaging in any ". . . political campaign on behalf of any candidate for public office." Under tax laws, an institution may lose its tax-exempt status for engaging in *partisan political activity*.

Of course, the Princeton plan was not advocating partisan political activity. It was merely releasing students to campaign for whomever they wished, if in fact they cared to campaign at all. Thus, the original Princeton plan had been

[7]See Howard Kahane, *Logic and Contemporary Rhetoric,* 2d ed. (Belmont, Calif.: Wadsworth, 1976), pp. 53–55.

associated with partisan political activity and the dire implications for tax-exempt institutions that adopted it. In brief, a marvelous straw man had been created.

And it worked; very few institutions adopted the Princeton plan. For whatever reason, they failed to see that giving students released time to campaign was not to engage in partisan politics. Failing to see that, the institutions rejected the Princeton plan on the basis of a straw man that Senator Thurmond had created.

STUDY HINT

Straw man deals with various arguments concerning a single issue (conclusion). Red herring is the introduction of a logically separate issue.

---

*EXERCISE 5-3 _____

Identify any fallacies of diversion (red herring, humor and ridicule, straw man, two wrongs, and common practice) you spot in the following passages.

1. There's been some criticism of this administration's support of the Star Wars defense system. It has been alleged that the technology is flawed. Let's study the issue. We can begin by pointing out that the defense industry is among the largest providers of jobs in this country. Imagine what would happen if we failed to provide funds for these jobs. Let's see some of the ways in which we all benefit economically from a healthy defense industry. . . .
2. MOM: I don't want you going to the movies tonight. It's a school night, and besides, you have an important algebra test in the morning.
   STUDENT: What! You're telling me that I can't go to the movies on week nights? That's unreasonable.
3. Ms. Norman argues that a woman has a right to decide what happens inside of her own body, and that the state has no business interfering in her right to abortion on demand. I say that we cannot stand by and simply allow pregnant teenagers to use abortion as a morning-after form of birth control, and Ms. Norman is wrong when she demands that right.
4. ANGRY TEACHER: Well, young lady, why did you kick Jenny?
   ANGRY PUPIL: She kicked me first, and you said we're not supposed to kick.
5. PUSHER: Here, try some of this crack. It'll really get you loaded.
   PAL: No, man, drugs are illegal.
   PUSHER: C'm on, it's okay. Everybody here does drugs, even the cops.
6. INTERVIEWER: Tell me, Slats, do you ever feel guilty for getting paid so much money to put a basketball through a hoop?
   SLATS: Look, everybody in the league with my ability gets paid as much.
7. FRED: Fudging on your taxes isn't anything to feel ashamed about. The tax structure in this country is unfair. It taxes us regular folks unfairly. In effect, it cheats us because it favors the wealthy. So a little padding of deductions here and there is just tit for tat.
8. BARNEY: Yeah, Fred! Besides, the IRS expects us to fudge. Nobody files a completely honest return. The system's built around a little good-natured cheating.

RELIANCE ON ASSUMPTION

Appeals to assumption are arguments that are logically inadequate because they presume as true key assumptions that must be independently verified to establish their conclusions.

Before studying various appeals to assumption, it will be helpful to consider a basic, illustrative pattern of this kind of irrelevant reasoning:

A is true because B is true.
B is true because C is true.
C is true because D is true.
D is true because A is true.

This pattern is a basic representation of circular reasoning. At first glance, it seems unlikely that anyone would be taken in by such thinking, since as the name implies, "it goes in circles." But consider a specific instance of this pattern:

Lying is wrong (A) because it's immoral (B).
Lying is immoral (B) because it's something we should not do (C).
Lying is something we should not do (C) because God forbids it (D).
God forbids lying (D) because lying is wrong (A).

The fallacious quality of all circular arguments is due to the fact that in one way or another they always assume too much, taking as given some essential claim that requires separate verification. Thus, they are actually assertions of a claim to truth rather than demonstrations of it.

Let's look at four of the most common forms of circular reasoning: begging the question, loaded epithets, complex question, and dismissal, as well as a close cousin, invincible ignorance.

Begging the Question

The fallacy of begging the question is an argument that uses some form of its own conclusion as part of the evidence offered to support that very conclusion. Begging the question is the most general of the five forms of circular reasoning we are going to review. The so-called "question" being begged is actually the conclusion. So it might help to think of this fallacy as conclusion begging: Instead of offering independent evidence capable of supporting the conclusion, a begged question merely asserts a crucial factor necessary to support its conclusion and then refers back to its own assertion as if it had been proven. We can do this in a number of ways.

The common element in each of the following fallacious strategies is that an aspect essential to proving the conclusion is "begged." Thus, since the proof of the conclusion depends on this essential aspect, the conclusion itself is begged. Here are three of the more common ways in which this occurs:

1. Using equivocated terms in the premise and conclusion

Example: Abortion is immoral because it's wrong.

In example 1, it is essential that we establish whether or not abortion is "wrong" *before* we can determine whether or not it is immoral. If "wrong" is used to mean "morally wrong," the premise "Abortion is wrong" means "Abortion is morally wrong," which, of course, is simply an equivalent way of saying "Abortion is immoral"—which is the premise! So this argument fails to establish its conclusion. It merely asserts it twice, once as its own premise.

2. Assuming as a premise a more general form of the conclusion

Example: Smoking marijuana is wrong because taking drugs is wrong.

Example 2 also fails to *establish* its conclusion. In this case, the premise already includes the conclusion, so if we accept the premise we have also accepted the conclusion. If taking any kind of drug is wrong, then certainly smoking marijuana is wrong, since it is a drug. But is it wrong to take drugs in general? The obvious answer is "no." What this argument requires is evidence that it is wrong to take one specific drug, marijuana. As in the case of example 1, example 2 fails to provide independent proof sufficient to support its conclusion. It merely asserts the same point twice: one as part of a sweeping general claim and once more specifically as the conclusion.

3. Using a questionable premise to support a favored conclusion

Example: Abortion is wrong because it's murder, and murder is wrong.

In example 3, the crucial issue is whether or not abortion is murder. *If* abortion is murder, it is wrong, because murder, by definition, is "wrong" in our culture— both morally and legally. The very term *murder* is only applied to the taking of human life when such an action is judged as morally or legally wrong. Since the concept of "wrong" is implicit in that of murder, to say that "abortion is murder" is essentially the same as saying "abortion is wrong." This argument reduces to "Abortion is wrong because abortion is wrong." What we have, then, is an "argument" only in a most trivial sense. When the premise and conclusion are logically the same, the argument is *trivially valid;* the truth of the premise entails the truth of the conclusion because it *is* the conclusion!

We see that in each of these examples, independent, sufficient proof for the truth of the conclusion is lacking. In its place we find only repetition and equivocation, so that the premises and conclusion are essentially the same. Rather than making a case, begged questions merely assert their conclusions twice: once as the conclusion and once disguised as a premise. (If you feel like gasping, "Whew! We're just going in circles," go ahead; you are absolutely correct. We are going in circles: hence the appellation, circular reasoning.)

Loaded Epithets

The fallacy of loaded epithets is an argument that substitutes questionable labels for reasons to advance a favored conclusion. In everyday terms, loaded epithets are name-calling.

An epithet is a word or phrase used to express some quality or characteristic of an object. An epithet is usually an adjective. Let's consider a few examples of epithets used to persuade without offering justification. A philosophy professor might announce, "And now class, let's take a look at Nietzsche's obviously juvenile moral philosophy." If this announcement is made before any discussion of Nietzsche, it is an example of using a loaded epithet ("obviously juvenile") in a way that advances the conclusion that Nietzsche's moral philosophy is juvenile without having to prove that it is, and which can be expected to bias subsequent analysis of it. (This is also an example of well poisoning.)

Expressions that "lead" us in the direction another prefers are especially dangerous: "It's *obvious* to any *knowledgeable* observer that this position is *clearly ludicrous,* but we'll look at it anyway." Terms with strong emotive charges like *reasonable, ludicrous, ridiculous, idiotic,* and so forth can often subtly (or not so subtly) color our perceptions of an issue by seducing us into accepting a position whose truthfulness is unproved.

Loaded epithets can be very effective. Carefully chosen for their subjective connotations, they can irretrievably alter our attitude toward something *before* we have a chance to investigate it. Once our attitude is tainted, we may never again look at the issue in question without bias. At any rate, well-chosen labels can and do substitute for argumentation and clear reasoning in too many cases.

"What do you think of the President's silly arguments about South Africa?" Are they silly? Labeling them so should not substitute for showing that they are. "Those godless humanists are at it again." A term like *godless* can have a very powerful effect—without any real reasoning to accompany it. So can *propaganda.*

A few years ago, a film entitled *If You Love This Planet,* produced by the National Film Board of Canada, won an Academy Award for best short subject. The film dealt with the effects of nuclear war. Not liking the film's viewpoint, the Reagan administration, through the Justice Department, won a Supreme Court decision upholding its right to label the film (and two others that dealt with acid rain) propaganda. In so ruling, the Court said *propaganda* is a neutral term. Is it?

You have probably gotten the point. When labels and name-calling are used to advance conclusions instead of reasons, we have in effect assumed those conclusions.

Complex Question

Sometimes an unestablished assumption is hidden in a question. When it is, it is a complex question. *The fallacy of complex question is an argument that in asking a question, assumes an answer to an unstated prior question.* A not so humorous example is found in the old vaudeville question "Have you stopped beating your husband (or wife) yet?" No matter how you reply, you're damned if you do, damned if you don't. The reason is that the questioner *assumes* that you are currently beating your spouse (or have in the past). This fallacious maneuver is known by many names: loaded question, trick question, leading question.

In a fashion similar to the way poisoned wells box us in, complex questions attempt to coerce us into "answering" unasked questions in a way favored by the asker. Thus, they are biased or loaded. "Are you still an alcoholic?" implies that you are now or once were one. In all fairness, however, the case that you are (or are not) an alcoholic should be made before this deceptive, leading, and loaded question is answered.

"When are we going to get married?" is really two questions, the first of which is "Are we going to get married?" If I want to marry you, I will try to "trick" you into assuming an affirmative answer to the unasked question. (This coerced answer is sometimes referred to as the "begged" conclusion.)

You can easily imagine the impact of complex questions in the courtroom. Thus, a prosecutor asks a murder defendant, "Tell me, Mr. Smith, what did you do with the knife after stabbing your ailing wife to death with it?" or "Who helped you manufacture your flimsy alibi for your whereabouts the night of the crime?" If it has not been previously established that Smith did in fact stab his wife or did in fact manufacture an alibi *and* with someone else's help, such questions are presumptive. (Note, too, the added presumptiveness of the loaded epithets *ailing* and *flimsy*.)

We want, also, to be cautious of all forms of circular reasoning in propaganda. For example, a proponent for increased tariffs on imported cars might begin a position paper or speech with this question: "Why do increased tariffs on imported automobiles strengthen the U.S. economy?" Do they? If this has not been established, the advocate is leading us before the point has even been demonstrated. Or a poll might ask, "How should we moderate our support of Israel to facilitate negotiating with Lebanese terrorists for the return of American hostages?" We will say considerably more about this kind of leading question when we study biased questions in polls and surveys later in our study.

We also want to watch for poisoned wells and loaded epithets in propaganda: "Of course the Russians say Nick Daniloff is a spy. What do you expect? They're commies." Which of course provokes this: "Of course the Americans deny that Daniloff is a spy. Governments always deny that spies are spies."

Dismissal

The fallacy of dismissal is an argument that uses the assumption of superiority to advance a conclusion. Many times we have heard a public figure respond to charges of misconduct with an indignant shrug: "I cannot believe that anyone would take these charges seriously. I refuse to stoop to the level of my accusers. I will not dignify such charges with a response."

An attitude is not a reasoned case. Simply acting hurt and indignant cannot substitute for a well-reasoned attack on a position or for a well-reasoned defense of one.

A professor asks a student taking an exam, "What's that you have there?" The student gathers up his books, including the suspicious notes the professor alluded to, huffily heads for the door, and announces, "I've never been so insulted. How could you think that *I* would cheat? Well, if you don't trust me any more than that, I'm not going to show you what I have here!" Slam goes the door!

A mother has reasons to suspect that sixteen-year-old Becky is using illegal drugs. One day, she presents her reasons for being suspicious to Becky and asks for an explanation. Becky begins to cry (pity) and then blubbers, "Oh Mom! You've hurt my feelings! I can't believe you'd just accuse me like that. You've really upset me. If you're going to think something like that about me, I refuse to stoop to your suspicious level. I won't discuss this anymore!"

Dismissal occurs when an issue is brusquely swept aside—rather than confronted. No amount of indignation can substitute for clear thinking. Our public figure, our indignant student, and poor suffering Becky all have one thing in common: They have brushed aside claims that warrant consideration. Other names for dismissal are pooh-poohing an argument and shrugging off an argument.

Dismissal is classified as a form of begging an issue because the shrugger's case is assumed—it is not supported by reasons.

Invincible Ignorance

One of the most frustrating fallacies of assumption occurs when we simply latch on to a point of view for any number of reasons, and then hang on to it for dear life. In other words, we adopt a rigid point of view in which we uncritically accept an idea, regardless of contradictory evidence.

The fallacy of invincible ignorance is an argument that insists on the legitimacy of an idea or principle despite contradictory fact. To illustrate, in recent years, Roscoe and Sweeney have engaged in a number of discussions about the wisdom of national health insurance. Roscoe has reached the point where he doesn't even want to discuss the issue any more because no matter what he says, Sweeney inevitably replies, "I don't care what you say about national health insurance, when the government starts meddling in private enterprise like that, no good can come of it."

In effect, Sweeney insists on the legitimacy of his position no matter what facts or points Roscoe might raise. But such insistence is irrelevant to the issue at hand, which is whether such a program is effective. Sweeney must demonstrate that it is ineffective. Simply to insist on the correctness of his position, no matter what, is to commit the fallacy of invincible ignorance.

A dead giveaway for this fallacy is the phrase "I don't care what you say" or some variation of it such as "All that's well and good *but* . . ." or "Be that as it may. . . ." Frequently what follows is a rejection of the opponent's position, not through justification but invincible ignorance. Thus, someone argues, "I don't know why everybody is so upset about this war. War is natural!" Or "Sure I know they look like tomatoes and feel like tomatoes and taste like tomatoes— even better than tomatoes! But they're hydroponic; they're not the 'real thing.' So they can't be any good for you." When faced with someone who's bent on invincible ignorance, perhaps the best thing for us to do is fold our tents and slowly steal away. And quickly! The reason's obvious: We're faced with someone whose mind is made up and who doesn't want to be confused with the facts— the ultimate form of begging the issue.

EXERCISE 5-4 _____

Identify the fallacies in the following passages. Choose from among these: invincible ignorance, begging the question, loaded epithets, complex question, and dismissal. If you think that more than one fallacy is present, explain.

1. ". . . and, no, I did not read the obscene books in question. I don't have to stick my head in the garbage can to know that it contains garbage." (passage from a letter to an editor)
2. How do you know that you can trust me, Dealin' Doug? Well, for one thing, I would never cheat you, and you can rely on that because you have my word on it.
3. Why do you think this is such a wonderful textbook?
4. Item number 4 on our agenda is the stale old proposal to restructure the income tax. It's not worth our time to hash it over yet another time. Let's go on to item 5.
5. TROUBLED HUSBAND: I'm worried about our marriage. You've been staying out till the wee hours of the morning for weeks. You won't say where you've gone. I'm worried that you're having an affair. Where do you go? What do you do?
   TRANQUIL WIFE: Me? Fool around? That's ridiculous. I'll see you later.
6. Shall we go out to a nice restaurant and have a fine dinner or stay home and split the tiny amount of greasy leftover roast—you know the roast you said was overcooked?

7. "Why I Am So Clever" (chapter title in Nietzsche's *Ecce Homo*)
8. UPTON: Black people are just not as bright as white people.
   SINCLAIR: Oh? What about Dr. Samuels? He's got a Ph.D.
   UPTON: He's not a typical black. He doesn't count.
9. "Why I Am So Wise" (chapter title in *Ecce Homo*)
10. JOYCE: What do you think of *Rambo*?
    GERARD: I don't. I never see Stallone films. I don't care what anybody says; I know they're violent junk!
11. What is it about me that's so loveable?
12. BERNIE: What do you think about Reagan's "workfare" idea of having people on welfare work for their money.
    TOD: Frankly, it reeks of socialism.
    BERNIE: How so?
    TOD: C'mon! It's obviously socialistic. It's the sort of socialistic thing you expect to find in Sweden.
13. RICH MAN: You know, people who make their own fortunes are superior to poor people.
    RICH WOMAN: How do you know that?
    RICH MAN: Because if we were not superior we wouldn't be able to make so much money.
14. JEFF: Putting money into space exploration is a waste of time. Nothing of real benefit to us here on earth has come from all that wasted time and money.
    JAN: Oh? What about weather satellites.
    JEFF: They don't count. Whatever's come from space exploration doesn't matter. It's still a waste of time and money.
15. OLD HIPPIE: I am proud that I refused to be drafted during the Vietnam War. In good conscience I could not raise my hand against another human being.
    YUPPIE: I suppose you wouldn't have fought in World War II against the Nazis.
    OLD HIPPIE: That's a stupid thing to bring up. By the way, what do you think about economic sanctions against South Africa?
16. WORRIED PARENTS TO ELOPING TEENS: But how will you support yourselves?
    TEENS: Don't worry; we'll do it.
17. "Why I Write Such Good Books" (This is the last one: a chapter from Nietzsche's *Ecce Homo*)
18. Everything happens for a purpose. If there were no purpose, nothing would happen.
19. PREACHER POPOVER: I can heal you if your faith is strong enough.
    SAD SINNER: But Preacher, my ulcer is as bad as ever.
    PREACHER POPOVER: See! There's your proof of what I say! Your faith is not strong enough.

SUMMARY

This chapter dealt with a number of fallacies of relevance, which are arguments containing premises that are logically irrelevant to their conclusions or to the purpose of demonstrating their conclusions. The irrelevancy arises out of a reliance on emotion, diversion, or assumption. Here is a list of the fallacies covered in this chapter:

Reliance on Emotion

1. *Ad hominem:* an argument that attacks the person who makes an assertion rather than the person's argument. Ad hominem can take three forms: The abusive ad hominem attacks the person's character, not the argument; the

circumstantial ad hominem attacks the circumstances of a person's life rather than the argument; the *tu quoque* ("you also") argument charges a person with behaving in a manner inconsistent with the position the person's advocating.

Example of abusive ad hominem: arguing that President Reagan's position on drug abuse can't be worthwhile because of his involvement in the arms-for-hostages deal with Iran.

Example of circumstantial ad hominem: arguing that Surgeon-General Koop's advice on safe sex practices can be ignored because his strong religious values will necessarily affect his thinking.

Example of tu quoque: Slim and B.J.'s reply to parental warnings about the dangers of drug abuse is "How can you tell us not to use drugs when you smoke and drink and take all sorts of pills?"

2. *Poisoning the well:* a fallacy that occurs when, prior to deliberation, we place an opponent in a position that excludes an unwanted reply.
   Example: Charles Kingsley's assertion that Cardinal Newman could not place high value on the truth because Newman was a Catholic priest.

3. *Mob appeal:* an argument that attempts to persuade by arousing a group's deepest emotions.
   Example: Mark Antony's oration over the corpse of Caesar (Chapter 3); the use of popular music in advertisements.

4. *Sex:* an argument that uses sexual feelings to advance its conclusion.
   Example: Paco Rabanne and Calvin Klein ads.

5. *Pity:* an argument that uses compassion to advance a conclusion.
   Example: Clarence Darrow's defense of Thomas Kidd.

6. *Fear or Force:* an argument that uses the threat of harm for the acceptance of a conclusion.
   Example: the lobbyist who justifies a position by reminding the legislator how many constituents she represents.

Reliance on Diversion

7. *Red herring:* an argument that uses the introduction of an irrelevant issue to avoid dealing with the original one.
   Example: "I have been accused of poor financial management in the matter of the Bidwell account. Let me point out that I have been very careful to file all my reports on time. Further, I have been an employee here longer than anyone. Then, too, I was awarded the Sterling Award for the cost-saving measures I introduced in Personnel."

8. *Humor or ridicule:* an argument that relies strictly on humor or ridicule in attacking a position.
   Example: the case of the member of Parliament named Thomas Massey-Massey.

9. *Two wrongs make a right:* an argument that attempts to justify what's considered wrong by appealing to other instances of the same or similar actions.
   Example: advice to the cheated-on spouse to have an affair to "even" things out.

10. *Common practice:* an argument that attempts to justify wrongdoing on the basis of some practice that's become widely accepted (or so it's claimed).
    Example: Regimen's defense of fraudulent advertising on the grounds that "thousands of other advertisers and agencies are doing the same kind of thing."

11. *Straw man:* an argument that so alters a position that the result is easier to attack than the original.
    Example: the Princeton plan.

Reliance on Assumption

12. *Begging the question:* an argument that assumes as a premise the very conclusion it intends to prove.
    Example: "Smoking marijuana is wrong because taking drugs is wrong."
13. *Loaded epithets:* an argument that substitutes questionable labels for reasons to advance a favored conclusion.
    Example: "And now let's take a look at Nietzsche's obviously juvenile moral philosophy."
14. *Complex question:* an argument that, in asking a question, assumes the conclusion at issue.
    Example: the prosecutor who asks the murder defendant, "Tell me, Mr. Smith, what did you do with the knife after stabbing your ailing wife to death with it?"
15. *Dismissal:* an argument that uses the assumption of superiority to advance a conclusion.
    Example: responding to an accusation that warrants a response by merely announcing, "I refuse to dignify that with a response."
16. *Invincible ignorance:* an argument that insists on the legitimacy of an idea or principle despite contradictory fact.
    Example: "I don't care what anybody says, no one will ever convince me that vitamin C has any effect on the common cold."

Summary Questions

1. Letters to the editor of your local paper are fertile sources of fallacies. Find an example of each of the three forms of ad hominem attacks.
2. A number of television commercials use appeals to fear to encourage us to buy their products. Such products as traveler's checks, smoke detectors, locks, diet and health foods, and life insurance are especially prone to this fallacy. Spot two or three of them. Are the fears they raise legitimate? Is there a way to advertise such products without fallaciously invoking fear? How?
3. Does the two-wrongs fallacy apply to arguments supporting capital punishment? Justify your opinion with your own fallacy-free argument.
4. What are some steps we might take to protect ourselves from fallacious and manipulative appeals to emotions?
5. Can you think of situations in which the "rational" thing to do might be to submit to a fallacious argument? Discuss.

ADDITIONAL EXERCISES

Identify any fallacies in each of the following passages. There may be more than one fallacy. Explain your choices. (If you spot any fallacies from Chapter 4, identify them also.)

1. Gauguin's paintings can't be very good. After all, he deserted his wife and family for a life in Tahiti.
2. Don't listen to Bowman when she talks about raises for police officers. She's a cop.

3. PROFESSOR: Why do you say that my teaching methods are ineffective?
   DEAN: Because the students say so—and they're the ones who pay the bills and keep us employed.

4. It's clear that the universe must have an order and purpose. Look around you: There is order and purpose in the human body, in nature, in the clockwork regularity of the stars, even in molecules and crystals. So surely the entire universe has order.

5. *"Don't risk letting a fatal accident rob your family of the home they love—on the average more than 250 Americans die each year because of accidents.* What would happen to your family's home if you were one of them?" (ad for Colonial Penn Life Insurance Company)

6. An antiabortion film called *The Silent Scream* contains ultrasound images of a twelve-week-old fetus being aborted. As the fetus draws away from the probes of the abortionist's suction tube, it appears to open its mouth and utter what the narrator describes as a "silent scream." The narrator talks about the "child being torn apart" and so forth.

7. My fellow Representatives, as you consider this new tax reform bill, please keep in mind that changes in it will fall squarely on the shoulders of the middle class. And the middle class is the largest single bloc of voters in this country. Do not be persuaded by the arguments of the poor: They rarely vote. It would be unwise to alienate the middle class—we must not anger those who elect us.

8. SKIP: Preacher Caldwell says we shouldn't take drugs.
   ROCK: Don't listen to him. He drinks coffee, and caffeine is a drug.

9. Do you think it's wise to turn down a date with a professor? Don't forget who determines your grade.

10. You know, Professor, I think you might want to consider raising my grade, what with all the concern there is on this campus about sex between students and faculty. I mean, not that we're doing anything wrong, but what if people get the idea that we are? You wouldn't want me to leave here upset, would you? Who knows what people might think upset me?

11. I wouldn't trust Mack's advice on what kind of car to buy—he's a Chevy dealer.

12. You honor, I know that my client was driving under the influence of alcohol. He's admitted it freely. But, your honor, he was just depressed over getting fired. He was worried about his young wife and two tiny children, one a mere babe in arms. Who will feed them? Who will clothe them? Who will comfort them if my client goes to jail? Look at that woman and those two little children, your honor. Can you deprive them of their daddy?

13. Sure, the so-called "right thing to do" is to love your neighbor. But they didn't have AIDS in the time of Jesus. I'm sure he didn't mean for us to jeopardize our own children's health by letting a child with AIDS attend school. What if your child has to sit next to him? What if he coughs on your daughter?

14. During a tax hearing, California Assemblyman Richard Floyd, D–Hawthorne, became impatient with a witness. The apparently exasperated Floyd demanded, "Do you think people are too damn dumb to throw out [officeholders] who vote for excessive taxes?" "You're living proof of that," replied Assemblyman Ross Johnson, R–La Habra. (reported in the *Sacramento Bee,* October 5, 1986)

15. A picture of a shabbily dressed child holding an empty bowl accompanies this caption: "Poor little Maria! Will she go to bed hungry again tonight?" (generic ad for various charities claiming to feed starving children)

16. President Reagan in a televised address during which he announced that American warplanes had just bombed Libya in retaliation for terrorist activities attributed to Moammar Kadafi: "He [Kadafi] counted on America to be passive. He counted wrong." (reported in the *Los Angeles Times,* April 16, 1986)

17. ". . . Since the Meese Report is graphically documented with pornography, and is therefore a carrier of the very plague it proposes to eradicate, Congress must order that all copies of the report be burned." (letter to the editor)

18. "'The Emotional Strain and Overspending Was Terrible,'... is a common statement after the funeral... *but there is a better way*." (opening lines in a mailer for National Memorial Plan; note: the passage set in single quotation marks was printed in blue ink—the body of text was in black—and in much larger type than the rest of the text)

19. "Nobody likes a phony. That seems to be especially so for folks like us who live in small towns. Maybe that's because our lives are simpler, purer than living in the city. I don't know. All I do know is that we should be able to depend on our state senators. That's why I'm so disappointed in Senator X. He took money from special interest groups and used it to pay his wife and then lived off of it. I think that's wrong; Senator X thinks it's all right. My name is _____ , and that's why I'm running for the state senate." (paraphrase of political radio commercial)

20. In 1974 Charles Evers, the then-mayor of Fayette, Mississippi, was indicted by the grand jury in Jackson on charges of evading payment of more than $53,000 in federal income taxes. In August 1974, he responded to the charges by saying, "They've tried everything else. Tried shooting me, starving me and breaking me, and they missed. Now they're trying this." (quoted in Ronald Munson's *The Way of Words*, 1976, p. 305)

21. I know $30,000 might seem like a lot of money to renovate my office. But, then, I am president of this company, and most executives of large companies spend more than that.

22. Cutting in on a man who was talking about drugs, *Today Show* host Bryant Gumbel asked; "Why should we care what you say—you're a junkie, right?" (*Washington Post*, January 4, 1986)

23. Judith Becker, a behavioral scientist at Columbia University was a member of the Meese Commission on Pornography. During a discussion over what constituted being a "victim of pornography," she asked, "What exactly is a victim of pornography?"
"Someone who has been raped," one member responded.
"That is a victim of the crime of rape," another member answered.
"Someone whose father or brother abused her."
"That is a victim of incest."
After more than an hour of wrestling over this, Becker finally concluded that "a victim of pornography [is] someone who sustains a paper cut while turning the pages of a sex magazine." (Carol Tavris, *Record-Searchlight*, Redding, Calif., July 12, 1986)

24. I don't trust all this talk about AIDS being difficult to catch through casual conduct. Don't forget, most of the organizations saying this are full of gay people.

25. WAYNE: I'm in favor of legalized gambling.
NEWTON: There are some strong reasons against legalizing it.
WAYNE: Yeah, but anyone who's opposed to legalized gambling is not worth listening to anyway.

Knowledge

6

The Meaning of Knowledge

No one is so wrong as the man who knows all the answers.

THOMAS MERTON

Dean was upset. He was worried about Nancy's cigarette smoking. But every time he brought the subject up, she claimed that she was just unable to quit, no matter how hard she tried. Dean didn't buy that: He *knew* that she could quit if she really tried.

Dean's logic teacher was annoyed with Dean. It was clear to him that Dean wasn't trying as hard as he could. Dean denied this, insisting, "Honest, Mr. Ross, I am studying and studying. I cannot work any harder." "That's not so," Mr. Ross countered. "I *know* you can do better."

Nancy was upset with her best friend Nola because Nola refused to take megadoses of vitamin C. Nola was concerned that overly large doses of the vitamin might harm her. Nancy tried to reassure her. "But, Nola, Linus Pauling is a Nobel Prize winner and a scientist! He has said repeatedly that large doses of vitamin C have many beneficial qualities."

"How do you *know* that he is right?" Nola asked. "Don't some other scientists question his claims?"

"It doesn't matter," Nancy answered. "You remember how many colds I had last year?"

"Yeah. You were sick pretty often."

"Well, this year I've been taking lots of vitamin C and I have fewer colds, and the ones I do have are not nearly so severe as those I had last year."

"How many colds did you have last year?"

"I don't *know* exactly, but it was a lot."

"Then how do you *know* if you've had fewer this year?"

"Well," an annoyed Nancy huffed, "I just *know,* that's all. And I also *know* that they aren't as bad this year. And I oughta *know;* I'm the expert on my own colds, aren't I?"

"Are you?" Nola asked. "How do you *know* whether or not you have a cold, an allergic reaction to something, a flu, a mild form of hepatitus, strep throat, or mononucleosis?"

Across the continent, the Meese Commission was announcing that it *knew* that exposure to pornography caused an increase in aberrant and criminal sexual conduct. Various other groups and coalitions were announcing that they *knew* that the Meese Commission was wrong.

Meanwhile, Secretary of Defense Caspar Weinberger was reassuring the public that Star Wars could work and that it would be operational in the not distant future, despite the totally contradictory judgment of physicists employed by the U.S. government.

Elsewhere, people claim to *know* that the Bible is the infallible word of God, whereas other people claim to *know* that it is not; that a monster earthquake will strike California within ten years; that reducing one's level of serum cholesterol could extend one's life. . . .

What *does* it mean to say you know something? Most of us go through life claiming all sorts of knowledge. Few ever seriously wonder what it means to know something. When you or I claim to *know* that the sun is about 93 million miles from earth or that a human first walked on the moon in the summer of 1969, just what do we mean?

Although the meaning of knowledge is a highly philosophical question, it's nonetheless important in our study of logic. Just think about it: Even the simplest argument expresses knowledge, for example, "Since every apple I've tasted from this bag is sour, every apple in the bag must be sour." The speaker claims to know that (1) a number of apples are sour and that (2) all apples in the bag are sour. Obviously the person knows (1) in a different sense from (2). You might say that the speaker can be certain about the apples tasted but not certain about the untasted ones. Yet the person claims to *know* both.

Whenever we formulate arguments, we are claiming to know something, premises, on the basis of which we claim to know something else, conclusions. Thus, any argument implies knowledge.

We can look at the connection between knowledge and argument in another way. Recall that we should be compelled only by sound arguments, ones that are justified or true and valid. Thus, we should accept the apple argument only if it's sound. But this presumes that we *know* when an argument is sound. In other words, in accepting an argument as sound, we are, in effect, claiming to *know* that it is. So whenever you accept an argument as sound, you are as much making a claim to knowledge as you are when you say, "I know that the sun is 93 million miles from the earth" or "I know that a human first walked on the moon in the summer of 1969." To accept an argument as sound is to say, "I *know* that this argument is sound."

Both the contents and the ultimate evaluation of arguments, then, are comprised of assertions of knowledge. This is why the meaning of knowledge is fundamental to a study of logic. When we ask, "What does it mean to *know* something?" we are not merely waxing philosophical. We are asking a question, the answer to which will help us sharpen our ability to analyze arguments, both in theory and in practice.

In this chapter, we'll see that any claim to knowledge implies at least three things: belief, truth, and justification. Indeed, *we may define knowledge as justified, true belief.* Lacking an understanding of belief, truth, and justification, we invite fallacies into argument. So in addition to explaining these three things, we'll also be considering some informal fallacies that result from a misunderstanding or an ignorance of belief, truth, and justification.

BELIEF

Belief refers to a person's attitude toward a particular statement. Thus, the astronomer Carl Sagan *believes* that extraterrestrial life exists; the chemist Linus Pauling *believes* that vitamin C can prevent the common cold.

There are several ways to understand what "believes" means in such cases. Let's consider Sagan's belief. One way to speak of his belief is to say that Sagan regards the statement "Extraterrestrial life exists" as being true. Another way is to say that Sagan has a high degree of confidence in the truth of the statement that extraterrestrial life exists. Either way of understanding belief statements is fine for our purposes. The key thing is that belief refers to an attitude that someone has toward a statement, that is, a proposition. And, of course, an attitude may be correct *or* incorrect. Our beliefs may be erroneous. Maybe extraterrestrial life does not exist. Or maybe vitamin C cannot cure the common cold.

Now, the connection between knowledge and belief is that when we claim to know something, we believe it. When we *know* something, we are not just guessing, musing, or speculating. "I know that *P*" (where *P* stands for *any* proposition, such as "Extraterrestrial life exists," "Vitamin C can cure the common cold," "I will be laid off") implies "I believe *P*" (that is, "I believe that extraterrestrial life exists" and so on).

Just imagine what you'd think if someone said, "I know that the earth is spherical, but I don't believe it" or "I know that humans have visited the moon, but I don't believe it." You'd think it odd, to say the least. How can someone *know* something but not believe it? They can't.

Of course, there are times, as when expressing emotion, that we say things like "I know the President has been assassinated, but I don't believe it!" or "I know that I'm looking at pictures of the planet Saturn, but I don't believe it!" But these are rhetorical utterances. We don't intend them to be taken literally. What we ordinarily mean is "Intellectually I know *P*, but emotionally I find it hard to accept *P*."

Since knowledge implies belief, where there is no belief, there can be no claim to knowledge. Thus, if a man does not believe he will be fired, he cannot be said to know that he will be fired. Even if subsequently he is fired, at most it could be said later that he should have known but never that he did know.

STUDY HINT

It is possible to believe something without knowing it, but it is not possible to know something without also believing it.

At the same time, belief is not sufficient for knowledge. Simply because a man believes he will be fired doesn't mean he actually will be fired. Similarly, simply because Sagan believes that extraterrestrial life exists doesn't mean that extraterrestrial life in fact exists; simply because Pauling believes that vitamin C can cure the common cold doesn't mean that vitamin C can actually cure it. No, knowledge implies something else—truth.

TRUTH

To say you know is to imply not only belief but also truth. If Sagan claimed to *know* that extraterrestrial life exists, he would be implying not only that he believes it but also that it is, in fact, the case. Although the distinction between belief and truth may seem obvious, many people confuse them. So let's look carefully at the differences between belief and truth.

When we term a proposition true, we mean that the proposition describes an actual state of affairs. By a "state of affairs," we simply mean some event, condition, or circumstance. Obviously, there are many states of affairs in the world. For example, if you're taller than 5 feet, that's a state of affairs; if the air temperature at present is 60 degrees or above, that's a state of affairs; if the current U.S. President is a Democrat, that's a state of affairs. A true proposition, then, describes some state of affairs. The state of affairs doesn't have to exist only in the present; it may have occurred in the past or will occur in the future. The following are examples of true propositions: "Washington, D.C., is the capital of the United States," "George Washington was the first U.S. President," "Water boils at 212 degrees Farenheit at sea level," "A spirochete causes syphilis." A false statement, in contrast, is one that does not describe a state of affairs. Just negate the four preceding examples and you'll have false statements.

The essential difference between a truth and a belief, then, is that a true statement reports an actual state of affairs, whereas a belief statement reports what someone *thinks* is a state of affairs. To illustrate, the propositions "Deeana is ill" and "I believe Deeana is ill" report two different states of affairs. The first reports what purportedly is the case; the second reports what someone thinks is the case. Notice that there's nothing contradictory about the first statement's being false and the second true. The truth of any belief statement depends simply on whether the speaker is accurately reporting the *belief.* The truth of "Deeana is ill," in contrast, depends on whether Deeana is actually ill.

It should be obvious that no amount of believing that Deeana is ill will alter one iota whether she is actually ill. But we often think and act as if belief does, in fact, mean truth. And because beliefs are relative, we sometimes assume that truths are as well. This simply isn't the case.

Truth Is Not Relative

When we ignore the difference between belief and truth, we're likely to assume that truth is relative. When we speak of the relativity of truth, we generally mean that persons themselves determine at least some truths and that these truths may vary from individual to individual. The error of this position takes root in a misunderstanding of what truth is.

Remember that truth is a characteristic of a proposition that's present when the proposition describes an actual state of affairs. Thus, "Humans have visited the moon" describes an actual state of affairs. That state of affairs is *independent* of what any one of us thinks or believes about it. Humans have either visited the moon or they have not. In this instance, humans have visited the moon. That's a fact, and facts are not relative, although beliefs certainly are.

What if the statement "Humans have visited the moon" were made before the summer of 1969, when the first person visited the moon? Then the statement would be false. But be careful. This doesn't mean that truths change, that what was not true yesterday may be true today. The error in thinking so arises from a failure to see that we must always evaluate propositions within their contexts. In part, this means we must take into account *when* the propositions are expressed. A proposition expressed before July 20, 1969, about humans visiting the moon is an altogether different proposition from one uttered today, even though the sentences' words and syntax remain constant. What we have here are two propositions, and one, uttered prior to July 20, 1969, was, *is*, and always will be, false. The other, uttered after July 20, 1969, *is*, and always will be, true. The meaning of a proposition, and therefore its truth value, cannot be separated from its context, including its historical context. Failing to realize this, we fall into the error of thinking that truth changes, that what may be true today may be false tomorrow, or that what's false today may be true tomorrow. Not fully understanding the meaning and nature of truth can also lead to a common informal fallacy, the argument from ignorance.

STUDY HINT

The truth itself is not relative, but belief is. This is why it sometimes *appears* as if the truth itself changes, when in fact our beliefs have changed.

The Fallacy of the Argument from Ignorance

The argument from ignorance fallacy is the argument that uses an opponent's inability to disprove a conclusion as proof of the conclusion's correctness. Such an argument is irrelevant because it shifts the burden of proof from an argument to the person hearing the argument. It claims that because the person can't disprove a conclusion, the conclusion must be true. A more calloused disregard of the meaning of truth would be hard to find.

We can see a good example of this fallacy in a running debate between Roscoe and Sweeney over the existence of God. Sweeney believes in God; Roscoe doesn't. But they rarely get far in their discussion because inevitably Sweeney claims, "Since you can't disprove God exists, then He must." In response, Roscoe insists that on the contrary, because Sweeney can't prove the existence of God, God must not exist. Both positions are arguments from ignorance. Our inability to disprove a conclusion doesn't make it true; nor does our inability to prove a conclusion make it false.

In fact, the argument from ignorance is a popular one in the Sweeney household. Here are other recent examples:

WILMA: Life in outer space doesn't exist because nobody has ever proved that it does.

SLIM: Who has ever proved that people have souls? Nobody. That proves that the whole concept of souls is just a religious superstition.

B.J.: Pot can't lead to hard-core drug addiction, for nobody has ever demonstrated that it can.

SWEENEY: These so-called psychics have never established a scientific basis for their concepts. So this whole question of psychic phenomena is silly. The fact is that so-called psychic experiences have no basis in science.

STUDY HINT

A lack of evidence is exactly that: A lack of evidence. Therefore, our opponent's lack of evidence is not of itself sufficient reason for us to reject the conclusion.

Each argument reveals that the arguer is misinformed about the nature of truth. There are lots of propositions that are false that we can't disprove; likewise, there are lots of statements that are correct that we can't prove. Our inability to prove or disprove a statement does not of itself warrant a conclusion about the statement's truth, although it would be relevant in helping us, together with other factors, to decide whether or not to *believe* something. Thus, if after repeated investigations, no causal connection between pot smoking and hard-core drug addiction has ever been established, that's certainly evidence to help support a *belief* that there may be, in fact, no causal connection. But it is not enough to warrant the conclusion that there is, in fact, no causal connection (because one has never been established). Perhaps tomorrow or the day after, maybe in the next series of experiments, such a connection will be discovered.

So far we've seen that knowledge implies belief and truth. But it implies something else as well, justification.

*EXERCISE 6-1 _____

1. Would you require anything more than the speaker's word before accepting the following propositions as true?
   a. I think I've got a cavity in a back molar.
   b. I have a cavity in a back molar.
   c. The restaurant is two blocks west of here.
   d. The restaurant, I believe, is two blocks west of here.
   e. Something tells me it's going to rain tomorrow.
   f. I'm going to be sick.

2. Why would you agree or disagree with the following?
   a. Until we know which it is, a proposition is neither true nor false. For example, since we don't know whether there is life in outer space, the proposition "There is life in outer space" is neither true nor false.
   b. A proposition may be true at one time but not another, as with "The United States is made up of forty-eight states." That proposition was true in 1950 but it is not true now.
   c. Sometimes a proposition may be true *of* one person but not *of* another, as with the proposition "I am 6 feet tall."
   d. Sometimes a proposition may be true *for* one person but not true *for* another, as with the sign that reads "Persons under twenty-one not admitted." Since I'm over twenty-one, the statement is not true *for* me.
   e. If you can't disprove a proposition, it's logical to consider that proposition true. For example, since no one can disprove the existence of ghosts, it makes sense to assume that ghosts exist.

JUSTIFICATION

To see how knowledge implies justification, let's rejoin Roscoe and Sweeney, as they discuss Sweeney's claim that he will be laid off.

ROSCOE: All right, Sweeney, how do you *know* you're going to be laid off?
SWEENEY: Because the word's around, that's how.
ROSCOE: What word?
SWEENEY: *The* word.
ROSCOE: Sweeney, can you be a little more specific?
SWEENEY: All right, I overheard Sheilah up in Personnel.
ROSCOE: And she said that you were going to be laid off?
SWEENEY: Not in so many words but . . .
ROSCOE: But what? What did she say exactly?
SWEENEY: That management's cutting back 15 percent across the board.
ROSCOE: You mean 15 percent in each department?
SWEENEY: She didn't say.
ROSCOE: Okay, so how are they going to determine who goes?
SWEENEY: How should I know? Probably on seniority.
ROSCOE: *Probably* on seniority.
SWEENEY: That's right. And there are plenty of people here with seniority on me.
ROSCOE: How many?
SWEENEY: Hey, Roscoe, what do I look like, some kind of computer? I don't have figures like that. I'm just a working slob like you, remember? I'm not management, you know.

What Roscoe wants is justification for Sweeney's claim that he will be fired. *Justification refers to the reasonableness of the evidence to support a conclusion.* Roscoe's trying to determine whether Sweeney has reasonable evidence for claiming to know that his job is in jeopardy. Generally the way to provide that is to assemble the facts, the data, to take a close look at what counts for a claim. Although Sweeney may think them nit-picking, Roscoe's questions are altogether understandable; for any claim to knowledge implies that there is justification, that is, reasonable evidence, for it.

So justification is needed for a claim to knowledge. If Sweeney believes he will be laid off, and even if he eventually is laid off, lacking reasonable evidence he cannot be said to *know* that he will be laid off. The reasonableness of evidence depends on having enough of the right kind of evidence for a claim. *Enough* and *right kind*—in other words, justification is rooted in both the quantity and quality of evidence. How much evidence and the nature of the evidence, in turn, depend largely on the kinds of statements we're evaluating, the nature of the proposition. Let's consider this subject more closely by examining the difference between subjective and objective claims.

SUBJECTIVE CLAIMS AND OBJECTIVE CLAIMS

A subjective claim is a proposition whose truth value is dependent on the knowledge, beliefs, and experiences of a specific individual. An objective claim is a proposition whose truth value is independent of any specific individual's knowledge, beliefs, or experiences. For example, the proposition "It's uncomfortably warm in this room" is subjective because its truth value depends on the individual asserting it. Distinguish this from a proposition such as "The temperature of this room is 98 degrees Farenheit." In the first example, the individual's preferences, physical condition, and so forth are essential components of the proposition. In the second example, the inner experiences of the person making the claim are irrelevant to it.

We want to use special care not to confuse subjective and objective claims. We must also use special care in assessing the truth value of subjective claims. This is not usually a matter of great difficulty when we are aware that a claim is subjective: "I really enjoyed the concert" or "I don't feel well" are clearly subjective. Often, however, subjective claims are presented in a fashion that suggests they are objective and independent of the observer making them.

This misrepresentation occurs most often when we express evaluations in art, morality, politics, religion, and other areas of controversy. Instead of saying, "Boy! I really like Coca-Cola a lot more than Pepsi-Cola," we might say, "Coke is better than Pepsi." This second way of expressing a subjective claim deletes any reference to the individual making it, and hence obscures its subjective nature. Thus, the impression given is that we are making a factual assertion about Coke and Pepsi when in fact we are reporting a personal preference. (For a more complete discussion of value judgments and logic see Part Six, "Evaluation and Values.")

A claim is subjective when its truth value cannot be determined without considering the knowledge, attitudes, moods, and feelings of the person making it. We should develop a sensitivity to subjective claims disguised as objective ones. The best way to do this is to demand clarity, precision, information about frames of reference, and other pertinent factors when we suspect that an apparently objective claim is actually subjective.

There is nothing wrong with subjective claims as such, but when they are treated as if they are objective, we often waste time and effort disputing their truth value. Suppose that your friend says, "The Chicago Cubs are a great baseball team." If her claim means something to the effect that, "I like the Chicago Cubs a great deal," its truth value is a function of her feelings. If, on the other hand, she means that considering such things as the earned run averages of the Cubs' pitchers, the overall rate of fielding errors per game, the win-loss record of the club, paid attendance averages, and so on, her claim is objective.

In the second case, its truth value is independent of any individual. In the first case, however, its truth value is dependent on a specific individual—her. We would, of course, treat the two kinds of claims differently in our analysis of them.

With experience, we can learn to recognize disguised subjective claims. If we do not, we are likely to engage in pointless wrangles of the "Is so!" "Is not!" variety. The treatment of subjective claims and evaluative judgments is so important that it is treated in a separate chapter in Part Six. At this point, we want to be clear about the difference between subjective claims and objective ones so that we can apply appropriate standards of evaluation to the knowledge claims we encounter.

EXERCISE 6-2 _____

Analyze each of the following claims and determine whether it is *most likely* objective or subjective. (If both possibilities are reasonable, recast the original statements into two new ones: one clearly objective and the other clearly subjective.)

1. *Hamlet* is the greatest drama ever written in the English language.
2. This soup is awful!
3. $2 \times 2 = 6$.
4. Homosexuality is wrong.
5. One-third of all teenage marriages are the result of unexpected pregnancies.
6. This room is too small for a class of 100 students.
7. This room is too big for a literature class. It makes it difficult to establish good rapport with students because of its size.
8. The Smith's house is orange.
9. You've got to be really sick to like that movie!
10. Pornography is really sick.
11. I feel the presence of Jesus.
12. Terrorism is morally wrong.
13. Christians believe in the divinity of Jesus.
14. St. Joseph is the capital of Missouri.
15. Say what you will, Mozart's music is superior to Beethoven's.
16. Among tribes of the Northeast Coast, the death of a family member demands the killing of a stranger.
17. I don't think that plan will work.
18. Wow! *Porky's XII* is the funniest movie ever made!
19. *Chez Barre* is the only place to eat if you want truly fine food.
20. You know, you're ruining Little Lester the way you spoil him.
21. No two ways about it: Oldsmobile makes the finest mid-size sedan available for under $15,000.
22. I just don't like that guy. There's something weird about him. I'm getting bad vibes.
23. This logic text is lousy.
24. I love you.
25. You're the kindest person I've ever known.

EVALUATING EVIDENCE

As we've seen, all arguments express knowledge. Knowledge implies three things: belief, truth, and justification. Justification of objective statements can present real problems. In general, a claim to knowledge is justified when there is enough of the right kind of evidence to support it. Just when is this? That is, when—

under what conditions—can I assume that I have enough of the right kind of evidence to accept an objective claim as justified?

In answering this question it's helpful to recognize that the essential ingredient in evidence is what scientists call observations. Whenever scientists weigh something, measure it, take its temperature, and record their findings, they are making observations. These observations frequently serve as a basis for the evidence in a subsequent argument. Thus, your family doctor concludes that you have a flu on the basis of observations she's made about your condition. Similarly, Carl Sagan might conclude that extraterrestrial life exists, and Linus Pauling might conclude that vitamin C can prevent the common cold, on the basis of observations they have made. So the question of sufficiency of evidence for a claim to knowledge is bound up with observations.

When may we accept an observation as correct? When we have satisfied ourselves about the conditions under which the observation was made and about the ability of the observer. Specifically, there are five key things to think about in evaluating observations: (1) the physical conditions under which the observations were made, (2) the sensory acuity of the observer, (3) the background knowledge of the observer, (4) the objectivity of the observer, and (5) the supporting testimony of other observers. Let's briefly consider each of these as well as some fallacies of relevance that arise in connection with them.

Physical Conditions

Physical conditions refer to the conditions under which the observations were made. For example, if your doctor diagnosed your condition solely on the basis of a telephone conversation with you, her diagnosis would be seriously in doubt. Contrast that with a diagnosis reached after a complete physical examination. In the latter case, the conditions under which the observations were made are much more conducive to a correct claim than a diagnosis reached under the conditions of a telephone conversation.

With respect to Sweeney's claims, Roscoe eventually asked him where he had overheard Sheilah say that layoffs were imminent. "Up in personnel," Sweeney told him.

"What do you mean, *up in personnel?*" Roscoe wanted to know. "There must be close to a dozen secretaries up there." Then he added, "I can hardly hear myself think up there, with the hum of all those typewriters."

Sweeney admitted it was difficult to hear, especially over the phone. "The phone!" Roscoe couldn't believe it. How Sweeney could have clearly overheard anything under such conditions was hard for him to accept.

The point's obvious enough: Before accepting any observation, ensure that the physical conditions were favorable. Where the conditions are unfavorable, as in Sweeney's case, the reliability of the observation is in doubt.

Sensory Acuity

Sensory acuity refers to the sensory abilities of the observer. Some people can see and hear better than others; some have a more sharply developed sense of smell and taste, even of touch. Observations always must be evaluated in the light of the observer's ability to have made the observations.

In science, where precise measurements are crucial, instruments heighten the observer's sensory acuity. As a result, in evaluating the reliability of scientific investigations where exact measurements of height, weight, volume, and temperature are crucial, we must evaluate the accuracy of the instruments, as well as the sensory abilities of the persons making the observations.

The technological extension of the human senses can be decisive in providing enough of the right kind of evidence to justify a conclusion. The classic example is probably found in the invention of the telescope, which allowed so many of the claims of the so-called Copernican revolution to be confirmed. In our own times, we can point to things such as the Pioneer XI spacecraft, which journeyed into outer space and, with the aid of marvelously sophisticated cameras, confirmed, for example, that Saturn is girded with radiation.

Necessary Background Knowledge

Necessary background knowledge refers to what an observer must already know to make a reliable observation. For example, at one time Sweeney had been convinced that he had cancer. As a matter of fact, it took Roscoe some time to dislodge Sweeney's belief. He finally did it by demonstrating to Sweeney that he, Sweeney, was in no position to diagnose cancer. Sweeney wasn't a doctor or a pathologist. To observe that he had a lump on his thyroid gland was one thing; he was in a position to observe this, and he obviously had the background experience to know a lump when he observed one. But to claim that that lump was malignant—that was an entirely different matter. Such a claim required a technical background, a highly trained pathological frame of reference. This, of course, Sweeney lacked.

We needn't go far today to see how often this factor in evaluating the reliability of observations is violated. People are paid handsomely for endorsing anything from automobiles to presidential candidates. More often than not, these endorsers lack the necessary background information to make their endorsements credible. We'll say considerably more about this practice when we discuss authority as a source of knowledge. Here it's enough to realize that we must ensure that observers have the needed background to make the observations they are claiming to make.

Objectivity

Objectivity refers to the quality of viewing ourselves and the world without distortion. No one of us can be absolutely objective, for as hard as we may try, we will always view things through the lens of our experiences, assumptions, and emotions. The best we can do is to become aware of these biases and minimize their impact on our observations. The same applies to how we evaluate the observations that make up the premises of other people's arguments.

Be aware of people's frames of references, their "taken-for-granteds." This doesn't mean that you should automatically dismiss the view of someone who may have a vested interest in a case, for that would amount to a circumstantial ad hominem fallacy. But you should be aware of how their loyalties, their built-in biases, may be coloring their observations and, as a result, coloring the evidence they present for a conclusion. Failing to do this, you easily can swallow, and of course formulate, all sorts of bogus arguments.

Supporting Testimony

Supporting testimony refers to the observations of other observers that tend to support the evidence presented. For example, after speaking with Sweeney, Roscoe asked a number of people, who might be in a position to know, whether they had heard of an impending layoff. Some had; others hadn't. Of those who had heard something, Roscoe asked whether they knew anything about who would likely be laid off or how a determination would be made. Not one of them claimed any such knowledge. In a word, there was no corroboration of Sweeney's claim. Lacking corroboration, Roscoe shouldn't accept Sweeney's claim, *even if it satisfied the other factors.*

What's more, had Roscoe found corroboration, he should have applied the preceding criteria to the observations of the others. Also, he should have considered *how many* corroborations he had received. In general, the more corroborative observations, the more reliable the observation at issue.

The five principles just discussed are extremely helpful in evaluating evidence in an argument. But we must be cautious. Even when an observation passes these tests, it ultimately may prove erroneous. Nonetheless, these principles do provide quick and immediate ways for determining whether we have enough of the right kind of evidence for making or accepting a claim to knowledge. In addition, they help us understand how several fallacies of relevance can easily arise in argument when these principles are ignored. Before concluding this chapter, let's take a look at two of these fallacies.

THE FALLACY OF UNKNOWABLE FACT

When an argument contains premises based on observations that are questionable because of unfavorable physical conditions, inadequate sensory acuity, or a lack of necessary background knowledge, the argument commits the fallacy of unknowable fact. So *the fallacy of unknowable fact is an argument that contains premises that are unknowable, either in principle or in this particular case.* Respecting things that are unknowable in principle, suppose someone told you that the blizzard of 1977 in the Northeast was greater than the blizzard there in 1947 because 5,483,221 more snowflakes fell there in 1977 than in 1947. You wouldn't take this argument seriously, because no one can know how many snowflakes fall in a blizzard.

Far more common than this sort of unknowable fact fallacy is the one that consists of a claim that, *in principle,* is knowable but probably is unknowable in this particular case. For example, the makers of Fleischmann's margarine have claimed, "Every fifteen seconds a doctor recommends Fleischmann's margarine." Now, even if this claim is knowable in principle (and you could easily argue that it isn't), it is highly unlikely that the makers of Fleischmann's know this for a fact. Just think what it would take to determine this fact—how much time, money, and personnel would have to be involved. Lacking the details of how Fleischmann's arrived at this observation, we'd best treat it as an unknowable fact.

Here's another example of what seems to be an unknowable fact. John W. R. Taylor, editor of *Jane's All the World's Aircraft,* claimed that President Carter's unilateral action in scrapping the B-1 bomber was probably the reason the

Soviets did not stage their usual display of air power in marking the anniversary of the October Revolution. Maybe that was the reason; maybe it wasn't. But was Taylor in a position to say? Far better trained and more astute Soviet watchers than Taylor weren't so bold as to try to explain Soviet behavior in this case. In fact, explaining Soviet behavior inevitably presents a real challenge, even to those who have studied Soviets the longest and appear to know them the best. In brief, Taylor was in no position to know why the Soviet Union had behaved as it had. Yet, later in his remarks, he made use of this likely unknowable fact to help advance the arguments that the United States was playing right into the hands of the Soviets, with respect to military preparedness. If our analysis is correct, that argument committed the fallacy of unknowable fact.

Sometimes an unknowable fact is signaled by a glaring inconsistency. Here, for example, is an excerpt from a Jack Anderson column, which deals with a so-called secret meeting held by business leaders, purportedly to kill the proposed Consumer Protection Agency. In reading the selection, keep in mind that the meeting was, by Anderson's own characterization, *secret*.

> Armstrong Cork's blunt-spoken Emmett, who presided over the secret session, was not interested in a compromise that would satisfy both sides. He just wanted to bury the Consumer Protection Agency. "The better the bill," he snorted, "the worse it is for us." Another participant also rejected any concessions, warning the assembled business tycoons to remember the "Trojan Horse" story. . . . Still another warned that the White House would throw its full weight behind the bill because, "There is a big need for a White House victory, and this could well be it." The assembled tycoons agreed to make a last ditch effort to defeat the consumer bill.

Some secret meeting! Actually, how secret could it have been when the column is replete not only with what apparently happened but with verbatim quotes, snorts, and warnings. If, in fact, the meeting was secret, it's doubtful that the columnist would know in such detail what went on. Notice that Anderson is not only reporting what occurred but is also characterizing the mood and identifying strategy. Was Anderson actually there? Did he have a source who attended the meeting? Did the source accurately record those quotes? These are important questions because the "facts" reported are advancing the conclusion that big business is conspiring to "kill" the Consumer Protection Agency. Readers can easily be seduced by these "facts" because the thesis is altogether reasonable; indeed it's probably most consistent with what business perceives as its own best interests. The thesis may even be accurate. But what concerns us as students of logic are the supposed facts that are advancing that thesis.

STUDY HINT

Meaningless claims rest on vague, ambiguous, and amphibolous uses of language. The fallacy of unknowable fact, however, rests on meaningful but untestable knowledge claims.

THE FALLACY OF PROVINCIALISM

When an argument lacks objectivity, it frequently commits the fallacy called provincialism. *The fallacy of provincialism is an argument that views things exclusively in terms of group loyalty.* People who argue by appeal to provincialism insist on seeing the world through the eyes of the group with which they identify. Thus, a salesperson who argues that you should buy a domestic car rather than an import because "it's only the American thing to do" is appealing to provincialism.

Many Americans were perfectly comfortable when we bombed Libya, hoping, apparently, to destroy Moammar Kadafi and/or his terrorist associates. Their reasoning apparently went like this: "It is all right to bomb Libyan women, children, and other noncombatants because we must stop terrorism." Of course, one of our objections to terrorism is that it involves the indiscriminate killing of innocent people. But what *we* do is "different."

When Nicholas Daniloff was arrested by the Russians for being a spy, most Americans simply refused to believe that one of "us" would lie about being a spy. We are often more than eager to help other countries with internal problems—El Salvador, Nicaragua, and so forth—yet preciously guard our own right to self-determination. The "Yes, but they are different" rationale is the tip-off to a provincial attitude. The white man who will only hire white men is loyal to a group. So is the family who always sides with Sister whenever she has a fight with her husband.

Athens in the fifth century B.C. was a masculine-dominated, chauvinistic society, in which homosexual friendships between male members of the citizenry were accepted as "the highest form of friendship." Today's history or philosophy students sometimes criticize the ancient Athenians by applying a twentieth-century, Judeo-Christian, American standard. When this is pointed out, some students insist on applying this standard anyway. By insisting on applying the moral standard of their group to an ancient, pagan culture, they exhibit a form of provincialism.

Of course, the fallacy of provincialism is not confined to examples of national loyalty. Sometimes the group identified with is considerably smaller, perhaps a professional or occupational group. Thus, an economist might argue, "The present administration deserves very low marks because it's quite clear that it knows nothing about introductory economics." Here a judgment about the administration's competence is made exclusively in terms of economics, the author's field. Similarly, an educator might favor the reinstitution of the military draft because it will help sagging college enrollments (the assumption being that many potential draftees will seek to avoid the draft by enrolling in college). Again, the arguer sees things exclusively through the lens of a particular group.

SUMMARY

In this chapter we examined knowledge. It's important to be clear on what we mean in claiming to know something because both the contents and our ultimate evaluation of arguments are comprised of assertions of knowledge. Knowledge implies belief, truth, and justification. Belief refers to a person's attitude toward a particular statement. Truth is characteristic of a proposition that describes a state of affairs. Ignoring the difference between belief and truth sometimes leads us to the erroneous assumption that truth is relative. Truth is *not* relative; beliefs are. Not understanding the nature and meaning of truth, we can easily commit the fallacy of the argument from ignorance. An argument from ignorance is one that uses an opponent's inability to disprove a conclusion as proof of the conclusion's correctness. For example, insisting that vitamin C cures the common cold because no one has ever proved it doesn't is an argument from ignorance. The third ingredient of knowledge, justification, refers to the reasonableness of the evidence to support a conclusion. Reasonableness of evidence depends on having enough of the right kind of evidence. What constitutes enough of the right kind of evidence, in turn, depends on the kind of statement we're dealing with. We've learned to distinguish between objective statements, in which the assumptions, experiences, and beliefs of the person making them are irrelevant, and subjective statements, whose truth value does depend on the subjective values and experiences of the individual who asserts them. Objective statements, which need justification outside ourselves—that is, in the world—raise the most serious questions of what constitutes enough of the right kind of evidence to warrant a claim of knowledge. The question of sufficiency of evidence is tied up with observations, which underlie the premises of arguments. We can accept observations as correct when we satisfy ourselves about the conditions under which they were made and about the abilities of the observer. Specifically, five key considerations should be introduced in evaluating observations and evidence: (1) the physical conditions under which the observations were made, (2) the sensory acuity of the observer, (3) the background knowledge of the observer, (4) the objectivity of the observer, and (5) the supporting testimony of others. Ignoring these factors, we can commit the fallacies of unknowable fact and provincialism. The fallacy of unknowable fact is an argument that contains an unknowable premise, either in principle or in a particular case. An example of a fact that's unknowable in principle would be the claim that a specific number of snowflakes fell in a blizzard. An example of a fact that's unknowable in a particular case is Fleischmann's claim that "every 15 seconds a doctor recommends Fleischmann's margarine." The fallacy of provincialism is an argument that views things exclusively in terms of group loyalty. An economist who argues that an administration is inept solely on the basis of its apparent ignorance of introductory economics would commit the fallacy of provincialism.

Summary Questions
1. Students sometimes say, "I know the answer to that question but I just can't think of it." Is it possible to "know" an answer and not be able to give it? Why or why not?
2. Restate the proposition quoted in question 1 in an unambiguous fashion.
3. Analyze the claim "It's all a matter of opinion anyway." Can you refute it?

*ADDITIONAL EXERCISES _____

Identify the fallacies in the following passages. Choose from among argument from ignorance, unknowable fact, and provincialism.

1. BETH: I'm prepared to accept the claim that astronaut gods visited earth a long time ago.

   BRAD: Really?

   BETH: Sure. Nobody has come up with any conclusive evidence that they didn't.

2. JIM (rushing around to open the car door for Susan): Here, let me get that for you.

   SUSAN: That's not necessary. I'm perfectly capable of opening my own door.

   JIM: No, I insist: It's the least I can do to show that chivalry isn't dead—it's just asleep.

3. Newspaper column: Russian deployment of troops in Afghanistan is strictly a diversionary tactic to conceal their number-one priority, which is expansion in Europe and Asia.

4. GENERAL: War has always been with us, Captain, and will continue to be.

   CAPTAIN: That's fortunate.

   GENERAL: I'll say it is. Otherwise we'd be out of a job.

5. Ad: Every ninety seconds, somewhere in America, someone reaches for a MacDingle's fishburger. Isn't it about time you joined them?

6. JOE: Despite the friendly overtures from the Red Chinese, they shouldn't be trusted.

   JAN: That's not a very constructive attitude toward easing East-West tensions.

   JOE: Maybe not, but I've yet to hear anyone demonstrate that friendly Red Chinese overtures aren't just camouflaging some insidious Maoist plot to expand its world influence.

7. TONY: If we were wise, we'd start right now to plan for an all-out confrontation with the nonindustrialized nations of the world.

   TOD: Why's that?

   TONY: Because by the year 2000, the relations between the industrialized and nonindustrialized nations will be so strained that a world war will be inevitable.

8. CONSUMER: The rising price of gas is really putting the pinch on my budget.

   AUTO DEALER: Well, you know these inflated fuel prices aren't really that bad. They'll probably get us all in fuel-efficient cars.

   CONSUMER: You carry some of them don't you?

   AUTO DEALER: *Some* of them? That's our whole line.

9. BARBARA: This Chernobyl episode has really got me thinking about the dangers of commercial nuclear power plants.

   TOD: Oh, I wouldn't worry about that. My dad says the dangers are greatly exaggerated.

   BARBARA: He works for a power company, doesn't he?

   TOD: Uh-huh.

   BARBARA: Well, he should know then.

10. Watergate trial judge John J. Sirica, commenting in retrospect about his feelings on learning of the involvement of President Nixon in Watergate-related events: "I never had any idea the President would be involved. . . . I was very sad when we found out, because, frankly, I had campaigned for Eisenhower and Nixon twice."

11. Lady Bird Johnson, explaining why she joined the women's movement in support of the Equal Rights Amendment: "People whom I respect and believe in and like were part of it. Particularly my two daughters—they thought it was right."

12. CAROLYN: Vitamin E really improves your sex life.

    JEANNINE: Oh, I don't know. I've never read anything that really establishes that.

    CAROLYN: Well, it's improved mine, I can tell you.

    JEANNINE: Who's to say it was the vitamin E? Maybe other things were involved.

    CAROLYN: Maybe so, but until somebody can convince me what they are, I'm going to go right on believing it's the vitamin E.

13. "Does the growing Cuban involvement in the Caribbean mean that Castro has revived his previously abandoned policy of 'export revolution' throughout the region? The answer appears to be yes. Reports *Time* Diplomatic Correspondent Strobe

Talbott: 'Officials at the State Department and National Security Council have no doubt—and indeed they have some evidence—that the Kremlin's department of global mischief-making, acting through its regional surrogates, the Cubans, are stirring up trouble in the once placid Caribbean, and then fishing in those troubled waters for political influence.' " (*Time,* October 22, 1979, p. 46)

14. According to James Ussher, sixteenth-century Anglican archbishop, and Dr. John Lightfoot, seventeenth-century chancellor of St. Catherine's College in Cambridge, creation occurred exactly 5,985 years ago, at 9 A.M., London time, October 23, 4004 B.C.

15. It's perfectly obvious: The universe must have had a beginning.

16. The Russians have never been able to prove that they are not conducting secret weapons tests. And since they can't, we can sure figure out why: They're conducting 'em!

17. ATTORNEY: Your Honor, please make the witness answer my question: Did you see your brother shoot at Mr. Hatfield?
WITNESS: Judge, I can't answer that. We McCoys always stick together—no matter what.

18. "This is a Christian business." (sign)

19. JOE: Boy, those Muslim terrorists really burn me up. There's just no excuse for terrorism of that sort.
JEAN: I tend to agree. But I suppose that some of them might truly believe that God—or Allah as they prefer—wants them to wage jihad, or holy war.
JOE: So what? They're heathens.

20. I don't care what you say.

21. This country is controlled by a few very powerful, very wealthy businessmen. They decide who gets elected, what gets into the news, what gets to Congress. And the most horrible thing about it is that nobody knows they exist. They are so clever and so powerful, no one can ever come up with proof of their influence. It's frightening.

22. Of course he's the best. He's my son!

23. DR. FROID: You see, you wrecked your mother's car last night as a way of punishing your mother.
PATIENCE: I don't understand. It was just an accident. I wasn't mad at my mother.
DR. FROID: Not consciously. Consciously, you are afraid to acknowledge your anger. So you have repressed it.
PATIENCE: But I don't feel angry.
DR. FROID: Of course not. We are never aware of our unconscious feelings while they are unconscious.

24. The sixth grade's better than the fifth grade, nyah, nyah! Everything we do is better.

25. CHAIRPERSON: The chair recognizes Ms. Malone.
MS. MALONE: Thank you. As a psychologist, I would like to point out that the issue of drug abuse is primarily a psychological one. Thus, we should look to a solution in that direction.
CHAIRPERSON: The chair recognizes Chief Parker.
CHIEF PARKER: Thanks. With all due respect to Ms. Malone, let me point out that the real consequences of drug abuse are felt in our legal system: courts, jails, and most of all at the level of the cop on the beat.
CHAIRPERSON: Reverend Edwards?
REV. EDWARDS: Thank you. And let me say that I agree with both Ms. Malone and Chief Parker—up to a point. What we're all overlooking, however, is, I'm afraid, the crux of the whole problem: America is suffering from a spiritual and religious crisis.

7

The Sources of Knowledge

Myself when young did eagerly frequent Doctor and Saint, and heard great argument about it and about; but evermore came out by the same door wherein I went.

OMAR KHAYYAM

"I can hardly breathe," Lisa moaned, dabbing at her nose with a tissue.

"Why don't you take some vitamin Cs?" Nicky asked.

"I don't need 'em. I eat a pretty balanced diet."

"That's not what I'm talking about. Vitamin C does great things for curing the common cold."

"I didn't think there was any way to *cure* the common cold," Lisa sniffled.

"Okay, okay! Not cure, exactly," a testy Nicky continued; "more like *prevent.*"

"I didn't know that," Lisa said.

"Well, it's common knowledge nowadays," Nicky insisted. "Where've you been, in a cave?"

"Hey, ease up; I'm sick, you know."

"Yeah? Well, I know how you can feel better quickly. Take megadoses of vitamin C. Linus Pauling began pointing out the benefits of massive doses of vitamin C over ten years ago. I first heard him on Johnny Carson."

"Who's he?"

"Who's Johnny Carson? Wow! You have been hibernating."

"No, stupid. Who's Linus Pauling?"

"Pauling is a scientist. And a Nobel Prize winner, too! He must know what he's talking about. He's been studying vitamin C for years. If he says it works—it works! Surely you don't want to disagree with a Nobel Prize–winning scientist."

"No," the aching Lisa admitted. "But . . ."

"But what?" Nicky snapped.

"But maybe he won a Nobel Prize for peace or for something unrelated to vitamins. How do I know?"

"That's right," a frustrated Nicky responded, "you don't know. After all, you never won any science awards."

"I don't even know if I have a cold or a flu or an allergic reaction. Maybe I should know that before I take massive doses of anything."

"Everybody knows when they've got a cold," a now exasperated Nicky sighed. "For heaven's sake, don't you want to get better? You don't know anything!"

"I know my head aches, my nose is running, and you've got me confused. All these health claims confuse me. So many people saying they know this works or that doesn't. Take your vitamin C as rose hips, they're 'natural vitamins.' Somebody else says a vitamin is a vitamin is a vitamin; take generic ones and save money. I am confused. I don't know who's right."

Lisa's confusion is understandable. In the last chapter we discussed the meaning of knowledge. We saw that knowledge requires belief, truth, and justification. But knowing that, we still have to face the inevitable issue of justification—and this invariably gives rise to questions about the sources of knowledge.

How do we come by what we know? In the preceding dialogue, chemist Linus Pauling is the chief source of Nicky's claim that vitamin C can prevent or mitigate the common cold. Similarly, Lisa could produce a battery of presumed experts to support her doubts about vitamin C. Whom do we believe? Under what circumstances may we take the word of so-called experts? When should we reserve judgment?

Such questions cannot be fully answered without investigating the sources of our knowledge. That's what this chapter will do. In discovering which sources are reliable, and which are not, we will be improving our chances of correctly evaluating the evidence presented in any argument.[1]

POSSIBLE SOURCES OF KNOWLEDGE

In their investigations of human understanding, many philosophers have noted the centrality of the question concerning the sources of knowledge. The English philosopher John Locke (1632–1704) is a good example.

[1]See Chapter 8, "Pseudoscience: Bogus Knowledge Claims," for a discussion of bogus experts.

In one part of his *Essay Concerning Human Understanding,* Locke reports how he and a group of friends had reached an impasse in a discussion. Unable to proceed, they realized that what they had to do was determine just what they were capable of knowing. This launched them into an investigation of the sources of knowledge, which they agreed was the first and fundamental question to be answered before they could make any progress in their argument. Here's Locke's account:

> Were it fit to trouble thee with the history of this Essay, I should tell thee, that five or six friends meeting at my chamber, and discoursing on a subject very remote from this, found themselves quickly at a stand, by the difficulties that arose on every side. After we had a while puzzled ourselves, without coming any nearer a resolution of those doubts which perplexed us, it came into my thoughts, that we took a wrong course; and that before we set ourselves upon inquiries of that nature, it was necessary to examine our own abilities, and see what objects our understandings were, or were not, fitted to deal with. This I proposed to the company, who all readily assented; and thereupon it was agreed, that this should be our first inquiry.[2]

Philosophers since Locke have been no less attentive to the issue of the sources of knowledge. They have inquired into where we get the beliefs we hold and whether there is one single source of knowledge or many sources. If there are many sources, they have wondered if some are more reliable than others. In modern discussions, philosphers generally recognize four sources of knowledge: reason, senses, authority, and intuition. We'll briefly examine each of these. Keep in mind that understanding these sources provides insights into the foundations of the premises of arguments. It also sharpens our ability to evaluate those premises, to determine whether they justify conclusions.

Senses

A primary source of knowledge is our senses. We know it's raining because we can *see* and *feel* the rain, maybe even *hear* it. We know that a food has spoiled because we can *smell* its stench; we know that milk has gone bad because we can *taste* its sour flavor. We can call such knowledge sense knowledge.

Philosophers sometimes debate the reliability of such sense knowledge. They wonder whether the five senses are dependable sources. To see why some people question the reliability of the senses, think about what a pencil in a glass of water looks like. It appears to be bent, but of course it isn't. Or consider that when we drive up a hill on a hot day, we seem to see a pool of water at the top of the hill. Or perhaps as a child you were frightened by what looked like a menacing figure on your bedroom wall but what in reality was no more than your father's overcoat. What about things like this? Do they show that the senses are unreliable sources of knowledge? Let's try to answer this question by distinguishing between two kinds of senses, outer and inner.

The Outer Senses.   The outer senses refer to the five senses of seeing, smelling, feeling, tasting, and hearing. Our preceding examples seem to suggest that our five outer senses can be deceived, that they are not always dependable sources of knowledge.

[2]From Sterlin P. Lamprecht, ed., *Locke Selections* (New York: Scribner's, 1928), pp. 84–85.

Before assuming this, consider for a moment how many times you were actually taken in by such illusions. Probably not more than once. Even though the pencil appears broken each time you see it in a glass of water, you are no longer fooled. You have learned to see through the illusion. This suggests that it is not the senses that mislead us, but our interpretations of the information the senses provide. Such perceptual errors, then, are more accurately termed *interpretive* or *judgmental errors*. Because we didn't wait until we received more information—which would have resulted from pulling the pencil from the glass of water, driving to the wet spot, turning on the light switch in the bedroom— we jumped to a conclusion.

So we can say that the outer senses are reliable sources of knowledge. It is in interpreting what these senses receive that we may commit judgmental errors and later express these errors in propositions and arguments.

One way to ensure that our judgments are accurate is to open them to public verification. *By public verification we mean that almost anyone wanting to could verify the claim.* If someone tells us it's raining we can verify this for ourselves. If someone tells us that the soup is too hot to drink, we can find out for ourselves. Such claims stem from sense experiences. Any of us—assuming that our outer senses are functioning adequately—can verify them.

The Inner Senses.   The inner senses refer to the unique, immediately experienced qualities of first-person experience. For example, only I know if I feel anxious, queasy, happy, indifferent, angry, loving, or vengeful. I know because of my inner senses, those capacities to experience pain, joy, sadness, fear, anxiety, and so on. Thus, if I say, "I'm really annoyed," I and I alone am in a position to verify that statement.

It's important to distinguish between a statement that reports strictly an inner state and one that reports something more than that. The former we call *subjective claims* and the latter *objective claims*. Take, for example, these two propositions: "I feel queasy" and "I feel that people are laughing at me." Both propositions report a feeling. But what are they stating? The first states that I feel sick to my stomach. Since this condition is strictly an inner state, my feeling is enough to verify the claim. That is, "I feel queasy" is identical to "I am queasy." This proposition reports a subjective claim.

But in the second objective claim, I am reporting more than strictly an inner state. True, I am feeling something, but that feeling is hardly enough in itself to verify that people are actually laughing at me. In "I feel queasy," my feeling is enough to verify my queasiness. But in "I feel that people are laughing at me," my feeling is not enough to verify that people are, in fact, laughing at me. What I am really voicing is a belief, an opinion, or even a conviction. But verification of that belief must be found outside me—in the real world. If I'm a nightclub comic or a clown, I have cause for such a feeling. If I'm a mortician, I should probably plan a long cruise to the islands.

*EXERCISE 7-1 _____

For which of the following propositions are the inner senses adequate sources of verification? For which are they not? Which, if any, need public verification? Explain.

1. I've got a toothache.
2. I have a cavity in a rear molar.
3. The person over there has a toothache.
4. I feel the presence of Jesus.

5. "Eureka!" ("I've got it." That is, "I have the solution to this problem.")
6. Every morning about this time I get terribly depressed.
7. I just know I've got high blood pressure.
8. You're lying.
9. I know you love me, even if you won't admit it.
10. The reason I like art so much is that I was a painter in a past life.

Reason

In general, reason is the capacity for rational thought, judgment, or discrimination. For our purposes, let's define *reason as the capacity to draw conclusions from evidence*. Reason, together with the senses, is another chief source of knowledge. We know a little bit about reason from our introductory remarks in Chapter 1, but it won't hurt to underscore some of that discussion.

If asked for the sum of 1 million and 1 million, what would you say? Two million. It's hardly likely you have ever seen 1 million things assembled at one time, so you mustn't be relying on your senses as the source of your knowledge. Then what is it that allows you to be so sure that 1 million plus 1 million equals 2 million? And what makes you so certain that if A is larger than B and B is larger than C, then A is larger than C? It's your reason that allows such claims. Earlier we spoke of two modes of reasoning: induction and deduction. Let's review them.

Say you go to the refrigerator wanting something to eat. You see a bag of apples. Picking up an apple and biting it, you find it's sour. You notice it's hard and green. You take up another and find it is also hard, green—and sour. You rummage through the bag and find that all the remaining apples are also hard and green. You conclude that they are also all sour. You have performed an *operation of induction*. Here, sense experience and reason are operating together. You found in two experiences that hardness and greenness went together with sourness. You reasoned that the remaining apples, all hard and green, would also be sour. Your premises are certain, based on direct experience. Your conclusion—as are all inductive conclusions—is probable. Scientists use the method of induction to discover the laws of nature. From precise experimental evidence, they induce general laws.

Reasoning inductively, you have arrived at a general law: "All the green and hard apples in this bag are sour." Suppose later someone opens the refrigerator and offers you one of the apples. Your mind, quickly and perhaps subconsciously, performs the following reasoning process: "All hard and green apples in this bag are sour; this is a hard and green apple from this bag. Therefore it is sour." Not liking sour apples, you refuse. You have reasoned *deductively*. Notice that all a valid deductive argument does is make plain the inferences already contained in its premises. But with more complicated arguments, these inferences are harder to see.

So by reasoning inductively, you have arrived at a *general* conclusion. Reasoning deductively from that general conclusion, you have arrived at a *particular* conclusion. If your reasoning is sound, it should predict future experience. If you have reasoned soundly and taste the offered apple, it should indeed be sour. If we were talking science instead of common sense, we would call this *experimental verification*.

In most cases, reason alone is insufficient to establish the truth of an argument's premises; to do this we must make careful appeals to the world of experience. To get at truth we often must leave pure reason and go to other areas: physics, chemistry, biology, social science, history. So, to determine the truth of the premises that make up an argument, we must frequently leave the realm of pure reason and find out if what the premises are reporting is an actual state of affairs. Logic in this sense is like a computer; it can certify the correctness of your reasoning about a given content, but it cannot by itself verify the accuracy or truth of that content. It simply says: "Give me *A* and *B*, and I'll tell you whether you can reasonably move to *C*; but I can't tell you whether *A* and *B* are true. That's up to you."

EXERCISE 7-2 _____

Indicate whether the following arguments are inductive or deductive.

1. Every student in this class is enrolled in the college. Carolyn is a student in the class. So Carolyn must be enrolled in the college.
2. Jack has never been to class on time yet. So we can expect him to be late today.
3. JUDY: I bet I'm not going to get paid what a man gets for doing this job.
   JERRY: That sounds pretty bitter.
   JUDY: It's just realistic. After all, most women still get less than men for doing comparable work.
4. GIL: There just has to be a cure for cancer.
   MERYL: I'm beginning to wonder.
   GIL: Look, every disease has a cure, doesn't it? We may not know what it is, but every disease must have a cure.
   MERYL: Well, I guess you're right then—cancer must have a cure.
5. DETECTIVE: You must have committed the murder.
   SUSPECT: Why?
   DETECTIVE: Because only the murderer would know the whereabouts of the victim's wall safe. And we've already established that you knew that.
6. CHERYL: Well, if you ask me, I think the President came on TV last night to shore up his political popularity and not at all to address the invasion of Grenada.
   CHARLIE: I don't know. He talked about a Cuban military brigade there.
   CHERYL: Yeah, but what was he doing on nationwide television at prime time? Just to show everybody how tough he is. He figures that will help him in the polls.

Authority

Authority refers to an expert outside ourselves. Authority is a most common source of knowledge. Just think about everything you know based on authority. World history, the state of your health, the condition of your car, the direction of the economy, the events of the day, the weather—the list goes on and on. Indeed, without reliance on authority, we would know very little of what we ordinarily take for granted. In fact, when you start thinking about how great a role authority plays in what you know, you can't help feeling a little nervous. After all, taking something on authority implies an act of trust. We just hope our trust hasn't been misplaced.

Since the time of Gutenberg's printing press, the printed word has been our most authoritative source of knowledge. What's between two covers, centered on a page and facing us in clear, bold print smacks of truth. We trust it. In many instances our trust is rewarded; we learn the truth. With the increase in publishing, however, with the great number of ghost-written books, and with the staggering economic possibilities of contemporary publications, we'd better be skeptical about accepting automatically the written word as a reliable source of knowledge.

In the area of self-improvement books alone, for example, there is a welter of publications, all making some claim to the truth. Many contradict others. Thus, for the physical-fitness buff there are authoritative sources that hold daily exercise as the key to long and healthful lives; other people espouse Mark Twain's dictum: Whenever you feel like exercising, just lie down until the feeling passes. For those concerned with their figures, there are high-protein, liquid, and low-carbohydrate diets allowing us to eat as much as we want; other sources would enforce meager food consumption with all the rigor of a medieval monastery. And for those who think their sex lives unexciting, there are manuals making sex sound as mechanically predictable as tuning a car; others maintain that continual sexual bliss is rare, if at all possible.

Determining the Reliability of Authority.   How do we determine when authority is a reliable source of knowledge? First and obviously, *we should ensure that the authority is just that—an expert in the field.* Perhaps the grossest violation of this principle is the practice of endorsements, all-pervasive in advertising. Enlisting the support of celebrities to sell products that have nothing to do with the celebrities' areas of expertise is a fallacious appeal to authority, a fallacy and practice we'll say considerably more about shortly.

Even when we're sure the authority is indeed an expert in a directly related area, we should not accept the viewpoint unquestioningly; often even the experts are divided. As a second criterion, then, we should ensure a concensus of expert opinion. Take, for example, the 1973 Supreme Court ruling on obscenity. By a margin of only one vote, the court found that obscenity should be determined by community standards and not by some universally applied standard stressing the social redemption of a piece of work. If we argue that we *know* this ruling is best because the Supreme Court has decided it, our appeal to experts ignores contradictory opinions of equal experts. Recognizing that such striking discord exists even among experts, we should realize that what we have is not knowledge but a belief that, at least for a time, is law. Understanding this point might make us less vulnerable to the uneasiness many people complain of in a modern society that's constantly shifting, changing, and rearranging; treating such positions as truths we *know* exposes us to degrees of insecurity hardly tolerable when these "truths" change. Obviously, authorities agree on many points: All agree that water boils at 212 degrees Fahrenheit at sea level; that Caesar was assassinated on the Ides of March in 44 B.C.; that George Washington was the first President of the United States. In basing our claims to knowledge of such things on the recorded word of scientists and historians, we're certainly within our rights. But where there is genuine disagreement among authorities on, for example, the health hazards involved in smoking marijuana or using birth-control pills, we should suspend our claim to knowledge and realize the best we can hold is a well-informed belief and opinion. Realizing this, we remain open to contradictory evidence, something B.J. is unwilling to do when he insists on considering only Linus Pauling's view. In fact, the experts are divided about the vitamin C and common cold connection.

Third, even in cases where the experts agree, we should ask ourselves, "Can I find out for myself?" This is a crucial question. It's asking if we could discover—if we had the time, interest, energy, and resources—this knowledge for ourselves, firsthand. With some authoritative claims, this presents no problem. Thus, we can boil water to find out if, in fact, it does boil at 212 degrees Fahrenheit at sea level; we can drop a large rock and a penny from the same height to see if weight affects the speed of a falling body; we can spray arsenic on insects to see if it's a poison. Of course, we hardly ever do these things to prove the truth of such propositions because it would be a waste of our time.

What about instances in which we cannot have a direct sense experience and in which unaided reason is insufficient, as in "Lincoln was assassinated"; "Napoleon was defeated by Wellington at Waterloo"; "The Battle of Hastings occurred in A.D. 1066"? In these cases we should easily be able to conceive of someone not so different from ourselves who could have had a direct sense experience of the claim. Then we should weigh corroborative sense experience, that is, identical sense experiences that other eyewitnesses have had. Under no circumstances should we maintain that in the last analysis the primary justification for holding that Lincoln was assassinated is that "it says so in the history books." Someone must have witnessed it or enough of the circumstances surrounding it to give the claim its ultimate and primary foundation.

In summary, faced with a barrage of arguments and opinions, unable to check out all facts for ourselves, we must often rely on *authority as a secondary source of knowledge*. There are dangers in relying on authority as a source of knowledge. Yet if we never did, we'd know very, very little. How do we know when to lend faith to the statements of a particular authority? We must ask ourselves, Is the authority a recognized expert in the field? Do the authorities in the field agree? Can we check the claims of authority for ourselves? This last criterion underscores an important fact to remember: Authority may never be the primary source of knowledge. Ultimately knowledge must be based on the senses and/or reason.

There are several fallacies of relevance connected with the use of authority as a source of knowledge. Let's consider them.

*EXERCISE 7-3 _____

Which of the following propositions would you feel confident to take on authority? Why? Why not?

1. $E = MC^2$
2. Hell exists (meaning the preternatural abode of evil and not, as Sartre suggests, "other people").
3. Many theologians believe that hell exists.
4. This Bible says that hell exists.
5. Sugar causes tooth decay.
6. The earth was once visited by astronaut-gods.
7. The U.S. Declaration of Independence was adopted on July 4, 1776.
8. Mercy killing is moral.
9. The *Mona Lisa* is an outstanding painting.
10. Democracy is the best form of government.
11. The Vietnam War was a necessary evil.
12. The Iran-Contra scandal is the result of a flawed presidential management style.
13. Taking the Shah of Iran into the United States caused Iranian students to seize the U.S. embassy in Teheran.
14. The crash of the space shuttle *Columbia* was due to faulty O-rings on the booster rockets.

15. Abortion is wrong.
16. All people of good taste prefer classical music to country music.
17. The stock market is headed for a steep decline in the next quarter.
18. That argument is invalid.
19. Beethoven is a better composer than Bruce Springsteen.
20. Too much exposure to the ultraviolet rays of the sun causes skin cancer.
21. Vitamin C is a cure for the common cold.
22. Herbalife products are safe.
23. Your car has a leak in its fuel pump.
24. The universe was created by a "big bang" eons and eons ago.
25. Violence on television causes violence in real life.

The Fallacy of False Authority. *The fallacy of false authority is an argument that violates any of the criteria for a justifiable appeal to authority.* Thus, if an argument uses as an expert a person who in fact is not an expert in the appropriate field, if there is not a consensus of expert opinion, or if we could not—even in theory— verify the claim for ourselves, the argument commits the fallacy of false authority.

Without doubt the commonest examples of false authority are found in product endorsements. Constantly we are bombarded by celebrities selling products about which they know as little as any of us, in some cases a lot less. But because of their names and reputations, they earn whopping fees for merchandising. Thus, sports heroes push everything from coffee makers to panty hose. Hollywood stars hawk everything from pickup trucks to political candidates.

Cybil Shepard and Bruce Willis, the two glamorous, "exciting" stars of the television show "Moonlighting," sell hair products and wine coolers, respectively. Former Oakland Raider Lyle Alzado sells subscriptions to *Sports Illustrated*. Ex-football tough-guy Dick Butkus and wrestling "baddie" King Kong Bundy pitch Chevys. Mickey Spillaine and Rodney Dangerfield sell beer. Charlton Heston and Cliff Robertson battle it out in the "long-distance wars," pitching long-distance phone service. We had James Coburn for MasterCard and Angela Lansbury, Robert Duvall, and Karl Malden, at one time or another, touting various credit cards.

George C. Scott is the latest in a long line of actors and personalities selling cars: Scott for Renault, James Garner for Mazda, Ricardo Montalban for Chrysler Cordoba, Telly Savalas for Toyota, even Grace Jones and Adam Ant for Honda motorscooters. Rod Stewart croons, "You're in my heart, you're in my soul," to a Mercury. Back in "the old days" of the 1950s and 1960s Milton Berle and Bob Hope would've sold us the gas: Texaco.

To our list we add Brooke Shields in her tight denim trousers, Catherine Deneuve, Joan Collins, Jacqueline Bisset, Martha Raye, Rosemary Clooney, Edward Hermann, and the venerable John Houseman— all selling something, trying to cash in on their images: beauty, glamour, sophistication, whatever.

Then there are Mary Lou Retton and Pete Rose for Wheaties, "what the big girls (boys) eat." The hawkers change over the years, to reflect the culture heroes of the times. But the song is the same. Just consider a meager list of some old chestnuts from the past:

> "Take it from Bruce Jenner: 'You need a good start to get in shape. And I can't think of a better start than a complete breakfast with Wheaties.' "

John Wayne for Datril 500: "New Datril 500. It's strong medicine for a headache, but gentle on the rest of your system."

"Elke Sommer knows watching her nutrition counts as much as watching her weight. So she's starting her day with the Special K Breakfast. That's good for Elke, and good for you, too."

Don Meredith for Lipton Tea: "What makes me a Lipton Tea lover? Lipton tastes so dang good."

Florence Henderson for TANG: "I'm glad my children love the taste of TANG because each glass contains a full day's supply of vitamin C."

"New! Clairol Short and Sassy Shampoo. The shampoo Dorothy Hamill uses."

Robert Young for Sanka: "I think it's important that we take care of ourselves. [Remember, he used to play Marcus Welby, M.D.] That's why doctors have advised millions of caffein-concerned Americans, like me, to drink delicious Sanka Decaffeinated Coffee."

That last ad, with its reference to "doctors," also illustrates how the prestige of a profession may be used in the false appeal to authority. Here's another from Anacin: "Doctors recommend one pain reliever most: the one you get in Anacin."

A recent variation of the false appeal to authority is the concoction of a character who embodies what all of us are supposed to desire. *Playboy* magazine, perhaps, pioneered in this psychology with its centerfolds. It's not so much that the centerfold embodies the fantasy that most American men are supposed to nurture about women (and possibly women nurture about themselves) but that the interview that accompanies the centerfold assumes an authoritative air because of the power of fantasy. The Playmate's comments about what constitutes the good life, how important it is to "relate" to others, how vital it is "to do your own thing," and how necessary it is "to love your fellow man" (no pun intended) would sound platitudinous coming from someone with a few less strategically placed inches. As theologian Harvey Cox pointed out, magazines of this kind often establish themselves as authorities of the "good life" for those young men—and perhaps women—who have acquired a certain affluence but don't quite know how to handle it. *Playboy* accordingly tells them what vacations to take, what food to eat and wines to drink, what stereo components to acquire, what books to read, what politics to pursue, what code of sexual morality to follow, and last but not least, what females to cultivate—and what females are cultivated. Appropriately, many of the ads in *Playboy* don't use the celebrity endorsement but instead capitalize on this ideal form of the "Perfect Playboy." Thus, a Dewar's Scotch ad shows a handsome young man, dressed smartly but casually, standing in the middle of a Playboy "pad," holding a glass of scotch. Beneath the picture is a thumbnail sketch:

Home: San Francisco
Age: 30
Profession: Produces rock-music specials.
Last book read: [usually the current best-seller]

Favorite quotation: "Winning isn't everything—it's the only thing."
Female preference: Bright, witty, beautiful, and unclinging.
Scotch: Dewar's, what else?

This ad, of course, has limitless variations.

The Fallacy of Positioning.   A new variation on the false appeal to authority has become so popular that it invites a special designation: the fallacy of positioning. *The fallacy of positioning is an argument that tries to capitalize on the earned reputation of a leader in a field to sell something.* Here's how it works.

Suppose a car-rental agency such as Avis advertises "We're the world's second largest car-rental agency. Since we're second, we must try harder." The car-rental agency here positions itself next to the leader, presumably Hertz, thus allowing it through transference to be identified with the most successful competitor. Goodrich has used this technique masterfully with its claim "We're the ones without the blimp," thus reminding us of a well-identified tire manufacturer, Goodyear.

Positioning creates a spot in the prospective buyer's mind for a company, a spot that considers not only the company's image but its competitor's as well. It's based on the assumption that the mind has become an advertising battleground. To be successful, a manufacturer must relate to what's already in the mind, what is fixed as authoritative. Thus, although RCA and General Electric failed in trying to buck IBM directly in the computer industry, the smaller Honeywell succeeded by using the theme of "the other computer company." Similarly, by attaching itself to another's star, Sabena Airlines has exploited Pan Am's claim to be the "world's most experienced airline" by itself advertising, "We started flying four years ahead of the world's most experienced airline." And 7-Up, realizing that half the soft drinks sold are colas, successfully wages an "Uncola" campaign. Finally, here are two manufacturers of copy machines that have gone after Xerox's top position in the field:

Ad for Pitney Bowes: "We don't have to make Xerox look bad to look good."

Ad for Toshiba: "O.K. Xerox, Try and copy this."

The Fallacy of Traditional Wisdom.   Fallacious appeals to authority can take still another form: the appeal to traditional wisdom. *The fallacy of traditional wisdom is the argument that uses the past to justify claims made in the present.* Thus, in answer to a student's question about why students must be tested, a teacher replies, "Why, students have been taking tests since the first school was built. That should tell you something about the value of tests and why you need to take them." Actually, the fact that students have always taken tests says nothing at all about their value or why students should continue to take them. The appeal is strictly to tradition to justify a practice in the present.

A former U.S. senator once committed the fallacy of traditional wisdom in justifying his opposition to the Equal Rights Amendment to the Constitution. Said Senator Sam Ervin (D–N.C.), "I tell them, 'Why ladies, any bill that lies around here for forty-seven years without getting any more support than this one has got in the past obviously shouldn't be passed at all. Why, I think that affords most conclusive proof that it's unworthy of consideration.'"[3] No, it doesn't.

Finally, recall the frequent appeals to traditional wisdom during 1974 when cries for President Nixon's impeachment resounded throughout the land. Many insisted that Nixon should not be impeached because a U.S. President never before had been successfully impeached. Thus, because we have never successfully impeached a President, we should not try to impeach one now.

The fact is that using tradition as the exclusive determinant of a present course is not only silly but potentially dangerous. By such logic, women still wouldn't be allowed to vote, blacks still wouldn't be allowed to eat in the restaurants of their choice, and sex education still wouldn't be taught in many places other than street corners and back alleys.

Common phrases that often invite an appeal to traditional wisdom are *the founding fathers, the earliest settlers, from time immemorial, tried and true, the lessons of history, it says so in, look at the record,* and others. Beware of them. Learn from tradition, but don't be enslaved by it.

The Fallacy of Popularity. Finally, a fallacious authority may take the form of an appeal to popularity. *The fallacy of popularity is an argument that tries to justify something strictly by appeal to numbers.* Thus, a bookseller tries to persuade you to buy a recent publication on the basis that *everyone* is reading it, or *thousands of copies* have already been sold. So what? Why should *you* read it? In such arguments, quantity constitutes authority.

Be cautious of the fashionable. Whatever's sought by many for a period of time frequently becomes the vehicle for fallacies of popularity. Thus, today what's "natural" is "in"; what's "artificial" is "out." Shrewd advertisers recognize this. They pitch their ads to this popular sentiment, hoping to reach a wide and sympathetic audience for their products. Also, they hope to profit by association with what appears to be a broadly held value.

The appeal to popularity is common outside advertising. President Johnson once replied to American and European critics of his war policy by pointing out that almost every country in Asia wanted the United States to remain militarily engaged in Vietnam. Did this justify our engagement there? Again, Johnson was known for carrying agreeable poll results in his pocket and using them to wall himself off from criticism. Both Johnson and Nixon used their overwhelming election "mandates" to justify policies that had become extremely unpopular and that caused both presidents great personal anguish and embarrassment. To an extent, President Reagan seems to have followed the same script with respect to Star Wars. And many members of Congress, when answering criticism of Congress's resounding vote to ban television blackouts of home football games providing tickets are sold out several days in advance, simply replied, "How many Americans do you think are upset?"

In concluding this section on authority as a source of knowledge, let's repeat that appeals to authority are legitimate when (1) the authorities are genuine experts in the pertinent field; (2) there is a consensus of authoritative opinion; and (3) when we can, at least in theory, verify the claims for ourselves. In the absence of any of these criteria, an argument that appeals to an expert commits the fallacy of false authority. Fallacious appeals to authority, however,

---

[3]Quoted in Howard Kahane, *Logic and Contemporary Rhetoric* (Belmont, Calif.: Wadsworth, 1976), p. 11.

may occur in a variety of other ways as well: by positioning, by appealing to traditional wisdom, by relying on popularity.

EXERCISE 7-4 _____

Identify the fallacies (false authority, positioning, traditional wisdom, popularity) in the following passages.

1. JOE: You know, I think I'm going to start banking at First Federal.
   JILL: Why's that?
   JOE: Well, I saw Fred Astaire do a commercial for them the other day. I figure a guy as successful as he is must know something about saving money.

2. REPORTER: Sir, there's been a lot of talk recently about migrant workers and particularly about how they are not receiving due process under the law.
   DISTRICT ATTORNEY: Well, I don't for a minute deny that there have been abuses. But you must remember that's how we do things in this state. I don't say it's right, mind you, but that's the way it's done.

3. "Subaru and Mercedes, two of the finest engineered cars around. One sells for eight times the price of the other. The choice is yours." (ad for Subaru)

4. "We were founded just a couple of years after the U.S. Constitution was signed, and by the same kind of people who signed the Constitution." (ad for insurance company)

5. FRANK: You know, I think all political parties should be entitled to TV time and not just the major ones.
   WINNIE: I don't see that at all. The major parties represent the significant viewpoints. The other parties don't.
   FRANK: Why do you say that?
   WINNIE: Well, by far the vast majority of Americans belong to the Republican or Democratic parties. So what those parties have to say is obviously important.

6. Ad for Equitable Life Assurance Society—written below a 1950-vintage picture of a father helping his son with his homework: "Nobody Else Like You Service. We stole the idea from your father." [Oh yes, Equitable has another ad, which is identical, except that Mama has replaced Papa.]

7. JOYCE: No TANG for me. I'd prefer something more nutritious.
   GEORGE: More nutritious? Don't you realize that NASA chose TANG for its astronauts?

8. BILL: There's no question that humans are inherently aggressive.
   JUNE: I disagree.
   BILL: If you do, you'll have to disagree with some pretty heavy thinkers, such as Darwin and Lorenz and Ardrey. As for me, their endorsement of the aggressionist view offers pretty good evidence for it.

9. JERRY: Educated people can't really believe in God any more.
   RITA: I disagree. I know plenty of educated people who hold deep religious beliefs.
   JERRY: Either they're faking them or they're not educated. For, as Freud pointed out in his *The Future of an Illusion,* religious belief is simply impossible for educated people today.

10. STAN: There's no question that the Golden Rule is a sound moral principle.
    STU: Why do you say that?
    STAN: Because it's basic to every system of ethics ever devised. I mean you can go back thousands and thousands of years and see some variation of the Golden Rule in society. Everybody has adopted it in one form or another.

11. PETE: Reincarnation explains why some of us have good lives and others have difficulties.
    KEN: I'm not sure. I don't see any good evidence to support belief in reincarnation.
    PETE: Oh, yeah? Well, just the other day I saw Shirley MacLaine on the "Phil Donahue Show," and she explained it. In fact, she's even written two books about

psychic phenomena, among other things. And they certainly wouldn't let her publish them if she didn't know what she was talking about.

12. STUDENT: I don't see why we have to have a term paper in this class. We write enough essays for you to evaluate us on.

     PROFESSOR: Term papers have always been part of college courses. They must be valuable learning aids to have withstood the test of time.

13. I know God must exist. For all recorded history billions of people have believed in some type of deity. If the vast majority of humankind has believed in God, who are we to doubt?

14. It is obvious that God does not exist, my biology teacher told me so, and she's a Ph.D.

15. The number one selling small truck in America today!

16. Kids ought to have jobs! I had a job when I was in school, and my Daddy had jobs. So you, my boy, should have a job too.

17. JOAN: I feel sorry for kids today.

     DORIS: Why's that?

     JOAN: Well, all these single parent "families." You know, that's not really a family. The family has always been Mom, Dad, and the kids. That's the way it's supposed to be.

18. ROSS: I'm getting a divorce.

     JIM: Why?

     ROSS: My therapist says that my marriage is unworkable, and he oughta know. He's an expert in marital relations.

19. GEORGE: Yep, I get to turn in my paper late. Barbara gave me permission, you know.

     RICH: Barbara?

     GEORGE: You know! Dr. Boyce. Oh, that's right, you don't know her well enough to call her Barbara.

20. But, Mom! You've got to get me Jordache jeans, Nike shoes, and Opium perfume. All the other girls have them.

Intuition

Actually, B.J. hasn't been completely forthright with Slim about his sudden interest in good health and particularly in vitamin C. The truth is he's met a girl—Wanda.

Some might call Wanda a "health nut." But that's unkind. Wanda simply takes a more serious interest in her health than most people her age, probably more serious than most people. And it was Wanda who really put B.J. onto vitamin C and introduced him to the work of Linus Pauling.

The funny thing, though, is that B.J. has developed implicit trust in Wanda. Why this happened is far too complex to go into here. But curiously, when B.J. met her for the first time, he seemed to know that she was someone he could trust. That impression has left an indelible mark, of which his new-born commitment to good health is just one example. He's also taken to reading certain books and seeing particular films on Wanda's recommendation. In effect, then, Wanda is functioning as a most influential authority in B.J.'s life. But even more noteworthy is how he came to invest such confidence in her. To repeat, he just seemed to know that she could be trusted.

Flashes of illumination, such as the one B.J. experienced on first meeting Wanda, occasionally happen to people. We encounter individuals, and before we've even spoken with them, we seem to know what they're like, whether they are trustworthy or not. You may have known what someone would say even before the person said it; or you may have known the solution to a problem even before you worked it out. Such experiences make us wonder if we have a sense that gives us immediate insight into situations, if there is a source of knowledge other than the inner and outer senses as conventionally understood, reason and authority.

A possible source of knowledge is intuition. *Intuition is the direct apprehension of knowledge that is not the result of conscious reasoning or of immediate sense perception.* Philosophers and scholars hold a variety of views regarding intuition.[4] Some speak of intuition as present in all knowledge. For example, before I can even begin to evaluate the soundness of an argument, I must directly apprehend the connection between the propositions that make up the various steps of the argument. In fact, reasoning itself seems to depend on some connection that we grasp or fail to grasp. Similarly, intuition apparently plays a part in our recognition of the beautiful, of the moral principles we accept, of the religious values we hold. Perhaps self-knowledge is the best case for such intuition, for knowledge of oneself seems to be present in all our knowledge of the world. As a simple example, consider that when you hear a phone ring, in addition to hearing it you are also aware of your hearing and of yourself as the one who does the hearing. Thought of this way, then, intuition refers to our awareness of the immediate data of consciousness, and as such, would be an element that's present in all our knowledge.

Other philosophers regard intuition as the accumulative result of one's past experience and thinking. In this sense valid intuitions are short-cuts to knowledge that the senses and reason eventually would disclose. Such intuitions, in effect, are the outcome of unconscious inductions and deductions. Bits and pieces emerge from our unconscious and fall together—we understand. Some psychologists refer to this as the "Aha!" experience, as in "Aha! I've got it!" or "Aha! I see it!"

Many creative people consciously utilize this process. The philosopher Bertrand Russell, in an article entitled "How I Write," tells of "planting" a problem in his subconscious and allowing it to work itself out there "underground."

> The most curious example of this process, and the one which led me subsequently to rely upon it, occurred at the beginning of 1914. I had undertaken to give the Lowell Lectures at Boston, and had chosen as my subject "Our Knowledge of the External World." Throughout 1913 I thought about this topic. In term time in my room at Cambridge, in vacations in a quiet inn on the upper reaches of the Thames, I concentrated with such intensity that I sometimes forgot to breathe and emerged panting as if from a trance. But all to no avail. To every theory I could think of I could perceive some fatal objections. At last, in despair, I went off to Rome for Christmas, hoping a holiday would revive my flagging energy. I got back to Cambridge on the last day of 1913, and although my difficulties were still completely unresolved I arranged, because the remaining time was short, to dictate as best I could to a stenographer. Next morning, as she came to the door, I suddenly saw exactly what I had to say, and proceeded to dictate the whole book without a moment's hesitation.

---

[4]See Harold H. Titus and Marilyn S. Smith, *Living Issues in Philosophy* (New York: Van Nostrand, 1974), pp. 240–44.

All difficulties are not so suddenly resolved. But as we said, many creative people consciously utilize the intuitive process. Eric Hoffer, writer and longshoreman, liked to unsettle his fellow dockworkers by announcing that he was going home to go to bed with a half-finished paragraph. As philosopher William James advised, have a well-stocked mind, then "get your mind whirling and see what happens." Many teachers have explained something in class and have suddenly seen connections and depths they hadn't seen before. These are moments of great joy. As the psychologist Abraham Maslow pointed out, it is not only thinkers and artists—people we term great—who are intuitively creative: Engineers, lawyers, electricians, and construction workers like Roscoe and Sweeney can be creative in the same way.

Still other philosophers view intuition as a higher kind of knowledge, different from the knowledge that the senses and reason disclose. The French philosopher Henri Bergson (1859–1941) is a good example of this view. For Bergson, intuition and intelligence are separate and distinct tools of knowing, even opposed tools. Intelligence, or the intellect, deals with things, with matter, and with quantitative relations. Intelligence solidifies whatever it deals with and is incapable of dealing with the nature of life. In contrast, intuition can penetrate the nature of life itself. Intuition points inward; it can allow us to discover the vital impulse in the world.

And there are those who regard intuition mystically, as a vehicle for receiving the inspirations of the supernatural and experiencing a unity with a supernatural reality. The founders of all the world's religions have declared to have had such mystical insights into what are termed the "deeper truths."

However we choose to regard intuition, there does appear to be an element of intuition in knowledge. But we must be careful. Used alone, intuition doesn't seem to be an adequate method of obtaining knowledge. Indeed, by itself it can be used, and has been, to advance some absurd positions. In the last analysis, intuition needs to be anchored by reason and the senses. Intuitions must be able to withstand rational criticism. When we attempt to explain our intuitions, we must rely on sense experiences and the concepts of reason. After the flash, after the flow, after the free play of fantasy and imagination comes reality testing: the cold, calculating, morning-after thoughts, the selections and rejections. Thus, Bertrand Russell, on completing his book, had to ask himself, "Is it true? Does it hold together? Will it be understood by others? Can I prove it?" If the creative intuition is accurate, it must in some sense hold up, be validated. If B.J.'s intuition about Wanda is correct, it must bear up in the arena of real life experience. To follow such an impulse blindly, unthinkingly, is to court an argument from ignorance.

RATIONALISM AND EMPIRICISM

We've seen that the two primary sources of knowledge are reason and the senses. For centuries philosophers and logicians have debated over which—if either— of these is *the* primary source of knowledge. Without necessarily being aware of it, many of us fall into one of the two major camps: *empiricism* and *rationalism*. Some of us are "hard nosed" and "scientific"; we demand "hard evidence." As Joe Friday used to say in the old radio and television series "Dragnet," "Just the facts, ma'am, just the facts." We are empiricists. Others of us take a different view of life, perhaps echoing Shakespeare's Hamlet: "There are more things in heaven and earth, Horatio, / Than are dreamt of in your philosophy." We find the empiricist's world lacking somehow. It seems to ignore the subtle, inner qualities of life, those areas wherein reside beauty, the soul, the meaning of life, perhaps even God. For us, science and the empirical approach are "crude." We are rationalists.

You probably know people who fall—broadly at least—into one category or the other. Perhaps you have a friend who always demands factual evidence: She must see, hear, taste, smell, touch, weigh, measure, analyze, graph, and chart every claim before accepting it. Another friend may prefer contemplation to chemistry, meditation to medicine, poetry to physics, and be more interested in personal psychology than in biology. More likely, most of us fall into one camp on some issues and into the other camp on others.

In its most general sense, *rationalism is the philosophical view that reason is the primary source of knowledge*. The first major exponent of rationalism was the seventeenth-century continental rationalist, René Descartes (1596–1650). The two other major exponents of this form of rationalism were Baruch de Spinoza (1632–1677) and Gottfried Wilhelm von Leibniz (1646–1716).

Rationalists believe that all knowledge stems from reason, not from experience. By this they mean that, ultimately, we come to the truth through the application of rational principles rather than from the "brute experience" of facts.

The second major epistemology in Western philosophy is known as empiricism. *Empiricism is the philosophical view that experience is the primary source of knowledge*. The chief exponents of what is called British empiricism were John Locke (1632–1704), George Berkeley (1685–1753), and David Hume (1711–1776). Contrary to the rationalists, empiricists believe that all knowledge and meaning are derived from experience based on perceptions of the five senses.

Rationalists subscribe to what is known as the coherence theory of truth. *The coherence theory of truth is the belief that truth value is a function of a statement's logical coherence with other statements*. Its primary concern is the "reasonableness" of claims. Certainly, rationalists take into account experience and the evidence of the senses, but they always test it against rational and logical principles for consistency. We might say, then, that when the evidence of our senses conflicts with what seems reasonable, the rationalist will always favor reason over the senses.

Empiricists subscribe to the second major truth test in Western thinking, the correspondence theory of truth. *The correspondence theory of truth is the belief that the truth consists of some form of correspondence between statements and facts*. For example, the proposition "*Practical Logic* weighs 9 ounces" is true if the actual weight of the book corresponds with the claim and false if it does not. Empiricists give precedence to observable facts when reason and the senses are in conflict. When the disciple Thomas insisted on touching the wounds and observing first-hand the figure of the apparently resurrected Christ, he was simply being a good empiricist.

In real life, we rely on both the senses and reason in determining the truth. The best rationalists are also superb observers and scientists, just as the best of the empiricists are first-rate reasoners. But it is important to be aware of the general theoretical differences between rationalism and empiricism because the standards of evidence acceptable to one are often unacceptable to the other. In order to enhance our general understanding of the meaning and sources of knowledge, as well as improve our analytic skills, let's see what difference being a rationalist or empiricist might make.

In our culture, to cite one example, a common idea of love tends to be "rationalistic" in the sense that it views "loving" as an inner state beyond and independent of empirically observable proof. A tragic consequence of holding this view can be found in cases of spousal abuse. When it is pointed out that their husbands abuse them physically, are often away from home without explanation, and so forth, some abused women are reported to reply, "But he loves me." Such a judgment is "rationalistic" in that it places more importance on a reasoned interpretation of events than on an empirical observation of the events themselves. It values conceptual knowledge above perceptual. It is, after all, *logically coherent* to assert that it is possible to love someone and at the same time hurt and ignore that person if one already accepts the prior belief that love is beyond empirical measure. The more "hard-nosed" empiricist might point out that a concept of love that depends on no observable, factual criteria is meaningless, and so reject it in favor of defining love in terms of empirically observable patterns of behavior.

On a less serious level, astrologers tend to be rationalists when they ignore such significant empirical factors as the enormous distances among heavenly bodies, the tiny size of the earth in relation to planets supposedly influential on our behavior, and so on. Issac Asimov points out that a typewriter exerts a greater physical force on a typist than does the position of Saturn, for example. His point is that we cannot empirically measure the effects of individual "stars" on different individuals, on New York City as opposed to New Orleans, and so on; and so, since what cannot be measured empirically does not exist, the empiricist rejects such astrological claims.

In such difficult and important matters as abortion, euthanasia, and the concept of death, empiricists define life in terms of measurable brain waves, heartbeats, respiration, and circulation. Rationalists, although not necessarily denying that these factors are important, will assert that there is a "qualitative" element missing from the empiricist's view. They will point out that empiricists can only deal with life on the level of observable facts, adding that the most important aspects of life go well beyond "what can be observed in a laboratory."

When we consider concepts such as the human soul, the meaning of life, and God, we can clearly see how an individual's basic epistemological orientation will influence what counts as evidence in his or her life and, finally, what counts as "real."

Though our discussion of epistemology is barely a beginning look at this fascinating, difficult, and important philosophical study of knowledge, it gives us a framework from which we can learn some basic analytic skills necessary for determining the adequacy of evidence offered to justify knowledge claims. These portraits of the rationalist and empiricist are admittedly broad and overly general. They are meant only to introduce us to the general difference between these two classic orientations toward knowing and to offer some examples of the ways our epistemological assumptions can have real-life consequences.

SUMMARY

This chapter dealt with four possible sources of knowledge: the senses, reason, authority, and intuition. The senses and reason are primary sources of knowledge. The outer senses refer to the five senses of seeing, hearing, tasting, feeling, and smelling. Generally speaking, what we term perceptual errors are actually judgmental errors. One way to ensure that our judgments are accurate is to open them to public verification. The inner senses refer to the unique, immediately experienced qualities of first-person experience. Reason is the capacity to draw conclusions from evidence. Induction and deduction are modes of reasoning. Induction leads to probable conclusions; deduction leads to logically certain conclusions. Authority, another source of knowledge, refers to an expert outside ourselves. In determining the correctness of an appeal to authority, we must ensure that the authority is, in fact, an expert in the field, that there is a consensus among the authorities, and that we can, at least in theory, verify the claim for ourselves. In the absence of any of these criteria, an argument commits the fallacy of false appeal to authority. Celebrity endorsements of products almost always rely on false appeal to authority. False authority has several variations. One is the fallacy of positioning, an argument that tries to capitalize on the earned reputation of a leader in a field to sell something. For example, Toshiba copy machines' ad reads, "O.K. Xerox, Try and copy this." Another variation is the fallacy of traditional wisdom, an argument that uses the past to justify claims made in the present. For example, Senator Sam Ervin dismisses the Equal Rights Amendment on the ground that it had lain around Congress for forty years, which according to Ervin, was proof that the proposal was unworthy of consideration. A last variation is the fallacy of popularity, an argument that tries to justify something strictly by appeal to numbers. For example, arguing for the purchase of a book because it's a best-seller. We also learned to recognize rationalism (the belief that reason is the primary source of knowledge) and empiricism (the belief that experience is the primary source of knowledge) and to recognize some of the practical consequences of favoring one over the other. Finally, intuition may be a source of knowledge. Intuition is the direct apprehension of knowledge that is not the result of conscious reasoning or of immediate sense perception. We must be careful to ground our intuitions in percepts of sense and concepts of reason; otherwise they can lead to unfounded claims.

Summary Questions

1. Just for fun, categorize your friends or family members as either empiricists or rationalists. Justify your choices in each case.
2. The issue of abortion is an important one. Suppose that you decide to consult an authority to help you form a reasoned point of view regarding "the issue of abortion." What kind of authority should you consult? What kind of issue is this? Moral? Legal? Religious? More than one? What approach would you take and why? (Note: this question is *not* about abortion but about the criteria for selecting an authority on a difficult and controversial issue.)
3. Positioning is often used to signify social importance. Some examples in-

clude having an office next to the boss's, standing close to the President or Senator in a photo, calling a professor by his or her first name to impress other students. Find a few examples of your own of the fallacious use of social positioning at school, in politics, and in advertising.

*ADDITIONAL EXERCISES

1. Identify the fallacies, if any, in the following passages. Choose from false authority, positioning, traditional wisdom, popularity. Explain.

   a. FERRIS: I really think we should terminate our mutual defense treaty with Taiwan.
   MARILYN: But a large portion of the Congress doesn't think so.
   FERRIS: But the President does.
   MARILYN: So what? The Congress represents the people. And if a majority of representatives think we shouldn't that's the will of the people and the wise thing to do.
   b. JUDY: Of course God exists.
   JUD: How can you be so sure?
   JUDY: Simple—every theologian says so.
   c. SAM: There's little question that the earth is about 93 million miles from the sun.
   SUE: I Agree. After all, astronomers agree on that.
   d. BART: You know, we really have to get rid of all these protective tariffs.
   LIL: But they protect domestic manufacturers.
   BART: Says you. I just finished an economics text that says protective tariffs only protect inefficiency.
   e. CAROL: The United States should get out of the United Nations.
   CARL: I don't think that sort of isolationism is wise.
   CAROL: Well, I can see you've forgotten the warnings of the Founding Fathers against entangling alliances.
   f. Julie Nixon, reacting to nationwide moral outrage at the content of the presidential Watergate-related transcripts: "I don't see how you can be shocked by the transcripts. It is a human being reacting to a situation where he saw all his dreams crumbling down around him and trying to weigh everything, to explore every alternative. To my mind I think that would have been the only human and natural thing to do." (*Los Angeles Times*, May 12, 1974, p. 12)
   g. Al Pollack, owner of The Shadows restaurant, reacting against the proposed San Francisco "truth in advertising" ordinance to require restaurant owners to identify food prepared off the premises and then frozen: "Three-quarters or seven-eights of the people who come into my place . . . don't give a good goddamn." (*Los Angeles Times*, July 4, 1974, p. 11)
   h. "Avis features cars engineered by Chrysler." (ad for Avis Rent-A-Car Systems, Inc.)
   i. "Can you put 2 and 2 together? Then use this Free Information Stamp to learn how you can add NEW INCOME, NEW PRESTIGE, NEW SECURITY to your life." (flyer advertisement from International Accountants Society)
   j. "NBA Players Association use and recommend Walgreen Vitamins." (ad for Circus Masters Vitamins)
   k. "Winston's Down Home Taste!" (ad for Winston cigarettes)
   l. Iran's Ayatollah Khomeini defending the paramount role the clergy plays in Iran's new constitution: "Since the people love the clergy, have faith in the clergy, it is right that the supreme religious authority should oversee the work of the Prime Minister or of the President of the Republic, to make sure that they don't go against the law, that is, against the Koran." (*Time*, October 22, 1979, p. 57)
   m. Pope John Paul II explaining that true academic freedom must balance independence with responsibility to the *magesterium* (the church's teaching office): "It is

the right of the faithful not to be troubled by theories and hypotheses that they are not expert in judging or that are easily simplified or manipulated by public opinion." (*Time,* October 22, 1979, p. 68)

n. JOYCE: I just read an article about how the quality of air can be a factor in lung cancer.
JIM: You don't believe everything you read, do you?
JOYCE: No, but I'm inclined to believe that.

o. "Take it from Ronson there is no better Flexible Head Shaving System than ours. Who do you think Schick took it from?" (ad for Ronson razors)

p. Clint Eastwood justifying the film roles he does: "A guy sits alone in a theater. He's young and he's scared. He doesn't know what he's going to do with his life. He wishes he could be self-sufficient, like the man he sees up there on the screen, somebody who can look out for himself, solve his own problems. I do the kind of roles I'd like to see if I were still digging swimming pools and wanted to escape my problems." (*Time,* January 9, 1978, p. 48)

q. The late congressional Representative William M. Ketchum, speaking against transferring the Canal Zone to the Republic of Panama: "Our forefathers at the turn of the century built that waterway through hazardous and hard work for the security and well-being of future generations. I refuse to stand on the sidelines and watch this resolve be destroyed. Consequently, you can be assured that I will do everything possible to see that the Congress defeats any bill which seeks to relinquish U.S. rights to the Canal." (form letter in response to a letter expressing support of the Panama Canal Treaty)

r. "Goodrich—we're the ones without the blimp."

s. I'm voting for Pat Robertson for President. He knows what he's talking about when he says that we have to take a tough stand against the Soviets. After all, he's an ordained minister.

t. Boy! I didn't realize that you were so important. Just look at the size of this office—and right next to the President's.

u. I don't like this idea of another major political party. The Republicans and Democrats are plenty. I mean, we've done okay with just two parties for over 200 years, haven't we?

v. *Iacocca* must be a great book. Millions of copies were sold in the first few months it was in print.

w. JUNIOR: I think I want to major in poetry.
DAD: Poetry? Are you nuts? What kind of job can you hope to get. Take it from me. Go into business. Look at how successful I am. I ought to know.
JUNIOR: You're right, Dad. You've sure made a lot of money. I guess you do know what you're talking about.

x. If Bruce Springsteen, Willie Nelson, Stevie Wonder, and Kenny Rogers all support We Are the World famine relief, I do, too. I'm sending my check today.

y. JOE: Hey, be careful. You'll pull a muscle exercising that way.
JOAN: What's wrong with the way I'm exercising.
JOE: Well, Jane Fonda says that you should do it like this.
JOAN: What does she know?
JOE: She's an expert. She's made a videotape and a record, she's written about exercising, and she's stayed in excellent shape herself.

2. Which of the following claims would you take on authority? Why or why not?

a. Light travels at 186,000 miles per second.
b. It's probably impossible for a body to accelerate to the speed of light.
c. Prolonged and concentrated marijuana usage produces a loss of sexual desire.
d. Fluoridated water is a health hazard.
e. A body will continue in a prescribed course until acted upon by some outside force.

f. The earth follows an elliptical orbit.

3. Do you think an appeal to intuition is enough to justify the following claims, or not?

   a. I'm not going to drink that water. My intuition tells me it's poisoned.
   b. My intuition tells me something is wrong at home. We should turn around and go back.
   c. Let's not leave yet. My intuition tells me the phone is about to ring.
   d. You want to know why I think we should approach this problem as I've suggested. Well, all I can say is that having spent months studying and pondering the problem, I'm convinced my proposal will solve it.

4. If you claim to know the following, what sources of knowledge would you probably rely on?

   a. The milk is sour.
   b. Washington is the capital of the United States.
   c. A thing can't be in two places at one time.
   d. Sodium and chloride combine to form salt.
   e. This object is either a book or not a book.
   f. That can't be his sister because he has no sister.
   g. Divorce is an emotionally trying experience.
   h. People fear dying.
   i. I feel that I'm possessed by a devil.
   j. Nightmares frequently remain with us for days afterward.
   k. Humans need oxygen to survive.
   l. This figure must be a polygon because it has many sides.
   m. The square of the hypotenuse of a right triangle is equal to the sum of the squares of the triangle's sides.
   n. $N + 1$ is always odd where N is even.

chapter 8

Bogus Knowledge Claims

We must always follow somebody looking for truth,
we must always run away from anyone who finds it.

ANDRÉ GIDE

It is the dull man who is always sure, and the sure
man who is always dull.

H. L. MENCKEN

"Wow!" said an obviously excited Slim, waving a copy of a book in front of Sweeney's face. "I've just found the neatest book. It's called *Dianetics*. It's by a guy named L. Ron Hubbard. One of my friends said that reading that book has made a wonderful change in her life. She said it really does explain how to be happy."

"Let me see that," Sweeney demanded, grabbing for the book.

"...However, I must caution you—if you're not prepared to accept the vows of 'proclivity,' 'nebulosity'
and 'luminescence,' then obviously we're not the religion for you."

"Sure," Slim said. "That's why I brought it home. I thought we should
all read it. My friend gave me this copy for free."

"Hmmm," Sweeney mused, reading from the back cover:

For thousands of years Man has been looking for the answers to his own mind,
what it is, how it affects him and what he can do about it.

At last, here is a book, DIANETICS: THE MODERN SCIENCE OF MEN-
TAL HEALTH which provides the answers to the problems of the human
mind. It also points the way, as well, to the possibility of real happiness for
every man, women and child on this planet.

THIS BOOK CAN CHANGE YOUR LIFE!
PERHAPS YOU COULD BE HAPPIER!
BUY THIS BOOK BY
L. RON HUBBARD TODAY

"I don't know," Sweeney said. "A couple of years ago you were into psychic
massage. After that it was the *I Ching,* then past-life regression and astral projection. Weren't you doing horoscopes there for a while, too? Then you bor-
rowed 500 bucks to go to that weekend seminar on enlightenment. Last month

you went to that trance-channeler who claims to be a 35,000 year old 'spirit' from Atlantis. You seem to believe everything you hear. Don't you ever stop and think? I mean, where's the proof? I just don't know. Seems to me that you're just off on another wild goose chase."

"Oh, Daddy!" a frustrated Slim sighed. "Lots of famous and well-educated people swear by *Dianetics*. At least read the first chapter."

Sweeney reluctantly agreed but was unable to get past the Synopsis before he got flustered.

In the Synopsis to *Dianetics,* Hubbard says such things as "The creation of dianetics is a milestone for Man comparable to his discovery of fire and superior to his invention of the arch" and *"The hidden source of all psycho-somatic ills and human aberration has been discovered and skills have been developed for their invariable cure."*[1]

To speak of the "science" of mind, to claim to have discovered *the* source of *all* psychosomatic ills and human aberration so that they can *invariably* be cured is to make a remarkable set of claims. Admittedly, *Dianetics* is a controversial book. Slim was correct when she told Sweeney that there are many people who willingly and exuberantly testify to its virtues. Accepting its claims would be simple if enthusiastic personal testimony were sufficient evidence to support such claims. But as we have seen, it is not.

Enthusiastic personal testimony—*by itself*—is as inadequate here as psychological sincerity is inadequate when offered as the sole justification for assenting to any truth claim. (See Chapter 2.) First, we have all the complications of any factual or causal claim. Second, the nature of the claims made by Hubbard is such that they are often so vague as to be meaningless.

For example, what is meant by saying that "Man is looking for the answers to his own mind"? What can it possibly mean to claim that the discovery of dianetics is "superior" to the invention of the arch? As so stated, such claims have no verifiable content; they only *feel* meaningful. And the controversy surrounding Hubbard's book and the Church of Scientology suggests, at the very least, that dianetic processing fails to live up to the claim that it *invariably* cures "*all* psycho-somatic ills and human aberration" since much of the unhappiness with the process apparently comes from people who have been through it.

Many systems, philosophies, religions, and theories make claims similar in kind to those in *Dianetics,* supported by exuberant personal testimony and criticized with equal exuberance.

Indeed, so charged is our culture with seemingly authoritative assertions, promises, advice, and belief systems that we are going to spend a little time surveying them under the general headings of "pseudoscience" and "sophistries." Our overview of these knowledge claims is a natural extension and application of our earlier discussion of what constitutes knowledge and legitimate authority and what doesn't.

PSEUDOSCIENCE

Pseudoscience, a term coined by Martin Gardner, *refers to a certain category of theories, systems, and explanations, which though claiming to be "scientific," in fact*

---

[1]L. Ron Hubbard, *Dianetics: The Modern Science of Mental Health* (Los Angeles: The Church of Scientology of California, 1950), p. ix; Hubbard's emphasis.

use only the trappings of genuine science and avoid the rigors of the checks and balances of the scientific method or the scrutiny of disinterested experts.[2] Invoking a certain caricature of scientific language and method, pseudosciences have proven to be highly lucrative to their founders and highly durable. What, then, are the basic characteristics of the pseudoscientist?

1. "First and foremost of these traits is that [they] work in almost total isolation from their colleagues . . . isolation in the sense of having no fruitful contacts with fellow researchers."[3]
2. The pseudoscientist submits his or her work not to bona fide experts in the field but to the general public, which is not qualified to evaluate it.
3. The pseudoscientist speaks through organizations he or she has founded, thus avoiding genuine peer review and conveying an aura of professional expertise.
4. The pseudoscientist considers himself or herself to be a genius (most likely misunderstood and persecuted).
5. The pseudoscientist regards colleagues to be, almost without exception, "blockheads" (Gardner's term).
6. The pseudoscientist compares himself or herself to Galileo, Bruno, Pasteur, or other well-known, well-respected scientists whose work met initial hostility and resistance. The pseudoscientist repeatedly cites comparisons between his or her own case and historical cases of the persecution of true scientific genius, which was initially misunderstood. (This functions as a form of the fallacy of positioning.)
7. The pseudoscientist exhibits a strong compulsion to focus criticism on the greatest scientists and/or best-established theories of the day.
8. The pseudoscientist tends to write in a complex jargon often making use of phrases, terms, and locutions he or she has coined. This rhetoric can be quite persuasive, creating a beautifully crafted jigsaw puzzle of assertions. Clever use of circular reasoning, equivocations, and other persuasive tricks makes it difficult to refute pseudoscience by logic and authentic scientific evidence.

Although we must take care not to slip into the error of dismissing every "isolated" theorist or iconoclastic thinker as a pseudoscientist, a little careful thought about the "scientific establishment" suggests that, *as a rule,* scientists do not "gang up" against each other. Galileo, for example, was persecuted for political and theological reasons by the church and by scientists who subsumed their science under what they believed were the demands of their faith. More importantly, it was scientists—*not laypeople*—who ultimately accepted Galileo's superior evidence. Throughout history, the ultimate validation of the misunderstood scientific genius has come from fellow scientists, as it must. As laypeople, we are usually not qualified to pass judgment on the scientific merits of such disputes. And this is to the advantage of the pseudoscientist, who would rather appeal to our sympathies, to our fears and hopes, and to our basic distrust

---

[2]See Gardner's *Fads and Fallacies in the Name of Science* (New York: Dover Publications, 1950) and *Science: Good, Bad, and Bogus: A Skeptical Look at Extraordinary Claims* (Buffalo, N.Y.: Prometheus Books, 1981), as well as James Randi's *Flim-Flam!* (Buffalo, N.Y.: Prometheus Books, 1982), for more detailed explanations and examples of this useful concept.

[3]Gardner, *Fads and Fallacies,* p. 8.

of "the establishment" than to a qualified, objective jury of genuine scientific experts.

In our own times, various best-sellers have extolled the theory that ancient "astronaut gods" visited pre-historic Earth in "chariots of the gods." Other popular books identify an area off the Florida coast as the deadly "Bermuda Triangle." Invariably, their authors rely on the general public for validation of their claims—not qualified experts.

To illustrate the practical importance of relying on legitimate authority in our daily dealings, we'll consider a hypothetical case: If the owner of the corner health food store tells me that "natural vitamins" are better for me than "artificial" ones, but my doctor and my chemistry professor both say that there is no significant difference, how am I to know which assertion to act on?

I can ask myself, "What kind of stake does each party have in the answer? What qualifications and experience does each party have relative to this issue?" In this hypothetical case, the store owner has a financial stake in what he or she says, and no verifiable expertise in vitamins, nutrition, or chemistry—only his or her own testimony and sincerity. My doctor and chemistry teacher, on the other hand, don't seem to have any stake that would be likely to bias their claims to the point of invalidating them. Thus, for me—*a nonauthority* on chemistry, biochemistry, nutrition, and vitamins—to reject the consensus of two qualified, unbiased authorities on behalf of the claim of a single nonexpert with a financial stake in the claim is rather foolish.

If my astronomy teacher asserts that astrological claims are untenable because the original observations on which they are (still) based were erroneous, but my astrologer tells me that I shouldn't marry you because our "sun signs are incompatible," whom should I trust?

Of course reading my horoscope is easier and, perhaps, more fun than learning enough physics and astronomy to make an educated assessment of astrological claims. It is also easier than making a serious attempt at an accurate and honest assessment of our current relationship and our chances for a long and healthy marriage. Then, too, pseudoscience sometimes appeals to our desire to be in touch with the mysterious forces of the universe, a desire to be in touch with guaranteed "inside information," perhaps even a need to feel special.

Pseudoscience also seems to thrive in part because of our basic distrust of "the establishment." We all know of professionals who refuse to consider any new theories until absolutely forced to. Science is conservative—it must be as a way of demanding quality evidence that can withstand rigorous testing and evaluation. And let's not overlook the widespread desire for hope. Science does not always provide enough hope fast enough. And it rarely provides the invariable "guarantees" of the pseudoscientist.

So it is that claims for psychosurgery, instant healing by the laying on of hands, or some other psychic process appeal to us. We want guaranteed hope where science offers only the possibility of hope. We want "magic"—a quick, easy, guaranteed way of making hard choices: Enter astrology, Tarot, palmistry, myriad "readings," mood rings, Kirlian photography, and other ways—we hope—of quickly and easily understanding life and choosing well.

A special species of pseudoscience involves spiritual gurus, financial gurus, social gurus, and healing gurus—all those characters lined up to sell us happiness, success, wealth, or health. They're called *sophists,* and they're all over the place. And since some of them can do us great harm, we'd be wise to get to know the species.

EXERCISE 8-1 _____

*1. Discuss the following in terms of pseudoscience and any other logical fallacies and principles that seem pertinent.

a. From the back cover of Joseph H. Cater's book *Awesome Force,* "A Private Publication of Cadake Industries," we read,

> This book will astonish the scientific community and shock the world. . . . In this book you will find one of the original thinkers of the 20th century relate information that will stun the layman and also the scientist. . . . He defiles [sic?] the orthodox scientist for keeping the status quo. . . . Not since Velikovsky has one man dared to reveal what orthodox scientists would like to bury under the rug.

We are also told that Cater, "disillusioned with academic physics," gave up his career in this field to develop "the awesome force"—"The Unifying Principles for All Physical and Occult Phenomena in the Universe." Cater says that "there is no known phenomena [sic] not taken in stride by these news ideas."[4] He says that his revelations can be expected to "make a shambles of currently popular, and universally accepted ideas of conventional science," adding that he is not likely to endear himself with the scientific community at large, and so on.[5]

In Chapter 1, Cater claims that the moon has a surface gravity much like Earth's, but that NASA has covered up that fact by using doctored television transmissions of moon landings. Cater claims that NASA slowed down the transmitted images so that objects appeared to fall slower than they really did, and so on. He also asserts that the astronauts' space suits do not really weigh the claimed 185 pounds, that the "research and evidence" indicate that the suits could only weigh 20 pounds or less.

b. When Simon & Schuster published the blockbuster diet book *Calories Don't Count,* it had not sent the manuscript to a single expert for evaluation. The original manuscript, written by Dr. Herman Taller a gynecologist, was simply rewritten by a free-lance sports writer, Roger Kahn.[6]

c. The late Carlton Fredericks was a very popular nutrition guru on radio who used the title "Doctor." He was a Ph.D., not an M.D. His dissertation was from the New York University School of Education, based on a thesis discussing how his female listeners responded to his own radio broadcasts.[7]

d. Scientists rarely debate publicly with pseudoscientists. Isaac Asimov says that one reason scientists rarely win such debates is because they often take place in front of audiences which have only the sketchiest of scientific backgrounds.[8] Elaborate on Asimov's point. Are there any other factors you can think of that might actually put the scientists at a disadvantage when dealing with refutations of pseudoscience?

2. Analyze the preceding *Dianetics* quotes in terms of the general characteristics of pseudoscience so far covered and for any other fallacies, ambiguities, and so on you find pertinent.

THE NEW SOPHISTS AND THEIR SOPHISTRIES

Does faith healing regularly occur in front of millions of viewers, as well-known television evangelists claim? Can we be personally transformed in a weekend?

[4]Joseph H. Cater, *Awesome Force* (Winterhaven, Fla.: Cadake Industries), p. 9.
[5]Ibid.
[6]Gardner, *Science: Good, Bad, and Bogus,* p. 55.
[7]Ibid., p. 54.
[8]See his interesting, succinct essay, "Losing the Debate," in *The Roving Mind* (Buffalo, N.Y.: Prometheus Books, 1983), pp. 29–30.

Is it possible for almost anyone to make a fortune with no experience and no money down? Can reading *Dianetics* help free us of past hangups? Can we really melt away tons of ugly fat while we sleep? Are there a few secret "power phrases" that will turn us into successful business dynamos? Can we improve our daily affairs by *Winning Through Intimidation?* Is "the government" secretly hiding proof of visits from extraterrestrials? Was the Holocaust an elaborate fraud? Have the big oil companies bought up the patent to the 200-mile-per-gallon carburetor? Is the greedy medical profession hiding a cure for cancer in order to make lots of money treating it? Can Madame Rosa read your future in the Tarot deck? Can Mr. Lucky's astrological reading help you save your marriage?

These and related claims are the fertile province of cranks, conartists, pesudoscientists, and myriad salespeople, who offer us hope when we are discouraged, easy schemes when we are overwhelmed, instant fixes for our instant era. Unreliable claims and the fraudulent characters who make them have certain basic characteristics that we can identify and then use to save ourselves from wasted time and money, from grief, from disappointment, from being used, even from an early death. All the time, money, and energy put into dishonest, unworkable, or truly harmful schemes are time, energy, and money that could more effectively be used to find reasonable and plausible solutions to our problems.

Over the last two decades, we have seen the rise of various systems, techniques, psychologies, therapies, and religions designed to offer a *quick fix, instant* enlightenment, the few *simple secrets (or keys) to success,* happiness, contentment, wealth, power, or health. Such claims are the special province of the "new sophists"—who are really not new at all.

This style of sophistry was identified in the West in Athens, in the fifth century B.C., and remains essentially unchanged today. Sophists deliberately used flattery, mob appeals, all sorts of fallacies and persuasive devices, to advance any claim they chose, regardless of its truthfulness. They would teach anybody anything if they were paid enough. They flattered their paying pupils and thrived on competition over who had the most disciples, who made the most money, and who had the most social connections. They believed in a dog-eat-dog world in which "it's not what you know but who you know." They curried favor with power and practiced as well as taught the arts of persuasion and manipulation. Sound familiar?

Because we are dealing with inductive reasoning here, we must judge each case on its own merits in light of the most likely evidence. Still, we can discern some general warning signs.

1. There's *always* money required—usually up front.
2. Virtually anyone with the fee is accepted—without insistence on any special abilities or qualities—under the guise of being open and democratic.
3. Overly simple or overly complex language is used to manipulate and obscure, not to communicate straightforwardly.
4. The group is often centered on a "dynamic personality" who "discovered" the system but who is (or becomes) increasingly isolated, hostile, paranoid, and inaccessible.
5. An air of secrecy creates an aura of both elitism and paranoia in followers, which makes it difficult, if not impossible, to analyze claims or origins of either the leader or the doctrine.
6. There is often an escalating system: a hierarchy in which success at one level "entitles" you to advance to a higher one—always with a new fee attached.

7. The group is hostile to critical questions, favoring instead groupthink and groupspeak.[9]

8. There is widespread use of fallacies, especially personal attacks, in response to criticism.

9. Often followers are isolated physically, emotionally, or intellectually by strictly controlling contact with unbelievers, censoring reading and friendships, and so forth.

Psychological Sophistry

Psychological sophistries include certain self-help books and systems that make grandiose, but mostly meaningless, claims involving an entire panoply of "warm-sounding" psychobabble (see Chapter 3).

One of the hallmarks of this contemporary sophistry is extreme self-centeredness. Social scientists refer to this as the "egocentric point of view." What we find here is the substitution of exuberance for information, the substitution of feelings for reasons.[10] (See Chapter 2.)

Psychobabble is always an early warning sign of the possible presence of sophistry: In the case of much new sophistry, this means inappropriately personal sounding, overly warm, "open," "life-affirming" language coupled with an excessive emptiness of content and ultimately impersonal behavior. The psychological appeal of such talk is obvious; the practical value of it—except as a kind of personal expression—is not. When claims to knowledge are made, rational analysis is appropriate. And rational analysis requires meaningful claims and rational discourse, which psychobabble can never provide.

In his study of psychobabble, R. D. Rosen reports that at one function of a popular weekend seminar-style system of the 1970s a man stood up and announced, "I am a fifty-three-year-old psychiatrist, and listening to you [the founder of the system], I've begun to think that I should give up my practice. What do you suggest?"[11] (According to Rosen, the psychiatrist was given an evasive and elliptical answer.)

That a *psychiatrist* would ask such a basic, profound question of a man he'd never met personally and at a public gathering is especially troubling. A fifty-three-year-old psychiatrist may have been practicing for as long as thirty years. The tragic irony here is compounded by the fact that the psychiatrist and other members of the audience apparently believed that a helpful, reliable answer to such an important, life-altering question could be given by a man with unknown credentials lecturing to a few hundred people, *and who did not even know the psychiatrist*.

Here we see an especially clear instance of the tragic element that often accompanies the new sophistry. Unhappy, confused people desperately seek anything that offers the slightest chance of help. For varying reasons, the kind of "help" they are drawn to in desperation is sometimes inappropriate, unreasonable, and even dangerous.

---

[9]For excellent literary treatments of groupthink and groupspeak see George Orwell's *1984,* Aldous Huxley's *Brave New World,* and Ira Levin's *This Perfect Day.* For a lucid philosophical treatment of the whole dynamic involved here, see, of course, Eric Hoffer's succinct classic *The True Believer.*

[10]See Christopher Lasch's *The Culture of Narcissism: American Life in an Age of Diminishing Expectations* (New York: W. W. Norton, 1979).

[11]*Psychobabble* (New York: Atheneum, 1978), p. 51.

When we are sold a system that deals with profound, personal concerns in a quick, "exciting," but impersonal way, we should suspect the presence of sophistry. When excessive profusions of love, empathy, openness, and so on are accompanied by inconsistently impersonal behavior, we should suspect sophistry. Consider, as an example, this sophistic remark once regularly made to thousands of people, many of whom viewed it as a revelation of a profound insight: "The self is fun to the self. The real self is actually satisfied. If you think you need something out there to be satisfied, you're in the wrong context."[12] Does this apply to hungry children who think they need food to be satisfied? Does it mean that the chronically mentally ill are "actually satisfied"? Are they "fun" to themselves?

No claim is made by the new sophists that requires more than unreflective inner evidence for verification—although a great deal of thought goes into creating the *impression* that meaningful claims are being made. By not actually saying anything meaningful, the sophist avoids the legal complication of having to substantiate the pseudoclaim—since no specific claim has been made. Thus, sophists are free to interpret their own words to their own advantage as circumstances require. Such empty claims allow their makers a perpetual escape clause: Sophists always take credit when we feel satisfied with their product. When we aren't satisfied, sophists always insist that the fault lies with us: *We* have somehow failed to try hard enough, to have enough faith, to think positively, and so forth. In either case, the system and the sophist appear to be beyond refutation. The sophist has used circular reasoning in a way that makes it impossible to ever seriously criticize the system: The begged assumption is that all failures are ours.

But not all of us seek personal transformation or enrichment. Some of us seek regular old "richment." We want to be wealthy, powerful, dynamic. We want to be *successful*. We need not fear that. For us, there is another kind of sophistry.

EXERCISE 8-2 _____

1. Analyze the following passage from a brochure entitled "The Possible Human: A Journey of Personal and Social Transformation," a workshop with Jean Houston, Ph.D. What kind of language uses can you find? Discuss in terms of logic and language, referring to what you've learned about sophistries, psychobabble, meaningfulness, and anything else from your logic studies that seems appropriate. What—specifically—is being said and promised?

   The premise of my teaching is that we cannot make the world work unless we are educated to do so. Most of us, unfortunately, are not being educated for the enormous complexity and challenge of our time. These educational workshops have been successful for so many people because we are providing them with an educational process whereby they develop dimensions of body, mind, spirit which gives them access to a far greater range of their own potentials. And with this they can deal creatively and even transformationally with problems, opportunities and challenges as these may arise. Thus, they can become change agents in their personal and professional lives—entrepreneurs of the possible, the ones who can, with the appropriate education, make a difference.

2. Werner Erhard, the controversial founder of est (Erhard Seminars Training) is now associated with Transformational Technologies. Analyze his following comment about Transformational Technologies. What do you think he is really saying? Discuss

[12]Ibid., p. 60.

in terms of logic and language, referring to what you've learned about sophistries, psychobabble, meaningfulness, and anything else from your logic studies that seems appropriate.

> What we intend that our work will do is to empower, facilitate and enable people to bring forth a new domain of possibility through which they will evolve on their own. Our work does not bring people to the end of that possibility but we intend it to bring them into a new possibility. So the work is a beginning rather than an end and it's true that people will come to new blocks in this new space of possibility.[13]

Success Sophistry

Success sophistries are chiefly concerned with selling us the secrets to quick, guaranteed success marked by money, power, or prestige. Although they may overlap with other kinds of sophistry, *success sophistries usually heavily rely on "powerbabble," a fusion of psychobabble, buzzwords, and puffery* (see Chapter 3). The chief function of this kind of language is to connote an aura of competency, power, and dynamism, a no-nonsense approach that "cuts to the heart of the matter and gets things done!"—without actually saying or doing much at all. Its style is usually overly simplified, nearly always vague, but "exciting."

Some of the hallmarks of success sophistries include

1. Promises of instant success
2. Simplicity almost anyone can follow
3. Use of power terms and language of dynamic action
4. Emphasis on money and social prestige
5. Promises of "secrets," "keys," "few simple principles" ways to manipulate other people or the marketplace
6. Stress on tricks and appearances more than development of substantive abilities
7. Unrealistic, absolute claims: "always," "inevitably," "without exception"
8. Demands money—usually up front

One of the cleverest devices for getting money way up front is used by Barrie D. Stern at the end of *How To Be NUMBER ONE Instantly!*, a slim volume that introduces us to "skinetics," a way of "causing" others to become our allies by the use of an "effective" two- to four-second touch.

At the conclusion of the book, Stern says, "Quite a few people have asked me about legitimate businesses that they can get into where the use of skinetics can make them rich quickly."[14] Stern claims to have become rich by using skinetics in a business that "never goes out of style," a business resting on a very simple and "unique" way to get started for less than $200. This business requires no showroom, no stocking of merchandise. "You can make as much as $1,000 to $2,000 per night! Yes . . . per night! It's one of the few businesses that I know about that you can legally charge anyone as much as you want—the sky is the limit and you can never get into any kind of legal trouble!"[15]

[13]Quoted in Mark Dowie's article, "The Transformation Game," *Image: The Magazine of Northern California,* reprinted in the *San Francisco Examiner,* October 12, 1986.
[14]Published by the author and copyrighted 1979, p. 62.
[15]Ibid., p. 63.

This sounds too good to be true. But Stern, as of 1979, was apparently writing a new book, which would cost $75 (the skinetics book, by the way, was only sixty-four pages long). Here's the truly clever part: We are told that because we have purchased the skinetics book, and because the business book, *How to Get into Almost Any Business You Want for $200 or Less!*, is not yet completed, we can reserve a copy for a "ten-dollar pre-publishing discount!" In other words, we are asked to send in $65 for an unfinished book. It will, we are promised, teach us " 'tricks' we've never seen or heard about before!"[16] (Like how to get people to pay $65 for an unwritten book?)

But perhaps you are more concerned with college. No problem; there are success sophistries for students, too. A flier for the Info/Quest Co. of Vancouver, Washington, announces, "A Great G.P.A. Is Within Your Grasp! Guaranteed! 3 Power Packed Volumes. OVER 450 PAGES! –Guide to Better Concentration –How to Make Better Grades –The Exam Secret. Order Today! Only $10 postpaid."

How can anyone legitimately "guarantee" a "Great G.P.A." to any student who sends in $10? But is it actually a great grade point average that is being guaranteed? Or is the guarantee, rather, that a great GPA is "within your grasp," whatever that might mean. Perhaps we are being guaranteed that there are really 450 pages in the three "power packed" volumes? And what is a "power packed volume"? How come this "exam secret" is a secret? In other words, is anything specific being claimed, and if so, is it reasonable?

You don't want to go to school anyway? You can still get rich by answering this ad: "Wealthy Man Wants to Give You His Wealth Secret Before It's Too Late!" This ad only asks for a postdated check or money order (difficult to postdate) for $12.95, so that we can see if the "secret" isn't truly as amazing as the full-page ad claims. Further, if we are unsatisfied, the ad says, we can get our $12.95 back *plus* a $20 "bonus." The ad headlines include "Fast Money," "Almost No-Risk," " 'Work' At Home," "Simple," "Age Doesn't Matter," "No Personal Selling," "Legal And Honest," "No Long Hours"—and we're given "proof" in the form of testimonials from people who claim to have made thousands of dollars by following the "secret" system.

There are, as you no doubt realize, countless ads for apparent sophistries dealing with business, personal health, or interpersonal success. They promise fantastic results for little or no effort or risk. They offer "guarantees" meant to suggest that the systems themselves are foolproof. Yet there is little verifiable evidence that such systems actually work.

Clearly, sales, interpersonal successes, breaking harmful habits, and the like require certain abilities. Some of these can be learned, but not all of them. Yet by stressing how "simple" their systems' requirements are, sophists imply that virtually anyone can succeed by using them. Many sophistic pitches use phrases such as "so simple almost anyone can follow this foolproof plan." Others, as we've seen, take great pains to encourage us that "no special education is needed," that results are "guaranteed," and so on.

But "simple" does not always mean "easy" or even "possible." For example, we could place our own elegant little ad in a national magazine: "SIMPLE 2-STEP PROGRAM FOR WEIGHT LOSS! SCIENTIFICALLY VERIFIABLE. GUARANTEED TO WORK. SO SIMPLE, VIRTUALLY ANYONE

[16]Ibid., p. 64.

CAN UNDERSTAND IT. $10." And what is our two-step "system"? (1) Eat less. (2) Exercise more. Though our claim is technically "correct," it is essentially deceptive (mixing mob appeal and concealed evidence).

The fact that millions of Americans are overweight indicates that actually being able to follow this "system" is dependent on quite complex causal conditions: individual environmental, physiological, and social factors make this "simple" system difficult to implement. Similar limitations and conditions might affect a given individual's abilities to find and make cheap real estate deals, to pick up dates, to stop smoking, to study more efficiently. By implying guaranteed results, the success sophists tip their hands: In their breezy, overly confident way, they oversimplify some of the most complex, important, and frustrating aspects of our lives for one ultimate purpose: to sell us something.

They offer us something unreasonable—and out of confusion or need, we buy it. Yet with just a bit of clear thinking, we can usually see these "secrets" for what they are: twentieth-century snake oil. We'll close with a look at one of the most offensive species of sophistry: spiritual and psychic deception.

*EXERCISE 8-3 _____

Analyze and discuss the following for signs of success sophistry.

1. Miscellaneous items from a full-page newspaper ad: "California Millionaire Wants To Share The Wealth." A California millionaire only wants a check for $10 postdated 60 days. And his system, as he says, does *not* require "education," "capital," "luck," "talent," "youth," or "experience." What, then, does it require? "Belief. Enough to take a chance. Enough to absorb what I'll send you. Enough to put the principles into *action*. If you do just that—nothing more, nothing less—the results will be hard to believe. Remember—I guarantee it   soon you'll be making enough money to |give up your job|—I guarantee it."

2. From an ad for Helen Gurley Brown's book *Having It All:* "Let Helen Gurley Brown Show You How to Have It All! Love, Success, Sex, Money—even if you're starting with nothing. . . ." Ms. Brown also states, "I'll scold you, support you, inspire you to become the best you can be—and that's enough to *guarantee* success. I promise!"

3. From an ad for Orgi-Nine: "New Pill Speeds Up Metabolism and Makes You Lose Weight Even While You Sleep!" We are cautioned, "As the pounds burn off, you should use good judgment and not let yourself become too thin."

4. Assess the comments from Jean Houston and Werner Erhard from Exercise 8-2 for signs of success sophistry.

Spiritual and Psychic Sophistry

Sophists exist in all areas of life. Some of the most unpleasant are found in religion, as has been recently demonstrated by James "The Amazing" Randi, a professional magician who publically debunks fraudulent healers and psychics.

Operating on the principle that "it takes one to know one," Randi believes that it takes a professional trickster to spot another professional deceiver. Hence, a magician can often spot what a layperson cannot. Martin Gardner, who coined the term pseudoscience, concurs, pointing out that according to magicians, scientists are actually among the easiest people for psychic frauds to deceive. "The thinking of a scientist is rational, based on a lifetime of experience with a rational world. But the methods of magic are irrational and totally outside a scientist's experience," Gardner says.[17] The habit of disciplined observation,

---

[17]*Science: Good, Bad, and Bogus,* p. 93.

which is so valuable under certain circumstances, is a liability when dealing with clever tricksters, for the typically trained scientist is very likely to look "where she's supposed to," meaning where the trickster wants her to look. A magician, on the other hand, is more likely to have the necessary background knowledge to look where she's not supposed to—at the source of the illusion.

Tricks of the Trade. Some of the common hedges against failure used by spiritual sophists might include

1. Manifestations of spiritual or religious "powers" occur only before true believers or under conditions controlled by the sophist.
2. Circular explanations are offered whenever a manifestation of psychic or spiritual power appears to fail: The most common is a charge of lack of faith on someone else's part, never a failing of the sophist's "gifts" or "powers."
3. Healings are carefully limited to conditions unverifiable to the immediate audience: ulcers, asthma, leukemia, and so on—never the straightening of arthritically deformed joints, healing of burns, restoration of missing limbs, or the like, which are much harder to fake.
4. Vague or deceptive predictions are made.
5. Money is usually involved, even if it is called a "love offering" or a "good-faith gift." One subtle ploy involves demanding money as a form of "sacrifice" on the part of the follower. Bhagwan Shree Rajneesh had over one hundred Rolls Royces at his ashram in Oregon, claiming that they were "symbols" of the unimportance of possessions.[18]

Electronic Wizardry. During 1986, psychic investigators James Randi, Paul Kurtz, Joseph Barnhart, and Philip Singer conducted surveys of various well-known, popular faith healers. Perhaps the most troubling item to come out of these investigations was Randi's discovery that the Reverend Peter Popoff was using a tiny, pink radio receiver inserted in his ear like a hearing aid to receive information sent to him on radio frequency 39.170 megahertz by his wife, Elizabeth.[19] Here is a sampling of what Randi's electronics expert, Alec Jason, recorded while Popoff was preaching in San Francisco: "Hello, Petey. I love you. I'm talking to you. Can you hear me? If you can't you're in trouble. 'Cause I'm talking. As well as I can talk. [Pause] I'm looking up names now."[20]

The "names," of course, were the names, street addresses, healing requests, and so forth that Popoff's wife and assistant had gathered from cards filled out by audience members before the service. Elizabeth Popoff and Peter's assistant strolled among the faithful, matching cards with faces. Later, as Popoff publicly prayed and preached, Elizabeth would direct him from a van stationed outside the auditorium, using a television monitor to spot the people who'd filled in the cards.

And when Popoff asked if *he* had ever met these people before, they could honestly say no. His wife and assistant had met them instead. He had "plausible deniability." Thus, Popoff apparently deliberately concealed information to im-

[18]See Frances FitzGerald's article, "Rajneeshpuram, Parts I and II," in the "Reporter At Large" column of *The New Yorker,* September 22 and September 29, 1986.
[19]James Randi, "Taking It on Faith," *Penthouse,* December 1986, p. 178.
[20]Ibid.

ply a false conclusion: Only divine knowledge could account for the remarkable accuracy of his claims.

In one of the most troubling of the recorded segments, Elizabeth laughingly says that they've got a "hot one"—referring to a prospect, an unfortunate woman with lumps in her breasts. According to Randi, there are recordings of Mrs. Popoff and a staff member laughing about the "big butts" of some of their temporary congregation, swapping recipes, and making small talk. What makes such callous deception especially reprehensible is that it occurs at the expense of desperate, seriously ill people, often seeking any last resort. We see graphically what can happen when unmet needs or powerful emotions dominate or block clear thinking.

Selective Cures.   Randi also discovered that none of the healers studied ever attempted to heal anyone in a customized wheelchair or who exhibited any evidence of a severe physical disability. In fact, Randi and his crew discovered that some faith healers cart around their own wheelchairs and put elderly or tired persons in them before the service begins. Then, during the heated frenzy of the show, the healer rushes over to the person, grabs them, shouts something like, "Show these folks how you can walk!" and sends the excited or bewildered individual scurrying up and down the aisles. Here, again, we have what clearly amounts to deception.

Randi reports that some healers go so far as to have people demonstrate their faith in God's healing power by throwing away their medications—insulin, digitalis, nitroglycerin tablets, for example. After the momentary excitement, most of these people find that they must return to their medications.

Concealing Wealth.   As an additional element of deception, sophistic characters of all types can create the appearance of being nonmaterialistic by publicly reporting relatively modest salaries. As "nonprofit" legal corporations they need only report whatever portion of their income they pay themselves as "salary"—the rest can be buried in the corporation. So it is that "the church" or "the foundation" may be the technical owners of a fine house, a luxury automobile, even a sharp wardrobe, but only the sophist (and his or her family) has free use of them. Thus, although technically true that a given individual earns only a modest "salary," his or her real income may be astronomical. By equivocating on terms like *salary* and *own,* and speaking the literal legal truth to a general audience, which may be unaware of these legal distinctions, such characters can effectively conceal evidence of their true earnings.

Crossroads Pitch.   A very common maneuver used by psychic sophists is a type of "reading" that we'll label the "crossroads pitch." Although there are variations, they usually follow a common theme: The psychic sees a vision, a dream, a spirit entity, or some other "psychic representation" of the person consulting them standing at a "crossroads." A typical reading might go like this: "I see a crossroads. One path is bumpy and heads downhill to a dark cloud. The other is steep and leads to a bright sun." If it's not a crossroads, it might be the bank of a stream or the foot of a mountain. The point is that it will involve *two clearly distinct choices*.

When are we most likely to seek psychic readings in earnest? Usually when we are confused, lost, or in need of assurance. It's a safe bet that *psychologically* the feeling of choice ("the crossroads") will strike a responsive chord. Then, if the psychic suggests that in the "near future" we will choose the sunlit, upward path, we feel more hopeful, confident, and pleased. We've been given just what we were looking for, told just what we hoped to hear. This simple, reassuring scenario may even have a placebo effect on our spirits, and our renewed self-confidence may then help us make better choices. But as clear thinkers, we do not want to settle for fallacious explanations of how the "reading" helped us.

Appeals to Clichés, Proverbs, and Common Sense. Another form of vague prediction involves disguised clichés, proverbs, and common sense. For example, a horoscope running near the Christmas season might read, "GEMINI: Watch matters of health. Family member plays important role." Yet this would be good, basic, general holiday-time advice for most of us. It is common for summertime (meaning vacation-time) horoscopes to say something like this: "LIBRA: change of location a possibility. Expect variety. Secure possessions." Again, note that this is basic, "commonsense" advice for most people anticipating a vacation. With the advent of the inexpensive personal computer, random generation of such vague "advice" has become a simple matter.

Popular astrology books are likely to contain elaborate descriptions of the basic "type" associated with each of the twelve zodiac signs. These descriptions usually contain enough variety of traits, couched in inconsistent and general language, to accommodate the selective identification of most people. The very same "description" will probably have enough variety (that is, inconsistencies) to fit anyone. On page 1 we might read, "The typical Aquarian needs to be alone at times." Page 2 informs us that "Aquarians are well liked and enjoy the company of good friends." Page 3 tells us, "Don't ever try to pin an Aquarian down," whereas page 4 says, "When he makes up his mind on a course of action, the Aquarian is among the most reliable of sun-types." Add to this mishmash such qualifications as "usually" or "typically" and the complications of ascending and descending planets, signs, cusps, and so on, and you have plenty of ways of modifying any astrological charting to accommodate any individual. Roger Culver and Philip Ianna studied 3,011 specific predictions made by well-known astrologers, and discovered that only 10 percent were realized.[21] Yet true believers will insist that there is a much higher rate of accuracy. They may be able to convince themselves because vague claims are susceptible to whatever interpretation is most desired, and because we have the ability to selectively recall only what supports our beliefs, ignoring what doesn't. (Connect this fact to material covered in Chapters 2 and 3.)

Causal Confusion. Note, too, the likely presence of causal fallacies. Many, if not most, "illnesses" and depressive moods are self-limiting, which means that we will recover from them in time without any treatment. So whether we consult a palmist, numerologist, "psychic surgeon," fortune teller, or bank teller today, we will be "cured" in the future (if nothing else interferes). However, we might be inclined to *attribute* our recovery to some noteworthy, prior event, such as our visit to the sophist. The psychic or faith healer who lays hands on

---

[21]Charles Downey, "Straightening Out the Mind Benders," *This World Magazine,* November 9, 1986, p. 9.

us Wednesday will most probably claim credit for "healing" us when our illness has run its natural course on Friday.[22]

We should not overlook those people claiming to be "cured" of self-diagnosed "cancers" and "ulcers" and so forth. As impartial observers, we cannot be sure that there ever was any organic condition to cure. What is glaringly absent in most such cases is any body of carefully controlled studies that support these remarkable claims. But as sophists from ancient times to the present are quick to point out, *scientists have been unable to disprove the successful sophist's claims of faith healing or psychic healing*—which is, we know, an instance of the argument from ignorance fallacy. That a major reason for the lack of such scientific criticism can be traced to the healers' refusal to cooperate in the acquisition of data, observations, and controls is, of course, not pointed out.

Faith and logic are not inevitable enemies—but fraudulent claims and clear thinking are. Sophists are reprehensible because they prey most successfully on people who are ignorant, unhappy, depressed, desperate, or just gullible. Why aren't cases like these investigated? Why don't people reveal that they have not been healed? There are probably many reasons, and we can draw only tentative conclusions about them. They most likely include some psychological denial (Chapter 2). People who strongly want to have a certain kind of faith, or to believe in a certain individual, can convince themselves that *their own* doubts are what block their chances at success. This is introjection (Chapter 2). Others sometimes insist—despite contradictory evidence—that they *are* being healed, *only very slowly*. Some simply deny the significance of serious inconsistencies (rationalization and psychological denial; see Chapter 2).

To a certain extent, we are perhaps sometimes responsible for our own gullibility. This does not, however, obviate the responsibility of those who deliberately and with great care fabricate claims designed to promise more than they deliver, and who deliberately take advantage of a person's feelings of inadequacy, financial fears, confusion, or suffering. We are justified in holding these sophists accountable because a great deal of *careful reasoning* has gone into crafting their fraudulent promises in ways that protect them from legal prosecution or from public exposure. We can conclude, therefore, that these misleading claims are deliberate.

Our best protection is to think clearly for ourselves and to use what we've learned in our logic studies. We should always look for the presence of fallacies, and we should always demand clarity of expression—especially when promises are made that affect our pocketbooks; our self-esteem; or our physical, mental, or emotional well-being. We must ask basic questions, using our own experience to test all claims where possible and consulting objective experts when our own knowledge and experience are inadequate guides.

Good thinking skills are at their most practical when the stakes are the highest.

EXERCISE 8-4 _____

1. The Amazing Randi reports that he once pretended to be an "astrographologist" on a call-in radio show out of Winnipeg, Canada. Listeners were asked to send in their

---

[22]This is an example of a casual fallacy called post hoc: Based *solely* on the fact that event *A* precedes event *B*, we conclude that event *A* *caused* event *B*. Post hoc is explained in Chapter 11, which deals with the concept of cause.

birthdates and samples of their handwriting during the week before Randi's appearance. During his appearance, Randi gave "readings" for three listeners, who were then asked to call in and evaluate their accuracy. Randi was judged to be quite successful, initially getting accuracy ratings of 9, 10, and 10 on a scale of 10. The 9 was changed to a 10 after the first listener objected when Randi said that he disliked hard work. The listener pointed out that he was a laborer and was accustomed to hard work. "But," Randi countered, "I said that you *disliked* hard work." "True," the listener said. "I guess you're right, I don't really *like* it."[23]

As Randi says, the most amazing thing about the whole experience is that he did not have any handwriting samples or birthdays with him. Instead, he read, word for word, three readings that had been given in Las Vegas months before by Sydney Omarr while on "The Merv Griffin Show." The readings were originally done for three members of Merv's audience.[24]

Analyze this incident using concepts you've learned regarding fallacies, persuasive language, psychic sophistries, and pseudoscience.

2. Some popular television evangelists announce what they call a "Word of Knowledge" about healings: "I see a tumor shrinking. I see someone with congestion clearing up now. I see a broken marriage being mended at this very minute." What, do you suppose, are the odds that in an audience of a million or more people someone, somewhere will fit these symptoms? If just a small percentage of those watching notice that their (self-limiting) diseases disappear and send in a note of thanks, our sophist has a batch of testimonials. (One percent of a million is 10,000, so the odds of hitting a few "predictions" are high.)

What steps could be taken to verify such claims? You might want to write politely to see if you can find any objective evidence supporting such claims for a particular healer. If you do, analyze whatever response you get.

SUMMARY

In this chapter, we have learned about pseudoscience and sophistry. We've discussed some of their general characteristics, applying what we've learned about knowledge and legitimate authority.

Pseudoscience, a term coined by Martin Gardner, refers to a certain category of theories, systems, and explanations, which though claiming to be "scientific," in fact use only the trappings of genuine science while avoiding the rigors of the checks and balances of the scientific method or the scrutiny of disinterested experts.

The *"new" sophistry* refers to the deliberate use of fallacies, persuasive language, "powerbabble," manipulative techniques, and personal charisma to sell success, health, salvation, or well-being.

We identified three general categories of sophistry in terms of their primary areas of interest, noting that all three may overlap: psychological sophistry, success sophistry, and spiritual and psychic sophistry.

Summary Questions
1. Scan a recent issue of one of the popular newspaper tabloids for examples of sophistry. Analyze your examples in terms of the list of characteristics covered in this chapter.

[23]Randi, *Flim-Flam!* p. 61.
[24]Ibid.

2. Why do you think sophistries in pseudoscience persist to the extent that they do today? Do you see this persistence as good, bad, or unimportant? Discuss.

ADDITIONAL EXERCISES

1. In April 1978, *Psychic News* reported that one Ingo Swann had made an "astral trip" to Mercury and Jupiter. Swann apparently described his "impressions" of these planets well before Mariner 10 journeyed past Mercury and Pioneer 10 past Jupiter. *Psychic News* quoted astronaut Edgar Mitchell as saying that Swann described things that were not known to earth scientists until *after* the Mariner and Pioneer probes.

   When careful analysis was made of Swann's thirty-one claims, six were true and four were probably true, eleven were wrong, one was probably wrong, three were unclear, and four were obvious.

   When his errors were pointed out in conversation with a British Broadcasting Corporation producer, Swann claimed that travel by astral projection takes place at such great speeds that it disorients the astral traveler. Swann then said that he had probably shot past Jupiter into another solar system: He had described another planet, not Jupiter.[25]

   Discuss this incident.

2. Martin Gardner reports that in his book *Superminds*, popular British "science personality" John Taylor, a mathematical physicist at King's College in London, reported that controversial "psychic" Uri Geller could bend spoons, keys, and other metal objects. According to Gardner, Taylor has, however, been unable actually to see anything bend or to videotape any actual bending. The reason for this is what Taylor labels the "shyness effect": Bending is most likely to occur when no one is looking.

   Among his many claims, Taylor asserted that hundreds of British "superkids" could duplicate Geller's psychic bending. He backed up this claim by giving children crudely sealed tubes containing a straight metal bar. The children took them home and returned with bent bars. Taylor was perplexed by the curious fact that bending did not occur when the children were given well-sealed tubes.[26]

   Discuss this incident.

3. Discuss the following assertions, which are part of a full-page ad headed "FROM DEBTS TO RICHE$, THE POOR MAN'S ROAD TO WEALTH"—A PROVEN METHOD TO ACHIEVE FINANCIAL FREEDOM!

   > "From Debts To Riches The Poor Man's Road To Wealth" will show you how you can achieve an income of up to $5,000.00 per month, just by spending a few hours per day following the easy to read instructions in my book. **In it YOU WILL LEARN:**
   >
   > —How to PASS any credit investigation.
   > —How to WIPE OUT all of your DEBTS, if you so wish, and still MAINTAIN AAA CREDIT.
   > —How to achieve FINANCIAL SECURITY, and a life of luxury, in less than 90 days.
   > —How to raise all the CAPITAL you need.
   >
   > To accomplish all of the things contained in "From Debts to Riches The Poor Man's Road To Wealth," **there are some things that you DON'T NEED.**
   >
   > —You don't need to be a genius
   > —You don't need to have an education

[25]Ibid., pp. 63–68.
[26]Gardner, *Science: Good, Bad, and Bogus*, pp. 93–94.

—You don't need to sell anything
—You don't need to visit anyone
—And you don't need to even move out of home."

4. What at first glance appears to be an article with the dateline (Peachtree City, Ga.) is headed "HIDDEN HEALTH SECRETS DISCOVERED." In small print, we notice that it is in fact an advertisement. Here's a sampling from that ad:

Amazing New Discoveries Give You Perfect Health And Help You Feel Great. (Special)
FC&A, a nearby Peachtree City, Georgia medical publisher announced today the release of a new, $3.99 book for the general public. *"Hidden Health Secrets."*

Look At Some Of The Secrets
Revealed In This Amazing
New Book
—Secrets that may help protect against gallstones, diverticulosis, some types of cancer, hardening of the arteries, varicose veins and hemmorrhoids [sic]
—A little known secret that can pep you up without pills
—A vitamin that cuts allergy and asthma attacks in half
—This secret may keep you from losing your teeth
—Headache . . . a mineral that may be helpful to migraine sufferers
—Ways to combat the common cold

Discuss this "article" in terms of the material covered in this chapter and any other fallacies, ambiguities, and so on that seem pertinent.

part FOUR

Induction

9

Inductive Reasoning: Generalization and Analogy

He who begins to count begins to err.

OSKAR MORGENSTERN

"College is a joke," Cooper announced loudly. He was waiting for his American Lit class to begin, and he was speaking loudly enough for people six rows in any direction to hear. "I mean," he went on, "most of the stuff we have to learn is irrelevant to real life, our instructors are mediocre at best, and I just read in the paper that fewer and fewer college graduates get jobs in their majors than ever before."

"Hold on," Nora said. "I kinda like college."

"Yeah?" Coop interrupted, "what do you know? You're just a freshman. Just wait till next year; you'll see."

"But you're only a sophomore," Nora pointed out. "You're only a year ahead of me."

"Only a year? That's 25 percent of a bachelor's degree! And besides, that's two semesters, or ten courses to your five. So my opinion is much more likely to be right."

"Well," Nora continued hesitantly, confused by Coop's point, "it still seems as if you're making a pretty big generalization even if it is based on ten courses."

"That's not all it's based on. My older brother, Ed, agrees with me, and he's taken hundreds of courses. He's got degrees in anthropology, history, engineering, and he's now gone back to school to study business. He ought to know."

At that point, Mr. Palmer arrived, and class began, cutting off Nora and Cooper's discussion. Out in the quad, however, an equally interesting "discussion" was heating up.

"Look! Men just want one thing," Betty nearly shouted.

"Oh, yeah? How do you know?" Norman shot back.

"Well, wiseguy, don't forget I've been married four times. And each time the guy let me down. All any of my exes wanted was somebody to baby them, to take care of 'em. So there!"

"Gee, that's only four guys out of billions."

"My mom's had the same experience, and so have lots of women."

"I don't doubt that," Norman replied, "but aren't you overlooking all sorts of factors?"

"Like what?"

"Oh, like the personality traits of the parties involved, childhood experiences, and so on. You know the kinds of things I mean."

"All I know is that every man I've married has been a male chauvinist baby, and that's true of my mother's husbands, and lots of our friends say it's true of their experiences. So there! Argue with numbers if you dare!"

Norman knew better than to argue with Betty when she was upset. But he also recognized that her arguments were full of hasty conclusions, sweeping generalizations, faulty causal reasoning, and in general, bad inductive reasoning. He remembered that much from his logic course. What he often overlooked, however, was his own tendency to think just as poorly as Betty. Why just the other evening, he had been really angered by Les.

"Blacks are just not as bright as whites."

"Whoa! Norm, old buddy, don't tell me you're a bigot," Les said with astonishment.

"Bigot? Hey, man, don't be rude. I worked with a couple of black guys last summer, and they were the slowest guys on the crew."

"What's that prove? All that shows is that those two guys were slow. You can't leap to conclusions about an entire race of people just because you worked with two of them. Do you even know any black people well?"

"I don't need to. I read a lot and pay attention to things. Look what a high percentage of blacks there are in prisons."

"Sociologists say that being poor, not being black, accounts for that— more poor people of all races go to jail than others, and then there might be a touch of racism in juries and cops and judges—just like there is in you," Les said.

"I'm no bigot. I'm just pointing out a fact. Statistics show that black people don't do as well on standardized tests like the SAT and Law School Admissions Test as whites. I can't help it."

"I'm not sure of your statistics, but even if they are accurate, they don't support your conclusion. You're looking at one variable—race—and overlooking such things as family background, income level, quality of available schooling—just like you do with your claims about criminal behavior. Your facts *may be* correct, but your thinking is sure muddled."

What interests us about each of these discussions is that they involve inductive reasoning and generalizations. As we learned in Chapter 1, in an inductive argument a conclusion is more or less probable, but not certain. We agreed to call a well-constructed inductive argument "justified" or "sound." A justified or sound inductive argument is one whose premises lend its conclusion a high degree of probability. The basic type of simple inductive argument is one whose conclusion is a generalization.

A generalization is a statement that covers many specifics, for example, "When seat belts are widely used, traffic fatalities decrease"; "If detected early enough, most cancers can be cured"; "Apple trees grow better in Washington than in Florida." These statements cover the specific instances of wearing seat belts, detecting cancer early, and growing apple trees in Washington and Florida. All are generalizations, as are many of the statements in the preceding "discussions."

The basic type of simple inductive argument is one whose conclusion is a generalization. This chapter, the first in our examination of inductive reasoning, deals with the inductive generalization and analogy.

As you might gather from the foregoing conversations, inductive generalizations are often unjustified; frequently they're unsound. When are inductive generalizations justified? When are they not? What criteria can we use in deciding? This chapter, the first of four dealing with induction, will answer these questions. It will also consider another common form of inductive logic: the analogy.

INDUCTIVE GENERALIZATION

An inductive generalization is an inductive argument whose conclusion is a generalization. It works as follows. On the basis of some cases known through experience, one draws an inference that applies to the whole collection of cases. Thus, having observed that some crows are black, I conclude that all crows are black. Or having observed that some basketball players are taller than 6 feet, I infer that most basketball players are taller than 6 feet, or that 99 percent of them are. Notice that in each case the generalization is based on observing a connection between two things—between crows and the color black, between basketball players and a height in excess of 6 feet. Having observed this connection on several or many occasions, I generalize that in the future the same connection will hold. The next crow I see probably will be black; the next basketball player probably will be taller than 6 feet. Again, a woman might observe that every time she eats zucchini she feels sick an hour later. After this phenomenon recurs, she might conclude that eating zucchini makes her sick, an inductive generalization that applies to all instances of her eating zucchini.

So in forming inductive generalizations, we start with specifics and end with a statement that will in the future apply to similar specifics. By so doing, we avoid past mistakes; we exercise greater control over our lives and actions. The woman in our example avoids zucchini.

Naturally, we don't always go through the process of forming inductive generalizations. Often we accept other peoples' generalizations. For example, you needn't go through the process of learning that foul-smelling, discolored meat is spoiled and not safe to eat. That generalization was formed long ago and passed on to us. But of course, we do form generalizations of our own, as Coop, Gloria, and Norm did. In forming our generalizations, it's important to ensure that we've observed enough specifics before generalizing. Thus, if you observed a couple of teachers at college being indifferent to their students' needs, you shouldn't immediately generalize that all teachers, or even most teachers, at the college are similarly indifferent. You simply wouldn't have enough specific instances of teacher indifference to form so sweeping a conclusion. You'd be guilty of a faulty generalization. We'll talk more about this later in the chapter when we discuss fallacies connected with generalizations.

First, let's look again at two of our examples of inductive generalizations: "All crows are black" and "Most basketball players are taller than 6 feet." Notice that in one we have used the word *all*; in the other we've used the word *most*. This suggests that generalizations can take two principal forms: the weak generalization and the strong generalization.

Strong Generalizations

A strong, or universal, generalization is a statement that asserts that something is true of all members of a class, for example, "All humans are vertebrates"; "All voters are citizens"; and "Every instance of human decapitation results in death." In each statement a property is attributed to every member of a class. Sometimes, of course, a universal quantifier such as *all* or *every* or *any* is not stated but is implied. Thus, "Humans are vertebrates" and "Voters are citizens" imply that we're speaking of every human and every voter.

Again, suppose you have a barrel of coffee beans. After mixing them up, you remove a sample of beans, ensuring that the sample is drawn from different parts of the same barrel. Upon examining the beans, you find that they are all grade A. You conclude, "The beans in the barrel are grade A." Clearly you mean *all* the beans. Incidentally, you could write your inductive generalization as follows:

> The beans in the observed sample are grade A.
> Therefore, the beans in the barrel are grade A.

Your premise states information about the observed beans in the barrel; your conclusion is a statement about all the beans in the barrel. It's a universal generalization.

Sometimes a universal generalization doesn't universally affirm membership of one class of things within another; it denies it. Thus, "No human can remain under water very long without oxygen" and "Men cannot bear children" are universal generalizations because they deny of *all* members of a class some property, characteristic, or attribute. In other words, no member of the class "human" will be found within the class of "things that can remain under water very long without oxygen"; no member of the class "men" will be found within the class of "humans who bear children."

Weak Generalizations

A weak, or particular, generalization is a statement that asserts that something is true of some members of a class. For example, "Nello's Ristorante serves good food," "As a rule, the younger two people are when they marry, the more likely they are to be divorced in five years," and "Students who come to class prepared do better than those who don't" are all examples of generalizations meant to assert only that something is true of some members of a class.

We must be careful not to confuse weak generalizations with strong ones. Often, students will mistake a weak generalization for a strong one by over-looking such key qualifiers as *usually, often, most of the time, rarely, as a rule,* and the like. Thus, when a sociology professor points out, "College graduates tend to make more money than high school dropouts," she might encounter this reaction: "But Miss Vargas, that's not true. My grandfather dropped out of school in the third grade, and he's a multimillionaire." Or a psychology teacher might carefully assert, "Most violent criminals were physically abused as children," only to hear this kind of objection: "Excuse me, Dr. Reich, but it's just not true. My cousin Bernie was physically abused as a child and he's a saint."

Generalizations involving human behavior and moral principles are often of the weak, or particular, form. They assert patterns ranging in degrees of probability from "rarely," or highly improbable, to "almost always," or highly probable. But they are not meant as universal statements.

Here, as we have so often seen, we must rely on context and signal words to help us out. We must be especially careful when qualifiers are implied but not stated, as in "Students who are prepared for class do better than those who are not" and "Republicans are richer than Democrats." In both cases, treating the statements as universal is incorrect. They are meant only to identify what the speaker asserts is a general pattern, which is sometimes true, perhaps even almost always true—but *almost* always is logically distinct from always.

If we fail to recognize that difference, we will be unable to analyze inductive arguments intelligently. And to analyze inductive arguments intelligently, we must also become aware of the uses of statistical generalizations, which are a particular form of weak generalization.

Statistical Generalizations

A statistical generalization is a statement that asserts that something is true of a percentage of a class. Being weak, statistical generalizations never speak of every member of a class, but only of some. "Seventy-five percent of the voters favor a reduction in property taxes," "Over half the fruit in this vineyard is rotten," "A large number of students today are majoring in business"—all qualify as statistical generalizations.

Back to our barrel of coffee beans. Suppose you notice that 80 percent of all the beans in the sample drawn are grade A. You conclude that 80 percent of the beans in the barrel are grade A. Your inductive generalizations might be written,

Eighty percent of the beans in the observed sample are grade A.
Therefore, 80 percent of the beans in the barrel are grade A.

Your conclusion is a statistical generalization. It asserts that something is true of a percentage of the beans in the barrel, not of every bean in it.

In both the strong and weak generalizations, we assert something about all or a percentage of the class members on the basis of enumeration, that is, observing some members of the class. For this reason, such generalizations are often referred to as inductions by enumeration.

Inductive generalizations, or inductions by enumeration, always consist of conclusions that go beyond their premises. Based on observed instances, we form a judgment about the unobserved. As a result, generalizations can yield false conclusions despite the truth of their premises. In other words, even though the premises of an inductive generalization describe an actual state of affairs (our definition of a true proposition), its conclusion may not describe an actual state of affairs. Thus, maybe the next crow you observe will *not* be black; perhaps only 60 percent of the beans in the barrel are grade A. This possibility of error in inductive generalizations shouldn't be surprising, however, for it's the characteristic of all inductive arguments that their conclusions are at best probable, never certain.

Our task, then, is to formulate sound generalizations, ones that are justified. We must try to construct generalizations in such a way that we reduce the chances of false conclusions following from true premises. Of great help here is an awareness of the factors involved in formulating reliable generalizations.

*EXERCISE 9-1 _____

Classify the following generalizations as weak or strong. Explain your choice.

1. Cigarette smoking causes lung cancer.
2. Women earn fifty-nine cents to every dollar a man earns.
3. Sound deductive arguments are valid.
4. Wearing seat belts reduces the chance of serious injury from automobile accidents.
5. More men than women die from heart attacks.
6. Being overweight is a risk factor for high blood pressure.
7. Most AIDS victims are gay.
8. The best time to fish for trout is in the early morning.
9. Nine out of ten people surveyed report that Bufferin doesn't upset their stomachs.
10. A 1985 survey by Ann Landers reported that 72 percent of American women would trade sex for cuddling.

RELIABLE GENERALIZATIONS

In Chapter 12 we will deal thoroughly with statistical fallacies as they apply to all forms of induction. Since what we say there will apply to generalizations, we'll be brief here in discussing the reliability of generalizations. It is sufficient to point to at least four factors to consider in determining the reliability of a generalization. Three of these deal with whether the sample is representative of the entire group. Specifically, it's important to consider whether the sample is comprehensive of the group, whether it's large enough, and whether it's random. The fourth factor deals with the margin for error in the generalization itself.

Comprehensiveness

In formulating or evaluating inductive generalizations, it's important to ensure that the sample that is the basis for the conclusion is comprehensive of the group. A small sample from a well-shaken bottle of milk will indicate whether the entire bottle is sour. But an accurate estimate of the size and quality of tomatoes in a truckload requires samples taken from different parts of the truck, including some from the bottom. The reason: in transportation, the smallest tomatoes invariably fall to the bottom of the load.

When a class of things consist of subclasses, numerous samples of the subclasses are needed to ensure comprehensiveness. This is especially true when people constitute the samples. For example, before a generalization is justified about the merits of a drug, the public's opinion of TV programs, or the political preferences of persons under thirty, considerable sampling must be done to account for the vast differences among the members of the class being generalized about.

Take, for example, the generalization "College graduates make more money in a lifetime than noncollege graduates." Obviously, the class "college graduates" includes a vast number of individuals who differ from one another in a multitude of ways. In other words, the category of "college graduates" includes many subcategories: "college graduates who majored in business," "college graduates who attended Ivy League colleges," "college graduates who entered a field directly related to what they studied in college," "female college graduates," and so on. A sample that overlooks the many subgroups within the group termed "college graduates" misrepresents the group itself. Any conclusion it suggests, therefore, must be considered unjustified—*even if it turns out to be true.*

Size

Directly related to the comprehensiveness of the sample is the sample's size. Ordinarily, the more instances observed, the more reliable the generalization. The reason is that large numbers tend to follow fixed laws.

You can easily demonstrate this tendency by tossing a dime. The chances of heads coming up on any toss is one in two. If you want a sample to serve as the basis for this generalization, don't flip the coin just twice. Heads could easily come up on both occasions, or not at all. To form an accurate generalization, you must toss the coin many times—hundreds, even thousands of times. The more tosses you include in your sample, the closer to the one-in-two split you'll observe.

The size of any sample is tied directly to the size of the group and the number of subgroups within it. Usually, the larger and more diversified the group, the larger the sample should be to ensure that it represents the group. Again, the generalization about the financial fortunes of college graduates is a good example. Since the class of "college graduates," as we saw, consists of many different subgroups, a relatively large sample is needed to justify any conclusion. If, on the other hand, we were interested only in the finances of graduates of a specific college, a smaller sample would be acceptable.

Randomness

Randomness means that each member of the group has an equal chance of ending up as part of the sample. A sampling technique that lacks randomness yields an unrepresentative sample.

To see how randomness works, suppose that in determining the size and quality of the tomatoes in the truckload, you sampled only the ones on the top. Because not every tomato had an equal chance of being picked, your sample would lack randomness.

Again, suppose you want to form a generalization about the percentage of the students at your college who believe in God. To do so, you query every student who has classes with you. Here again, your sample would lack randomness because not every student had an equal chance of being queried.

Each of the preceding factors clearly deals with whether a sample accurately represents the group being generalized about. A sample can be unrepresentative by not being comprehensive, by being too small, or by lacking randomness. Even when a sample is comprehensive, large enough, and random, the generalization that follows it may be risky because of the breadth of its claim. This point is directly related to its margin for error.

Margin for Error

Be sensitive to the breadth of the claim made by any generalizations. Ordinarily, the greater the margin for error, the more reliable is the generalization.

On first glance, this may seem an odd principle. After all, how can a generalization that carries a greater margin for error be more reliable than one that carries a smaller margin for error? Perhaps the confusion arises because it sounds as if we're saying that the more likely a generalization is wrong, the more reliable it is. Of course, that would be absurd. What we *are* saying is that the greater the *allowance* for error in the generalization, the more reliable the generalization is. A simple example will clarify the point.

Let's return to your interest in finding out what percentage of students believe in God. This time let's restrict your curiosity to the students in your logic class, of whom, we'll say, there are thirty-three. You want to find out what portion of this thirty-three believes in God.

To form your generalization, let's suppose you randomly sample twelve of your classmates. You find out that ten believe in God; two don't. Thus, your sample indicates that those who believe in God outnumber those who don't by a ratio of six to one. As a result, it would be very safe for you to generalize, "The *majority* of students in my logic class believe in God."

The reason this is so safe a generalization is that your sample allows a substantial margin for error. Just think, of the remaining twenty-one classmates, only seven would have to believe in God to verify your generalization. In other words, even if the ratio of believers to nonbelievers flips from six to one to one to three, your generalization is still true.

Now, contrast such a generalization with this one: "Eighty-three percent of the students in my logic class believe in God." You based this, of course, on the original sample: 83 percent of the original twelve believed in God. But the margin of error for this generalization is considerably smaller than for the first one about the majority. Remember that in generalizing about the majority, only seven of the remaining twenty-one students would have to believe in God to verify your generalization. But in the 83 percent generalization, a full seventeen must believe in God to verify it: $33 \times .83 = 27.4; 27.4 - 10 = 17.4$—thus, the seventeen figure. Clearly, then, the majority generalization, because it provides a greater margin for error, is the safer of the two, although both could be justified. (Of course, a generalization about more than 83 percent believing in God wouldn't even be justified.)

So the margin for error a generalization carries is important in evaluating its reliability. The greater the margin for error, the more reliable the generalization. But keep in mind that a generalization that carries the tiniest margin of error may, nonetheless, be *justified*. You'd be wise, however, to reduce the breadth of its claim to be on the safe side.

When we overlook the preceding four factors, we probably formulate unreliable generalizations.

EXERCISE 9-2 _____

The following arguments are inductive generalizations. Identify premises and conclusions and criticize the arguments in terms of the four factors relative to their reliability.

1. I know a half dozen college graduates who are making over $50,000 a year in their jobs. That just goes to prove that college graduates are paid handsomely in their occupations.

2. BILL: I think our next class president is going to be Lydia.
   TONY: I think Myra has a much better chance.
   BILL: Myra? I just can't believe that a sizable number of our 7,500 student body even knows who Myra is.
   TONY: Are you kidding? The school paper just conducted a poll. They set up a booth over in the cafeteria last Wednesday afternoon. And guess what? Sixty-two percent of the 112 students they asked said they were voting for Myra.

3. Member of committee supporting tax levy for schools: I think the public is squarely behind this measure. After all, every member of the PTA and school board supports it.

4. To find out what percentage of their income a family of four spends for food, a sample is taken. Fifteen hundred phone calls are made to 1,500 different families. Of these, a thousand indicate that they spend at least 25 percent of their income on food. The conclusion is drawn that two-thirds of American families of four spend at least 25 percent of their income on food.

5. In every case of syphilis we have ever observed, a certain spiral shaped bacterium called a spirochete has been present. This proves that a spirochete, and only a spirochete, is the cause of syphilis.

6. GEORGE: There's no question that farmers think that government is giving them the shaft.
   RUTH: My father's a farmer and he thinks he's getting a pretty square deal.
   GEORGE: Oh sure, you're always going to find the isolated exception. But a recent poll of farmers in the San Joaquin valley in central California reveals widespread discontent with government farm policies.

7. A jar contains a thousand jellybeans. After the jellybeans are thoroughly mixed, a handful of them is taken out. Twenty-eight of them are green, twenty-seven red. It's concluded that (1) the jar contains only green and red jellybeans and (2) that at least half are green.

8. ALYSON: All men are fickle.
   AL: Honey, I have something to tell you.
   ALYSON: Why, you didn't hear a word I said.

AL: I'm sorry, I have this other thing on my mind. What did you say?

ALYSON: I said that all men are fickle.

AL: Oh, come on now.

ALYSON: I mean it. Every guy I've ever dated has thrown me over for somebody else. . . . Now what is it you have to tell me?

AL: Well, I . . . uh . . . I've met somebody else.

ALYSON: See!

9. A man has a bucket of gravel. He notices the big, smooth rocks on the top. But he's no fool. He realizes that the ones below may not be big and smooth, so he gives the bucket a thorough shaking. Lo and behold, big, smooth rocks are still on top. That satisfies him—the bucket of gravel contains big, smooth rocks.

10. MADGE: You know, the courts are really too lenient in granting paroles.

MIKE: Why do you say that?

MADGE: Because a day doesn't go by when I don't read of some paroled convict who's committed a crime.

MIKE: Hmm, you have a point there.

11. Report to the Downtown Mall Association: The results of our report are based on a survey conducted the week of September 9, from 1 to 3 P.M., M–F. Over 63 people answered our simple 6-question form. Here, then, is our report on the attitudes of the typical mall shopper.

12. Dr. Boswell must be a great instructor. The results of his student evaluations are consistently excellent. Of the 38 percent of the students responding, over half rate Dr. Boswell as excellent.

13. LEE: There's no point in seeing if you want to go skating.

GAIL: Why do you say that?

LEE: I asked you to go twice this month, and both times you refused.

14. I demand that Dr. Boswell be fired. I've talked to a number of my friends, and they all think she's a lousy lecturer.

15. To Whom It May Concern: Enclosed please find the manuscript of my two-thou-sand-page saga. I know that it is a good book because I've let my friends and family read it, and they are unanimous in their praise.

16. Virtually every heroin addict ever studied has been found to have begun abusing drugs by smoking marijuana. Thus, we see that marijuana usage always lead to heroin addiction.

17. Look, I'm tellin' ya, Fords are all lemons. I had two myself—both lemons. And my brother had one, a lemon. Trust me in this; I am giving you the benefit of my experience.

18. Ladies and gentlemen of the jury, how else can we explain the presence of this fiber at the scene of the crime? After all, chemical analysis shows that this fiber is identical to fibers in the jacket found in the defendant's car. And even though the defendant claims that this is not his jacket, let us ask ourselves how likely it is that somebody else's jacket would be in his trunk. No, ladies and gentlemen, the conclusion is obvious: The only explanation for the presence of that fiber at the scene of the crime is that the defendant was wearing this jacket when he broke into the parlor that awful night.

19. I'm never going back to House of Steaks. The last time I was there I had to wait twenty minutes for my meal. Their service is horrible.

20. Boy, this Spielberg film will be just great. Every Spielberg film I've ever seen has been great, so this one will be too!

ANALOGY

When we draw an analogy between things, we indicate one or more respects in which they are similar. Sometimes we draw analogies in description to help create a picture in the reader's mind. Thus, someone writes, "The universe is populated by billions of galaxies, which are receding from one another, *like raisins in an expanding pudding.*" Other times analogies help an explanation by making the unfamiliar understandable by comparison with the familiar. For example, somebody says, "Thinking is like swimming. Just as in swimming our bodies naturally float on the surface and require great physical exertion to plunge to the bottom; so in thinking it requires great mental exertion to force our minds away from the superficial down into the depths of weighty problems." Here a comparison is made between thinking and swimming to make the point about the nature of thinking comprehensible. Both the descriptive and the explanatory analogies are nonargumentative analogies.

But, of course, we frequently use analogies in argument. *An argument from analogy is an inductive argument in which a known similarity that two things share is used as evidence for concluding that the two things are similar in other respects.* Thus, "If entity A has characteristics w, x, y, and z; and entity B has characteristics w, x, and y; then entity B must also have characteristic z." In any argument from analogy, we extend what is known to be true about members of one class to new objects standing outside the class. So an argument from analogy is really a form of inductive generalization. Similarly, in every inductive generalization we assume that the objects to which the statement is being applied are analogous to the objects in the observed sample. Thus, every inductive generalization implies an analogy.

Let's look at an example. Sweeney has gotten particularly good service from a number of Volkswagens he's owned over the years. In fact, based on his good fortune, he's formed the generalization that Volkswagens are very dependable cars. So, naturally enough, when B.J. needs to get a car, Sweeney suggests a Volkswagen. Technically speaking, we could say that Sweeney extends his generalization to apply to B.J.'s case on the basis of the known resemblances between his own VWs and B.J.'s. Letting w, x, y, and z represent the characteristics of a VW Rabbit model, being a standard transmission, a brand-new car, and finally, dependable, we could diagram Sweeney's analogical argument as follows:

Sweeney's VWs: w, x, y, and z
B.J.'s VW: w, x, y—therefore, z.

As is true of all inductive inferences, conclusions drawn from analogy are never certain. At best they provide probability or likelihood. There's no guarantee that B.J.'s VW will prove as dependable as Sweeney's, but if the analogy is a sound one, it's likely that the VW will be as dependable. The question then is, what counts for an analogy and what counts against it? What factors should we consider in evaluating the soundness of any analogical argument?

*EXERCISE 9-3 _____
Indicate whether the following are argumentative or nonargumentative uses of analogy.

1. It's so hot today you could fry an egg on the sidewalk.
2. A family is like a nation. Both consist of individuals related by blood, culture, and interests. And just as a nation is best governed by an elected head, so is a family. Let the family members decide who will govern it.
3. BRAD: Have you heard Willie Nelson's latest LP?
   BELLE: I don't have to to know I'll like it. He's never done an LP I haven't liked.

4. "The bees have only one king, the flocks only one head, the herds only one teacher. Can you believe that in heaven the supreme power is divided and that the entire majesty of that true, divine Authority is broken up?" (Prudentius)

5. INSTRUCTOR: I have no doubt that the vast majority of students will pass this test. They've passed the last three tests I've given, haven't they?

6. "In nearly all of the non-Communist world, socialism, meaning public ownership of industrial enterprises, is a spent slogan. Like promises to enforce the antitrust laws in the United States, it is no longer a political program but an overture to nostalgia." (John Kenneth Galbraith, *The New Industrial State*)

7. "One of the pleasures of science is to see two distant and apparently unrelated pieces of information suddenly come together. In a flash what one knows doubles or triples in size. It is like working on two large but separate sections of a jigsaw puzzle and, almost without realizing it until the moment it happens, finding that they fit into one." (John Tyler Bonner, "Hormones in Social Amoebae and Mammals, *Scientific American,* vol. 221, no. 5, November 1969)

8. "The objections which have been brought against a standing army, and they are many and weighty, and deserve to prevail, may also at last be brought against a standing government. The government itself, which is only the mode which the people have chosen to execute their will, is equally liable to be abused and perverted before the people can act through it." (Henry David Thoreau, "On the Duty of Civil Disobedience")

9. "We are seeing the end of our adolescence. In its reincarnation as guardian advisor and donor to half the world the United States is emerging from its teens. A certain glow begins to fade. The hard, gray thoughts of maturity take possession and there is some danger of the cynicism that is itself immature." (Eric Sevareid, *This is Eric Sevareid,* New York: McGraw-Hill, 1964)

10. "We have waited for more than 340 years for our constitutional and God-given rights. The nations of Asia and Africa are moving with jetlike speed toward gaining political independence, but we still creep at horse-and-buggy pace toward gaining a cup of coffee at a lunch counter." (Martin Luther King, Jr., "Letter from Birmingham Jail")

11. "One of the most popular [explanations for student revolt]—too many students still live in an adolescent stage of parent rejection, and if a university insists on maintaining its role of parental substitute, it must be prepared to face rebellious offspring." (Bill Ward, "Why Students Revolt," *The Nation,* January 25, 1966)

12. "Father was always a bit sceptical of this story, and of the new flying machines, otherwise he believed everything he read. Until 1909 no one in Lower Binfield believed that human beings would ever learn to fly. The official doctrine was that if God had meant us to fly He'd have given us wings. Uncle Ezekiel couldn't help retorting that if God had meant us to ride He'd have given us wheels, but even he didn't believe in the new flying machines." (George Orwell, *Coming Up for Air*)

13. "If a single cell, under appropriate conditions, becomes a man in the space of a few years, there can surely be no difficulty in understanding how, under appropriate conditions, a cell may, in the course of untold millions of years, give origin to the human race." (Herbert Spencer, *Principles of Biology*)

14. "Amidst all the earnest wringing of hands, nobody is so impolite as to point out that the taking of stands against drugs is like taking a stand against death, communism, or the rain." (Lewis H. Lapham, *The Sacramento Bee Forum,* September 21, 1986)

15. "Accepting the claims of astrology is much like accepting the laws pertaining to property rights and slavery set up over three thousand years ago by the rulers of Babylon, and using their theories of medicine as well, for that is when the rules that are still used by modern astrologers today were devised." (James "The Amazing" Randi, *Flim-Flam!* Buffalo, N.Y.: Prometheus Books, 1982)

EVALUATING ANALOGICAL ARGUMENTS

In evaluating an analogical argument, we're really interested in determining how strong the connection is between the things compared. The stronger the connection, the more likely the conclusion; the weaker the connection, the less likely the conclusion. And of course, the more likely the conclusion, the better the analogical argument; the less likely the conclusion, the poorer the analogical argument. Four factors affect the strength of analogies: (1) the number of entities involved in the comparison, (2) the number of relevant likenesses between the entities, (3) the number of differences between the entities, and (4) the strength of the conclusion relative to the premises. Let's consider each.

Number of Entities Involved

Ordinarily, the more instances lying at the base of the analogy, the greater the likelihood of its conclusion. Thus, the more VW Rabbits Sweeney had owned that performed well, the stronger his analogical argument that B.J. should buy a VW because it probably would be dependable. This point is obvious when you recall what we said about generalizations: Ordinarily, the larger the sample, the more representative of the class it is. Likewise, the greater the number of instances in the analogical argument, the better the chances that the sample is representative and, thus, accurately forecasts the next instance. Naturally, then, every instance of a dependable VW Rabbit that Sweeney could muster would strengthen his analogy.

Number of Relevant Likenesses

The more relevant likenesses among the instances, the stronger the analogical argument and more likely its conclusion. In his original argument, Sweeney had in mind three relevant likenesses, stemming from the fact that B.J. intended to buy (1) a brand-new car, (2) a standard transmission, (3) the Rabbit model. Suppose that, in addition, Sweeney had driven his Rabbit primarily on the highways, and B.J. would, too. Moreover, the mechanic who had worked on Sweeney's would also work on B.J.'s. These additional relevant likenesses would strengthen the analogy. Of course, if both Rabbits happened to be yellow and contained an AM/FM radio, these likenesses would have no bearing on the analogy since they are irrelevant to a car's dependability.

Number of Differences

Frequently the things being compared differ in a number of aspects. Some differences can strengthen an analogy; others can weaken it, even void it.

The more strengthening differences between the things compared, the stronger the analogical argument itself. For example, suppose Sweeney knew of a number of people, and not just himself, who had found the Rabbit dependable. The fact that different drivers all had good luck with the new car would speak more highly for the analogical inference than if Sweeney alone had. Similarly, suppose these cars had been purchased from different dealerships and subsequently worked on by a variety of mechanics. Again, such differences would strengthen the analogical argument because they pointed up the inherent dependability of the car itself rather than some accidental accompanying features. Differences that strengthen analogical conclusions are termed *disimilarities*. They should be distinguished from *disanalogies,* differences that weaken analogies.

The more weakening differences, or disanalogies, between the things compared, the weaker the analogical argument itself. For example, suppose that although Sweeney had limited the driving of his Rabbit to the highway, B.J. would do mostly city driving. Since the stop-and-go kind of driving characteristic of city driving is ordinarily harder on a car than is highway driving, this would constitute a difference that weakens the argument. Again, suppose that only Sweeney had driven his cars. In contrast, B.J., Slim, and Wilma would drive the new Rabbit. Generally speaking, a car performs better when driven by one driver. So the fact that several drivers would drive the new Rabbit weakens the analogy. Finally, suppose that Sweeney's Rabbits didn't have the pollution control devices required of the later models, such as B.J.'s. There's no evidence that cars run better with these devices but ample evidence that many of them run worse. So we'd have to consider the inclusion of a pollution control device a weakening difference in the analogy.

Strength of the Conclusion Relative to the Premises

A final criterion in evaluating analogical arguments is the strength of their conclusions relative to their premises. This criterion, in effect, is the same as the one we applied to generalizations: The greater the margin for error in the analogical conclusion, the stronger the argument.

Suppose, for example, that Sweeney had averaged 27 miles per gallon with his VW Rabbits. Given a number of likenesses and no significant disanalogies between his and B.J.'s, Sweeney would be justified in expecting B.J. to average over 20 mpg. But his argument would be much weaker if he concluded that B.J. would average 27 mpg, because now he'd be allowing for no margin of error.

EXERCISE 9-4 _____

A. Each of the following analogical arguments is followed by several additional premises. Indicate whether the premises would strengthen, weaken, or have no effect on the conclusion. In all cases use the criteria for evaluating analogies.

1. On two separate occasions you have bought a pair of shoes at Naturalizer. The shoes wore exceptionally well. So now that you're in the market for another pair of shoes, you infer you'll again get a good pair at Naturalizer.
   a. Suppose you'd bought shoes there on four occasions, rather than three.
   b. Suppose a number of your friends also had bought shoes there that wore well.
   c. Suppose that two sweaters you'd bought there also wore well.
   d. Suppose that you expect to get a full three years' wear from your new shoes, although the others lasted only two years.
   e. Suppose you expect to get at least a year's wear from your new shoes, again assuming the other two pairs wore well for two years each.

2. The first three films by Woody Allen you saw were comedies situated in New York, starring Allen and Diane Keaton. When you hear that Allen has come out with another film, you assume it's a comedy situated in New York and stars Allen and Keaton.

   a. Suppose that the film, unlike the others, was made after the off-the-screen Allen-Keaton romance had cooled off.

   b. Suppose that you merely infer that the film is a comedy.

   c. Suppose you read that Allen had spent considerable time in California during the time the film was shot.

   d. Suppose that you merely infer that there is a female lead.

   e. Suppose you infer that the film is a comedy situated in New York and stars Keaton but not Allen.

3. Several of Myron's relatives, including his mother and father, have died of heart disease. Myron is therefore convinced that at some point he, too, will develop heart disease.

   a. Suppose that Myron smokes, but none of his relatives did.

   b. Suppose that Myron is the only member of his family ever to be consistently underweight.

   c. Suppose Myron jogs two miles a day, whereas his relatives were sedentary.

   d. Suppose Myron prefers the diet of his parents.

   e. Suppose Myron is the only college graduate in his family.

   f. Suppose Myron merely infers that he probably has a tendency to develop heart disease.

4. Stella has taken three philosophy courses and found them very stimulating and worthwhile. So she enrolls for a fourth, fully expecting to enjoy and profit from it.

   a. Suppose her previous philosophy courses were in ethics, epistemology, and religion.

   b. Suppose all her previous courses had been taught by the same professor who is scheduled to teach the present one.

   c. Suppose Stella had found the three previous courses the most exciting intellectual experiences of her collegiate life.

   d. Suppose the three previous courses were in general ethics, business ethics, and medical ethics, whereas the present one will be in metaphysics.

   e. Suppose the three previous courses had all met at 10 A.M., and the present one is scheduled to meet at 7 P.M..

   f. Suppose Stella expects the course will prove to be the most enriching of any course she'll take in college.

B. Evaluate the following analogical arguments in terms of the criteria previously explained.

   1. Children are very much like puppies—they have to be trained and taught how to behave. Otherwise, they'll grow up to be wild and troublesome.

   2. Of course limiting property taxes will result in the curtailment of many social services. But that can't be helped. Remember: If you want to make an omelet, you must break some eggs.

   3. A college education is like the foundation of a house. Both must be solid and adequate to support what will rest on it. And just as you'd not think of laying a foundation without regard to the structure it must support, you should not commence a formal education without knowing what it is you want to do with your life.

   4. People shouldn't be any more critical of advertisements than they are of poetry. Just as a poem deals in fantasy, hope, and promise, so does the well-crafted ad. In fact, the purpose of the ad, like the poem, is to go beyond reality and offer illusion.

So the next time you criticize an ad as foolishly unrealistic, ask yourself if you'd say the same of your favorite poetry.

5. "If you cut up a large diamond into little bits, it will entirely lose the value it had as a whole; and an army divided up into small bodies of soldiers loses all its strength. So a great intellect sinks to the level of an ordinary one, as soon as it is interrupted and disturbed, its attention distracted and drawn off from the matter in hand: for its superiority depends upon its power of concentration—of bringing all its strength to bear upon one theme, in the same way as a concave mirror collects into one point all the rays of light that strike upon it." (Arthur Schopenhauer, "On Noise")

6. "Sentiment is all right up in the part of the city where your home is. But downtown, no. Down there the dog that snaps the quickest gets the bone. Friendship is very nice for a Sunday afternoon when you're sitting around the dinner table with your relations, talking about the sermon that morning. But nine o'clock Monday morning, notions should be brushed aside like cobwebs from a machine. I never took stock in a man who mixed up business with anything else. He can go into other things outside of business hours but when he's in the office, he ought not to have a relation in the world—and least of all a poor relation." (Dan Drew, founder of Drew Theological Seminary)

7. Where are wars won or lost? On the gridiron, that's where. For the gridiron is a battlefield where the many learn to function as a single, well-oiled fighting machine. It's where a man learns to sacrifice self for the good of the team and to endure pain, even perform with it. And mostly the gridiron is where men learn to hold on to what's theirs, even if only a few inches of mud. Sure, football may be brutal, perhaps barbarous. But what's war—a Sunday-school picnic?

8. Sex is just as natural as eating. And just as we don't regard an appetite for variety in diet as strange or unnatural, why should we consider any less normal a desire for a variety of lovers?

9. Americans have become energy junkies. We need our energy fix on a regular basis and we're willing to pay anything for it. That's why the Arabs can so successfully taunt, insult, even blackmail us. They're our neighborhood pusher, and as long as they can satisfy our addiction, we'll do their bidding.

10. "If the nature of the work is properly appreciated and applied, it will stand in the same relation to the higher faculties as food is to the physical body. It nourishes and enlivens the higher man and urges him to produce the best he is capable of. It directs his free will along the proper course and disciplines the animal in him into progressive channels. It furnishes an excellent background for man to display his scale of values and develop his personality." (J. C. Kumarappa, *Economy of Permanence*)

THE VALUE OF ANALOGICAL ARGUMENTS

To see how analogical arguments can provide valuable insights, even suggest a viewpoint, consider the evolution of scientific knowledge about the atom. The earliest problem scientists faced was figuring out how the atom's positive and negative electric charges were arranged so that atoms could exist as stable entities and not simply fly apart. Experiments by English physicist Ernest Rutherford indicated that the atom's positive charge was highly concentrated. So Rutherford and, later, Niels Bohr suggested that the atom was analogous to the solar system. An atom, they said, is like a miniature solar system. Just as the sun is in the center of the solar system, so all of the positive charge is in the center of the atom. Similarly, just as the planets orbit the sun, so electrons move around the center of the atom while carrying the negative charge.

In effect, then, Rutherford and Bohr saw the solar system as a model for the atom, arguing that the structure of the atom is analogous to the structure of the solar system. Even today this model is used in elementary discussions of atomic physics.[1]

In fact, the history of science is studded with examples of how instructive analogical reasoning can be. The classic illustration, perhaps, is Archimides' discovery that a body immersed in fluid loses in weight an amount equal to the weight of the fluid it displaces. Supposedly the discovery occurred while Archimides was trying to help solve a problem for King Hieron. It seemed the king wanted to know what metals had been used in his crown. But he didn't want to destroy the crown by melting it down to find out. Archimides solved the problem by using an analogy. Having observed that the water in his bath rose as his body displaced it, the brilliant Greek mathematician reasoned by analogy that a certain weight of gold would displace less water than silver of the same weight, because gold was smaller in volume. He tested the crown, and found that it was, in fact, made of impure gold.

A similar example of analogical reasoning underlay Copernicus's revolutionary theory of a sun-centered universe. Boating near the bank of a river one day, Copernicus is said to have been struck by the illusion that the bank, and not his boat, was moving. Could a similar illusion produce the common belief that the sun moves around a stationary earth? The thought intrigued Copernicus. Subsequently, he went on to overturn our understanding of the universe.

These examples notwithstanding, *most analogies are not good ones*. Even when analogies are good, they don't prove anything. They must be tested, proved. Recall that Benjamin Franklin, having observed a number of resemblances between electric sparks and lightning, wondered if lightning possibly could be a form of electricity. But he didn't stop there. He saw this insight as an explanation, a hypothesis, that needed to be tested and proved. Of course, he subsequently did just that. He conducted a test with his kite-and-key experiment. It proved that lightning was, indeed, electric. The analogy itself *proved* nothing.

INDUCTIVE FALLACIES

Although we might consider numerous fallacies associated with simple inductive and analogical arguments, we'll restrict our discussion to four: hasty conclusion, accident, guilt by association, and false analogy. These are very common fallacies that have their roots in faulty induction. You may find them called by other names in different texts.

Hasty Conclusion

The fallacy of hasty conclusion is an argument that draws a conclusion based on insufficient evidence. Sometimes the insufficient evidence in a hasty conclusion takes the form of isolated cases, which a person uses to force the conclusion. For example, on the basis of having been "ripped off" by a used-car salesperson,

---

[1]See Ronald N. Giere, *Understanding Scientific Reasoning* (New York: Holt, Rinehart and Winston, 1979), p. 79.

one concludes, "All used-car salespersons are ripoff artists." The single isolated case is not sufficient to warrant the conclusion. We could say that the sample in question, the isolated case, is too small to justify the inference. Again, one argues that every member of the National Organization of Women is a socialist on the basis that a half dozen of them are known socialists. The evidence here is not enough to support the conclusion; the sample is far too small.

An arguer would be guilty of a hasty conclusion if, on the basis of a handful of college and noncollege acquaintances, he or she concluded that people going to college to improve themselves financially stand a better chance of learning than those not so motivated. Obviously, people go to college for all sorts of reasons: for knowledge, for status, for social interaction, and so on. What motive is best for learning? No one knows. Certainly, such a tiny sample doesn't warrant that conclusion.

Sometimes the hasty conclusion results from basing an inference, not so much on isolated cases, but on exceptional ones. For example, someone argues, "Jones must have been an athlete at one time, for he's built so well" or "I bet Smith recently inherited a lot of money; otherwise he wouldn't have been able to afford that brand-new Mercedes." Although it's true that people with good builds often are or were athletes, there are exceptions: Many well-built people aren't and never were athletes. Similarly, a recent inheritance sometimes explains the purchase of a new Mercedes. But there are exceptions: Many people who have not recently inherited a lot of money also buy Mercedeses. In both cases, the specific cases are related to the generalization in an unessential way. There is no logical basis for assuming a connection.

Sherlock Holmes was at times guilty of the hasty conclusion. Take, for example, his conclusions about Dr. Watson, which Holmes formed immediately upon being introduced to him:

> Here is a gentleman of a medical type, but with the air of a military man. Clearly an army doctor, then. He has just come from the tropics, for his face is dark, and that is not the natural tint of his skin, for his wrists are fair. He has undergone hardship and sickness, as his haggard face says clearly. His left arm has been injured. He holds it in a stiff and unnatural manner. Where in the tropics could an English army doctor have seen much hardship and got his arm wounded? Clearly in Afghanistan.[2]

Holmes is, of course, correct. But that's irrelevant. Recall our earlier discussion of Holmes's powers. Here, too, his deduction rests on poor induction. The question is, does the evidence warrant his conclusion, or is the evidence insufficient to warrant it? Certainly Watson could have a military bearing without ever having been in the military, let alone having been a military doctor. And certainly he needn't have acquired his tan in the tropics. And surely a "haggard face" doesn't always mean "hardship and sickness"; nor does holding the arm in a "stiff and unnatural manner" always result from an injury. Nonetheless, Holmes not only forms these hasty conclusions but also uses them as the basis for his final hasty conclusion: that Watson was in Afghanistan! And, oh yes, you and I might use this seemingly impressive incident to form a hasty conclusion of our own: that Holmes has brilliant powers of ratiocination. More likely, the author, Arthur Conan Doyle, was a most clever bloke.

[2]Arthur Conan Doyle, "A Study in Scarlet," *The Adventures of Sherlock Holmes* (New York: Berkley Publications, 1963), pt. 1, ch. 2.

Accident

The fallacy of accident is an argument that applies a general rule to a particular case whose special circumstances make the rule inapplicable. For example, suppose that someone argues, "People have the right to go where they want. Therefore, if a convicted murderer wants to leave prison, the authorities have no right to stop him." The first premise in the argument is a general principle that we usually accept. But it doesn't apply to the specific case of a convicted murderer. The argument contains the fallacy of accident.

The word *accident* is used in designating the fallacy because of the "accidental" circumstances, that is, special or exceptional conditions, that make the rule inapplicable. Again, suppose someone argues, "Since exercise is good for health, Rita Gomez, who has a serious spinal injury, ought to exercise." Generally speaking, exercise is good for one's health. But not in Rita Gomez's case. There, the accidental circumstances make the general rule inapplicable.

> **STUDY HINT**
>
> The fallacy of accident treats a weak generalization as if it were strong.

What sometimes makes the fallacy of accident persuasive is that it resembles sound arguments in which specific cases do, in fact, fall under a general rule. Thus, "All citizens over eighteen may vote. Therefore, thirty-five-year-old citizen Brown may vote." Now this is a perfectly correct application of a general rule. But if Brown is currently locked up in prison, then even though he's a citizen and over eighteen, he may not vote. The point to remember is that a generalization is designed to apply to the individual cases *that fall under it,* not to all individual cases.

A judge who once released a woman arrested by an officer for passing heroin to young children on a school playground seemed aware of the fallacy of accident. As a general rule, people committing this crime are stiffly punished. The judge accepted this rule and recognized that the woman had indeed committed the crime. But one thing about her, the judge pointed out, made her an exception to the general rule: She was ninety years old!

Before concluding our remarks about the accident fallacy, we should distinguish it from a fallacy we spoke of under fallacies of ambiguity: the fallacy of division. (See Chapter 4). Although similar—and sometimes even treated as the same fallacy—the fallacy of accident and the fallacy of division are different. As we've just seen, in the accident fallacy one argues that since most members of a class have a specific property, any member of the class must also have that property, even though it's an exception. In the accident fallacy, then, we're always talking about *individual class members*.

In contrast, in the fallacy of division, we argue that, since the *class itself* has a specific property, any member of the class must also have that property. An example of each fallacy should clarify the difference:

Accident fallacy: Since most of the members of this club are rich, member Jones, who has just applied for welfare, must be rich.

Division fallacy: Since this club is rich, Jones must be rich.

In the accident fallacy, we moved from a statement about the *members* of a class to a statement about an individual member of it. In the division fallacy, we moved from a statement about the *class itself* to a statement about one of its members.

While we're on the point, we might as well draw a similar distinction between the hasty conclusion and the composition fallacies. Remember that in one form of the hasty conclusion, we argue that because some atypical members of the group have a specific property, all or most members of the group do. Here again we're talking about *individual members* of the group.

In contrast, in the fallacy of composition, we argue that since all members of a class have a specific property, the *class itself* must have that property. Here's an example of each:

> *Hasty conclusion:* Three members of this club are rich. Therefore, every member of this club must be rich.

> *Composition:* Every member of this club is rich. Therefore, the club itself must be rich.

Notice that in the hasty conclusion, the reasoning moves from a statement about a property of some atypical members to a property of every *member*. In the composition example, the reasoning moves from a statement about a property of every member to a property about the *class itself,* the club.

Guilt by Association

The guilt by association fallacy is an argument in which people are judged guilty solely on the basis of the company they keep or the places they frequent.

For example, on a number of occasions, Frank Sinatra has had to defend himself against charges that he has underworld connections. Why? Because at least one or more persons of his acquaintance were involved in organized crime. Even if Sinatra did know such a person, that didn't mean that he himself was involved, as many of his critics intimated.

Those who prejudge by association assume that likes always attract likes, that birds of a feather always flock together. They use such generalizations as a basis for judging someone guilty by association. The way to help someone see the error involved in this fallacy, then, is to demonstrate that the generalization on which it is based is faulty. Likes don't always attract likes; birds of a feather don't always flock together. Seeing that, we should realize that association is not a sound basis for inferring guilt.

Before inferring another's guilt, we should have irrefutable evidence of complicity in wrongdoing. We would be wise to apply this maxim when judging not only the guilt or innocence of persons but also their characters, motives, personalities, and behavior.

But clearly we often do judge others guilty by their looks or dress. Thus, a Brazilian soccer team once canceled a match in Lusaka, Zambia, when officials there demanded that the Brazilians cut their (the Brazilians') long hair. It seems the Zambians had a "mind set" about long-haired people. Since the Brazilians had long hair, the Zambians judged them guilty by association with all the negative qualities they connected with long hair. Zambia and other African countries also assume that those wearing short skirts or tight-fitting trousers are disreputable.

Closer to home, a Texas football coach once wrote an article beseeching his fellow coaches to dismiss long-haired players because they are effeminate and godless. Presumably, the coach had never heard of Samson.

In all these cases, the arguer generalizes that because something is sometimes the case, it is always the case. Because long hair sometimes accompanies unpopular lifestyles and views, long hair is judged to be in and of itself an indication of those lifestyles and views. Similarly, because acquaintances of criminals are themselves *sometimes* criminals, it's assumed that acquaintances of criminals are *always* criminals. Having formed such faulty generalizations, we then apply them to people, judging them guilty by association with the object of disdain: long hair, criminals, and so forth.

*EXERCISE 9-5 _____

Identify the fallacies in the following. Choose from hasty conclusion, accident, guilt by association, division, and composition. In all cases, explain.

1. JACK: I think Uncle Bill should be allowed to own that lot on Main Street.
   BETTY: But Uncle Bill has been declared insane.
   JACK: I know. But everybody has the right to own property.
2. STAN: I wouldn't trust any more union representatives.
   OLLIE: Me neither—not after seeing the last two we had put in jail for embezzling union funds.
3. MUDCAT: I just bet twenty bucks on the Wildcats in the big game today.
   MOOSE: I think you made a good bet, Mudcat. I've talked to every Wildcat, and to a man they're ready.
   MUDCAT: I knew it! As a team, the Wildcats couldn't be more prepared!
4. FRED: There's no doubt in my mind that our former U.N. Ambassador Andrew Young is anti Israeli.
   MONA: Why do you say that?
   FRED: Well, because of that party he attended where there were people from the Palestine Liberation Organization. And you know how the PLO feels about the Israelis.
5. The sole purpose of an army is to defend its nation from aggression. So it follows that the sole purpose of any soldier should be the same.
6. JUNE: I just know that Professor Macbeth must have studied drama.
   JODY: You mean because she wears so much makeup?
   JUNE: Don't be silly. Because she speaks so eloquently.
7. People should work for what they get. So this business of providing food stamps for those in need is really immoral.
8. CLERK: Stop! Thief!
   CUSTOMER: Who me?
   CLERK: Yes, you. You haven't paid for those sweaters.
   CUSTOMER: I don't owe you anything. The sign says "Sweaters—20% off regular price." Well, I have five sweaters. Five times 20 percent off equals 100 percent off. So they're free.
9. JANICE: I think it was unconscionable of you to ask me to help you cheat on your logic test.
   JERRY: Oh, yeah? Well, I'm sorry you don't have more appreciation for the Golden Rule.
   JANICE: The Golden Rule! You call cheating on a test living by the Golden Rule?
   JERRY: Sure. The Golden Rule tells us to do unto others as we would have them do unto us. Well, if our positions were reversed, I'd help you cheat. . . . You know, I really thought you were more moral than that, Janice.
10. STUDENT: Tell me, Professor. What can I do to improve my comprehension of this material.

PROFESSOR: You should plan on reading the material at least twice, coming to class prepared, and studying for an hour a day.

STUDENT: That doesn't work. I've tried it all week, and I still don't understand what's going on.

False Analogy

The fallacy of false analogy is an argument that makes an erroneous comparison. Generally, we make erroneous comparisons by ignoring significant disanalogies between the things compared. In other words, we commit the fallacy of false analogy when the things we compare are alike in unimportant ways and unalike in very important ones.

For example, consider this argument that B.J. once voiced to Slim, only half in jest. "Students should be allowed to use their texts during examinations," he told her, "since lawyers can use their law books in preparing a case and doctors can use their medical books in making a diagnosis. So why shouldn't students be allowed to use their textbooks during exams?"

On first look, Slim had to admit that B.J.'s argument seemed to have some merit. There is a similarity in the cases compared: Like doctors and lawyers, students are seeking information to resolve a question or problem. But this similarity is trivial compared with the outstanding difference between the compared cases, and it wasn't long before Slim spotted it.

"What you forget," she told her brother, "is that doctors and lawyers aren't taking tests to see what they've learned, but students are."

Notice that in the false analogy the things compared are made to appear more similar than they really are. Students' use of texts during exams is made to appear more similar to doctors' and lawyers' use of texts than it really is. For this reason we can say that the false analogy makes an unjustifiable presumption; it distorts facts.

As another example of the false analogy, consider this argument an evangelist once voiced on television. "We must do everything possible," he said, "to get people to accept Christianity for their own good—in the same way that we'd do everything possible to stop a madman from killing himself. For just as we should do everything possible to keep a lunatic from killing himself, so we should do all we can to keep people from killing themselves spiritually by rejecting Jesus Christ as their personal Saviour."

The comparison made here is between (1) saving seriously demented people from killing themselves and (2) saving people from killing themselves spiritually. Even if we concede that a "spiritual self" exists and that those who do not accept Jesus Christ as their personal Saviour destroy themselves spiritually, the argument is unsound because of the false analogy it employs. In case 1 the issue centers on people who are insane; but in case 2, presumably, the people are not insane.

Of course, the evangelist might claim, "Those who do not accept Jesus Christ as their personal Saviour are obviously insane." But such an argument is guilty of provincialism. It also begs the question, as follows:

EVANGELIST: That man is a lunatic.

SKEPTIC: Why is that?

EVANGELIST: Because he won't accept Jesus Christ as his personal Saviour.

SKEPTIC: But how do you know that a man who doesn't accept Jesus Christ as his personal Saviour is a lunatic?

EVANGELIST: Because anyone who doesn't accept Jesus Christ as their personal Saviour must be a lunatic.

To spot the false analogy, you must notice that the things compared share insignificant similarities while differing in significant ways. Take as another example Slim's argument in favor of legalizing suicide: "There shouldn't be any law against trying to take your own life," she insisted, "any more than it's illegal to change the course of a mighty river. Why should it be a crime to divert a few ounces of blood from their natural course?"

When Sweeney heard her express this argument, he walked out of the room. Too bad he didn't criticize the analogy, because it's a weak one. In redirecting the course of a mighty river, we don't destroy it. But in redirecting an arterial channel of the human body, we do destroy the body. Quite a difference. But Slim shouldn't feel bad. A similar argument was voiced by the eighteenth-century Scottish philosopher David Hume in his famous essay "On Suicide":

> It would be no crime in me to divert the Nile or Danube from its course, were I able to effect such purposes. Where then is the crime of turning a few ounces of blood from their natural channel?

Coming from a philosopher doesn't make the analogy any better.

Again, Sweeney has argued analogically: "People shouldn't allow pornographic magazines into their homes any more than they'd serve their families contaminated food." Perhaps people shouldn't permit filthy reading material in their homes. But Sweeney's analogy does nothing to advance that position. Contaminated food makes people physically ill, and presumably that's why Sweeney wouldn't serve it to his family. But there's no substantial evidence that pornographic reading material makes a person mentally ill, let alone physically ill. So although Sweeney's proposition may have merit, his analogy does not justify it because it is a false analogy.

EXERCISE 9-6 _____

Identify the analogies in the following passages and determine whether they are sound or false.

1. JAY: I think student government is not only a waste of time but can actually be counterproductive.
   JAN: But shouldn't students have a say about what goes on at their school?
   JAY: Look, I've seen what's happened in houses where parents let their kids run things their own way.

2. TED: You know, this whole $1.5 billion bailout of Chrysler by the federal government is a real ripoff.
   PAT: Why do you say that?
   TED: For one simple reason. Imagine what the government's reaction would be if I asked it to subsidize my antique business during the rough times.
   PAT: It'd probably tell you to get lost.
   TED: Exactly.

3. TRISH: All this talk about reducing foreign aid—I think it's downright irresponsible.
   TOM: "Irresponsible"? That's pretty strong, isn't it?
   TRISH: I don't think so. You'd call a parent who wouldn't care for their children

irresponsible, wouldn't you? By the same token, if we don't take care of the less fortunate nations of the world, we're being irresponsible.

4. BUDDY: I'm convinced that Venus is habitable.
   BERTHA: I doubt it.
   BUDDY: Think about it for a minute. Venus is roughly the same radius as Earth. And it has approximately the same mass. You can't say that about any other planet in our galaxy.
   BERTHA: So, you're saying that since there's life on Earth, there probably is life on Venus?
   BUDDY: Right.

5. GEORGE: I'm convinced that the mind really can produce physical changes in the body.
   GINGER: Oh that's ridiculous. Does the smoke from a locomotive have any influence on the movement of a train?
   GEORGE: Well, no, but—
   GINGER: Well, then, there's your answer.

6. PHILLIP: Cigarette?
   MORRIS: No thanks.
   PHILLIP: What! You've given up smoking?
   MORRIS: You said it. Yesterday I took a good long look at my fingers. They're yellow! Can you imagine what my lungs must look like?
   PHILLIP: Wow!—I never thought of that. Pass me that ashtray, will you?

7. STUDENT LEADER: I think it's time colleges started paying students for high scholastic achievement.
   DEAN OF STUDENTS: Paying? As in dollars and cents?
   STUDENT LEADER: You said it. Business gives its top people bonuses and commissions doesn't it? And look at the performances it gets out of them.

8. DISILLUSIONED TEACHER: I've had it. No more teaching for me. I'll pump gas first.
   COLLEAGUE: Oh, come now. You're just a little discouraged today.
   DISILLUSIONED TEACHER: A little discouraged? The hell you say! I'm desperate! What I do every day in the classroom is tantamount to casting real pearls before real swine.

9. COMMUNITY COLLEGE BOARD MEMBER: I think we should start charging students tuition.
   COLLEGE PRESIDENT: I'm unequivocally opposed to that. Why it would be like charging for withdrawing books from the library.
   COMMUNITY COLLEGE BOARD MEMBER: Is that so? Well, I make my children pay for their toys and treats. And believe me, they appreciate them all the more because they have to pay for them. I think that's pretty clear evidence that we should start charging tuition.

10. CARMEN: You're not going to put that saccharine in your coffee, are you?
    CARL: Sure, I'm on a diet.
    CARMEN: But don't you realize that saccharine has caused cancer in laboratory rats?
    CARL: Really? Pass me the sugar, will you?

SUMMARY

This chapter dealt with two of the simpler forms of induction, the generalization and the analogy. A generalization is a statement that covers many specifics. The basic type of simple inductive argument is one whose conclusion is a generalization. Such an argument is termed as inductive generalization. Thus, on the basis of some cases known through experience, we draw an inference that applies to the whole collection of cases, for example, "All the crows I've observed have been black. Therefore, crows must be black." It's convenient to divide generalizations into strong, weak, and statistical. A strong generalization is a statement that asserts that something is true of all members of a class, for example, "All humans are vertebrates." A weak generalization as a statement that asserts that something is true of some members of a class, for example, "Some humans are vertebrates." A statistical generalization is a statement that asserts that something is true of a percentage of a class, for example, "Over half the fruit in this vineyard is rotten." The conclusion of an inductive generalization always goes beyond the argument's premises. As a result, conclusions of inductive generalizations can be false, even though the premises are true. To avoid false conclusions, be conscious of the factors affecting reliable generalizations. There are four factors to be especially aware of: (1) comprehensiveness—that is, the sample must account for the various subgroups within the group; (2) size—ordinarily, the more instances observed, the more reliable the generalization; (3) randomness—each member of the group must have an equal chance of ending up as part of the sample; (4) margin of error—ordinarily, the greater the allowance of error in a generalization, the more reliable it is. Overlooking these factors, we commit fallacies. Three fallacies are particularly noteworthy: (1) The hasty conclusion is an argument that draws a conclusion based on insufficient evidence, for example, Sherlock Holmes's conclusions about Watson. The hasty conclusion should be distinguished from the fallacy of composition. (2) The accident is an argument that applies a general rule to a particular case whose special circumstances make the rule inapplicable, for example, arguing that because people, generally speaking, have a right to go where they want, a convicted murderer should be permitted to leave prison at the prisoner's request. The accident fallacy should be distinguished from the fallacy of division. (3) Guilt by association is an argument in which people are judged guilty solely on the basis of the company they keep or the places they frequent, for example, Sweeney's insistence that Slim must be smoking pot because she happens to date someone who occasionally smokes pot.

We also studied another basic form of inductive reasoning: the argument from analogy. An argument from analogy is an inductive argument in which a known similarity shared by two things is used as evidence for concluding that the two things are similar in *other* respects. An analogical argument is actually a form of inductive generalization. In every analogical argument, we extend what is known to be true about members of one class to new entities standing outside the class. We assume that the entities to which the statement is being applied are analogous to the entities in the observed sample. The stronger the connection between the things compared, the more likely the analogical argument's conclusion. Four factors bear on the soundness of analogical arguments: (1) the number of instances involved in the comparison, (2) the number of relevant likenesses between the entities, (3) the number of relevant differences between the entities, and (4) the strength of the conclusion relative to the premises. Analogies are weakened by significant differences between the things being compared; these differences are called *disanalogies*. The fallacy of false analogy is an argument that makes an erroneous comparison, for example, claiming that students should be allowed to use their textbooks during examinations because doctors use their medical books in making diagnoses. Analogies can provide valuable insights and viewpoints, especially in science. But in the last analysis, even good analogies prove nothing: They must be tested and proved before they can be taken as truths.

Summary Questions

1. Find a few examples of hasty conclusion. Fertile sources include prejudicial claims made about racial or gender characteristics and vague attributions such as "the humanists," "the fundamentalists," and so forth. The more sweeping such claims are, the more difficult they will be to justify.
2. Find some examples of accident involving moral and behavioral maxims (rules of conduct). Here's a case to start with:

> Bob and Ray are good friends. Bob has borrowed Ray's car with the promise to return it whenever Ray asks. Late one evening, Ray shows up obviously drunk, so drunk that he can barely walk or talk coherently. He demands the keys to his car. Bob hands them over without hesitation. Later, after Ray has been hurt in an auto accident that very night, Bob justifies giving him the keys by saying. "Well, we should always keep our promises."

Explain why Bob's attempt at justifying his action is a case of the fallacy of accident.

See if you can find other examples of accident involving moral or behavioral rules misapplied or taken too literally.

ADDITIONAL EXERCISES _____

*1. Identify the fallacies, if any, in the following passages. Choose from hasty conclusion, accident, and guilt by association.

a. ANNA: I see you're on that liquid protein diet.
ANDY: Yes, I'm really enthusiastic about it.
ANNA: But haven't you heard that it can be really dangerous?
ANDY: Oh, I don't know about that. After reading a book on liquid protein diets, I don't think they're all that dangerous.
b. FATHER: There's no way Suzy can learn in that school.
MOTHER: Why not?
FATHER: Because the classes are large and the school district's poor. And you know what that means.
MOTHER: Sure, that the school can't provide an opportunity that could do justice to Suzy's ability to learn.
c. DALE: Roy, why don't you take an aspirin for that terrible headache?
ROY: You know that nature's way is best, Dale. It's not wise to interfere with Mother Nature.
DALE: So you're just going to sit there and suffer?
ROY: I'm just going to let nature take its course, because that's obviously best.
d. PAIGE: You say commercial nuclear power plants are safe. Why?
LEE: Because there are over fifty of them operating in the United States. Collectively they've produced two thousand years of reactor operation. And there are more than one hundred nuclear submarines operating in the U.S. Navy.
PAIGE: So?
LEE: So, none of these has ever injured or killed a member of the public. That proves without doubt that commercial nuclear power plants are safe.
e. "According to folk wisdom in many cultures, redheaded people tend to be a bit temperamental. An Israeli researcher believes there may be something to the ancient

prejudice. At the Honolulu conference, psychiatrist Michael Bar, of Israel's Shalvata Psychiatric Center, reported a study showing that redheaded children are three or four times more likely than others to develop 'hyperactive syndrome'—whose symptoms include overexcitability, short attention span, quick feelings of frustration, and, usually, excessive aggressiveness.

Bar arrived at his conclusion after matching the behavior of 45 redheaded boys and girls between the ages of six and twelve against that of a control group of nonredheaded kids. Though the evidence was far from conclusive, Bar believes the study points to a genetic connection between red hair and hyperactive behavior." (*Time,* September 12, 1977)

f. Part of an ad by the Kellogg Company to establish the nutritional value of "ready-sweetened cereals": "FACT: READY-TO-EAT CEREAL EATERS SKIP BREAKFAST LESS THAN NON-READY-TO-EAT CEREAL EATERS. In a study which surveyed the breakfast eating habits of 250 children, it was established that breakfast skipping occurred three times as often among noneaters of ready-to-eat cereal."

g. EVA: Barbados must be the island in the Western world where Europeans first landed.

ED: How come you're so sure?

EVA: Because the great explorer Thor Heyerdahl has successfully crossed the Atlantic in a papyrus raft and landed on Barbados.

h. Journalist Nicholas von Hoffman, on the television program "Sixty Minutes," April 21, 1974, said he hoped President Nixon would not be impeached so that the electorate could reverse Nixon's 1972 mandate by turning every Republican out of office that November.

i. A congressional seat is on the line. An unpopular but important politician insists on campaigning for his party's candidate. Party officials do not want the politician to come to their state to campaign, but he does and the candidate loses. Party officials say that that proves the politician was a liability.

j. DEFENSE ATTORNEY: Now, your honor, you know as well as I that mothers love their children. Knowing that, how can you find my client guilty of callously abandoning her children?

k. MICK: I think it's terrible that a court sentences a man to five years in jail for stealing a loaf of bread to feed his family.

BIANCA: Don't you believe that thieves should be punished?

MICK: Of course I do, but—

BIANCA: But nothing. The guy stole—now let him pay the price.

l. "By permitting our highest elected officials and those they appoint to administrative posts to classify information as confidential, and by placing no constraints on those public servants, we deny the public information necessary for proper decision making in the democratic process." (Robert C. Jeffrey, "Ethics in Public Disclosure," speech delivered at the 59th Annual Meeting, Speech Communications Association, New York, November 11, 1973)

m. Judge Marvin Frankel's reaction to a politician's charge that "the time has come for softheaded judges . . . to show as much concern for the rights of innocent victims of crime as they do for the rights of convicted criminals": "One case I remember vividly was of an orchestra leader, a devoted father, whose first conviction was clearly going to be his last—a judgment shared by the prosecution as well as the probation officer and me—and whom no jury would have convicted in the first place if it knew he faced anything like five or ten years in prison." The judge inferred on the basis of this and one other similar example that leniency is necessary. (*Los Angeles Times,* May 20, 1973)

n. FRAN: I think students should be allowed to use their textbooks during examinations.

EMIL: I'd sure go for that.

FRAN: Sure, just think about it. A key function of a textbook is to provide students with information in a field. Well, when do we need the information more than on an exam?

EMIL: I see what you mean. I'm going to ask Professor Emerson to let us use textbooks on the next exam.

o. MURRAY: You know, even if I thought she had something worth listening to, I'd tune out Jane Fonda.

BEA: But why? She often makes a lot of sense.

MURRAY: Maybe so. But you know who she's married to? That socialist Tom Hayden.

BEA: Oh, I didn't know that. I'd better reconsider my opinion of her.

p. TYLER: Personally, I don't think we citizens have any right to decide whether our country goes to war.

TRUDY: Are you mad?

TYLER: No, just logical. Think about it—no citizen has a right to decide whether their fellow citizens should die, does he or she?

TRUDY: Probably not.

TYLER: Then it follows that we shouldn't have the right to decide such crucial matters as war and peace.

q. Phyllis Schlafly, leading anti-ERA spokesperson, of the boycott against cities that have not ratified the ERA: "This boycott is a conspiracy against innocent people who have nothing to do with the issue. I think this boycott is conclusive proof that the proponents can't pass the ERA on its merits."

r. UCLA Dean of the Graduate School of Management, J. Clayburn LaForce, arguing that the business of corporations does not include achieving the "wider goals of society": "If the 'corporate governance' and 'responsibility' issues succeed as other political fads have, and bureaucrats or their appointees enter the board room, the free market, or what is left of it, will be damaged beyond repair." (from a speech delivered to a group of executives, August 1979)

2. Analyze the structures of the following analogical arguments. Evaluate the arguments in terms of the criteria for a sound analogy. If the analogy is a false one, explain.

a. "Scuba diving, roller skating, jogging and tennis are all part of today's life-style that's full of life. A style that is shared by the sporty and efficient Chevy Monza." (ad for 1980 Chevy Monza)

b. INTERVIEWER: Your honor, do you think you can fairly rule on motor accidents when, in fact, you yourself have never driven a car?

JUDGE: Certainly. Remember, I also try rape cases.

c. "There is absolutely no reason for . . . any . . . presidential candidate to apologize for raising the matter of Chappaquiddick vis-à-vis Senator Kennedy. To the contrary Chappaquiddick is as much a part of Senator Kennedy's background as is the date of his birth. Considering its implications it merits serious discussion and consideration." (Letter to *Time,* November 5, 1979, p. 5)

d. "Let no one belittle coaching experience in preparation for a position as college president. As coach, you must win or leave. I suggest this is similar to the president's position." (McNeese State University athletic director Jack Doland on the occasion of being elected the university's new president)

e. "A judge once said: 'The death penalty is a warning, just like a lighthouse throwing its beams out to sea. We hear about shipwrecks but we do not hear about the ships the lighthouse guides safely on their way. We do not have proof of the number of ships it saves, but we do not tear the lighthouse down.'" (FBI director J. Edgar Hoover)

f. "I am the father of two daughters. When I hear this argument that we can't protect freedom in Europe, in Asia, or in our own hemisphere and still meet our domestic problems, I think it's a phony argument. It is just like saying that I can't take care of Luci because I have Lynda Bird. We have to take care of both of them and meet them and we have to meet them head on." (President Lyndon B. Johnson)

g. Former governor of Texas John Connally, calling for increased U.S. military presence around the world: "The growth in the size and capability of Soviet strategic forces exceeds the Nazi buildup of the '30s." (*Time,* November 11, 1979, p. 33)

h. "It can run a mile cheaper than you can. The Rabbit Diesel runs a mile, and burns about 1.4 cents worth of fuel. Compared to that you're a guzzler. If you weigh 150 pounds, you'd burn around 90 calories per mile. Figure that as a mere fourth of a fast-food cheeseburger, and comes to about 18 cents. Fact is, if you were a car, you couldn't afford *you.* So, don't walk. Run for a Volkswagen Rabbit Diesel." (ad for Volkswagen Rabbit Diesel)

i. Fundamentalist Muslim defense of state executions of those convicted of adultery, prostitution, or homosexuality: "If your finger suffers from gangrene, what do you do? Letting the whole hand and then the body become filled with gangrene, or cutting the finger off? . . . Corruption, corruption. We have to eliminate corruption." (*Time,* October 22, 1979, p. 57)

j. Apartment tenant commenting on landlords' "no children allowed" policies: "When I first moved into this complex, the ages of the tenants varied from twenty-one to thirty-five. Then the older generation moved in and most of my friends said how the place was going to pot. Well, today do you know that the place is a better one because of them? That's why I think it would not be bad to allow children here. I think it would be a better place because of them." ("Sixty Minutes," January 22, 1978)

k. Spokesperson for the Golden Empire Transit District explaining why residents should be willing to subsidize the district's transportation service: "GET provides a service the same as police and fire departments do. Think of it this way; how often do you need the fire department or police, on the average? Sometime the average person is going to need a transit system that serves his needs . . . especially if the energy crunch becomes real enough to force people to consider riding the buses all the time."

l. Argument against the Panama Canal Treaty: The American Canal in Panama is a part of the United States just as any one of the fifty states and in no way should our country forfeit its right to unconditional control of the territory.

m. Letter to the editor opposing the Panama Canal Treaty: "In 1803, we bought the land that now makes up the states of Louisiana, Arkansas, Missouri, Illinois, Wisconsin, Minnesota, North and South Dakota, and parts of Montana, Wyoming, Kansas, Nebraska and Oklahoma from the French for $15 million. If the French threatened us with war today, should we give them back this land?"

n. Political commentator about to evaluate a freshman Senator's first year in office: The Senator has been in Congress for some nine months. Since this is the normal human gestation period, it is time to see what new policies he has given or is about to give birth to and to grade these policies.

o. "A reporter covering a political trip to Poland was amazed at the numerous monuments to freedom and independence he witnessed throughout the land, obviously erected prior to the Communist takeover there. . . . The situation in Poland should serve as a serious warning to us here in the United States, where too many naively believe that as long as Old Glory waves over the land and the Statue of Liberty hovers over New York Harbor we can rest assured that our freedoms are still intact." (Letter to the Editor, *Los Angeles Times,* January 11, 1978)

p. Former Los Angeles Police Chief Ed Davis defending capital punishment as disallowing the murderer from murdering again: "It's like shooting a rabid dog— you don't kill it as a warning to other dogs. You kill it so innocent people will be protected." (Editorial, *Bakersfield Californian,* November 2, 1977)

q. "One of woman's most natural attributes is the care of children. Since the ill and infirm resemble children in being physically weak and helpless as well as psychologically dependent and narcissistically repressed, women are also especially qualified to care for the sick." (*Sociological Review,* 1950)

r. "The fact that for a long time Cubism was not understood and that even today there are people who do not see anything in it means nothing. I do not read English, but this does not mean that the English language does not exist. I cannot blame anyone but myself if I do not appreciate that which I know nothing about." (Pablo Picasso, quoted by Mario Zayas in "Picasso Speaks," *Arts*)

s. "Just as the mass of water of the sea presses with its weight the earth beneath it, and just as, if it covered the whole earth instead of a part of it only, it would press with its weight the whole surface of the earth; so since the mass of the air covers the entire surface of the earth, this weight presses its every part." (Blaise Pascal, *The Weight of the Air*)

t. "In Sweatt v. Painter . . . in finding that a segregated law school for Negroes could not provide them equal educational opportunities, this Court relied in large part on 'those qualities which are incapable of objective measurement but which make for greatness in a law school.' In McLaurin v. Oklahoma State Regents, 339 US 637 . . . the Court, in requiring that a Negro admitted to a white graduate school be treated like all other students, again resorted to intangible considerations: 'his ability to study, to engage in discussions and exchange views with other students and, in general, to learn his profession.' Such considerations apply with added force to children in grade and high schools. To separate them from others of similar age and qualifications solely because of their race generates a feeling of inferiority as to their status in the community that may affect their hearts and minds in a way unlikely ever to be undone." (U.S. Supreme Court decision, Brown v. Board of Education of Topeka, 1954)

u. "One natural question often raised is, how do we even get new verbal creations such as a poem or a brilliant essay? The *answer is that we get them by manipulating* words, *shifting them about* until a new pattern is hit upon. . . . How do you suppose Patou builds a new gown? Has he a 'picture in his mind' of what the gown is to look like when it is finished? He has not. . . . He calls his model in, picks up a new piece of silk, throws it around her; he pulls it in here, he pulls it out there. . . . He manipulates the material until it takes on the semblance of a dress. . . . Not until the new creation aroused admiration and commendation, both its own and others, would manipulation be complete—the equivalent of the rat's finding food. . . . The painter plies his trade in the same way, nor can the poet boast of any other method." (John B. Watson, *Behaviourism*)

v. "Suppose that someone tells me that he has had a tooth extracted without an anesthetic, and I express my sympathy, and suppose that I am then asked, 'How do you know that it hurt him?' I might reasonably reply, 'Well, I know that it would hurt me. I have been to the dentist and know how painful it is to have a tooth stopped without an anesthetic, let alone taken out. And he has the same sort of nervous system as I have. I infer, therefore, that in these conditions he felt considerable pain, just as I should myself." (Alfred J. Ayer, "One's Knowledge of Other Minds," *Theoria,* vol. 19, 1953, p. 51)

w. In an article entitled "The linguistic gap between men and women," sociolinguist Deborah Tannen discusses how different language patterns can create communication difficulties between men and women. Tannen asserts that men and women learn different ways of communicating, which though not better or worse, are different enough to create problems. She illustrates this with the following analogy: ". . . Whenever linguistic habits differ, each person is likely to make the other feel manipulated simply in an attempt to get comfortable in the situation. For a nonverbal analog, imagine two people who have slightly different senses of appropriate distance between conversants. The one who feels comfortable standing farther away keeps backing off to adjust the space, but the conversational partner who expects to stand closer keeps advancing to close up the space, so they move together down the hall until one is pinned against a wall." (*The Sacramento Bee Forum,* October 26, 1986)

x. "The proposed economic sanctions against South Africa, now being bruited about in Congress and the media, bear comparison to the sprinkling of holy water on money received in plain brown envelopes from the purveyors of munitions and pornography." (Lewis H. Lapham, "End Paper," *San Francisco Chronicle's World,* July 27, 1986)

y. "X-rated movies are boring. Generally it's a novelty buy. But it's like peanut butter—a little goes a long way." (Arthur Morowitz, *Sunday Punch,* October 19, 1986)

z. "An astronomer is somebody who can tell you about faraway worlds that are hostile to human safety and well-bein'. In that sense, he's like a Washington correspondent." (Oxnard N. Thorpe, quoted by Richard K. Morse, *Sunday Punch,* October 19, 1986)

aa. President Reagan suggesting a way to pacify those who object to the sight of oil rigs off their beaches: "Maybe we ought to take some of those liberty ships out of mothballs and anchor one at each one of the oil platforms between that and offshore, because people never object to seeing a ship at sea." ("Reagan Supports Watt Stand," *Santa Barbara Evening News Press,* August 5, 1981, p. A21)

Scientific Method and Hypotheses

The formation of hypotheses is the most mysterious of all the categories of scientific method.

ROBERT PIRSIG

"I feel awful about missing your wedding." Ted had finally screwed up the courage to call his old pal Jim—two weeks after Jim and Pam returned from their honeymoon.

"Yeah, well, I was kinda hurt. No, I was really hurt. I mean, we've been friends for years. You're the last person I would expect to miss my wedding."

"I know. I feel sick about it. I think I've got a problem. . . ."

"I'll say you've got a problem. You don't know how to be a friend."

"Hey! That's unfair. It's just that I can't seem to make it to any of my friends' weddings."

"What?"

"Remember how I missed Larry's wedding? I overslept."

"Oh, yeah, I do remember. We all thought it was pretty funny the way you showed up halfway through the reception looking like a drowned rat."

"I missed Gene's wedding, too. I marked the wrong week on my calendar."

"Right," Jim mused, "I'd forgotten that one. And you missed Jack's too. Said you were sitting in the matinée when you remembered."

"See? That's what I mean," Ted wailed. "I'm worried. I honestly planned to go all those weddings. I had my suit cleaned and pressed, the wedding gifts, everything. And I forgot! In every case it completely slipped my mind."

"Aw, c'mon."

"No, really. That's what freaks me out. It's like I had a blackout or something. Bam—no hint of the weddings until they're over."

"Boy," Jim said, "it sounds like you've got some pretty heavy hangups about marriage."

"Whadda ya' mean?"

"Well, look at it scientifically. In each case you consciously intended to attend a friend's wedding. In the past—in spite of what I said before—you have been a good friend. You never fail to show up when the group has plans; you're helpful and energetic. So we must conclude that your subconscious mind does not want you to go to weddings. The key is *weddings*—they're the only commitments you fail to make. And besides, you're the only one in our crowd who's never been engaged and who's parents are divorced. It all adds up, don't you see: You hate marriage!"

"Gee," Ted said admiringly, "I never realized it. I guess I hate marriage without knowing that I hate marriage!"

Ted has a problem, a factual pattern he can't explain. He's missed every one of his close friends' weddings. He feels bad about this, and his friends are hurt by it. Like most of us with problems, Ted's seeking an answer to his, an explanation. A fancy name for such an explanation is *hypothesis*, the chief subject of this chapter.

The term *hypothesis* often is used to mean any unproved or untested assumption. But in this chapter we're going to use *hypothesis* in a more restricted sense to refer to *a tentative conclusion that relates and explains a group of different items of information*. For example, on coming home one day, you find your front door ajar, some muddy footprints on your carpet, your possessions rummaged, and your stereo missing. To explain these facts you hypothesize, "A thief has broken into my house and stolen my stereo."

Contrast this form of inductive argument to hypothesis with generalization and analogy. In the latter, we start out with a set of similar specifics on the basis of which we draw a probable conclusion. As we saw in the theft example, an argument to a hypothesis ordinarily involves a number of dissimilar specifics we're trying to explain.

Again, with generalizations and analogies, we try to *apply* what we've observed. In forming hypotheses we try to *explain* what we've observed.

STUDY HINT

Generalizations and *analogies* seek to *apply* what we observe. In forming *hypotheses*, we try to *explain* what we observe.

To understand the hypothesis as a form of inductive argument it's useful to have some appreciation of scientific method. Scientific method refers to a sequence of steps used in science to make discoveries. Hypothesis is the core of scientific method. So in addition to discussing inductive argument to hypothesis, this chapter looks at scientific method and the role hypothesis plays in it. But don't be misled into thinking that the chapter will offer nothing of everyday, practical use. The fact is that hypotheses, as well as scientific method, play a vital part in common problem solving—even in solving problems like Ted's.

SCIENTIFIC METHOD

Broadly speaking, *we may define scientific method as a way of investigating a phenomenon that's based on the collection, analysis, and interpretation of evidence to determine the most probable explanation*. Since this definition pretty much captures the essence of induction, you can readily understand why scientific method is thought of as synonymous with sound inductive procedure.

As a simple illustration of how scientific method works, let's suppose that one morning your car fails to start. In trying to explain why your car won't start, you'll probably check everything that can be part of the problem: battery, battery cables, distributor, spark plugs, points. Of course, you won't check your tires or bumpers; their condition is irrelevant to the problem; that is, they can't explain the car's failure to start. Once you've collected all the relevant information, you'll analyze and interpret it and ultimately explain the car's failure to start on the basis of the observations.

Before getting to the steps involved in scientific method, let's see what this simple example suggests about science and scientists. First, notice how you assume that an explanation exists that accounts for the problem. Also you assume that some things need to be checked, whereas others do not. You check relevant criteria, which, by and large, are determined by common sense or background knowledge. But so-called common sense and background knowledge are selective in that they present a frame of reference, a frame of expectations. When a car doesn't start, anyone who's familiar with cars presumes certain things while ignoring others. In other words, the person views the problem within a frame of reference, a frame of expectations. Where do these expectations come from? Experience—yours and that of others. In this simple example, the expectations are drawn from the catalog of human knowledge about cars and why they fail to start.

Think about it. Before we're even aware of our own existence, we are profoundly influenced by our relationships with all sorts of people, who themselves have complex histories. And they, in turn, are parts of society, which of course has an even more complicated and evolved history. The point is that by the time we make conscious choices, we already are using a set of expectations about the world and the things in it. In short, we make use of tradition.

Scientists use tradition, too. They employ hypotheses, assumptions, and expectations that have evolved within their own discipline. They observe through hypotheses and networks of empirical generalizations as well as through many philosophical assumptions. Sir Karl Popper, often considered the greatest philosopher of science, develops this very point in his *Conjectures and Refutations:*

> All this means that a young scientist who hopes to make discoveries is badly advised if his teacher tells him, "Go round and observe," and that he is well advised if his teacher tells him, "Try to learn what people are discussing nowadays in science. Find out where difficulties arise, and take an interest in disagreements. These are questions which you should take up." In other words, you should study the *problem situation* of the day. This means that you pick up, and try to continue, a line of enquiry which has the whole background of the earlier development of science behind it; you fall in with the tradition of science. . . . From the point of view of what we want as scientists—understanding, prediction, analysis, and so on—the world in which we live is extremely complex.[1]

Charles Darwin, the great biologist and author of the modern theory of evolution, once made a similar comment. "All observation," Darwin wrote, "must be for or against some view, if it is to be of any service."

These important scientific thinkers, and others too numerous to mention here, realized that there are simply too many facts in the world for one to become familiar with them all. Even the most painstaking investigator must pick and choose among the available data. This is as true of seeking a cure for cancer as it is of trying to figure out why your car won't start or why a person like Ted misses weddings. In short, we must collect data to support or contradict some explanation or hypothesis. And the data we collect will be influenced by the appropriate point of view, the frame of reference and expectations, the tradition we bring to the problem.

The Five Basic Steps in Scientific Method

Having made these preliminary comments about scientific method, let's now get more specific and look at the five basic steps of which it generally consists. The five-step pattern is not inviolable. Sometimes there are earlier or later steps; often there is overlapping. But these steps do get at the essence of what scientific method involves and, most important here, show the centrality of the hypothesis in scientific method. As an illustration of the scientific method, of the application of these steps, we'll be referring to a milestone in the development of medical biology: the discovery of the cure for beriberi, a disease caused by the deficiency of vitamin B_1, characterized by paralysis of the extremities and emaciation.

Statement of the Problem.   As we've already seen, any scientific inquiry begins with a problem, that is, a fact or facts that need to be explained. "Why is the universe expanding?" "Is there extraterrestrial life?" "Why have so many aircraft and boats vanished in the area known as the Bermuda Triangle?" "Who is responsible for the assassination of Martin Luther King, Jr.?" "How come there are more suicides during the Christmas season that at any other time of the year?" "What's the cause of AIDS?" "Why is it that black males on the average have a higher incidence of high blood pressure than white males?" The problems go on and on, and they cut across all areas of human interest. Just because we're talking of scientific method doesn't at all mean that the problems must exist only in the realm of pure science.

---

[1]Karl Popper, *Conjectures and Refutations* (New York: Basic Books, 1965), p. 129.

Invariably such problems can be stated in the form of a question, as illustrated by the foregoing. But it's important that the question be clear and precise because the question inevitably directs the research. An inexact question can misdirect research. In contrast, an exact question-formulation of a problem focuses research. Consider, for example, the problem of beriberi, which for the longest time literally plagued medical researchers. The problem, of course, could be put quite simply: "What's the cause of beriberi?" Having formulated the question, researchers were then able to implement the second step of scientific method.

Collection of Facts.   After the problem is expressed in question form, scientific method then entails further observations and fact collection. Respecting beriberi, it was observed that the disease was largely infecting people on a rice diet. For example, the Japanese navy, for whom rice was a staple, had an enormous incidence of beriberi. But when barley was substituted for the rice, incidence of the disease among sailors dramatically declined.

In 1890, the Dutch government sent medical researcher Christian Eijkman to study the disease. Eijkman took note of the assembled facts and made additional observations of his own. One observation he made was that chickens fed only rice sometimes developed a disease like beriberi. But it wasn't just any rice. The chickens contracting the disease were fed on polished rice, rice from which the husks have been removed. Those that were fed on unpolished rice did not contract the disease.

Formulating a Hypothesis.   Together with the other facts, Eijkman's crucial observation suggested to him an explanation, a hypothesis, which is the next step in scientific method. In other words, he was now in a position to formulate a hypothesis for the various facts he had observed. Specifically, he could connect the eating of polished rice with beriberi. The hypothesis: Something in the rice husks helps prevent beriberi.

This hypothesis was at least plausible. It accounted for the puzzling facts; the facts could be inferred from the hypothesis. If something in the rice husks did help prevent beriberi, then chickens and people that ate polished rice should contract the disease far more often than people who ate unpolished rice. Indeed, this fact had been widely observed.

But even when a hypothesis such as this one explains the observed facts, scientific inquiry does not rest. The obvious reason is that, as with any inductive argument, an argument to a hypothesis is at best probable. In any investigation, what's desired is the highest probability attainable. And what makes a hypothesis increasingly probable is its capacity to account for more and more facts.

Making Further Inferences.   A hypothesis such as Eijkman's shouldn't account only for the observed facts. It should also imply and then explain further facts. For example, if suspect A is thought to have committed a robbery, it follows that suspect A would not have a good alibi for his whereabouts when the crime was committed, that he would have a motive, that the weapon involved in the crime could be traced to him, and so on.

One big fact that could be inferred from Eijkman's hypothesis was that people who ate unpolished rice would be far less susceptible to beriberi than those who ate polished rice. If this could be confirmed, the strength of the hypothesis would be greatly increased, just as the contention that suspect A committed the crime would be increased if the inferences drawn could be confirmed. Of course, in the case of the suspected thief, the inferences don't lend themselves to any confirmatory experiment. But in many instances, tests can be conducted to verify the inferences. Eijkman's hypothesis is an example.

Verifying the Inferences. If the inferences made in step four are verified, the hypothesis is thereby supported. If the inferences are not verified, the hypothesis is discredited. For example, hypotheses about planetary motion lead to inferences about eclipses. If the predicted eclipses occur, our hypotheses are borne out. If the eclipses don't occur, we must go back to the drawing board.

A stroke of good fortune enabled Eijkman to confirm the chief inference from his hypothesis. By chance, local custom in Java decreed that some prison inmates received unpolished rice whereas others got polished rice. What better way to test the inference that polished-rice eaters should contract beriberi more often than unpolished-rice eaters? In fact, the inference was confirmed: Of some 300,000 prisoners, about 2.5 percent of those who ate polished rice had beriberi; but almost no one who ate unpolished rice had the disease.

Eijkman made other predictions that were subsequently confirmed. He inferred, for example, that if the diet of chickens fed on polished rice was supplemented with ground-up rice husks, they would not contract the disease. They didn't. He also inferred that if chickens were fed this identical diet *less* the ground-up rice husks, they would develop beriberi. They did. Other inferences were also borne out. Subsequent research, of course, isolated the rice husk ingredient that prevents beriberi: vitamin B_1.

Although scientific inquiry is conducted as systematically as this episode suggests, it would be inaccurate to view scientific method as a bloodless, mechanical operation that generates hypotheses. After all, facts suggest hypotheses to all but the lame-brained. But whether of a purely scientific or everyday variety, the compelling hypothesis springs from a vast repertoire of knowledge, considerable insight, imagination, and yes, intuition.

The history of science records a marvelous example of the important roles all these ingredients play in formulating hypotheses. For some time, professor of chemistry Friedrich Kekulé had been pondering the structure of benzene, but he couldn't explain it. Then, one afternoon in 1865, Kekulé turned his mind away from his work. As he subsequently told it,

> I turned my chair to the fire and dozed. Again the atoms were gamboling before my eyes. This time the smaller groups kept modestly in the background. My mental eye, rendered more acute by repeated visions of this kind, could now distinguish larger structures, of manifold conformations; long rows, sometimes more closely fitted together; all twining and twisting in a snakelike motion. But look! What was that? One of the snakes had seized hold of its own tail, and the form whirled mockingly before my eyes. As if by a flash of lightning I awoke and this time also I spent the rest of the night working out the consequences of the hypothesis.

Kekulé had found his clue to the structure of benzene in his dream of the snake gripping its own tail: Carbon compounds can form rings.[2]

---

[2]See Vincent Barry, *Philosophy: A Text with Readings* (Belmont, Calif.: Wadsworth, 1980), p. 233.

*EXERCISE 10-1 _____

Identify the steps in scientific method that are evident in the following passages.

1. Professor Rinehart was puzzled. She couldn't figure out how student Ronald, who had miserably failed every logic test in the term, could suddenly turn in a near-perfect test. She looked at her seating chart and noticed that Bill, who sat next to Ronald, had also turned in a near-perfect paper on the same test. In fact, both had missed the same question. Rinehart hated to think it, but she suspected that Ronald had cheated from Bill. So on the next test she insisted that the students so space themselves that they couldn't possibly cheat from another's paper. In addition, she so monitored Ronald that he couldn't possibly cheat. Sure enough, Ronald flunked the test, whereas Bill turned in a perfect paper. Professor Rinehart was confirmed in her suspicions.

2. "I can't believe it!" Mindy said, looking at the new gold necklace her boyfriend Mork had given her for her birthday. She gave Mork such a big hug that it made him wince. Then she ran to a mirror, where she stood for some minutes admiring how beautiful the necklace looked.

   But after the initial excitement wore off, Mindy began to wonder just how Mork could afford such a beautiful present. Why, he wasn't even working and couldn't even afford the price of a decent dinner.

   So Mindy decided the necklace wasn't real gold at all but an imitation. She knew that imitation gold necklaces were cheap enough even for Mork to afford. And everyone knew that today such necklaces could be made to look like the real thing. In fact, the more she looked at it, the more it resembled the costume jewelry she'd seen around the necks of many of her friends. "Oh, well," Mindy decided, "it's the thought that counts."

   But she didn't think that for long. A couple of days later she hotfooted it down to a neighborhood jewelry shop. The jeweler examined the necklace, smiled benignly and said, "Lady, this ain't the real thing."

   "I didn't think so," said Mindy, nonetheless disappointed.

   She was halfway out the door when the jeweler called to her. "But one thing," he said, "on you it looks *better* than the real thing."

   That made Mindy feel better, and she skipped on home, thinking what a marvelous man was Mork.

3. RESEARCHER MYSHKIN: This is quite amazing, Friedrich. Our yogurt-fed rats have gained about 30 percent more weight.
   FRIEDRICH: So what's so amazing about a fat rat?
   MYSHKIN: The 30 percent isn't just extra weight. It's an overall increase in size, including bigger bones.
   FRIEDRICH: You don't say. So how do you account for that?
   MYSHKIN: I'm inclined to think the bacteria in the yogurt produces a growth factor—call it, uh, factor Myshkin.
   FRIEDRICH: *Myshkin?* Not on your life! We'll call it factor *Friedrich*.
   MYSHKIN: All right, all right—for the time being, let's call it factor *X*.
   FRIEDRICH: Very well. Now, tell me, what about the strength of these fat rats?
   MYSHKIN: They're much stronger and healthier than those that didn't get the yogurt.
   FRIEDRICH: But maybe feeding rats milk would produce the same effect. Remember, Myshkin, yogurt's made of skimmed cow's milk and milk solids.
   MYSHKIN: You think I don't know that? I was eating yogurt before you were born! . . . Besides, we've not only fed a group of rats milk but loaded the milk with vitamins.
   FRIEDRICH: And the yogurt-fed rats are larger?
   MYSHKIN: They are.
   FRIEDRICH: Hmm, well, then, it must be the bacteria that's added to the milk and

milk solids to cause fermentation that explains these rotund little rodents.

MYSHKIN: My sentiments exactly.

FRIEDRICH: Perhaps *exactly,* but not *originally.* That's why we'll call the mysterious ingredient factor Friedrich.

4. Was cannibalism ever a universal practice? Most sociobiologists believe it was. Indeed, some have argued that cannibalism is evidence of what they believe is the human's inherent aggressiveness. What's more, anthropologists have classified different kinds of cannibalism or depicted it as a ritualistic denial of death (the victim lives on by being ingested as food). Well, anthropologist William Arens believes otherwise. According to Arens, cannibalism was never a universal practice. In fact, in his *The Man-Eating Myth,* he argues that cannibalism never existed anywhere as a regular custom. How, then, did the myth originate? Arens believes it's because of the tendency of every group to accuse its neighbors of this rather unneighborly practice. But what about all the evidence to the contrary—the eyewitness testimonies, the reports of such notable explorers as Christopher Columbus? Arens claims that these people were hoodwinked, that their testimonies were largely the result of misinterpretations of unfamiliar tribal languages or of their own gullibility at the hands of enterprising natives who, for the right price, would readily oblige the copy-hungry European. For example, sixteenth-century accounts of cannibalism among the Tupinamba, a now extinct Brazilian tribe, all use similar wording, which according to Arens, would be highly unlikely were these accounts accurate. As for Columbus, Arens believes he was simply passing on meaty tales about the Caribbean natives to his Spanish masters to help establish the slave trade.

5. One of the most celebrated cases in all American jurisprudence is the kidnapping and murder of the Lindberg baby. After the famed aviator Charles Lindberg had paid a $50,000 ransom for the return of the baby, its body was found in the woods behind the Lindberg home. A man named Bruno Hauptmann was subsequently arrested and charged with the crime. Although Hauptmann insisted he was innocent, the state assembled an array of particulars to establish its charge. Among the facts were these:

a. The ransom note indicated that the author was a German; Hauptmann was a German.

b. Hauptmann worked near the Lindbergh home.

c. An auto spotted shortly before the kidnapping fit the description of Hauptmann's.

d. Hauptmann had a criminal record in Germany.

e. A handwriting expert identified the ransom note as Hauptmann's handwriting.

f. The handwriting on a note left in the nursery after the kidnapping was identical to the writing on the ransom notes.

g. When arrested, Hauptmann had $20 of the ransom money in his pocket; $14,600 more was found in his garage. (Hauptmann claimed that a friend named Fisch, who since had died, had left the money with him for safekeeping.)

h. Although Hauptmann had little money before the kidnapping, immediately after that event, both he and his wife quit their jobs and took trips costing $35,000.

i. The ladder used in the kidnapping was made from lumber from Hauptmann's attic floor and from lumber bought at a company where Hauptmann worked.

j. The nails used in the ladder showed the same defects as nails found in Hauptmann's home.

k. Ground marks made after the kidnapping indicated that the kidnapper might have injured his leg. For several weeks after the kidnapping, Hauptmann walked with a cane.

l. The telephone number and address of the man who was to transfer the ransom money was found written on the back of a closet door in Hauptmann's home. Hauptmann said he'd copied it from a newspaper ad; however, that information was never in a newspaper.

CRITERIA FOR EVALUATING HYPOTHESES

Having briefly discussed scientific method and the place of hypotheses in it, we should now ask how hypotheses are to be judged. Recall that we raised a similar question about generalizations and analogies: What counts for a good generalization, a good analogy? Just as there are helpful criteria for determining the strength of those inductive forms, so there are criteria for evaluating hypotheses.

Before discussing these criteria, we should note their importance. Because there is usually more than a single explanation for a fact, we must have some way of distinguishing between alternative hypotheses. Ted's problem, for example, may be explained by simple forgetfulness; some general, unconscious anxiety; or something else. How do we decide which is the best hypothesis? Again, in the realm of science, the expansion of an object when heated can be explained by both the caloric theory of heat and the kinetic theory. The caloric theory considers heat as an invisible, weightless fluid, called "calorie." This fluid could penetrate and expand or dissolve bodies, even dissipate them in vapor. In contrast, the kinetic theory regards heat as consisting of the random motions of a body's molecules. Both of these alternative hypotheses explain some of the phenomena of thermal expansion. The question is, which better accounts for the phenomena?

To answer that question and to decide between hypotheses generally, we need a list of conditions that a good hypothesis should be expected to fulfill. But we shouldn't think of such a test as a formula for *constructing* good hypotheses. Hypothesis formulation, as we've already seen, is as much an art as a science. It requires talent and imagination; it can't be reduced to some instant recipe. This said, let's turn to some accepted criteria to which a hypothesis should conform.

Relevance

Any good hypothesis must be relevant; that is, it should explain the problem directly. Suppose someone stood you up for a date. The next time you meet, the person explains, "Sorry about the other night, but Pearl Harbor was bombed on December 7, 1941." An absurd explanation; it has nothing to do with what it proposes to explain—why the person didn't appear. On the other hand, suppose the person explained, "I didn't make the date because of the fuel shortage." Although this explanation alone doesn't account for the absence, it might explain it in combination with other relevant reasons. Thus, perhaps the person's car was out of gas, and because the gas stations were out of gas or were closed because of the gas shortage, the person couldn't make the date. The point is that this second explanation, although incomplete and possibly not even satisfying to you (why didn't the person plan for such an eventuality?), is at least relevant. From that information you can infer a possible explanation for the absence.

When the fact to be explained can be inferred from the hypothesis, the hypothesis is relevant. Put another way, the fact to be explained must be deducible from the proposed hypothesis alone or in combination with other highly probable suppositions.

In theory any scientific hypothesis is potentially irrelevant because it is falsifiable. By calling scientific hypotheses falsifiable, we simply acknowledge that, by definition, such statements are incomplete. Although generally unnoticed or unexpressed, qualifiers are implied in every scientific statement, such as "according to the evidence available," "based on my studies," or "given these conditions." Thus, scientific statements are never unamendable. They're always open to revision based on new data or on a new interpretation of the old data. This is another way of saying that scientific statements are falsifiable. Respecting scientific hypotheses, if just one of the deductions the hypothesis offers is, in fact, falsified, the hypothesis no longer is a credible explanation; it no longer is relevant. An example will illustrate.

If you observe the sky at night, you'll notice that the stars move gradually toward the west as the night progresses. You will notice, as you watch night after night, that the same patterns of stars appear regularly but not at the same place at the same time. Each night a given pattern appears at a given place in the sky about four minutes earlier than the previous night. You'll also notice that "peculiar stars" appear near the same place in relation to other stars on successive days but change their positions radically over a longer period of time. These are the planets. How do we explain these events?

The Greek philosopher and logician Aristotle (384–322 B.C.) offered an early explanation. He suggested that the earth is a stationary sphere in the center of the universe. The heavenly bodies are on huge, clear spheres that circle the earth. The sun, the moon, and each planet have their own spheres that circle the earth; beyond them is a single sphere containing all the fixed stars.

Now was Aristotle's explanation at least relevant? Could it explain the facts? Could the facts be inferred from the hypothesis? Yes. From Aristotle's hypothesis we can infer why the same patterns generally exist among the stars: Most of the stars are spots on the same sphere. We can also infer why five stars (planets), the sun, and the moon don't remain in the same place among the other stars. Each follows its own circular orbit around the earth at its own rate, which is slightly lower than the rate of the stars' revolution.

Of course, problems arose in subsequent centuries when astronomers tried to plot the paths of the planets more exactly so that they could determine their speed. Observations indicated that none of the planets moved at a constant speed. Thus, Aristotle's explanation no longer fit the major facts. Put another way, what was deducible from his explanation no longer squared with what was observable. The explanation was no longer relevant. This didn't mean, however, that Aristotle's hypothesis was junked. It needed reexamination and perhaps modification and amendment. And in later centuries, it received just that.

The point is simple but important. Any relevant explanation is potentially irrelevant in the sense that it is (and *should be*) falsifiable. Thus, eventually it might fail to account for the problem under investigation. What's more, just because a hypothesis is relevant doesn't make it a good one or the best of what's available. It must meet other criteria.

Compatibility

Compatibility refers to whether or not a hypothesis fits in with a body of knowledge that is already accepted as true. To draw out the meaning of this criterion, let's join Roscoe and Sweeney. Sweeney's seeking an explanation for why he's having nightmares that keep him from sleeping.

SWEENEY: All right, wise guy, you're so bright. Tell me, why do you think I'm having nightmares?

ROSCOE: What do you do before you go to bed?

SWEENEY: Hey! That's personal, huh?

ROSCOE: Okay, but if you want me to help you. . . .

SWEENEY: All right, all right. Let's see, I, uh, well I brush my teeth. Yeah, I do that every night.

ROSCOE: Forget it. Teeth don't have anything to do with nightmares. What else?

SWEENEY: Ah, c'mon, will you? How should I know what else?

ROSCOE: If you don't, who does? Now think. What else do you do? Do you eat, maybe?

SWEENEY: Sure I eat—a small pepperoni-sausage pizza.

ROSCOE: Every night?

SWEENEY: Doesn't everybody?

ROSCOE: How long you been doing that?

SWEENEY: Who's counting? For as long as I've had the tube, I guess—forever. Why?

ROSCOE: Well, that rules out the pizza. Otherwise you would have been having these nightmares all along, I figure. Tell me something. Sween, do you watch the tube while you're eating the pie?

SWEENEY: I eat the *pie* while I'm watching the *tube*. Let's keep the old cart before the horse, huh? Geez, you make me sound like one of those guys that lives to eat.

ROSCOE: Okay, okay, don't be so sensitive. Tell me, what do you watch?

SWEENEY: What do you mean what do I watch? What do people watch on the tube?

Roscoe seems to be implying that Sweeney's television viewing could explain his nightmares. The explanation is at least relevant. Together with other facts it could explain Sweeney's problem. After all, if Sweeney is susceptible to suggestions just before drifting off to sleep, perhaps the programs he's watching account for the nightmares he's having.

In addition, the explanation fits in nicely with other established hypotheses about dreaming, especially the one that holds that visual stimulation before retiring can produce dreams. When a hypothesis, such as this one, is compatible with existing thought on an issue, its probability is strengthened.

Nonscientists frequently regard this compatibility criterion as strictly an appeal to traditional wisdom. Why should an explanation be evaluated on the basis of how it fits in with accepted thought, they ask, since the history of science glitters with examples of how inaccurate and incomplete thought can be?

In fact, compatibility is an altogether reasonable criterion when we remember that science, in trying to encompass additional facts, seeks to achieve a system of explanatory hypotheses. But such a system must be self-consistent. Surely, a set of self-contradictory statements can't be true, let alone intelligible. Ideally, scientists hope to perfect such a system by expanding their hypotheses so that they account for more and more facts. But to make any progress, scientists must attempt to fit new hypotheses to hypotheses that have already been confirmed. There's no good reason for us to depart from this standard in our everyday lives. After all, do we wish less intelligibility in the resolutions of our personal affairs than scientists seek in explaining the workings of the universe?

At the same time, it is true that many important new hypotheses were not compatible with existing accepted hypotheses. Consider, for example, the historical development of the explanation of astronomical phenomena that attracted Aristotle's interest. In the second century, Ptolemy, a Greek astronomer, modified Aristotle's position by claiming that the planets traveled in little circles (epicycles) on their orbits around the earth. By assuming that the centers of the orbits of the planets were not always the earth, Ptolemy could predict where the planets would be at any given time. Ptolemy's explanation held sway until modern times.

In the sixteenth century, Copernicus, a Polish astronomer, studied and plotted the paths of the planets but couldn't fit the planets' locations over time to Ptolemaic system. So to account for these differences, Copernicus hypothesized that the sun, *not* the earth, was the center of the universe; that the earth went around the sun and spun on an axis, and so did the other planets. Clearly Copernicus's explanation was not compatible with the accepted Ptolemaic hypothesis, which had not only scientific but religious approval as well. Nonetheless, Copernicus's insistence on the sun's centrality was justified, although taken as a whole his explanation was not entirely satisfactory.

Other scientific hypotheses have been inconsistent with older explanations. The hypothesis that radium could spontaneously disintegrate redefined the principle that matter could neither be created nor destroyed. And then there's Einstein's theory of relativity, which unmoored many Newtonian suppositions.

But even in these dramatic instances a compatibility criterion prevails. After all, each of these hypotheses could account for the same facts as well as or better than the older hypotheses could. They thus became the appropriate prevailing standard against which other hypotheses must be measured, with which other hypotheses must prove to be compatible.

So science does not develop capriciously. Neither should we in our every day lives formulate hypotheses helter-skelter. Any change in an accepted hypothesis should represent an improvement by making an explanation more comprehensive. The criterion of compatibility, therefore, is a vital part of this organic development. As a result, it is quite correct to say that if a hypothesis is consistent with the prevailing thought in a field, the reliability of the hypothesis is thereby strengthened.

Testability

Testability refers to whether or not a hypothesis offers observations that will confirm or disconfirm it. A good hypothesis is testable, as Roscoe suggests in his unending quest for the explanation for Sweeney's nightmares.

ROSCOE: Do you watch movies on the tube before turning in?

SWEENEY: Absolutely. I mean there's no way I'm going to listen to a lot of half-wits beat their gums on those talk shows.

ROSCOE: What kind of movies?

SWEENEY: You know, you're really something, Roscoe. I'd swear you were applying for a job with the Nielsen ratings.

ROSCOE: Look, Sweeney, it's no skin off my nose if you never sleep again.

SWEENEY: All right, all right. Let's see, I watch whatever movies are on. Right now Channel Nine is running. . . . Wait a minute!

ROSCOE: What's wrong?

SWEENEY: How could I be so dumb!

ROSCOE: What's the matter?

SWEENEY: That's it! It's got to be! I can't believe I didn't think of it before!

ROSCOE: What?

SWEENEY: Those horror flicks!

ROSCOE: The news? I thought you were watching movies.

SWEENEY: Not the news! You think I'm going to watch the news when Channel Nine's running a week of "creature features"?

ROSCOE: Creature features?

SWEENEY: You know—the kind where a hand crawls out of a grave and turns a guy into a cornflake? That's all I've been watching for a week, Roscoe, those creature features!

ROSCOE: That could be it, all right.

SWEENEY: What do you mean—*could* be? That *has* to be it!

ROSCOE: There's only one way to find out for sure.

SWEENEY: Do you know what this *means*, Roscoe?

ROSCOE: Now calm down, Sweeney. It means you won't be watching any creature features tonight.

SWEENEY: What are you talking about? It means I can still have my pizza every night!

Although Sweeney isn't listening, Roscoe's proposing a test for the hypothesis that the horror films are contributing to Sweeney's nightmares. If this is true, if Sweeney doesn't watch the films before retiring, he shouldn't have the nightmares. Like this hypothesis, all hypotheses should be testable. They should allow for observations that will confirm or disconfirm them.

Of course, not all hypotheses can be tested directly. Newton's laws of gravitation and motion, Darwin's theory of evolution, Einstein's theory of relativity, the "big bang" theory—these cannot be tested directly. But they are, and should be, testable indirectly. In other words, if these explanations of phenomena are sound, certain other things should follow. And these other things, these other inferences, *are* testable.

Take, for example, Newton's inertia hypothesis— that a moving body will maintain its line of direction unless disturbed by an external force. If this hypothesis is true, it follows that when you fully apply the brakes to a car traveling forward at 55 miles per hour, the car should skid forward, the people in the car should thrust forward, and a parked car struck by the skidding car should move. These inferences we can test directly; if they occur, the inertia hypothesis is strengthened.

Again, the theory of evolution in part hypothesizes the gradual development of organisms from simple to increasingly complex forms. Now scientists have long known that Cambrian formations (rock formations assumed to be 500 to 600 million years old) contain highly developed fossil forms. If evolution is a sound theory, pre-Cambrian formations should contain simpler fossil forms. In fact, in 1947 fossil traces of simple forms were found in pre-Cambrian rock formations in Australia. Subsequent discoveries have further borne out the theory of evolution.

Testability is the main difference between scientific and nonscientific explanations. For an explanation to be scientific, there must be the possibility of making observations that would tend to confirm or disprove the explanation. So any hypothesis that allows for this proof is said to be a scientific explanation. And of course, such explanations are *not* confined exclusively to the world of science.

Predictability

Frequently, two hypotheses are relevant, compatible, and testable. As a result, we decide which is the better on the basis of their predictability powers. *Predictability refers to the explanatory power that a hypothesis has*. A hypothesis that has great explanatory power—that is, we can deduce many testable facts from it—is said to have considerable predictive power. The more predictive power a hypothesis has, the stronger the hypothesis is.

Take, for example, Newton's law of gravity. The law allows for numerous deductive facts; it explains not only why apples fall from trees but also why tides move as they do, why great booster rockets are needed to put an object into space, why an astronaut in space had better hold onto that glass of TANG, and why the universe may have begun with a "big bang."

What about Roscoe's hypothesis? Well, it certainly helps explain why a film can sadden or elate us. It also helps explain why a film can remain with us for days after we've seen it, why we rate films unsuitable for children, why subliminal advertising can be so effective, and why the blind do not dream in a visual mode.

Sometimes two or more hypotheses are not only relevant, compatible, and testable but are also highly predictive. It may be possible to decide between them by deducing *incompatible* propositions and then setting up a crucial experiment designed to eliminate one or more of the hypotheses.

In Book II of his *The New Organon*, Francis Bacon (1561–1626), a seminal scientist-philosopher in the development of scientific method, illustrates the value of crucial experiments in unlocking the nature of things. For instance, is the weight of a body due to the body's own nature or to the attraction of the earth? To find out, says Bacon, test the rate of a pendulum clock. He suggests that the pendulum clock be placed at the top of a tall steeple and its rate observed to see whether it goes slower because of its diminished weight. He then suggests repeating the experiment, this time at the bottom of a mine to see if the clock goes faster because of its increased weight. "If the virtue of the weights is found to be diminished on the steeple and increased in the mine, we may take the attraction of the mass of the earth as the cause of the weight."

Of course, such crucial experiments are not always easy to carry out. Sometimes the required circumstances are difficult or impossible to effect. For example, the choice between Newtonian theory and Einsteinian general theory of relativity could not be made until a total eclipse of the sun occurred, which, of course, is beyond human power to produce. In other cases, we may simply have to await the development of new instruments or technology. Astronomy is replete with examples of this kind. In still other cases, where hypotheses of a high level of generality are involved, no observable testable predictions can be deduced from just one of them. Instead, a whole group of hypotheses must be used as premises. If the observed facts contradict what the group predicts, at least one of the hypotheses must be false. But determining which one is another matter.

To illustrate, Copernicus held that the earth was spherical, not flat. In *On the Revolutions of the Heavenly Bodies,* he writes, "That the seas take a spherical form is perceived by navigators. For when land is still not discernible from a vessel's deck, it is from the masthead. And if, when a ship sails from land, a torch be fastened from the masthead, it appears to watchers on the land to go downward little by little until it entirely disappears, like a heavenly body setting." In effect, Copernicus is suggesting a crucial experiment to decide between the two rival hypotheses.[3]

The experiment seems to prove the flat-earth hypothesis false. But the experiment is not decisive because it is possible to accept the observed facts and still maintain that the earth is flat. The reason is that the testable prediction that Copernicus makes is not deducible from the rival hypothesis alone but from it together with the added hypothesis that light travels in a straight line. So even if the earth is spherical, the decks will not necessarily disappear before the masthead does unless light rays follow a rectilinear path. The point is that an experiment can be crucial in showing that a given set of hypotheses is untenable. When this is the case, further tests must be designed to determine which hypotheses of the set are wrong.

Simplicity

Finally, a hypothesis must be judged on the basis of simplicity. *Simplicity refers to a hypothesis's capacity to account for the facts and data in the most economical way of all the alternatives*. This criterion is most important when alternative hypotheses are equal according to all other criteria.

To understand the relevance of simplicity in weighing hypotheses, remember that scientists try to take the data in a given area and invent a general principle or set of principles with which these data are compatible. Scientists attempt to develop a framework within which they can approach events and data and understand them. Generally speaking, the greater the number and variety of events that an explanation accounts for, the better the explanation. In addition, science attempts to adopt the smallest set of hypotheses or principles that accounts for the greatest diversity of events. In other words, all things being equal, the simpler explanation is preferred.

In science, this simplicity criterion is often referred to as the principle of parsimony. Among other things, the principle of parsimony suggests that a person take the simplest explanation as the most likely one. This postulate is a check against unnecessary intricacy. It rightly warns about complicated explanations. You will sometimes see the parsimony principle referred to as "Occam's razor," since William of Occam, a fourteenth-century English philosopher, warned, "Entities should not be multiplied beyond necessity."

A good example can be seen in the choice between the Ptolemaic theory of an earth-centered universe with rotating planets and the Copernican theory of a sun-centered universe with rotating planets. A significant factor in deciding in favor of the Copernican theory was that it offered fewer "epicycles" in its explanation than did the Ptolemaic. Translated, this meant fewer complications. In effect, then, Copernicus had done everything Ptolemy had done, but had done it *more simply*.

This simplicity criterion is a commonsensical one. We use it all the time when deciding between equal rival hypotheses. Think how a jury often accepts the explanation that seems "more natural" and less complicated, that accounts for things more "elegantly" than rival explanations. At the same time, it's important to emphasize that the simplicity criterion is extremely vague and can

[3]See Irving Copi, *Introduction to Logic* (New York: Macmillan, 1972), pp. 449–52.

easily lead to error when used indiscriminately or exclusively. But when other factors are equal, simplicity does determine the more reliable explanation.

EXERCISE 10-2 _____

1. Suppose you're trying to explain why we as voters can be so easily taken in by political rhetoric. Which among the following hypotheses would you consider at least relevant? Explain.

   a. The news media do not do an adequate and accurate job in presenting the news.
   b. Americans are indifferent to the political process.
   c. Americans are great sports fans.
   d. Traceable back even to our frontier origins is a gift for rhetorical exaggeration.
   e. The United States is so big that politicians can't possibly visit each and every town.

2. Suppose that you're trying to explain why we've cut back on the space program. Which among the following hypotheses would you consider at least relevant? Explain.

   a. Americans are bored with television coverage of space shots.
   b. There are more pressing domestic needs.
   c. Life has not been discovered in outer space.
   d. Americans have an inherent suspicion of science and particularly of science fiction.
   e. Some of the astronauts have turned their space ventures into personal financial gain.
   f. Since no one is threatening us in outer space, we don't feel the need to explore space further.
   g. We're approaching the end of the twentieth century.
   h. We can travel as fast as we want in airplanes.

3. Suppose that you're trying to explain why your most recent romantic relationship has fallen apart. Which of the following hypotheses would you consider least relevant? Explain.

   a. Your astrological sun sign is incompatible with your ex's.
   b. Your ex does better in school than you do.
   c. You knew your ex in a past life and had some karma to work out, but that's all taken care of now.
   d. Your ex has moved 1,800 miles away to finish college.
   e. Over half the romantic relationships in America end in the first year.

4. Suppose that you're trying to explain why you're having trouble understanding logic. Which among the following hypotheses would you find at least relevant? Explain.

   a. Your text is unclear.
   b. Your instructor is a woman.
   c. The room is too hot.
   d. You are taking six solid courses and working twenty-five hours a week at MacDonald's.
   e. You are the creative, poetic sort, not the logical, scientific type.

5. Suppose you're trying to explain why no one has discovered any physical evidence that Bigfoot exists. Which among the following hypotheses would you find at least relevant? Explain.

   a. There is no Bigfoot.
   b. Bigfoot has superior senses to our own, and so hides effectively.

 c. There has been evidence, but someone or some group has systematically destroyed it.

 d. We've been looking in the wrong places.

 e. The public's lost interest in Bigfoot.

6. Of the hypotheses you thought relevant in the previous exercises, which do you think fit in with existing thought? Explain.

7. Which of the hypotheses in exercises 1 through 5 that are relevant and compatible are also testable? How would you go about testing them?

8. Which of the hypotheses that are relevant, compatible, and testable also have vast predictive or explanatory power? Explain.

9. Of the hypotheses that you've decided are relevant, compatible, testable, and predictive, which seem to meet the criterion of simplicity?

EXERCISE 10-3 _____

Discuss the following cases, answering the questions asked about each in terms of the criteria for evaluating hypotheses.

1. The psychic Uri Geller was scheduled to appear on the "Tonight Show" some years ago. As there was some controversy concerning whether or not Geller was a psychic or a magician, Johnny, who is a first-rate magician himself, asked Orson Welles to appear on the same show. Welles was also a fine magician. Geller claimed that using special psychic powers he could "sense" which film cannister in a tall stack was the only one that contained film. He said that he could do this without touching the cannisters in any way. He would simply walk around them to "sense" which was the one cannister containing film.

  Before Geller appeared, Johnny discussed this feat with Welles. Both men pointed out that this purported "psychic feat" resembled a magic trick in which the magician surreptitiously brushed against the stack of containers in a way that revealed—by the weight of the many empty versus one full container—which was the full box, cannister, or whatever.

  They reasoned that if Geller were truly psychic, he would indeed "sense" which cannister contained the film, but that if he were merely a clever magician pretending to be a psychic, he would at some point have to touch the stack of metal film cannisters to determine which was the heavy, or full, one.

  To test their hypothesis, the two amateur magicians filled one cannister with film and the others with water so that the weight of each was identical. They discussed this on the air, prior to Geller's appearance, pointing out that the weight of the containers should have no effect on Geller's psychic powers, but that it would interfere with a magician's trick.

  Geller refused to come out from the greenroom claiming that he was insulted and so forth.

 a. Analyze the Welles and Carson hypothesis according to the five criteria for evaluating hypotheses.

 b. Psychics sometimes claim that the presence of hostile or skeptical "vibes" interferes with their powers. Suppose Geller made such a claim. Would it be testable? Explain.

2. It was once believed that diseases were caused by the presence of "evil humors" in the body. This was the reason that physicians bled patients. The theory was that the "bad blood" containing the disease-causing humors would be drained away.

  In 1828, French physician Pierre Charles Alexandre Louis decided to test this hypothesis. Using patients suffering from pneumonia, Louis discovered that when patients were bled within the first three days after the onset of pneumonia, the mortality rate was 50 percent. Patients who were not bled until seven to nine days had passed from the onset of the disease had a mortality rate of only 16 percent. (See Robert Paul Churchill's *Becoming Logical: An Introduction to Logic*. New York, 1986, p. 377.)

a. What did Louis's experiment suggest in regard to the practice of bleeding in general? in regard to bleeding in pneumonia cases?
b. Why is the number of days after the onset of pneumonia significant to this hypothesis?
c. If the "evil humors" theory had been viable, what results could Louis have expected? What do his actual results tell us?

SUMMARY

This chapter dealt with another inductive form: the argument to hypothesis. The term *hypothesis* often refers to any unproved or untested assumption. We defined *hypothesis* as a tentative conclusion that relates and explains a group of different items of information. To understand the hypothesis as a form of inductive argument, we found it useful to be acquainted with scientific method because the hypothesis is the core of scientific method. Scientific method refers to a way of investigating a phenomenon that is based on the collection, analysis, and interpretation of evidence to determine the most probable explanation. Scientific method consists of (1) statement of the problem, (2) collection of facts, (3) formulation of a hypothesis, (4) making further inferences, and (5) verification of inferences. How beriberi was cured is a good example of scientific method in action. It also illustrates that the good hypothesis springs from vast knowledge, insight, imagination, and even intuition (as in Kekulé's discovery of the structure of benzene). We can expect a good hypothesis to conform to five criteria: (1) It should be relevant; that is, it should explain the problem directly. All scientific statements are potentially irrelevant in that they are falsifiable; that is, they are always open to revision or new interpretation. (2) A hypothesis should be compatible with the accepted body of knowledge. (3) A hypothesis should be testable; that is, it should generate observations that will confirm or disconfirm it. Testability is the main difference between scientific and nonscientific explanations. (4) A hypothesis should have predictive value; that is, it should allow us to infer many testable facts from it. Frequently, crucial experiments can determine the better of two otherwise equal hypotheses. (5) A hypothesis should be simple; that is, it should account for the facts and data in the most economical way of all the alternatives. This simplicity criterion is sometimes referred to as the principle of parsimony or Occam's razor.

Summary Questions
Study the following statements to see which are true and which are false. Explain what is wrong with those that are false.

1. A hypothesis is relevant if it can in any way explain the problem, either directly or indirectly.
2. A hypothesis that allows us to infer many testable facts is said to have predictive value.
3. A truly groundbreaking hypothesis will be so revolutionary in its scope that it is no longer compatible with the accepted body of knowledge.

*1. In each of the following passages, (1) what problems or data are to be explained?
(2) What hypotheses are suggested to explain them? (3) How good are the hypotheses,
in terms of the five criteria discussed?

a. "A common explanation of suicidal attempts is that the person who attempts
suicide is making an appeal for sympathy. One would, therefore, at least expect suicide
attempts to be rare in a society indifferent or hostile to its individual members. No
such society now exists. However, not long ago there existed a society which was
openly hostile to its members, i.e., German concentration camps. Several reports
about the behavior of the inmates have been published by medical observers who
were themselves members of those communities. All of them noted the rarity of
suicidal attempts." (Erwin Stengel, *Suicide and Attempted Suicide*)

b. "For many years Trisomy 21 was believed directly and simply correlated to maternal age, because the incidence of Trisomy 21 was found to increase gradually from
.04% in mothers under 30 years of age to more than 3% in those over 45 years old.
These data seemed to correlate closely with results of studies made on *Drosophila,* in
which nondisjunction was shown to increase with maternal age. The cause of the
condition may be more complex than previously suspected, however, as suggested
in recent studies undertaken in Australia. These studies indicate that the mutation
occurs in epidemics that show a distinctive time pattern and that disseminate from
cities into rural areas. Hence the disease now appears to be induced by a virus infection
that resembles infectious hepatitis." (Lawrence S. Dillon, *Evolution, Concepts and
Consequences*)

c. "Darwin admitted that he was unable to find an explanation for the extermination
of the mammoth, an animal better developed than the elephant which survived. But
in conformity with the theory of evolution, his followers supposed that a gradual
sinking of the land forced the mammoths to the hills, where they found themselves
isolated by marshes. However, if geological processes are slow, the mammoths would
not have been trapped on the isolated hills. Besides this theory cannot be true because
the animals did not die of starvation. In their stomachs and between their teeth
undigested grass and leaves were found." (Immanuel Velikovsky, *Worlds in Collision*)

d. "It be a matter of daily observation that infinite numbers of worms are generated
in dead bodies and decayed plants. However, I am inclined to believe that these
worms are all produced by insemination and that the putrefied matter in which they
are found has no other purpose than to serve as a place, or suitable nest, where
animals deposit their eggs at the breeding season, and in which they also find nour-
ishment; otherwise, I assert that nothing is ever generated therein. . . . I was confirmed in this belief by having observed that, before meat grew wormy, flies had
hovered over it, of the same kind as those that later bred in it. Belief would be
groundless without support of experiment. Hence, in the middle of July I put a snake,
some fish, some eels of the Arno, and a slice of milk-fed veal in four large, wide
mouthed flasks; having well closed and sealed them, I then filled the same number
of flasks in the same way, only leaving these open. It was not long before the meat
and the fish, in these second vessels, became wormy and flies were seen entering and
leaving it at will; but in the closed flasks I did not see a worm, though many days
passed since the dead flesh had been put in them." (Francesco Redi, *Experiments on
the Generation of Insects*)

e. "Like multiple sclerosis, poliomyelitis in its paralytic forms was a disease of the
more advanced nations rather than of the less advanced ones, and of economically
better-off people rather than of the poor. It occurred in northern Europe and North
America much more frequently than in southern Europe or the countries of Africa,
Asia or South America. Immigrants to South Africa from northern Europe ran twice
the risk of contracting paralytic poliomyelitis than South-African-born whites ran,
and the South-African-born whites ran a much greater risk than nonwhites. Among

the Bantu of South Africa paralytic poliomyelitis was rarely an adult disease. During World War II in North Africa cases of paralytic poliomyelitis were commoner among officers in the British and American forces than among men in the other ranks. At the time various wild hypotheses for the difference were proposed; it was even suggested that it arose from the fact that the officers drank whisky whereas men in the other ranks drank beer!

We now understand very well the reason for the strange distribution of paralytic poliomyelitis. Until this century poliomyelitis was a universal infection of infancy and infants hardly ever suffered paralysis from it. The fact that they were occasionally so affected is what gave the disease the name "infantile paralysis." With the improvement of hygiene in the advancing countries of the world more and more people missed infection in early childhood and contracted the disease for the first time at a later age, when the risk that the infection will cause paralysis is much greater.

This explains why the first epidemics of poliomyelitis did not occur until this century and then only in the economically advanced countries." (Geoffrey Dean, "The Multiple Sclerosis Problem," *Scientific American,* vol. 223, no. 1, July 1970)

f. "Nearly everyone has seen sleeping pets whimper, twitch their whiskers, and seemingly pump their legs in pursuit of dream rabbits. But are they really dreaming? Since animals can't wake up the next morning and describe their dreams, the question seemed unanswerable. But recently, Dr. Charles Vaughan of the University of Pittsburgh devised an ingenious experiment so animals could tell us, at last, that they were indeed dreaming. Rhesus monkeys were placed in booths in front of a screen and taught to press on a bar every time they saw an image on the screen. Then the monkeys were wired to an electroencephalograph machine and placed back in their special booths. Eventually they fell asleep. Soon the EEG was recording the special tracings produced by the dreaming brains of the moneys. But most important—the sleeping moneys were eagerly pressing the bars. Clearly they were seeing images on the screens of their minds—they were dreaming. Or so Dr. Vaughan believes." (Bob Gaines, "You and Your Sleep," *Ladies Home Journal,* March 1967, p. 5)

g. Between 1844 and 1846, the death rate from a mysterious disease termed "childbed fever" in the First Maternity Division of the Vienna General Hospital averaged an alarming 10 percent. Curiously, the rate in the Second Division, where midwives rather than doctors attended the mothers, was only about 2 percent. How could the difference be explained? More important, did the explanation account for the disease itself? Despite heroic efforts for two years to account for the higher rate of childbed fever in the doctor-supervised division, medical researcher Ignaz Semmelweis remained thwarted. Then one day a colleague accidentally cut himself on the finger with a student's scalpel while performing an autopsy. Although the cut seemed innocuous enough, the man died shortly thereafter, exhibiting symptoms identical to childbed fever. A thought struck Semmelweis. Perhaps doctors and medical students, who spent their mornings doing autopsies before making their division rounds, were unwittingly transmitting the disease to the women by something they picked up from the cadavers. If he was right, the disease could be checked by requiring the doctors and students to cleanse their hands before examining patients. So Semmelweis insisted that they do just that: Doctors and students were forbidden to examine patients without first washing their hands in a solution of chlorinated lime. *Voilà!* In 1848 the death rate in the First Division was less than 2 percent.

h. The field of molecular biology is today one that rightly receives considerable attention. But it's actually a very young science, its beginnings going back only to the 1940s. In that decade geneticists Salvador Luria and Max Delbruck dramatized the importance of molecular biology of solving a major problem concerning the production of mutations in living organisms. Now, it was widely known at that time that certain viruses, termed bacteriophages, could attack and kill bacteria. What puzzled researchers, however, was that bacteriophages could not kill all bacteria; some resisted the bacteriophages. Not only that, the resistance proved to be a genetic trait, since the descendants of the bacteria also were resistant. So the question was, Were the mutations in the genetic material that lead some of the bacteria to be resistant produced by the attacking bacteriophages, or did they just arise spontaneously in the bacteria population? To decide which it was, Luria and Delbruck produced a number of bacteria cultures from a small number of bacteria. They then introduced bacteriophages into each culture. They reasoned that if the attacking bacteriophages produced the mutations leading to resistance, all the cultures should have about the same number of resistant bacteria because each was roughly the same size. But if the mutations arose by chance, the number of resistant bacteria should vary from culture to culture, depending on when the mutation appeared in the culture. After introducing the bacteriophages, Luria and Delbruck examined the cultures. They found great variance from culture to culture in the number of resistant bacteria.

i. How does the human memory work? In the 1950s, researchers speculated that the memory changes and stores certain chemicals in the brain. If memory is indeed a kind of chemical storage system, it might be possible to transfer memory from one organism to another simply by transferring chemicals from one brain to another. In the 1960s experiments were conducted to determine this conjecture. A group of rats were taught to get a small drink of milk by pressing a lever on the opposite side of their cage from where the milk was dispensed. Not much of a skill for a human, but a difficult task for a rat, taking a typical group about twenty-five hours to master. Chemicals were then taken from the brains of the trained rats and injected into the brains of similar, though untrained rats. At the same time, other untrained rats were injected with the chemicals from still other untrained rats. Researchers reasoned that untrained rats injected with the chemicals from trained rats should learn faster than untrained rats injected with the chemicals of other untrained rats. In fact, the rats injected with the "smart" chemicals mastered the task in an average of three hours. The others took about twenty-five.

j. Today we have tables and charts that give the positions of the various planets. But in the early 1800s, astronomers were still working them out. Of great aid, of course, was Newton's theory until the outermost planet, Uranus, raised some curious questions. Not only did Uranus's position differ from what Newton's theory predicted it should be, but the difference was too great to be attributed to inaccurate measurements. The conclusion seemed unmistakable: Either Newton's theory was wrong or something was interfering with the orbit. Because of its vast number of past accurate predictions, astronomers were most reluctant to abandon Newton's hypothesis. Then, in 1843, the English astronomer J. C. Adams and the French astronomer Le Verrier independently calculated that Uranus's unpredicted orbit could be accounted for if there was an additional planet beyond Uranus. This farther planet would exercise a gravitational force on Uranus that would explain its deviations from Newtonian predictions, which assumed no such planet. Assuming that the new planet was Newtonian in all respects, Adams and Le Verrier calculated where it should be at a particular time. In 1846 the planet was observed. Le Verrier named it Neptune.

2. Keeping in mind the criteria for a good hypothesis, construct a hypothesis to explain

   a. the increase in the divorce rate over the past ten years.
   b. why the candidate defeated in the last presidential election lost.
   c. the rise of the commune as a way of life for many people.
   d. the decline of membership and participation in institutional religion.
   e. the increase in terrorist activity over the past ten years.
   f. why there are so few female medical doctors in the United States as compared with Russia.
   g. the increase in crimes of violence against individuals over the past ten years.
   h. the increase in the number of working women over the past ten years.
   i. waning student interest in sociology and the humanities as college majors.

j. the increase in the rate of venereal disease over the past ten years.

k. the decrease in the past ten years of the average American male's life expectancy.

l. the increase in lung cancer among females.

m. the increase in the number of registered Independents, as opposed to Democrats or Republicans.

n. burgeoning interest in "self-care" as an alternative to conventional medical care.

o. why the universe is expanding.

3. Read a Sherlock Holmes story or view a television detective mystery. Analyze the hero's use of hypothesis to solve the crime.

4. In his book *An Inquiry Into the Human Prospect*, economist Robert Heilbroner detects three disquieting facts of contemporary life: (1) the population explosion, especially in underdeveloped countries; (2) the growing number of nations that have an H-bomb; and (3) the depletion of the world's natural resources. He contends that these will probably cause (A) future wars that will attempt to redistribute the world's wealth and (B) the rise of strong-armed leaders, even in the United States. Symbolically we could represent his hypothesis as follows: "If (1), (2), and (3) continue unchecked, then (A) and (B) will follow." By applying the criteria for a good hypothesis, evaluate Heilbroner's thinking.

Cause

To know truly is to know by causes.

FRANCIS BACON

"Whew!" Lucianna exclaimed, "that was some sermon Reverend Ed delivered. I'm relieved to see that more and more people recognize the dangers of pornography."

"Aw, c'mon," Gina groaned. "Everybody knows Reverend Ed is a fuddy-duddy. He thinks those ads for Jordache jeans are obscene."

"Yeah? Well the Meese Commission has just released its massive report on pornography. And after thousands of hours of careful study, they have identified *causal links* between pornography and sexual crimes against women and children, between pornography and homosexuality, and between pornography and all sorts of other sick forms of behavior. I'm with Reverend Ed— pornography *causes* sexual deviance and sexual violence."

"Hold on, now," Gina said. "Some researchers point out that countries like Sweden have fewer cases of rape and molestation than we do, and yet pornography is widely available there. How can pornography *cause* rape and stuff if Sweden has fewer sex crimes than we do?"

"Maybe the Swedes are too sick to notice how deviant they are," Lucianna countered. "Maybe they're just used to deviance."

"Hey! You took logic. Now you're arguing in circles, begging the whole question."

"Begging the question, am I? How come there are more pornographic bookstores, 'Adult Bookstores' they euphemistically call 'em—how's that for remembering my logic?—now than there were in the 1930s? And how come our national rates of rape and child molestation are going up? First, more dirty books, then more sexual deviance. Seems pretty clear to me that the more pornography there is in society, the more rapes and so forth."

"I can explain the increase in rapes," Mick butted in.

"Oh? Okay, if you're so smart, tell us," Lucianna said.

"Please, oh enlightened one, do tell us," Gina chimed in.

"Simple," Mick proclaimed, "women's lib!"

Gina and Lucianna looked on increduously as Mick continued. "Sure. You'll notice that the rate of both divorces and rapes has increased since the women's movement began in the '60s."

"Hold it right there," Gina said. "The women's movement began thousands of years ago. . . ."

"I mean *this* women's movement," Mick continued. "So-called sexual equality has really *caused* the breakdown of the family, as evidenced by our high divorce rates, by our increased sexual unhappiness, as evidenced by our high rates of promiscuity, venereal diseases, sexual abuse, and the like. I mean, open your eyes! The *cause* of all these problems is clear: feminism."

Is Mick right? Or Reverend Ed? Does rock and roll cause teenage delinquency? Does smoking marijuana lead inevitably to heroin addiction? Does an unhappy childhood *cause* an unhappy adulthood?

Before we can answer such questions, we must come to a clearer understanding of what we mean by "cause." We make causal claims daily, even though we don't necessarily use the term *cause* itself. Such terms as *make, prevent, produce, lead to,* and the like can and often do imply causal connections. There are literally thousands of such expressions and terms, all of which carry the idea of causation.

Such terms become part of what are called causal statements or causal hypotheses. *Let's define a causal statement as a statement that asserts a relationship between two things, such that one is claimed to effect the other.* Thus, "Vitamin C prevents the common cold," "Saccharin causes cancer," "Penicillin can cure syphilis"—all are causal statements or hypotheses asserting causal relationships.

Naturally, we'd be pretty foolish to accept or formulate a causal statement without reasons, that is, without causal arguments. *A causal argument is an argument that attempts to support a causal statement.* Causal arguments are another common form of inductive reasoning, and they abound. Just think about the countless commercial and public service messages you've seen, causal arguments about anything from toothpaste to nuclear energy. In your reading you come across causal arguments that relate to economics, politics, education, the arts— every field.

So given the centrality of causal argument in our lives, we should take a close look at this form of inductive reasoning. That's what this chapter aims to do. We're going to find out what makes for a good causal argument and consider some common informal fallacies associated with causal reasoning. But before we do that, we must look at this slippery idea of causation and precisely what a causal statement is asserting.

THE IDEA OF CAUSE

As we just saw, *a causal statement is a statement that asserts a relationship between two things, such that one is claimed to effect the other.* A simpler way to say this is that a casual statement is one that reduces to the claim that A causes B. But just what does it mean to say that A causes B—that the use of marijuana leads to heroin addiction, that cigarette smoking causes lung cancer, that oral contraceptives cause fatal blood clots? There is perhaps no more elusive a question in the philosophy of science.

To begin with, let's recall from Chapter 10 the problem of trying to discover the cause and cure of beriberi. At various stages in the research, rice, polished rice, and the lack of vitamin B_1 were thought to be the causes of beriberi. And in a sense each was. Put in the context of what medical scientists knew at the time about the prevention and treatment of beriberi, each of these rightly could have been termed a cause of the disease.

A case like this underscores an important point in understanding cause: A connection often exists between cause and control.[1] And a sound causal argument recognizes this connection. In the case of beriberi, the control interest is obvious: extermination of the disease. At one research stage, scientists observed widespread cases of beriberi where rice was a dietary staple. Conversely, no rice, no disease. The conclusion seemed unmistakable: If you want to avoid beriberi, avoid rice. Fine, but what of the society that is largely sustained by rice? Although beriberi is bad, starvation is worse. So, while people had an interest in controlling beriberi, they had a greater interest in avoiding starvation.

In this sense, the second hypothesis—"Polished rice is the cause of beriberi"—was a more satisfactory answer. It provided control over the disease while at the same time responding to the more pressing need to avoid starvation. But the lack of vitamin B_1 was the best causal explanation in the sense that it had the greatest potential for the prevention and cure of beriberi; *the hypothesis allowed for the most control.* At the same time it respected dietary interests. Thus, today we can in effect eat what we want, supplement our diet with B_1, and forget about beriberi.

The point is that, in general, a causal statement implies an interest in control. "Vitamin B_1 can prevent beriberi" implies that we have an interest in controlling that disease. Furthermore, any attribution of cause depends on what we know at a particular time. Thus, "Rice is the cause of beriberi," "Polished rice is the cause of beriberi," and "Lack of Vitamin B_1 is the cause of beriberi" illustrate the connection between what we assign as cause and where we stand relative to what we understand and know. What we assign as cause also is influenced by our own individual interests.

STUDY HINT

Any causal statement generally implies an interest in control.

---

[1]See Perry Weddle, *Argument: A Guide to Critical Thinking* (New York: McGraw-Hill, 1978), pp. 162–65.

To illustrate how idiosyncratic interests affect our attribution of cause, let's take the case of Pete's being late for a very important project-planning meeting at work. It seems that one morning Pete was deflected from his normal route to work by a fire that left the route cordoned off and traffic detoured. As a result, he arrived in the plant parking lot at 8:55, five minutes before the meeting. Now, ordinarily, this would be ample time for him to park and be punctual. But his usual parking place was occupied. That didn't surprise Pete because everyone in his section knew that unless they arrived by 8:45, they'd have to park in a remote area of the lot; the nearest parking spots were always occupied by that time. Had traffic not been detoured, Pete would have been in the lot by 8:45. As it turned out, he didn't even find a parking space until 9:00 A.M. He arrived at the meeting five minutes late.

Before he even got there, Pete knew what he was in for. Supervisor Severer was a stickler for punctuality. No excuse for tardiness ever satisfied him. Sure enough, when Pete walked in late, Severer jumped all over him. Pete claimed that he couldn't find a parking space. Severer insisted that it was poor planning on Pete's part that caused him to be late. "You should have given yourself more time!" the supervisor told a red-faced Pete.

Who was right—Pete or the supervisor? Well, it's not a matter of right or wrong. It's a question of one's interest, or viewpoint. In one sense, you could say that Pete's lateness was caused by the lack of a parking space. We might call that the *proximate cause* of his tardiness. In the view of many at the meeting, that represented a true and complete statement of cause. And they told Pete as much afterward. But obviously that cause didn't wash with Severer. In an attempt to calm him down, Pete explained to him about the fire and detour. And rightly so, for in another sense, these were the causes of his lateness as well. They are what might be called *remote causes,* as distinguished from the proximate cause.

Where there is a causal sequence of several events, say *A* causing *B*, *B* causing *C*, *C* causing *D*, and *D* causing *E*, *E* can be regarded as the effect of any or all of the preceding events. The *nearest* of them, *D*, is considered the proximate cause; the others are considered more and more remote. Thus, *A* is more remote than *B*, *B* is more remote than *C*, and so on.

STUDY HINT

The *proximate cause* is the one "nearest" the effect. Any other causes are *remote causes*.

The remote causes that Pete added to his initial proximate-cause explanation didn't impress Severer. He insisted that the lateness was caused by Pete's imprudence. And in a sense Severer was right, for this was a still more remote cause. Pete knew about the importance of the meeting. What's more, he knew how finicky Severer was about punctuality. He should have given himself more time, just in case an emergency arose. But he didn't, and, yes, *as a result,* he was late. The point is simple but important: *causes are not discrete.* One's interest and viewpoint frequently suggest different causes in a causal sequence or chain of several events.

So causation is associated with control and diverse interests. To understand the idea of cause is to recognize control and interest as integral parts of it.

Because of this connection, it's not surprising that we entertain many causal concepts that accommodate the degree of control we wish to exercise and the interests we have. Let's look at some of these concepts.

CAUSAL CONCEPTS

As we just saw, what makes the idea of cause so elusive is that cause may have different meanings under different circumstances. It's convenient to view causal statements, and supporting arguments, as possibly involving four different relationships between cause and effect. These relationships are generally termed *necessary, sufficient, necessary and sufficient,* and *contributory.* Although in some ways similar, these four relationships are different enough to be considered separate causal concepts.

Necessary Cause

A necessary cause is a condition that must be present if the effect is to occur. Thus, if in "*A* causes *B*" the term *causes* implies a necessary condition, then *A* must be present for *B* to occur. In other words, in the absence of *A*, *B* cannot occur, or simply "If no *A*, no *B*." In this sense, electricity is a necessary cause for light in a bulb; without electricity the light will not occur.

Sufficient Cause

A sufficient cause is any condition that, by itself, will bring about the effect. Thus, if in "*A* causes *B*," the term *causes* implies a sufficient condition, then when *A* is present, *B* will always occur. In other words, the presence of *A* is always enough to bring about *B*, or simply "If *A*, then *B*." In this sense, a blown fuse is a sufficient condition for a light to go out. If the fuse blows, the light will go out. But of course, a blown fuse is not a necessary condition for the light to go out; for should the fuse not blow, the light could still go out, perhaps because the power company turned off the current when you failed to pay the electric bill.

Necessary and Sufficient Cause

A necessary and sufficient cause is any condition that must be present for the effect to occur and *one that will bring about the effect alone and of itself.* Thus, if in "*A* causes *B*," the term *causes* implies a necessary and sufficient condition, then *B* will occur *when and only when A* occurs. In other words, *A* and only *A* is enough to bring about *B*.

Instances of a single necessary and sufficient condition are understandably rare, but they do occur. For example, a spirochete is a necessary and sufficient condition for syphilis. When and only when this spirochete occurs is there an instance of syphilis. Far more common are occasions of several necessary conditions that, taken together, constitute a sufficient condition and sometimes a necessary *and* sufficient condition. For example, taken together, current, bulbs in working order, correct current for the bulbs, and satisfactory wiring constitute a necessary and sufficient condition for an electric light to burn.

Contributory Cause

A contributory cause is a factor that helps create the total set of conditions, necessary or sufficient, for an effect. Thus, a violent storm can be a contributory cause to your room's suddenly being pitched into darkness. The violent storm can help create the conditions that cause the lights to go off. But obviously the light may go off without a storm; and the lights may remain on in the presence of a storm. So to say that *A* is a contributory cause of *B* is to say that *B* is more likely to occur when *A* occurs than when *A* does not occur. The lights in your room are more likely to go off in the presence of a violent storm than in its absence.

Usually we speak of contributory causes when we wish to emphasize the complexity of a problem. Thus, in discussing the cause of the fall of the Roman Empire, historians often cite a number of contributory causes: the rise of Christianity, moral decay, economic chaos, and so on. Of course, speaking of contributory causes doesn't rule out the possibility of focusing on one chief or sole cause. Thus, while mentioning the nexus of contributory causes to explain the fall of the Roman Empire, some historians have concentrated on the rise of Christianity, others on economic disorder. Once again, then, we are reminded of the role that one's interests and viewpoint play in the attribution of cause.

The danger in formulating any causal argument is the same danger we observed previously in discussing analogy and generalization: observing only the instances that confirm the causal hypothesis and ignoring violations of it. For example, a person might take notice only of those instances that confirm the hypothesis that vitamin C can prevent the common cold and ignore those instances that disconfirm it or tend to suggest that it may be just a contributory cause. In the same vein, another danger is to focus on a single cause, when in fact there are many contributory causes that account for a phenomenon. Failing to recognize and appropriately deal with the elusiveness of the whole idea of cause, we overlook these dangers and commit fallacies. We must look at these fallacies. But before we do, let's try to illuminate the problem of establishing probable causation. Let's try to devise some method of determining that *A* is the probable cause of *B*.

EXERCISE 11-1 _____

Is the relationship of the items that of necessary cause, sufficient cause, necessary and sufficient cause, or contributory cause, or is it noncausal?

 1. no sleep / fatigue
 2. overeating / illness
 3. deciding to raise your hand / raising your hand
 4. writing an essay / reading that essay
 5. bullet penetrating the heart / death
 6. Ayds (diet candies) / weight loss
 7. speaking / listening
 8. unscrewing a light bulb / no light
 9. friction / heat
10. infection / fever
11. increase in the prime interest rate / tighter money
12. fear / increase in adrenaline
13. sexual intercourse / sexual pleasure
14. increase in oil consumption / increase in oil prices

15. mature female / child
16. oxygen / fire
17. capital punishment / fewer capital offenses
18. saccharin / cancer
19. college education / earning potential
20. adaptability / survival
21. DNA / eye color
22. verbal skill / occupational success

METHODS FOR ESTABLISHING PROBABLE CAUSE

In evaluating any causal argument, we face two tasks. One is to determine whether a relationship between *A* and *B* actually does exist; the other is to determine whether the relationship is that type of causal relationship claimed to exist.

For example, Helen's college offers a number of television courses. One is called "The Long Search," a marvelous journey into the world's religions. Here's how the course is set up. "The Long Search" consists of about fifteen one-hour TV segments on different religions. Students enrolled in the course are expected to view the programs and complete reading assignments in conjunction with them. The only time the class ever meets as a group is for the final examination.

Helen's college offers a review session one week before the final. Students are invited, but not required, to attend this review. In the literature it mails to enrollees, the college claims that those who attend the review are more likely to perform better on the exam than those who don't attend. In effect, the college is claiming a causal relationship between review attendance and exam performance.

If we're to deal with such claims intelligently, the first thing we must do is to determine whether a relationship between review attendance and test performance does, in fact, exist. We might do this by monitoring the performance of review attenders over several terms. If, as a group, they perform better than those who don't attend the review, we have reason to suspect a relationship between attendance and performance. But this is *not* enough evidence to infer a causal relationship. The better performance could be caused by any number of things: Maybe the students who turned out for the review watched the programs more faithfully and did the assignments more conscientiously than the others; perhaps these students are better test takers to begin with; possibly review attenders could be superior students overall. The point is that considerably more is needed to establish a causal relationship.

Suppose the college randomly selected students enrolled in "The Long Search" and gave only these students the review. In each of several terms, this group as a whole outperformed those who didn't get the review. Assuming that the college *controlled relevant variables,* it would now be justified in inferring a *contributory* causal relationship between review attendance and test performance. But it would not be justified in claiming a *necessary* relationship.

In short, in formulating and evaluating causal arguments, we must judge whether the evidence establishes a relationship between a phenomenon and an alleged cause. In addition, we must determine whether the evidence establishes the relationship as the particular type supposed to exist. This is no mean undertaking. But the process is aided by several methods for establishing causal relationships. These methods are usually associated with the nineteenth-century English philosopher John Stuart Mill, who formalized them. We'll consider three: the method of agreement, the method of difference, and the method of concomitant variation.

Agreement

The method of agreement states that if two or more instances of a phenomenon have only one circumstance in common, *that circumstance is probably the cause (or the effect) of the phenomenon.* For example, suppose that in a particular section of the country a small group of twelve people contracts a lung disease. We wish to determine "the cause." We might begin our investigation by looking for any possible candidates for necessary conditions of contracting this lung disease. We collect basic information about our sample, which we represent on the following table, using *yes* to signify the presence of the following potentially significant conditions: working in the local coal mine, living near the paper mill, or having a history of tuberculosis in the family:

Case	Mine Worker	Paper Mill	TB in Family
1	yes	yes	yes
2	yes	yes	
3	yes		yes
4	yes	yes	
5	yes		
6	yes	yes	yes
7	yes		yes
8	yes	yes	yes
9	yes	yes	yes
10	yes	yes	yes
11	yes	yes	
12	yes	yes	yes

We see at a glance that the one common relevant antecedent condition is working in the local mine. Based simply on the method of agreement, we have a strong case for identifying that condition as the probable cause of this lung disease.

But our chart concerns only three variables. What if in addition to working in the mine all those with the disease also smoked? Is it working the mine, smoking, or some combination of the two which causes this lung disease? We need to add another method to the method of agreement.

Difference

The method of difference states that if an instance when the phenomenon occurs and an instance when it doesn't occur have every circumstance in common except one, *and that circumstance occurs only in the former, then that circumstance is probably the cause (or the effect) of the phenomenon.* The essence of this method is the elimination of all except one difference between the instances when the phenomenon occurs and those when it doesn't. Thus, to resolve the lung disease case, we interview other inhabitants of the area who have every relevant factor in common with the victims save one: They don't work in the coal mine. We isolate a difference. If none of the other people in the area—including smokers—has the disease, we can conclude that working in the coal mine is an indispensable part of the cause of the lung disease.

So using the method of agreement, we found that men having the lung disease shared two characteristics: They worked in the coal mine and they were heavy smokers. Using the method of difference, we found that working in the coal mine was an indispensable part of the cause of the disease. Clearly, it is not a sufficient condition, for not every coal miner contracted the disease. Taken together with heavy smoking, which itself may be an indispensable part of the cause, working in the mine *could be* a sufficient condition. Indeed, working in the mine and heavy smoking might turn out to be a necessary and sufficient condition. But more investigation is needed.

At the same time, our conclusions may turn out erroneous. Perhaps something else is causing the disease, something that we haven't yet detected. In other words, our causal argument is *probable, not certain*. This is why, when it is appropriate, both the method of agreement and difference are applied in testing for cause; we want as much probability as possible.[2] What's more, since in such cases we're really dealing with a hypothesis—a causal hypothesis—the factors we mentioned in the last chapter for judging hypotheses come into play. Of particular relevance in this lung disease case would be testing the inferences that can be drawn from the hypothesis that working in the mine is an indispensable part of the cause of the lung disease. Thus, if we gave every miner an air-filtration mask and ensured that they used it, we could at the least expect a marked decline in the incidence of the lung disease. Also, if the hypothesis is sound, we could expect to find an occurrence of this same disease among miners who work in substantially the same environment. Were these expectations borne out, the probability of our causal hypothesis would increase dramatically.

Whether agreement or difference, or a combination, it's clear that elimination is an integral part of establishing cause. The application of these methods, then, demands the presence or absence of certain circumstances or the occurrence or nonoccurrence of a specific circumstance. But what if this isn't the case?

For example, how would we establish a causal connection between air pollution and lung cancer? Since fresh country air no longer exists, we'd be hard pressed to eliminate polluted air, as called for by the method of difference. By the same token, we couldn't use the method of agreement, since polluted air is common to all the instances of lung cancer involved; that is, no matter who we are or where we are, we breathe air that is to some degree polluted. We need another method.

Concomitant Variation

The method of concomitant variation states that whenever a phenomenon varies in a particular way as another phenomenon varies in a particular way, a causal relationship probably exists between them. For example, the faster you drive your car, the greater the distance you need to stop it; the faster you drive your car, the fewer miles per gallon of gas you get. In the case of lung cancer and polluted air, we might be able to show that there's a direct relationship between an increase in air pollution and an increase in lung cancer.

[2]Mill called this combination of both methods "The Joint Method of Agreement and Difference."

A direct relationship means that as one thing increases, the other increases proportionately; or as one thing decreases, the other decreases proportionately. Speed and safe following distance would be an example of two things that bear a direct causal relationship to each other. The opposite of direct relationship is inverse relationship. *An inverse relationship means that as one thing increases, the other decreases proportionately; or as one thing decreases, the other increases proportionately.* Speed and fuel efficiency would be an example of this kind of causal relationship, generally speaking.

Clearly, the method of concomitant variation is based on a repeated, regular connection between one phenomenon and another. The fact is that such a connection is an integral part of the idea of cause and naturally plays a significant role in all methods of establishing causal relationship. Such a connection is often called a *correlation*. Do correlations establish causes? This question naturally arises in any discussion of causation, but it's especially present when concomitant variation is relied on to establish cause. The reason is that concomitant variation more overtly deals in statistical correlations than do the other methods. And there always exists the temptation to infer causation from a statistical correlation. Although sometimes a statistical correlation indicates a genuine causal factor, often it does not. When it does and doesn't, that is, the difference between a correlation and a causal relationship, is something we must now look at very closely. Failing to distinguish them, we invite fallacy into attribution of cause.

CORRELATIONS AND CAUSES

A correlation is a connection between properties that members of a group or population have. To elaborate on this definition, let's imagine a single population with two properties, each represented by a different variable. In any such case, we can always ask whether there's a correlation between the two variables.

Specifically, consider the student population at Helen's college. Respecting this population, sex is a variable with two possible values: male and female. Now, as our second property, let's take the course we mentioned earlier, "The Long Search." We may look on "The Long Search" as also having two variables: students who enroll in the course, whom we'll call "searchers" for short, and students who do not enroll in the course, whom we'll call "nonsearchers." Now, let's say that over several terms, the following statistical facts are established:

> Sixty percent of the female students are searchers. Fifteen percent of the male students are searchers.

Using these two statements, we may infer that sex and taking the "The Long Search" are correlated in the student population at Helen's college.

We may infer further a *positive* correlation between searchers and females in the student population. We call the correlation positive because the percentage of searchers among females is *greater* than among males. By the same token, we may say that there's a *negative* correlation between searchers and males. This means that the percentage of searchers among males is less than among females. If the percentage of searchers were identical for both females and males, then we could say that there was *no* correlation between searchers and sex in the student population at Helen's college.

We can use this example to generalize about these concepts. In any population, let *A* be a variable standing for any property that the members of the population might or might not have. For each member of the population, this variable has value *A* or Not *A*, which means the population is divided into two groups, the *A*'s and the Not *A*'s. (Thus, letting *A* stand for female, we get females and nonfemales, or simply males). Likewise, we can let *B* be another variable that divides the population into two groups, *B*'s and Not *B*'s (searchers and nonsearchers). Finally, we must have some percentage of the *A*'s (females) that are *B*'s (searchers) and some percentage of the Not *A*'s (males) that are *B*'s (searchers). Now we can say that B *is positively correlated with* A *if and only if the percentage of* B's *among the* A's *is greater than the percentage of* B's *among the Not* A's. (Being a searcher is positively correlated with being female if and only if the percentage of searchers among the females is greater than the percentage of searchers among the males.) On the other hand, B *is negatively correlated with* A *if and only if the percentage of* B's *among the* A's *is less than the percentage of* B's *among the Not* A's. (Being a searcher is negatively correlated with being female if and only if the percentage of searchers among the females is less than the percentage of searchers among the males.) Finally, B *is not correlated with* A *if and only if the percentage of* B's *among the* A's *is the same as the percentage of* B's *among the Not* A's. (Being a searcher is not correlated with being female if and only if the percentage of searchers among the females is the same as the percentage of searchers among the males.) Statisticians generally represent the strength of a correlation numerically on a scale from -1 to $+1$, with 0 representing no correlation, that is, no strength at all. The strength of the correlation between *B* and *A* is the fraction of *A*'s that are *B*'s minus the fraction of Not *A*'s that are *B*'s.

All the preceding is necessary to show why correlation is *not* necessarily causation. To see why, let's pretend, for simplicity, that there are just 200 students at Helon's college, equally divided between males and females. Based on the figures previously given, sixty females (60 percent) and fifteen males (15 percent) are searchers. Since the percentage of searchers among females is greater than the percentage of searchers among males, there is a positive correlation between searchers and females.

Now let's turn this around. Instead of determining whether being a searcher is positively correlated with being a female, let's ask whether being a female is positively correlated with being a searcher. To find out, we must divide the student population into searchers and nonsearchers. There will be 75 searchers (60 females + 15 males) and 125 nonsearchers (200 − 75). Of the searchers, 80 percent are females (60 of 75); of the nonsearchers, 32 percent are females (40 of 125). We can infer from this that being female is positively correlated with being a searcher.

Now, this kind of symmetrical relationship can be generalized to any positive or negative correlation. In other words, if *B* is positively correlated with *A*, then *A* will be positively correlated with *B*; if *B* is negatively correlated with *A*, then *A* will be negatively correlated with *B*. But causal relationships are *not* symmetrical relationships. Yes, increasing your speed *causes* you to get fewer miles per gallon; but getting fewer miles per gallon does *not* cause you to increase your speed. Again, decapitation is a *cause* of death; but death does *not* cause one to be decapitated. Similarly, smoking may be a *cause* of lung cancer; but lung cancer does *not* cause one to smoke. Putting the causal relationship abstractly: Where *A* causes *B*, *B* does not necessarily cause *A*. Clearly, then, when we assert a causal relationship, we are saying something quite different than when we assert a simple statistical correlation.[3]

The thing that's confusing, and often leads us astray, is that causation inevitably involves a connection between two things. For example, if we say that cigarette smoking causes lung cancer, implied in that is that there is a connection between smoking and getting cancer. But the connection is not just a correlation that holds that there are, in fact, more cases of lung cancer among smokers than among nonsmokers. To assert a causal relationship between smoking and lung cancer is to say that there *would be* more cases of lung cancer in the population if everyone smoked than if no one smoked, other factors remaining constant. And that is an entirely different statement.

To sum up, *a correlation is a relationship between properties that exist in some actual population.* In contrast, a causal relationship is defined in terms of a connection between two *hypothetical* versions of the real population. Failing to distinguish between a correlation and a causal relationship, we can grossly distort Mill's method of concomitant variation. Notice that the method of concomitant variation says that *whenever* a phenomenon varies in a particular way as another phenomenon varies in a particular way, a causal relationship probably exists between them. That "whenever" is crucial. Implied in it is that hypothetical version of the real population just mentioned. For example, let's say that there is a positive correlation between taking vitamin C and cold prevention. If on the basis of concomitant variation, you assert a causal relationship between vitamin C and cold prevention, what you're saying is that if everyone in the population took vitamin C, there would be fewer colds than if no one took vitamin C. Such statements relative to diseases are possible as, for example, with vaccinations and small pox or vaccinations and polio, or more analogously, with vitamin B_1 and beriberi. But to conclude that vitamin C can prevent the common cold, exclusively on the basis of a positive correlation, is not at all a proper application of the method of concomitant variation. Indeed, to argue that way is to commit the fallacy of questionable causation.

In fact, there are several common fallacies associated with causal arguments. Now that we've deepened our understanding of cause and considered some of the ways of establishing probable causation, let's take a look at these fallacies.

*EXERCISE 11-2 _____

1. Illustrate through a hypothetical example how you'd establish probable causation in the following cases by using Mill's methods of agreement and difference.

   a. food poisoning in a college cafeteria (a phenomenon, of course, that we all know is pure fantasy)
   b. a disproportionately large number of men to women enrolled in a philosophy course
   c. the failure of your car to start on a chilly morning
   d. your occasional but recurring tendency to stutter, stammer, or be at a loss for words.

2. Using capital letters (*A*, *B*, and so on) to indicate circumstances and small letters (*a*,

---

[3]We are indebted to Ronald N. Giere for his lucid discussion. See his *Understanding Scientific Reasoning* (New York: Holt, Rinehart and Winston, 1979), ch. 9.

b, and so on) to indicate phenomena, can you symbolically represent Mill's methods of agreement and difference?

3. Explain the difference between asserting a simple correlation and a causal relationship in the following cases:

   a. Christmas and an increase in suicides
   b. violence on television and violence in life
   c. the decline of membership in institutional religion and growing interest in the occult
   d. the women's liberation movement and an increasing number of working women

FALLACIES OF CAUSATION

Questionable Causation

The fallacy of questionable causation is an argument that asserts that a particular circumstance produces (that is, causes) a particular phenomenon when there is, in fact, little or no evidence to support such a contention. For example, when the Borana tribe in Kenya witnessed the solar eclipse of June 30, 1973, they claimed it was caused by the white men, who having landed on the moon, had learned the secrets of the heavenly bodies and were, presumably, tampering with them. Similarly, in Nigeria's Islamic Neth, emirs have waged *jihad,* holy war, on single women because the emirs believed the women had brought on a drought in western Africa. These are two obvious examples of questionable causation.

Questionable causation inevitably pops up when we infer causation from correlation. A classic example is found in anthropology. Anthropologists studying a South Seas tribe found its members believed that body lice advanced good health. In fact, every healthy person had some lice. In contrast, most sick people didn't. Clearly, then, there was a positive correlation between having lice and being healthy. But the lice didn't promote health. Being healthy caused a person to have lice! After all, lice aren't dummies. They don't want to leach off sick, feverish bodies. That's why the ill didn't have lice whereas the healthy did.

In questionable causation we mistake what is not the cause of a given effect for its real cause. But taking for a cause what is not a cause may occur in a less general way.

Post Hoc

The post hoc fallacy[4] *is an argument that asserts that one event is the cause of another from the mere fact that the first occurred prior to the second.* As an absurd example, suppose that after breaking a vase, a person fell and broke a leg. If we inferred that breaking the vase caused the accident, we'd be guilty of the post hoc fallacy. A more serious example is found in Egyptian history. Egyptians used to worship a bird named the ibis because each year, shortly after flocks of ibis had migrated to the banks of the Nile, the river overflowed its banks and irrigated the soil. The Egyptians believed the ibis caused the flood water, when of course both the birds' migration and the river's overflow were attributable to the change of season.

---

[4]The fallacy's full name is *post hoc, ergo propter hoc,* which literally means "after this, therefore because of this." It's better known simply as the post hoc fallacy.

The basis for post hoc fallacies is understandable. Causes precede events. So it's tempting to associate causally events occurring near one another. But neither immediate temporal succession nor more remote temporal succession is enough for establishing a causal relationship. Simply because the Roman Empire declined after the appearance of Christianity does not demonstrate that Christianity caused the decline of the Roman Empire. By the same token, just because Norman Cousins's collagen disease abated after massive doses of vitamin C doesn't mean that vitamin C caused the remission of the disease. True, such occurrences may suggest an association that should be further investigated. But temporal relationships alone are insufficient for establishing causal relationships, in the same way that correlations alone are insufficient for establishing causation.

Slippery Slope

The fallacy of slippery slope is an argument that objects to a position on the erroneous belief that the position, if taken, will set off a chain of events that ultimately will lead to undesirable action. For example, Sweeney opposes the legalization of marijuana primarily because he believes that such action will lead to the legalization of heroin and other "hard" drugs, which in turn will eventuate in America's becoming a drug culture. The fact is that legalization of marijuana does not have to lead to those things at all. The subsequent legalization of other drugs is a separate and distinct issue from the legalization of marijuana. What Sweeney fails to realize is that the legalization of marijuana is in no way a sufficient condition for the legalization of other drugs. Indeed, people who rely on slippery slope appeals don't understand what constitutes a cause. Whenever one can refuse, resist, or prevent *B* from occurring after *A*, then *A* cannot be said to produce *B* inevitably, inalterably, unequivocally.

Yet many celebrated arguments ignore this fact. A glaring example is the Vietnam War. How many times did we hear that if Vietnam went, Thailand would follow, then Burma, India, and so forth? But why a stand couldn't be taken at any one of these junctures—indeed, perhaps a strategically *better* stand—was never mentioned. Similarly, a U.S. Vice-President once defended a state governor's refusal to meet with prisoners at their request during a prison riot by insisting that had the governor met with them and refused to surrender the state, the prisoners would have demanded that the President of the United States meet with them. Obviously, if that scenario occurred, the President simply could have refused.

During the controversial property tax initiative campaigns in California in 1978, slippery slope appeals rang out on both sides. Those sponsoring the initiative insisted that, if it weren't passed, owning a home would quickly become a thing of the past. Those opposing the initiative claimed that, if passed, it would destroy education and the social welfare program and would cripple vital services such as police and fire protection. As scare tactics these ploys are pretty obvious. But as versions of questionable causation, they may not be.

Magical Thinking

The fallacy of magical thinking is an argument that uncritically attributes causal power to thoughts and words. For example, in a fit of anger, little Nick hollers at his brother Harry: "I hope you break your neck!" Later that same afternoon,

Harry falls off his bike and sprains his wrist. Nick is consequently consumed with guilt, believing that his angry words and thoughts somehow "caused" Harry's accident.

Psychologists sometimes refer to this pattern of thinking as "imminent justice." By that they mean that we assume that there will be an "instant accounting" for whatever we do or think—and that the act of thinking something is sufficient to trigger its occurrence. So the magical thinker who in a moment of temporary rage wishes you were dead, feels somehow responsible when you do, coincidentally, die a short time later.

In the examples we've just seen, magical thinking is a variation of post hoc. But sometimes, magical thinking occurs in other forms. Perhaps your parents used to warn you to watch what you say "or else it might come true." Here, even though nothing has as yet happened, the fear that just saying or thinking something might have the power to cause its occurrence is still an instance of magical thinking.

The origins of this fallacy are probably rooted in our primitive past, in which shamans, witch doctors, priests, and priestesses claimed to be able to control nature through the utterance of secret, powerful incantations. Thus, we "knock on wood" as we say something positive to assuage ancient Celtic and Druid gods and demons thought to have lived in trees ("wood"), we cross our fingers, and so on.

Growing evidence shows the importance of how we think to how we feel and even to physiological well-being. But these claims are based on careful, controlled observations; they do not attribute magical omnipotence to thinking or speaking. Whenever we *uncritically* attribute causal power to words or thoughts, we are guilty of magical thinking.

Oversimplification

The fallacy of oversimplification is an argument that treats a situation as if it involved only a few significant factors when in fact it involves a complex of many significant, interrelated facets. Consider this all-too-common example: You've just asked your logic instructor for tips on improving your grade. She responds with: "Well, it's really very simple. Just study more." Let's assume that in this case "more" won't help. You need a more detailed answer, such as: identify key concepts in the reading, take better notes, review your notes daily, ask questions in class. "Just study more," is too simple in this case (but not in every case!)

When we oversimplify our view of a situation, we deprive ourselves of enough information to make a reasonable analysis of it, and, thus, we deprive ourselves of any realistic chance of adequately dealing with it.

"The Republicans have caused our gross national debt." "The Democrats always cause inflation." Such statements are overly simplistic—and that is their appeal. They allow us the illusion of analysis without the effort, and they often encourage and reinforce stereotypes, prejudices, and faulty frames of reference.

Moore, McCann, and McCann point out that "Chronic oversimplifiers are easy to spot. They have a breezy, self-assured way of speaking and hold strong opinions on every subject. They are fond of such expressions as 'That's the situation in a nutshell'—as if any complex situation would fit into a nutshell."[5]

[5]W. Edgar Moore, Hugh McCann, and Janet McCann, *Creative and Critical Thinking* (Boston: Houghton, Mifflin Company, 1985), p. 313.

ADMINISTRATION WAR AGAINST DRUGS IN BOLIVIA...   AND IN U.S.A.

Copyright © 1986, Conrad for the *Los Angeles Times*. Reprinted with permission of Los Angeles Times Syndicate.

A dogmatic, overly exaggerated manner of speaking often accompanies oversimplification because, to the oversimplifier, everything is clear—too clear. "I don't see why the Russian people can't see that they're being lied to by the Kremlin. All they have to do is use a little common sense." Expressions such as "all they have to do" or "it's simple, just . . . " are warning signs, too. "My wife left me 'cause she didn't love me" may sound like an adequate explanation of a marriage's demise, but it usually isn't. To learn from such a tragedy, we need to delve more deeply into the myriad aspects that make up any marriage. "Losing weight's simple—just eat less and exercise more." To be helpful, such advice must dig deeper: It must deal with why it is so difficult to change dietary or behavior patterns, what food does that makes compulsive overeating addicting, and so forth.

One last class of examples here: hyperbolic (extremely exaggerated) claims. "That's my favorite movie of all time,"—uttered without reflection immediately upon leaving the theatre, or, "It was all your fault that we went broke," and the like, almost always signal oversimplification, in addition to whatever other fallacies they may involve: meaningless claims, provincialism, and others.

We see, then, that many fallacious arguments include some faulty causal assumptions and claims. These may be present in addition to, and as contributors to, other more easily spotted fallacies.

*EXERCISE 11-3 _____
Explain whether or not the following passages commit the fallacies of questionable causation, post hoc, slippery slope, magical thinking, or oversimplification.

1. "Impeach the Press!" (bumper sticker popular during times of intense domestic turmoil)

2. PHIL: That's the last time I'll leave that bedroom window open at night.
   PAT: But it's good to sleep in a roomful of fresh air.
   PHIL: Are you kidding? My throat's killing me!

3. INTERVIEWER: Three hundred people on board and all are killed but one—you. How do you feel about that?
   SURVIVOR: All I can say is it's a miracle.

4. JERRY: Of course we've been visited by astronaut-gods.
   ANNA: That's absurd.
   JERRY: Okay, know-it-all, how would you explain airstrips thousands of years old in primitive and remote areas of the earth?

5. CARRIE: You know, Don, you should get married.
   DON: Really?
   CARRIE: Sure. Married men on the average live longer than single men.
   DON: So what?
   CARRIE: So that proves that for men marriage is more conducive to a longer life than bachelorhood.
   DON: Okay, you've talked me into it. Let's get married.
   CARRIE: Don't be ridiculous. Within a month we'd be fighting, within a year we'd be separated, and within two years I'd have all your money.
   DON: Phew! I'm glad you mentioned that. I'd rather die young and rich than live old and poor.

6. MAURICE: So you're opposed to a national health insurance program, eh?
   MILLIE: And if you had any sense you would be, too. Who wants to live in a country where all its institutions are socialized? And that's what's going to happen if we pass this thing.

7. MYRA: Oh, don't bother offering Fred another cup of coffee. He never has more than a single cup.
   SUE: Oh really?
   MYRA: Ever since the night he had two cups and didn't sleep a wink, he never has more than one cup after dinner.

8. SHERYL: You know that expression "There are no atheists in foxholes"?
   TOD: Sure. I think it's probably true.
   SHERYL: Oh me, too. That's why I believe that deep down all people really do believe in God, even if they say they don't.

9. In every single case I've ever investigated, men convicted of rape have had pornographic magazines in their homes. It's clear that pornography causes sexual violence.

10. RYAN: You know, I really think we should encourage Israel to return any Libyan prisoners to the Libyans.
    ROSS: Why is that?
    RYAN: To ensure the safety of Americans currently held hostage there.
    ROSS: Don't be foolish! The next thing, we'd have every radical group in the world kidnapping Americans and making outlandish demands. Once you give in to any terrorists, you've set up a pattern of no resistance.
    RYAN: Wow! I never thought of that.

11. I kept hoping you'd call. I sat here and thought, "Call me! Call me!" And you did! I guess I've got more psychic powers than I realized.

12. It's clear to me that Dr. Duck is a miracle worker. For days I had these awful headaches. Then I went to Dr. Duck. He gave me a few of his secret formula injections. In a couple of days, I felt better.

13. "If you [sic] could get rid of drugs [in the work place], we'd be far ahead of other countries in productivity." (Ira Lipman, quoted in Stanley Penn, "Losses Grow from Drug Use at the Office," *Wall Street Journal,* July 29, 1981, p. 27)

SUMMARY

This chapter dealt with causation and causal argument. A causal argument is an argument that attempts to support a causal statement, that is, a statement that reduces to the claim that *A* causes *B*. In understanding the idea of cause it's important for us to remember that causes are not discrete; they are associated with control and various interests. This association results in several concepts of cause. It's convenient to view causal statements, and supporting arguments, as possibly involving four different relationships: necessary, sufficient, necessary and sufficient, and contributory.

A necessary cause is a condition that must be present if the effect is to occur. Electricity is a necessary cause for light in a bulb.

A sufficient cause is any condition that by itself will bring about the effect. A blown fuse is a sufficient cause for a light bulb to go out.

A necessary and sufficient cause is any condition that must be present for the effect to occur and one that will bring about the effect alone and of itself. A specific spirochete is a necessary and sufficient cause of syphilis.

A contributory cause is a factor that helps create the total set of conditions, necessary or sufficient, for an effect. A violent storm can be a contributory cause for your room's suddenly going dark.

The danger in formulating any causal argument is observing only the instances that confirm the causal hypothesis and ignoring violations of it. In evaluating a causal argument, we must determine (1) whether a relationship between *A* and *B* actually exists and (2) whether the relationship is that type of causal relationship claimed to exist. Helpful here are Mill's methods of establishing probable causation, of which we discussed three: agreement, difference, and concomitant variation.

The method of agreement states that if two or more instances of a phenomenon have only one circumstance in common, that circumstance is probably the cause (or the effect) of the phenomenon.

The method of difference states that if an instance when the phenomenon occurs and an instance when it doesn't occur have every circumstance in common except one, and that the circumstance occurs only in the former, then that circumstance is probably the cause (or the effect) of the phenomenon.

The method of concomitant variation states that whenever a phenomenon varies in a particular way as another phenomenon varies in a particular way, a causal relationship probably exists between them.

The subject of correlations naturally arises in connection with the method of concomitant variation, although correlations are an integral part of all causal statements and arguments. A correlation is a connection between properties that members of a group have. *B* is positively correlated with *A* if and only if the percentage of *B*'s among the *A*'s is greater than the percentage of *B*'s among the Not *A*'s. *B* is negatively correlated with *A* if and only if the percentage of *B*'s among the *A*'s is less than the percentage of *B*'s among the Not *A*'s. *B* is not correlated with *A* if and only if the percentage of *B*'s among the *A*'s is the same as the percentage of *B*'s among the Not *A*'s.

Correlations do not necessarily imply causation. A symmetrical relationship can be generalized to any positive or negative correlation. But causal relationships are not symmetrical. Furthermore, whereas a correlation is a relationship between properties that exist in some actual population, a causal relationship is defined in terms of a relationship between two hypothetical versions of the real population. Failing to distinguish between correlations and causal relationships, we often commit the fallacy of questionable causation: an argument that asserts that a particular circumstance produces a particular phenomenon when there is, in fact, little or no evidence to support such a conclusion, for example, the claim that body lice causes good health.

Another fallacy connected with causation is post hoc: an argument that asserts that one event is the cause of another from the mere fact that the first occurred earlier than the second, for example, the ancient Egyptians' belief that the ibis caused the Nile to overflow.

Still another causation-related fallacy is the slippery slope: an argument that objects to a position on the erroneous belief that the position, if taken, will set off a chain of events that ultimately will lead to undesirable action, for example, insisting that the legalization of marijuana will inevitably lead to the legalization of hard drugs and ultimately to the United States' becoming a drug culture.

An additional causal fallacy is known as magical thinking: an argument that uncritically attributes causal power to thoughts and words; for example, you yell at your friend, "I hope you fall off your bike and break your neck!" Shortly thereafter she falls and sprains her wrist. You conclude that your wish caused her accident.

The last causal fallacy we studied was oversimplification: an argument that treats a situation as if it involved only a few significant factors when in fact it involves a complex of many significant, interrelated facets. Example: "The Democrats cause inflation."

Summary Questions

1. "If one hundred police officers testify that every drug addict they arrested was found to have milk in the refrigerator at home, why can't we conclude that drinking milk leads to drug addiction?" (Carol Travis, "Porn Panel Report Doesn't Give Complete Analysis of Sexual Abuse," *Los Angeles Times;* reprinted in the *Redding Record-Searchlight,* July 12, 1986)
2. Discuss Gaffney's First Law of Nomenclature (named in honor of Wilbur G. Gaffney of the University of Nebraska): "You become what your name is." Examples used to "support" Gaffney's Law include a linebacker named Quash, an offensive lineman named Heavyside, an animal psychologist named Fox. (reported in Charles Osgood's column in *USA Weekend,* October 24–26, 1986)

ADDITIONAL EXERCISES _____

1. What are the explicit or implied conclusions in the following? Where appropriate, indicate which of Mill's methods are being used. Do you think the conclusions are strong? If they could be strengthened, explain how.

   a. "On August 23, 1948, individual tagged fruits of Rome Beauty apples and adjacent spur leaves were sprayed at the Plant Industry Station, Beltsville, Maryland, with aqueous solutions of 2, 4, 5-T at 10-, 100-, and 200-ppm concentrations. Fruits that received either the 100- or the 200-ppm spray concentration developed red coloration and were maturing rapidly by September 13. This same stage of maturity on unsprayed fruits was not attained until one month later, October 12, the usual harvest date for this variety. At 10-ppm concentration, the spray had no observable effect. Measurements on fruit softening were made on September 27 with the aid of a fruit pressure tester. At this time the untreated fruits showed an average pressure reading of 25.9 lbs., whereas the fruits sprayed with 10-, 100-, and 200-ppm concentrations of 2, 4, 5-T tested 24.8, 19.8, and 18.9 lbs., respectively." (P. C. Marth et al., "Effect of 2, 4, 5 Trichlorophenoxyacetic Acid on Ripening of Apples and Peaches," *Science,* vol. 3, no. 2883, March 31, 1950)

b. "It has long been assumed that a diet low in saturated fats (meaning mostly animal fats) can reduce the risk of cardiovascular disease. Direct evidence for this assumption, however, has been scarce. Such evidence is now provided by a study made at a veterans' hospital in Los Angeles. The study shows that the incidence of cardiovascular disease in a group of 424 veterans with a diet high in unsaturated fats for eight years was 31.3 percent, whereas a control group of 422 men with a normal diet high in saturated fats had a cardiovascular disease rate of 47.7 percent." ("Science and the Citizen," *Scientific American,* vol. 221, no. 3, September 1969)

c. ABE: There's no question that the Democrats are the "war party."

TOM: That's absurd!

ABE: Is it? Wilson, a Democrat, was President when the United States got into World War I. Roosevelt was in charge when we entered World War II. And who was President when we sent troops to Vietnam? Kennedy—another Democrat! Now I ask you—what other conclusion can you draw but that American wars are caused by Democratic administrations?

d. MARIE: I sure wish I could get my coleus to grow.

MATT: Have you tried talking to it?

MARIE: What?

MATT: I mean it. I have two coleuses. A month ago they were just about the same size and color and in the same state of health. Which stands to reason, because they're in the same room where they get the same amount and degree of light. Well, for the past month I've been giving both the same amount of water and plant food, and I've been spraying them in the same way. The only difference is that I speak softly to one, but not the other.

MARIE: And now I suppose you're going to tell me that one's bigger, brighter, and healthier.

MATT: If looks are any indication, the one I talk to is—a full 8 inches longer, much brighter, and apparently thriving, compared to the other.

e. "The commissioners are convinced that many more inmates should be paroled. For prison experience unquestionably boosts the chance that an offender will break the law again. In one experiment, conducted by The California Youth Authority, a group of convicted juvenile delinquents were given immediate parole and returned to their homes or foster homes, where they got intensive care from community parole officers. After five years, only 28 percent of the experimental group have had their paroles revoked, compared to 52 percent of a comparable group that was locked up after conviction" ("Crime and the Great Society," *Time,* March 24, 1967, p. 21)

f. CHAD: All this talk about vitamin C preventing colds—I think it's a lot of bunk.

CAROL: Not me. I'm taking about 2,000 milligrams of it a day and I haven't had a cold all year.

CHAD: Big deal. There's nothing scientific about that. But let me lay this on you. Researchers recently carried out a mass experiment on 2,500 army conscripts. They were randomly divided, with half receiving 200 milligrams of ascorbic acid a day and the other half receiving placebos. And guess what—absolutely no difference was noted in the frequency or duration of colds or diseases of any description in the two groups!

g. "Aristotle believed a moving object could continue in motion only as long as something moved it. In the case of a projectile, air displaced by compression in front of the object came around behind it and pushed it along. The new medieval theory of 'impetus' insisted that a moving object continues to move until it is stopped by resistance: air has nothing to do with motion except insofar as it is a cause of friction. The anti-Aristotelian scientists of the fourteenth century used the rotary grindstone (a device that, as we have seen, was unknown to Aristotle) as a favorite nonspeculative proof of their position. The grindstone still turned for a time after the grinder's hand left the crank, but its motion, unlike the motion of a traveling projectile, displaced no air. Therefore the grindstone moved not by pressure of air but by impetus until the resistance of friction at the axle stopped it." (Lynn White, Jr., "Medieval Uses of Air," *Scientific American,* vol. 223, no. 2, August 1970)

h. MAUDE: Don't tell me you're ordering a cheeseburger.

HARRY: Sure, why not?

MAUDE: Because meat contains large amounts of cholesterol and saturated fat, which stimulates the production of cholesterol. And cholesterol contributes to heart attacks.

HARRY: How do you know so much about all this?

MAUDE: I just read a study conducted on Seventh-Day Adventists. They don't eat meat at all, you know. Well, the study reports that Seventh-Day Adventist males suffered only 60 percent as much heart disease as other American males. And even where they did develop it, it was much later in their lives.

HARRY: Wow! . . . Hey, waiter! Cancel that cheeseburger, will you? I'll have the soybean burger with alfalfa sprouts on the side and a small plate of mash.

i. "Two ads were prepared, set in editorial style with no pictures, two columns, 100 editorial lines. The last paragraph a phone number. Ad number 1 differed from ad number 2 only in headline. Number 1's read, "It's not the heat it's the humidity. New room coolers dry the air.' Number 2's headline read, 'How to have a cool home. Even on hot nights.' Number 1 was run one Friday in May in the local daily (circ. 400,000) and number 2 was run the following Friday. Number 1 produced 75 calls, number 2 produced 160 calls. Obviously number 2 was more effective at generating response." (Perry Weddle, *Argument: A Guide to Critical Thinking.* New York: McGraw-Hill, 1978, p. 187)

j. "It's not hard to demonstrate the key role that the love song plays in mating. Remove the male fly's wings and he will court with the same persistence as before, but his courtship is seldom successful. It is apparent that the male's wing display, at least, is a prerequisite to mating. Indeed, one species (D. obscura) sings no song and courts only by means of a silent wing display. This, however, is one of the few fruit fly species that will not mate in the dark. Since most species breed successfully at night, one must conclude that visual display alone is not enough to win female acceptance. The importance of sound to the female is also easy to demonstrate. Our colleague A. W. G. Manning has shown that when the antennae of a sexually responsive female are immobilized with glue, she ceases to be receptive." (H. C. Bennet-Clark and A. W. Ewing, "The Love Song of the Fruit Fly," *Scientific American,* vol. 223, no. 1, July 1970)

k. MOTHER (to teenage daughter): Judy, I wish you wouldn't start smoking.

JUDY: Oh, I don't intend to, Mom. I know it's bad for your health.

MOTHER: It's not just that. I just read a study that links smoking to having sex.

JUDY: You're kidding!

MOTHER: Uh-uh. Two hundred and fifty boys and girls were interviewed at random. Fifty-seven percent of the boy smokers reported engaging in sexual intercourse, whereas only 23 percent of nonsmokers said they had. Of the girls, 31 percent of the smokers had had sex. Only 8 percent of the nonsmokers had.

JUDY: On the other hand, Mom, I'm inclined to think that the health hazards associated with smoking have been greatly exaggerated.

l. CITY COUNCIL MEMBER: Chief, every year you come before us and ask for more money to fight crime.

POLICE CHIEF: But, believe me Councilman, it's necessary.

CITY COUNCIL MEMBER: How can you say that? In 1978 we budgeted $30,000 for law enforcement and that year you reported a total of 200 crimes. In 1979, we gave you $35,000 and you reported 275 crimes. Last year we upped the ante to $40,000 and you have just reported that a whopping 380 crimes were committed!

POLICE CHIEF: What are you getting at?

CITY COUNCIL MEMBER: What I'm getting at is a *reduction* in your budget to $25,000.

POLICE CHIEF: You can't be serious!

CITY COUNCIL MEMBER: On the contrary. It's obvious to me that that's the only way we're going to reduce the annual crime rate in this city.

m. "Dew, the deposit of moisture on the outside of a cold glass, and the condensation of steam on the inside of a teacup all have one thing in common: air containing moisture is cooled to the point where it can no longer contain it all. This, then, is the cause of the phenomena: temperature dropping below the point of supersaturation." (Gerald Runkle, *Good Thinking: An Introduction to Logic.* New York: Holt, Rinehart and Winston, 1978, p. 255)

n. ANDY: Gimme a straight whiskey, will you?

BARTENDER: No water this time?

ANDY: No way. I've tried scotch and water, vodka and water, brandy and water, even whiskey and water—and every time I get kind of wobbly in the knees. No more water for me.

BARTENDER: Makes sense to me.

o. BILL: I think they should lower the speed limit to 40.

BUCK: That's pretty low. Lots of people favor raising it from 55.

BILL: I know, but don't you realize that traffic fatalities declined after the national speed limit was reduced to 55 mph?

BUCK: Yeah, but maybe cars or roads are safer or somethin'?

BILL: Naw! It's pretty clear: lower the speed limit, lower the death rate.

p. Sin causes punishment: AIDS is spread by homosexuals, and the Bible condemns homosexuality.

2. State the correlations that can be drawn in the following passages. Is there any reason to think that the correlation provides any support for a causal hypothesis? Explain.

a. The results of a nationwide poll indicate that 68 percent of females older than eighteen favor the equal rights amendment, and 41 percent of males older than eighteen favor it.

b. U.S. Bureau of the Census statistics indicate that in the fifty-to-sixty-five-year-old age bracket five of every six divorced males marry for the second time; three of every four divorced women do.

c. A survey indicates that 57 percent of college students with below-average grades smoke pot; 21 percent of non-pot-smokers have below average grades. Opponents of the legalization of marijuana claim that these figures prove that pot smoking causes one to get below-average grades. Others argue that getting below-average grades causes one to smoke pot. Is there reason to think that the correlation provides more justification for one causal hypothesis than for the other?

d. A study indicates that 52 percent of those earning in excess of $22,500 a year favor gasoline rationing, whereas 33 percent of those earning less than that figure favor gasoline rationing.

e. A study is conducted to find out whether people think that a government should give in to terrorist demands if that is the only way to save the lives of hostages. Eighty-eight percent of those who have been hostages say a government should; 11 percent of those who have never been hostages say it shouldn't.

f. A survey indicates that considerably more people who earn in excess of $30,000 a year believe that the United States should take whatever means necessary to secure enough industrial resources from third-world countries to ensure "the American way of life" than people making less than $30,000 a year.

g. Fifty-seven percent of "regular church or synagogue goers" are found to believe that at least some UFOs are extraterrestrial space travelers, as opposed to 21 percent of those who don't regularly attend a church or synagogue.

h. Teenage suicides often occur in clusters.

i. Various studies show that virtually all heroin addicts have smoked marijuana.

j. Records indicate that crime rates increase during periods of the full moon.

k. Records indicate that crime rates decrease during cold spells.

l. Male children of alcoholics are four times more likely to be alcoholics than are male children from nonalcoholic homes.

m. Every time I wash my car it rains.

n. A study of thirty celebrated American authors over fifteen years by University of Iowa psychiatrist Nancy C. Anderson finds that 80 percent were treated for mood disorders (compared with 30 percent of a control group), 43 percent experienced manic-depression (compared with 10 percent of the control group), 30 percent suffered alcoholism (compared with 7 percent of the control group), and two of the authors committed suicide. (reported in *Psychology Today,* April 1987)

3. Identify the fallacies, if any, in each of the following: questionable causation, post hoc, slippery slope, magical thinking, oversimplification.

a. CRAIG: This bread you baked is great!

JAN: It must be the sea salt. I ran out of regular salt for this batch.

CRAIG: What a difference! You should use it all the time.

b. "Everybody I talked to there (in Vietnam) wants to know why they can't go in and finish it, and don't let anybody kid you about why we're there. If we weren't, those Commies would have the whole thing, and it wouldn't be long until we'd be looking off the coast of Santa Monica [at them]. [Bob Hope, quoted in Anthony J. Lukas, "This is Bob (Politician-Patriot-Publicist) Hope," *New York Times Magazine,* October 4, 1970, p. 86]

c. The women's liberation movement is partly responsible for the energy crisis because it's encouraged more women to enter the job market. This means more people are consuming energy on highways and at jobs than there used to be. (a paraphrase of General Electric's energy systems manager John C. Fischer in a speech to the National Academy of Science, January 29, 1973)

Reactions to Fischer's remarks: "It's an incredible distortion. It's convulsive. We are becoming energy gluttons not because women are out working but because companies like G.E. are pushing energy-consuming appliances down our throats." (Ellen Zawell, head of National Consumer Congress) "The energy crisis started because of incredibly poor planning on the part of men." (Karen De Crow, author of *Sexist Justice*) "Women certainly have been wasteful. They have been taught to be ostentatious, to be the consumers. . . . But it's predominately a male-oriented values system. Women were taught to please men." (all quoted in the *Los Angeles Times,* January 30, 1974, p. 10)

d. Every millionaire in this city has blue eyes. Who would think the color of a person's eyes affects how much money they have?

e. If marijuana is legalized, then sure as shootin' heroin and cocaine are on the way.

f. PARENT: I hope there's not going to be any beer at that party tonight.

EIGHTEEN-YEAR-OLD SON: There may be. Why?

PARENT: Please don't have any son. Taking the first drink is the surest way to end up an alcoholic.

g. While General Grant was handily winning battles in the West, President Lincoln received lots of complaints about Grant's drinking. One day a delegation told the President, "Mr. President, the General is hopelessly addicted to whiskey." To which Lincoln is said to have replied, "I wish General Grant would send a barrel of his whiskey to each of my other Generals!"

h. SAM: Did you know that a greater percentage of men in America smoke than women?

LIL: That just goes to show that being a male is a contributing factor to smoking.

i. MARSHALL: There's no question that if a person wants to be wealthy they should enroll in an Ivy League college.

LAVERNE: Why? Are they giving away bushel baskets full of money to jack up their enrollments?

MARSHALL: Almost. A study just released shows that twenty years after graduation, Ivy League graduates have an average income five times that of people who have no college education.

j. "I've always reckoned that looking at the new moon over your left shoulder is one of the carelessest and foolishest things a body can do. Old Hank Bunker done it once, and bragged about it: and in less than two years he got drunk and fell off the shot-tower and spread himself out so that he was just kind of a layer, as you may say; and they slid him edgeways between two barn doors for a coffin, and buried him so, so they say, but I didn't see it. Pap told me. But anyway it all come of looking at the moon that way, like a fool." (Mark Twain, *Huckleberry Finn*)

k. "Fascism thus repudiates the doctrine of pacifism—born of renunciation of the struggle and an act of cowardice in the face of sacrifice. War alone brings up to its highest tension all human energy and puts the stamp of nobility upon the people who have the courage to meet it. All other trials are substitutes that never really put men into the position where they have to make the great decision the alternative of life or death." (Benito Mussolini, *Encyclopedia Italiana*)

l. "Is it really a coincidence that the height of the Pyramid of Cheops multiplied by 1,000 million corresponds approximately to the distance between the earth and sun? That is to say, 93 million miles?" (Eric von Daniken, *Chariots of the Gods*)

m. Letter to the editor on the subject of high apartment rents: "The high rents are the result of our officialdom neglecting to plan ahead, and just spending merrily, including pay raises and pensions for themselves, that resulted in these usurious property taxes. Now they want to use the apartment owner as a scapegoat to pacify the outraged senior citizens," presumably by controlling rents, limiting increases, and so on (*Los Angeles Times*, December 1, 1977)

n. INTERVIEWER: Why do you think [rapes are up]?

L.A. POLICE CHIEF ED DAVIS: I don't know. I'm trying to find out. I had a meeting with a bunch of policemen recently and I asked them how many had arrested rape suspects, and all of them had. How many of them had found any unusual quantity of pornographic literature in the rape suspects' homes? All of them had. Pornography gets into the hands of socially inadequate people who can't express themselves normally and be attractive, in love, or go through the courting routine and all that sort of thing." (*New West*, December 19, 1977)

o. " 'Before he took B-15 he (her husband) could barely get up for his meals (because of a severe heart condition),' said Jaye Link, a 51-year-old Glen Cove, New York, widow. 'Two weeks after he started taking the vitamin pill he was completely changed.' Then Bill stopped taking the vitamins. Three months later he was dead—victim of a fifth heart attack. . . . Now Mrs. Link takes B-15 herself for arthritis. 'I take it constantly, three 50 milligram tablets a day,' she said. 'I have a slipped disc in addition to the arthritis. I tried everything under the sun to relieve the pain. But nothing else has worked.' " (*Globe*, September 11, 1979, p. 22)

p. RHETA: That chicken should taste a lot less oily than usual.

ROB: Really? Why's that?

RHETA: I used Wesson this time. You've seen their commercial, haven't you?

ROB: The one where the actor returns the oil to the bottle after frying the chicken and the oil measures only a tablespoon less than it did to start with?

RHETA: That's the one.

ROB: Did you test it for yourself?

RHETA: Not this time, but I intend to.

q. TRACY: I think it would be terrible if the state legalized gambling.

TROY: But think about the revenue it would generate. That would really help out social services.

TRACY: Maybe. But do you want drugs, prostitution, and organized crime?

TROY: Well, no.

TRACY: Then you better think again about the merits of legalized gambling.

r. My wife left me because I wouldn't go to her mother's for Christmas; can you believe it?

s. After Baba Bubba touched my head I felt such a healing peace that I cannot doubt his holy powers.

t. "Order today: The Seven Magic Words to Guarantee Success! Learn the seven magic words to use to retrieve lost objects, to mend broken relationships, to get a job—and more!" (ad for cassette tape)

u. After his team lost the sixth game of the 1986 World Series, Dwight Evans said, "We've got to come back and win one ball game. Nothing more. It's as simple as that." (Lowell Cohn, *San Francisco Chronicle,* October 27, 1986)

12

Statistics

There are three kinds of lies—lies, damned lies, and statistics.

BENJAMIN DISRAELI

One of the most heated and controversial political campaigns in recent California history was the 1986 campaign for the reelection of the Chief Justice of the California Supreme Court, Rose Bird. Opposition to the then-Chief Justice was intense, centering primarily on the fact that virtually every capital punishment verdict sent before the Bird court had been overturned. This led Bird's detractors to accuse her of being "prodefense." Surprisingly, however, the *California Journal* reported that "85 percent of Chief Justice Rose Bird's decisions tend to favor prosecutors," and *Time* magazine reported that Bird's "backers claim that she sided with the prosecution 90 percent of the time."[1]

What were the "facts"? Was the Chief Justice inclined to "favor" either

---

[1] Thomas Sowell, "Painting Bird as 'Pro-Prosecution' Is to Use Fine-Haired Brush Indeed," Scripps Howard News Service, October 16, 1986.

the prosecution or the defense? One way to answer the question is to consult the statistics.

But there is a problem. If we consider *all* the petitions coming before any supreme court, virtually *every* supreme court is "proprosecution"—because most of the cases petitioning review are initiated by defendants. And since most cases are denied a hearing by most supreme courts, most decisions are "against" defendants—or "proprosecution." And so it was that Bird's opponents, citing only capital cases, were able to claim that the Chief Justice was "anti-victim" and "anti-law and order," whereas her defenders, using a data base of all petitions presented to the court, were able to claim that her court was predominately "proprosecution."

It's precisely this kind of statistical sleight-of-hand that confuses and frustrates so many of us and mocks sound inductive process. Both Bird's supporters and her opponents based their claims on statistical samples. And each faction, not surprisingly, chose the sample that best suited its purposes. But since we are often unaware of all of the relevant factors involved in statistical claims, most of us have fallen victim to the misuse or misunderstanding of a statistical sample.

One reason for our vulnerability to statistics is that ours is a fact-minded culture. Graphs, averages, trends, relationships—all feed our hunger for facts. When someone claims that "Violent crimes have increased 12½ percent in the last six months" or "Zombie aspirin has been found 25 percent more effective in relieving pain than any other nonprescription analgesic," we listen. The language of statistics impresses us; it sounds authoritative. And the more precise the statistic, the more convincing. In a word, even the most absurd claims sound plausible when propped up with a statistic.

In one sense all inductive arguments rely on statistics since they base their conclusions on a number of observed specifics. But things like studies, polls, and surveys supposedly use statistics in precise, scientific ways to generate inductive conclusions. It's this use of statistics, and the common devices that rely on them, that concerns us in this final chapter devoted to inductive reasoning.

We are considering this topic last in our look at induction to emphasize that statistics can be associated with any form of inductive conclusion: generalization, analogy, hypothesis, or cause. For example, someone might decide to buy an Aquarius compact car because it will have a high resale value. The belief about the resale value of the Aquarius is based on using statistics in an analogical argument: Statistically, the Aquarius has had a higher resale value than any other comparable compact. Another person could argue to a hypothesis that since a certain percentage of colds clear up after treatment with antihistamine pills, antihistamine pills can cure colds. This final example is, of course, also an illustration of how statistics can be used in causal reasoning.

By the time you complete this chapter, you'll have a good idea of how statistics are used in inductive arguments. More important, you'll know what to watch out for in statistical arguments, the common fallacies that such arguments often commit. Although we can't promise that you will never again be hooked by statistics, you will be a tougher fish to land.

STUDIES, SURVEYS, POLLS

"Two out of three doctors recommend Bayer," "By 1991 more women will be contracting lung cancer than breast cancer," "Eighty-four percent of Golden

Lights smokers switch from higher-tar brands and stay," "More people watch CBS in a given week than any other network," "Sixty-one percent of the American people believe the President is doing a mediocre or poor job," "Studies prove that saccharin can cause cancer." "By 1995 every person in the United States will personally know someone who has AIDS." Our world is alive with statistics. In the battle for our minds we may be the casualties. We must be careful.

Before considering the common fallacies associated with statistics, let's take a brief and admittedly superficial look at the usual spawning grounds for statistics: studies, polls, and surveys.

Studies

Probably there are no research studies that bombard us more on a daily basis than those associated with aspirin. Aspirin advertisers, regardless of the brand, continue to make claims for their product's superiority. Some even "back up" their claims by quoting "studies conducted by a major university." The makers of Bayer and Tylenol have even taken out full-page ads disputing, and supposedly refuting, the claims made by the other. It has reached the point that whenever a white-smocked individual with stethoscope appears on the TV screen pushing some brand of aspirin, some of us are tempted to launch into a profanity-peppered diatribe against misleading commercials. The upshot, of course, is that we're often left with, well, a splitting headache. It seems as if such commercials exist, not to offer relief, but to produce pain!

Our consternation is understandable. For one thing, tests independently conducted some years ago by Robert C. Batterman at the New York Medical College and Dr. G. A. Cronk at Syracuse University have shown that "there are no significant differences in speed of absorption, promptness of pain relief, or safety between plain and buffered aspirin."[2] In addition, the amount of food in the stomach and the user's emotional state determine absorption rate more than an antacid that may be in an aspirin. Obviously, until consumers know what the aspirin companies' studies entail—including the mental and physical state of the subjects in the study—they're unwise to accept the product's claim on the basis of some authoritative-appearing figure.

The fact is that in the case of aspirins we're probably better served by reading a report of a comparative study of Bayer Aspirin, St. Joseph's Aspirin, Bufferin, and Excedrin in the December 1962 issue of the *Journal of the American Medical Association*. There we learn *specifics* of the study and can thus evaluate the truth of the conclusion that no significant differences were found among the products in their effectiveness and speed in easing pain.

Cold remedies advertised on television and in magazines are another thing that can drive the concerned consumer right up the wall—especially when he or she has a cold. And rightly so. Cold remedies also make questionable claims based on dubious research. As sincere as much of the research may be, it's still difficult to diagnose accurately the cause of acute nasal and throat congestion. Nor is it any easier to determine the effect a person's mental state plays in relieving cold symptoms. And since very little is known and understood about the common cold, it's tough to forecast the course of a virus-induced cold. In

[2]The Editors of Consumer Reports, *The Medicine Show* (Mount Vernon, N.Y.: Consumers Union, 1972), p. 14.

short, no available evidence provides probability high enough to justify some antihistamine claims that a particular product *causes* symptomatic relief. Indeed, in controlled clinical trials, antihistamines have been found only as effective as placebos (inert pills) in relieving cold symptoms. "Over the long haul, the antihistamines have proved of no real value against the common cold; further- more, they produce in many users such side effects as drowsiness, dizziness, and headache."[3]

What can we say, then, about these kinds of studies that are used to sell products? Before accepting their findings as justification for buying and using a product, we should satisfy ourselves on a number of points. These can be put in the form of questions:

1. Who were the subjects involved in the study?
2. For how long was the research conducted?
3. Who conducted the study—the company itself or some independent agency such as the National Institutes of Health, the Food and Drug Adminis- tration, the Federal Trade Commission, a nonpartisan university?
4. Who participated in the study—physicians, medical centers, hospitals?
5. To which stage of reseach does the claim refer—test tube, animal, human?
6. How was the study conducted; were all the variables accounted for; what methods were used to establish causation between product usage and claimed results?
7. How extensive was the testing?
8. How many subjects were involved; what were their backgrounds; were they always under control during the testing; how were they selected?
9. Were follow-up studies conducted; for how long?
10. Did the subjects report side effects; at what stages; did they report cures or relief; how were their reactions different from those using conventional treatment or products?

EXERCISE 12-1 _____
From your television viewing and from reading compile a list of ads that include studies or findings. How many are documented? Write to an advertiser and ask for the specifics of a study. Include in your letter questions from the preceding list.

Polls and Surveys

We should ask similar questions of what can be another great source of unre- presentative generalizations: the poll or public opinion survey. So common have these become in our society that most politicians automatically write into their campaign budget amounts for poll taking. As Roll and Cantril pointed out in their fine, succinct work on the subject, sometimes this figure is staggering, as it was in the 1972 presidential election: Candidates spent in excess of $1.5 million just taking polls.[4] (Now, such a figure is not uncommon in *state* elec- tions!) The money is often well spent, however; for despite criticism, polls, if properly conducted, are extremely accurate in their predictions. Of course they cannot predict the outcome of an election with certainty; but by using the

[3]Ibid., p. 19.
[4]Charles W. Roll, Jr., and Albert H. Cantril, *Polls: Their Use and Misuse in Politics* (New York: Basic Books, 1972), p. 31.

inductive method together with sound statistical procedures, they can make highly probable predictions. Unfortunately, people conducting polls do not always use sound procedures, as they didn't in the notorious *Literary Digest* poll of 1936, which predicted a Landon victory over Roosevelt. Just as erroneous were the polling methods that led to the prediction of a Dewey victory over Truman in 1948 and a Wilson victory over Heath in Britain's 1970 elections.

People harbor several misconceptions about polls and surveys, which sometimes make us more gullible, sometimes more skeptical, than we should be. First, many of us believe that the size of the group sampled *substantially* affects the accuracy of the poll. For example, we think that a poll or survey that reports how 1 million people feel about an issue is far more likely to be accurate than one that reports how 100,000 people feel. Statistically, the margin of sample error, which is the numerical designation in percentage of how inaccurate a poll may be, is identical in both cases, when the sample size is the same. So the size of the group may not be a significant factor. What is a factor is how *accurately* the sample represents the group.

A second misconception is that the group size must determine the sample size. Thus, for accurate results, we must draw a larger sample if we want to find out how 1 million feel about an issue than we must if we want to find out the feelings of 100,000. As Table 12.1 indicates, sample size is a significant factor in polling but not as significant as many of us think. Statistical analysis shows that beyond a 1,500 probability sample, we reach a point of diminishing returns—the costs of additional interviews outweigh their advantages in accuracy. (See Table 12.1.) Of course, the difference between 100 interviews and 1,500 is significant. Nevertheless, people continue to be impressed by large numbers. But remember, the *Literary Digest* poll of 1936 involved 2 million respondents. The results were nonetheless inaccurate because the sampling technique was imperfect.

A third misconception about polling is that the interviewee or respondent must be handpicked to typify a group or subgroup member. Actually, the accuracy of the sample depends largely on the *randomness* of the sampling. As we saw in the chapter on generalization, randomness means that each member of the group has an equal chance of being sampled. When a poll or survey is conducted through a random sample, nothing but chance determines the instances selected.

TABLE 12.1   Sample Size and Sampling Error

Number of Interviews	Margin of Error (%)
4,000	±2
1,500	±3
1,000	±4
750	±4
600	±4
400	±5
200	±6
100	±11

Source: Roll and Cantril, *Polls,* p. 72.

But selecting a purely random sample isn't easy—or cheap. For example, if a television rating service interviewed every fifteenth person who passed the busiest corner of a city during school hours, it wouldn't be getting a random sample. Among other groups underrepresented would be children. If the television service wants a purely random sample, it will have to devise a way of selecting persons such that *everyone in the population has an equal chance to be selected*. And that could end up being a lot more expensive than just spending a few hours on a street corner.

Just how closely a sample approximates pure randomness depends in part on the purpose of the sample. Consider the case of a local newspaper, for example, that predicts local election results on the basis of samples composed of every tenth name on an alphabetic roster of registered voters. Now that procedure is fairly close to random for predicting an election. Unfortunately, the paper uses the same technique for rating the popularity of television programs. What the paper fails to realize is that the directory, in excluding all people below voting age, excludes an important segment of the television audience.

Another thing: A haphazard selection is not necessarily random. For example, suppose that your math teacher, Mr. Hrasta, occasionally likes to select a half dozen students in the class to get an idea of how well the class as a whole has prepared an assignment. Hrasta does this by letting his eyes roam the room and selecting people. It all seems random enough, but it's not, and everyone in the class realizes this except Hrasta himself. Everyone knows that Mr. Hrasta is influenced by his moods: If he's feeling grouchy, he'll probably pick students who will be unprepared; if he's feeling good, he'll probably pick those who will be prepared. Mr. Hrasta does this subconsciously, not by design. Nevertheless, his sample is biased; it is not random but haphazard. One way to make the selection random would be to assign each student a number, put all the numbers in a hat, shake up the numbers, and then pick a half dozen of them.

Of course, when you're dealing with large groups, ensuring randomness is not this simple. And as mentioned, it can be very expensive. Of great help in such cases is the so-called stratified sample. *A stratified sample is a sampling technique in which relevant strata within the group are identified and a random sample from each stratum is selected in proportion to the number of members in each stratum.* For example, if the local newspaper were genuinely interested in determining the popularity of television programs, it would establish relevant strata on the basis of the characteristics of people that could influence their program preferences, characteristics such as age, sex, educational level, and geographic region. Having established these strata, it would then randomly select persons from each stratum in direct proportion to the number of people within it. So three steps are necessary in a stratified sample: (1) Identify the strata within the population; (2) determine the number of instances in each stratum; and (3) select randomly the same proportion from each stratum.[5]

A final misconception worth noting relates to the so-called "barometer" areas, areas of the country that supposedly have so accurately reflected the whole population in, say, past elections that they can be taken as accurate indicators of how the country will vote: thus, "As goes Maine; so goes the nation." As Roll and Cantril demonstrate, however, the record does not justify such lofty

[5]See W. Edgar Moore, Hugh McCann, and Janet McCann, *Creative and Critical Thinking*, 2d ed. (Boston: Houghton Mifflin, 1985), pp. 119–120.

assumptions. For example, if one had taken barometer counties Clay (Indiana), St. Francis (Kansas), Guilford (North Carolina), and Carroll (Tennessee), one would have predicted a Nixon victory over Kennedy in 1960. The forecaster could have pointed to the reliability of those counties in having forecast Republican percentages within 1 percent in 1948, 1952, and 1956. But in 1960 these barometers were off by a whopping 10 percentage points. Obviously, the more barometer areas polled, the more accurate the forecast. But conditions change from election to election. No amount of barometer-area polling can account for the idiosyncrasy of each election. Only the stratified random sample has a good chance of doing this.

Having spoken generally of studies, polls, and surveys, let's now get specific. Let's look at some informal fallacies frequently associated with statistics.

STATISTICS AND FALLACIES

Although just about any of the informal fallacies that we've already discussed could turn up in a statistical argument, several warrant special consideration because they occur so often. We'll focus on five: the biased sample, equivocation, the biased question, the false dilemma, and concealed evidence.

The Fallacy of Biased Sample

The fallacy of biased sample is an argument that contains a sample that is not representative of the population being studied. We came across this fallacy earlier in discussing generalizations. Here we want to specify just how bias can creep into a sample. Three ways bear mentioning: (1) through the pollster, (2) through the sampling technique, and (3) through the respondent.

The Pollster.   In guarding against sample bias, the first thing to look out for is pollster bias. If the poll is one of the many so-called private polls we read about, be suspicious. The private poll is often conducted by an individual, group, party, or manufacturer whose vested interests in the findings can taint the poll's objectivity.

For example, the makers of Zest soap wished to find out what consumers thought of their product. Predictably enough, Zest found that consumers thought highly of its soap. The only problem with the survey was that the people interviewed were Zest loyalists to begin with.

Similarly, Alpha Beta supermarkets used to sponsor a commercial that showed AB spokesperson Alan Hammel knocking on people's doors and soliciting their opinion about Alpha Beta. The opinions were, to say the least, most complimentary of Alpha Beta. The inherent pollster bias in such a sample needs no further comment; the lack of randomness couldn't be any more obvious than if a "warning" to that effect accompanied the commercial.

In brief, be suspicious of the results of surveys that support the positions of the very people who conducted the surveys. Since the investigator's objectivity is in question, the survey and its results must be in question as well.

The Sampling Technique.   *The sampling technique is the method or procedure used to generate a sample.* The most accurate techniques, as we've seen, are the random and stratified samples. When interviewers use other techniques, they introduce bias into the sample.

For example, in the aforementioned case of Zest, interviewers decided to use a sample of people who lived in Jacksonville, Florida, and who were loyal Zest users. This could hardly be considered an unbiased sampling technique. If Alpha Beta decides to feature only endorsements of their supermarket, thus giving the impression of consumer consensus of approval for AB, its sampling technique is biased.

The *Literary Digest*'s prediction of the presidential election of 1936 was guilty of biased sampling technique in two ways. First, it sent ballots mainly to people listed in telephone books and city directories. In so doing, it introduced a decided socioeconomic bias into its sample: Only the relatively well-to-do had telephones in 1936. Second, the *Digest* counted *only* the ballots that were returned. Experience indicates that ballots or questionnaires voluntarily returned are likely to "load" the sample: Those with an interest in the result are more likely to go to the trouble of filling out and returning a ballot/questionnaire than those without such an interest.

Polls reporting the results of telephone interviews have their own problems, even though they are cheaper and quicker than the mail format and guarantee dispersion. First, it's often difficult to extract necessary personal information from someone during a telephone interview. Information about income, race, religion, and age is something few people are willing to disclose to a faceless voice on the other end of a phone. Yet such information may be crucial for stratification. The same reservation applies to answering controversial questions. People simply are less inclined to be open and candid with someone they cannot see. The obvious drawback with the telephone poll, however, is the one the *Literary Digest* discovered: The interviewer cannot reach those without a phone, a group that still makes up about 10 percent of the U.S. population.

Though the telephone is quicker and cheaper than polling by mail, important segments of the desired sample may be over- or underrepresented. Certain low-income communities; some nonwhite communities; communities of immigrant groups who—though citizens—speak little English; rural pockets, especially in parts of the South; and so on are likely to be underrepresented.

Even where stratification is properly done, bias can creep in via interviewer selection of respondents. Suppose, for example, an agency wants to find out what people think of child-care centers. The agency decides that one of the strata within the population is the category of "young mothers," let's say those between eighteen and thirty years old. Now it's important that the interviewer equally represent the various interests within this stratum. If, say, the interviewer questions only twenty-three-year-old "young mothers," the sample is bound to overrepresent that group and underrepresent the others. Such a sample would lack randomness.

The Respondent.   People who respond to polls, respondents, can bias a sample. Why? Blame it on human nature if you want, but people often tell us what they expect we want to hear and not what they *actually* think, prefer, or do. A classic example is seen in a house-to-house survey made some years ago purporting to study magazine readership. The question asked respondents was "What magazines does your household read?" The replies indicated that a large percentage of households read *Harper's,* but not many read *True Story.*

This was odd, since publishers' figures clearly showed that *True Story* sold millions of magazines, whereas *Harper's* sold hundreds of thousands. When pollsters eliminated all other possible explanations, they faced an unmistakable conclusion: A good many respondents had lied. And those lies biased the sample and led to an erroneous conclusion.

A humorous footnote to this study occurred some time afterward when a worldly wise pollster set out again to determine people's reading preferences. The question asked respondents dealt with the kinds of books they usually read. An overwhelming number indicated that they read the classics: Shakespeare plays, Dickens novels, O. Henry stories, and so forth. As a token of appreciation for their participation, the pollster offered each respondent a choice of any book from among a vast array of titles and subject matter, which included of course, many of the "beloved" classics. Curiously, the work most selected was hardly a classic, except perhaps in the field ecdysis. Its title: *Diary of a Stripper,* authored by the most famous ecdysiast of all time, Gypsy Rose Lee. Thus, not in what people said, but in what they did, was to be found the naked truth.

The television program "Candid Camera" once went even further to show that people's responses can be highly misleading. As a stunt, a man pretending to represent a soft-drink concern asked respondents to sample two colas and to indicate which they preferred. A number of people had little trouble deciding, even going to lengths to detail why one was decidedly better than the other. In fact, the two colas were identical.

EXERCISE 12-2 _____
Examine for bias the sample used in each of the following arguments. Explain.

1. A poll is being conducted to determine whether the students at a college are for or against the construction of commercial nuclear power plants. A sample is taken in the library on a Wednesday between 8:00 A.M. and 9:00 P.M.. Every tenth person passing through the turnstile at the main entrance is asked his or her opinion. The results indicate that 61 percent of the students oppose the construction of commercial nuclear power plants, 37 percent favor it, and 2 percent have no opinion either way. The student government is thinking about using these findings as the basis for asking the administration to put the college on record as opposing the construction of nuclear power plants.
2. To predict the next election, candidate Smythe's forces take a sample. They phone at random 2 million registered voters. It is found that 1.5 million are expecting to vote for Smythe, in an election that figures to have a voter turnout of 50 million. Smythe's people are elated!
3. The Target Public Opinion Agency wants to find out how widespread coke snorting is among U.S. college students. To do so it uses a stratified random sample of 1,500 college students. The results indicate that a minority of students snort coke on a regular basis (at least once a week). In publishing its findings, Target editorializes that the incidence of cocaine use among U.S. college students is greatly exaggerated and uses its survey to back up its claim.
4. Ad for Ford LTD: "63 percent of those who tested a Ford LTD and a Chevy Impala chose LTD. Recently 50 Ford and 50 Chevy owners selected at random in the L.A. area rated both a Ford LTD and Chevrolet Impala for overall styling, interior and exterior features, roominess, trunk space, parking and driving under city, freeway and residential conditions. There were 55 separate tests in total. At the conclusion of these tests, all were asked if they had to choose, which of these cars they would be more likely to buy. The answer? 63 percent, or nearly 2 out of 3, chose a Ford LTD. See why at your Ford Dealer."

5. Harris Gallup has been hired by the Valley Shopping Mall Association to take a sample. The members want to know why the number of shoppers at the mall has been steadily declining for the last year. After determining that a sample of 350 shoppers is ample, and after careful preparation of a questionnaire, Harris Gallup tells his pollsters to be very sure not to interfere with the randomness of the sample. They are to set up a table with a big sign, "OPINION POLL," in the center of the main floor of the mall, Monday through Friday from 10:00 A.M. to 10:00 P.M. (the mall's weekday hours of operation), and they are to interview the first 350 people who randomly approach them. Gallup was very careful to impress on his poll takers that they were in no way to encourage or discourage anyone from responding to the questionnaire. This approach seemed unbiased, random, and professional to the association. Was it? Explain.

6. In an effort to improve his teaching, Professor Stallone decides to sample his home economics class. He prepares a questionnaire with the help of Ms. Pascal, the college statistician. He then calls each of his students into his office—one at a time—and has them answer the questions as he asks them. Professor Stallone is very careful to make sure that each student is interviewed.

7. Well-known pollsters Rowland Evans and Robert Novak have built a formidable reputation on, among other things preelection polls. Typically, they poll fifty to seventy-five voters in "key" districts and then generate a statewide prediction. Howard Kahane reports the case in which they rated the chances of Democratic State Senator Sander Levin to become the governor of Michigan. They concluded that his chances were poor because only 42 percent of those polled in a key Democratic precinct favored Levin (36 percent favored his opponent; 22 percent were undecided). The entire sample consisted of sixty-four blue-collar workers living in the suburb of Warren, Michigan. (Howard Kahane, *Logic and Contemporary Rhetoric,* 4th ed., Belmont, Calif., Wadsworth Publishing Company, Inc., 1980, pp. 103–104)

The Fallacy of Equivocation

In discussing fallacies of ambiguity in Chapter 4, we defined the fallacy of equivocation as an argument that uses a word or phrase in such a way that it carries more than a single meaning. Equivocation occurs frequently enough in statistics for us to consider it again here. Generally, the fallacy of equivocation in statistics takes one of two forms: verbal or visual.

Verbal. Often a statistic includes a word that equivocates; that is, it can be taken to mean different things. A good example is the word *average*.

For example, one reason Sweeney bought the home the family currently occupies was that the "average" income in the neighborhood impressed him and Wilma. Until the realtor mentioned the average income, the Sweeneys were indecisive about the purchase. But when the realtor casually said to Sweeney and Wilma one afternoon, "I don't know if you're aware of this, but the average income in this neighborhood is $30,000 per year," well, that did it. There was just enough snobbery in the Sweeneys to hook them with that bait.

Interestingly, a few years later Wilma joined a local taxpayer's committee that actively sought to curb the steady increase in property taxes. One of the committee's arguments was that the "average" income in the Sweeney's neighborhood was $15,000. Although Wilma went along with the committee, she couldn't help wondering about the disparity between the committee's "average" and the realtor's. When she told Sweeney about it, he simply said, "Somebody's lying."

Actually, as Slim was fast to point out, nobody was lying. "That's the beauty of statistics," she told her parents; "you can use them to do your lying for you." What Slim meant was that the word *average* was being used differently in the two instances.

The fact is that in statistics, *average* can carry one of three meanings: as the mean, median, or mode. The mean is an arithmetic average. You derive it by adding up the value of items and dividing by the number of items. Thus, add up the income of all the people in the neighborhood and divide by the number of people. The result is the mean. That's the figure the realtor gave the Sweeney's.

The median is the figure right in the middle of all the items. Technically, in any distribution the median is the figure above which 50 percent falls and below which 50 percent falls. That's the figure the tax committee used.

To illustrate, let's consider just five incomes:

1. $100,000
2.   20,000
3.   15,000
4.   7,500
5.   7,500

Add all those figures, divide by five, and you get $30,000, the average taken as the mean. But the average taken as the median is the figure right in the middle, $15,000.

Actually, if the tax committee were dealing only with these figures, they'd be better served by claiming that the "average" income was $7,500. That would be the average taken as the mode. The mode refers to the figure in a distribution that occurs most frequently. Here it's $7,500.

When Slim pointed out to her parents these various uses of the word *average,* they decided to do a little investigating of their own. They acquired figures on the incomes of wage earners in their neighborhood. They learned that the disparity between the $30,000 and the $15,000 figures could be explained simply: The neighborhood included two millionaires, which boosted the total income of the neighborhood and thus the arithmetic average, the mean. Actually, everybody else in the neighborhood was making far less. All of which gave Sweeney pause. "This word *average,*" he mused, "it doesn't tell you much, does it?" No, it doesn't. When we find it in a statistic, we better find out in what sense it's intended. If we don't, then rest assured that on the *average* we'll be duped.

Statistical verbal equivocation arises with other words. For example, almost any claim containing a superlative—*best, finest, most*—is using the word equivocally, and perhaps even meaninglessly. Thus, Armour-Dial once advertised, "Dial is the most effective deodorant soap you can buy." Now you might take that as a claim to superiority over any other soap. But when pressed by the Federal Trade Commission (FTC), Armour-Dial insisted that the claim simply meant that Dial soap was *as* effective as other soaps. So why not say that? The fact is that even if Armour-Dial had said "as effective as," that wouldn't be much of an improvement; for the phrase "as effective as" is itself hopelessly obscure. "As effective as" in what sense—cleaning, perfuming, softening?

And, oh yes, let's not forget "weasel" words in statistical equivocation. *Weasel words are words used to evade or retreat from a direct or forthright statement or position.* They are advertisers' buzzwords. They allow somebody to say something without really saying it. The weasel *help* is a good example. *Help,* of course, means "aid" or "assist" and nothing else. Yet as one author has observed, "'Help' is the one single word which, in all the annals of advertising, has done the most to say something that couldn't be said."[6] What he means is that, since *help* is used to qualify, once it's used, almost anything can be said after it. Thus, we're exposed to ads for products that "*help* us keep young," "*help* prevent cavities," "*help* keep our houses germ free." Just think about how many times a day you hear or read phrases like these: "*helps* stop," "*helps* prevent," "*helps* fight," "*helps* overcome," "*helps* you feel," "*helps* you look." Of course, *help* isn't the only weasel. Here are some others: *like, virtual* or *virtually, can be, up to* (as in "provides relief *up to* eight hours"), *as much as* (as in "saves *as much as* one gallon of gas"). Such words and phrases function to say what really can't be said because, in most cases, the statistical studies necessary to back up a specific claim just aren't available; if they were, rest assured that the advertiser would happily boast of them. Lacking hard data, advertisers—as well as those in other fields, of course—enlist the weasels to give the *impression* of substantial claim support.

Visual.   Statistical equivocation need not come only in words. Graphs, charts, pictographs, and other visual aids used to represent statistical claims can also commit the fallacy of equivocation. If a picture is worth a thousand words, in statistics it may be worth considerably more than that.

Take, for example, the common two-axis graph, consisting of a vertical ascending linear scale and a rightward extending horizontal linear scale.[7] All sorts of trends and data are plotted on this most common visual aid. But be careful. The two-axis graph can be used to misrepresent.

To illustrate, let's represent a region's increasing unemployment in the course of a year (shown in the graph at the top of page 269). Now this graph is clear enough. It shows what happened with unemployment, month by month through the year. The graph is in proportion. There's a zero line at the bottom for comparison. The 10 percent increase in unemployment during the year looks like 10 percent. In short, the unemployment picture is conveyed clearly, quickly, accurately, and unemotionally.

But suppose you wanted to alarm readers, convince them that the situation was very serious. If you did, the chart at the top of page 269 wouldn't be nearly dramatic enough. The one below it is a more effective one for that purpose. Notice that the figures and curve are the same. But by chopping off the graph we've changed its impression. The reader now sees an unemployment line that has climbed halfway up the chart in one year! What is actually a relatively modest rise now appears enormous.

You say you're still not satisfied? That you want something even more dramatic because you have an even bigger axe to grind? Very well. Simply alter the proportion between the vertical and horizontal axes by letting each mark up the vertical line represent only one-tenth as many people as before: thus, the

---

[6]See Paul Stevens, "Weasel Words: God's Little Helpers," in *Language Awareness,* eds. Paul A. Eschhol, Alfred A. Rosa, and Virginia P. Clark (New York: St. Martin's Press, 1974), p. 156.

[7]See Darrell Huff, *How to Lie with Statistics* (New York: W. W. Norton, 1954).

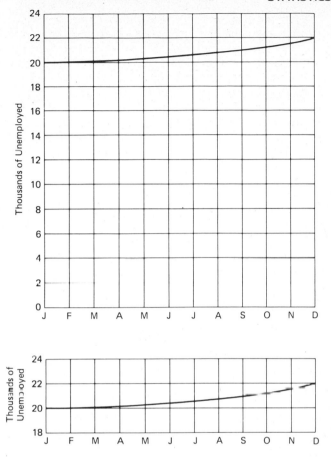

graph on page 270. Now, that should produce a cardiac skip in the most lion-hearted chest. In fact, this graph represents a subtle, visual way of editing "Unemployment rose 10 percent" into "Unemployment climbed a whopping 10 percent!" And the beauty of it is that the graph contains no words that might betray slanting. Indeed, it appears completely objective, unless of course you know what to look for and think about.

Technically speaking, such graphic distortions are a form of equivocating on relative terms. Bases of comparison get shifted. The standard of comparison is obscured by truncating or compressing the graph. Interpretation is served up with information. In short, the data the graph represents carry more than one meaning. In that lies the equivocation.

Other statistical visuals can equally mislead. The pictograph is a good example. Pictographs are little pictures used to present data: a picture of a man carrying a lunch pail to represent labor, a picture of a woman in a gingham dress to represent housewives, a picture of a barrel to represent amounts of oil. Imagine, in fact, a graphic that attempts to portray increasing American oil consumption since World War II by depicting a series of increasingly large barrels, one at each regular interval along a horizontal axis. Ambiguity arises

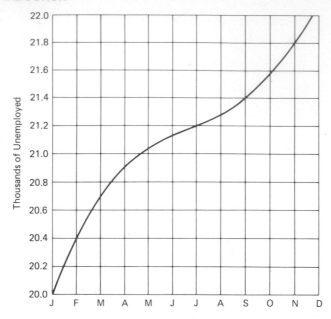

when we interpret the pictograph. Do we compare the barrels' relative heights, areas, volumes? Because we generally underestimate increases in areas resulting from increases in height and width and increases in volume resulting from increases in areas, we can easily downplay our increasing oil consumption. The point: Look skeptically on pictographs that change their lengths and widths while representing a single factor or that present three-dimensional objects whose volumes are hard to compare.

EXERCISE 12-3 _____

Are there any fallacies of equivocation in the following passages? Explain.

1. BONNIE: Wow! I feel a lot better after reading that article in *Psychology Today*.
   BART: I thought you might. I knew how you'd been struggling with those unresolved feelings of hostility toward your parents.
   BONNIE: And now this article says I'm perfectly normal!
   BART: That's what I've been trying to tell you—the average person feels the same way you do.
   BONNIE: That's exactly what the article says.

2. "Alka Seltzer: the best antacid you can buy without a prescription." (ad for Alka Seltzer)

3. FERN: You know, the cavalier way that peoples' political freedoms are treated around the world is really outrageous.
   STU: I guess you're talking about Russia, huh?
   FERN: I'm talking worldwide. Did you know that in the past year the political liberties of 823.3 million people were violated?
   STU: No, I didn't know that.
   FERN: Then here, read this article. I think it's about time this country did something about this outrage.

4. BETH: Can I use your phone?
   BURT: Sure, if I had one.

BETH: No phone?

BURT: I just ordered one.

BETH: Well, lots a luck! Did you know it takes anywhere from 90 to 180 days to get a phone installed in this area?

BURT: Oh, no!

5. WIFE: Well, you're running true to form—having a drink before dinner.

HUSBAND: What's that supposed to mean?

WIFE: According to the latest survey, more middle-aged men have at least one drink before dinner than any other age group of males or females.

6. Every ninety seconds a woman gives birth in America: We've got to find that woman and stop her!

7. There's no more effective analgesic on the market today.

8. You'll be surprised at how well it works.

9. MOE: Why're you so depressed, Larry?

LARRY: I just got my Archeology 1A midterm back—I got an F.

CURLEY: Oooooo! Ooooooo! That's awful!

LARRY: Yeah, I'll say. But I'm not alone; over half of the class flunked.

MOE: Hey! Don't feel so bad then; you got an average grade.

10. JERRY: I object to my children studying Einstein.

JIMMY: Why? He was a genius.

JERRY: That's what I mean. He was deviant, abnormal.

The Fallacy of Biased Question

The fallacy of biased question is an argument based on the answer to a question that is worded to draw a predetermined reply. For example, suppose a pollster asks respondents this question: "Should the United States continue to spend millions of dollars annually on foreign aid while neglecting needed domestic problems?" The results: 77 percent "no," 23 percent "yes." You'd be unwise, however, to accept this conclusion because the question that generated it is biased. It is worded to draw a predetermined reply, in this case "no." Such questions are commonly termed *loaded.*

Sweeney received a loaded question in the mail recently. It was part of a "survey" purportedly to determine how people felt about reinstating the death penalty. The question read, "Should we reinstate capital punishment, or continue to allow the potential murderer and rapist to operate without even the threat of death?" Psychologically, a respondent is made to feel that a "no" reply is a vote for murder and rape. The question is calculated to elicit a "yes" reply.

Sometimes question bias can result when alternatives aren't clear. Consider, for example, this question: "A proposal has been made in Congress to require the U.S. government to bring home all U.S. hostages from the Middle East before the end of this year. Would you like to have your representative vote for or against this proposal?" Without a follow-up question, the results can be misleading. Those responding "yes" to this question might change their minds when subsequently asked, "Some people say that the United States should bring home all its hostages from the Middle East by the end of the year, regardless of what happens there. Do you agree or disagree?"

Question bias can result from the substitution of one word for another. For example, here are several questions that the makers of Alamo Brand pet food asked respondents in a "Pet Owner's Opinion Study." Observe how the word *that,* when really *whether* or *if* should have been used, biases the questions.

1. Did you notice that Alamo Brand looks meatier than the dry dog food you have been using?
2. Did you notice that Alamo Brand has a meatier feel than the dry dog food you have been using?
3. Did you notice that your dog preferred and enjoyed Alamo Brand more than his usual dry dog food?
4. Did you notice that your dog appeared more contented and satisfied after eating Alamo Brand?

Are they serious? Apparently so. The respondent is asked to return the survey to Manufacturers Marketing Research Services in Chester, Pennsylvania. And just to confound matters, Alamo promises to conduct a follow-up study based on the responses to this questionnaire! As they put it: "Based upon the responses to this questionaire (sic), we are going to choose a select group of consumers for a 30 day Use and Opinion Study of ALAMO BRAND. The purpose of this study will be to see if consumers notice an improvement in their dog's general condition and health when they feed (sic) ALAMO BRAND for a long enough time. If you are selected for this study, would you agree to give us your opinions?" The worst part of this sort of thing is that we'll all have to suffer through the annoying ads and commercials that this "study" is bound to generate.

Just as unreliable in statistical arguments as the biased question is the ambiguous one. "Do you think it's a good practice for a woman to be paid less for doing the same job that a man does?" Well, probably that depends on what is meant by "a good practice." From the viewpoint of employers, or maybe even men, it might well be "a good practice." From the viewpoint of women, it wouldn't be. Again, the question "Do you think it's possible that we'll discover life in outer space by the year 2000?" is ambiguous. Does the interviewer mean empirical, technical, or logical possibility? The respondent has no way of knowing; indeed, the interviewer may even mean "likely" or "probable," and not "possible" at all. The problems with such questions are twofold. First, the respondent doesn't know which meaning is intended. Second, the pollster has no way of knowing that all the respondents understood the question in the same way. Hence, any conclusion drawn from an ambiguous question is fallacious.

EXERCISE 12-4 _____
Are the following survey questions biased or ambiguous or are they not? Explain.

1. Do you favor more educational programs on television?
2. Should the United States support the Israelis in its dealings with the Arab countries?
3. Many people believe that we are spending far too much on national defense. Do you agree?
4. Do you usually have a ready-to-eat cereal for breakfast?
5. Do you think the United States should accept Russian influence in Cuba?
6. Do you think the government should ration gasoline?
7. To which class do you feel you belong: white collar, blue collar, or some other?
8. Which of these questions is less biased? Why?

a. Do you think most manufacturing companies that lay off workers in the slack periods could avoid layoffs and provide steady work right through the year?
b. Do you think most manufacturing companies that lay off workers in the slack

period could avoid layoffs and provide steady work right through the year, or do you think layoffs are inevitable?[8]

The Fallacy of False Dilemma

The fallacy of false dilemma is an argument that erroneously reduces the number of possible positions or alternatives on an issue. To argue, for example, that one should either support our government's policies or leave the country is to commit a false dilemma. There is ample middle ground, alternatives, between these two extremes. A bank commits a false dilemma fallacy when it suggests, "A logical alternative to the stock market: MADISON SAVINGS AND LOAN." The bank implies that there are just two ways to invest: either in the stock market or in Madison Savings and Loan.

Of course, there are times when such either-or choices are appropriate. One of Aristotle's three laws of thought is the law of the excluded middle: A thing is either *A* or not *A*. Thus, the object before you is either a book or not a book. It can't be both. Similarly, a question like "Is the flower in your hand a rose or not a rose?" poses a genuine dilemma, not a false one. Surely the flower either is a rose or not a rose. Notice that the question did not ask, "Is the flower in your hand a rose or a carnation?" Unless it had been established previously that the flower was, in fact, one or the other, that question would be a false dilemma; the flower might be neither one.

The false dilemma is a ploy. Arguers use it when they wish to eliminate your range of choices and thereby lead you to a predetermined conclusion. In this sense, a question that poses a false dilemma is a variation of the biased question. Statistics frequently have as their source results that have been generated by a false dilemma.

For example, a poll that asks, "Are you for or against the women's liberation movement?" creates a false dilemma. You may be indifferent to the women's liberation movement. (Of course, the question is ambiguous as well: Just what constitutes being "for" or "against.") Here's another false dilemma question: "Do you think the United States should support the Arabs or the Israelis in the Middle East?" Maybe you feel the United States should "support" neither or perhaps both equally. It's true that most polls do provide a "no opinion" choice. But the trouble with this category is that it's hopelessly ambiguous. After all, in addition to those who genuinely have no opinion are those who have an opinion that wasn't listed and those, perhaps logicians, who refuse to answer such a fallacious question. All are treated as having "no opinion," which surely must qualify as the fallacy of hasty conclusion.

*EXERCISE 12-5 _____

Are the following genuine or false dilemmas?

1. Directions for an essay exam: Write an essay entitled "Captain Ahab—Fanatic or Idealist?"
2. Poll question: Do you favor or oppose increased military spending?

---

[8]Quoted in S. L. Payne, *The Art of Asking Questions* (Princeton, N.J.: Princeton University Press, 1951). Question **a** elicited far more affirmative replies than **b**, although the questions are essentially the same.

3. Political commentator on the 1979 seizure of the American embassy in Teheran by Iranian students: The entire episode goes to prove that the United States is a paper tiger. Otherwise we would have exercised our military muscle to free the U.S. citizens being held hostage. The fact that we didn't demonstrates that we no longer have the will to stand by our principles. And it also shows something else: In a real showdown we will put our material interests, oil in this case, before the lives of Americans abroad.

4. "Coffee, Tea or Vivarin?" (ad for Vivarin Tablets)

5. "At Mercedes Benz, they engineer a great car, without regard for price. Subaru engineers a great car, with great regard for price. . . . Subaru and Mercedes, two of the finest engineered cars around. One sells for 8 times the price of the other. The choice is yours." (ad for Subaru)

6. SALLY: Well, the evidence is in. Business leaders continue to discriminate against women on the job.

   SAM: Why do you say that?

   SALLY: Because the results of a study prove it. Look, a thousand business leaders were picked at random and asked, "If you had to choose between a male and a female for a job with your firm, and the two happened to be equally qualified, which would you choose—the male or the female?" And guess what? Sixty-eight percent said they'd pick the male.

7. Following are questions from a course evaluation designed by the instructor:

   The best thing about this course is (a) the instructor, (b) lectures, (c) the tests, (d) weekly practice quizzes, (e) a–d are equally effective.

   The worst thing about this course is (a) time it meets, (b) day it meets, (c) book, (d) room, (e) none.

   What grade would you give this instructor? (a) A, (b) B, (c) not sure.

8. Christ was either a madman or who he said he was. (paraphrase of C.S. Lewis's oft-quoted assertion)

The Fallacy of Concealed Evidence

Recently the Sweeneys were victimized by a "numbers game." It seems they were in the market for an automatic fruit juicer. In their shopping, they came across one that claimed to extract 30 percent more juice. That sounded pretty good, so they bought it. Only afterward did they find out that the manufacturer meant 30 percent more juice than the old-fashioned hand-reamer juicer. Since the Sweeneys had never intended to buy such a juicer, the advertised claim was totally irrelevant for their purposes. This kind of hidden or suppressed information constitutes one of the most common, and potentially dangerous, fallacies associated with statistics: the fallacy of concealed evidence.

The fallacy of concealed evidence is an argument that presents only facts that are favorable to its conclusion while suppressing relevant but nonsupportive facts. Before showing this fallacy in a statistical context, let's see how widespread its use is in nonstatistical contexts.

Nonstatistical. By far one of the most dramatic examples of nonstatistical concealed evidence concerns a product called Pertussin Medicated Vaporizer.[9] Between 1968 and 1973 eighteen persons apparently died from inhaling its contents. Some deaths resulted from product abuse; some did not.

[9] For the related facts, see the *Los Angeles Times,* July 2, 1973, p. 1.

On July 2, 1973, a decade after the product first appeared on merchants' shelves, the Food and Drug Administration removed Pertussin from the market.

In that ten-year interim, anyone reading the can's label read nothing alarming about the product's contents. On the contrary, Pertussin spray supposedly built "a roomful of relief" from colds and hay fever. The directions called for spraying the contents on handkerchiefs, in rooms, and even on pillows and sheets. "Repeat as often as necessary" and "safe even in the nursery" made the unsuspecting shopper even more confident of the product's merit. Pertussin even had the blessing of *Parents* magazine (an appeal to authority), its seal indicating that the spray had been tested by the FDA. It had not. Even the most suspicious consumer was reassured by the harmless ingredients listed: menthol and oil of eucalyptus. In short, consumers seemed safe in buying and using this product. They might have reasoned that any medicated vaporizer containing the ingredients Pertussin claimed it did was versatile enough to be used on handkerchiefs, in rooms, and even on pillows and sheets; had been proved effective; and was moderately priced and a product they should buy. As it turned out, such an argument was tragically unsound; evidence had been concealed.

A couple of ingredients and related facts about them went unmentioned on the can. First, the manufacturers made no mention that menthol and eucalyptus made up only 12 percent of the total ingredients. The remaining 88 percent consisted of propellants and solvents. Nor did the manufacturers mention that the propellants and solvents were about equally divided between flurocarbons and trichloroethane, which tend to upset the heartbeat and depress other vital activities such as breathing. The combination proved fatal, and a tragic example of how dangerous concealed evidence can be. As Daniel Webster once noted, "There is nothing so powerful as the truth, nothing so dangerous as a half-truth."

From our discussion in Chapter 1, we know that a proposition is either true or it is not; it cannot be half true and half untrue. But we include that term *half-truth* because the term's popular connotation is that of incomplete picture or omission of pertinent facts, details, or information. Understood this way, *half-truth* becomes a useful phrase, suggesting the common characteristic of all the fallacies of concealed evidence: They result from relying on incomplete or inaccurate evidence.

To generalize correctly we need all relevant facts—not just some of them. We've already touched on the information explosion and how difficult it is for us to obtain certain knowledge, even under the best of conditions. But added to this difficulty is the fact that we must often evaluate and act on our evaluation of highly technical and specialized claims, in many cases for our physical survival.

The most common examples of concealed evidence are in advertising. Because most of us have so little knowledge of the product, we can't begin to detect the fallacy in the appeal. Many advertising executives nevertheless insist that the primary purpose of advertising is not to sell a product but to educate the public. Certainly many ads do this. Mounting evidence, however, contradicts the claim that this is generally the case. In fact, one very influential advertising president, David Ogilvy, admits, "Surely it is asking too much to expect the advertiser to describe the shortcomings of his product."[10] This is little more

[10]David Ogilvy, *Confessions of an Advertising Man* (New York: Atheneum, 1963), p. 158.

than a defense of concealed evidence. In *The Permissible Lie,* Samm Sinclair Baker, who spent many years in advertising, makes the point more forcefully:

> Inside the agency the basic approach is hardly conducive to truthtelling. The usual thinking in forming a campaign is first, what can we say, true or not, that will sell the product best? The second consideration is, how can we say it effectively and get away with it so that (1) people who buy won't feel let down by too big a promise that doesn't come true, and (2) the ads will avoid quick and certain censure by the Federal Trade Commission.[11]

In defending concealed evidence, advertisers often like to say that the public is too smart to be duped, that it's impossible to "put one by" as sophisticated an audience as a product is likely to find in contemporary America. This may be so. But at a gathering of the American Marketing Association in the spring of 1973, Seymour Lieberman—president of Manhattan-based Lieberman Research Inc.— reported that "deceitful ads can be far more persuasive than promotions that tell the simple truth."

> Lieberman enlisted the aid of the Kenyon & Eckhardt agency to create one deceptive and one truthful television commercial for each of six fictitious products. A panel of 100 largely middle-income consumers watched the truthful commercials and another group of the same size, income and education level saw the dishonest versions. Both sets of commercials used the same actors, and except for the misleading bits, the same language. Yet in four of the six tests, the cheating commercial placed well ahead of the honest promotion in coaxing the audience into a buying mood. More people were persuaded to buy the mythical Pro Gro plant fertilizer when the commercial stressed that it contained protein—*though protein is of absolutely no help to plants* [italics added to show concealed evidence]. A bunion remedy, D-Corn, drew more buyer interest when it was touted as having four times as much methylglyoxal as its competition; yet *no evidence was offered to support the notion that increasing the amount of methylglyoxal might be in the least beneficial* [italics added to show questionable claim].[12]

The sample used in this test is hardly large enough to provide conclusive findings. Nor is the evidence we've provided sufficient to conclude that the advertiser is primarily motivated by a desire to sell, not to inform.

But we neither desire nor intend to indict the advertising industry. We only want to be alert to those areas in which concealed evidence in argument constitutes a real and present threat to argument. Consumerism is one of those areas, a vital one.

Colgate-Palmolive for a long time showed its Rapid Shave Cream being used to shave sandpaper: "To prove Rapid Shave's super moisturizing power, we put it right from the can onto this rough, dry sandpaper." It was: "Apply, soak, and off in a stroke." The "proof" of such a claim appeared, but the concealed evidence made it impossible to sustain—the sandpaper was actually Plexiglas. "Tests showed that actual sandpaper had to be soaked in Rapid Shave for about eighty minutes—not for the few seconds depicted in the commercial—to be shaved."[13] Similarly, automobile advertisers, to show how little the glass

[11]Samm Sinclair Baker, *The Permissible Lie* (New York: World, 1968).
[12]*Time,* May 14, 1973, p. 96.
[13]Baker, *The Permissible Lie,* p. 16.

of their cars distorts vision, aren't averse to filming their cars with the windows rolled down; and manufacturers of "one-swipe" floor cleansers don't object to covering the floor with graphite before wiping.[14] In each case the advertiser "forgets" to tell you something important: that the sandpaper is really Plexiglas, that the windows of the car are really rolled down, or that the floor is really covered with graphite. What the advertiser "forgets" to tell you in the interest of preserving the persuasiveness of the argument or demonstration usually falls under the heading of *concealed evidence*. This evidence, of course, would make the stated or implied conclusions less forceful and, in some cases, highly improbable.

The whole area of labeling is rife with concealed evidence. For example, the so-called "feminine deodorant sprays," which have mushroomed into a $55 million annual sales industry, never mention that the products are unnecessary. (Any gynecologist will verify that normal daily cleansing is much more hygienic than any cosmetic application.) Nor does the label mention the undesirable side effects that such products have: itching, burning, blistering, and urinary infections. The Food and Drug Administration has finally proposed the following warning on all such products:

> CAUTION—For external use only. Spray at least eight inches from skin. Use sparingly and not more than once daily to avoid irritation. Do not use this product with a sanitary napkin. Do not apply to broken, irritated or itching skin. Persistent or unusual odor may indicate the presence of a condition for which a physician should be consulted. If rash, irritation, unusual vaginal discharge or discomfort develops, discontinue use immediately and consult a physician.

Even with this warning, the mind boggles at the millions of cans already sold without this information. As Joseph A. Page, associate professor of law at Georgetown University, wrote in a letter to FTC Chairman Lewis A. Engman, "Up to now the FTC by its inexcusable inaction has served as a silent partner in a giant 'ripoff' conjured up in the caldrons of Madison Avenue and foisted upon American women by means of massive, cleverly conceived advertising."[15] Even after extracting the emotive language from the statement, the charge is clear and difficult to refute.

Past advertising of intrauterine devices was no less clever. Unlike producers of birth control pills, manufacturers of IUDs are not required by law to provide the FDA with premarket evidence of effectiveness and safety. Pamphlets accompanying such devices often suppressed the fact that among users there was significant evidence of perforation of the uterus and infection, excessive menstrual bleeding, and ovarian and tubal pregnancies. The A. H. Robins Company of Richmond, Virginia, in a pamphlet that accompanied its Dalkon Shield, said that the cramps that some women had for a short time following insertion were "generally mild and usually pass in a few minutes." Appearing before a congressional hearing, obstetrician-gynecologist Major Russel J. Thomsen disagreed. Such claims, he said, border on falsehood. "I [have] seen a number of women faint following IUD insertion and particularly from Dalkon Shield insertion."[16]

---

[14]Ibid.
[15]*Los Angeles Times,* June 21, 1973, p. 25.
[16]*Los Angeles Times,* May 31, 1973, p. 12.

Moreover, sometimes the IUD could become dislodged, in which case X-rays of the entire pelvis must be taken, "a practice followed 20,000 times a year in the United States alone."[17] The threat to future generations is clear. Yet as Thomsen pointed out to the Congress, "This significant IUD complication is studiously ignored in medical literature."[18]

The dangerous thing about concealed evidence is that before we recognize it, we've been persuaded to accept a conclusion and we're acting on it. Avis Rent-a-Car, for example, in 1973 advertised a car-rental plan variously entitled "Avis $7-a-Day Plan," "The 7-11 Rate," or "The 7-11 Plan." Across the country the plan offered a car for $7 a day and 11¢ a mile. What went unsaid, however, was that in resort areas like Las Vegas or Palm Springs—where rental demands are greater than in nonresort areas—the plan offered: *$11 a day and 7¢ a mile*. But there's little we can do once we're there.

With many of us conscious of our weight, concealed evidence also turns up in the selling of low-calorie foods or diet-control products. Some diet aids claim to depress appetite; by eating a caramel candy before meals, it's claimed, our blood-sugar level rises enough to stifle appetite. What's concealed is that candies don't bring about a great rise in blood sugar. But even more important, there is no clinical evidence to show that an increase in blood sugar inhibits appetite! In a similar way, bulk-producing products taken before meals allegedly swell in the stomach (by absorbing water), thus depressing appetite. Unfortunately, most of these products contain methylcellulose, originally sold to relieve chronic constipation. Consequently, rather than swelling the stomach, such products quickly pass into the small intestine. But even if this mass does inhibit hunger contractions, as advertised, it does nothing to curb appetite. Appetite is a learned way of behaving, associated with a complex network of pleasurable physical and psychological feelings. It's appetite, not hunger, that causes obesity. Hunger is caused by normal, natural stomach contractions signaling the body's need for food; satisfying these signals hardly ever causes obesity. Then there are those products that would persuade us to purchase diet aids by using "before" and "after" photos. Often, however, as in the case of Regimen tablets,[19] the photos have been as touched up as the centerfold of *Playboy*.

With errors of concealed evidence or half-truths, then, the conclusions seem to follow from the evidence, but we should not be persuaded to accept those conclusions. The reason is that we don't have all the relevant evidence, the whole truth. To put it another and precise way, such arguments omit evidence bearing directly on the conclusions they're trying to force. As a result, the arguments are not *sound*. And an unsound argument should never persuade us.

Statistical.   Turning to the statistical uses of concealed evidence, let's consider a simple example. Some years ago it was reported that the number of deaths chargeable to steam railroads in one year was 4,712. If you were around then, you might have considered that as ample reason to stay off trains. But if you'd taken the time to investigate what the figure was all about, you would have learned that nearly half of those victims were people whose automobiles

[17]Ibid.
[18]Ibid. (Note: The Dalkon Shield has been removed from the U.S. market.)
[19]Baker, *The Permissible Lie*, p. 23.

had collided with trains at crossings. And the great part of the rest were riding
the rods. In fact, of the 4,712 people killed, only 132 were passengers on trains.
(Even that figure doesn't mean much until you know how many passenger miles
trains traveled that year.)[20]

Look for statistically concealed evidence in the profit pictures that large
corporations try to paint. For example, a big company might report that in a
given year it made only one cent in profits out of every sales dollar. Sounds fair
enough. After all, to replace a two-dollar typewriter ribbon, the company would
lose the profit on two hundred sales dollars. Makes you feel guilty about making
"typos," doesn't it? But the truth is that what a company reports as profits is
only a fraction of the overall profit picture. Hidden depreciation, special depreciation, reserves for contingencies—all make up the part of the profit picture
that goes unreported.

Appeals for rate increases for everything from utilities to insurance often
rely on concealed evidence. An insurance company, for example, might argue
that it's paid out 3 billion dollars more in claims than it has collected in premiums
over the past eight years. Sounds like reason enough for a rate increase, doesn't
it? Well, don't be so sure. Remember that the profit standing of an insurance
company is hardly determined by subtracting claims from premiums. After all,
premiums don't lie buried in an office vault somewhere. They're banked and
invested, whereby they generate additional income. So before believing that the
increase is justified, find out the total income and total expenditure, for that
will reveal total profits.

Sometimes because statistics conceal evidence, we feel we're getting something for nothing. For example, a supermarket once advertised a price reduction
on over 7,500 products.[21] What it didn't report was that its original prices were
for the most part higher than prices in competitive chain markets. Beware of
this kind of "prices slashed" advertising. It may be concealing evidence.

A final word about concealed evidence. Obviously, before you're able to
detect the concealed evidence fallacy, you must know what it is an argument is
suppressing. This means that we as practical logicians must constantly be expanding our repertory of information in economics, politics, consumerism, history, nutrition, medicine, science—indeed in every field imaginable. Otherwise,
we're just asking to be duped and ripped off. Think about it—think about the
times we've wondered about the usefulness of all those "other" courses, the ones
outside our majors that we must take in college. Forget about all the high-
blown justification for those courses. Think of them in terms of simple survival.
The person who knows nothing about politics, consumerism, history, science,
and so on stands a greater chance of perishing financially, emotionally, intellectually, even spiritually, than the one who keeps informed of these and other
fields. So when a college curriculum requires us to take courses outside our
major field, it's not punishing us; it's protecting us. End of sermon.

EXERCISE 12-6 ⎯⎯⎯⎯⎯⎯⎯⎯

1. The fallacy of concealed evidence is often present in textbooks. Choose one of the
   following subjects from American history. Then consult an American history textbook

---

[20]Huff, *How to Lie with Statistics*, p. 79.
[21]See *Accurate Pricing Book,* Marketing Service Corporation, Central Valley, Calif., September 1,
1972.

and see if the author has omitted information incompatible with the impression he or she is trying to create.

a. Indians
b. blacks
c. women
d. U.S. Presidents
e. wars and the need for them

2. Pretend that you've just attended a party and that you're about to transcribe what you witnessed. First, write precisely what you saw. Then write an account that by omitting pertinent information misrepresents what occurred.

3. Document three cases of advertising that conceal evidence for the purpose of persuading.

4. For the next two weeks, read two newspapers. Do you find that they report the same event differently? Is concealed evidence involved?

5. Carefully read the speeches and comments of leading politicians for the next two weeks. How many times do you catch them concealing evidence to persuade? (Undoubtedly there will be some students who lack sufficiently masochistic tendencies to do this exercise.)

6. Equivocation, meaningless claim, and other fallacies of ambiguity are often used to conceal evidence. For example, some years ago Ocean Spray Cranberry Juice ran a campaign in which they touted the fact that their cranberry juice contained "more food energy" than orange juice. "Food energy," it turned out, meant calories. Find two or three current examples of fallacies of ambiguity used to conceal evidence.

7. *Consumers Reports* has a feature called "Once Over," which carefully scrutinizes products and claims. This is an excellent source of examples of concealed evidence. Find three or four cases of concealed evidence from recent editions of the "Once Over" column.

SUMMARY

This chapter dealt with statistics. Statistics can be associated with any form of inductive argument: generalization, analogy, hypothesis, or cause. The usual spawning grounds for statistics are studies, polls, and surveys. Before accepting the results of a study, you should satisfy yourself on a variety of questions dealing with who conducted and participated in the study and the methods used.

The same applies to polls. Polls can be reliable when proper sampling procedures are followed. The accuracy of any sample depends largely on randomness, which means that each member of the group has an equal chance of being sampled. Selecting a purely random sample can be difficult and expensive. Of great help is the stratified random sample, a sampling technique in which relevant strata within the group are identified and a random sample from each stratum is selected in proportion to the number of members in each stratum.

Three steps are necessary in using a stratified random sample: (1) Identify the strata within the population, (2) determine the number of instances in each stratum, and (3) select randomly the same proportion from each stratum.

A number of fallacies are associated with the improper use of statistics: biased sample, equivocation, biased question, false dilemma, and concealed evidence.

The fallacy of biased sample is an argument that contains a sample that is not representative of the population being studied. Sample bias can originate with the pollster, sampling technique, or respondent. An example of pollster bias is Zest selecting only Zest loyalists to find out what people think of Zest soap. An example of sampling technique bias is *Literary Digest*'s sample consisting of people listed in the telephone book and city directories and its counting *only* returned ballots. An example of respondent bias is people telling the pollster what they think the pollster wants to hear and not what they actually believe or do, as in indicating what magazines they prefer.

The fallacy of equivocation, discussed in Chapter 4, can take two forms in statistics: verbal and visual. An example of verbal equivocation in statistics is the ambiguous use of the word *average*. An example of visual equivocation in statistics is a two-axis graph that not only conveys information but an interpretation as well; as when, in presenting unemployment statistics, an illustrator so compresses the graph that it conveys alarm along with statistical information.

The fallacy of biased question is an argument based on the answer to a question that is worded to draw a predetermined reply, for example, "Should the United States continue to spend millions of dollars annually on foreign aid while neglecting needed domestic problems?"

The fallacy of false dilemma is an argument that erroneously reduces the number of possible alternatives or positions on an issue, for example, "Should the United States support the Israelis or the Arabs in the Middle East?"

The fallacy of concealed evidence is an argument that presents only facts that are favorable to its conclusion while suppressing relevant but nonsupporting facts. Concealed evidence takes a nonstatistical as well as statistical form. An example of nonstatistically concealed evidence is Pertussin failing to mention the potentially dangerous ingredients in its medicated vaporizer. An example of statistically concealed evidence is a company's report of its profit picture that conceals such profits as hidden and special depreciation and reserves for contingencies. Of all the informal fallacies, concealed evidence is potentially the most harmful. To detect it, one must have a vast repertory of information, which suggests a solid reason for practical logicians to school themselves in as many fields of knowledge as they possibly can.

Summary Questions
1. Products are often sold "below list price." For example, records and cassette tapes often sport stickers showing, say, a $9.95 list price and—in bolder print or different colors—"Our Price: $7.95." Find out (if you can) what "list" the famous list price refers to. Do many stores sell at list price? Try to find out.
2. Similar to the "list price" in question 1 is the notorious phrase "Nationally Advertised at $X—Now Only $Y." Pick a product you are suspicious of, and try to find out what is behind the claim "Nationally Advertised at. . . ."
3. Words such as *natural, organic, artificial,* and so on are often used ambiguously. Find three or four examples of concealed evidence in health-oriented claims.
4. One way to raise prices without appearing to do so involves leaving the

dollar amount constant but decreasing the amount of product. Recent examples: Coffee sold in 13-oz. containers virtually indistinguishable from previous 16-oz. ones—at the same price; candy products becoming thinner and lighter—while the cardboard backing remains the same size—thus creating the illusion that the amount of candy is constant; spray deodorants decreasing from 12 oz. to 10 oz., while the can and box remain exactly the same size (in one case, the package even said "NEW!"—meaning *less!*). Find a few current examples from among products with which you are familiar.

5. Speaking of satisfaction surveys, many colleges conduct instructor evaluations based on surveys taken of students currently enrolled in an instructor's courses to evaluate his or her teaching. What do you think of such evaluations? Are these biased samples or not? What factors need to be considered in evaluating such evaluations? Have you ever taken or avoided a course based on student evaluation results? If so, what factors were most important in your decision? In your opinion, are such evaluations generally reliable? Discuss.

*ADDITIONAL EXERCISES

Identify the fallacies, if any, in the following passages. Choose from biased sample, equivocation, biased (or ambiguous) question, false dilemma, and concealed evidence. In all cases explain.

1. Test question: Is Freud's libidinal drive explanation an oversimplification of human motivation or an adequate explanation of it?
2. MORTON: Did you know that it's safer to take a trip across country than to drive into town for a movie?
   MEL: I didn't know that.
   MORTON: Amazing, but true. Half of all auto accidents occur within five miles of the driver's home.
3. Gallup Poll question: "In politics, as of today, do you consider yourself a Republican, Democrat, or Independent?"
4. WYATT: I think it'd be unconstitutional to restrict an American's right to own a handgun. And plenty of Americans would agree.
   ELLEN: Oh, come on now. How do you know how many Americans would agree?
   WYATT: Are you kidding? A survey was just conducted that backs up what I'm saying.
   ELLEN: Is that a fact? Who conducted it?
   WYATT: The American Rifle Association.
   ELLEN: I rest my case.
5. RELUCTANT AUTO BUYER: I don't know. The sticker price doesn't seem like such a deal to me.
   SALESPERSON: Okay, tell you what I'm going to do. I'm going to slash three hundred bucks off the sticker price. How's that?
   RAB: Now you're talking.
6. "The extra strength non-aspirin in Datril 500 worked better than 2 leading prescription pain relievers." (ad for Datril 500)
7. TONI: I'm definitely going on Dr. Linn's high-protein diet.
   JULIE: I don't blame you. It's the quickest way ever to lose weight. And much safer than fasting.
8. Gallup Poll question: "How would you describe yourself—as very conservative, fairly conservative, middle of the road, fairly liberal, or very liberal?"

9. "Incredible. Almost 50 percent of America's children don't get their recommended daily allowance of vitamin C. That's why I'm glad my whole family loves the fresh taste of TANG Instant Breakfast Drink. It gives us a full day's supply of vitamin C." (Florence Henderson, ad for TANG)

10. Administrators at Hudson State College are interested in determining why Hudson graduates attended Hudson and what factors contributed to their successful completion. So they devise a questionnaire, which they send to their graduates. Among the questions asked is this one: "How important does each of the following items appear to you now that you have graduated? (PLEASE CHECK EACH ITEM THAT APPLIES.)" The respondents are asked to react to the items as follows: Not Important, Important, Very Important, No Opinion/Not Applicable. Here are some of the items: writing emphasis, logic course, math course, science courses, behavioral science courses, humanities courses.

11. "News Industry—Responsible or Reckless?" (cover of *U.S. News & World Report,* April 29, 1974)

12. Gallup Poll question: "Many states have tenure laws, which means that a teacher cannot be fired except by some kind of court procedure. Are you for giving teachers tenure or are you against tenure?"

13. "Here's 7 cents to try a cereal that's big with kids. Save 7 cents when you buy Post Honeycomb cereal. It's a big, nutritious cereal kids love to eat. . . . Fortified with 8 essential vitamins." (ad for Post Honeycomb)

14. STU. What a fraud!
    JAY: What are you so hot about?
    STU: You remember that "winner-take-all" tennis match on TV last spring?
    JAY: Sure. That was great. I hope they televise something like that again this year.
    STU: Oh, yeah? Well, what if I told you that it wasn't a winner-take-all proposition at all?
    JAY: What?
    STU: That's right—everybody who participated got handsomely paid for it.
    JAY: Why, if I had known that I wouldn't have watched it.

15. "Why do doctors recommend Tylenol more than all leading aspirin brands combined? The reason is simple. Tylenol reduces pain and fever as effectively as aspirin but is far less likely to cause side effects. What are some of the common aspirin side effects? Heartburn, nausea, and allergic reactions are just a few. But perhaps the most common aspirin side effect is stomach bleeding." (ad for Tylenol)

16. Gallup Poll question: "Do you know what the metric system is?"

17. "*Fact:* Ready-to-eat cereals do not increase tooth decay in children.
    Fact: Ready-sweetened cereals are highly nutritious.
    Fact: There is no more sugar in a one-ounce serving of a ready-sweetened cereal than in an apple or banana or in a serving of orange juice.
    Fact: The per capita sugar consumption in the United States has remained practically unchanged for the last 50 years." (part of a two-page ad entitled "A Statement from Kellogg Company on the Nutritional Value of Ready-Sweetened Cereals")

18. "The American Funeral: Useless tradition for the dead . . . or useful therapy for the living?" (ad for Clark Metal Funeral Vaults)

19. RON: Smoking pot definitely leads to heroin addiction.
    ROY: Oh, I don't know.
    RON: Figures don't lie. A report by the U.S. Commission of Narcotics on a study of 2,000 narcotics addicts in a prison shows that well over two-thirds smoked marijuana before using heroin.
    ROY: Hmm, I guess I can't argue with that.

20. "When you start an IRA or Keogh retirement program at Glendale Federal, you'll get an immediate substantial deduction. But that's only part of your tax relief. For example, IRA, the Individual Retirement Account, can earn *tax-sheltered* interest of

7.75 percent a year. So if you were to contribute the allowable $1,500 each year, you would have:

After	With a Tax-Sheltered Plan	Without a Tax-Sheltered Plan	Extra Money for Retirement
10 years	$25,548	$15,758	$7,790
20 years	$74,670	$44,098	$30,571
30 years	$185,653	$95,067	$90,586"

(ad for Glendale Federal Savings and Loan Association)

21. Gallup Poll question: "There's always much discussion about the qualification of presidential candidates—their education, age, race, religion, and the like. If your party nominated a generally well-qualified man for president and he happened to be a black, would you vote for him?" (Do you think that Gallup should have asked this other question to put the results of the preceding one in proper perspective: "How likely do you think it is that your party will nominate a black for the presidency some time in the next twenty years?")

22. "150% raise for Redding council studied" (This headline in the Redding, Calif., *Record Searchlight,* November 4, 1986, is for an article about an increase in city council salaries from $200/month to $500/month; the last pay increase for the council was $150 to $200 in January 1977.)

23. A 2-oz. jar of *Royal Kona* freeze-dried instant coffee sold for $7.34 in October 1985. (Hint: What does that cost per pound?)

24. "A vigorous lifestyle puts extra demand on your body. So if you play golf or tennis or swim, walk, jog or bike, you should know about our formula." (ad for Activi-tamins)

25. "Over $33\frac{1}{3}$% Larger!" (copy on wrapper of 0.78-oz. candy bar)

part F I V E

Deduction

13

Categorical Syllogisms

I readily own, that all right reasoning may be reduced to Aristotle's forms of syllogism.

JOHN LOCKE

Having just completed a rather heated "discussion" about the science of deduction with his new friend Sherlock Holmes, an annoyed Dr. John Watson tries to change the subject by calling Holmes's attention to a fellow walking slowly down the opposite side of Baker Street. Glancing out the window, Holmes says, "You mean the retired sergeant of Marines."

This further annoyed Watson, who thought to himself, "Brag and bounce! He knows I cannot verify his guess."

But as things tend to happen in the world of Holmes and Watson, the good Doctor was indeed given the chance to verify Holmes's "guess"—and guess what? The Great Deducer was right again. But how? What mysterious powers did Holmes possess that Watson (and most of the rest of us) lacked?

Let Holmes himself explain it in "A Study in Scarlet":

> "Even across the street I could see a great blue anchor tatooed on the back of the fellow's hand. That smacked of the sea. He had a military carriage, however, and regulation side whiskers. There we have the marine. He was a man of some amount of self-importance and a certain air of command [evidenced by] the way in which he held his head and swung his cane. A steady, respectable middle-aged man, too, on the face of him—all facts which led me to believe that he had been a sergeant."
> "Wonderful!" Watson ejaculated.
> "Commonplace," said Holmes. . . .[1]

Wait a minute! What's going on here? Surely Holmes is being hasty when he concludes that only seamen have great blue anchor tattoos. And how does one recognize "an air of command"? Why couldn't this fellow have been a sailor who just happened to have a "military bearing"? And couldn't a middle-aged man still be a private? Or a lieutenant?

These are all reasonable questions. And it is possible that Holmes had other bits of information that would substantiate these *inductive inferences*. But it is his *deduction* of which he seems most proud. *A deductive argument is an argument whose premises, it is claimed, logically entail its conclusion.* This means that when the premises of a valid deductive argument are considered as true, they provide certain logical grounds for its conclusion: You cannot logically accept the premises of a valid deduction and reject its conclusion. Thus, if it is accepted as true that "All mothers are females" and that "The bank's loan officer is a mother," *logically speaking* it must also be the case that "The bank's loan officer is a female." Likewise, if it's considered as true that "All red objects are apples" and that "The object I am wearing on my head for warmth and fashion is red," then it follows with *logical* (versus factual) certainty that "The object I am wearing on my head for warmth and fashion is an apple."

Of course not all deductive arguments are correct. There are some whose conclusions do not logically follow from premises accepted as true, as in the following:

> All mothers are females.
> Two-year-old Amy is a female.
> _____
> Therefore, two-year-old Amy is a mother.

The conditions under which deductive arguments are valid will constitute a major part of our study of deductive inference.

If we attempt to reconstruct part of Holmes's deductive reasoning, it might go as follows:

> I: a. All those with great blue anchor tatoos are somehow
>   associated with the sea.
>   b. This fellow has a great blue anchor tattoo.
>   _____
>   Therefore, this fellow is somehow associated with the sea.
>
> II: c. All those with "regulation" side whiskers are military
>   personnel.

[1]Arthur Conan Doyle, *The Complete Sherlock Holmes,* vol. 1 (Garden City, N.Y.: Doubleday & Company, 1930), pp. 25–26.

d. This fellow has "regulation" side whiskers.

Therefore, this fellow is a military man.

III: e. No sailors have a military bearing.
f. This fellow has a military bearing.

Therefore, this fellow is not a sailor.

IV: g. There are only two types of military services associated with the sea: sailors and marines.
h. This fellow is a military man associated with the sea.
[*h* comes from the conjunction of the conclusions deduced in I and II]

Therefore, this fellow is either a sailor or a marine.

V: i. This fellow must be either a sailor or a marine.
[*i* is the conclusion of IV]
j. This fellow is not a sailor. [*j* is the conclusion of III]

Therefore, this fellow is a marine.

And of course Holmes would also have arguments supporting his claim that the man is retired, and so on.

We see how Holmes has strung together a series of simple deductive arguments consisting of two premises and one conclusion. Such arguments are called *syllogisms*. Note, too, how he used the conclusion of one argument as a premise in another. Most complex arguments can be broken down into such a series of smaller arguments. This makes the task of analysis manageable. But just as a chain is no stronger than its weakest link, so, too, a complex argument is no better than each of its parts.

We see also that Holmes's arguments consist of three basic deductive types, called *forms*.

1. All X is Y.	2. No X is Y.	3. Either X or Y.
This is X.	This is X.	Not X.
Thus, this is Y.	Thus, this is not Y.	Thus, Y.

Arguments I, II, and IV are examples of the first form, argument III is an example of the second form, and argument V is an instance of the third type. As we proceed, we shall see that *validity is a function of form* and that it is useful to be able to translate arguments from ordinary language into their basic formal "shapes."

Whether or not this string of syllogisms is precisely Holmes's reasoning, it illustrates how induction and deduction work together in so much of our thinking. Both kinds of reasoning are involved in Holmes's claims. Reasoning inductively, he draws factual inferences, such as *a, c,* and *e*. These strong generalizations are actually the conclusions of inductive arguments, and as such are judged as true or false within varying degrees of probability. They are then used as premises to help logically entail conclusions in deductive arguments. (Induction is covered fully in Part Four.)

So, the "Science of Deduction" of which Holmes brags involves the use of these inductive inferences, plus factual observations, to construct *deductive arguments*. Arguments I through V are deductive arguments. That is, they are attempts to establish the truths of their conclusions with *logical certainty*. Holmes refers to deduction as a "science" because the principles of deduction are fixed.

Thus, for example, *any* argument of the first form will be valid—without exception. If we ignore—for the moment—whether or not the premises are in fact true, we can evaluate deductive arguments on purely logical grounds. We can analyze them in terms of whether or not they establish an airtight logical connection between their premises and conclusions.

There are good reasons for studying deduction. First, we will not need to be experts in history, social customs, military fashions, physics, chemistry, or any other factual matters. We can analyze deductive arguments on purely logical grounds by using certain deductive rules and principles. Second, deductive arguments are either valid or invalid: There is no middle ground to frustrate or confuse us. Next, the concept of *logical form* is an essential part of all logical analysis, and the study of deductive arguments is an excellent way to learn to distinguish the form of an argument from its content. Last, as we become proficient logicians, we discover that we can *quickly* analyze arguments for the presence of deductive fallacies because we do not have to get involved in the often difficult task of evaluating their factual claims. If they prove to be invalid, we are relieved of the burden of factual testing, since no matter what the facts may be, an invalid argument remains invalid, and therefore unsound.

This chapter begins our study of deductive reasoning and argument. One of the most common forms of deductive argument is the syllogism, a few examples of which we have just seen. Actually, there are several kinds of syllogisms, which are distinguished according to the types of propositions they contain. In this chapter we'll focus on the categorical syllogism and learn a way of determining when categorical syllogisms are valid. But first we'll contrast induction and deduction and review some crucial concepts connected with these complementary modes of reasoning.

INDUCTION AND DEDUCTION

If someone said to you, "There are two persons inside and only one is a male," what would you infer about the other person? If a church bell *only* tolls the hour, what can you infer if the church bell, working accurately, is tolling? If everyone who studies logic stands a good chance of not being "gouged" in the marketplace, what can you infer if you're studying logic? One thing is true of all your inferences: They're logically *certain*. By logically certain it is meant that if the premises are true, the conclusion follows necessarily. *The reasoning process that leads to logical certainty is called deduction.*

With induction our conclusions are at best highly probable, never certain. But as we saw in the Holmes illustration, deduction and induction are not incompatible. On the contrary, consider this example. Assuming you're dealing with an ordinary deck of fifty-two playing cards, you know the chances of drawing a red card are one in two. And you know this with logical certainty— there just aren't any other possibilities. What you don't know with certainty, of course, is the outcome itself: whether you will actually draw a red card. Your chances of doing this are fifty-fifty; they're uncertain. Through deduction you *know with logical certainty* what your chances are; through induction you *know with probability* what the outcome will be. So the two methods—deduction and induction—are as intimately joined as two sides of the same card.

Related to the idea that deductive arguments lead to logically certain conclusions is the notion of validity. Given the premises "All apples are fruits" and "This object is an apple," you would certainly conclude that "This object is a fruit." It is logically impossible—given the truth of the premises—that any other factor, condition, or circumstance could intervene between these two premises and that conclusion, just as it was logically impossible for the chances of drawing a red card from an ordinary playing deck of fifty-two cards to be anything but one in two. *When the premises of an argument logically entail a conclusion, the argument is called valid.* Validity, strictly speaking, applies only to deductive arguments. Again, remember that in our study of induction we observed that inductive conclusions are never certain because more complete, accurate, and relevant evidence affects the reliability of such arguments. Thus, if we reason that "Since all the planes have been on time, the next one probably will be on time," we are reasoning inductively to a probable but not certain conclusion. In other words, nothing about that premise makes its conclusion necessary. So we shouldn't apply the term *valid* to inductive arguments but should instead reserve it for deductive arguments whose premises, when assumed true, entail or logically guarantee their conclusions.

Another point to note about deduction and induction: Often deduction is described as reasoning from the general to the specific. This means that we move from a statement describing a condition that holds true in all or almost all instances to a statement describing a particular extension of that condition; from "All apples are fruits," we move to "This apple is a fruit." It's true that deductive reasoning usually takes this form, but not exclusively. Although it may sound peculiar, we could deductively reason from the general statement "All apples are fruits" to another general statement: "Therefore, no nonfruit is an apple." Or we could deduce from the specific "This apple is a fruit and a dessert" to the equally specific "This apple, therefore, is a fruit." Similarly, although induction is frequently described as moving from the specific to the general—which it often does—we could move from the general to the specific, as in "All the planes have been on time, so the next plane probably will be on time." To talk in terms of moving from the general to the specific or from the specific to the general is, then, an inexact way of distinguishing deductive from inductive arguments. *The precise difference between these two methods of reasoning is that in a valid deductive argument the conclusion necessarily follows from the truth of its premises; in a proper inductive argument the conclusion follows with a high degree of probability but not with logical certainty.*

When we call a deductive argument valid, we don't make any comment about the actual truth of its premises or conclusion. Consider this argument: "All things with legs are humans. This spider has legs; therefore, this spider is a human." This deductive argument is valid; its premises entail its conclusion. But is it empirically true? No. Validity has nothing to do with empirical truth, although "soundness" does. *A deductive argument that is sound is one that is true and valid.* In discussing induction and informal fallacies, we learned much about evaluating premises for truth. And we'll have ample opportunity to apply this knowledge in determining *sound* deductive arguments. But we must first learn more about the other dimension of soundness in deduction: validity.

There are precise rules of correct reasoning that determine whether a deductive argument is valid. These rules pertain to the *form* the argument takes, that is, how the argument appears. In dealing with inductive arguments, we were concerned primarily with an argument's *content*. In evaluating deductive arguments, we'll focus initially on form, for with deductive arguments it's not a question of what is said but of *how* it is said. Before getting technical about this subject of argumentative form, let's simply illustrate what we mean. Consider these two arguments:

> All apples are fruits.
> This object is an apple.
> _____
> Therefore, this object is a fruit.

and

> All apples are fruits.
> This object is a fruit.
> _____
> Therefore, this object is an apple.

We need no course in logic to tell us the first argument is correct and the second is not. But not all arguments are this simple. Some are very complex. Nevertheless, the errors they make are frequently of the same kind as the error this second argument makes: a *formal* error, an error in the way the terms relate to one another. If we can learn to spot these formal fallacies quickly and easily, we can separate the valid deductive arguments from the invalid ones. This is important, for if an argument is invalid, it is unsound—even if it is true. And if an argument is unsound, we shouldn't be persuaded by it.

Before we can hope to evaluate deductive arguments, we must know how they appear. Deductive arguments, such as the ones about the apples, appear as *syllogisms*. A *syllogism is a deductive argument containing two premises and a conclusion*. In this chapter we'll study what is perhaps the commonest expression of the syllogism: the standard-form categorical syllogism. The basic building block of all syllogisms, particularly this kind, is the *categorical proposition*.

CATEGORICAL PROPOSITIONS

In Chapter 1 we defined an argument as a group of statements, one of which, it is claimed, logically follows from the others. We call these statements propositions. Propositions are statements that are either true or false. Just as propositions make up inductive arguments, so they make up deductive arguments, too. And just as in inductive arguments, some deductive propositions relate two classes, *a class being a group of things having a common property or characteristic*. The proposition "All apples are fruits" relates the class *apples* with the class *fruits*. *Apples* is that class of things sharing the common characteristic of being an apple; *fruits* is that class of things sharing the common characteristic of being a fruit. In speaking of classes, Aristotle, "the father of logic," used the word *category*. So naturally enough, *any proposition that asserts that one class is included in whole or in part within another class* (such as the proposition "All apples are fruits") *is referred to as a categorical proposition*.

The statement "All apples are fruits" asserts that the whole class *apples* is included within the class *fruits*. Propositions of similar form are "All mothers are females"; "All humans are vertebrates"; "All dogs are carnivores." Sometimes a class is composed of several words, as in: "All *U.S. Presidents are persons who are at least thirty-five years old*" and "All *children too old to qualify are spectators for this event*." And of course, some categorical propositions are blatantly false:

"All giraffes are animals of prey"; "All swimmers who wear caps are women"; "All things that fly are birds." But in studying deductive validity, as we noted, we're not concerned with the empirical truth of an argument's premises but with the argument's form. It's an argument's form that ultimately determines whether or not the argument is *valid*.

All the propositions we've mentioned so far take the form "All something is something." If we merely substitute S for the first *something*, or class term, and P for the second *something*, or class term, we have a form that reads: "All S is P."

*EXERCISE 13-1 _____

1. Name completely the classes that are being related in the following propositions.

    a. All Californians are citizens.
    b. All baseball players are athletes.
    c. All those breaking the law are criminals.
    d. All newspapers that suppress news are inadequate sources of information.
    e. All commercials that rely solely on persuasive techniques to communicate are vehicles of noninformation.
    f. All nonvoters are citizens who should not complain when things don't go as they'd wish.
    g. All nonparticipants in the finals held over the weekend in Washington are non-enrollees in next year's competition, to be held on July 4 at a yet-to-be-designated city.

2. Can you name completely the classes being related in the following propositions?

    a. No police officer is a thief.
    b. Some police officers are thieves.
    c. Some police officers are not thieves.
    d. No non-police officer is a thief.
    e. No non-police officer is a nonthief.
    f. Some nonthieves are not police officers.
    g. Some non-police officers who are chronically complaining about the lack of law and order are themselves violators of the law.
    h. No police officer who takes the oath seriously and does the best he or she can is a person who must ever fear a charge of noncompliance with the law.

Propositional Form

When we speak of a proposition's form, we refer to the manner in which the proposition speaks of its classes. The form "All S is P" is the form of any proposition that relates one class to another in exactly this way.

Each member of the statement "All S is P" is performing a job. The *all* is telling us *how many* of S we're talking about. For this reason, *all* is said to quantify or to be the *quantifier* of this form. Here *all* speaks of S in a universal way; that is, it includes every single S. Because *is* links or couples the S and the P, *is* is said to be the *copula* of the propositional form.

Notice that *is* is affirmative. We speak of a form as having quality; *the quality of a proposition indicates whether the proposition is affirmative or negative.* In this instance *is* obviously affirms something between S and P; therefore, this particular form, All S is P, is affirmative.

What about S and P? We already know they stand for classes. *But if we define the subject as whatever appears between the quantifier and the copula, S represents the subject as well. And if we define the predicate as whatever follows the copula, P represents the predicate.* So we can see that S and P stand not only for class terms but also for the subject and predicate of the proposition itself.

Since we can put any proposition of this type into the form "All S is P," we may call this form *standard,* which is to say it's a conventional designation of all propositions that speak of their class terms in this way. "All S is P," then, simply says that every member of the class S is included within the class P (that is, "All apples are fruits"; "All humans are vertebrates"; "All mothers are females"). Since the quantity signified by *all* is *universal*—it includes every member of the S class—and since the quality of the proposition is affirmative—it affirms something of the subject class—this standard-form categorical proposition ("All S is P") is called a *universal affirmative*.

Aristotle observed four ways to relate the same subject and predicate of a categorical proposition. We've spoken of one; now let's consider the other three.

Consider the proposition "No apples are fruits." This relates the same subject and predicate as the proposition "All apples are fruits," but it relates them in a different way. Likewise, we could say "No humans are vertebrates" or "No mothers are females." We could represent such propositions symbolically as follows: "No S is P," in which S and P again signify class terms as well as subject and predicate of the given proposition. Like the universal affirmative, "No S is P" also says something about every member of its subject class. The quantifier *no* really means that every single member of the S class (apples) is excluded from the P class (fruits). So its quantity is certainly universal. Since "No S is P" is denying membership of one class within another, its *quality* is negative. So we can conclude that *"No S is P" is a universal negative standard-form categorical proposition.*

We can speak of the same subject and predicate in still another way. This time we'll not speak of all the members of a class but only of some; thus, "Some apples are fruits." Unlike the two standard-form universal propositions we spoke of, this form—"Some S is P"—does not speak of its subject term universally. The proposition says that there exists at least one particular instance of the subject and it will be found within the predicate class. In other words, "Some S is P" is affirming *partial* membership of S within P. Is it affirmative or negative? Affirmative. Such a propositional form that *affirms particular* membership of the subject within the predicate we call, appropriately enough, a *particular affirmative* standard-form categorical proposition.

As we saw, we can have both universal negative and universal affirmative propositions. Likewise, we can have particular negative as well as particular affirmative propositions. This is the fourth standard way of expressing a relationship between a subject and predicate class. The proposition "Some apples are not fruits" is an example of a particular negative proposition. As was true of the particular affirmative, this propositional form—"Some S is not P"—talks about some but not all members of the subject class. This is why we call it a particular proposition. Rather than affirming partial subject class membership within the predicate class, this form denies it. We call such a proposition that denies partial membership of one of a class within another a *particular negative* standard-form categorical proposition.

These, then, are the four standard-form categorical propositions:

All *S* is *P*—universal affirmative
No *S* is *P*—universal negative
Some *S* is *P*—particular affirmative
Some *S* is not *P*—particular negative

In each, the *S* and *P* stand for subject and predicate and for class terms. The *all* and *no* mean that every member of the class is being referred to; the *some* means that at least one existing member of the class is being referred to. For simplicity we refer to the four standard forms by these letters: *A* (universal affirmative), *E* (universal negative), *I* (particular affirmative), and *O* (particular negative). These letter designations come from the Latin words *affirmo* ("I affirm") and *nego* ("I deny"), *affirmo* supplying the *A* and *I* and *nego* the *E* and *O*.

Since we are dealing with the form—and not the content—of the propositions at this stage, we should take advantage of this simplification. Every single *A, E, I,* or *O* type proposition will have the preceding form. No matter how long and complicated the class terms may be, the basic form remains the same. For example, the proposition "All students with short hair, but without moustaches, who have gone to college for one semester, but whose GPA is between 2.3 and 3.4, with one older brother and two younger sisters, whose last name begins with *M* are Democrats" is a basic *A* proposition. The subject term begins after the quantifier (*all*) with the word *students* and ends with *M*, before the copula (*are*).

STUDY HINT: PRACTICE REDUCING CATEGORICAL PROPOSITIONS TO STANDARD FORM BY KEYING IN ON THE QUANTIFIER AND COPULA.

Whatever falls between the quantifier and copula is always the subject. Whatever comes after the copula is the predicate.

A good way to familiarize yourself with the four forms is to underline the quantifier and copula of a proposition. This will immediately isolate the subject and predicate.

EXERCISE 13-2 _____

1. Name the subject and predicate terms of the following propositions; indicate their quantity and quality.

   a. Some women are not members of the women's liberation movement.
   b. No desirable leader is a coward.
   c. All business people are rugged individualists.
   d. All educators for capital punishment are nonhumanitarians.
   e. No Christian is a believer in abortion.
   f. Some students are either arts or science majors.
   g. Some candidates who are not heavily financed are not potential pawns of big-money interests.
   h. No one who believes in premarital sex is a nonsponsor of premarital cohabitation.

i. Some ecologists are nonopponents of offshore drilling.

j. No father who cares about his child's welfare is one who'd take his child to an X-rated film!

k. Some patients exhibiting all the symptoms of schizophrenia are manic-depressives.

l. No companies doing business in the Middle East are secure firms.

m. Some feathered things that fly are not birds.

n. Some stockbrokers who work for E. F. Hutton are not partners in companies whose securities they recommend.

o. All physicians who are licensed to practice in this state are medical school graduates who have passed special qualifying examinations but are not necessarily internists.

p. Some politicians who are not highly respected by the people are, without doubt, honest people.

q. No serious musician—stereotypes notwithstanding—is a dullard whose interests lie in nothing more than what's contained in a musical score.

r. Some women, despite what men say, are workers who are capable of outperforming their male counterparts.

s. No thing that is long lasting and productive of great long-term pleasure is an object that we should treat in a cavalier fashion.

t. Some occasions of intense suffering, though seemingly pointless, are opportunities for the growth that is necessary to achieve maturity.

2. By giving the letter and name, designate the form of each of the preceding propositions.

Distribution

There's one other point to remember about the standard-form propositions—*A, E, I, O*—and that concerns the question of their *distribution.* We know that when a proposition speaks *universally* of one of its terms it talks about every single member of that class, or *distributes* that term. *A proposition distributes a term if it refers to all members of the class designated by that term.* An *A* proposition ("All *S* is *P*") distributes its subject term because it speaks universally of *S.* Do you think it distributes its predicate? If it does, *S* and *P,* with respect to distribution, are being spoken of in the same way. In a proposition that handles its subject and predicate in the same way—distributes both or does not—the subject and predicate can be interchanged with no loss of logical meaning. Is "All fruits are apples" the logical equivalent of "All apples are fruits"? Obviously not. Let's use a diagram to see why not.

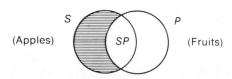

The circles represent all members of both the *S* and the *P* classes. Since the propositional form claims that every instance of *S* is also an instance of *P,* let's indicate that the class of *S* without *P* is empty. We do this by shading out the appropriate area. The diagram now shows that "All *S* is *P,*" as in "All apples are fruits." But is every instance of *P* an instance of *S*? No. Some portion of *P* exists apart from *S*: Some fruits are not apples. So *an A proposition distributes its subject but does not distribute its predicate.*

In speaking of *E* propositions ("No *S* is *P*"), we saw how they distribute their subject terms, that is, exclude every member of the subject class from the predicate class. Does an *E* proposition distribute its *P* term? Is "No fruits are apples" the logical equivalent of "No apples are fruits"? Yes, these are equivalents. The following diagram illustrates the point.

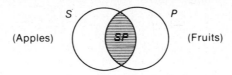

The circles again represent all members of both the *S* and *P* classes. The diagram shows that the class *SP* is empty, as the proposition "No *S* is *P*" prescribes. We see that *S* and *P* have no members in common (the shaded area *SP* is unoccupied), that every member of each class excludes every member of the other. This is why "No apples are fruits" has its equivalent in "No fruits are apples." We are speaking of the classes in the exact same way. *In an* E *proposition, we are distributing both* S *and* P.

The particular affirmative proposition, *I*, obviously does not distribute its subject term because it speaks of *some,* not *all.* It says that there exists at least one member of the subject class that is a member of the predicate class. This is the meaning of *some: There exists at least one member.* But it also says only some members of the predicate class are members of the subject class. In other words, it doesn't distribute its predicate either; it speaks of its predicate in the same partial terms that it speaks of its subject, as the following diagram illustrates:

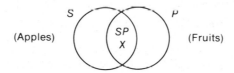

The form "Some *S* is *P*" claims that at least one member of the *SP* class exists. *X* represents the existence of this one member. Notice that only part of each circle is excluded from the other, which illustrates that neither term is spoken of universally. Since the subject and predicate are spoken of in precisely the same way, that is, as undistributed terms, we can interchange them and have a proposition equivalent to the original. So "Some apples are fruits" is logically equivalent to "Some fruits are apples." In other words, both propositions share the same portions of the interlocked circles shown.

Finally, in discussing the *O* form, "Some *S* is not *P*," we saw that the *S* term is spoken of particularly; therefore, *O* propositions do not distribute their subject terms. A superficial look at an *O* proposition suggests that the *P* term is undistributed as well. But is it? Actually, in the proposition "Some *S* is not *P*," aren't we saying that *every member of the* P *class will exclude the particular members of the* S *class of which we're speaking?* In other words, "some *S*" is excluded from *all* of *P*; there is "some *S*" that is not identical with *any* member of *P*; every instance of *P* will exclude "some *S*." This is perhaps difficult to grasp. A good way to see it is, again, with the help of a diagram.

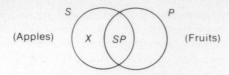

The diagram illustrates what "Some *S* is not *P*" is really saying. It says there exists at least one member of *S* (*X*) that is excluded from *P*. In other words, *every* instance of *P* will exclude the particular member of *S* that falls outside it ("some *S*"). Again, "some *S*" is always outside the *entire* class *P*. To see this in an actual proposition, consider "Some females are not mothers." If we try to interchange the subject and predicate here, we do not come up with an equivalent to the original proposition. Instead, we come up with "Some mothers are not females." This proves that the terms are not being spoken of equally: One is being distributed, but the other is not. (It is only by chance that many propositions, such as "Some males are not politicians," seem to produce an equivalent when we interchange the subject and predicate terms: "Some politicians are not males." This should impress on us the importance of *form*, not content, in determining the validity of a deductive argument. Distribution is vital in proving arguments valid.) The terms in boldface are always distributed—and only those terms—according to the following pattern:

A: All **S** is P.
E: No **S** is **P**.
I: Some S is P.
O: Some S is not **P**.

STUDY HINT

In determining subject, predicate, and distribution in standard-form categorical propositions, the key factor is *where* the term occurs and *not what* it says.

The following chart will help us master what we've discovered so far about standard-form categorical propositions.

Categorical Proposition	Designation	Quantity	Quality	Distribution
All S is P	A	universal	affirmative	subject only
No S is P	E	universal	negative	subject and predicate
Some S is P	I	particular	affirmative	neither subject nor predicate
Some S is not P	O	particular	negative	predicate only

*EXERCISE 13-3 _____

Name the form of each of the following propositions and what it distributes.

1. Some children are lovers of ice cream.
2. No revolutionary is a believer in the status quo.

3. All men in combat are soldiers under extraordinary pressure.
4. All noncombatants earning combat pay are shameless individuals.
5. Some film projectionists are not members of a union.
6. Compared with foreign automobile manufacturers, some American automobile manufacturers, despite various pressures, are reluctant observers of the public interest.
7. Some nonmartial arts are not exercises that are lacking in physical courage.
8. All students, some of whom are under twenty-one, are advocates of more tax money spent on education.
9. Some colors of the rainbow are not hues seen anywhere else.
10. Some lives are tragedies that we write, direct, and star in.

We've learned what a categorical proposition is and the forms that it can take. We're now ready to turn to the deductive arguments containing such propositions.

Since syllogisms often appear in deductive arguments, we must find out what a syllogism is, how we can construct one, and what role the syllogism plays in argument. Again, our goal is to be able to distinguish the valid deductive argument from the invalid one, the one whose premises logically imply its conclusion from the one whose premises do not. In short, we'll learn to recognize and use correct deductive reasoning. Of course, correct deductive reasoning alone does not guarantee truth, but it *can* guarantee true conclusions *if* our premises are actually true, as this argument illustrates:

> All mothers are females.
> Some students are not females.
> Some students are not mothers.

Here both of our premises are actually true and we have reasoned correctly from those premises to our conclusion. Our argument is valid, our conclusion true; the argument is sound. But if our reasoning is invalid, no amount of true premises will *guarantee* true conclusions:

> All mothers are females.
> Some students are females.
> Some students are mothers.

Here both our premises are again true, but we have reasoned incorrectly from those premises to a conclusion. Our argument is invalid and our conclusion, although it might be true, doesn't logically follow from our premises.

Both of these deductive arguments are syllogisms. *Like all syllogisms they contain two premises and a conclusion.* Because these syllogisms contain only categorical propositions, they are called categorical syllogisms.

STANDARD-FORM CATEGORICAL SYLLOGISMS

To understand what a standard-form categorical syllogism is, let's consider this argument:

> All cigarettes are hazards to health.
> All Marlboros are cigarettes.
> All Marlboros are hazards to health.

This is a categorical syllogism. From it we can note a number of things that are characteristic of arguments like these. First, a categorical syllogism contains three categorical propositions. Second, the syllogism has *exactly three terms—cigarettes, hazards to health,* and *Marlboros*. Third, *each of the terms appears in exactly two of the propositions.* Fourth, *the propositions are in a certain order—the conclusion coming last and the premises coming first.* We can specify even further the order of the propositions when we realize that the *predicate term* of the conclusion (*hazards to health*) is called the *major term* of a syllogism, and the *subject term* of the conclusion (*Marlboros*) is called the *minor term.* The premise containing the major term is called the *major premise;* the one with the minor term is the *minor premise.* (The term common to both premises is called the *middle term;* here it's "cigarettes.") Like this one, a categorical syllogism should always appear in this order: major premise, minor premise, conclusion. These, then, are the defining characteristics of any standard-form categorical syllogism: (1) It consists of three categorical propositions; (2) it has exactly three terms; (3) each of its terms appears in exactly two of the propositions; and (4) it appears in the order of major premise, minor premise, and conclusion. To determine the validity of such an argument, we must know about its form.

We can summarize what we've so far learned about syllogistic form as follows:

1. The conclusion determines the major and minor terms of a categorical syllogism.
2. The *major term* is always *the same term as the predicate* of the conclusion.
3. The *minor term* is always *the same term as the subject* of the conclusion.
4. The *middle term is not in the conclusion but is common to each premise.*

Remember, look to the conclusion to determine the major and minor term. Once we have identified the components of the syllogism, determining its form is a mechanical matter.

*EXERCISE 13-4 _____

In the following syllogisms (1) state the three terms; (2) state the major and minor terms; (3) state the major and minor premises; and (4) order them correctly, assuming the last statements in **1** through **5** are the conclusions.

1. All political candidates are seekers of offices.
   Some political candidates are Republicans.
   Some Republicans are seekers of offices.
2. No true sportsman is a cheater.
   All cheaters are dishonest persons.
   No dishonest person is a true sportsman.
3. Some animals are not endangered species.
   All endangered species are precious creatures.
   Some animals are not precious creatures.
4. Some epicureans are lovers of wine.
   Some epicureans are lovers of women.
   Some lovers of wine are lovers of women.
5. All pollutants are disease carriers.
   All cigarettes are disease carriers.
   All cigarettes are pollutants.
6. All men are equal citizens and all equal citizens are persons entitled to due process.
   Therefore all men are persons entitled to due process.

7. Some countries are belligerents and no belligerents are peace lovers. It follows that some countries are not peace lovers.
8. No sprinters are slow runners, because no slow runners are members of the track team, and all sprinters are members of the track team.
9. Since some TV programs are bores and all bores are wastes of time, some TV programs are wastes of time.
10. Some airlines are poor means of transportation, for all airlines are expensive enterprises and some expensive enterprises are poor means of transportation.

Form

A syllogism's form consists of its mood and its figure. The mood of a syllogism is the order in which the propositions occur when the syllogism is in standard form. We determine the *mood* of a standard-form categorical syllogism by noting the order of the standard-form categorical propositions it contains. In our sample syllogism

> All cigarettes are hazards to health.
> All Marlboros are cigarettes.
> ─────────────────────────────
> All Marlboros are hazards to health.

the order is AAA, that is, the major premise is an A proposition, the minor premise is A, and the conclusion is A.

The figure of a syllogism is determined by the location of the middle term, the middle term being the term that appears in both premises. There are four and only four possible figure arrangements for the middle term. We can represent them as follows:

Figure 1			Figure 2			Figure 3			Figure 4	
M	P		P	M		M	P		P	M
S	M		S	M		M	S		M	S
S	P		S	P		S	P		S	P

In figure 1, the middle term appears as the subject in the major premise and predicate in the minor premise. The middle term, *cigarettes,* in the preceding argument occupies this position; so the argument is in figure 1. In figure 2, the middle term appears as the predicate of the major premise and minor premise. In figure 3, the middle term appears as subject of major and minor premises. And in figure 4, the middle term appears as the predicate of the major premise and subject of the minor premise.

If we study this chart we see a basic pattern emerge for identifying each of the four figures.

If we draw a real or imaginary line connecting the middle terms in each figure, we see the following:

Figure 1			Figure 2			Figure 3			Figure 4	
M	P		P	M		M	P		P	M
S	M		S	M		M	S		M	S
S	P		S	P		S	P		S	P

Combine a syllogism's mood and figure and you have its form. The form of the preceding syllogism, therefore, is AAA-1. The following categorical syllogisms also have form AAA-1:

> All vertebrates are creatures with spines.
> All humans are vertebrates.
> _____
> All humans are creatures with spines.

> All identical medications are drugs producing the same results.
> All aspirin are identical medications.
> _____
> All aspirin are drugs producing the same results.

> All persons with needs are potential thieves.
> All consumers are persons with needs.
> _____
> All consumers are potential thieves.

All these arguments are valid. In fact any syllogism in AAA-1 form is valid. There are 256 possible forms; only a handful are valid. Knowing that a syllogistic form is valid, we know that any argument of the same form is also valid. Likewise, knowing that a syllogistic form is invalid, we know that any argument in that form is invalid.

But before we can test a syllogism for validity, we must first be able to identify its form. One of the most important steps in this process, no matter which method of testing we ultimately use, is correctly identifying the conclusion of the syllogism. If this crucial step is missed, any subsequent analysis will be futile.

Spotting the Conclusion

In testing a syllogism, we must be sure that we have correctly identified its form. That is, we must be sure that we correctly arrange the syllogism in the standardized way: major premise, minor premise, conclusion. Initially, it is easy to confuse the order of the premises or to misidentify the conclusion. To guard against this error, concentrate on finding the conclusion.

There are usually a number of signals, or clues, which can aid us in this task. For example, consider the *grouping* of the propositions. In the syllogism "All apples are red. All apples are sweet fruit, and all sweet fruit is red," we notice that one proposition is isolated from the other two. This is our signal that it is the conclusion. (Note that such an arrangement not only isolates one proposition but also groups the other two together, suggesting that they share some common feature.)

We should also look for *signal words*. For example, the same syllogism might be expressed this way: "Since all apples are sweet fruit, and since all sweet fruit is red, all apples are red." Here, the two premises are identified by the signal word *since*. *As a general rule, signal words always precede the propositions they signal.*

If the syllogism were presented as "It follows, because all sweet fruit is red, that all apples are red, for all apples are sweet fruit," we must use both grouping and signal words to unpack this syllogism. The structure of this syllogism might be simplified like this:

It follows, because _____, that _____, for _____.

Each of the blanks represents one of the three propositions. Simplified in this way, we see that two of the propositions are identified by the premise indicators *because* and *for*.

The key in all cases is to pay attention to grouping, punctuation, and signal words. Using all the information available, we can correctly distinguish the premises of a syllogism from its conclusion with accuracy. *Identification of the conclusion is the first important step in testing syllogisms for validity.*

STUDY HINT: **DETERMINING SYLLOGISTIC FORM**

To identify the form of a standard-form categorical syllogism, follow these steps:

1. Identify the conclusion of the syllogism.
2. Find the predicate of the conclusion, and then find the premise tht contains the same term.
3. List that premise (the major premise) first.
4. List the remaining premise next. (If the syllogism is truly standard form, this premise will contain the same term as the subject of the conclusion.)
5. List the conclusion last.
6. Give the letter names of the premises and conclusion in standard-form order (major premise, minor premise, conclusion). This identifies the *mood*.
7. Find the pattern created by the middle term in each premise, and identify it according to the information on *figure* from above.
8. *Combine mood and figure to get form.*

ᴬEXERCISE 13-5 _____

1. Identify the conclusions of the following syllogisms, using grouping, punctuation, and signal words as your guides.
2. Rewrite each of the syllogisms in standard form.
3. Give the mood and figure for each of the following syllogisms:

a. Some animals are objects of worship since all cows are animals and some objects of worship are cows.

b. Some Republicans are not opponents of deficit spending since no opponents of deficit spending are Keynesians and some Republicans are Keynesians.

c. Because no biologist who believes in Darwinian evolution is a literal interpreter of Genesis, no literal interpreter of Genesis is a college graduate, since all biologists who believe in Darwinian evolution are college graduates.

d. Since all toothpastes with fluoride are cavity fighters and some peppermint toothpastes are cavity fighters, some peppermint toothpastes are toothpastes with fluoride.

e. All males interested in females only for sex are male chauvinists, and all male chauvinists are persons insecure in their sex roles. So some men interested in females only for sex are persons insecure in their own sex roles.

f. Some nonparty members are nonvoters, for all nonparty members are officers and some officers are nonvoters.

g. All married persons are consumers, so since some individuals are not married persons, some individuals are not consumers.

h. It follows, because no one signing a Living Will is a believer in suffering for suffering's sake, that no one signing a Living Will is a theist, for all believers in suffering for suffering's sake are theists.

EXERCISE 13-6 _____

Using S = minor term, P = major term, and M = middle term, construct standard-form categorical syllogisms for each of the following forms. Here's a sample, using IAI-2:

> Some P is M
> All S is M
> _____
> Some S is P

Now you try:

1. AAA-3
2. III-2
3. IOE-4
4. IOE-1
5. OIE-1
6. AEA-2
7. EEE-1
8. EEE-2
9. EIO-3
10. IAI-4

LOGICAL ANALOGIES

A good way to prove an argument *invalid* is by logical analogy. Whenever we try to prove a syllogism invalid in this way, we set up an argument that has the *same form* as the original and that has true premises. When we construct such an analogy that leads to a patent falsehood, we know that we have an invalid form. For if the form were valid, true premises should *always* entail (logically guarantee) a true conclusion. Let's see how this works.

Suppose that you expect to be cheated nearly every time you take your car to a mechanic. Your reasoning might run something like this:

> All thieves are people out to con us.
> Some mechanics are people out to con us.
> _____
> Some mechanics are thieves.

The form of your argument is AII-2.

If this form is valid, it will be impossible to set up a counterargument of the same form, one that has true premises and a false conclusion. Again, the reason is that any valid deductive argument with true premises must—of logical necessity—have a true conclusion. In other words, *it is logically impossible for a valid argument with true premises to entail anything but a true conclusion.* So if we can set up a counterargument of the form AII-2 that has true premises and a false conclusion, we will have proven that *any* argument of the AII-2 form is invalid.

Here's such a logical analogy:

> All mothers are females.
> Some infants are females.
> _____
> Some infants are mothers.

Notice that this argument's form is AII-2. It contains true premises and an obviously false conclusion. We can, therefore, conclude that the AII-2 form is invalid; and of course, that your original argument is invalid because it is *AII*-2. Notice, again, that we didn't say that the conclusion is *untrue*. Undoubtedly you could demonstrate that your premises and conclusion are true propositions. But a sound deductive argument must be *valid* as well; the premises must logically entail the conclusion. The premises of your argument, as we've shown, do not logically entail its conclusion, even when we accept them as true. And so, no matter how much we may agree with the *content* of this argument, we should not accept the *argument* as sound. If we do, we are allowing ourselves to be victimized as much by a formal fallacy as we have previously seen we can allow ourselves to be victimized by any number of informal fallacies.

To illustrate further, let's look at an argument that Slim recently zipped by Sweeney. Ever since she was in high school, Slim's been campaigning for the passage of the Equal Rights Amendment (ERA), which will ensure women equal rights under law. She's still at it. Recently she's become profoundly discouraged by the seemingly intractable opposition the ERA has met, especially among women. In fact, Slim's decided that some women, actually quite a few, she believes, just aren't aware of the "viciousness of sexism."

One day as she was expressing these feelings around the house, Sweeney decided to turn the tables on her—to test the logic of Slim's position, as she was accustomed to doing of Sweeney's. "Just what makes you think some women aren't aware of the 'viciousness of sexism,' as you call it?" he asked her.

"For two reasons," she quickly replied. "First, it's obvious that any ERA supporter is aware of the viciousness of sexism. And second, it's also obvious that a lot of women don't support the ERA." As Sweeney was thinking that over, she said to him, "Now you don't have to be a logician to see that a lot of women simply aren't conscious of how bad sexism really is."

Slim's statement is ironic—not only don't you need to be a logician to draw her conclusion, you'd better not be! The argument's invalid. We can prove this by logical analogy.

First, let's set up Slim's argument as follows:

> All ERA supporters are individuals who understand the viciousness of sexism.
> Some women are not supporters of the ERA.
> ___
> Some women are not individuals who understand the viciousness of sexism.

The form of the argument is *AOO*-1.

Now let's set up a logical analogy, ensuring that its premises are true and its conclusion false.

> All mothers are females.
> Some girls are not mothers.
> ___
> Some girls are not females.

This analogy has the same form as the original, *AOO*-1. Since its premises are true, its conclusion should also be true—if the form is valid. But its conclusion is false. Therefore, form *AOO*-1 is invalid, and Slim's argument is invalid as well—even though each of its assertions may be true.

Although logical analogies can be quick and easy ways for proving *inva-*

lidity, they aren't adequate for providing *validity.* To see why, let's set up another analogy of the *AOO*-1 form.

> All mothers are females.
> Some humans are not mothers.
> Some humans are not females.

In this *AOO*-1 categorical syllogism, the premises are true, and *so is the conclusion.* Here's another:

> All apples are fruits.
> Some hard, green objects are not apples.
> Some hard, green objects are not fruits.

Again, an argument in *AOO*-1 form with true premises and conclusion. But even if we set up a thousand such syllogisms, they would not prove the form *AOO*-1 valid, for all it takes is *one* exception. In short, if we can't think up an analogy that proves a form invalid, we can't assume that it is valid. It may be that we just haven't hit on the right analogy.

By the same token, we may be dealing with a valid form. Consider, for example, this argument:

> All events must have a cause.
> The big bang is an event.
> The big bang must have a cause.

In a subsequent chapter you'll learn why propositions such as "the big bang is an event" and "The big bang must have a cause" are actually *A* propositional forms; they're the same as saying "All *S* is *P*." So what we have here is an argument in the *AAA*-1 form. Now this form is valid. But if you didn't know that, you couldn't prove it by logical analogy. True, after several thousand analogies, you'd be inclined to think you were dealing with a valid form. But would you know *for sure?* Would you know for certain that you wouldn't eventually strike the analogy that would prove it invalid? You wouldn't.

So the logical analogy is fine for proving invalidity; it's a handy, and effective, way of demonstrating to someone the error of his or her deductive ways. So practice it; sharpen your analogical powers. In so doing you'll hone your analytical skills, and likely deflate a lot of people's arguments. But at the same time, realize that the logical analogy is inadequate for proving validity. For that we can use other techniques, which we'll learn in the next chapter.

EXERCISE 13-7 _____
Determine the forms of the following categorical syllogisms. Then, by constructing a logical analogy, prove them invalid.

1. Some books are not artworks and some artworks are not paintings; so some books are not paintings.
2. No successful surgeon is a poor person and some doctors are successful surgeons; hence, some poor persons are not doctors.
3. All capitalists are believers in the free-enterprise system, because all believers in the free-enterprise system are supporters of open competition and all supporters of open competition are capitalists.
4. No patriots are chauvinists; therefore, no patriots are fanatics, for all chauvinists are fanatics.
5. No deterrent to crime is a form of capital punishment, so because all deterrents to

crime are penalties worth preserving, no form of capital punishment is a penalty worth preserving.
6. Since some organizers of crime are respectable citizens, it follows, because some men are not respectable citizens, that some organizers of crime are not men.

SUMMARY

This chapter dealt with the categorical proposition and the standard-form categorical syllogism. A categorical proposition is a statement that relates two classes. A standard-form categorical proposition is one that relates two classes in one of four ways, as the following symbolic expressions designate: "All *S* is *P*"; "No *S* is *P*"; "Some *S* is *P*"; "Some *S* is not *P*." Each of these forms has quantity and quality: quantity pertaining to whether it's universal or particular, and quality pertaining to whether it's affirmative or negative. When a proposition speaks universally of a term, it's said to distribute it. For simplicity, these propositions are referred to by the letters *A*, *E*, *I*, and *O*.

The categorical proposition is the building block of all syllogisms. In particular, it constitutes one kind of syllogism: the standard-form categorical syllogism, which consists of three categorical propositions; has exactly three terms that appear in exactly two of its propositions; and appears in the order of major premise, minor premise, and conclusion. The major premise of a categorical syllogism is the premise containing the major term, the predicate of the conclusion. The minor premise is the premise containing the minor term, the subject of the conclusion. The remaining term of the syllogism, the one that occurs in both premises, is the middle term.

Every standard-form categorical syllogism has form: mood and figure. Its mood is the order in which it appears when properly arranged (major, minor, conclusion); mood is designated by the letters of the propositions.

The figure is the position of the middle term in the premises: figure 1, middle term in the subject position of the major premise and the predicate position of the minor premise; figure 2, middle term in the predicate position of both premises; figure 3, middle term in the subject position of both premises; figure 4, middle term in the predicate position of the major premise and subject position of the minor premise. A common way to prove a syllogistic argument invalid is to set up a logical analogy—a syllogism with the same form as the original but with true premises and a false conclusion. The logical analogy, however, is inadequate to establish validity.

A final reminder: To analyze any standard-form categorical syllogism correctly, we must accurately represent its form. The first step in doing so is to identify the conclusion. We do this by looking for signal words and grouping.

Summary Questions
1. What is the mood of a standard-form categorical syllogism with a universal affirmative minor premise, a particular negative major premise, and a conclusion that only distributes its predicate?
2. What is the figure of the syllogism described in question 1 if the major premise distributes the middle term and the minor premise distributes the minor term?

3. What is the figure of a standard-form categorical syllogism if the minor term is the predicate of the minor premise and the major term is the predicate of the major premise?

ADDITIONAL EXERCISES _____

1. Following are fifteen propositions. Give their form and tell what they distribute.
   a. No spoiled children are candidates for self-reliance.
   b. Some careless husbands are inattentive lovers.
   c. All predators are animals of prey.
   d. Some futile affairs are tragedies.
   e. All of the students are biology majors.
   f. Some candidates for self-reliance are snobs.
   g. Some predators are not threats to life.
   h. No students are males.
   i. No inattentive lovers are romantics.
   j. All wars are tragedies.
   k. Some spoiled children are snobs.
   l. No careless husbands are romantics.
   m. Some threats to life are not animals of prey.
   n. Some wars are futile affairs.
   o. No biology majors are males.

2. Assume that propositions **k** through **o** in the preceding exercise are conclusions to arguments that include as premises propositions **a** through **j**. Construct the appropriate syllogism for each conclusion, name its form, and prove it invalid by logical analogy.

3. Refute the following arguments by constructing logical analogies.
   a. All investment counselors are active opponents of restrictive mutual-fund legislation, for all active opponents of restrictive mutual-fund legislation are stockbrokers, and all stockbrokers are investment counselors.
   b. No Republicans are Democrats, so some Democrats are liberals, since some liberals are not Republicans.
   c. No scholarship winners are persons having an IQ less than 90, but all persons having an IQ less than 90 are less than average minds, so no scholarship winners are less than average minds.
   d. Some specialists are not cardiologists, so some general practitioners are not specialists, since some general practitioners are not cardiologists.

Testing Categorical Syllogisms for Validity

*The value of deduction is grounded in its emptiness.
For the very reason that the deduction does not add
anything to the premises, it may always be applied
without a risk of leading to a failure.*

HANS REICHENBACH

In the period immediately after World War II and into the era of the Korean War, many Americans were troubled by the Cold War—a period of increasing tension between the non-Communist Western world and the Communist bloc countries headed by Russia. This was a period in which schoolchildren were taught to be wary of the "Red Menace," and during which the notorious House Un-American Activities Committee, under its florid and aggressive leader Senator Joseph McCarthy, went on what has been described as a witch hunt for Communists and "fellow travelers."

Most Americans knew that Marxist-Leninist doctrine is materialistic and atheistic, denying the existence of any supernatural order. Thus, they understood that all Communists must also be atheists. From this, it seemed to follow that if "All Communists are atheists," and if a given individual were an atheist, that person must also be a Communist. This argument has its adherents even today. But is it valid?

Consider a different case. Mary Beth Sweet announces that she is going to marry Bob Slick. Asked why, she answers that Bob loves her. And how does she know that he loves her? Well, to Mary Beth, it's obvious: He is generous and attentive to her. Her reasoning is as follows: "If you love someone, you are generous and attentive to them. Bob is generous and attentive to me. Therefore, Bob loves me."

And apparently Mary Beth is not alone in accepting this argument as valid. The pattern of "winning" one's love by giving gifts (candy, flowers, records, tapes, rings, Teddy Bears, and so on) and attention (calls, dates, dinners, strolls in the park) is so well entrenched in our culture that it is easily stereotyped in movies and on television.

Although most of us probably do agree with Mary Beth that love (at least of the "romantic" variety) does *involve* such generosity and attentiveness, it is not clear exactly what the relationship between loving and generosity is from Mary Beth's argument. Is this good reasoning?

> If X loves Y, then X gives to Y.
> X gives to Y.
> _____
> Therefore, X loves Y.

Mary Beth seems to think so—and her happiness and well-being may be affected by her conclusion. Perhaps this argument "feels okay," to you too. What can you conclude from your hunch? Suppose, on the other hand, that it "doesn't seem right." Does that mean that it is invalid? Obviously, such feelings are worth pursuing—but how? It is important to separate good arguments from bad ones for many practical, social, and ethical reasons.

If we cannot do so, we might be susceptible to seduction, like Mary Beth is (her argument is an example of the *fallacy of affirming the consequent,* which we'll study in Chapter 16), if not into marriage perhaps into a "relationship" or purchase or favor. If we cannot reason clearly, we might mistake our neighbor's atheism for anti-Americanism; they are, of course, not the same thing. (The atheist/Communist argument is an example of the *fallacy of the undistributed middle term,* which we will study in this chapter.)

We might test categorical syllogisms for invalidity by using the logical analogies test we learned in Chapter 13. But using logical analogies has two serious drawbacks. First, we are not always able to think of an analogous argument; second, the use of logical analogies can be time-consuming and frustrating.

Fortunately, there are other methods for evaluating syllogisms that avoid the ambiguity and frustration of logical analogies. The charm of such "mechanical" tests is that they are "elegant": They quickly and straightforwardly reveal whether or not an argument is valid without any wasted motion. If each of their steps is correctly followed, these methods exhaust all possibilities and tell us clearly and with certainty that a given argument is valid or that it is invalid.

This chapter deals with testing categorical syllogisms for validity. We'll learn two useful and straightforward methods: the use of Venn diagrams and the use of a set of rules.

By the time you complete this chapter, then, you'll have a working knowledge of some basic syllogistic forms and of ways to prove their validity. This means, as we'll demonstrate, that you'll be able to dissect arguments and determine their correctness.

VENN DIAGRAMS

The Venn diagram method of proving syllogisms valid is certain and relatively simple and quick. With it, we construct circles to represent the class terms in a syllogism. The method is particularly helpful because it makes the syllogistic argument and the relation between class terms clearly visible. The adage "A picture is worth a thousand words" is literally true as applied to the Venn diagram, for we can actually see why a particular argument is valid or invalid. Many students, especially those who shy away from mathematics, often shudder at the thought of having to use any diagrams whatever. But when we keep in mind a few simple principles, the use of Venn diagrams becomes almost as simple as drawing circles with a dime. It's even fun. And for those who think the Venn diagram is completely strange, it might come as a surprise to learn that we've already used a modified Venn diagram to see how propositions distribute their terms. Let's now take a closer look at that diagram.

Consider the interlocking circles that we used before in speaking of distribution:

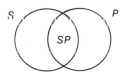

This diagram represents every instance of S and P. It also represents every instance of SP—where S and P come together. If we examine this diagram, we observe (1) that a portion of the S circle excludes a portion of the P circle, (2) that both S and P share a portion of the diagram, and (3) that a portion of the P circle excludes a portion of the S circle. We know we can represent (2) by placing SP where we have, or PS since they are equivalent (the same as 3 times 2 is the equivalent of 2 times 3). How in the diagram would you present (1) and (3)? To do this let's introduce the term *complement*.

Complement means that which *completes*. If S represents a class, the complement of that class will be everything else it takes to complete the whole universe of things. Everything that isn't S: non-S. Taken together, S and non-S complete everything that is. So do P and non-P. Put another way: The complement of a term is everything that the term is not. What would the complement of apples be? Nonapples. And the complement of nonhouses? Houses. Non-S and non-P, for simplicity, are represented by the symbols $\bar{S}$ (read S-bar) and $\bar{P}$ (read P-bar). The complement of S, then, is $\bar{S}$ (S-bar); the complement of P is $\bar{P}$ (P-bar). And the complement of $\bar{S}$ is S; the complement of $\bar{P}$ is P. That's all the information we need to know how to fill in (1) that portion of the S circle that excludes a portion of the P circle and (2) that portion of the P circle that excludes a portion of the S circle.

Using what we know about a term's complement, we can make interlocking circles:

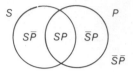

And notice that we can represent anything outside the circles by $\overline{S}\overline{P}$.

Let's now see what a proposition looks like on this diagram. "No mothers are males." This is an *E* form: No *S* is *P*. It's saying that no instance of a mother is an instance of a male. Applied to our circles, the proposition asserts that the portion of the circle signified by *SP* (mothers and males) does not have even one member. If we wanted to represent this very simply by using an equation, we might write *SP* = 0. To show this on the diagram, let's shade in the portion of the circle marked *SP*. Thus, the diagram now appears as

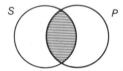

This simply means that where there is an *S* there is not *P*, and where there is a *P* there is not *S*. Since this diagram represents the *form* "No *S* is *P*," we can infer that the diagram represents *any E* proposition. And also, since the equation *SP* = 0 represents the form "No *S* is *P*," we can infer that the equation represents *any E* proposition. Thus

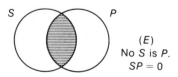

We can handle the other forms in a similar diagrammatic way. Let's consider the contradiction of *E*:*I*. "Some females are mothers" is an *I* proposition. This *I* proposition says that some of the members of *S* are included within the class *P*, and some of the members of *P* are included within the class *S*. *S* and *P* share a portion of the interlocking circles. Another way of saying this is that there exists at least one member of the class *SP*. If we put this into an equation, we'd have *SP* ≠ 0. This is the contradiction of the *E* equation *SP* = 0, as well it should be because *I* contradicts *E*. So this time, rather than shading a portion of the circles to show that a class is empty, we should show that a class has at least one occupant. Let's signify this by placing an *X* in the appropriate portion

of the circles. Thus

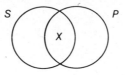

This diagram represents all I propositions, as does the equation $SP \neq 0$. Thus

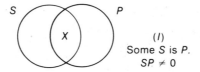

(*I*)
Some *S* is *P*.
$SP \neq 0$

What about the A proposition "All mothers are females"? This time the proposition says that every instance of S (mothers) includes an instance of P (females). Another way of stating this is that S never appears without P or that S and non-P are incompatible. Looking at our circles,

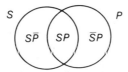

we see that we're talking about the area marked $S\overline{P}$. And we're saying that there can never be a member in that section. In equation form this would be $S\overline{P} = 0$. And on our diagram we show this by shading in the appropriate section to show that it has no membership. Thus

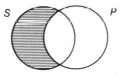

This diagram, then, represents all A forms, as does the equation $S\overline{P} = 0$.

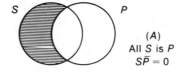

(*A*)
All *S* is *P*
$S\overline{P} = 0$

Finally, we can do the same thing with an O proposition: "Some females

are not mothers." This proposition says some members of S are excluded from P, that is, that sometimes an S is a non-P. Looking at our circles,

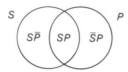

we see we're talking again about the area $S\overline{P}$. But this time, as is not the case with the A proposition, we are saying there is at least one member of this class. In equation form this would be $S\overline{P} \neq 0$. It is the denial of the A equation, $S\overline{P} = 0$, for O is the contradiction of A. On our diagram we show $S\overline{P} \neq 0$ by placing an X in the appropriate section, indicating that it has at least one member. Thus

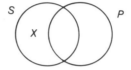

This diagram represents all O forms, as does the equation $S\overline{P} \neq 0$.

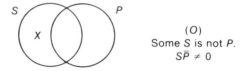

(O)
Some S is not P.
$S\overline{P} \neq 0$

So the four equations for the standard-form categorial propositions are $S\overline{P} = 0$ (A); $SP = 0$ (E); $SP \neq 0$ (I); $S\overline{P} \neq 0$ (O). If the P comes before the S in a proposition—as we know in syllogisms it can, since the conclusion dictates what the S and P terms of the argument are—we adjust the equations appropriately. Thus, if "All P is S," our equation is $P\overline{S} = 0$; if "No P is S," our equation is $PS = 0$; if "Some P is S," our equation is $PS \neq 0$; if "Some P is not S," our equation is $P\overline{S} \neq 0$.

The diagrams for these would be

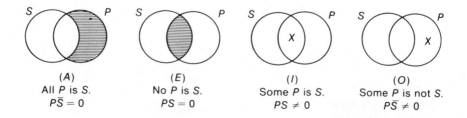

(A)	(E)	(I)	(O)
All P is S.	No P is S.	Some P is S.	Some P is not S.
$P\overline{S} = 0$	$PS = 0$	$PS \neq 0$	$P\overline{S} \neq 0$

Notice that the diagrams for "No *P* is *S*" and "No *S* is *P*" are the same, as are the ones for "Some *P* is *S*" and "Some *S* is *P*."

We have, then, the Venn diagrams, named after the nineteenth-century English mathematician John Venn. There are, in all, six different diagrams representing eight possible equations. They, in turn, stand for the eight possible ways that a subject and predicate class can be related to each other in a proposition. Thus

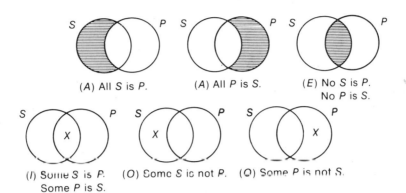

(A) All S is P.   (A) All P is S.   (E) No S is P.
                                          No P is S.

(I) Some S is P.   (O) Some S is not P.   (O) Some P is not S.
    Some P is S.

STUDY HINT: READING EQUATIONS

A simple way to read, and hence to write, equations is to begin "inside," reading from the "= 0." Read "= 0" as "There is nothing" and "≠ 0" as "there is something" (literally, "there is not nothing").

A equations: $S\overline{P} = 0$ reads, "There is nothing which is *S* and not *P*." This means, "There is nothing which is *S* without *P*." Alternatively, it means, "Any *S* must also include *P*." This is, of course, "All *S* is *P*."

E equations: $SP = 0$ reads, "There is nothing which is *S* and *P*." This means "There is nothing that is both *S* and *P* together." Alternatively, this means, "No *S* can mingle with *P*." This is, of course, "No *S* is *P*."

I equations: $SP \neq 0$ reads, "There is something which is *S* and *P*." This means, "There is at least one thing which is both *S* and *P*." Alternatively, this means, "Something is both *S* and *P*." This is, of course, "Some *S* is *P*."

O equations: $S\overline{P} = 0$ reads, "There is something which is *S* and not *P*." This means, "There is at least one thing which is *S* without *P*." Or, "Some *S* exists with no *P*." Or, "Some *S* is not *P*."

Practice familiarizing yourself with the form and meaning of the equations for the standard-form categorical propositions.

---

*EXERCISE 14-1 _____
1. Give the letter names for the following propositions.
2. Using *S* and *P*, write their equations.
3. Use a Venn diagram to graph each of them.

a. No trafficker in dope is an ethical person.
b. All friends are jewels to be cherished.
c. Some nonstudents are brilliant readers.
d. No drinkers are smokers.
e. All travelers who are alert are witnesses to the wonders of the world.
f. All nonchronic television viewers are intelligent users of spare time.
g. Some nonpersistent coughs are not now signs of serious illness.

USING VENN DIAGRAMS

Now, just how can Venn diagrams be used to prove categorical syllogisms valid? To see, let's consider this argument:

> All cigarettes are hazards to health.
> All Marlboros are cigarettes.
> _____
> All Marlboros are hazards to health.

Is this argument valid? Let's find out by means of a Venn diagram. First, we should draw interlocking circles:

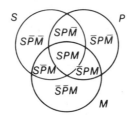

Observe that we've had to add another circle to account for the middle term. This bottom circle, M, represents the middle term, *cigarettes*. *Marlboros* is the subject of the syllogism, and *hazards to health* is the predicate. For clarity, let's place the letters S, P, and M—signifying the minor, major, and middle terms of the syllogism—over the appropriate terms in the syllogism. Remember: S here designates the minor term or *subject* of the conclusion. P designates the major term or *predicate* of the conclusion. We find them in the conclusion, then locate them in the premises. Thus

> M P
> All cigarettes are hazards to health.
> S M
> All Marlboros are cigarettes.
> _____
> S P
> All Marlboros are hazards to health.

Is the syllogism in the proper order: major premise, minor premise, conclusion? It is, and its mood is AAA. What about its figure? Since the middle term occupies the subject position of the major premise and the predicate position of the minor premise, the syllogism's figure is 1. Thus, its form is AAA-1. We're now ready to test its validity through a Venn diagram.

To diagram the syllogism we must first translate the premises and conclusion into equation form. The easiest way to do this is to bring down the letter designations from the ordered argument. Thus

MP
SM
SP

Then we make equations of these appropriate to their propositional forms. Since each of these propositions is A form ($S\overline{P} = 0$), the equations become

$M\overline{P} = 0$
$S\overline{M} = 0$
$S\overline{P} = 0$

We are now ready to diagram the premises. The major premise, $M\overline{P} = 0$, in effect reads "M outside P is empty,"[1] so we should shade in the portion of the diagram $M\overline{P}$ (remember $\overline{P}M$ is the same as $M\overline{P}$):

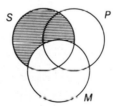

Since the minor premise, $S\overline{M} = 0$, reads "S outside M is empty," we should shade in the area designated $S\overline{M}$:

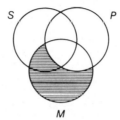

The completed diagram then becomes

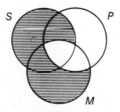

[1] Using such phrases will prove helpful when you become familiar enough with the diagrams that you needn't write in the letter designations at all. You should equate *empty* with *shade in* and *not empty* with *X*. Thus, *M outside P is empty* means that any place on the diagram where there is an *M outside a P* should be shaded in; *M outside P is not empty* would mean that an *X* should be inserted in the $M\overline{P}$ area.

At this point, if the syllogism is valid, *the premises have provided the conclusion on the diagram*. The conclusion, $S\overline{P} = 0$, reads, "*S* outside *P* is empty." If this syllogism is valid, any section designated $S\overline{P}$ should *already* be shaded in. It is. Therefore, the syllogism is valid. Remember, *we do nothing more with the conclusion than see if the diagrammed premises entail it. We do not graph the conclusion on the diagram.* (Of course, simply because the argument is valid doesn't make it sound. Soundness also depends on the truth of its premises; to determine that, we can apply inductive methodology to see if its premises commit any fallacies that would flaw the conclusion. This subject was discussed in Part Four.)

Now let's consider another syllogism, this one invalid:

> Some scientists are not engineers.
> Some astronauts are not engineers.
> Some scientists are not astronauts.

Again, let's draw three interlocking circles to represent the three terms *S*, *P*, and *M*:

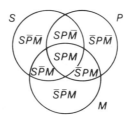

Next, let's write the letter of each syllogistic term above the appropriate word:

$$\begin{array}{cc} S & M \\ \end{array}$$
Some scientists are not engineers.
$$\begin{array}{cc} P & M \\ \end{array}$$
Some astronauts are not engineers.
$$\begin{array}{cc} S & P \\ \end{array}$$
Some scientists are not astronauts.

Since the syllogism is not in proper order; let's reorder it:

$$\begin{array}{cc} P & M \\ \end{array}$$
Some astronauts are not engineers.
$$\begin{array}{cc} S & M \\ \end{array}$$
Some scientists are not engineers.
$$\begin{array}{cc} S & P \\ \end{array}$$
Some scientists are not astronauts.

Now that we've ordered it properly, we can determine its mood as *OOO*, and because the middle term functions in the predicate slot in both premises, its figure is 2. It's form, then, is *OOO-2*.

Bringing down the letters, we get

PM
SM
SP

Making equations of these adjusted to an O form ($S\overline{P} \neq 0$), we get[2]

$P\overline{M} \neq 0$
$S\overline{M} \neq 0$
$S\overline{P} \neq 0$

We may now diagram the syllogism.

Since the equation of the major premise, $P\overline{M} \neq 0$, means "P outside M is not empty," we should place an X in the area designated $P\overline{M}$. But what do we find? Couldn't this be in two sections: $\overline{S}P\overline{M}$ or $SP\overline{M}$? Since the premise does not tell us exactly where to put the X, we place it on the line between these two portions of the circle:

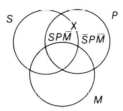

The minor premise, $S\overline{M} \neq 0$, means "S outside M is not empty," so we should place an X in the area designated $S\overline{M}$. Again, however, this could be in either of two sections: $SP\overline{M}$ or $S\overline{P}\overline{M}$. So we must place the X on the portion shared by these two sections:

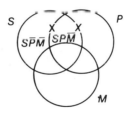

The conclusion, $S\overline{P} \neq 0$, means "S outside P is not empty." If the conclusion is contained in the premises, the diagram should show X unequivocally in a section that contains $S\overline{P}$. But this is not the case. The only possibility is the X that sits on the line between $S\overline{P}\overline{M}$ and $SP\overline{M}$, but we don't know *for sure* that the X actually belongs to $S\overline{P}\overline{M}$. Couldn't it as easily belong in $SP\overline{M}$? Since the conclusion of such a form does not follow with *certainty* from its premises, we call *OOO-2* an invalid form.

When an argument contains a universal and a particular premise, always diagram the universal first. That way you'll eliminate the uncertainty evident in the preceding example. Thus

> Some humans are vertebrates.
> All humans are mammals.
> _____
> Some mammals are vertebrates.

---

[2]This step will become automatic once you are familiar with the A, E, I, O diagrams and the Venn test.

Again, we'll first draw three interlocking circles to represent the terms S, P, and M. We needn't continue to fill in the sections:

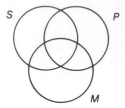

Next, let's write the letter of each syllogistic term above its appropriate word.

$$\begin{matrix} M & & P \end{matrix}$$
Some humans are vertebrates.
$$\begin{matrix} M & & S \end{matrix}$$
All humans are mammals.
$$\begin{matrix} S & & P \end{matrix}$$
Some mammals are vertebrates.

The syllogism is in the proper order; its form in IAI-3.

Bringing down the letter designations, we get

MP
MS
SP

Adjusting these to the appropriate model-form equations for I ($SP \neq 0$) and A ($S\bar{P} = 0$), we get

$M\underline{P} \neq 0$
$M\bar{S} = 0$
$SP \neq 0$

Since the major premise, $MP \neq 0$, means "MP is not empty," we should place an X in the area designated MP. But again we notice that the X can go in either of two sections: $\bar{S}PM$ or SPM. Before trying to diagram this premise, let's consider the minor one. Since the minor premise, $M\bar{S} = 0$, reads "M outside S is empty," we should shade in the area designated by $M\bar{S}$. Thus

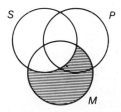

Since the minor premise has eliminated on the diagram the area designated $\bar{S}PM$, there remains only one section in which to place the X of the major

premise, that is, in *SPM*. The completed diagram shows the form *IAI*-3 to be valid.

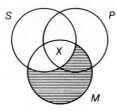

This teaches us an important lesson in diagramming: *Whenever we have a universal and particular proposition as the premises of a syllogism, we must diagram the universal first.*

Let's summarize the Venn diagram procedure for establishing the validity of standard-form syllogisms.

CRESCENTS AND ELLIPSES

Venn diagrams of standard-form categorical propositions consist of only two basic shapes: two semicircles and the elliptical shape created by the intersection of the *S* circle with the *P* circle. Thus, each diagram of a single proposition consists of two *crescents*, the semicircles, and one *ellipse*, the union of the circles.

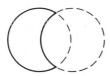
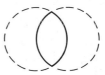

Crescents and ellipses are either shaded in or *X*-ed, depending on what the proposition says.

By reducing Venn diagrams to crescents, ellipses, shading, and *X*-ing, they are easier to learn. And since we actually graph only the two premises on our three-circle diagram, we know that our diagramming will always take place on one of two diagonals created by the *SM* circles (for the minor premise) and the *SP* circles (for the major premise). Thus, it is helpful to learn to recognize these two diagonals.

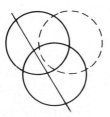
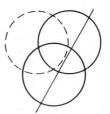

After we have diagrammed each premise, we look to see if the conclusion is clearly represented. The conclusion area of the three-circle diagram is the horizontal created by the *S* and *P* circles.

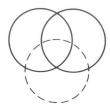

In A *diagrams, always shade the subject crescent.* It does not matter whether or not the subject circle is on the left, right, top, or bottom.

In E *diagrams, always shade the ellipse.* Since there is only one ellipse per diagram, finding the right area to shade is simple.

In I *diagrams, put an* X *inside the ellipse.* Once again, there is only one ellipse; we simply make sure that we put the X *inside* it.

In O *diagrams, put an* X *inside the subject crescent.* Although there are two crescents, we *always use the subject crescent.* It does not matter whether the subject crescent is left, right, top, or bottom.

Where to put the X?

1. Diagram the universal premise if there is one.
2. Determine the basic shape you will be working with: subject crescent or ellipse (refer to the figure on page 321).
3. Find the corresponding area on the diagram.
4. Put the X *inside* the crescent or ellipse: If there is an unshaded line *inside* the crescent or ellipse, put the X on it. If there is a shaded line, put the X *inside* the unshaded area left within your main crescent or ellipse.

Simplified Steps for Venn Testing of Standard-Form Categorical Syllogisms

1. Arrange the syllogism in standard-form order.
2. Draw three interlocking circles, one each for the major, minor, and middle term.
3. Diagram the premises/diagonals one at a time. (Diagram universals first.)
      (Caution: You want to see if the premises together produce the conclusion, so be very sure not to diagram the conclusion. You will only diagram two propositions: the major premise and the minor premise.)
4. Always use the subject crescent.
5. If there is an unshaded line *inside* an area where an X goes, put the X on that line.
6. *Stop!* After diagramming each premise, stop.
7. Determine whether or not the resulting minor term–major term diagram (see figure above) reflects the conclusion of the tested syllogism. If it does, the syllogism is valid. If it "could" or "might" or "suggests" or "almost means" what the conclusion asserts, the syllogism is invalid. (Remember: The truth of the premises of a valid deductive argument guarantees

the truth of the conclusion with logical certainty. This means that "almost" or "maybe" isn't enough.)

EXERCISE 14-2 _____

1. Test the validity of each of the following arguments by means of a Venn diagram.

a. No professional athletes are welfare recipients because no professional athletes are low-income earners, and all welfare recipients are low-income earners.

b. Some politicians are persons of integrity. Thus some entertainers are politicians, for some entertainers are persons of integrity.

c. All victims of injustice are members of oppressed groups, so because all blacks are members of oppressed groups, all blacks are victims of injustice.

d. It follows that some American Indians are not exponents of the traditional account of American history because no American Indians are people dealt with fairly in American history books, and no one dealt with fairly in American history books is an exponent of the traditional account of American history.

e. Some explosives are chemicals, from which it follows that some purchasable items are not chemicals because no explosives are purchasable items.

f. Some wealthy people are millionaires, because some millionaires are possessors of large sums of money and all possessors of large sums of money are wealthy people.

g. Some persons without sin are ones who should cast the first stone. So no person is one who should cast the first stone because no person is a person without sin.

h. Some newspapers are not true accounts of what's happened, for all true accounts of what's happened are complete and accurate sources of information, and some newspapers are not complete and accurate sources of information.

i. Because some movies are films for adults, some movies are not films for children, as no films for adults are films for children.

j. All roads are ways that lead to Rome and all roads are potential dead ends. Thus, all ways that lead to Rome are potential dead ends.

*2. By means of a Venn diagram, test the validity of these forms:

a. _AAA_-4
b. _IOO_-3
c. _AII_-4
d. _OAO_-2
e. _EOO_-1
f. _OAI_-1
g. _AEE_-2
h. _OIO_-3
i. _IOI_-1
j. _IAI_-3

RULES OF VALIDITY

There is another, less technical, method of proving the validity of a standard-form categorical syllogism. It involves applying six simple rules of correct deductive reasoning. An argument that violates any one of these rules is invalid. If it does not violate any of them, it is valid.

Rule 1: *A valid standard-form categorical syllogism must contain three, and only three, class terms, each being used in the same sense throughout the argument.* Any syllogism having more than three terms commits the *fallacy of four terms*.

Look at this argument:

> Any fast runner makes a good halfback. Since Smith is a good long-distance runner, Smith is a good halfback.

Fast runner, a good halfback, Smith, a good long-distance runner—four terms. This argument commits the fallacy of four terms; it's invalid.

It's not likely that anyone would ever argue in such a blatantly invalid way. But the fallacy can occur in more subtle ways. Consider this argument:

> Unlikely things happen all the time. But what happens all the time is likely. So, unlikely things are likely.

The fallacy, and the amusement, of the argument can be found in its equivocal use of the phrase *all the time*. In the major premise ("what happens all the time is likely"), *all the time* means "usually," "ordinarily," or "generally." But in the minor premise ("unlikely things happen all the time"), *all the time* means "frequently," as in "frequently enough to be alert to them." So the fallacy of four terms can occur when a term is used equivocally.

Sweeney committed the fallacy of four terms in one of the arguments he laid on Roscoe opposing government financing of abortion clinics. His reasons were that such a thing would mean the government was officially supporting abortion, and according to Sweeney, a government ought never to do that. We could set up his argument as follows, allowing for the awkwardness of the translation, which at present is necessary to see precisely what forms we're dealing with:

> All instances of a government's financing abortion clinics are instances of a government's officially supporting abortions.
> No government should be an instance of a government's officially sup-porting abortion.
> ___
> No government should be an instance of a government's financing abortion clinics.

After a quick first look, this argument may appear to be *AEE*-2, which happens to be a valid form. But be careful. The phrase *officially supporting* in the middle term, "instances of a government's officially supporting abortions," seems equivocal. In the minor premise it carries the meaning of taking an official position *in favor of* abortion, whereas, in Sweeney's view, abortion is strictly an individual, moral decision; a "private affair," as Sweeney says. But in the major premise, *officially supporting* means "providing the financial wherewithal" to establish abortion clinics and making them available to those who may wish their services. Looked at this way, the argument commits the fallacy of four terms.

Of course, Sweeney may intend only a single meaning, that of the minor premise: favoring abortion. If so, his major premise is guilty of a *straw man fallacy*. After all, financing abortion clinics merely provides people, especially the poor, an opportunity to have an abortion, *if they so choose*. Looked at another way, individuals and institutions could consistently *oppose* abortions while *supporting* abortion clinics. "Supporting," that is, *financially* supporting, the abortion clinic could be viewed as a tangible recognition of everyone's right—and not just the rich's—to have an abortion if one wants one; a recognition of the principle that in matters like these, people should have equal opportunity rights and that these rights are violated when they're contingent on financial condition. Thus, one who opposes abortion could favor financial support of abortion clinics.

So, either way, Sweeney's argument is unsound. It is either invalid because it commits the fallacy of four terms, or it is unsound because its major premise presumes what simply is not the case.

But Sweeney needn't feel bad. Even philosophers have been known to commit the fallacy of four terms. Consider this argument from David Hume's *A Treatise of Human Nature:*

> Since morals . . . have an influence on the actions and affections, it follows, that they cannot be deriv'd from reason; and that because reason alone, as we have already prov'd, can never have any such influence.

We can set up Hume's argument as follows:

> All moral sentiments are influences on actions and affections.
> No acts of reason are influences on actions and affections.
> No moral sentiments are things derived from acts of reason.

If we're not careful, we might take this to be an *AEE*-2 form, which we just said is valid. But look again. The major term of the argument, "things derived from acts of reason," is not the same major term that appears in the major premise. There the term is "acts of reason." So the premises provide no basis for Hume's conclusion. What he could have inferred, of course, was that "No moral sentiments are *acts of reason*." But when he sneaked in *"things derived from acts of reason,"* he committed the fallacy of four terms; after all, there's nothing in his premises that precludes moral sentiments being *derived* from acts of reason.[3]

Rule 2: *In a valid standard-form categorical syllogism, the middle term must be distributed in at least one premise.* Consider this argument:

> All mothers are females.
> Some students are females.
> Some students are mothers.

Although the premises and the conclusion are true, the argument is invalid. By means of logical analogy and Venn diagram, we have already proved this form *AII*-2 invalid. In this example the minor premise includes some students within *some females*. But since the major premise is not speaking about *every female*, we don't know whether the particular ones spoken about in the minor premise are the same ones spoken about in the major premise. So we cannot conclude that "Some students are mothers."

Compare this argument with

> All mothers are females.
> Some students are mothers.
> Some students are females.

---

[3] See Gerald Runkle, *Good Thinking: An Introduction to Logic* (New York: Holt, Rinehart and Winston, 1978), pp. 152–53.

This *AII*-1 form does not commit the error that *AII*-2 does. In its minor premise it includes *some students* within the class *some mothers*. And the major premise speaks of *all mothers*. So we know that everything said of *all mothers* also applies to *those students who are mothers*. Thus, the premises entail the conclusion, making the syllogism valid.

Let's consider this argument:

> Some astronauts are engineers.
> Some astronauts are scientists.
> Some scientists are engineers.

This argument, an *III*-3 form, assumes that the very same astronauts who are scientists are also engineers. But should it? Maybe the engineers it's talking about exclude the scientists it's talking about. Therefore, the premises do not logically guarantee the conclusion, and the syllogism is invalid. If, on the other hand, the argument read

> All astronauts are scientists.
> Some astronauts are engineers.

we could validly conclude

> Some engineers are scientists.

Why?

In each of the two invalid syllogisms, the invalidity occurred because the middle term was not spoken of universally in at least one premise. In other words, the middle term wasn't distributed at least once. When a syllogism fails to distribute its middle term at least once, it commits the *fallacy of the undistributed middle*. This always produces an invalid argument. Thus, again,

> Some females are vertebrates.
> All mothers are females.
> Some mothers are vertebrates.

Although the premises and conclusion are true, this argument is invalid—it does not distribute its middle term. Thus, the form *IAI*-1 is invalid.

Rule 3: *No valid standard-form categorical syllogism may distribute in its conclusion any term not distributed in its premises.* Consider this argument:

> All mothers are females.
> Some students are mothers.
> All students are females.

The conclusion obviously overstates the premises, saying more than the evidence allows. The same holds true for this argument:

> All milk-giving animals are mammals.
> Some cats are milk-giving animals.
> All cats are mammals.

The conclusion speaks of *all cats*. Although the conclusion is true, the premises do not allow us to speak of *all cats* but of only some. What about this argument?

> All doctors are college graduates.
> Some doctors are not golfers.
> _____
> Some golfers are not college graduates.

It's a little harder to see the flaw here. But remembering that *O* propositions distribute their predicate terms, we see that this conclusion is speaking of *all college graduates*. But the major premise doesn't speak of *all college graduates*. Therefore, the argument is invalid.

So in concluding more than their premises allow them to, arguers commit fallacies called *illicit major* and *illicit minor* terms. *Illicit major means that the predicate is distributed in the conclusion but not in the major premise; illicit minor means that the subject is distributed in the conclusion but not in the minor premise.* In the first example given, about mothers, this *AIA*-1 form commits the fallacy of illicit minor term, as does the next one about cats, an *AIA*-1; the final example, *AOO*-3, commits the fallacy of illicit major term.

Rule 4: *No valid standard-form categorical syllogism may contain two negative premises*. The reason for this rule becomes clear when we look at some illustrations:

> Some females are not mothers.
> Some politicians are not females.
> _____
> Some politicians are not mothers.

As tempting as such a conclusion may be, we cannot logically draw it because the subject, *politicians*, and the predicate, *mothers*, are excluding from their classes the middle term, *females*. As a result, the premises allow us no way to relate the classes *mothers* and *politicians* as the conclusion attempts to do. In other words, the premises don't show that these two classes have a common bond since it's impossible to know whether they are excluding the same females. A logical analogy will point up the error:

> Some politicians are not females.
> Some mothers are not politicians.
> _____
> Some mothers are not females.

Again, the conclusion must relate the classes *mothers* and *females*. But the minor premise excludes from the class *mothers* every instance of politician. The major premise excludes every instance of the class *females* from the particular politicians it's addressing. The classes *mothers* and *females*, then, share no basis for a relationship. Hence, no valid conclusion is possible.

In brief, whenever the premises of a syllogism are both negative, no valid conclusion can be drawn. *If we draw a conclusion from two negative premises we commit the fallacy of exclusive premises.*

Rule 5: *If either premise of a standard-form categorical syllogism is negative, its conclusion must be negative.* Consider these premises:

> No mothers are males.
> Some males are politicians.

Logically, the only conclusion we could draw here is the negative one:

Some politicians are not mothers.

The major premise excludes the class *mothers* from the class *males*. The minor premise, on the other hand, includes part of the class *males* within part of the class *politicians*. The only possible relationship that could exist between *politicians* and *mothers*, then, is one of exclusion, in which some politicians are excluded from the class *mothers*. In other words, the conclusion must be a negative one. Whenever either premise of a syllogism is negative, the conclusion must be negative. An affirmative conclusion can only follow premises in which the middle term includes one term (*S* or *P*) and is itself part of another (*S* or *P*), that is, from affirmative premises. When we exclude this middle term from either premise, we force the conclusion to exclude, or to be negative. *Whenever we draw an affirmative conclusion from a negative premise, we commit*—appropriately enough—*the fallacy of drawing an affirmative conclusion from a negative premise.* The corollary is this: *If the conclusion to an argument is negative, one of its premises must be negative as well.*

Rule 6: *No valid standard-form categorical syllogism with two universal premises may have a particular conclusion.* If you remember when we introduced the particular propositions, *I* and *O*, we said that *some* means that there exists at least one member (*exists* taken to mean in the past as well as the present). We can say, then, *some* has *existential import*: It makes a comment about existence. *No* and *all*, on the other hand, carry no such meaning; they make no comment about existence at all. Thus, "All trespassers are persons who will be prosecuted" does not in itself imply the existence of any trespassers. But if we said "Some trespassers are persons who will be prosecuted," we would be logically implying the existence of at least one trespasser. What if someone says, "No lawbreaker is a good citizen"; does this imply the existence of a lawbreaker? No, it doesn't. But "Some lawbreakers are not good citizens" does logically imply the existence of at least one lawbreaker.

The existential implications of propositions show up dramatically when we try to diagram a syllogism having two universal premises and a particular conclusion, as in

No lawbreakers are good citizens.
All speeders are lawbreakers.
Some speeders are not good citizens.

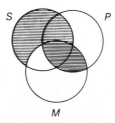

The premises do not provide membership, signified by an *X* in the section designated *SP̄*, as the conclusion demands. *Thus, the argument is invalid.* It's invalid because the conclusion makes an existential claim that its premises just do not allow; the conclusion states that there exists at least one speeder, but the premises don't contain any such implication. The argument is said to commit the *existential fallacy. Any syllogism whose premises consist of universal propositions (A or E) and whose conclusion is a particular proposition (I or O) commits the existential fallacy and is thereby invalid.*

Summarizing, the six rules and their accompanying fallacies are

Rule 1: *A valid standard-form categorical syllogism must contain three, and no more than three, terms; otherwise it commits the fallacy of four terms.*

Rule 2: *A valid standard-form categorical syllogism must distribute its middle term at least once; otherwise it commits the fallacy of undistributed middle term.*

Rule 3: *A standard-form categorical syllogism must not say more in its conclusion than its premises allow. If it distributes its major term (P) in the conclusion but not in the major premise, it commits the fallacy of illicit major term; if it distributes its minor term (S) in the conclusion but not in the minor premise, it commits the fallacy of illicit minor term.*

Rule 4: *A valid standard-form categorical syllogism must not contain two negative premises; otherwise it commits the fallacy of exclusive premises.*

Rule 5: *A valid standard-form categorical syllogism must not draw an affirmative conclusion from a negative premise; otherwise it commits the fallacy of drawing an affirmative conclusion from a negative premise.*

Rule 6: *A valid standard-form categorical syllogism must not draw a particular conclusion from two universal premises; otherwise it commits the existential fallacy.*

So much for standard-form categorical syllogisms. At the beginning of our study of the syllogism, we mentioned that the categorical syllogism is only one kind of syllogistic argument and that there are two other kinds as well. These are easy to handle, but they do occur frequently enough for us to be alerted to them. So in Chapter 16 we'll take up validity as it applies to disjunctive and conditional syllogisms. But before that, we must consider the important topic of argument reconstruction.

*EXERCISE 14-3 _____

1. Determine the validity of the following syllogisms by means of rules and fallacies. If a syllogism breaks a rule, identify the broken rule and the fallacy.

a. No refined foods are nutritional foods. So no white flour is a nutritional food because no nutritional food is a white flour.

b. Some people who believe in astronaut-gods are gullible readers and all gullible readers are fans of the book *Chariots of the Gods?*; therefore, some fans of the book *Chariots of the Gods?* are people who believe in astronaut-gods.

c. Some extrasensory experiences are not just the products of imagination, because some products of imagination are things explained through sense data, and no things explained through sense data are extrasensory experiences.

d. Some professors are not idealists and all professors are college graduates. Therefore, some idealists are not college graduates.

e. Since some ministers are not happy men, some ministers are not alcoholics, for no alcoholics are happy men.

f. All good teachers are good administrators, because all good teachers are compassionate individuals and all compassionate individuals are good administrators.

g. It follows that some Americans are coffee lovers from the facts that some Americans are not tea lovers and no tea lovers are coffee lovers.

h. All horses are quadrupeds; so, because some horses are faster runners than humans, some quadrupeds are faster runners than humans.

i. Some inventors are people who know how to make money, for all inventors are imaginative individuals and all imaginative individuals are people who know how to make money.

j. All missionaries are altruists and some altruists are women. Thus, some missionaries are women.

2. By means of rules and fallacies, determine the validity of the following forms:

    a. *OAO*-2
    b. *EAO*-1
    c. *IAA*-3
    d. *OEO*-4
    e. *AAA*-3
    f. *IOO*-1
    g. *EEO*-3
    h. *AEE*-4
    i. *AEO*-4
    j. *EIO*-3

SUMMARY

This concludes our study of the two methods of proving standard-form categorical syllogisms valid. What have we seen?

    First, by using Venn diagrams we can determine with certainty a standard-form categorical syllogism's validity. Specifically, we should follow these steps:

1. Draw three interlocking circles designated by *S, P,* and *M.*
2. Place the letters *S, P,* and *M* over the appropriate syllogistic terms in the argument.
3. Order the syllogism and establish its form.
4. Bring down the letters of each proposition and, if necessary, make of them equations appropriate to their propositional forms.
5. Diagram the premises, universal first.
6. See if the diagram indicates the conclusion; if it does, the syllogism is valid; if not, it's invalid.

With respect to step 4 we learned that the equations for the four standard-form categorical propositions are

$$S\overline{P} = 0 \ (A)$$
$$SP = 0 \ (E)$$
$$S\underline{P} \neq 0 \ (I)$$
$$S\overline{P} \neq 0 \ (O)$$

    But the quickest and simplest way to determine validity is to use the following rules and fallacies:

Rule 1: A valid standard-form categorical syllogism must contain three, and only three, class terms, each being used in the same sense throughout the argument. Any syllogism containing more than three terms commits the fallacy of four terms.

Rule 2: In a valid standard-form categorical syllogism, the middle term must be distributed in at least one premise. A syllogism that fails to do this commits the fallacy of the undistributed middle term.

Rule 3: No valid standard-form categorical syllogism can distribute in its conclusion any term not distributed in its premises. A syllogism that distributes its predicate in the conclusion but not in the major premise commits the fallacy of illicit major term; a syllogism that distributes its subject in the conclusion but not in the minor premise commits the fallacy of illicit minor term.

Rule 4: No valid standard-form categorical syllogism can contain two negative premises. A syllogism that does commits the fallacy of exclusive premises.

Rule 5: If either premise of a standard-form categorical syllogism is negative, its conclusion must be negative. A syllogism that violates this rule commits the fallacy of drawing an affirmative conclusion from a negative premise.

Rule 6: No valid syllogism can draw a particular conclusion from two universal premises. A syllogism that does this commits the existential fallacy.

We also learned to spot the two basic diagram shapes, the crescent and ellipse:

And we learned that the premises are always diagrammed on one of two diagonals created by the three-circle configuration,

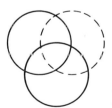 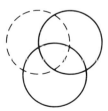

whereas the conclusion is always represented on the horizontal diagram:

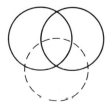

Summary Question

1. Using the rules and Venn diagrams, determine for yourself which of the possible 256 combinations of mood and figure are valid. (This is not as time-consuming as it seems. For example, we know that any syllogism with two *E* premises commits the fallacy of exclusive premises, so *EEA, EEE, EEI,* and *EEO* are invalid moods from just that one rule. Since the moods themselves are invalid, each figure is also invalid. Thus, *EEA*-1, *EEA*-2, *EEA*-3, and *EEA*-4 are all invalid. Ditto for the other three *EE* syllogisms. We have just eliminated four moods × four figures, or sixteen forms. This is a problem of logical organization.)

ADDITIONAL EXERCISES _____

Determine the validity of the following syllogisms by using Venn diagrams and the rules. Identify the rule(s) violated for all invalid syllogisms.

1. Since no barbers are qualified to practice medicine, all those qualified to practice medicine have been to college, because no barbers have been to college.
2. Since some apples are fruits and some apples are red objects, some red objects are fruits.
3. If some women are college graduates, and all college graduates are high school graduates, then some high school graduates are women.
4. Some professional organizations that charge dues are not organizations worth belonging to. Some organizations worth belonging to are elite clubs. Consequently, some elite clubs are not organizations worth belonging to.
5. Some Chevrolets are overpriced lemons, and some overpriced lemons are selling like hot cakes, so some Chevrolets are selling like hot cakes.
6. If we assume that no signs of forced entry were present at the scene of the crime, we can conclude that the defendant is innocent.
7. All horses are quadrupeds. No humans are horses. Thus, no humans are quadrupeds.
8. All horses are quadrupeds. No horses are human. Thus, no quadrupeds are human.
9. All flour fit for consumption is ground. All places on which houses are built are ground. Therefore, all places on which houses are built are fit for consumption.
10. All Communists are atheists. No atheists are good citizens. So some Communists are not good citizens.
11. *AEE*-3
12. *IOE*-2
13. *OOI*-1
14. *IOI*-2
15. *AAA*-4
16. *AAA*-3
17. *AEA*-2
18. *EAA*-2
19. *IAI*-3
20. *EIO*-4

chapter 1 5

Reconstructing Arguments

The mass of mankind will never have any ardent zeal for seeing things as they are.

MATTHEW ARNOLD

"T.G.I.F.—Thank goodness it's Friday." After a couple of grueling weeks of categorical propositions, syllogisms of all sorts, equations, and Venn diagrams, a bunch of Ms. Ponen's Logic 1A students were ready to unwind at the college pub, jokingly named "Steady Hall." There'd been some local controversy about serving alcohol on a college campus, and the pub's operation was only temporary. The Board of Trustees decided to adopt a wait-and-see attitude—but not Ms. Ponen's logic crew. They were ready to party.

Phil and Sandy got there first. Sitting at the bar, chatting about this and that, they glanced now and again at the TV set behind the bar. Instead of the early news, the President came on to make one of his monthly addresses to the nation.

"Oh, no," groaned Phil. "Not him! Not now! I'm trying to relax."

"Maybe he's got something important to say," Sandy suggested.

"The President never has anything important to say," Phil insisted.

"You don't know what he's going to say," Sandy replied.

"Well, I know this much: *Only nitwits pay attention to these talks."*

"That's just not so," Sandy said. *"Not all those who pay attention to the President's talks are nitwits."*

"Maybe not, but *most of them are nitwits."*

"Be quiet! He's speaking, and I want to listen."

"My fellow Americans," the President began, "we face a serious challenge. Today, I am calling on each of us to enlist in my War on Drugs. *No concerned citizen can ignore the seriousness of drug abuse in our society.* Studies show that *almost all fifth-graders experiment with drugs at least once. Many of them go on to become addicted to hard-core drugs.* Everyone listening to me now has an obligation to fight this pernicious menace."

"He's right, you know," Sandy said.

"No, he's not. I know lots of people who have experimented with drugs without becoming addicted to hard-core stuff."

"He didn't say that *everybody who experiments with drugs becomes addicted to them,* only that *most of them do."*

"Most, shmost. He meant everybody."

"I assume you. . . ."

"Don't assume! When you ASSUME, you make an ASS out of U and ME."

"Ha, ha. Very funny. What I was trying to say was that I assume that you've completely forgotten what Ms. Ponen told us about disguised categorical propositions occurring in ordinary language."

"Whoa!" groaned Phil. "That's it. Enough! I came here to forget about logic and stuff. Let's get back to reality and forget that academic stuff. I'm tired of being lectured to. First, by Old Lady Ponen. Then by the President. Now by you. I know how to think for myself, and I don't take drugs. . . . Hey! Here comes the rest of the gang. Bartender! More beer!"

Although there is some merit in Phil's admonition about assumptions, we need to take a closer look. Often, what we assume does make fools of us. But assume we must. In fact, if we take the word *assumption* to mean something that is taken for granted in argument but not explicitly asserted, it's a safe bet that most of the arguments we encounter are built on assumptions. They consist of premises and conclusions that are implied but not overtly stated.

For example, suppose someone says, "You shouldn't eat that apple because all the apples from that bag are sour." Clearly the speaker assumes "That apple is from that bag." Likewise, should someone argue, "Some of these students must be juniors because they're taking American literature," the speaker must be assuming that "All students taking American literature are juniors."

The ability to see precisely what is being assumed in an argument is crucial, because determining validity depends on it. Take, for example, that fragment of an argument about the students. It's valid, of course, if the premises entail the conclusion. Given only one premise, we must reconstruct the other to determine the argument's validity. And we'd better be accurate in our reconstruction; otherwise we'll misrepresent the argument by, in effect, setting up a straw man, an argument that looks like the original but significantly differs from it.

To illustrate how we might misrepresent this argument, suppose we assume that the missing assumption is "All juniors are students taking American literature." Using this premise in the argument, we get

> (All juniors are students taking American literature.)
> <u>Some of these students are students taking American literature.</u>
> Some of these students are juniors.

The form here is *AII*-2. The argument commits the fallacy of the undistributed middle term and so is invalid. But the original argument *isn't* this form at all; we've set up a straw man. We misrepresented the argument by misrepresenting its assumption, which actually is "All students taking American literature are juniors." Using this premise, we get an argument that reads,

> (All students taking American literature are juniors.)
> <u>Some of these students are students taking American literature.</u>
> Some of these students are juniors.

The form here is *AII*-1, and it's valid.

How do we know what's being assumed in fragmented arguments? That's what this chapter is about. It concerns techniques for correctly reconstructing arguments when they come in incomplete form. The President's speech is a good example. It contains all sorts of assumptions. Phil and Sandy have different views on what these assumptions are and on their implications. Their interest is laudable, for the only way to judge the validity of the President's arguments is to unearth the assumptions underlying them. When we do, we'll find that some of his arguments are invalid. The same applies to any argument: Dig into its assumptions. It is in the "taken for granted" that invalidity often lies.

Another problem concerns what is openly expressed in an argument. Rarely do real-life arguments contain statements that appear in standard propositional form. Indeed, they almost always contain statements expressed in ordinary, everyday language and syntax. Consider, for example, the italicized statements in the Phil and Sandy story at the beginning of this chapter. Actually, all these statements are categorical propositions; they are of the *A, E, I,* or *O* variety. If we're to evaluate ordinary-language arguments like these, we must know how to translate orginary-language statements into standard propositional form. So this chapter deals with that subject before going on to consider argument reconstruction.

TRANSLATING CATEGORICAL PROPOSITIONS INTO STANDARD FORM

All the arguments we've dealt with so far have been clean ones; they've neatly fallen into syllogistic form. Most arguments, however, contain propositions that at first glance don't resemble any of the standard propositional forms. Take these propositions, for instance: "The New York Mets defeated the Boston Red Sox in the World Series," "Mature people don't insist on having things their way all the time," "A vandal broke the lock," "Not all people believe in an 'open' universe." Could you recognize these as *A, E, I,* or *O*? They are. And if we are going to insert them into a standard-form categorical syllogism, they need to be translated into those forms. We'll consider seven variations the standard-form categorical proposition often takes and show how these can be translated.

These variations will be propositions that (1) contain a singular reference; (2) contain adjectival phrases; (3) lack the verb *to be*; (4) have irregular quantifiers; (5) lack subject and predicate terms; (6) use *only* or *none but*; and (7) consist of two statements, one affirmative, the other negative. But first let's look at arguments that appear to have more than three terms but actually don't.

Arguments with Logical Equivalencies

What if you were evaluating the validity of this argument?

> All humans are vertebrates.
> Women are humans.
> _____
> Therefore, women are creatures with spines.

At first glance you might judge this argument to be invalid because it commits the fallacy of four terms. But two of the terms mean the same thing—*vertebrates* and *creatures with spines*. Simply by replacing one with the other, we can produce a standard-form syllogism.

> All humans are creatures with spines.
> Women are humans.
> _____
> Therefore, women are creatures with spines.

Now what about this argument?

> No human is a nonvertebrate.
> All snakes are nonvertebrates.
> _____
> All humans are nonsnakes.

Not only do we appear to have four terms—*human, nonvertebrate, snakes,* and *nonsnakes*—but we also seem to have an affirmative conclusion following from a negative premise. But two of the terms—*snakes* and *nonsnakes* are merely complements. We can eliminate one of the complements by restating one of the propositions in terms of its logical equivalent.[1] Thus, the logical equivalent of "All humans are nonsnakes" is "No humans are snakes." The syllogism now has three terms and a negative conclusion drawn from a negative premise. Since the syllogism commits no fallacy, it is valid. So whenever we find an argument appearing to have more than three terms, we should look for synonyms and complements. We should then eliminate one of the synonyms and employ a logical equivalent to eliminate the complement.

> **STUDY HINT: IF AN ARGUMENT APPEARS TO HAVE MORE THAN 3 TERMS,**
>
> 1. Identify any synonyms and complements.
> 2. Eliminate one of the synonyms (if present).
> 3. Employ a logical equivalent to any complement.

Now let's consider the seven kinds of propositions that don't appear in standard *A, E, I,* or *O* form.

---

[1]We do this through the process called *obversion:* changing the quality of a proposition and substituting the complement of its predicate for the predicate itself. Thus, "Some *S* is *P*" obverts to "Some *S* is not non-*P*," "Some *S* is not *P*" obverts to "Some *S* is non-*P*," and so forth.

Propositions Containing Singular Terms

Sometimes a proposition takes this form: "Reagan is a U.S. President." Because it speaks of an individual, such a proposition is called *singular*. The proposition "This Harley-Davidson runs well" is another singular proposition. Singular propositions affirm or deny that a specific individual is in a class. *The individual is considered the sole occupant of its class.* So, since in mentioning the individual we are really speaking of the whole class, we consider singular propositions to be universal propositions *A* or *E*. The first two singular propositions, then, are universal affirmative and therefore *A* form. If the singular proposition is negative, its form is *E*. Thus, the argument

> All U.S. Presidents are male.
> Jeanne Kirkpatrick is not a U.S. President.
> Jeanne Kirkpatrick is not a male.

has the mood *AEE*.

STUDY HINT

   Treat propositions containing singular terms as universals (*A* or *E*).

Propositions Containing Adjectival Phrases

In addition to arguments containing synonyms, complements, or singular propositions, some arguments appear with adjectival class terms. Thus,

> All fast runners are team members.
> "Toes" Larsen is really fast.
> "Toes" Larsen is a team member.

To get the minor premise into standard propositional form, you can change the adjective into a noun: " 'Toes' Larsen is a fast runner." Consider this argument:

> What's obsolete and decrepit is an eyesore.
> All the buildings are obsolete and decrepit.
> Therefore, all the buildings are eyesores.

Translating the adjectives into class terms, we get

> All obsolete and decrepit *objects* are eyesores.
> All the buildings are obsolete and decrepit *objects*.
> All the buildings are eyesores.

STUDY HINT

   Change adjectival phrases to nouns.

Propositions Lacking the Verb to Be

Related to the problem of translating adjectival phrases into noun class terms is translating the proposition's verb into a form of the verb *to be* (*is, are, was, were, have been, has been, should be, will have been,* and so on). What's the simplest way to translate such a proposition as "Some men lust after their neighbors' wives" into standard form? Simply insert, immediately after the subject, a phrase consisting of (1) a form of the verb *to be,* (2) an appropriate class term, and (3) the relative pronoun *who* or *which*; then finish the proposition. This proposition becomes "Some men *are persons who* lust after their neighbors' wives." "All persons who defend themselves have fools for lawyers" becomes "All persons who defend themselves *are persons who* have fools for lawyers" (or simply "persons with fools for lawyers").

Propositions Containing Irregular Quantifiers

Sometimes the quantity of a proposition is not designated by the standard quantifiers *all, no,* and *some*. Thus, "Anyone present heard him make the remark"; "Everyone is late"; "Whoever votes is a citizen"; "Anything you bring to the picnic we'll appreciate." *Any, everybody, whoever, anything,* and similar words mean *all,* and we should handle them accordingly. Some confusion may arise, however, regarding the indefinite article *a*. In "A man is a vertebrate," the *a* obviously means all humans are vertebrates; therefore, it should be considered a universal quantifier, making this proposition an *A* form. And "A snake is not a vertebrate" obviously means *no* snake is a vertebrate. But *a* can also mean "some," as in "A ball came crashing through the window" or "A question interrupted his speech." Because they refer neither to every member of a class nor to singular members, these uses of *a* should be considered particular quantifiers, thus making their propositions particular ones. The two preceding propositions, then, are *I* form. (Remember: *Some* means at least one.) What about "A ball did not crash through this window"? This is *O*.

The article *the* is similar to *a* in this respect, but significantly different. For example, the proposition "The lion is a carnivore" obviously speaks of all lions; so *the* functions as a universal quantifier, making the proposition *A* form. On the other hand, "The lion escaped from the St. Louis Zoo" refers, not to all lions, but to this singular lion. Still *the* serves as a universal quantifier, making this proposition, like singular ones, *A* form.

> **S T U D Y   H I N T**
>
> *A* can be a universal or particular quantifier. *The* is *always* a universal quantifier.

Propositions Lacking Subject or Predicate Terms

Some propositions begin with *wherever* or *whenever*, as in "Wherever there's smoke, there's fire" and "Whenever the means are outrageous, we must resist them." In addition to providing the quantifier *all* in such propositions, we must also provide a class term to complete its sense. Since *wherever* suggests a place, the word *place* itself becomes a convenient term to substitute for *wherever* and like terms; and since *whenever* suggests time, the word *time* is convenient to substitute for *whenever* and related words. Thus, in standard form, the preceding propositions become "All *places* there's smoke are *places* there's fire" and "All *times* the means are outrageous are *times* we must resist them."

Similar to *wherever* and *whenever* are *where, unless, never,* and *when*. Consider this proposition: "The Draculas will not come to a party unless blood pudding is being served." Translated into standard form this becomes "All *times* the Draculas come to a party are *times* that blood pudding is being served." We handle syllogisms containing such words by translating the propositions in which the words appear into standard form.

> Since the baby cries whenever the phone rings, the phone mustn't be ringing because the baby is quiet.

Translated, this argument becomes

> All times the phone rings are times the baby cries.
> This time is not a time the baby's crying.
> ───
> Therefore, this time is not a time the phone is ringing.

The argument is valid. It is an *AEE*-2, a valid syllogistic form.

Propositions Using *Only* and *None But*

Sometimes categorical propositions specify the members of a class they're speaking about, as in "Only sophomores are entitled to a free bus ride." The use of *only* here restricts those entitled to a free bus ride to a special group known as *sophomores*. Such a proposition is said to be *exclusive*. Exclusive propositions can be deceiving; this one *seems* to be speaking universally of *sophomores* and thus appears to translate as "All sophomores are students entitled to a free bus ride." But this misrepresents the meaning of the sentence. The word *only* is really specifying *sophomores* within a larger unmentioned group, probably *students*. To translate this exclusive proposition faithfully, we should show that any instance of a student who is entitled to a free ride is an instance of a sophomore. Simply put, this means, "All those (students) entitled to a free bus ride are sophomores." Consider this example: "Only men are priests of the Roman Catholic Church." Does this mean that all men are priests of the Roman Catholic Church or that all priests of the Roman Catholic Church are men? Obviously the latter. So the *only* in an exclusive proposition is actually distributing the *apparent* predicate.

In translating an exclusive proposition into standard form, then, it's necessary to interchange the *apparent* subject and predicate and then treat the proposition as a universal one. Thus, "Only those younger than eighteen cannot vote" becomes "No voter is one less than eighteen years old." Similar to *only* is the phrase *none but,* as in "None but the most needy will be fed." This becomes "All those who will be fed are those who are most needy."

Look on the translation of exclusive propositions as consisting of three steps. First, drop the "only" or "none but." Second, translate what remains into standard form. Third, interchange "subject" and "predicate." What remains is the proper translation. Let's apply this procedure to Phil's statement "Only nitwits pay attention to these talks." Thus

Step 1: Nitwits pay attention to these talks.
Step 2: All nitwits pay attention to these talks.
Step 3: All persons who pay attention to these talks are nitwits.

The error that students usually make in translating exclusive propositions is to end the translation at step 2. Make sure that having completed step 2, you then interchange "subject" and "predicate." That provides the correct meaning of the exclusive proposition. Consider, for an additional example, this statement: "None but the brave deserve glory." Applying the three steps, we get

Step 1: The brave deserve glory.
Step 2: All brave persons are persons who deserve glory.
Step 3: All persons who deserve glory are brave persons.

> **STUDY HINT: WHEN TRANSLATING EXCLUSIVE STATEMENTS:**
>
> 1. Drop *only* or *none but.*
> 2. Translate what remains into *A* or *E.*
> 3. Interchange "subject" and "predicate."

Propositions Containing Two Statements: Affirmative and Negative

The quantifiers *almost all, only some, not quite all, all but,* and the like often introduce propositions that need translation into standard form. Such phrases really imply *two* statements, not one. They are called *exceptive* propositions.

Take, for example, the statement "We grant that almost all the students' demands are justifiable." This statement means that some of the demands are justifiable and that some of the demands are not justifiable. The statements differ in quality, and a difference in quality may affect the validity of a syllogism. Thus

> All demands that are justifiable are ones the university should meet.
> Almost all the students' demands are justifiable.
> ―――
> Some of the students' demands are ones the university should meet.

Now, translating the minor premise, we could have either "Some of the students' demands are not justifiable" or "Some of the students' demands are justifiable." Let's test each:

> All demands that are justifiable are ones the university should meet.
> Some of the students' demands are not justifiable.
> ―――
> Some of the students' demands are ones the university should meet.

This *AOI*-1 syllogism draws an affirmative conclusion from a negative premise, and is therefore invalid. But

> All demands that are justifiable are ones the university should meet.
> Some of the students' demands are justifiable.
> ―――
> Some of the students' demands are ones the university should meet.

This syllogism commits no fallacy. Therefore the original syllogism, as demonstrated by this *AII*-1 form, is valid.

So in dealing with exceptive premises, we must test both implied statements to determine the validity of the syllogism. If at least one of the implied statements helps entail a valid version the original argument is considered valid.

Now consider this argument:

All but the stubborn are willing.
No one willing is present.
No one present is stubborn.

The major premise is actually composed of two propositions: "No stubborn person is a willing person" and "All nonstubborn persons are willing persons." Let's try each in the syllogism.

No stubborn person is a willing person.
No willing person is a person present.
No person present is a stubborn person.

EEE-4

This argument is invalid because of its exclusive premises. But before declaring the original syllogism invalid, we must test its other version:

All nonstubborn persons are willing persons.
No willing person is a person present.
All persons present are nonstubborn persons.

AEA-4

Notice that we used a logical equivalent of the original conclusion to ensure three terms in the syllogism.[2] Having done that, we proved that the syllogism even in this form is invalid because it draws an affirmative conclusion from a negative premise. Therefore, the original argument is invalid.

The phrase *not quite all,* as in "Not quite all the members were on time," introduces an exceptive proposition. We can handle this just as we did *about all,* that is, by translating it into two propositions, one beginning *some are* and the other beginning *some are not*. In the argument

Everyone on time received an award.
Not quite all the members were on time.
Some members received an award.

we can translate the minor premise into "Some members were persons on time" or "Some members were not persons on time." Substituting the second, we get

All persons on time were persons who received an award
Some members were not persons on time.
Some members were persons who received an award.

AOI-1

This argument draws an affirmative conclusion from a negative premise and is therefore invalid. But what about using the other implication of the "not quite all" proposition?

[2]To repeat, this process is called *obversion*. It involves changing the quality of the original proposition and substituting for its predicate the complement of the predicate. Obversion always results in a logical equivalent. The obverted form of "All *S* is *P*" is "No *S* is non-*P*"; of "No *S* is *P*," "All *S* is non-*P*; of "Some *S* is *P*," "Some *S* is not non-*P*"; of "Some *S* is not *P*," "Some *S* is non-*P*."

> All persons on time were persons who received an award.
> Some members were persons on time.
> _____
> Some members were persons who received an award.
>
> *All-1*

This argument commits no fallacy and is therefore valid. Thus, the original argument is valid.

Now let's consider the case of an exceptive proposition serving as the conclusion.

> All Republicans are registered voters.
> Some Republicans are businesspersons.
> _____
> Not all voters are businesspersons.

Remember what we said about deductive arguments: The premises must entail, or logically guarantee, the conclusion. An exceptive conclusion implies either "Some *S* is *P*" and "Some *S* is not *P*" or "No *S* is *P*" and "All non-*S* is *P*." These are the only possible translations of exceptive propositions. So when we draw an exceptive conclusion from two standard-form premises, at the least we will commit either the fallacy of drawing an affirmative conclusion from a negative premise or a negative conclusion from an affirmative premise. So in the preceding argument, the premises can't logically entail both conclusions: "Some registered voters are businesspersons," and "Some registered voters *are not* businesspersons." We can conclude that any syllogism whose premises are standard form and whose conclusion is exceptive is an invalid syllogism. Of course, if a syllogism contains both exceptive premises and an exceptive conclusion, it can be valid if it entails both conclusions.

These methods, then, enable us to deal with propositions that do not appear in standard form. But what about propositions that are missing, that remain partially or fully unstated? Most arguments we encounter, in fact, come in this incomplete form. How do we handle such arguments? This we must consider next.

> **STUDY HINT**
>
> In dealing with exceptive *premises*, always test both implied statements, and if one of them produces a valid argument, the argument is valid.
>
> If a syllogism contains standard form (nonexceptive) premises and an *exceptive conclusion*, it is always invalid.

EXERCISE 15-1 _____

1. Translate the following propositions into standard form.

   a. Flowers are fragrant.
   b. Onions are not sweet.
   c. Many a party goer awakens to regret "the night before."
   d. Not every opportunity lost is a catastrophe.
   e. Nothing is both educational and frivolous.
   f. If it says "Government Approved," you can feel safe.
   g. Only the best teams play in the title game.

   h. Not quite everything that's green is grass.
   i. Not everything that's green is grass.
   j. "You can be sure if it's Westinghouse."
   k. Not all mammals are nonhumans (eliminate "nonhumans").
   l. "Let he who is without sin cast the first stone."
  m. Only the good die young.
   n. He who defends himself has a fool for a lawyer.
   o. Some nonvoters are not noncitizens (eliminate "noncitizens").
   p. None but the eager volunteer.
   q. Not all that glitters is gold.
   r. None think the rich happy but the rich themselves.
   s. To know her is to love her.
   t. I go where I want.
   u. If he's telling jokes, he's drunk.
   v. He jests that he never felt a wound.
  w. Whatsoever a man soweth, that shall he also reap.
   x. A thing of beauty is a joy forever.
   y. They also serve who only stand and wait.
   z. None but the indifferent would hurt someone's feelings.
 aa. Almost all complaints are referred to upper management.
 bb. Not quite all dates always order the most expensive items on the menu.
 cc. People are never so likely to appreciate life as when they're about to die.
 dd. He'll say nothing unless you ask him.

2. Translate the President's italicized assertions into standard form.
3. Translate the following arguments into standard form; then test their validity.

   a. All countries wanting war are threats to world peace. No threat to world peace is a member of the UN. So no member of the UN is a belligerent country.
   b. Since some males are not chauvinists and some sexists are proponents of the Equal Rights Amendment, some proponents of the Equal Rights Amendment must be men.
   c. Not all the victims were adults. Some of the dead were musicians. So some of the adults must have been musicians.
   d. Smith must be a college graduate because he can apply and only college graduates can apply.
   e. Whenever the President can't explain something he's done, he attributes it to national security. I guess he's at a loss again because he's attributing the wiretapping to national security.
   f. None but the brave should volunteer for harzardous duty. Nothing personal, Jones, but you shouldn't be volunteering—you're a coward!
   g. The competition for places at medical schools is fierce because there are so few places available, and the competition is never easy when there aren't many places available.
   h. Since nothing relevant is immaterial and some relevant things are interesting, some immaterial things are uninteresting.

THE ENTHYMEME

An argument in which a premise or conclusion is suppressed or missing is called an *enthymeme*. In the argument "Since I'm riding in a car I'll get sick," the major premise remains unstated. How do we know it's the major premise that is unstated? Basically, by asking ourselves, "What is the speaker assuming in order to draw the conclusion?" To see this argument more clearly, we can use what we've already learned to put it into standard form:

> (All occasions I ride in a car are occasions I get sick.)
> This is an occasion I'm riding in a car.
> ───────────────────────────────────
> This is an occasion I'll get sick.

Since the unstated premise, in parentheses, contains the predicate of the argument, it is the major premise. *An enthymeme suppressing its major premise is called a first-order enthymeme.* Another example of one is "He must be guilty. He has the gun." The conclusion is obvious: "He must be guilty." Since the stated premise does not contain the conclusion's predicate term, the missing premise must; this makes the missing premise the major premise and the enthymeme first order. The reconstructed argument appears,

> (The person with the gun is the guilty person.)
> He is a person with the gun.
> ───────────────────────────────────
> He is a guilty person.

Sometimes the minor premise is missing, as in the argument "Jefferson must have been a male because all U.S. Presidents have been males." The stated premise, "All U.S. Presidents have been males," contains the predicate of the conclusion; therefore, it is the major premise. The minor premise must therefore be missing. *An enthymeme suppressing its minor premise is called a second-order enthymeme.* The reconstructed argument reads,

> All U.S. Presidents have been males.
> (Jefferson was a U.S. President.)
> ───────────────────────────────────
> Jefferson must have been a male.

Another example of a second-order enthymeme is this argument: "Anyone who wasn't present for roll call has been marked absent. So Casper has been marked absent." Since the predicate of the conclusion, "Casper has been marked absent," appears in the stated premise, the missing premise must be the minor premise, thus making this argument a second-order enthymeme. The reconstructed argument reads,

> All persons not present for roll call are persons marked absent.
> (Casper is a person not present for roll call.)
> ───────────────────────────────────
> Casper is a person marked absent.

Sometimes an enthymeme suppresses its conclusion, as in the argument "Anyone who voted is a citizen, and Jean voted." The conclusion is obvious: "Jean is a citizen." *An enthymeme suppressing its conclusion is called a third-order enthymeme.* Another example would be "Where there's smoke there's fire. There's smoke pouring out of that store!" The conclusion? "The store is on fire!"

The premises and conclusions were omitted from the preceding arguments because they were obvious, too obvious to be stated. That's often why in writing and speaking we do not always state an argument in complete form. Sometimes, however, the reason is that the unstated premise or conclusion is offensive, crass, impolite, or plainly absurd. Take, for example, this first and third-order enthymeme ad:

> Star athletes drink milk.

The purpose of such a message is to persuade us to buy and drink milk. As is true of all ads, the implied conclusion would have us do something: "Milk is a liquid you should drink." If we rewrite but preserve the meaning of the stated premise, we can see the subject of the conclusion in it: "Milk is a liquid star athletes drink." So it's the major premise that remains unstated. Stating the major premise and subsequently the whole argument, we get

> (A liquid that star athletes drink is a liquid that you should drink.)
> Milk is a liquid that star athletes drink.
> _____
> (Milk is a liquid you should drink.)

Pretty absurd, isn't it? Here's another ad enthymeme:

> Bayer brings fast headache relief.

Again, a premise and conclusion go unstated. The conclusion would have us buy Bayer; so we can safely enough reconstruct the conclusion to read, "Bayer is the aspirin you should buy." Since the stated premise contains the subject of the conclusion, we are again missing the major premise. Reconstructing it and the whole argument we get

> (An aspirin that brings you fast headache relief is an aspirin you should buy.)
> Bayer is an aspirin that brings you fast headache relief.
> _____
> Bayer is an aspirin you should buy. (Spot the concealed evidence here?)

At times an enthymeme can take twists, as in

> All models are attractive women.
> Attractive women have good figures.
> No woman with a good figure is shy.
> No model is shy.

This argument actually consists of two enthymemes, not one. Such a multiple argument is a *sorites*. Let's next see what a sorites is.

*EXERCISE 15-2 _____

Name the order of the following enthymemes, complete them, and test their validity.

1. Some books are thrillers; so some thrillers must be mysteries.
2. Not all advertisements are geared to inform, which means that some ads warrant scrutiny.
3. Whatever threatens privacy threatens justice. That's why subjecting people to polygraph tests as a condition of employment is so serious.
4. Knowledge is power and education means knowledge.
5. Only ambitious people succeed in politics. As a result, the country is run by self-serving individuals.
6. "The United States and the Soviet Union are the two most powerful nations on earth, and the relationship between us is complex because it involves strong elements of both competition and cooperation." (President Jimmy Carter addressing the nation on the presence of Soviet troops in Cuba, October 1, 1979)
7. "Senator Edward M. Kennedy asserted Sunday that he had always acted responsibly under pressure, which has, in addition to his long, in-depth involvement in government, made him uniquely qualified to be president." (B. Ayres, Jr., *New York Times*, November 1, 1979)

8. "Of the five great liqueurs in the world only one is made in America. Wild Turkey Liqueur." (ad for Wild Turkey Liqueur)

9. "There is no doubt the United States has the power to obliterate Khomeini [Iranian revolutionary leader Ayatollah Ruhollah Khomeini, who came to power when the Shah of Iran was ousted], his forces and his oil installations overnight. There is equally no doubt military action would be the wrong response. It would risk the safety of every American and westerner in the Middle East." (*London Daily Mirror*)

10. Resident reacting against a mobile-home park's becoming part of the neighborhood: I have nothing against mobile homes as a way of living, but it's unthinkable to put a mobile-home park right in the middle of a residential area. After all, they're usually in outlying areas.

11. "I have asked my own White House staff . . . to protect the integrity of their family. . . . We need a stable family life to make us better servants of the people." (Jimmy Carter, February 1977)

12. Political commentator George Will, criticizing *The Brethren,* a scalding view of the Supreme Court under Chief Justice Warren Burger, which relied substantially on the information leaked by the Court's clerks: "*The Brethren* became sources in violation of trust, and so must be considered somewhat untrustworthy." (George F. Will, "The Injudicial Justices," *Newsweek,* December 10, 1979)

13. Many doctors welcome a patient's informed consent as protection against malpractice suits.

14. ". . . anyone who needs an X-ray shouldn't be afraid to have one; the potential benefits usually outweigh any possible damage." ("Screening Unnecessary X-Rays," *McCalls,* November 1979, p. 10)

15. Former U.S. Attorney General Ramsey Clark on the execution of convicted murderer Jesse Walter Bishop: "Each execution makes it easier to kill the next time."

16. "Strong hair is beautiful hair. Wella Balsam Conditioner actually helps build new strength into your hair." (Cheryl Ladd, ad for Wella Balsam)

17. "Imperialist is a dirty word all right, but it hardly fits a nation like the United States which, with all our faults, is ready to give millions of dollars to help starving and dying Cambodians. . . ." (William Randolph Hearst, Jr., "Editor's Report," *Los Angeles Herald Examiner,* November 4, 1979, p. F3)

18. Former Michigan Governor George Romney in describing the Equal Rights Amendment as "moral perversion": "Surely this resolution and its supporting statements are designed to legitimize sex and social relationships other than those that form the basis of divinely ordained marriage, parenthood and home." (AP release, January 2, 1980)

19. "The building trades must ally . . . with the other groups in society who share . . . basic political interests. We will seek to join the diverse groups which represent consumers, women, blacks, Hispanics, the elderly and small business." (Robert A. Georgine, president of the Building Trades Department of the AFL-CIO)

20. "Malaysia prides itself on religious tolerance—freedom of worship is guaranteed by the constitution—and thus far the Moslem reformers have not aimed their moral guns at non-Malays, except in cases where a non-Malay might be involved in a sexual offense with a Malay or Moslem partner." (Keyes Beech, "The Rise of Moslem Puritanism," *Los Angeles Times*)

THE SORITES

The preceding argument actually consists of two arguments:

All models are attractive women.
All attractive women are persons with good figures.

(All models are persons with good figures.)

AAA-4

No woman with a good figure is a shy person.
(All models are women with good figures.)

No model is a shy person.

EAE-1

An argument like this one, which states one or more premises and a main conclusion but conceals conclusions in between, is called a sorites.
Let's look at another sorites:

All persons who climb mountains are physically fit.
No one physically fit is a chronic smoker.
Only chronic smokers develop respiratory problems.
No mountain climber develops respiratory problems.

To conclude that "No mountain climber develops respiratory problems," as these premises do entail, we have to construct two syllogisms, not one. Thus

No physically fit person is a chronic smoker.
All mountain climbers are physically fit persons.

(No mountain climber is a chronic smoker.)

EAE-1

Not stated in the original argument, this conclusion is now used by the speaker as the minor premise for the second syllogism:

All persons with respiratory problems are chronic smokers.
(No mountain climber is a chronic smoker.)

No mountain climber is a person with respiratory problems.

AEE-2

How do we know when a sorites is valid? By testing the validity of the syllogisms it contains. The first syllogism above is *EAE*-1 and the second is *AEE*-2. Since both are valid, the sorites is valid. *All reconstructed syllogisms must be valid for the sorites to be valid.*

Sometimes a sorites can become quite involved, having many premises and a conclusion. For example,

All mountain climbers are physically fit.
No one physically fit is a chronic smoker.
All respiratory diseases develop in chronic smokers.
Lung cancer is a respiratory disease.
All persons with lung cancer die soon.
Some persons who die soon are reckless persons.

Some reckless persons are not mountain climbers.

How many syllogisms would you say are needed to reconstruct this sorites? Let's see.

1. No physically fit person is a chronic smoker.
   All mountain climbers are physically fit persons.

   (No mountain climber is a chronic smoker.)

   EAE-1

2. All persons with respiratory diseases are chronic smokers.
    (No mountain climber is a chronic smoker.)

    (No mountain climber is a person with a respiratory disease.)

    AEE-2

3. All persons with lung cancer are persons with a respiratory disease.
    (No mountain climber is a person with a respiratory disease.)

    (No mountain climber is a person with lung cancer.)

    AEE-2

4. All persons with lung cancer are persons who die soon.
    (No mountain climber is a person with lung cancer.)

    (No mountain climber is a person who dies soon.)

    AEE-1

5. (No mountain climber is a person who dies soon.)
    Some persons who die soon are reckless persons.

    Some reckless persons are not mountain climbers.

    EIO-4

Is this sorites valid? It is only if each of its five syllogisms is valid. The fourth syllogism, *AEE*-1, contains an illicit major term, thus invalidating the sorites.

We can now generalize about the sorites. Before testing the validity of any sorites, we should

1. Put all its propositions in standard form.
2. Make sure each term appears twice.
3. Make sure that every proposition except the last one (the conclusion) has a term in common with the proposition that immediately follows it.

What have we learned from discussing the enthymeme and sorites? Simply that what remains unstated in an argument is often crucial. Such assumptions aren't always crucial from the viewpoint of the persons arguing since they're interested in persuading us, and unstated premises and conclusions often help them do this. Unstated propositions are more frequently crucial from the viewpoint of the reader and listener, who are the targets of persuasive techniques. If we are to protect ourselves from being manipulated, we must be able to see an argument for what it is. This involves not only the ability to recognize an enthymeme or sorites when we see one—that's relatively easy—but also the skill of reconstructing the argument into a manageable syllogistic form. This is not always easy. But it's a vital skill to master.

To illustrate, let's look at an excerpt from another speech made by the President. At one point he said, "Furthermore, those governments that condone acts of terrorism and blackmail within their borders are themselves no better than terrorists. The reason is obvious: None but terrorists would give aid and comfort to acts of terrorism. So let there be no mistaking the United States' resolve on this point: The United States will hold the new revolutionary government accountable for the terrorists' actions." Editing out the strictly rhetorical, which is perfectly all right to do since what is strictly rhetorical doesn't advance the logic of the argument, we see that there are essentially three propositions here:

1. Governments that condone acts of terrorism and blackmail within their borders are terrorists.

2. Countries that give aid and comfort to acts of terrorism are terrorists.
3. The new revolutionary government is a group that the United States will hold accountable.

The President's argument is actually a sorites, which may be constructed as follows, noting once again that statements in parentheses are unexpressed premises:

> Countries that give aid and comfort to acts of terrorism are terrorists.
> (Governments that condone acts of terrorism and blackmail within their borders are countries that give aid and comfort to acts of terrorism.)
>
> Governments that condone acts of terrorism and blackmail within their borders are terrorists.
>
> AAA-1
>
> Governments that condone acts of terrorism and blackmail within their borders are terrorists.
> (The new revolutionary government condones acts of terrorism and blackmail within its borders.)
>
> (The new revolutionary government consists of terrorists.)
>
> AAA-1
>
> (Terrorists are groups the United States will hold accountable.)
> (The new revolutionary government consists of terrorists.)
>
> The new revolutionary government is a group that the United States will hold accountable.
>
> AAA-1

Here we have a sorites consisting of three arguments, each in the valid *AAA*-1 form. So the President's argument is valid. You'd likely admit that reconstructing this argument wasn't the easiest thing in the world to do. Look at some of those assumptions. How do we know that the President is making them? Have we misrepresented him? Answering these questions is important not only from the aspect of faithfully reconstructing what someone says but also from the view of critically analyzing it. For example, we might ask whether the President's remarks put the United States on record as "unilaterally holding *any* government responsible for *any* act of terrorism that it condones within its borders." Yet this might be reading more into the President's remarks than the President intended. But if our reconstruction is accurate, the major premise of the final argument states that *all* terrorists are groups that the United States will hold accountable. Now that assumption warrants scrutiny. Does the President have in mind *any* act of terrorism, occurring in *any* country, aimed at *any* goal? In Ireland, say? In South Africa? In Nicaragua and El Salvador? If our reconstruction is accurate, these are legitimate, indeed pressing, concerns that the President's assumption invites and that concerned citizens should raise. Otherwise, they might find themselves enmeshed in international conflicts without understanding their nation's involvement, even deploring it.

So the skill of argument reconstruction is no frivolous one. Much is at stake for us as individuals and as a nation. That's why the rest of this chapter is devoted to it. We won't be able to exhaust the subject, but we can provide useful techniques for reconstructing and cataloguing some common pitfalls.

EXERCISE 15-3 _____

Translate each of the following sorites into standard form. Test its validity.

1. No one who studies logic is stupid.
    Anyone who is dull makes a bad writer.
    Stupid persons are dull.
    _____
    No one who studies logic makes a bad writer.

2. Only the brave are rewarded.
    Some who are not promoted are not females.
    Some who are rewarded are females.
    _____
    Some who are not promoted are not brave.

3. None but the ambitious need apply.
    No one not applying should expect a check.
    Smith's not ambitious.
    _____
    Smith shouldn't expect a check.

4. Some who should know better tread on thin ice.
    A dog doesn't really know better.
    Anyone treading on thin ice is bound to drown.
    _____
    No dog is bound to drown.

5. All my brothers are athletes.
    All persons prone to diabetes are overweight.
    No athlete is overweight.
    All who must take insulin are persons prone to diabetes.
    _____
    No brother of mine must take insulin.

RATIONAL RECONSTRUCTION AND VALIDITY

The expression _rational reconstruction_ refers to the process of exposing the logical (hence, "rational") structure of an argument for purposes of analysis. We do this when we encounter arguments couched in extraneous rhetorical devices, or which for some reason or other are confusing and incomplete. We may, for example, have to translate statements into standard form or infer implied premises and conclusions.

Since our purpose is to analyze the argument as it is made—and not to create the argument ourselves—we must take care not to change it for the worse. To do so would be to generate a straw man, the refutation of which is unhelpful since it does not touch the original argument anyway. Further, as rational individuals, we seek the truth—not merely the defeat of an opponent's position. Indeed, an essential characteristic of being rational is a willingness to accept the conclusions of the best available arguments—even when they conflict with our personal preferences.

It is tempting and all too easy to unwittingly weaken an argument in the process of reconstructing it if we violate the guidelines discussed so far. One way to decrease the likelihood of this is to rely on the principle of charity.

Principle of Charity

The principle of charity in rational reconstruction is the rule that whenever two possible interpretations of an argument are equally likely, choose the one that most strengthens the argument.

Why should we do this? In the first place, we assume that others—just as we do—attempt to reason well. Thus, the author of an argument can, in general, be assumed to have intended a sound argument. If an argument is presented in a fragmented, vague, or ambiguous manner, we must select the most likely interpretation *consistent with* what is given. Since most of us intend to reach true conclusions derived from sound arguments, we are warranted in assuming that the best of the reasonable interpretations is the intended one.

Additionally, in some cases, we will spot ways to improve an opponent's argument. This means that even though he or she has failed to present a worthwhile argument to support a particular claim, we are aware that one exists. Although we may proceed to refute our *opponent's argument*, we have not really refuted the *best argument* (the one most likely to be sound). We have bested our opponent without thoroughly analyzing the issue.

Though, technically, we have not created a straw man, the effect is the same: We are refuting an inferior argument while ignoring a more compelling one of which we are aware. This does not mean to suggest that we must do others' thinking for them. Our obligation is really to our own search for truth. In those cases in which two or more equally plausible interpretations of an argument are possible, we are on safer ground when we choose the better. In so doing, we diminish the chances of distorting the argument in favor of our own beliefs and we diminish the chances of overlooking the truth in that particular case.

Three Steps to Rational Reconstruction

Since most of the research dealing with argument reconstruction has focused on the standard-form categorical syllogism, we will concentrate on that argument form.

To call any syllogism incomplete or fragmented means that it leaves one or more of its premises or its conclusion unexpressed. An incomplete categorical syllogism is what we have previously termed an enthymeme. First- or second-order enthymemes are fragments that have not expressed their major or minor premises respectively, and a third-order enthymeme is a fragment that has not expressed its conclusion. The challenge of argument reconstruction, therefore, consists in making these missing parts explicit.

Missing premises usually test our reconstruction skills far more than missing conclusions. That's why we're going to focus on reconstructing first- and second-order enthymemes in this discussion.

The theory behind reconstructing missing premises in categorical syllogisms is direct enough. To begin, consider this form stripped of its quantity and quality:

$$
\begin{array}{cc}
P & M \\
M & S \\
\hline
S & P
\end{array}
$$

As you know, the middle term, M, is the bridge term in any categorical syllogism. It provides the link between S (minor term) and P (major term), which in turn logically entails a relationship between S and P as expressed in the conclusion. By definition, an enthymeme, in not expressing the middle term twice, does not provide an explicit bridge for relating S and P.

For example, in enthymematic form, the preceding complete form would appear as either

First order		*Second order*	
(unexpressed)		P	M
M	S	(unexpressed)	
S	P	S	P

In each of these fragmented forms, the stated premise provides no explicit justification for asserting a relationship between S and P in the conclusions. In the first-order version, the P term isn't even mentioned in the evidence (premise), and in the second-order version, the S term isn't expressed in the evidence. Therefore, there are no explicit grounds for accepting either version. Reconstructing such arguments, therefore, consists of restoring these terms in a way that allows one to infer a logical relationship between S and P. And the only way to do this is with the help of the bridge term, M.

If we are reconstructing a first-order enthymeme, then, we are expressing a premise that connects P and M. If we are reconstructing a second-order enthymeme, we are expressing a premise that connects S and M.

In reconstructing into standard form a fragmented argument that has left a premise unexpressed, follow these three steps:

1. Determine the conclusion of the fragmented argument and any stated premise(s).
2. Determine the middle term of the fragmented argument.
3. Reconstruct the missing premise by relating the middle term with the argument's predicate (in the case of a missing major premise: first order) or subject (in the case of a missing minor predicate: second order).

Let's see how this procedure works with a simple argument: "Sam is a student, so he is a participant." (1) What's the conclusion here? "He is a participant." The stated premise is "Sam is a student." (2) Since *Sam* (*he*) is the subject and *participant* is the predicate, *student* must be the middle term. (3) Since the major premise is missing, we must reconstruct the major premise by relating the middle term, *student*, with the major term, *participant*. Thus, "All students are participants." We can now reconstruct the whole argument:

```
(All students are participants.)
Sam's a student.
─────────────────────────────
Sam's a participant.
```

AAA-1

But not all arguments are this simple. Consequently, a number of pitfalls await us in reconstruction. We must careful. Following the preceding three steps will help us avoid these pitfalls, but even more is required.

In reconstructing fragmented arguments, it's vital to preserve the spirit and intent of the original argument. We have called this the *principle of charity*. Often we have to make judgements about the spirit and intent of an argument. For example, in the simple preceding argument, technically we had a choice between reconstructing the missing premise as we did or reconstructing it as "All participants are students." But this reconstruction would have resulted in an invalid AAA-2 argument. When we have such a choice, we should reconstruct the premise that entails validity.

Of course people can and do use enthymemes that, when reconstructed, are invalid. So we must be careful. Sometimes all possible relevant reconstructions result in invalidity. Suppose, for example, Sweeney argues, "The premier of Russia can't be a capitalist because only capitalists believe that the means of production should be privately owned." His argument affords two possible reconstructions:

> All who believe that the means of production should be privately owned are capitalists.
> (No premier of Russia believes that the means of production should be privately owned.)
> _____
> The premier of Russia can't be a capitalist.

The form here is AEE-1; it's invalid because of an illicit major term. The other possible reconstruction is

> All who believe that the means of production should be privately owned are capitalists.
> (No person who believes that the means of production should be privately owned is a premier of Russia.)
> _____
> The premier of Russia can't be a capitalist.

The form here is AEE-3, which is invalid, again, because of an illicit major term. Since invalidity results either way, we are justified in calling Sweeney's argument invalid.

The point is that in reconstructing, we should give the arguer the benefit of the doubt when, not knowing for sure what the arguer's assumption is, we have a choice between a reconstruction that entails validity and one that does not. However, when no possible reconstruction that's relevant entails validity, we should consider the argument invalid. Having made these general remarks, let's now look closely at some cautions in reconstructing.

Two Things to Avoid in Reconstruction

There are two major pitfalls in argument reconstruction that lead to a misrepresentation of the original argument: (1) misrepresenting the quantity of the terms, (2) misrepresenting the positions of the terms. Even scrupulously avoiding these pitfalls does not guarantee accurate reconstruction; there are no foolproof, hard-and-fast rules to guarantee that. But being aware of these pitfalls increases our chances of faithful reconstructions.

Misrepresenting the Quantity of Terms. In reconstructing arguments, we sometimes create a bogus issue, a straw man, by misrepresenting the quantity of certain terms. Take, for example, the President's argument we met earlier:

> The United States will hold the new revolutionary government accountable because it's made up of terrorists.

Translating this argument into standard form, we get

S M

The new revolutionary government is one made up of terrorists.

S P

The new revolutionary government is a group that the United States
will hold accountable.

The form of this argument is

(unexpressed relationship between P and M)
All S are M. (minor premise)

All S are P.

(Before proceeding, make sure you understand why these are A propositions.)
Since the major premise is unexpressed, this is a first-order enthymeme.
To complete this argument, we must express a major premise. That is, we must
relate P and M. Here's one possible version:

(Some M are P.)
All S are M.

All S are P.

This IAI-1 form is invalid because it does not distribute its middle term. But
we'd be hasty—and incorrect—to call this fragment invalid on the basis of this
initial attempt because another version is possible that is perfectly consistent
with what the fragment states. Thus,

(All M are P.)
All S are M.

All S are P.

This AAA-1 form does distribute its middle term and follows all the other rules
for valid deductive reasoning. Restoring this version to ordinary language we
get

M P

(Terrorists are groups the United States will hold accountable.)

S M

The new revolutionary government is one made up of terrorists.

S P

The new revolutionary government is a group that the United States
will hold accountable.

So the guideline here is simple but important: Given a choice between competing
versions of a missing premise that differ in their quantity, choose the one that
helps logically guarantee the conclusion—not the one that doesn't.
Here's another simple fragment:

Some of these defendants cannot be guilty, for they have alibis.

Translated into standard form we get

S M

Some of these defendants are persons with alibis.

S P

Some of these defendants are not guilty persons.

The form of the stated argument is

> (unexpressed relationship between *P* and *M*: first order)
> Some *S* are *M*.
> _____
> Some *S* are not *P*.

By connecting *P* and *M*, while keeping in mind that we have a negative conclusion, two versions emerge:

> (Some *M* are not *P*.)
> Some *S* are *M*.
> _____
> Some *S* are not *P*.

This *OIO*-1 form is invalid because it fails to distribute the middle term. The other version—which is valid—is

> (No *M* are *P*.)
> Some *S* are *M*.
> _____
> Some *S* are not *P*.

The form of this version is *EIO*-1, which is valid. Expressed in ordinary language, the original argument is

> M P
> (No persons with alibis can be guilty persons.)
> S M
> Some of these defendants are persons with alibis.
> _____
> S P
> Some of these defendants cannot be guilty persons.

Of course not all arguments are as simple and straightforward as the preceding, although the principles of reconstruction are identical in all cases. Indeed, most fragments we encounter every day are decidedly more complex. As a result, reconstructive skills often require intense contextual analysis—a close inspection of the language; a keen sensitivity to the arguer's probable intended meaning; and to be sure, a good measure of creative thought. Such skills are not easily or quickly acquired. They demand painstaking concentration, constant practice, and commitment to rational thought and truth. So don't be too disheartened if at first you find yourself struggling to reconstruct more difficult arguments accurately. Everyone experiences such difficulties at some level of argument analysis.

As an illustration of a challenging fragmented argument—but by no means the most difficult we could select to illustrate the point—consider this passage:

> What the poet Robert Browning said of one of his poems perfectly expresses the problem with modern art: "When I wrote this poem, two people knew what it meant—God and I. Now only He does." Take for example that painting over there in the corner. . . .

To reconstruct such an argument, we must first cut through what is non-informational and irrelevant. Browning's statement is informational but does not of itself advance the argument. Yet the *point*, the intent, of the quotation does. Browning seems to be saying that some poems are so esoteric that nobody can understand them—sometimes not even the poet. (Since even if we accept the existence of God, it's impossible to say what's in His mind, we assume that

Browning and the person quoting him are using this allusion as humorous exaggeration to make a point.) The speaker wants to make this point about modern art in general and "that painting" specifically. His conclusion, then, seems to be "That painting hanging over there in the corner is one that nobody can understand—not even the painter." From this analysis, we're able to construct a syllogism that faithfully represents the argument:

> (Modern art is something that no one can understand—not even the
>   painters.)
> That painting in the corner is modern art.
> _____
> Therefore, that painting in the corner is one that no one can under-
>   stand—not even the painter.

This syllogism of *AAA*-1 form is valid, providing that the speaker is using *modern art* in precisely the same way in each premise. But if we disagree with the speaker's argument, we might be tempted to qualify the major premise generalization and thus misrepresent the argument:

> (Some works of modern art are paintings that no one can under-
>   stand—not even the painters.)
> That painting hanging over there in the corner is a work of modern
>   art.
> _____
> That painting hanging over there in the corner is a painting that no
>   one can understand—not even the painter.

This *IAA*-1 form does not distribute its middle term and is therefore invalid. But this reconstruction does not faithfully represent the intent of the original argument, which implies not *some* modern art but *all* modern art.

Misrepresenting the Position of the Terms.   Sometimes we misrepresent an argument by misrepresenting the position of its terms. As an example, consider the President's argument reconstructed earlier:

> Countries that give aid and comfort to acts of terrorism are terrorists.
> (Governments that condone acts of terrorism and blackmail within
>   their borders are countries that give aid and comfort to acts of
>   terrorism.)
> _____
> Governments that condone acts of terrorism and blackmail within their
>   borders are terrorists.
>
> AAA-1

Suppose that rather than reconstructing the missing premise as we did, we took it to be "Countries that give aid and comfort to acts of terrorism are governments that condone acts of terrorism and blackmail." Reconstructing the argument with this version, we get

> Countries that give aid and comfort to acts of terrorism are terrorists.
> (Countries that give aid and comfort to acts of terrorism are govern-
>   ments that condone acts of terrorism and blackmail within their
>   borders.)
> _____
> Governments that condone acts of terrorism and blackmail within their
>   borders are terrorists.
>
> AAA-3

The form here, *AAA*-3, is invalid because of the illicit minor term. But to so represent the President's argument would be to misrepresent it by misrepresenting the position of the terms.

Let's suppose that at the end of his speech, the President said, " . . . only the weak-willed and morally bankrupt cave in to blackmail. And, I can assure you, the United States will not cave in to blackmail." Presumably, these two premises entail the conclusion: "The United States is not weak-willed and morally bankrupt."

Let's see if such a conclusion validly follows from the President's premises. Reconstructing his argument we get

> All those who cave in to blackmail are weak-willed and morally bankrupt.
> The United States will not cave in to blackmail.
> _____
> (The United States is not weak-willed and morally bankrupt.)
>
> AEE-1 or AEE-3[3]

Neither of the possible forms of this argument, AEE-1 or AEE-3, is valid because both commit the fallacy of illicit major term. Now it is possible to take the conclusion in a logically equivalent sense of "No weak-willed and morally bankrupt nation is the United States." In that event, the argument would read,

> The United States will not cave in to blackmail.
> All those who cave in to blackmail are weak-willed and morally bankrupt.
> _____
> (No weak-willed and morally bankrupt nation is the United States.)
>
> EAE-3 or EAE-4[4]

Neither of these forms, EAE-3 or EAE-4, is valid because both commit the fallacy of illicit minor term. In short, the President's argument is invalid; he inadvertently misrepresented the terms. His implied conclusion, that the United States is not weak-willed or morally bankrupt, would follow if he had used "all" instead of "only" in " . . . only the weak-willed and morally bankrupt cave in to blackmail." But chances are that few in the President's audience picked up the invalidity, especially since they probably were very sympathetic to his remarks. Lack of objectivity, as we have seen previously, colors our perception, as well as the formulation of arguments.

*EXERCISE 15-4 _____

Reconstruct the following arguments in standard form, being sure not to misrepresent the quantity or the terms. Be certain to preserve the spirit and intent of the argument.

1. Some of these guys can't be golfers. They're not carrying golf clubs.
2. Chances are the next President will be a male, since all the rest have been males.
3. I know she's got great legs. But do you think I'm madly in love with every girl with great legs?

---

[3]The figure here could be either 1 or 3 because the minor premise conceivably could be translated, "No instance of those who cave in to blackmail is the United States" or "No instance of the United States is an instance of those who cave in to blackmail."

[4]The figure here could be either 3 or 4 because the major premise again could be translated, "No instance of those who cave in to blackmail is the United States" or "No instance of the United States is an instance of those who cave in to blackmail."

4. California pays its counties an incentive for every prisoner they don't sentence to a county jail. Economy can't be the root of all virtue.
5. The United States is contributing to the population explosion in underdeveloped countries by refusing to provide economic assistance only where there's a birth-control program.
6. How can you expect me to know the answer? I haven't even read the question.
7. Some natives are unfriendly because they're suspicious of outsiders.
8. Only those who are willing can be rehabilitated. So you can write off some of these inmates.
9. If capital punishment isn't a deterrent to crime, how come the rate of violent crime has increased since capital punishment was outlawed?
10. Of course Jack is bright, loyal, and experienced. But he's not a party member. So, he qualifies as a consultant but not as a candidate.

Four Things to Do in Reconstruction

There are at least four things we can do to help provide accurate reconstructions. We can make sure that the reconstructed statements are (1) relevant, (2) self-supporting, (3) appropriately strong, and (4) contextually accurate. Ignoring even one of these will invite a straw man.

Relevant Reconstruction. We can consider an unstated premise as an assumption, a statement speakers don't make explicitly but use to help entail a conclusion. As such, it must be directly related to the rest of the argument. It's crucial that we remember this if we're to avoid misrepresenting the original argument.

For example, suppose Sandy argues, "He married mostly for sex; his marriage won't last long." What's the missing premise here? What's she assuming? We're apt to list among the possibilities "Anyone who marries just for sex is unwise"; "The person is not interested in a long marriage"; "People should marry for other things besides sex"; "Sex is a temporary value; something more enduring is necessary to preserve a marriage"; and so on. Sandy may very well agree with any one of these statements. She may even consider them the assumptions underlying her premises. But they are *not* the assumptions that lead directly to the conclusion of her argument. That's why being clear about the conclusion of an argument is the key to uncovering its unstated premise. Unless we consider *where* an argument goes, we're likely to reconstruct irrelevant premises.

Using the three-step method, operational reconstruction, let's first locate the conclusion: "His marriage (is one that) won't last long." The stated premise is "He married mostly for sex." Next, we can determine the middle term by putting the stated premise into standard form: "His marriage is a marriage entered into mostly for sexual reasons." Since *his marriage* is the subject of the conclusion, the minor term, it can't be the middle term; and since we know that the predicate, the major term, is *one that won't last long,* the middle term must be *a marriage entered into mostly for sexual reasons.* Reconstructing the major premise, we now get "All marriages entered into mostly for sexual reasons are ones that won't last long." Since this premise contains the middle term and the predicate of the argument, we know it must be relevant. Now we should ensure that the quantity of the reconstruction is accurate and that the terms are related correctly. Reconstructing the entire argument, we get

(All marriages entered into mostly for sexual reasons are ones that
   won't last long.)
His marriage is a marriage entered into mostly for sexual reasons.

His marriage won't last long.

AAA-1

Let's consider another argument, one that Phil expressed recently: "Any
time the superpowers are talking to each other increases the chances of world
peace. The very fact that the Iceland summit took place at all signals hope for
world peace." Let's assume that one of these statements is intended as the
conclusion but that we're not sure which. How can we decide?

We can usually find the conclusion in such cases by inserting the phrases
it follows that and *for the reason that* before the propositions, each in turn. As
we know, *it follows that* signals a conclusion; *for the reason that* indicates a premise.
So one possible version of Phil's argument is "(It follows that) any time the
superpowers are talking to each other increases the chances for world peace,
(for the reason that) the very fact that the Iceland summit took place at all
signals hope for world peace." Here, we leap to a generalization from one event.
As a result, the generalization does not follow, and if we grant Phil any intelligence, it cannot be the conclusion of his argument. But there is another possible
version of his argument: "(It follows that) the very fact that the Iceland summit
took place at all signals hope for world peace, (for the reason that) any time
the superpowers are talking to each other increases the chances of world peace."
This argument makes more sense, and following what we have learned about
rational reconstruction and the principle of charity, we should attribute this one
to Phil. Having determined Phil's probable conclusion, we can now go about
reconstructing the unstated premise.

We can restate the conclusion as "The Iceland summit is an occurrence
that increases the chances for world peace." Since the predicate of the conclusion,
an occurrence that increases the chances for world peace, is suggested in the stated
premise, the stated premise must be the major premise. Since the subject of the
conclusion, *the Iceland Summit,* does not appear in the stated premise, the
unstated premise must be the minor premise. There's still one term to be accounted for: *any time the superpowers are talking to each other;* this must be the
middle term. We can fairly substitute *an occurrence of* for *time.* Notice how this
information forces us to reconstruct a relevant assumption. Phil's reconstructed
argument thus appears

All occurrences of the superpowers talking to each other are occurrences that increase the chances for world peace.
(The Iceland summit is an occurrence of the superpowers talking to
   each other.)

The Iceland summit is an occurrence that increases the chances for
   world peace.

AAA-1

By making the minor premise, the unstated one, adhere strictly to the *content*
of the stated premise and conclusion, we have made it relevant to the argument.
Having reconstructed the argument, we should now check the quantity and the
subject and predicate to ensure that they too reflect the spirit and intent of the
original fragmented argument.

Self-Supporting Reconstruction.   In addition to ensuring that the assumption we reconstruct is relevant to the fragmented argument, we should also be certain that it is self-supporting. *A self-supporting premise is one that the arguer does not state (even indirectly) in the fragmented argument but is one taken for granted as helping to entail the conclusion.* If we merely reconstruct what the arguer is already expressing, we don't provide an additional premise to entail the conclusion.

Take, as an example, this argument:

> Because today's TV violence is portrayed in graphic detail, it contributes to real-life violence.

That today's TV violence is portrayed in graphic detail does not—of itself— demonstrate that today's TV violence contributes to real-life violence. A missing premise is needed to link the idea of today's TV violence portrayed in graphic detail, *M*, with today's TV's contribution to real-life violence, *P*. Here are two candidates for the missing premise:

Candidate 1: Any violence portrayed in graphic detail contributes to real-life violence.
Candidate 2: Any television violence portrayed in graphic detail contributes to real-life violence.

Each of these premises helps the expressed premise entail the conclusion. Is one preferable?

Although both premises are relevant, they clearly differ in the breadth of their claims. Candidate 1 in effect asserts that *anything* that portrays violence in graphic detail contributes to real-life violence. Candidate 2 connects only TV violence and real-life violence. Although candidate 2 sticks closer to the argument's content, it really just repeats the argument without illuminating it. Anyone who argues, "Because today's television violence is portrayed in graphic detail, it contributes to real-life violence" obviously believes that the expressed premise leads to the expressed conclusion. That's how arguments and reasoning work: Premises entail conclusions; if the premises are accepted as true, a conclusion's supposed to follow logically. All candidate 2 does, then, is make explicit what is implied about the nature of arguments and the reasoning process. Candidate 2 is, in effect, merely an expression of the general principle that leads any arguer from any premise to any purported conclusion: "If you accept my premise, you logically must accept my conclusion." But candidate 2 doesn't tell us anything about the reasoning behind the argument; it doesn't show *how* the arguer moved from stated premise to conclusion. If we fill in the missing premise with candidate 2, we can still ask, "But *why* does television violence contribute to real-life violence?" Candidate 2 doesn't come near answering that question— but that is precisely what the reconstruction must answer if it is to help entail the conclusion.

Of the two possibilities, candidate 1 is preferable because it does not merely repeat what is already explicit in the argument. It illuminates; it shows how the arguer moved from expressed premise to conclusion. It answers the question of why TV violence contributes to real-life violence.

Appropriate Strength of Reconstruction.   *In determining a missing premise, choose one that is strong enough to help entail the conclusion but not stronger. Strong enough—but not too strong.* There are good reasons for this advice.

If the reconstruction is not strong or general enough, it won't help provide conclusive support for the deduction. On the other hand, if it's too strong, it will misrepresent the argument; it will say more than the *arguer* intended. Either way, the reconstruction would be inadequate to the task of correctly completing the argument.

To understand this guideline, consider this argument:

Since Frances is a police officer, she probably favors collective bargaining.

The missing premise must connect "police officers," the middle term, with "people who probably favor collective bargaining," the major term.

The word *probably* in the major term is significant in distinguishing the asserted class from "people who *definitely* favor collective bargaining" and from "people who *may* favor collective bargaining." Since the stated premise—"Frances is a police officer"—does not express this likelihood, it's crucial that the reconstructed premise does. In a valid argument, the conclusion cannot contain more than is given in the premises. In this argument, likelihood must be introduced in one of the premises if it is to be entailed in the conclusion.

Thus, "All police officers are people who probably (or likely or typically or generally) support collective bargaining" reflects the notion of probability called for by the conclusion. On the other hand, to reconstruct the missing premise as "All police officers are people who support collective bargaining" is too strong. It calls for a stronger conclusion—"Frances is a person who (definitely) supports collective bargaining"—than the one stated. But to express the missing premise as "All police officers are people who *may* (or might or sometimes do or possibly) support collective bargaining" is too weak to support the *probably* in the conclusion.

In reconstructing missing premises, then, we need to be especially sensitive to words in the conclusion that imply certainty, probability, or possibility. We want to be sure to reconstruct missing premises that accurately reflect the degree of likelihood or certainty expressed in the conclusion—no more and no less. Missing premises need to reflect appropriate statistical conditions to be accurate.

Contextually Accurate Reconstruction

So far we've learned to be careful to make our reconstructed premises relevant, self-supporting and strong. Our final note of caution concerns the context of an argument. *The context refers to the physical as well as the rhetorical surroundings of an argument. The physical context of an argument concerns such things as who voices it, where, when, and why—in short, the complexity of circumstances under which the argument was made.* These can prove vital in accurate reconstruction.

As an illustration, consider this simple argument, voiced by a judge in a beauty contest. Ordinarily this judge bases her decision on physical beauty alone. But in this contest, the beauty of the finalists is of comparable merit, so she's still left with the problem of deciding the winner. The finalists are asked to show any talents they have; after they do so, the judge announces to the audience,

"The beauty of these finalists I've adjudged equal. What's made up my mind in this case is talent. The singer, finalist number three, is the winner." How would you reconstruct this argument?

The judge's conclusion is obvious: "Finalist number three is the winner." What about the premises? It might be best here to derive the unstated assumption before using the given ingredients to reconstruct the stated premise. What's the judge assuming? We might at first think, "Any finalist who sings should win a beauty contest." But it's more likely that she means that *in this particular case* singing has decided the contest for her. Does the context indicate that the judge feels a beauty-contest winner must have singing ability? Hardly. Perhaps she means, "Talent *must* be a factor in all beauty contests in which the beauty of the finalists is of comparable merit." But such an assumption would lead to the conclusion that talent must be a factor in *this* contest, not that finalist number three is the winner, the conclusion of this argument. The context seems to demand an assumption of this sort: "The most talented finalist should win this beauty contest, in which the beauty of the finalists is of comparable merit." Someone might argue that the judge says nothing of "talents" but only of singing. But again, inspect the *context. Under these circumstances* doesn't it make better sense to assume that the judge regards singing as simply one talent and that she would consider other talents? In other words, judging from the physical surroundings (no double meaning intended), we show little sense in reconstructing such a narrow assumption as "The finalist who sings the best should win this beauty contest, in which the beauty of the finalists is of comparable merit."

Let's reconstruct the argument in standard form, using our more likely assumption:

> (The most talented finalist should be the winner of this beauty contest
>   in which the beauty of the finalists is of comparable merit.)
> The finalist who sang, number three, is the most talented finalist.
> _____
> Therefore, the finalist who sang, number three, is the winner of this
>   beauty contest.
>
>   AAA-1

Let's now look at a simple example of how *rhetorical* surroundings, language, can affect an argument's reconstruction. "I'd prefer the cheaper car if it weren't so small," B.J. tells a car dealer. The implied conclusion here is "I don't prefer the cheaper car." Would it be fair to say that B.J. is assuming, "Any inexpensive car is one I prefer, as long as it's not small"? We certainly can view this premise as relevant and self-supporting enough to find its way into the argument:

> (All cars that are inexpensive but not small are cars that I prefer.)
> This car is inexpensive but small.
> _____
> Therefore, I do not prefer this car.
>
>   AEE-1 (Can you explain why?)

But before reconstructing the argument in this way, let's consider the context of the statement. When B.J. says, "I'd prefer the cheaper car if it weren't so small," he's deciding on the basis of a comparison; the word *cheaper* gives that much away. But our reconstruction ignores this fact. The standard of comparison is a larger and more expensive car. What B.J. means, then, is that in having compared the two cars, he'd prefer the cheaper one if it were not so small. In other words, as far as he is concerned, the difference between the two cars that makes him shy away from the cheaper one is that the cheaper one is so small. Does this mean that he would take any larger car for the same price? No, only one that meets the qualities of his standard of comparison, which is the bigger and more expensive car implied in the statement. So we'd faithfully serve B.J.'s argument by reconstructing the following premise:

> All cars that are not so small and have the characteristics of car X but are cheaper are the cars that I prefer.

We can then use this premise and our conclusion to formulate the argument:

> (All cars that are not so small and have the characteristics of car X and are cheaper are cars that I prefer.)
> Car Y is not a car that is not so small and has the characteristics of car X and is cheaper.
> _____
> Therefore, car Y is not a car I prefer.

AEE-1

*EXERCISE 15-5 _____

1. Reconstruct the following fragmented arguments. Be certain the reconstructions are relevant, self-supporting, appropriately strong, and contextually accurate. Are the arguments sound, i.e., valid and free of informal fallacies? Where necessary, use parenthetical information.

   a. Dogs are not ruminants, because they don't chew the cud.
   b. Jacques Penf is the largest-volume furniture mart in America. You know you'll get the best deal there on new furniture.
   c. "Winston tastes good like a cigarette should." (ad for Winston cigarettes)
   d. Inasmuch as all voters are citizens, some of the people leaving the polling station probably aren't voters.
   e. "If you've seen Perry Como describe the new Sylvania color set on TV, you know what we have here." (ad for Sylvania GT-Matic, self-adjusting color television)
   f. The Senator has something to hide. After all, only people hiding something refuse a polygraph test.
   g. LULU: Government spending may contribute to inflation.
   LOLA: Why do you say that?
   LULU: Because government spending helps the employment situation.
   h. Not all persuasive devices are reliable. Plenty of them are invalid arguments.
   i. "In 1977 Washington and Lafayette may well have planned strategies over a glass of Martell." (ad for Martell brandy, *not* for the American Historical Society or Alcoholics Anonymous)
   j. That meat must be very good. The label says "U.S. Certified Grade A."
   k. "Lose ugly bulges. Be more feminine." (ad for Waistlets gum)
   l. It must have rained today, for the game was postponed.
   m. "Yond Cassius has a lean and hungry look . . . such men are dangerous."
   n. "It's only natural." (ad for Salem cigarettes)
   o. "California has already done more for farm workers than any other state." (California State Senator Clare Berryhill opposing unemployment compensation for farm workers)
   p. Maria can't be employed here. Her name isn't listed in the employment directory.
   q. Not all people benefit from exercise. So I'm not going to start jogging without first consulting my physician.

r. JACK: Uh-oh, it must be tax time again.
DEL: Why's that?
JACK: Pop's groaning.
s. The president never expresses an opinion unless asked to. He must be very wise or very empty-headed.
t. Poker players are thinkers, simply because they're people.
u. "Liberty means responsibility. That is why most men dread it." (George Bernard Shaw)

2. Just to sharpen your recognition of *informal* fallacies, reexamine the preceding arguments for informal fallacies in the stated or assumed premises.

SUMMARY

This chapter concludes our treatment of translating propositions into standard form and reconstructing fragmented arguments. In handling the non-standard-form argument with more than three terms, we learned ways of handling synonyms and complements. Also, we can now translate into standard-form propositions arguments that (1) contain a singular reference, (2) contain adjectival phrases, (3) lack the verb *to be*, (4) have irregular quantifiers, (5) lack the subject and predicate terms, (6) use *only* or *none but*, and (7) consist of two statements—one affirmative, the other negative.

Before we discussed the fragmented argument, we learned that the best way to determine the conclusion and premises of an argument is through the context of the argument—the argument's rhetorical and physical surroundings. Signal words are helpful but can be misleading, as they don't always indicate arguments.

The fragmented argument is called an *enthymeme*. A first-order enthymeme, we saw, suppresses its major premise; second-order, its minor premise; and third-order, its conclusion. Often a string of enthymemes appear together, their conclusions suppressed except for the last one. Such an argument is called a *sorites*. A sorites is valid only if each argument it contains is valid.

Finally, we considered the important subject of reconstruction and validity. View this discussion as cautionary and advisory. We suggested a three-step method that's helpful in reconstructing fragmented arguments: (1) determine the conclusion, (2) determine the middle term, and (3) reconstruct the unstated assumption by relating the middle term with the subject (in the case of a missing minor premise) or the middle term with the predicate (in the case of a missing major premise). We reviewed two pitfalls in reconstruction: (1) misrepresenting the quantity of the terms, and (2) misrepresenting the terms themselves. In reconstruction, it's important to produce statements that are (1) relevant, (2) self-supporting, (3) appropriately strong, and (4) contextually accurate. Throughout this section on reconstruction, we emphasized one thing above everything else: fidelity to the spirit and intent of the original argument. Only conscious commitment to this principle of charity can help us avoid misrepresenting arguments.

Summary Questions
Reconstruction self-test: Answer the following questions for yourself. Then check your answers by referring to the text.

1. Whenever we find an argument appearing to have more than three terms, we _____ .
2. For propositions containing singular terms, the individual is considered _____ .
3. Treat adjectival phrases as _____ .
4. Give an example of a proposition in which the article *a* means "some."
5. When dealing with *only* and *none but,* we follow these three steps: (1) _____ , (2) _____ , and (3) _____ .

ADDITIONAL EXERCISES _____

1. Reconstruct the following fragments and determine whether they are valid.

a. "The job of the White House press office is to convey questions on the positions that we take on the issues. I do not intend to go through 1986 dwelling on . . . the so-called Daniloff affair."

b. "You can't dismiss the rock groups as 'far out.' The fact that their music succeeds suggests that their ideas are widely circulated and probably accepted by a lot of people." (ad for Dewar's White Label Scotch)

c. "The best-selling menthol has 17 mg. 'tar.' Iceberg has only 10. Buy Iceberg." (ad for Iceberg 10 cigarettes)

d. "The ordinary citizen usually sees the policeman in an authoritarian position. . . . Therefore, people often do not deal with policemen as people." (Dr. John Telzel, quoted in "Police Find New Esteem in Mufti," *Los Angeles Times,* June 18, 1973, p. 19)

e. "The Food and Drug Administration plans to keep secret in the future the recall of certain defective and potentially deadly medical devices and drugs. In a series of interviews, FDA officials said they are concerned that public warnings may literally frighten people to death." (Associated Press release, September 17, 1973)

f. "To believe that law is breaking down in the U.S. because the Supreme Court for a short span of time went 'soft on crime' is to duck the issue. Did all the supreme courts in all the other nations suddenly and at the same time decide to coddle criminals?" (Alvin Toffler, "The Future of Law and Order," *Encounter,* June 1973, p. 15)

g. "Détente is an idea, a perception of intentions among countries. As such, it is not an objective fact." (General Creighton W. Abrams, Chief of Staff, U.S. Army, in a speech before World Peace Luncheon, October 22, 1973)

h. "The society we live in doesn't give you permission to have psychic abilities. That is one reason that so much talent is suppressed." (Spokesperson for Stanford Research Institute, quoted in "Boom Time on Psychic Frontier," *Time,* March 4, 1977, p. 72)

i. ALICIA: Rover must be hungry.
ART: Hungry? I just fed him.
ALICIA: But he's barking.

j. JOYCE: Smith and Jones can't be good reporters.
JOE: Not good reporters! But they exposed the Walker espionage affair.
JOYCE: That's my point. Most good political reporters wouldn't have used a story so damaging to the national interest.

k. Ted Kennedy will always have to accept questions on Chappaquiddick gracefully. A hypersensitive politician doesn't remain a presidential contender.

l. STAN: The nations of the world unanimously condemned Russia when it seized journalist Nick Daniloff and took him hostage.
LUPE: Not so. Albania didn't.
STAN: Okay, a mere technicality. So just about every nation did. And as far as I'm concerned that establishes the righteousness of the U.S. position.

m. We can't possibly have any idea of divine attributes and operations because we have no experience of them.

n. TAYLOR: Why do you call yourself an idealist?

TRISH: Because I believe that all that exists is spiritual.

TAYLOR: But that makes you a spiritualist.

TRISH: Not necessarily. Not everyone who believes in the primacy of the spiritual is a spiritualist.

o. "I do not believe we can have any freedom at all in the philosophical sense, for we act not only under external compulsion but also by inner necessity." (Albert Einstein)

p. "Man tends to increase at a greater rate than his means of subsistence; consequently he is occasionally subject to a severe struggle for existence." (Charles Darwin)

q. PAUL: I can't see how you can abandon the biblical theory of creation.

SAUL: Because there's no scientific evidence for it.

PAUL: But that's irrelevant. Don't you realize that only demonstrable proof should be able to shake your belief in the biblical theory?

r. The best way to avoid error is to cultivate objectivity, for only those who ignore the facts are likely to be mistaken.

s. Lying still [in the face of an iniquitous government], you are considered as an accomplice in the measures in which you silently acquiesce. Resisting, you are accused of provoking irritable power to new excesses. The conduct of a losing party never appears right." (Edmund Burke)

t. Wealth is not an evil. So it must be a good.

u. "It is clear that we mean something, and something different in each case, by such words (e.g., "substance," "cause," "change"). If we didn't we could not use them consistently. . . ." (C. D. Broad)

2. Reexamine the preceding arguments for informal fallacies.

Symbolic Logic: Disjunctive and Conditional Syllogisms

Though syllogisms hang not upon my tongue,
I am not surely always in the wrong!
'Tis hard if all is false that I advance—
A fool must now and then be right, by chance.

WILLIAM COWPER

As we saw in Chapter 15, having a "sense" about the validity of an argument is not very reliable. And just as Cowper's fool "must now and then be right, by chance," so, too, must he be wrong.

Even if we always can't be right, we have reduced the likelihood of being wrong by learning how to prove the validity or invalidity of standard-form categorical syllogisms. But not all syllogisms are standard-form categorical syllogisms, and, thus, don't lend themselves to the methods of proving validity. We've discussed so far methods that apply only to standard-form categorical syllogisms. Consider, for example, this argument:

> If all syllogisms are standard-form syllogisms, we have adequate means available for proving their validity.
> Not all syllogisms are standard-form categorical syllogisms.
>
> We do not have adequate means available for proving their validity.

Is it valid? Perhaps we can figure that out if we think about it carefully. But there is a better, more efficient, way of analyzing such syllogisms than just trying to "figure them out," which is the subject of this chapter. (By the way, the syllogism in question is invalid. It is an example of a commonly committed fallacy, called *the fallacy of denying the antecedent,* which we will learn about as part of our study of nonstandard syllogisms.)

In this chapter we'll discuss two of the most common patterns of deductive reasoning—patterns we naturally use as part of our everyday reasoning. We will also reinforce and add to our understanding of the concept of logical form. We will learn to recognize the forms of three nonstandard syllogisms and also how to simplify them through the use of a few basic symbols. In Chapter 15 we learned how to "translate" or reconstruct syllogisms in ordinary language into standard-form categorical propositions. Thus, with the completion of this chapter, we will have a firm grasp on the basics of deductive reasoning and a supply of some basic analytic tools for handy reference.

To understand and reveal more fully the nature of deductive reasoning, as well as to avoid some of the pitfalls of imprecise expression, logicians often turn to *artificial symbolic languages.* Such languages are carefully constructed in a way that avoids certain problems of meaning that can occur when arguments are expressed in ordinary language.

Great progress has been made in modern logic since the introduction of these symbolic languages. I. M. Copi compares the changes in the power and efficiency of modern logic over ancient and medieval logic with the change in mathematics that occurred with the switch from Roman to Arabic numerals.[1] (If you don't believe that's progress try doing some simple division with Roman numerals.)

Those of you familiar with computer languages are already familiar with artificial symbolic languages. Indeed, the so-called "thinking machine" is in part a product of a symbolic language deliberately created to serve a special function. We will see that through the use of special logical symbols, it is possible to represent the "shape" (form) of two common non-standard form syllogisms, disjunctive and conditional, in a way that allows us to distinguish quickly and easily invalid ones from valid ones. To do so we need to take a basic look at some of the essential components of something called the statement calculus. Ours will be only a summary look—but even so we'll quickly recognize the power and utility of contemporary symbolic logic.

THE STATEMENT CALCULUS

The *statement calculus* is sometimes known as *sentential logic* or the *logic of truth functions.* Don't let the jargon throw you. *The statement calculus is just a way of*

---

[1]I. M. Copi, *Introduction to Logic,* 5th ed. (New York: Macmillan, 1978), p. 264.

analyzing an argument's form in terms of the simple affirmative statements it contains and analyzing the logical relationships that exist among those statements.

Consider this statement: *"Either* the woman is a voter *or* she's a foreigner." This is a *compound statement;* that is, it is composed of two simple statements: "The women is a voter" and "She's a foreigner." The statement *"If* it rains, *then* you'll get wet" is another example of a compound statement. It is made up of these two simple statements: "It rains" and "You'll get wet."

Statement Variables

In general, the language of the statement calculus expresses simple affirmative statements in lowercase letters from the latter half of the alphabet, conventionally beginning with p: p, q, r, s, and so forth. These letters are called *statement variables*. Statement variables are *symbols* for which we can substitute *any* statement.

Logical Operators

But what about the expressions in our two examples—*either . . . or* and *if . . . then?* They are called *logical operators, usage of which expresses or shows the particular logical relationship among the simple statements that make up a given compound statement.* There are special symbols for logical operators, too. The basic logical relationships (called *logical operators*) that we will use in this chapter are represented by the following symbols:

not: ∽ (called the curl)
and: · (called the dot)
or: ∨ (called the wedge or "vee")
if . . . then: ⊃ (called the horseshoe)

Using this basic information, we will be able to contrast clearly simple affirmative statements such as "The woman is a voter" with compound statements such as "Either the woman is a voter or she's a foreigner." The difference is simply this: *A compound statement contains a logical connective; a simple statement does not.*

STUDY HINT

Compound statements contain logical operators—simple statements do not.

Punctuation

Written English requires many punctuation marks to ensure clarity. Consider this ambiguous statement: "Joan will travel abroad or go to work and have a family." The statement could mean either (1) "Joan will travel abroad, or she will go to work and have a family" or (2) "Joan will travel abroad or go to work, and she will have a family." The proper placement of commas makes all the difference to us—and to Joan as well. To eliminate such ambiguity, we need adequate punctuation. Symbolic logic uses a system of parentheses, brackets, and braces (in increasing order) to meet this need. They help us group related parts of compound statements in unambiguous ways. For example,

1. Joan will travel abroad or (she will go to work and have a family).

has a quite distinct meaning from

2. (Joan will travel abroad or go to work) and she will have a family.

In statement 1, the main logical operator is *or;* in 2, it is *and.*

Now let's take a closer look at these symbols and see how they relate to syllogistic reasoning.

NEGATION

The symbol ~ is called a *curl* (or *tilde*). It corresponds to the English word *not,* or more precisely, to *it's not the case that* or *it's false that.* Thus, ~*p* can be read "not *p,*" "it's not the case *p,*" or "it's false that *p.*" Because ~ functions to contradict or deny, it is the symbol of *negation.*

Note that statements such as "The task is unnecessary," "The supply is insufficient," and "The student is irresponsible" are treated as negations. Such prefixes as *un-, in-, ir-,* and so forth deny, that is, negate, the root term they precede, and, in effect, mean *not.* Thus, for example, *unnecessary* means *not necessary.* "The task is unnecessary" is symbolized as the negation of the statement variable *p,* where *p* stands for "the task is necessary": ~*p* ("It's *not* the case that the task is necessary").

Since *any statement like this is expressed the same way* (~*p*), this symbolic expression is called a *statement form,* or *formula.* Therefore, *any case in which a simple affirmative statement is being denied is represented by* ~p.

You should be able to detect a relationship between *p* and ~*p,* between "The task is necessary" and "The task is not necessary." One denies the other. In other words, if *p* is true, ~*p* is false; if *p* is false, ~*p* is true. If we represent the truth values "true" and "false" as T and F, we can represent the truth values of *p* and ~*p* as:

p	~*p*
T	F
F	T

T and F represent the possible combinations of truth values *p* and ~*p* might have. Such a *table,* one *that accounts for all the possible truth values of the variables, is called a truth table.*

Given as true the statement "The New York Yankees are a baseball team," from the truth table for negation we can see that its denial—"The New York Yankees are not a baseball team"—is false. Given as false the statement "Oxygen is not necessary for fire," we see that its denial ("Oxygen is necessary for fire") is true. Although we hardly need a truth table in such simple cases, in more complex ones the truth table is an economical aid.

*EXERCISE 16-1 _____
Which of the following are negations?

1. Nothing is certain but uncertainty.
2. Nonexisting things are unimaginable.
3. Christ was not a philosopher.
4. No cats are vegetarians.
5. Jones is a noncommissioned officer.

CONJUNCTION

The logical connective _and,_ which is used to conjoin statements, is represented here by the symbol ·, called the _dot._ Statements that are conjoined are called _conjuncts,_ and the compound statement they compose, a _conjunction._

There are several ways to express a conjunction in English. Besides the obvious _and,_ you might be surprised to learn that _but, moreover, however, yet,_ and other such expressions often represent the logical operator we're calling a conjunction. When they do, they are symbolized by ·.

STUDY HINT

Do not confuse ordinary language conjunctions (such as _but, yet, however,_ and _nevertheless_) with negation.

For example, the logical form of each of the following statements would be symbolized by $p \cdot q$:

Plato was a rationalist _and_ Locke an empiricist.
Plato was a rationalist, _but_ Locke an empiricist.
Plato was a rationalist; Locke was an empiricist.
Plato was a rationalist, _yet_ Locke was an empiricist.
Plato was a rationalist; Locke, _however,_ was an empiricist.

A conjunction is true if and only if both its conjuncts are true. Consider the preceding statements: If both p and q are true individually, the conjunction $p \cdot q$ is also true. But if either p or q is false, $p \cdot q$ is false. We can see why from the truth table that expresses all the possible combinations of truth values for two variables in conjunction:

p	q	$p \cdot q$
T	T	T
T	F	F
F	T	F
F	F	F

Thus, the only time $p \cdot q$ can be true is when the conjuncts p and q are both true.[2]

---

[2]It should be pointed out that the truth-functional connective · fails to express temporal order (as in "The students married and had a baby"), arithmetical operations ("Three and four is seven"), and certain other ordinary language uses of the conjunction.

> **STUDY HINT: TREAT CONJUNCTIONS AS ASSERTING
> THAT *BOTH* CONJUNCTS ARE TRUE.**
>
> Thus, if either conjunct is false, the conjunction is, too.

*EXERCISE 16-2 _____

Which of the following can be represented by $p \cdot q$? Keep in mind that p and q symbolize simple affirmative statements.

1. The automobile was expensive, but it was gaudy.
2. Hemingway wrote *A Farewell to Arms* and "The Snows of Kilimanjaro."
3. The Athletics and the Angels are in the same league.
4. Although wet, the field was playable.
5. He won't be present, for he's the president.

DISJUNCTION

The symbol **v**, called the *wedge* or *vee,* stands for *or*. In English we use the single word *or* in two senses. For example, in a statement on a restaurant menu such as "Dinner includes soup or salad," *or* means clearly *either* soup *or* salad *but not both*. This meaning, termed the "exclusive sense of *or*," is clear to most of us from the context: in this case, the context of a restaurant menu. But in "All those eligible for welfare are unemployed *or* infirm," *or* is used in a "weaker" sense known as the *inclusive* sense. In this example of the "weaker" sense, the statement asserts that one could be either unemployed *or* infirm and allows for the possibility of being *both* unemployed *and* infirm. The inclusive *or* asserts that *at least one of the alternative statements is true*. Thus, "All those eligible for welfare are at least unemployed or infirm." Symbolic logic uses this second, weaker, or inclusive, sense of *or*.[3]

The statements joined by the inclusive *or* are called *disjunctions. The statement including both disjuncts and the logical operator* or *is called a disjunction.* Symbolically, we can represent any disjunction as $p \lor q$. *If either disjunct is true, the disjunction is true.* The truth table representing disjunction looks like this:

p	q	$p \lor q$
T	T	T
T	F	T
F	T	T
F	F	F

Obviously, *only when* p *and* q *are both false is the disjunction* p $\lor$ q *false.* In other words, if either p or q is true or if both are true, $p \lor q$ is true.[4]

---

[3]Note that this sense allows for the greatest usefulness of our symbols. We can express the strong sense of *or* by the following: $(p \lor q) \cdot \sim(p \cdot q)$. This means "At least one of the disjuncts but (and) not both."

[4]Treat *neither . . . nor* as a conjunction. Thus, "They are neither officers nor candidates" means "They are not officers *and* they are not candidates."

> ***STUDY HINT:*** **INCLUSIVE OR ASSERTS THAT AT LEAST ONE OF THE DISJUNCTS IS TRUE.**
>
> A disjunction is false in only one case: when both disjuncts are false.

EXERCISE 16-3 _____

Which of the following can be represented as $p \lor q$?

1. The book is either a novel or a history.
2. Either parent will represent the child.
3. The current President is either a Republican or a Democrat.
4. He wants a hamburger with fries or a milkshake.
5. The fare is a hundred dollars or less.

MATERIAL IMPLICATION

The symbol $\supset$, called the *horseshoe*, is read "if . . . then." Certain "if . . . then" statements are called *conditionals, hypotheticals,* or *implications. We call the statement that occurs between* if *and* then *the antecedent of the conditional, and we call the statement that follows* then *the consequent.* This is a special kind of conditional, known as a *material conditional.*[5]

Let's see when a material conditional statement is true by considering the following example: "If it's raining, the game is cancelled." This conditional is true provided that "the game is cancelled" is not false at the same time that "it is raining" is true. *A conditional statement is true if and only if the consequent is not false and the antecedent true.* If we let $p \supset q$ represent any material conditional statement, the truth table for the *horseshoe* looks like this:

p	q	$p \supset q$
T	T	T
T	F	F
F	T	T
F	F	T

From this table we can see that any conditional $p \supset q$ is true if and only if q is not false when p is true. Observe that the *only* time $p \supset q$ is false is when p is true and q is false.

> ***STUDY HINT***
>
> The only time a conditional statement is false is when the antecedent is true and the consequent is false; otherwise the conditional is true.

---

[5]Other conditionals are logical, definitional, causal, and decisional; we are concerned only with material conditionals.

Every conditional statement—whatever else it may mean—asserts this relationship: It denies that its antecedent is true and its conditional false. Although this may seem odd, remember that we are talking about only one type of conditional statement, the *material conditional,* as logicians call it. *This* common meaning, the negation of the conjunction of the antecedent with negation of the consequent, $\sim(p \cdot \sim q)$, is what we mean by the symbol $\supset$, the *horseshoe.*

    With these introductory remarks behind us, we can now look at disjunctive and conditional syllogisms.

EXERCISE 16-4 _____

Express the following statements as material conditionals in the form $p \supset q$ (if p then q). Think carefully about the relationships being asserted by these propositions, keeping in mind that the material conditional denies the possibility of both the antecedent being true and the consequent false.

1. If it's Monday, this is logic.
2. You must be careful, if you're crossing that street.
3. Assuming you're present, you'll see the visitor.
4. I'll be there unless something terrible happens.
5. Either that's the thief or I'm a monkey's uncle.
6. I'll leave my phone number in case you forget.
7. The records will be available only if you're authorized to see them.
8. I'd like to see her, providing she's willing.
9. In the event that the old man dies, you will inherit his fortune.
10. Only if the plane is late will you have to wait.

DISJUNCTIVE AND CONDITIONAL SYLLOGISMS

Disjunctive Syllogisms

Recall that a syllogism consists of two premises and a conclusion. When a disjunction occurs as a premise in a syllogism, the syllogism is called a *disjunctive syllogism. Disjunctive syllogisms contain a disjunction and a standard-form categorical proposition (A, E, I, O) as premises.* Here's an example:

> Either some students are scholars or they are athletes.
> Some students are not scholars.
> _____
> Then some are athletes.

Notice that the second proposition negates (or denies) one of the disjuncts, and the conclusion affirms the other. Since, as we have seen, to assert a disjunction is to assert that at least one of the disjuncts is true, we may validly infer such a conclusion if both premises are treated as being true. In our example, the conclusion "Then some are athletes" must logically follow. Let's look at another example:

> Either the plane has crashed or it's been delayed.
> The plane has not been delayed.
> _____
> Therefore, the plane has crashed.

Here, too, the second premise denies one of the disjuncts and the conclusion affirms the other. This is the same logical pattern—or form—as the first example.

It, too, is valid.

On the other hand, consider this argument:

> Either the plane has crashed or it's been delayed.
> The plane has been delayed.
> _____
> Therefore, the plane has not crashed.

Notice that the second premise does not deny either disjunct; instead it affirms one of them. Is it possible for both disjuncts to be true? Yes—that's the meaning of disjunction. It allows for the possibility that the plane has been delayed *and* also crashed: Our categorical assertion is merely telling us that at least one of those two disjuncts is true. The meaning of disjunction, as defined in the preceding truth table, only says that *at least one disjunction must be true*—it also always allows for the possibility that both might be. Consequently, the conclusion in this example does not follow inevitably from the premises—it goes beyond them. So this example is invalid.

Last, consider this example:

> The Senator is qualified to be either President or Vice President.
> The Senator is qualified to be President.
> _____
> Therefore, she's not qualified to be Vice President.

As we've already noted, affirming one of the disjuncts does not deny the other. The conclusion, because it does not necessarily follow from the premises, is invalidly drawn. This argument, too, is invalid.

A valid disjunctive syllogism, then, is one in which one premise denies one of the disjunctions of the disjunctive premise, and the conclusion affirms the other disjunct. An invalid disjunctive syllogism *always* results when the categorical premises affirm one of the disjuncts.

We may symbolize any *valid disjunctive syllogism* as follows:

$$p \lor q \qquad\qquad p \lor q$$
$$\dfrac{\sim p}{q} \quad \text{or} \quad \dfrac{\sim q}{p}$$

We can show the validity of this disjunctive syllogism form by constructing a truth table as follows:

p	q	$p \lor q$	$\sim p$
T	T	T	F
T	F	T	F
F	T	T	T
F	F	F	T

The first two columns show all the possible different truth values of statements which may be substituted for the variables p and q. We filled in the 3rd column simply by referring to the first two, and the 4th by referring to the first. Notice that the third row is the only one which contains T for both premises (3rd and 4th columns) and the conclusion (2nd column). According to the table, this disjunctive form has no substitution instances consisting of a true premise and a false conclusion. Thus, this disjunctive form is valid. What's more, any other disjunctive form is invalid, such as the following two:

$$
\begin{array}{c}
p \lor q \\
\underline{p } \\
\sim q
\end{array}
\qquad
\begin{array}{c}
p \lor q \\
\underline{p } \\
q
\end{array}
$$

(To see why the first syllogism is invalid, look at row 1 of the truth table. To see the invalidity of the second, consult row 2.)

We see that whenever a disjunctive syllogism affirms one of the disjuncts as its second, categorical, premise, it is invalid regardless of the truth value of its conclusion.

Symbolizing Specific Arguments.   If we want to symbolize a specific disjunctive syllogism, we use upper-case letters to represent each specific proposition that occurs in it, rather than p, q, r, s, and so on, which represent any statement whatsoever. Recall that p, q, r, s, and so on are the letters traditionally used to represent *statement variables*. Upper-case letters are used when we want to represent specific propositions; these upper-case letters are called simply *statements*. For example, we might represent the rather pessimistic disjunction "Either I flunk logic or I drop it" as $F \lor D$, letting F stand for the statement "I flunk logic," and D for "I drop logic." As a matter of convention and convenience, let's use as statements letters that reflect some essential aspect of the propositions they represent. In this case, for example, F and D remind us of *flunk* and *drop*. (A helpful rule of thumb is to use the first letter of the main verb in the represented statement.)

Thus, the argument "Either I flunk logic or I drop it, but I can't drop it, so I flunk it" can be symbolized as:

$$
\begin{array}{c}
F \lor D \\
\underline{\sim D } \\
F
\end{array}
$$

The argument that results from substituting statements for statement variables is known as a substitution instance of that argument. Our example is a substitution instance of

$$
\begin{array}{c}
p \lor q \\
\underline{\sim q } \\
p
\end{array}
$$

And since that form is valid, any substitution instance of it is valid.[6] We can determine the validity of any disjunctive syllogism by comparing its form to the valid form we've defined on the preceding truth table.

Whatever letters we choose to represent specific statements, we must be sure not to use the same letter to represent more than one statement in a given argument. To do so would render our symbolization ambiguous and useless.

[6]Demonstrating precisely why this is so goes beyond the scope of our survey of basic deductive principles.

STUDY HINT

Be very sure to use the same letter for every occurrence of a statement in any given argument. Never use the same letter to represent more than one statement in any given argument.

It is also a very good idea to jot down a "dictionary" of statement constants not only to remind us which letter represents which simple proposition but also to help keep us from using the same letter to stand for two different propositions. For example, we would be unwise to choose the letter I to represent both "I flunk logic" and "I drop logic." Although a written dictionary may not be necessary in the case of a very simple argument, it is indispensable in more complex cases.

To convey as much meaning as possible, we always symbolize negation with the *curl*. We do not use N, for example, to symbolize "I do not flunk" but rather ~F, where F represents "I flunk," and the ~ negates it.

Three-Step Procedure for Determining Validity.   Let's symbolize this disjunctive syllogism: "Either you're for me or you're against me. You're not for me, so you must be against me."

1. We create our dictionary: F—"you're for me"
$\qquad\qquad\qquad\qquad\quad$ A—"you're against me"

2. We symbolize the argument:

$$F \lor A$$
$$\underline{\sim F}$$
$$A$$

3. We compare the form of the symbolized substitution instance to the form of any valid syllogism (in this case, to the form of a valid disjunctive syllogism):

$$
\begin{array}{ll}
p \lor q & \quad F \lor A \\
\underline{\sim p} & \quad \underline{\sim F} \\
q & \quad A
\end{array}
$$

Following these three steps, we see immediately that our argument is valid. Let's try one more for practice: "We'll go to the movies either tonight or Saturday. We'll go tonight, so it follows that we won't go Saturday."

1. Create a dictionary: T—"we'll go to the movies tonight"
$\qquad\qquad\qquad\qquad\quad$ S—"we'll go to the movies Saturday"

2. Symbolize the substitution instance:

$$T \lor S$$
$$\underline{T}$$
$$\sim S$$

3. Compare with valid form:

$$
\begin{array}{ll}
p \lor q & \quad T \lor S \\
\underline{\sim p} & \quad \underline{T} \\
q & \quad \sim S
\end{array}
$$

In this case, we see that the argument under analysis is invalid. This three-step procedure for testing for validity works for simple deductive syllogisms of the sorts we will confine ourselves to in this text. There are more sophisticated procedures for testing more complex deductive arguments, but they rest on basic principles we're learning here.[7]

EXERCISE 16-5 _____

Using the three-step procedure, determine the validity of the following disjunctive syllogisms.

1.   There's either a fuel shortage or the government is lying.
     There is a fuel shortage.
     _____
     Therefore, the government is not lying.

2.   Either the general is guilty of obstructing justice or he's a patriot.
     The general is no patriot.
     _____
     Then the general is guilty of obstructing justice.

3.   The United States either supports the Israelis or the Arabs in the
        Middle East.
     The United States supports the Israelis.
     _____
     Therefore, the United States does not support the Arabs.

4.   Whether we like it or not—and we probably don't—we must either
        become energy self-sufficient or resign ourselves to international
        blackmail.
     We must not resign ourselves to international blackmail.
     _____
     Hence, we must become energy self-sufficient.

5.   The matter of the universe will continue to expand to extinction, or it
        will begin to contract, in which case another "big bang" will even-
        tually occur.
     The matter of the universe will continue to expand.
     _____
     So the matter of the universe will not begin to contract and, thus,
        another "big bang" will not eventually occur.

6.   Either all S is P or no S is P.
     Some S is not P.
     _____
     It follows that no S is P.

7.   Either some S is P or some S is not P.
     No S is P.
     _____
     Therefore, some S is not P.

8.   Either all S is P or some S is P.
     Some S is not P.
     _____
     So some S is P.

9.   Either no S is P or some S is not P.
     No S is P.
     _____
     Then some S is not P.

[7]Many good symbolic logic texts are available that more fully develop the basic principles we are
    only surveying here. But with even this rudimentary introduction, we can begin to realize
    how special symbols can help us "see" the nature of logical forms and quickly assess the
    validity or invalidity of basic argument forms.

(Can you explain your answer to this final exercise by making use of the existential fallacy?)

Conditional (Hypothetical) Syllogisms

Consider the following argument:

> If Deanna watches "Creature Features," then she's having nightmares.
> Deanna's watching "Creature Features."
> _____
> Therefore, she's having nightmares.

Such an argument form is called a *mixed-conditional syllogism*. It is "mixed" because it contains a conditional premise and a categorical premise. If we look carefully at this argument, we notice that the categorical premise affirms the antecedent of the conditional premise and the conclusion affirms the consequent. Any substitution instance of this form is valid. Such arguments are said to be in the *affirmative mood;* they are commonly referred to by their Latin name: *modus ponens. Any time the categorical premise of a mixed-conditional syllogism affirms the antecedent of the conditional premise and the conclusion affirms its consequent, the syllogism is valid.* Let's symbolize *modus ponens:*

$$p \supset q$$
$$p$$
$$q$$

Modus ponens can be shown valid by means of the following truth table:

p	q	$p \supset q$
T	T	T
T	F	F
F	T	T
F	F	T

Columns 1 and 3 represent the true premises of the *modus ponens* form; column 2 represents the conclusion. Only row 1 represents substitution instances in which both premises are true. In such arguments, the conclusion is also true, as represented in Column 2. The *modus ponens* form is thus established as valid, which means that any argument of this form is valid. There's a fallacy that superficially resembles *modus ponens:*

> If Deanna watches "Creature Features," then she's having nightmares.
> She's having nightmares.
> _____
> Therefore, she's watching "Creature Features."

Even if this conclusion is, in fact, true, it does not logically follow from the premises. (To see why, look at the third row of the preceding truth table.) And a deductive argument is only valid when the premises entail the conclusion—a condition not met by this second example of a mixed-conditional syllogism. Such an argument is said to commit *the fallacy of affirming the consequent.* Let's compare *modus ponens* to affirming the consequent:

modus ponens	*fallacy of affirming the consequent*
$p \supset q$	$p \supset q$
p	q
p	p

STUDY HINT

Modus ponens is always valid; affirming the consequent is never valid.

Besides *modus ponens,* another valid form of mixed-conditional syllogism denies the consequent as its categorical premise and denies the antecedent as its conclusion. Here's an example:

> If Deanna's watching "Creature Features," then she's having nightmares.
> Deanna's not having nightmares.
> _____
> Then Deanna's not watching "Creature Features."

Valid mixed-conditional syllogisms of this form are called *modus tollens,* or *denying the consequent.* Again, we can use a truth table to demonstrate the validity of the *modus tollens* form:

$p \supset q$
$\sim q$
_____
$\sim p$

Thus,

p	q	$p \supset q$	$\sim p$	$\sim q$
T	T	T	F	F
T	F	F	F	T
F	T	T	T	F
F	F	T	T	T

Columns 4 and 5 are derived from negating columns 1 and 2. The premises of the *modus tollens* form are represented by columns 3 and 5, the conclusion by column 4. Only row 4 represents substitution instances in which both premises are true. And in such arguments the conclusion, column 4, is also true. The truth table, therefore, demonstrates the validity of any argument of form *modus tollens.*

Just as we have to be wary of confusing *modus ponens* with the fallacy of affirming the consequent, we must be careful not to confuse *modus tollens* with the fallacy of denying the antecedent. Here's an example of the fallacy of denying the antecedent:

> If Deanna's watching "Creature Features," then she's having nightmares.
> Deanna's not watching "Creature Features."
> _____
> Then Deanna's not having nightmares.

(To see why this syllogism is invalid, consult row 3 of the preceding table.) Let's symbolize *modus tollens* and the fallacy of denying the antecedent to see how they clearly differ:

modus tollens	*fallacy of denying the antecedent*
$p \supset q$	$p \supset q$
$\sim q$	$\sim p$
$\sim p$	$\sim q$

Sometimes, a conditional syllogism contains only conditional propositions, for example:

> If Lisa has nightmares, then Nicky wakes up.
> If Nicky wakes up, then Lina goes bonkers.
> If Lisa has nightmares, then Lina goes bonkers.

Since the syllogism contains only conditional propositions, we call it a *pure conditional* (or *hypothetical*) *syllogism*. Note three things about this particular argument that make it—and any argument with the same form—valid: (1) The consequent of the first premise is the same as the antecedent of the second premise; (2) the antecedent of the first premise is the same as the antecedent of the conclusion; (3) the consequent of the second premise is the same as the consequent of the conclusion. We can represent this valid form symbolically:

$$p \supset q$$
$$q \supset r$$
$$p \supset r$$

Any *pure* conditional syllogism of this form is valid; if it does not follow this form it is invalid. (You can see why, if you so desire, by means of still another truth table.)

*EXERCISE 16-6 _____

Using the three-step procedure, determine which—if any—of the following conditional syllogisms are valid.

1. If the Vice President was not guilty of wrongdoing, he would not resign from office.
   The Vice President did resign from office.
   Therefore, the Vice President was guilty of wrongdoing.

2. If there's life in outer space, it's probably superior to us.
   If it's superior to us, it will contact us.
   If there's life in outer space, it will contact us.

3. If a thing precedes itself, it is its own cause.
   A thing cannot precede itself.
   Thus, a thing is not its own cause.

4. If this is Brussels, today is Tuesday.
   Today is not Tuesday.
   Therefore, this is not Brussels.

5. If a President is impeached, then no one benefits.
   A President is impeached.
   Then no one benefits.

6. If the witness is either the criminal or the criminal's accomplice, he'll lie.

The witness is neither the criminal nor the criminal's accomplice.
Therefore, he'll not lie.

7. If Joanne knows what she's talking about, I'm a monkey's uncle. And
    since I'm obviously not a monkey's uncle, Joanne doesn't know what
    she's talking about.

8. If taxes rise, consumer purchases decline. If consumer purchases de-
    cline, the economy suffers. If taxes rise, the economy suffers.

9. If the President knows what he's doing with this Star Wars thing, I'm
    not your wife. Since you're my husband, the President doesn't know
    what he's doing with this Star Wars thing.

10. If Harry goes to town on payday, he'll come home broke. Harry comes
    home broke, so we can conclude that he goes to town on payday.

The Dilemma

The dilemma is a syllogism that contains conditional and disjunctive propositions. Specifically, *the dilemma is a syllogism that contains a conditional premise
and a disjunctive premise and either a categorical proposition or a disjunctive for a
conclusion.* If a dilemma contains a categorical proposition for a conclusion, it's
termed a *simple dilemma;* if it contains a disjunctive for a conclusion, it's termed
a *complex dilemma.*

To illustrate the simple dilemma, let's look at an argument that most
students lapse into now and again. It goes like this:

If I study, I don't have any fun; if I'm idle, I don't have any fun.
Either I study or I'm idle.

Therefore, I don't have any fun.

Letting S stand for "I study," I for "I'm idle," and $\sim F$ for "I don't have any fun,"
we can symbolize our argument thusly:

$(S \supset \sim F) \cdot (I \supset \sim F)$
$\underline{S \lor I}$
$\sim F$

We notice that our dilemma combines two instances of *modus ponens:*

$S \supset \sim F \qquad\quad I \supset \sim F$
$\underline{S} \qquad\qquad\quad \underline{I}$
$\sim F \qquad\qquad\quad \sim F$

Given the conditional $S \supset \sim F$, and given S, $\sim F$ must necessarily follow; on the
other hand, given the conditional $I \supset \sim F$, and given I, $\sim F$ must necessarily
follow. In other words, given the two conditionals, each of the antecedents
would logically entail one of the consequents. The basic form of a valid simple
dilemma is as follows:

$(p \supset q) \cdot (r \supset q)$
$\underline{p \lor r}$
q

Any simple dilemma of this form is valid; otherwise it is invalid. *A simple dilemma contains a simple statement for its conclusion; a complex dilemma contains a disjunction for its conclusion.* Let's look at a complex dilemma:

> If I get married, then I lose my freedom; if I stay single, then I am lonely. I either get married or stay single.
>
> Therefore, I either lose my freedom or I am lonely.

Symbolized, we get this:

M—I get married; S—I stay single; F—I lose my freedom; L—I am lonely

$$(M \supset F) \cdot (S \supset L)$$
$$\underline{M \lor S}$$
$$F \lor L$$

The basic form of this argument—and of any valid complex constructive dilemma—is

$$(p \supset q) \cdot (r \supset s)$$
$$\underline{p \lor r}$$
$$q \lor s$$

Any complex constructive dilemma of this form is valid; otherwise it is invalid.

STUDY HINT

Simple dilemmas contain simple statements as conclusions; complex dilemmas contain disjunctions as conclusions.

Our example of a complex dilemma illustrates an important point: The frustration we so often feel when confronted with an apparent dilemma is usually compounded by the fact that most of the dilemmas we encounter in our daily dealings are valid. So we often feel the frustration of being "caught on the horns of a dilemma." In fact, you may have noticed that the everyday use of the term *dilemma* is almost entirely confined to circumstances in which someone seems to be confronted with an inevitably unattractive outcome. There are times, as we'll see, when the inevitable isn't at all bad; but generally the dilemma poses an undesired and unpleasant conclusion.

When simple and complex dilemmas deviate from valid form, they present no problem of rebuttal. We simply can dispose of them as being invalid. But what about dilemmas that are valid? What can we do to avoid being impaled on the horns of simple and complex dilemmas?

As is true of any valid argument, before accepting it as sound we should examine its premises for truth. There are two ways to challenge the truth of dilemmas. One is to take the dilemma by the horns; the other is to escape between the horns. Let's illustrate what we mean by focusing on the student's argument.

By "taking the dilemma by the horns," we mean attacking the truth of the conditional premise. Respecting the student's dilemma we can ask, Why are studying and having fun mutually exclusive? Can't studying *be* fun? In fact, the best kind of learning takes place when we're enjoying what we're studying—when we're "having fun." The point is that if we successfully attack one of the conditionals (by perhaps showing that it is a questionable cause fallacy or a hasty conclusion), we destroy the dilemma it sets up.

On the other hand, rather than attacking the conditional proposition, we might *"escape between the horns" of the dilemma by attacking the disjunction*. Thus, perhaps we can be both studious and idle. Surely there are times when the mind must turn away from intense work to restore itself for more work. Undoubtedly, a healthful combination of study and idleness—rest and relaxation—is the best guarantee of success. Reasoning in this way, we in effect contend that the disjunction poses a false dilemma, an either/or situation where, in fact, none exists. If our contention is correct, we destroy the disjunction and the dilemma with it.

Taking a dilemma by the horns or escaping between the horns are the best ways to refute a dilemma. There is a third way, however, that is marvelously entertaining, though usually inadequate to the task.

The Counterdilemma

A counterdilemma is a dilemma whose conclusion is opposed to the conclusion of the original. Ideally the counterdilemma should contain the same propositions as the original dilemma. A celebrated lawsuit between the ancient Greeks Protagoras and Eulathus provides a classic example of such a counterdilemma and how rhetorically devastating it can be.

Protagoras was a fifth-century B.C. teacher who specialized in pleading cases before juries. Eulathus was his student. Lacking the required tuition for his training, Eulathus arranged with Protagoras to defer payment until he, Eulathus, won his first case. Unfortunately for Protagoras, Eulathus delayed going into practice after he finished his training. Fed up with waiting for his money, Protagoras decided to sue his former student for the tuition. At the beginning of the trial, Protagoras posed his case in the form of a dilemma:

> If Eulathus loses this case, then he must pay me (by judgment of the court); if he wins this case, then he must pay me (by terms of the contract). He must either lose or win this case. Therefore Eulathus must pay me.

What could be harder to imagine than Eulathus's avoiding the horns of this dilemma? As unpromising as his situation seemed, Eulathus was nonetheless up to it; evidently he had learned his rhetorical lessons well. He offered the court a counterdilemma:

> If I win this case, I shall not have to pay Protagoras (by judgment of the court); if I lose this case, I shall not have to pay Protagoras (by the terms of the contract, for then I shall not yet have won my first case). I must either win or lose this case. Therefore, I do not have to pay Protagoras!

Notice that the beauty of Eulathus's counterdilemma is that its conclusion explicitly denies the conclusion of Protagoras's dilemma. Genuinely to rebut a dilemma requires such an explicit denial in the conclusion. When it occurs, the counterdilemma is most effective. But rarely do we come across such counterdilemmas. More often than not, the counterdilemma, although enormously crowd pleasing, logically does nothing to refute the dilemma.

To illustrate an entertaining but logically inert counterdilemma, let's again dip into Greek history. An Athenian mother who was attempting to persuade her son not to enter politics is said to have argued,

> If you say what is just, men will hate you; and if you say what is unjust, the gods will hate you; but you must either say the one or the other; therefore you will be hated.

To which her son replied,

> If I say what is just, the gods will love me; and if I say what is unjust, men will love me. I must say either the one or the other. Therefore I shall be loved!

Although such a counterargument is extremely clever and bound to win many debating points, its conclusion is not an explicit denial of the dilemma's conclusion. Recall the Protagoras-Eulathus debate. Protagoras's conclusion was "Eulathus must pay me." Eulathus's conclusion was "I do not have to pay Protagoras." These two statements are incompatible; to accept one is to deny the other; one is the contradiction of the other. But believe it or not, the Athenian youth's conclusion, "I shall be loved," is *not* incompatible with his mother's conclusion, "You will be hated." The reason is that the mother is, in effect, concluding, "You will be hated by men or by the gods." And the son, in effect, is concluding, "I shall be loved by the gods or by men." Since the son could end up being hated by men and loved by the gods, or hated by the gods and loved by men, the conclusions of mother and son are perfectly compatible. The son has not refuted his mother's argument. He'd be much better served to attack the horns of its dilemma or try to escape between its horns. And thus we all would when faced with a dilemma.

But daily, as politicians and advertisers prove, we are taken in by flashy rhetorical devices. And the counterdilemma can be one of them. Not only can the counterdilemma win over an audience, but it can even convince arguers that their shrewdly constructed dilemmas are unsound. Take Roscoe, for example.

Roscoe thought he had Sweeney right where he wanted him. He had loaned Sweeney twenty dollars to bet on a horse, and according to their agreement, Sweeney either owed him twenty dollars or a share of the winnings. Maybe so. But with uncommon deftness, Sweeney counterattacked. He posed a counterdilemma of essentially this form:

> If the horse wins, then I don't owe you twenty dollars (for in that event, I'd owe you a share of the winnings); if the horse loses, then I don't owe you a share of the winnings (because obviously there would be no winnings).
> Either the horse wins or loses.
> _____
> Either I don't owe you twenty dollars or I don't owe you a share of the winnings.

And then, with a flourish of his hand, he added, "Either way we're even." Whereupon Roscoe did what any rational person would do under the circumstances: He threatened to rip Sweeney's ears off if he didn't get his money back.

EXERCISE 16-7 _____

Use the three-step method to determine the validity of the following dilemmas. If invalid, refute by either taking the dilemma by the horns or by escaping between the horns. Construct a counterdilemma for each original dilemma.

1. If the speech is just informative, it will bore me; if it is just entertaining, it will not educate me.
   The speech will be either informative or entertaining.
   _____
   Therefore, the speech will either bore me or not educate me.

2. If there is a God, he will reward me for my virtuous deeds; if there is no God I will sleep a peaceful, uninterrupted sleep.
   There is either a God or there is not.
   _____
   Thus, I will either be rewarded for my virtuous deeds or I will sleep a peaceful, uninterrupted sleep.

3. If she rejects me, I'll be crushed; if she accepts me, I'll be terrified.
   She'll either reject me or accept me.
   _____
   I'll be either crushed or terrified!

4. If the United States modifies its Middle East position, it will offend a good many American Jews; if the United States does not modify its Middle East position, it will jeopardize its fuel supplies in Arab countries.
   The United States must either modify its position in the Middle East or not.
   _____
   As a result, the United States will either offend a good many American Jews or jeopardize its fuel supplies in Arab countries.

5. If I study my logic tonight, then I will not get to go to the movies; if I don't study my logic tonight, I will worry.
   I either study my logic tonight or I don't.
   _____
   I either don't get to go to the movies or I worry.

6. If I vote, then I must choose between two evils. If I don't vote, then I am not a good citizen.
   Either I vote or I don't.
   _____
   So I either choose between two evils or I am not a good citizen.

7. If I pay my rent, then I can't pay my utilities and they will be turned off. If I don't pay my rent, then I will be evicted.
   I either pay my rent or I don't.
   _____
   I am either evicted or they turn off my utilities.

8. If I get married, I lose Midge; if I don't get married, then I lose Louise.
   Either I get married or I don't.
   _____
   I lose either Midge or Louise.

9. If I tell the truth, you will be angry with me; if I lie, I will be angry with myself.
   I either tell the truth or I lie.
   _____
   One or the other of us is angry with me.

10. If I keep this old clunker, I must spend a fortune on repairs; if I buy a new car, then I must spend a fortune on payments and insurance.
    Either I keep this old clunker or I buy a new car.
    _____
    Either I spend a fortune on repairs or I spend it on payments and insurance.

SUMMARY

In this chapter, we learned the rudimentary concepts of the statement calculus and the logical operators' negation, conjunction, disjunction, and material implication, summarized as follows:

Operator/Connective	Symbol (Name)	Truth Value
Negation	~ (curl)	Opposite of original statement
Conjunction	· (dot)	True if and only if both conjuncts are true
Disjunction	v (vee/wedge)	False if and only if both disjuncts are false
Material Conditional	⊃ (horseshoe)	False if and only if antecedent true and consequent false

We also learned about

The statement calculus: We can analyze an argument's form in terms of the simple affirmative statements it contains and analyze the logical relationships that exist among those statements.

Compound statements: This is any statement that contains a logical connective (operator).

Statement variables: The letters p, q, r, s, and so on, are used to represent any statement in symbolic logic.

Statements and substitution instances: Upper-case letters are used to represent specific propositions; the letters used as statement constants usually represent some key term in the proposition, often the first letter of the main verb. The resulting symbolized argument is a substitution instance of a specific argument form. Every substitution instance of a valid argument is valid.

Punctuation: Using parentheses, brackets, and braces, we can punctuate symbolized statements. We follow two rules of punctuation: (1) Assume that the curl applies to the smallest statement the punctuation allows, and (2) when working with complex statements, always remove the innermost parentheses first and work outward.

We have also learned about two kinds of syllogisms—disjunctive and hypothetical—and an argument form that combines them both, the dilemma.

Using our symbols, we can represent the valid forms of disjunctive and conditional syllogisms and simple and complex dilemmas as follows:

Valid

disj. syllogism	modus ponens	modus tollens	pure hyp.	simple dilemma	complex dilemma
$p \lor q$	$p \supset q$	$p \supset q$	$p \supset q$	$(p \supset q) \cdot (r \supset q)$	$(p \supset q) \cdot (r \supset s)$
$\sim p$	p	$\sim q$	$q \supset r$	$p \lor r$	$p \lor r$
q	q	$\sim p$	$p \supset r$	q	$q \lor s$

We also studied two fallacious (invalid) conditional syllogisms:

Invalid

fallacy of *affirming the consequent*	*fallacy of* *denying the antecedent*
$p \supset q$ q ───── p	$p \supset q$ $\sim p$ ───── $\sim q$

Last, we learned a simple *three-step procedure* for determining the validity of certain disjunctive and conditional syllogisms:

1. Create a dictionary.
2. Symbolize the argument.
3. Compare the form of the substitution instance to those just shown; if it exactly matches one of the valid forms, it is valid; otherwise it is not.

Summary Questions

Determine whether or not the following syllogisms are valid. Then translate them into ordinary language, using the dictionary provided. B = Bob goes to college, M = Mom gets mad, D = Dad steps in, F = Fredilyn changes her mind about marriage.

1. $M \supset \sim D$
    D
    ─────
    $\sim M$

2. $B \supset F$
    B
    ─────
    F

3. $(B \supset F) \cdot (\sim B \supset M)$
    $B \vee \sim B$
    ──────────────
    $F \vee M$

4. $(\sim B \supset D) \cdot (B \supset \sim M)$
    $\sim B \vee B$
    ──────────────
    $D \vee M$

*ADDITIONAL EXERCISES ──────────────

Apply the three-step procedure for determining validity of the following. Identify any fallacies that may be present.

1. Reagan either forgot that he approved of trading arms for hostages, or he lied. He didn't lie, so he must have forgotten.
2. If secular humanism is a religion, then it should not be taught in public schools. But secular humanism is taught in public schools, so it must not be a religion.
3. If I study for my logic final, then I'll lose my sweetheart.

If I lose my sweetheart, then my life's empty and futile.
If I study for my logic final, my life's empty and futile.

4. If I go to the movies, then I enjoy myself; if I stay home, then we have fun together. I'm either going to the movies or I'm not, so I'll either enjoy myself or we'll have fun together.

5. God either exists or I'm a fool. God exists. Therefore I'm not a fool.

6. If you think De Niro's a better actor than Stallone, then I'm a nitwit, and I ain't no nitwit!

7. If you love me, then you give me gifts. You give me gifts, so I know that you love me.

8. If I love you, then I want to marry you. But I don't love you, so I don't want to marry you.

9. If it rains, the crops will die; if it doesn't rain, the stock will die. Either the crops will die or the stock will die, since it either rains or it doesn't.

10. If this is question 10, then we're through with this exercise. We're not through with this exercise, so this isn't question 10.

Evaluation and Values

1 **7**

Evaluating Arguments: Normative and Nonnormative

Come now, and let us reason together.

ISAIAH 1:18

Bob and Linda were having dinner with their best friends, Stan and Sue, when Sue began to complain about the way science was being taught in high schools across the nation.

"I know what you mean," Linda said. "Our kids just can't compete with graduates from other countries in science and math. They're really deficient I guess."

"That's not what I meant," Sue corrected. "My objection is to the fact that they teach only evolution. They entirely ignore creationism."

"Oh, no" thought Stan, "Here we go." So he said, "Hey, everybody! How 'bout a game of Trivial Pursuit?"

"Trivial Pursuit? That's old hat," Bob laughed. "Let's play Uno or Scruples."

"C'mon, guys," a serious Sue continued. "You shouldn't try to change the subject. This is an important subject, and so we ought to discuss it."

"I agree," Linda said. "With discussing it, I mean, but not with Sue's point."

"I haven't even finished my point."

"Well," Linda went on, "I just figured that you were going to take the stock creationist position and argue that it's not fair to teach only one side of the issue."

"Yeah? Well you're doubly wrong. In the first place, I have a right to express my opinion before you attack it. I think it's lousy of you to just assume what you think I'm going to say without listening to me. Second, I was going to argue—if you'd only wait and listen—that science is a religion, a secular religion, and that it should not be taught at all."

"Are you serious?" Stan nearly shouted. "That's the silliest thing you've said in days."

"Oh?" a hurt Sue nearly sobbed. "I thought you loved me! I thought you were my husband, but now I don't know."

"What do you mean now?" an annoyed Stan asked.

"I just mean that a husband should always support his wife in public, that's what I mean. A husband should never criticize his wife in front of their best friends."

"There, there," consoled Linda, putting her arms around Sue's shoulders and glaring at both Stan and Bob. "You know, Stan, Sue's right," Linda said, staring intently at Bob. "A good husband—Bob are you listening?—a good husband never criticizes his wife in front of other people."

"Yeah," an angry Bob growled. "Just like a nice wife never drops veiled criticisms of her husband in front of other people, huh, Linda?"

As you can imagine, the discussion didn't end here. It grew into a full-blown brouhaha about who decided what was right, what "a right" was anyway, what made a good wife or husband, what obligations friends had to jump into or stay out of disputes between husbands and wives, and more.

It seemed that everybody had a view. Sometimes they overlapped, sometimes they conflicted. But underlying all the views were assumptions of worth and value. Occasionally, values were overtly expressed, but more often they went unexpressed. Instead, they were implied. They were used as the foundations of arguments without being analyzed, discussed, or acknowledged *as values*. They were simply asserted as facts, buttressed with conviction and fury—but without much else.

Value statements are especially slippery. We've just run across a whole slew of them in the preceding discussion: "You *shouldn't* try to change the subject"; "This is an important subject, and so we *ought* to discuss it"; ". . . it's *not fair* to teach only one side of the issue"; "I have *a right* to express my opinion before you attack it. I think it's *lousy* of you to just assume what you think I'm going to say without listening to me"; ". . . a husband *should always* support his wife in public. . . . A husband *should never* criticize his wife in front of their best friends . . ."; ". . . A *good husband* . . . *never* criticizes his wife in front of other people . . ."; and ". . . A *nice wife never* drops veiled criticisms of her husband in front of other people. . . ."

Value statements are slippery because they report more than facts, more than mere information. They report often subtle and usually complex value judgments. It's one thing to verify a factual claim: Stan said to Sue, "That's the silliest thing you've said in days." It's quite another to verify a value judgment:

"Stan *should* not have said that." This chapter is about one of the most difficult yet interesting and important aspects of argument in real life: values in arguments.

In fact, many of the most important questions we face, as individuals and as a society, involve values and value judgments. Daily we must formulate and respond to discourse on issues that involve assessments of worth. Our job is to deal with them most intelligently.

Because such arguments constitute a large and vital part of our lives, and because they raise unique problems of analysis, we're devoting this chapter to them. The primary object of this chapter is to broaden the scope of our practical logic, to show how what we've thus far learned can and should be used in what is the most meaningful aspect of our lives: values and value judgments.

In a real sense, then, this chapter begins our commencement. It keynotes ways that we can use to bring our practical logic to bear on the bread-and-butter issues of life. Its intention, of course, is not to impart values or to present a theory of value. Instead the chapter aims to provide an outline of how we can start to deal intelligently with value arguments—an outline that's broad enough to entertain a panoply of values and value systems yet narrow enough for immediate use.

But before getting into this important and intriguing subject, let's draw together what we've covered so far by presenting a handy method of argument evaluation. What we present will provide a basis for evaluating any argument, including those expressing values.

EVALUATING ARGUMENTS: AN EIGHT-STEP PROCEDURE

In the preceding chapters we learned what correct inductive procedure is, what informal fallacies are and their great variety, and what valid deductive procedure is. We now have all we need to evaluate almost any argument we confront. (See the list headed Fallacies Covered in Text on pages 397–398.) Although we needn't be conscious of the process we use in such evaluation, it might prove helpful to ponder it in a step-by-step fashion. The following eight steps are offered as a framework for analyzing and evaluating arguments. Your instructor probably will wish to adapt these to his or her own coverage of the text.

1. Clarify meaning.
2. Identify conclusion and premises.
3. If appropriate, restructure into syllogistic form.
4. Fill in missing premises.
5. Determine the syllogism's validity.
6. Examine premises and support for truth and justification.
7. Check for informal fallacies.
8. Give an overall evaluation.

Let's elaborate a bit on each of these steps.

1. The first thing we must do is make sure that we clearly understand what is being claimed. We begin with a linguistic and contextual overview. At this stage, we apply what we've learned about context, intention, and language. We want to make sure that we understand what is intended, not just what is said. To do this fairly and thoroughly, we must consider the context in which

the argument occurs and carefully scrutinize it for unclear or misleading language. With experience, we need not consciously delineate each of these concerns; rather, we develop a sensitivity to the nuances of argument.

Before even attempting to clarify meaning, read a passage all the way through. This will give you a feel for the argument as a whole. If you happen to disagree with the position advanced, don't allow your disagreement to color your interpretation. If you don't understand some words, consult a dictionary. Beware of the blocks to critical thinking in the passage itself and in your own reaction. Recall and use what you've learned about stress and clear thinking, defense mechanisms, and methods of distortion. (See Chapter 2.) Be alert for: (1) obscure or ambiguous language, including jargon; (2) shifts in word meaning; (3) bias communicated by highly emotive words and loaded epithets; and (4) euphemism. If the passage includes a definition, note what kind it is— denotative, objective or subjective connotative, stipulative, persuasive. Be particularly alert to the use of persuasive definition—redefining a term while trying to preserve its old emotive impact. (See Chapter 3.)

2. Recall that signal words such as the following are helpful in identifying premises and conclusions. (Chapter 1):

> **Conclusion signals:** then, therefore, consequently, it follows that (and so forth)
> **Premise signals:** since, because, for, insofar as (and so forth)

When an argument contains no such words, ask yourself, What is being advanced? What is the arguer trying to demonstrate as true? The answer to these questions most probably is the argument's conclusion. Similarly, to locate premises in the absence of signals, ask yourself, Why is this conclusion claim so? What bases does the arguer give for drawing the conclusion?

3. If necessary, reconstruct the argument into some syllogistic form— standard-form categorical, disjunctive, conditional. (See Chapters 15 and 16.) This includes minor or "mini" arguments, consisting of premises and their support, as opposed to the main argument, which consists of main premises and a main conclusion.

4. Fill in missing premises whenever an argument is incomplete and its missing premise is not exactly obvious. An argument is incomplete when the stated premises are insufficient to logically entail the conclusion. In other words, the conclusion in a fragment argument (enthymeme or sorites) is asserting more than the expressed premises logically warrant. (See Chapter 15.)

5. Determine the syllogism's validity by using Venn diagrams or rules for correct deductive inference, as they apply to standard-form categorical syllogisms, disjunctive syllogisms, and conditional syllogisms. (See Chapters 14 and 16.)

6. In testing the argument's premises and support for truth and justification, recall that a statement is true if it describes an actual state of affairs. Justification refers to the reasonableness of the evidence to support an assertion. Whether or not an argument contains enough of the right kind of evidence is crucial in determining its soundness. In assessing an argument's evidence, distinguish between objective and subjective assertions. And keep in mind that the justification of objective statements hinges on the observations that underlie them. The legitimacy of the observations, in turn, depends upon: (1) the physical

conditions under which they were made, (2) the sensory acuity of the observer, (3) the background knowledge of the observer, (4) the objectivity of the observer, and (5) the corroborative testimony of others. (See Chapter 6.)

7. In checking the argument for informal fallacies, be familiar with the many emotional and psychological appeals that we've studied. While these devices are psychologically persuasive, they are irrelevant, presumptuous, or confusing, and therefore, illogical. (See the accompanying list headed "Fallacies Covered in Text," with chapter references.)

FALLACIES COVERED IN TEXT

The numbers in parentheses indicate the chapters in which the fallacies are discussed.

Informal Fallacies

Ambiguity
  eupehmism (3)
  slang (3)
  jargon (3)
  buzzwords (3)
  puffery (3)
  vague language (4)
  equivocation (4)
  amphiboly (4)
  accent (4)
  composition (4)
  division (4)
  meaningless claim (4)
  cliché thinking (4)
  hairsplitting (4)
Emotion
  ad hominem (5)
  poisoning the well (5)
  mob appeal (5)
  sex (5)
  pity (5)
  fear or force (5)
Diversion
  straw man (5)
  red herring (5)
  two wrongs (5)
  humor and ridicule (5)
Assumption
  circular reasoning (5)
  loaded epithets (5)
  complex question (5)
  dismissal (5)
  invincible ignorance (5)

Authority
  argument from ignorance (6)
  unknowable fact (6)
  provincialism (6)
  false authority (7)
  positioning (7)
  traditional wisdom (7)
  popularity (7)

Fallacies Connected with Induction

  hasty conclusion (9)
  accident (9)
  guilt by association (9)
  false analogy (9)
  questionable causation (11)
  post hoc (11)
  slippery slope (11)
  magical thinking (11)
  oversimplification (11)
  biased sample (12)
  statistical equivocation (12)
  biased question (12)
  biased order (12)
  false dilemma (12)
  concealed evidence (13)

Formal Fallacies (Deductive Fallacies)

  four terms (8)
  undistributed middle term (8)
  illicit major term (8)
  illicit minor term (8)
  exclusive premises (8)

Formal Fallacies (Cont)
    drawing an affirmative
    conclusion from a negative premise (8)
    existential fallacy (8)
    faulty disjunctive (16)
    denying the antecedent (16)
    affirming the consequent (16)

8. Give an overall evaluation. Having completed the preceding steps, you are now in a position to give the argument an overall assessment. Does it have force? If so, how much? Are you ready to go with the argument on balance, or against it? Has the arguer won you over? To answer questions like these, return to your criticisms, especially to Steps 5, 6 and 7. Are the argument's essential premises so flawed that they provide little or no support for the conclusion? Or are the flaws contained in premises not essential to the claim? Rendering an overall evaluation is an important part of the evaluative process, for—if nothing else—it keeps critical thinking from becoming a bloodless, abstract exercise. It allows you to decide whether or not to believe, to endorse, and possibly to act on a claim. It also gives you an opportunity, which you should take, to show how the argument could be improved. Finally, it allows you to clarify your own beliefs as you respond to the argument in a creative and constructive way.

Of course, not every argument requires a complete application of these steps. Very brief arguments with glaring falsehoods, highly questionable assertions, or obvious fallacies can and should be disposed of quickly by indentifying the problem and, on that basis, judging the argument unsound. Other more complex or less clearly inadequate arguments require more detailed evaluation. The eight-step procedure constitutes a conceptual framework which is intended to ease, not tax, the task of analysis and evaluation. It is best to use these steps prudently, in light of your own rational skills and your instructor's counsel.

Now, let's look at some specimen arguments.

Argument 1: "I reject Ms. Wilcox's arguments in favor of the Equal Rights Amendment because she's a member of the women's liberation movement and therefore, cannot be objective in what she says."

Analysis:
Step 7: The argument relies on an ad hominem appeal and is, therefore, unsound.

Argument 2: "The Association of Law Enforcement Officers has just completed a study that indicates that capital punishment is, indeed, a deterrent to crime. The findings of such a prestigious body compel any thinking person to accept the thesis that capital punishment truly is a crime deterrent."

Analysis:
Step 7: The argument relies on a false appeal to authority because the experts are not in agreement on the claim. Also, the research methods must be examined before the findings can be accepted. The argument is, therefore, unsound.

Argument 3: "Since no one has disproved Von Daniken's theory that the earth was visited by astronaut-gods, there is considerable reason to believe it."

Analysis:
Step 7: The argument relies on an argument form ignorance and is, therefore, unsound.

Argument 4: "Smith must be an AMA member because she's a physician."

Analysis:
Step 4: Reconstructed the argument reads

(All physicians must be AMA members.)
Smith is a physician.
———————————————————————
Smith must be an AMA member.

The major premise is a faulty generalization: Physicians need not be AMA members; many aren't. Therefore, the argument's unsound.

Argument 5: "Only citizens are voters. So Jones is definitely a voter."

Analysis:
Step 4: Reconstructed the argument reads

All voters are citizens.
(Jones is a citizen.)
———————————————————————
Jones is a voter.

There are no informal fallacies in the reconstruction.
Step 5: The form of the argument in *AAA*-2. It commits the fallacy of the undistributed middle term. The argument, therefore, is unsound.

Argument 6: "Man tends to increase at a greater rate than his means of subsistence. Consequently he is occasionally subject to a severe struggle for existence."

Analysis:
Step 4: Reconstructed, the argument reads

(Whatever tends to increase at a greater rate than its means of subsistence is occasionally subject to a severe struggle for existence.)
Man tends to increase at a greater rate than his means of subsistence.
———————————————————————
Consequently man is occasionally subject to a severe struggle for existence.

The reconstruction contains no informal fallacies.
Step 5: The syllogism is valid.
Step 6: The premises are justified.
Step 7: No informal fallacies.
Step 8: Sound.

Argument 7: "That the sun will rise tomorrow is a hypothesis; and that means that we do not know whether it will rise."

Analysis:
Step 1: Know will be taken to mean "to know with certainty."

Steps 3 and 4: The argument is a sorites consisting of the following reconstructed arguments:

(No hypothesis is certain knowledge.)
That the sun will rise tomorrow is a hypothesis.
_____
(That the sun will rise tomorrow is not certain knowledge.)

(If that the sun will rise tomorrow is not certain knowledge, then we
    don't know whether it will rise.)
(That the sun will rise tomorrow is not certain knowledge.)
_____
Then we don't know whether it will rise.

There are no informal fallacies in these reconstructions.
Step 5: The form of the first argument is *EAE*-1, valid. The second argument, a hypothetical syllogism, affirms the antecedent (*modus ponens*) and is, therefore, valid.

Step 6: The premises are true.
Step 7: No informal fallacies.
Step 8: Sound.

The preceding arguments have one thing in common: They contain statements that are *value neutral*. This means that their premises neither express nor are intended to express a value judgment. Contrast this argument:

> Hiring people by quota is unfair because it introduces non-job-related criteria into the decision process.

Now the assumption behind this argument is "Whatever introduces non-job-related criteria into the hiring process is unfair." This is obviously a value judgment. How do we evaluate it? How do we determine whether it's true, whether it contains informal fallacies?

Again, consider this argument: "As the major economic instrument of production in our society, business is justified in intruding into ecosystems." The assumption here is "The major economic instrument of production in our society is justified in intruding into ecosystems." Again, the statement expresses a value judgment. How can we assess the truth of this value claim? The question is obviously important because determining the soundness of the argument depends on it, not to mention the integrity of the environment.

So as we mentioned at the outset, many arguments express value claims. Before examining these kind of arguments, let's consider a complex argument which, while containing value claims, can nevertheless be evaluated in terms of these eight steps.

> **Argument 8:** "In the fury that surrounds the debate about school prayer, it is sometimes forgotten that prayer is an essential part of religion. To permit school prayer is virtually the same as endorsing religion. What can be said, then, for religion? Not much, I'm afraid. Indeed, religion is dangerous. It has spawned numerous wars throughout history. Today it continues to sow the seeds of discontent and destruction in Northern Ireland and the Middle East. It divides people by emphasizing their differences rather than their similarities. It breeds intolerance of people of opposed views. Is there any doubt, therefore, that the responsible citizen should oppose school prayer?"

Step 1: Clarify meaning.

"Prayer" and "religion" and ambiguous. We will take "prayer" to mean a spiritual communion with God or an object of worship and "religion" to mean an organized system of belief in and worship of that God or object of worship. "Virtually" is a weasel. Every assertion made about religion in this argument is an unqualified generalization. "Spawns," "breeds," and "sows the seeds" are emotive. The last sentence is a persuasive definition.

Step 2: Identify conclusion and main premises.
Conclusion: The responsible citizen should oppose school prayer.
Premise: To permit school prayer is virtually the same as endorsing religion.
Premise: Religion is dangerous.

Step 3: If appropriate, restructure into syllogistic form.
The main argument consists of the aforementioned two premises and conclusion, which can be expressed as a fragment standard-form categorical syllogism (actually a sorites):

To permit school prayer is virtually the same as endorsing religion.
Religion is dangerous.
___
The responsible citizen should oppose school prayer.

Both main premises are themselves supported, thereby forming two mini arguments within the main argument. Mini argument 1, again, can be expressed as a fragment standard-form categorical syllogism:

Prayer is an essential part of religion.
___
To permit school prayer is virtually the same as endorsing religion.

Mini argument 2 can be viewed as consisting of an inductive generalization. Thus,

It (religion) has spawned numerous wars throughout history.
Today it continues to sow the seed of discontent and destruction in Northern Ireland and the Middle East.
It divides people by emphasizing their differences rather than their similarities.
It breeds intolerance of people with opposed views.
___
Religion is dangerous.

Of course, it's possible to consider each piece of support separately as constituting, together with "Religion is dangerous," a standard-form categorical syllogism, actually an enthymeme. But this seems to undercut the spirit of the argument, which is to have the four pieces of evidence taken as a set or cluster of support data for the generalization that "Religion is dangerous."

Step 4: Fill in missing premises.
Mini conclusion "To permit school prayer is virtually the same as endorsing religion" follows from "Prayer is an essential part of religion," plus the unexpressed assertion "To permit an essential part of religion to be practiced in school is virtually the same as endorsing religion." The reconstructed mini argument 1, therefore, reads:

Prayer is an essential part of religion.
(To permit an essential part of religion to be practiced in school is virtually the same as endorsing religion.)
___
To permit school prayer is virtually the same as endorsing religion.

The main argument, which consists of the two main premises and conclusion, is a sorites that can be reconstructed as follows:

To permit school prayer is virtually the same as endorsing religion.
Religion is dangerous.

(To permit school prayer is dangerous.)

(To permit school prayer is dangerous.)
(The responsible citizen should oppose anything dangerous.)

The responsible citizen should oppose school prayer.

Step 5: Determine the syllogism's validity.
All syllogisms are valid.

Step 6: Examine the premises and support for truth and justification.
It's difficult to evaluate "Prayer is an essential part of religion" because "prayer" and "religion" are ambiguous. But if these terms are stipulated, as in Step 1, then the assertion can be considered true on definitional grounds. However, the unexpressed premise of this mini argument, "To permit as essential part of religion to be practiced in school is virtually the same as endorsing religion," is ambiguous and misleading. "Endorsing" literally means "supporting." If the state allows school prayer and if prayer is an essential part of religion, then it could be argued that the state "supports" religion in the sense that it provides a constitutional basis for the practice of religion in the classroom. We will say considerably more about this unexpressed assertion in the next step when we consider informal fallacies.

Mini argument 2 contains a value judgment, "Religion is *dangerous*," that needs much support, which presumably is provided by the four pieces of data expressed. An evaluation of this support is, again, best left to the next step. The same applies to the unexpressed assertions in the main arguments "To permit school prayer is dangerous" and "The responsible citizen should oppose anything dangerous." In short, the only acceptable assertion at this point is "Prayer is an essential part of religion."

Step 7: Check for informal fallacies.
Returning to mini argument 1, we find "endorsing" loaded with subjective connotations. An example will illustrate. The state permits the publication and sale of pornographic materials. Can it be said, then, that the state "endorses" pornographic enterprises? Yes, but only if "endorses" is taken to mean "support," and "support" in turn is taken to mean providing a judicial basis for the manufacture and sale of pornographic materials. But "endorsing" carries the subjective connotations of "approval" or "actively advancing the interests of." But the state does not endorse pornographic enterprises in either of these senses. In fact, if you read the Supreme Court rulings on pornography, you'll find that the justices who comment without exception express revulsion toward pornography. The court's "permission," then, is based not on approval, and certainly not on active support of the interests of pornographers, but on an interpretation of the constitutional right to freedom of expression. Therefore we'd be inclined to think that, at the very least, to say that the state "endorses" pornography is misleading. Similarly, it seems just as misleading to argue that permitting school prayer is tantamount to endorsing religion in the sense of approving of or actively supporting the interests of religion. For this reason we're calling "endorsing" a loaded word.

But even if the arguer insists that "permit" implies "endorse" and "endorse," in turn, implies "approval of" or "actively advancing the interests of," then we must be clear about what it is that's being approved or advanced. It isn't religion but individual freedom, specifically the opportunity for the individual to say (or refrain from saying) a prayer in a public classroom, so long as that practice does not conflict with the constitutional doctrine of church/state separation. Stated another way, if school prayer does not violate church/state separation, then there is no constitutional basis for restricting individual freedom to worship. Consider the pornography example again. If the manufacture and sale of pornographic material is permitted, what is being approved of and actively advanced is the individual right to freedom of expression. To say that what is being underwritten is the pornography industry is a distortion, a straw man. It is as much a straw man, in our judgment, to say that permitting school prayer is tantamount to endorsing (that is, approving or actively advancing) religion. And the straw lies in the subjective connotations of "endorsing."

Our judgment that the arguer has introduced a straw man is supported by what follows in the argument, namely, an attack on religion. Having identified prayer with religion, the arguer then attempts to show why religion is dangerous. The diversionary tack here is to discredit school prayer by discrediting religion. Whether or not this strategy proves effective very much depends on the audience's preceptions of religion. But it's easier to "blow over" religion, and with it school prayer, than it is to repudiate school prayer on legitimate grounds, namely, by attempting to show how school prayer violates the doctrine of church/state separation. In other words, even if religion is dangerous, so what? How does this address the school prayer issue? The arguer undoubtedly will point to the first syllogism in the sorites that is intended to identify prayer with religion and school prayer with endorsing religion. At this point we would reintroduce our criticism of that mini argument on the grounds of ambiguity, loaded language, and straw man.

But if we wanted to be saintly charitable, we could concede the legitimacy of mini argument 1, and then closely inspect mini argument 2. The mini premises of that argument are generalizations that need qualification. They are also half-truths, for they omit to mention that religion also has contributed to understanding and human betterment, to the establishment and maintenance of social services (such as schools, orphanages, hospitals, and disaster relief agencies), and the formulation of humanity's highest ideals. Moreover, all are causal oversimplifications. Beyond this, in the context of the main argument, all these mini premises are diversionary appeals to fear and slippery slope, such that if school prayer is permitted, presumably those dreadful things associated with religion will inevitably follow.

As for the two unexpressed main premises that make up the sorites, "To permit school prayer is dangerous" is vague—Just what is meant by "dangerous"?—and "The responsible citizen should oppose school prayer" is a persuasive definition.

Step 8: Give an overall evaluation.
The argument is unsound: The premises and their support use various appeals of omission, diversion, and confusion, namely concealed evidence, straw man, fear, causal oversimplification, and loaded and vague language. When the premises and support are stripped of these ploys, they collapse, thus rendering the conclusion unwarranted. It seems that any compelling argument against school prayer must establish that permitting school prayer violates the doctrine of church/state separation and perhaps that this doctrine is worthwhile. The preceding argument doesn't do this, nor does it develop an alternatively compelling argument against school prayer.

*EXERCISE 17-1
Use the eight steps prudently to determine the soundness of the following arguments. Be alert for the sorites.

1. As there is no direct evidence against Frank, we can't prove him guilty. So we can be confident of his innocence.
2. Communists read the *Daily Worker*. The *Daily Worker* used to be Fred's favorite newspaper. You can draw your own conclusion.
3. There's no question that members of the Jonestown community weren't capable of thinking for themselves. Why I remember one incident when a Jonestown member was told to beat a three-year-old. And sure enough, that's exactly what he did.
4. Clearly the teller didn't push the alarm button. For if she had, the police would have arrived within five minutes, in plenty of time to have caught the robbers.
5. Sarah must be a Christian because none but Christians believe in the doctrine of the Trinity.
6. Respecting the Nazi leaders, it's obvious that justice has never been meted out because not quite all of them have been brought to trial for their crimes.
7. Students who study at all will study each of their courses equally or study some more than others—which means that students who study at all will either get low grades in all their courses or fail some of them. Not a pretty picture.
8. The professor said she didn't want anybody unprepared for class. But obviously she didn't mean me, because I'm not just anybody—I'm the student council president!
9. Not all moneymaking films are made by the Hollywood studios. After all, some pornographic movies are moneymakers.
10. The number of people in the United States turning to Eastern religions is increasing at an astonishing rate—which goes to prove that not everything that's exotic by our own standards is outside our grasp.

VALUES AND VALUE JUDGMENTS

People value all sorts of things: health, wealth, power, time, friendship, love, prestige, leisure time—the list is endless. Sometimes the values are quite specific: We value a particular object such as a family heirloom or a stray dog. Other times the value is more general: We value a successful business career. We can value something in and of itself, as perhaps we value pleasure or knowledge; or we may value something because it leads to other things, as perhaps we value money or power. However we choose to talk of value, one thing's for sure: A value, any value, is an assessment of worth. If we value something, we consider it to have worth. Specifically, we view it as good or bad, better or worse, ought to be or not ought to be.

Frequently we express values, that is, assessments of worth, in statements. For example, B.J. claims, "Huey Lewis and the News is a sensational rock group." Wilma insists, "*Moby Dick* is a masterpiece." Slim asserts, "The Strategic Defense Initiative should be passed." Sweeney says, "Cocaine should not be legalized." And Roscoe observes, "The state of the world is revolting." Each of these statements reports the worth that the speaker attaches to something. Such statements express our value judgments; they are ordinarily termed normative statements, as opposed to nonnormative statements.

Normative and Nonnormative Statements

Normative statements are assertions that express value judgments. Normative statements come in many varieties. In our study of logic we have encountered and formulated many normative statements. Technically speaking, every time we termed an argument "bad," we were expressing a value judgment. Indeed, our whole study of logic is based on a value judgment: that knowing and using the rules of correct argument, we stand a better chance of surviving and prospering than if we didn't know them.

But ordinarily we think of normative statements as expressing our values in ethics, aesthetics, and social and political philosophy. Thus, in ethics someone might claim, "I shouldn't lie," "Keep your word," or "Murder is immoral." In aesthetics, "Picasso is a great artist," "Beethoven's Fifth Symphony is his best," "Neil Simon's latest plays are flawed." In social/political philosophy, "Democracy is the best form of government," "Abortion-on-demand ought to be legalized," "The United States should evenly distribute its wealth among its citizenry."

In contrast to normative statements stand nonnormative ones, which are not intended to express value judgments. *Nonnormative statements are true or false assertions used to express matters of empirical or logical fact.* A statement expresses a matter of empirical fact when its truth can be determined by appeal to sense observations. "Water boils at 212 degrees Fahrenheit at sea level," "George Washington was the first U.S. President," and "Many citizens don't vote" are nonnormative statements of the empirical variety. A statement expresses a matter of logical fact when its truth can be determined solely by appeal to reason. Thus, "Squares have four sides," "The form AAA-1 is valid," and "X must be greater than Z, if X is greater than Y and Y is greater than Z" are nonnormative statements of the logical kind.

When an argument contains only nonnormative premises, it's a nonnormative argument. In applying our eight-step method for argument evaluation, we confined ourselves to this kind of argument. But numerous arguments, even the most important we formulate and encounter, are normative arguments; that is, they contain a normative statement as a premise.

EXERCISE 17-2 _____

1. Identify the following statements as normative or nonnormative.

   a. Stealing is wrong.
   b. Shakespeare is the most effective dramatist in the English language.
   c. Shakespeare wrote comedies, histories, and tragedies.
   d. Oxygen starvation can result in brain damage.
   e. Education is the surest ticket to occupational success.
   f. Sexism is a function of acculturation.
   g. Trading weapons to Iran in return for American hostages is based on a narrow and short-term view of national best interest.
   h. Sex without love is sin.
   i. Never give a sucker an even break.
   j. Honesty is the best policy.
   k. Polygamy is illegal in California.
   l. If two candidates are equally qualified for a job and one is a woman or member of a minority group, we should give the job to the woman or minority member.
   m. Photography isn't really an art.
   n. Our criminal justice system is a national disgrace.
   o. In part, philosophy studies issues that science cannot fully answer.
   p. Alcoholism results from a character flaw.
   q. Birth control pills, which can cause blood clots, shouldn't be taken over a long period of time without medical supervision.

r. Let the government stay out of business.

s. Although the law is a guide to proper behavior, sometimes what's legal is not what is moral, and what's illegal is not what is immoral.

t. The cooler the light, the less energy it wastes.

2. Write two statements about each of the following, one normative and one nonnormative.

    a. political parties
    b. sex education
    c. legalization of marijuana
    d. advertising
    e. American military preparedness
    f. genetic engineering
    g. pornography
    g. active voluntary euthanasia
    i. premarital cohabitation
    j. lesbian/gay liberation
    k. children with AIDS attending school
    l. parental influence on textbook selection in grade school
    m. the government's right to "lie" in the interest of national security
    n. warning labels on rock albums

NORMATIVE ARGUMENTS

A normative argument is one that contains at least one normative statement as a premise. Here's an example:

> Selling illicit drugs to children is reprehensible.
> Smith sells illicit drugs to children.
> _____
> Smith does something reprehensible.

This is a normative argument because one of its premises, "Selling illicit drugs to children is reprehensible," is a normative statement. Here's another example:

> If ours is a just society, then women have equal opportunities.
> Women don't have equal opportunities.
> _____
> Ours is not a just society.

Again, a premise contains a normative statement: "If ours is a just society, then women have equal opportunities." A final example:

> Any movie with Dan Ackroyd is worth seeing.
> *Ghostbusters* stars Dan Ackroyd.
> _____
> *Ghostbusters* is worth seeing.

Here the major premise, "Any movie with Dan Ackroyd is worth seeing," is a normative statement. The argument, therefore, is a normative one.

Now let's take the same issues these arguments deal with and see how they might appear in *nonnormative* arguments. Notice that none of the following arguments contains a normative statement as a premise:

> Selling illicit drugs to children is a felony.
> Smith sells illicit drugs to children.
> _____
> Smith commits a felony.

> If women can't vote, then our society doesn't give them a voice in the
>   electoral process.
> Our society does give women a voice in the electoral process.
>
> Women can vote.

> Any movie with Dan Ackroyd is usually popular.
> *Ghostbusters* is a Dan Ackroyd movie.
>
> *Ghostbusters* will probably be popular.

The eight-step method for argument evaluation applies equally to normative and nonargumentative arguments. But to make effective use of this method with normative arguments, you must be aware of peculiar problems that pertain to them and know how to deal with these problems.

*EXERCISE 17-3 _____

Identify the following as normative or nonnormative arguments. Reconstruct assumptions.

1. Reverse discrimination should be allowed because it can promote social justice.
2. Reverse discrimination sometimes occurs in the workplace. So it's clear that in some instances people are judged on criteria that are not directly job-related.
3. Mercy killing seems advisable in cases of terminal diseases, to save the patient and loved ones from heroic suffering.
4. "When in Rome, do as the Romans do" is a time-honored tradition. So we shouldn't restrict our multinational firms from bribing foreign officials when that's the accepted practice in the country.
5. American businesses often behave overseas differently from how they behave at home, as indicated by the admissions of Gulf and Lockheed to paying millions of dollars in bribes and "grease payments" abroad.
6. Given the fact that between 10 and 20 percent of American adults are homosexual, it's safe to say that America is a very sick society.
7. Inasmuch as art is a form of human expression, all art is in one way or other a statement.
8. As a taxpayer, I have a right to decide what my child reads in school, and if it goes against my personal beliefs, I have an obligation to protect my child from reading it.
9. We should always keep our promises. That's why I'm so upset to learn that the United States secretly sold arms to Iran.
10. The primary obligation of the United States is the protection of its citizens. That's why I'm so glad to learn that President Reagan sold weapons to Iran in the hopes of freeing American hostages there.

The Problem of Truth

To begin with, reconsider the normative argument

> Selling illicit drugs to children is reprehensible.
> Smith sells illicit drugs to children.
>
> Smith does something reprehensible.

Now we know that this syllogism, like any other, is sound if, and only if, both premises are true and the argument is valid. Since the argument's form is *AAA-1*, it's valid. As for the truth of its premises, we can easily ascertain the truth of the minor premise, "Smith sells illicit drugs to children," by determining whether this statement describes a state of affairs. But what about the major premise? What must be the case for the statement "Selling illicit drugs to children is reprehensible" to be true? Just what state of affairs do we measure this statement against, indeed any normative statement, to determine its truth?

Such a question clearly stimulates philosophical concerns about the nature of truth and normative statements. But it also provokes questions about argument evaluation that are downright practical. Just how do we evaluate the truth of value judgments? Indeed, can we logically speak of truth at all in connection with such statements? Some people believe that normative statements are essentially meaningless. Others hold that they make sense but that they can't be justified. Still others believe that normative statements make sense and can be justified but that their justification does not extend beyond the society in which one lives. Since so many important arguments we face and devise are normative ones, we must know how to deal with such arguments. Otherwise, we'll remain unequipped to deal rationally with a significant, perhaps the most significant, aspect of human existence.

If you're still unconvinced of the importance of this issue, reflect on your bedrock assumptions about morality, religion, art, politics, government, sex, education, child rearing, law—on any human concern. You'll see that they all reflect value judgments. Nothing goes untouched by values and value judgments. And they inevitably inform the arguments that we and others compose and accept to direct our lives, to fashion our dealings with other people, to chart our national and international course, and so on. Thus, if we can't make logic "work" in these areas, we'll remain mentally impoverished to deal with life's momentous concerns. And on the personal and collective levels, there's ample and frightening evidence that many individuals and institutions are currently in that state of logical bankruptcy.

So assessing the truth of normative statements is of pressing practical concern. We must find out how to handle them. In fact, there are several things we can do to meet this challenge. But first let's briefly confess and explain our own assumptions here.

A main thesis of this chapter is that value judgments can be evaluated. Now that doesn't sound like much of a claim. But without getting into all the philosophical subtleties that enshroud it, rest assured that the claim is far from being "obvious" in a philosophical sense. Just to give you the thrust of contentious views, be aware that some insist that only things that can be "counted" or "measured" can be evaluated. Since normative statements make assertions that cannot be so quantified, such statements cannot be evaluated. In short, generally speaking, only nonnormative statements can be evaluated.

Now, it's undoubtedly true that value judgments can't be weighed and measured with scientific precision. But it doesn't necessarily follow that they therefore cannot be evaluated at all. The fact is, as we've just seen, people can, do, and must evaluate normative statements constantly. Simply because we can't count on laboratory precision in our evaluations doesn't in the least make our task less trivial, surely not meaningless. Indeed, it could be argued that the inevitable inexactness of our evaluations makes it even more urgent that we carefully consider just how we go about the evaluations.

Probably the key thing for our purpose is to recognize and acknowledge that values and value judgments crowd in on us. Like it or not we must accept some, reject others, probably keep an open mind about most. And this presupposes evaluation. We must weigh the reasons that count for a normative claim and the ones that count against it. When there are more of the right kinds of reasons for it, we consider it warranted, that is, justified. When there are more of the right kinds of reasons against it, we consider it unwarranted, that is, unjustified. And we make up our minds accordingly.

It's in this sense of warranty, then—of more counting for a normative claim than against it—that we seemingly can connect truth with normative statements. At least for our purposes this seems a most efficacious way of speaking about evaluating normative statements. In brief, when we speak of evaluating normative statements, we have in mind a rational process that aims to determine whether there are more reasons for accepting a value judgment than for rejecting it. Now let's consider just how we can evaluate normative statements.

Assessing Normative Statements

Language Clarification.   The most important thing to do in assessing the truth of normative statements is to *clarify their language*. Value words such as *good, ought, wrong, superb, should not,* and *inferior* are vague; they invite numerous interpretations. So if we're to avoid fallacies of ambiguity, and if we're going to determine whether a normative statement is warranted, we must know how the argument intends its value words. Take these normative statements from ethics: "Abortion is wrong," "Mercy killing should be legalized," "Forced sterilization is evil." *Wrong, should be, evil*—each of these must be clarified before we can begin to evaluate the statements that contain them.

Value words can carry several meanings, only some of which we'll cover here. Generally speaking, the ordinary value arguments we encounter carry a meaning that can be translated into nonnormative form and then evaluated. Specifically, when appearing in ordinary normative arguments, value words usually carry the meaning of (1) personal preference; (2) social preference; or (3) conformity with a principle, standard, or law.

1. *Personal preference.* It's possible that value words are intended as expressions of personal approval or disapproval. Take, for example, the normative statement "Abortion is wrong." It's possible that those claiming this are expressing only personal disapproval of abortion. Thus, "Abortion is wrong" is equivalent to "I disapprove of abortion." Likewise, "The *Mona Lisa* is a great painting" translates to "I like or I think highly of the *Mona Lisa*." And "Everyone should get a college education" would mean "I'm in favor of everyone's getting a college education." In each instance the value word is intended as an expression of personal preference. This allows a translation into a nonnormative form that no longer reports a value but merely a feeling. Such a translation is perfectly legitimate if that's the meaning the arguer intends, for then the person is not commenting about the nature or quality of the act or thing itself.

As for the truth of such statements, having translated them, we need only ensure that they accurately report the person's feelings. If we realize that value words carry only this autobiographical meaning for some people, we can save ourselves much time and exasperation in fruitless debates over normative issues. Even more important, we can direct the discussion to a far more constructive plane.

To illustrate, suppose someone argues, "Abortion on demand should be legalized." You find out that by "should be" the person intends personal approval. So the argument reads, "I approve of abortion on demand being legalized." Now you're in a position to ask the person why he or she approves of it. It may be that the person knew of someone who was legally obliged to carry a fetus to term, which ultimately produced great hardship and suffering for everyone. The arguer's approval may rest largely on that one episode. If so, you're then in a position to spot the faulty generalization. Better still, the arguer may see the flimsiness of his or her own argument.

The point is that once you've established an autobiographical interpretation of the value words, you're in a position to pin the person down on what generated the preference. This is crucial, for as we stated earlier, we're ultimately interested in how much counts for the claim, how much against it. Thus, the only way we can evaluate the normative statement is to find out what supports it. And having established a personal-preference interpretation of value words, we can then find out what, if anything, supports it.

One other point, this one on a philosophical level: This personal-preference view raises a number of philosophical questions, which we're justified in asking. First, since normative statements presumably express only personal preference, does that mean that no acts are right or wrong in themselves, that no things are good or bad in themselves? Second, does this view imply that something can be "right" for you and "wrong" for me under identical circumstances? Is this sensible? Third, doesn't this view imply that debating the merit of normative arguments is foolish because such arguments are merely expressions of personal opinion?

Such questions may seem irrelevant. But that's not so. After all, anyone who assumes that a value word is only the equivalent of an expression of personal preference takes a lot for granted. Surely the "taken for granted" should be introduced in evaluating whether more counts for the normative claim than against it.

2. *Social preference.* Frequently people don't mean that only they approve or disapprove of something when they use a value word but that society does. In other words, value words can carry the meaning of social preference. Thus, "Abortion is wrong" may be interpreted as meaning "Society disapproves of abortion."

If a normative statement carries this meaning of social preference, our job of verifying it simplifies. All we need do is verify that a majority approves or disapproves of the view. Determine the majority view and we determine the truth of the statement.

But again, as is true in personal preference, having established a sociological bias, we can now ask trenchant questions about its assumptions. Thus, is nothing right or wrong, good or bad in itself? Can't the individual be right and the majority wrong? After all, the German theologian Dietrich Bonhoffer, having spoken out against Hitler, was imprisoned and later hanged. Was he wrong and the majority right? The nineteenth-century American writer and naturalist Henry David Thoreau refused to pay taxes to a government that, supported by the majority, sanctioned slavery. One day his friend and fellow artist, Ralph Waldo Emerson, came to visit him in jail. "What are you doing in there?" Emerson asked. "What are you doing out there?" Thoreau answered. Was Thoreau wrong? Was Emerson? Was Christ wrong? And just what "majority" do we have in mind anyway—the community, state, nation, world? Maybe the majority is within one's own ethnic group, sex, profession, or economic stratum.

These questions are not trivial. In equating value words with social preference, we invite profound questions about the highly controversial assumptions underlying that equation. At the very least, such a translation seems to beg for charges of appeals to popularity and provincialism. So anyone confronting this kind of rationale has a perfect right to raise the foregoing questions. What's more, such persons shouldn't be discouraged and intimidated by charges of "nit-picking" and "hair-splitting." They are doing no such thing, and those who insist they are are themselves relying on an ad hominem to discredit the questioner.

3. *Conformity with principle, standard, or law.* In addition to translating value words into expressions of personal or social preference, we sometimes identify them with conformity to principle, standard, or law. For example, suppose someone says, "Sexism is wrong." They don't mean "wrong" in the sense of personal or social disapproval but in the sense of nonconformity with the principle of justice as fair play and giving to others what they deserve. Similarly, by "Abortion is wrong" one might mean that abortion doesn't square with the law of God. Likewise, in painting, someone might consider Rembrandt's *Night Watch* a "great" painting because it conforms with artistic standards of light, color, proportion, and harmony. Respecting the evaluation of such normative statements, all we need do is determine whether the statement actually does conform with the principle, law, or standard. If it does, we can accept the statement as true; if it doesn't, we can reject it as false.

But again, and most important, having ascertained this interpretation of the value words, we're then in a position to raise important philosophical questions about its underlying assumptions. For example, what makes the particular standard or principle itself doubtless? Take justice, for instance. In the preceding example, someone took justice to be a principle of fair play or just desert. But why not consider justice as a principle of efficiency? Lots of people do. They consider what's fair as what produces the most happiness for the greatest number of people, even if certain individuals suffer. Similarly, if "right" means that something squares with the law of God, what if one doesn't believe in God, or at least not with the God whose law is intended? Can such people be moral? In a similar vein, standards of beauty, success, morality and other things frequently vary from person to person. Often these differing standards conflict. What makes one standard more credible than another?

Again, these questions are anything but irrelevant. They cut to the foundational assumptions of a normative argument. So we should ask them; for if there's a serious doubt about the legitimacy of the principle, law, or standard, conformity to it might be inconsequential, nothing more than an appeal to traditional wisdom or provincialism.

As we indicated earlier, these are only a few of the interpretations people place on value words. Reading in specialty fields such as ethics and aesthetics will reveal more. The key thing to remember is that the meanings affect our assessment of the truth of normative statements and, ultimately, of the soundness of normative arguments. Faced with any normative argument, then, you should first find out just what interpretation of the value word is intended. Having done this, you should do other things to minimize the difficulty of evaluating the argument itself. Let's see what these are.

*EXERCISE 17-4 _____

Pick out the value words in each of the following statements and indicate what possible interpretations can be put on those words. In the light of each meaning, show how the truth of the statements would be assessed.

1. Needlessly inflicting pain is wrong.
2. Infanticide is evil.
3. A doctor ought never operate on people without their informed consent.
4. Poetry is the highest artistic form.
5. Hypocrisy is immoral.
6. The best form of government is the one that allows the most personal freedom.
7. Einstein's theory of relativity is the greatest scientific development of the twentieth century.
8. A government should not underwrite research dealing with in vitro fertilization.
9. No war is ever morally justifiable.
10. You should never disobey your parents or persons in authority over you.
11. The Iranian seizure of American hostages was an act of political desperation.
12. Communism is godless.
13. The women's liberation movement threatens the survival of the family as we've traditionally known it.
14. The ends justify the means.
15. That was a lousy movie.

Evaluation. Just as people can give a variety of interpretations for value words, they can give many reasons for their normative claims. We have just seen that the key thing in ensuring the warrantability or truth of normative statements is to clarify the meaning of the value terms. Once we do this, we can ask for reasons to support that meaning. In doing so we are, in effect, acknowledging what we've already learned: that the strength of any argument, normative or nonnormative, depends on the strength of the premises offered in support of the conclusion. *Because normative statements, as we've seen, can't be weighed and measured with the precision that nonnormative statements frequently can, the need for justification in normative arguments looms large.* Until we hear enough of the right kind of reasons for the normative premises, we're simply not in any position to intelligently stake out our own reaction to the argument.

For example, consider this case involving a friend of Slim's, Anna. Anna worked in a day-care center for over a year before she decided to take another job to supplement her income. Because it offered good money, and she was reasonably good at it, Anna decided to work nights as an exotic dancer at a local club. For several months, things went well. Then the manager of the day-care center found out. In the manager's view, working as an exotic dancer was an unsavory occupation. And since that job could reflect unfavorably on the day-care center, the manager gave Anna an ultimatum: Choose one job or the other.

Now the manager's claim that working as an exotic dancer is an unsavory occupation is a normative statement. Before we can rationally respond to it, and to the argument it's in, we need reasons. Maybe there are compelling reasons for the judgment. But maybe there aren't; maybe the manager's imposing an idiosyncratic evaluation on something she really knows very little about. Whatever the case, the wisdom or folly of the judgment depends on justification.

Another word for justification, as we know, is reasons. But just what kinds of reasons are we looking for in support of normative statements? In general, we're seeking reasons that would persuade objective, informed, rational people that the normative claim is beyond any reasonable doubt. Specifically, it seems reasonable to expect normative arguments in whatever field to satisfy at least these two criteria: (1) that what's offered in support of the normative premise is, in fact, a justification of it and not merely a pseudojustification; (2) that the purported justification meets the minimum adequacy requirements in the appropriate field.[1]

1. *Pseudojustification.*[2] We already know enough about correct and incorrect arguments to know that people frequently confuse all sorts of things with reasons. People appeal to emotions, to irrelevancies, to presumptions, thinking they're giving reasons in the sense of justification for their claims. We've spent considerable time cataloging these informal fallacies. Indeed, a big step in our eight-step method is a consideration of informal fallacies. Recognition of these informal fallacies is no less important in evaluating normative arguments. In fact, it's probably more important; for the temptations to "fudge" on rational justification for normative arguments is greater than with the nonnormative because the former can't be carted into a lab and demonstrated as true to all but the soft-headed.

For some reason, far too complex to go into here, there's evidently a decided inclination to cast reason to the winds in dealing with normative claims, to substitute phony or pseudojustification for the real thing. For example, not too long ago at work, Sweeney heard a fellow worker confess that recently he had banged into a parked car in a parking lot and then left without leaving a note for the driver. What's more, the fellow insisted that what he did was right.

"Right!" Sweeney exclaimed. "How can you say something like that is right?"

"I was scared," the man said. "I wasn't carrying any insurance and I couldn't cover the costs—not with the wife sick and two kids in college."

And on he went, enriching his appeal to pity to the point where Sweeney was sorry he'd asked the fellow to justify his action. In fact, the person had substituted motivation for justification; he explained what had motivated him to do the act, but he did not offer justification for it. There's a big difference. Giving motivation, when justification is sought, results in pseudojustification.

Just as justification is confused with giving motivation, it can also be confused with rationalization. Recall that *rationalization refers to giving reasons for a choice after the fact, after we've already decided what to do*. To rationalize is to choose first and look for reasons later. When we rationalize, we endorse or reject reasons because they support or weaken a predetermined choice.

A local politician in Sweeney's town recently endorsed an "antismut" bill because, he said, "We must protect the young and vulnerable against the onslaught of pornography." He added that that was why he intended to vote for the bill. If the truth were known, the reason he endorsed the antismut bill is that he believes his endorsement will look good to his constituents. The public reason is sheer rationalization, nothing more than pseudojustification. Beware of rationalization in normative arguments and of the informal fallacies that often accompany it, such as questionable cause and concealed evidence.

[1]See Peter A. Facione, Donald Scherer, and Thomas Attig, *Values and Society: An Introduction to Ethics and Social Philosophy* (Englewood Cliffs, N.J.: Prentice-Hall, 1978), pp. 26–31.
[2]See also Chapter 3.

So *providing one's motivation or rationalizations is not providing justification.* Neither is providing excuses. Excuses, although relevant in assigning blame or praise, are irrelevant for justification. Generally speaking, we don't hold people accountable for their actions when circumstances were beyond their control or when they had no other alternative than what they did or when their freedom to choose was so constrained that they couldn't be said to have chosen freely. But a good excuse provides a reason we shouldn't be blamed, punished, or held accountable. It *does not alter* what we did.

To illustrate, a firm doesn't meet the Environmental Protection Agency's air pollution standards within the time prescribed. Now there's no altering the fact that the firm didn't comply with the standard. But there may be reasons to exonerate the company from blame: Maybe the costs for the antipollution devices were more than the business could bear; maybe the time allotted was simply insufficient to complete the job; maybe any number of things. But none of these reasons, taken alone or together, can be considered justification; they're excuses, and excuses are not justification. Indeed, when the EPA or government chooses not to prosecute or fine the firm, but to extend the deadline, it in no way condones what the firm did. It simply recognizes that there are compelling reasons to *excuse* the firm from blame.

When a responsible defense attorney argues that a client committed a technically illegal act under extreme stress or duress, he is not condoning the *action* but rather attempting to mitigate his client's *responsibility*. In one famous case some years ago, a woman was *not* sent to prison for burning to death her violently abusive husband, though she was placed on probation after being convicted of involuntary manslaughter. At the time, some people were outraged because they saw anything short of a severe prison sentence as condoning homicide as a way of dealing with spousal abuse. Sometimes the lines between explaining a motive and excusing a specific individual's specific action, or condoning it, blur together. It helps if we distinguish justification from excusing in terms of individual responsibility.

In short, an excuse is not a justification for conduct but from accountability for the conduct. Similarly, to excuse someone is not to justify the person's behavior but to free the person from responsibilities. In introducing excuses where justification is called for, we introduce irrelevant reasons into our argument.

So the tendencies to confuse motivation, rationalization, and excuse with justification result in a variety of informal fallacies in normative arguments, especially ones in ethics. Be alert to these tendencies. Focusing on them will take you a long way toward clarifying normative claims and evaluating normative arguments.

EXERCISE 17-5 _____

Following are ten situations. For each situation, give two examples of (1) giving motivation, (2) rationalizing, and (3) offering an excuse.

1. Every Monday morning Myra's late for work.
2. A teacher fails to return student exams on the next meeting of the class, which is one week after the exam is given.
3. A doctor raises her fees for an office visit.
4. The government limits wage and price increases to 7 percent.
5. The draft is reinstituted.

6. A wife has an extramarital affair.
7. A politician suddenly shifts his position and endorses a property-tax-limit initiative.
8. A consumer, already heavily in debt, purchases a new car.
9. A state government makes all its residents carry an identification card at all times.
10. The personnel director of an advertising firm asks female applicants about their marital status.

2. *Minimum adequacy requirements.* In addition to expecting a normative argument to provide justification, not pseudojustification, we're certainly right in expecting it to meet the minimum adequacy requirements appropriate in the field. To get at what this means, let's consider the case of a nonnormative argument. Suppose Dr. McGee, renowned astronomer, insisted that the expanding universe could be accounted for by something other than the big bang theory. Now Dr. McGee wouldn't be much of a thinker or scientist if she hadn't assembled as much factual support for her claim as she could. And her fellow scientists, as well as we ourselves, wouldn't be very rational if we didn't insist on such factual support for her remarkable claim. Indeed, those in and outside science take for granted the obvious need to support claims with factual data. Providing such support is, after all, a minimum requirement for any sound argument, which is readily acknowledged and acted on in all nonnormative arguments.

But along comes a normative argument, and often rationality is put on a back burner. For some reason, many of us act as if a normative argument in, say, ethics or aesthetics or social philosophy is exempt from such minimal requirements of a sound argument. Well, it's not. We as much need *factual* support for claims such as "Prostitution ought not to be legalized" and "The government should take over the oil industry" as we admittedly do for "Vitamin C can prevent the common cold" and "Humans are innately aggressive."

Now let's dwell on those last two nonnormative statements for a minute. Suppose you asked the claimant, "Why do you think that vitamin C can prevent the common cold?" and suppose the claimant responded, "I just think so, that's all." Or suppose, in the second instance, the claimant "justified" the claim by saying, "Humans are innately aggressive because I feel that they are." Surely, you'd tell these people to go peddle their papers elsewhere. Or if you were kinder, you might insist that the persons were begging the question and press them about why they feel as they do. And if they persisted in such circularity, you'd rightly dismiss their arguments as absurd.

When it comes to normative arguments, however, it's amazing how often we not only tolerate but also endorse arguments that have no more to say for them than personal whim, prejudice, feeling, hunch, or fancy. Don't misunderstand. As we've already established, normative statements do indeed differ from nonnormative ones, and thus normative arguments differ from nonnormative arguments. But they don't differ so radically that the minimal requirements of good reasoning and sound argument don't apply to normative claims.

It's true that when a person expresses a value judgment, the person may be intending it strictly as an expression of personal preference. Thus, "Lying is wrong" could be interpreted as "I disapprove of lying" and no more than that. And "Picasso is a great painter" might be interpreted as "I really like Picasso" and no more than that. But *meaning* isn't justification any more than motivation, rationalization, or excuse is. Thus, if you ask a claimant, "Why is lying wrong?"

and the claimant replies, "Because I disapprove of it," you won't be any more satisfied with that reply than the comparable ones given in "justification" of the nonnormative statements about the expanding universe and the aggressive human. The reason for your dissatisfaction is that you realize that you're asking for justification, but the claimant is giving you meaning or interpretation. As we saw, that's a nice first step. But now that you understand what the claimant means by the value word, you'll likely ask, "Okay, so why do you disapprove of it?"

At this point, it's mind boggling, and downright disconcerting, how many people take such warranted persistence as aggressive behavior and summarily dismiss the interrogator as a "real pain." And this from otherwise intelligent people! Don't allow yourself to be cowed. Explain that you realize that one can't expect the scientific confirmation for the value judgment that one could muster, say, for the nonnormative assertion that cigarette smoking is a contributory cause of lung cancer. You realize that you're not dealing with such a statement to begin with. But at the same time explain that you do expect, and the person should be able to provide, supporting facts that make an endorsement of the value judgment more advisable than not. Surely that isn't being unreasonable or being a "real pain."

Unfortunately, it seems that in more cases than not people simply don't have the supporting facts to substantiate their value judgments. As a result, in everything from sex to social justice, *opinion passes as justification*—and one opinion is thought to be as good as the next. Respecting nonnormative claims, no one would be so foolish as to make such an assertion that one opinion is as good as the next. But not so for normative claims. More often than not, opinion, not justification, charts our thinking and actions. Thus, I'm of the opinion that extramarital sex is good, so I am justified in engaging in it; I believe that marijuana shouldn't be legalized, so that justifies the claim that marijuana shouldn't be legalized; I think *Star Trek* is the greatest science fiction film ever made, so the issue is closed. Fallacies such as hasty conclusion, questionable cause, invincible ignorance, and provincialism should leap out at you from the snarls that constitute such claims.

But there's more to it than just committing informal fallacies. At issue is a whole mind set that really has relegated the normative to the realm of the irrational. Think about the countless hours consumed on talk shows by people pontificating on some very important issues of the day. With rare and refreshing exceptions, these folks offer little more to support their barrage of value judgments than that they believe what they're saying, that they're of a certain opinion. Dietary habits, religious affiliations, child rearing, criminal justice, nuclear power, sexual preferences, government spending—nothing escapes the value judgments of some talk-show guests. The fact that these people rarely know what they're talking about is only one affront to rationality. Compounding this is that the talk-show host, in the vast majority of cases, doesn't require any more justification of the guest's claims than that the claims are "interesting," "provocative," or "controversial." Can you imagine some medical researcher's claims for a cancer cure receiving serious scientific coverage simply because they're "provocative"? And just to make matters insufferable, the studio audience is left to evaluate the claims largely on the provincial basis of its own approval or disapproval, like or dislike, of them. So is the television audience, except that its evaluation probably carries the additional bias of having been colored by the resounding studio aplause that greeted popular claims.

But it needn't be like this—at least not for you. Like Candide, Voltaire's indomitable pragmatist, you can tend to your own garden. You can protect yourself from the onslaught of the inane. The fact is that there is generally available to anyone taking the time to consult it a vast array of intelligent, insightful, often profound scholarship in any field. And this scholarship, in many cases the distilled wisdom of the ages, represents a rich source of the factual support needed to ground value judgments.

So familiarize yourself with political philosophy, economics, and psychology; with ethics and aesthetics; and with the various arts—poetry, music, literature, and painting. This doesn't mean that you need to be an expert before formulating or responding intelligently to a value claim. But surely you must be informed, for if you're not, you stand no chance of meeting the minimum adequacy requirements appropriate in a field or of detecting when the arguments of others don't.

SUMMARY

This chapter sketched an eight-step method for evaluating arguments: (1) Clarify meaning. (2) Identify conclusion and main premises. (3) If appropriate, restructure into syllogistic form. (4) Fill in missing premises. (5) Determine the syllogism's validity. (6) Examine the premises and support for truth and validity. (7) Check for informal fallacies. (8) Give an overall evaluation. This method can be used with normative and nonnormative arguments alike. A nonnormative argument is one that contains only nonnormative statements, that is, true or false assertions that express matters of empirical or logical fact. In contrast, a normative argument is one that contains a normative statement as a premise. A normative statement is an assertion of a value judgment. Because normative statements can't be verified with scientific precision, they raise special problems in arguments. In encountering any normative statement, always determine how it's being used, what interpretation the value words are carrying. Having established the meaning, you can assess the statement for warrantability or truth. Similarly, in evaluating normative arguments, always ensure that the reasons being offered are indeed justification for the claim and not pseudojustification. Motivations, rationalizations, and excuses are pseudojustification, not justification. Finally, normative arguments, like nonnormative ones, must meet the minimum adequacy requirements in the appropriate field. In brief, this means that they need factual support.

Summary Questions

1. See if you can spot two or three examples of apparently factual statements that are, in actuality, disguised value judgments.
2. Sportscasts contain myriad value judgments. Just for fun, make a list of a few from a typical game.
3. Commercials and advertisements—obviously—express value judgments as well as appeal to our current values. Some of these are widely noted: youthfulness, being trim, sexuality, success, and so on. Identify some of the specific ways in which advertisers express and foster value judgments. See if you can find some less obvious ones than those listed.

Use the eight-step method to evaluate the following arguments. In the case of normative arguments, indicate what you'd have to do to assess the truth of the normative statements.

1. ". . . the American government leaves business 'on its own.' A government that lets business alone is said to be a *laissez-faire* government." (Richard E. Gross and Vanza Devereaux, *Civics in Action*)

2. JESS: The United States needs trade and military help. That's why the United States needs the friendship of other countries.

   JANE: Sure. But the United States has forgotten something really important: that it must also help other countries. And that's precisely why we're losing some of our friends.

3. "Whatever triumph the TV-movie genre had scored over cinematic religiosity with [director] Franco Zeffirelli's remarkable *Jesus of Nazareth* in 1977 is vitiated by this three-hour film [*Mary and Joseph: A Story of Faith*]. The art with which Zeffirelli destroyed 'myth' is missing in this pedestrian and pretentious work." (Judith Crist, *TV Guide,* December 8–14, 1979, p. A-6)

4. ROGER: The best offense is a good defense.

   RUTH: No question about it. That's why a woman today has to take courses in judo and karate—so she can get ahead in the world.

5. "Under a government which imprisons any unjustly, the true place of a just man is also in prison." (Henry David Thoreau defending his being in jail, in *Civil Disobedience*)

6. ". . . we must not regard what the many say of us: but what he, the one man who has understanding of just and unjust, will say, and what the truth will say. And therefore you begin in error when you advise that we should regard the opinions of the many about just and unjust, good and evil, honorable and dishonorable." (Socrates in Plato's *Crito*)

7. "It is true also of journeys in the law that the place you reach depends on the direction you are taking. And so, where one comes out on a case depends on where one goes in." (Glanvill Williams, *The Sanctity of Life and the Criminal Law*)

8. WYATT: The value of Dali's work is bound to appreciate when he dies.

   PEARL: Is that why you're buying all his stuff now?

   WYATT: Not quite. His work isn't only a good investment, it's pure genius.

9. "If I am mobilized in a war, this war is *my* war; it is in my image and I deserve it. I deserve it . . . because I could always get out of it by suicide or by desertion." (Jean-Paul Sartre, *Being and Nothingness*)

10. PROFESSOR: What if I said that I am thinking of a primate that shares food and is monogamous? What would you say?

    STUDENT: I'd say you were thinking of a human, a gibbon, or a marmoset.

    PROFESSOR: Why?

    STUDENT: Because among primates only humans, gibbons, and marmosets share food and are monogamous.

11. "[Chief Justice Warren] Burger is not the only Justice on the Supreme Court who lacks a coherent, identifiable judicial philosophy. . . . 'There are no strong philosophical bents on this court,' says University of Virginia Law Professor A. E. Dick Howard. 'Most of them are independent pragmatists who take each case as it comes.'" ("Inside the High Court," *Time,* November 5, 1979, p. 64)

12. "If we can justify the infliction of imprisonment and death by the state 'on the ground of social interests to be protected,' then surely we can similarly justify the postponement of death by the state. The objection that the individual is thereby treated not as an 'end' in himself but ony as a 'means' to further the common good was, I think, aptly disposed of by [Justice Oliver Wendell] Holmes long ago. 'If a man lives in society, he is likely to find himself so treated.'" (Yale Kamisar, arguing

against a relaxation of euthanasia laws, in "Some Non-Religious Views Against Proposed 'Mercy Killing' Legislation")

13. "Evolution is a scientific fairy-tale just as the 'flat-earth theory' was in the 12th century. Evolution directly contradicts the Second Law of Thermodynamics, which states that unless an intelligent planner is directing a system, it will always go in the direction of disorder and deterioration. . . . Evolution requires a faith that is incomprehensible! Biblical Creation is the only sensible alternative." (Dr. Edward Blick, professor of aerospace, mechanical and nuclear engineering at the University of Oklahoma, in *21 Scientists Who Believe in Creation*)

14. ". . . one of the distinct inconveniences or tragedies of human sexuality is that it endows us, and perhaps particularly the males among us, with a propensity to become exceptionally involved and infatuated with members of the other sex whom, had we no sex urges, we would hardly notice. That is too bad; and it might well be a better world it if were otherwise. But it is *not* otherwise, and I think it is silly and pernicious for us to condemn ourselves because we are the way that we are in this respect." (Albert Ellis, *Sex Without Guilt*)

15. "Young people can no longer get a bootlegged feeling of personal identity out of the sexual revolt, since there is nothing left to revolt against." (Rollo May, *Antidotes for the New Puritanism*)

16. "If a being suffers, there can be no moral justification for refusing to take that suffering into consideration, and, indeed, to count it equally with the like suffering (if rough comparisons can be made) of another being. So the only question is: Do animals other than man suffer? Most people agree unhesitatingly that animals like cats and dogs can and do suffer, and this seems also to be assumed by those laws that prohibit wanton cruelty to such animals." (Peter Singer, "Animal Liberation")

17. " 'If you don't break your neck,' said Garnett, 'you'll be the laughing stock of the expedition when we get back to the base. That mountain will probably be called Wilson's Folly from now on.'

" 'I won't break my neck,' I said firmly. 'Who was the first man to climb Pico and Helicon?'

" 'But weren't you rather younger in those days?' asked Louis gently.

" 'That,' I said with great dignity, 'is as good a reason as any for going.' "
(Arthur C. Clarke, *The Sentinel*)

18. "Working at a paid job, any job, a woman is no longer just a family creature. . . . Hence, for women to work means relieving at least some part of their oppression." (Susan Sontag, *Partisan Review*, XL, 1973, 199)

19. "Experience indicates that purely voluntary efforts at self-regulation are not likely to be successful. There must be some enhancement mechanism by which violations of regulatory norms can be punished through collective action against the violator." (David A. Aaker and George S. Day, *Corporate Responses to Consumerism Pressures*)

20. "Keep up with the latest developments in alternative technology, environmental issues, holistic health, and human potential. . . . Listen in on conversations with humanistic innovators such as Margaret Mead, Frederick Leboyer, Daniel Ellsberg, Allen Ginsberg, Elisabeth Kübler-Ross, and Bucky Fuller. . . . Look into *New Age*, the monthly magazine for people who want to make a difference in the world." (ad for *New Age* magazine)

21. "When you join DSOC [Democratic Socialist Organizing Committee], you're joining people like Michael Harrington, Representative Ronald Dellums, Gloria Steinem, Machinists Union President Bill Winpisinger, Irving Howe, James Farmer, Joyce Miller, president of the Coalition of Labor Union Women, Harry Britt, San Francisco Commissioner, and Ruth Messinger, NYC Council Member. Most important you're joining thousands of people you'll want to meet and work with in the struggle for a just society." (ad for the Democratic Socialist Organizing Committee)

22. "Global Corporations, with their worldwide network of subsidiaries, high technology and marketing systems, far outstrip the puny regulatory efforts of a government that considers corporate crime a minor nuisance at worst. Nothing short of a complete moral transformation of the corporate ethos will stop dumping [the practice of exporting products banned in the U.S.]." (Mark Dowie, "The Corporate Crime of the Century," *Mother Jones*, November 1979, p. 49)

23. ". . . according to modern physics, radio is our only hope of picking up an intelligent signal from space. Sending an interstellar probe would take too long—roughly 50 years even for nearby Alpha Centauri—even if we had the technology and funds to accomplish it. But radio is too slow for much dialogue. The most we can hope from it is to establish the existence (or, more accurately, the former existence) of another civilization." (Patrick Moore, "Speaking English in Space: Stars," *Omni*, November 1979, p. 26)

24. "Primroses and landscapes, he [the Director] pointed out, have one grave defect: they are gratuitous. A love of nature keeps no factories busy. It was decided to abolish the love of nature . . . to abolish the love of nature, but *not* the tendency to consume transport. For of course it was essential that they [the lower classes] should keep on going to the country, even though they hated it. The problem was to find an economically sounder reason for consuming transport than a mere affection for primrose and landscapes. . . . 'We condition the masses to hate the country,' concluded the Director. 'But simultaneously we condition them to love all country sports. At the same time, we see to it that all country sports shall entail the use of elaborate apparatus." (Aldous Huxley, *Brave New World*)

25. "We are asked to notice that the development of a human being from conception through birth into childhood is continuous; then it is said that to draw a line, to choose a point in this development and say 'before this point the thing is not a person, after this point it is a person' is to make an arbitrary choice, a choice for which in the nature of things no good reason can be given. It is concluded that the fetus is, or anyway that we had better say it is, a person from the moment of conception. But this conclusion does not follow. Similar things might be said about the development of an acorn into an oak tree, and it does not follow that acorns are oak trees, or that we had better say they are. Arguments of this form are sometimes called 'slippery slope arguments'—the phrase is perhaps self-explanatory—and it is dismaying that opponents of abortion rely on them so heavily and uncritically." (Judith Jarvis Thomson, "A Defense of Abortion")

26. "Language is the symbolic repository of the meaningful experience of ourselves and our fellow human beings down through history, and, as such, it reaches out to grasp us in the creating of a poem. We must not forget that the original Greek and Hebrew words meaning 'to know' meant also 'to have sexual relations.' . . . The etymology of the term demonstrates the prototypical fact that knowledge itself—as well as poetry, art, and other creative products—arises out of the dynamic encounter between subjective and objective poles." (Rollo May, *The Courage to Create*)

27. "There is one law only which, by its nature, requires unanimous consent; I mean the social compact: for civil association is the most voluntary of all acts; every man being born free and master of himself, no person can under any pretense whatever subject him without his consent." (Jean Jacques Rousseau, *The Social Contract*)

28. "Just as a modern European economist would not consider it a great economic achievement if all European art treasures were sold to America at attractive prices, so the Buddhist economist would insist that a population basing its economic life on nonrenewable fuels is living parasitically, on capital instead of income. Such a way of life could have no permanence and could therefore be justified only as a purely temporary expedient. As the world's resources of nonrenewable fuels—coal, oil, and natural gas—are exceedingly unevenly distributed over the globe and undoubtedly limited in quantity, it is clear that their exploitation at an ever-increasing

rate is an act of violence against nature which must almost inevitably lead to violence beween men." (E. F. Schumacher, *Small Is Beautiful: Economics as if People Mattered*)

29. "It is the belief of this writer that *ecology is a profoundly serious matter, yet most of the solutions suggested for environmental quality will have, directly or indirectly, adverse effects on the poor and lower income groups.* Hence, economic or distributive justice must become an active component in all ecology debates." (David R. Frew, "Pollution: Can the People Be Innocent While Their Systems Are Guilty?")

30. ". . . Man is condemned to be free. Condemned, because he did not create himself, yet in other respects is free, because, once thrown into the world, he is responsible for everything he does." (Jean-Paul Sartre, *Existentialism and Human Emotions*)

chapter 18

The Extended Argument: A Strategy

Histories make men wise; poetry, witty; the
mathematics, subtle; natural philosophy, deep . . .
logic and rhetoric, able to contend.

FRANCIS BACON

"Wow! What a movie!" Lina whispered, dabbing her eyes with a tissue. "I hope that if I'm ever paralyzed, you'll love me enough to help me end it all."

Lina and Mike had rented the movie *Whose Life Is It, Anyway?* the powerful story of a sculptor who is paralyzed from the neck down in an accident and who decides that he wants to die rather than live without being able to create his art. Lina was obviously moved by the story they'd just watched; Mike was silent at first. Finally, he spoke.

"Aw, c'mon, Lina. Don't ask that. You know I couldn't do anything like that."

"Don't you believe in euthanasia, Mike?"

"You mean 'mercy killing'? Naw. I sure don't."

"Okay, maybe you don't. But what about me? I do. So I should have the right to die if I'm ever in circumstances that destroy the quality of my life."

"So," said a troubled Mike, "who's stopping you?"

"Who's stopping me! Why you are! Everybody is! Don't you remember that '60 Minutes' segment on Elizabeth Bouvier that we watched, and how upset I got?"

"Oh, yeah. She's the woman with cerebral palsy who's been trying to get the courts to rule that she has the right to have doctors in a hospital help her die."

"Yes. Remember how frustrated we both were? After all, she's a bright woman, but she's trapped in a body that is slowly decaying. She can't feed or clean herself; she has trouble speaking."

"Right. And they force-fed her and stuff. Boy, that steamed me."

"Then how can you say you're against euthanasia?"

"I don't know. It just feels wrong. Besides, maybe I'm just against you dying, maybe I just don't want to think about death," Mike said, beginning to get a little teary-eyed himself.

Lina reached over and held his hand, and they both sat silently for a moment.

Voluntary euthanasia refers to a direct action to terminate a patient's life because the patient has requested it. It's an issue that won't go away as medical technologies make early diagnosis and prolonged treatment likely for more and more debilitating, often terminal, illnesses. Involuntary euthanasia is already a controversial and important issue, as it becomes possible to keep comatose patients "alive" almost indefinitely and as the desire for organ transplants grows. Both forms of euthanasia have sparked a volatile public debate ever since the tragic case of Karen Ann Quinlan received public attention in the mid-1970s.

You'll recall that on an April night in 1975, shortly after drinking a gin and tonic with friends, twenty-one-year-old Karen Ann Quinlan mysteriously collapsed. Earlier she had taken some tranquilizers. The combination caused her to "nod out," according to one of her friends. Attempts to revive her failed.

A year later, in a hospital in New Jersey, Karen Ann Quinlan lay curled in a fetal position and fell to less than half of her normal weight of 120 pounds. Her eyes were open but she did not see. Every few seconds her body convulsed slightly; an artificial respirator connected to her windpipe forced her lungs to work, which enabled her to be maintained in what doctors described as a "chronic vegetative state." Her heart continued to beat; her brain, though permanently damaged, emitted faint but steady signals visible on an electroencephalogram (EEG).

The upshot of the whole tragic affair was that Karen Ann's father appealed to the N.J. Supreme Court to be allowed permission to suspend life-sustaining apparatus and let nature "take its course." He was given permission, and shortly thereafter ordered that the artificial respirator be removed. It was. Karen Ann Quinlan lived for ten years, presumably being maintained by her own natural processes, before she finally died.

In the midst of such events the public's attention understandably turned toward the complex question of euthanasia. Responding to this interest, a local paper had run a series of articles on the subject, specifically on the issues of legalizing voluntary euthanasia. Apparently one reader felt so strongly that euthanasia shouldn't be legalized that he wrote a letter to the editor. Here's what it said:

Against Legalizing Euthanasia

Your recent series once again has raised the issue of euthanasia. A number of voices have been heard advocating the legalization of voluntary euthanasia. While the agonizing plight of many of our terminally ill makes this proposal understandable, there are good reasons to resist liberalizing our euthanasia laws.

First of all, no matter how you look at it, euthanasia is killing and killing is wrong. The Bible is clear on that point, and our society has always forbidden it. The fact that somebody voluntarily requests to be killed doesn't make it right. Anyone who says it does is assuming that we have absolute rights over our bodies. But this just isn't so, and to think it is is simply foolish.

But even if terminal patients did have a right to a mercy death on request, there's still a question about whether a terminally ill patient is capable of making such a decision "voluntarily." I guess those who advocate voluntary euthanasia believe that patients should be allowed to die on request when they've developed a tolerence to narcotics. Okay, but exactly when are those patients to decide? When they're drugged? If so, then surely their choice can't be considered voluntary. And if they're to decide after the drugs have been withdrawn, this decision can't be voluntary either. Anyone who's had a simple toothache knows how pain can distort judgment and leave us almost crazy. Imagine how much more likely to be irrational we'd be if we were suffering from some terminal disease and suddenly had our ration of morphine discontinued.

Even granting that such a decision could be completely voluntary, is it really wise to offer such a choice to the gravely ill? I remember how, before she died of stomach cancer, my mother became obsessed with the idea that she was an emotional and financial burden on her family. Why, she actually kept apologizing to us that she went on living! Had she the option of euthanasia, she might have taken it—not because she was tired of living, but because she felt guilty about living!

I shudder to think of the stress that such a choice would have put on us, her family. Surely, we would have been drawn into the decision. And just as surely we'd have been divided. Some of us would have said, "Yes, let mother die," while others would have resisted out of a sense of love or devotion or gratitude, even guilt.

Then there's the whole question of mistaken diagnoses. Doctors aren't infallible. Even the best of them errs. The story is told of the brilliant diagnostician Richard Cabot who, when he was retiring, was given the complete medical histories and results of careful examinations of two patients. The patients had died and only the pathologist who'd seen the descriptions of their post-mortems knew their exact diagnoses. The pathologist asked Cabot for his diagnoses. Guess what—the eminent Dr. Cabot blew both of them! Now if a brilliant diagnostician can make a mistake, what about a less accomplished doctor? Let's face it: There's always the possibility of a wrong diagnosis. But once a person dies, there's obviously no chance of correcting it.

But suppose we could be sure of diagnoses. Even so, there's always the chance that some new pain-relieving drug, even a cure, is just around the corner. Many years ago the president of the American Public Health Association made this point forcefully when he said, "No one can say today what will be incurable tomorrow. No one can predict what disease will be fatal or permanently incurable until medicine becomes stationary and sterile."

But I think the thing that frightens me the most about legalizing voluntary euthanasia is that it will open the door for the legalization of *involuntary* euthanasia. If we allow people to play God and decide when and how they'll die, it won't be long before society will be deciding when and how defective infants, the old and senile, and the hopelessly insane will die as well.

A few days after they'd watched *Whose Life Is It, Anyway?* Mike read the letter to the editor. He asked Lina to read it and tell him what she thought.

"I don't agree with that letter," she said, putting down the paper. "I don't agree at all."

"Figures. You never agree."

"Hey, that's not fair. You did ask me what I thought of it."

"Okay, okay. Let's get this over with so we can have some peace. What'd you think of it?" an annoyed Mike asked, sorry he'd been dumb enough to bring the whole thing up.

"I think it's wrong to make people suffer."

"So who said anything about making people suffer?"

"Not in so many words. But the guy who wrote that letter must be a sadist. He's implying that it's wrong to save sick people from suffering."

"Aw, c'mon. You know better than that. All the letter says is that a lot of the people who make a big deal of people's rights don't see the whole picture. All they see is the part of it with somebody in bed suffering. Sure that's awful. But killing is even worse. And I agree with the letter: No matter how you try to disguise it, euthanasia is killing."

"Mike, you weasel. You're just arguing to make me mad, aren't you?"

"Why do you say that?"

"Why? Because you're Mister Law and Order, that's why. Always talking about your right to kill in self-defense, always in favor of capital punishment. Capital punishment is killing; self-defense killing is still killing."

"Cut it out," Mike said, dismissing Lina's last point with a wave of his hand. "Even you ought to be smart enough to see that capital punishment's a different issue. It's what you'd call justifiable killing."

"And euthanasia isn't?" Lina shot back.

"No! Besides, so what if it is? The issue is whether to legalize it or not. And that letter just demonstrated that it shouldn't be legalized. Maybe you should read it again—and try to follow it this time."

"Hmmmph," Lina growled. "I'm not the one who needs to learn how to think clearly."

The preceding scenario isn't exceptional. Faced with an argument longer than a simple ad or brief paragraph, we often respond through the filter of our own preconceptions, biases, and other provincial reference points. What's more, we can easily allow ourselves to be overwhelmed by the extended argument. We don't quite know what to make of it—how to approach it, what to look for and react to. As a result, we never completely come to grips with what's been written or spoken; we never formulate any intelligent response to it; we never deepen our own understanding of and opinion on the issue. For all they got out of it, Lina and Mike might as well never have read the letter.

But they did read it. And we did. In fact, we read, hear, or formulate extended arguments constantly. It's a rare week that goes by when we don't come across some essay, article, editorial, review, or commentary that argues for or against something. Indeed, the extended argument is a most common argumentative form, which happens to present unique problems for us. It's important that we learn how to manage these problems, for through the extended argument people try to win our support and loyalty for an infinite variety of views.

So no practical logic would be complete without considering the extended argument. That is what we'll do in this final chapter. Most important, we'll develop a strategy for dealing with this kind of argument, a strategy that capitalizes on the eight-step method of argument evaluation developed in Chapter 15.

By the time we've completed this chapter, we'll have a systmatic method for coping with any extended argument. We'll no longer be like our likable but logically floundering fictitious friends, ill equipped to deal with life's argumentative tugs and pulls.

THE EXTENDED ARGUMENT

A useful way to develop some strategy for dealing with the extended argument is to consider what such an argument generally consists of. But before we do this let's specify precisely what kind of discourse we have in mind when we speak of the extended argument.

Argument and Persuasion

There are several modes of discourse, which are familiar to anyone who's ever taken a basic course in composition: narration, description, exposition, and so forth. One of these modes is ordinarily termed *argument and persuasion*.

Both argument and persuasion are written forms of debate originating in the public forums and law courts of ancient Greece and Rome. In those times, argument meant a fixed form of public speech designed to present a rational, logical appeal on some important issue. Persuasion developed as a variation to argument, as Athenian lawyers sought acquittal for their clients. Although persuasion, like argument, seeks to compel, it differs from argument in its use of emotional techniques. Nonetheless, at its best, persuasion is grounded in the same rational approach that defines argument.

Currently what we term "argument" or "persuasion" in fact combines both methods. We have seen many examples in the preceding pages. But most of these have been brief, such as the ad or the political pitch. But frequently the argument and persuasion combination takes the form of a relatively long essay, which brings us to the extended argument.

By an extended argument we mean a longer piece of discourse that combines argument and persuasion to compel the listener or reader to adopt another position, another manner of thinking, or another solution to a problem. Curiously, all good extended argument still rests on the basic forms of ancient times, which require the inclusion of four essential elements: (1) an analysis of the problem; (2) a proposed solution that is developed or supported by factual and logical details and evidence; (3) a refutation of the opposing position, if there is one; (4) a concluding restatement of the proposed solution. Not every extended argument will include each of these elements, nor will it necessarily take them up in this order. But it will include most of them, and being familiar with the format is a good first step toward effectively evaluating the argument. Also, realizing that today the extended argument usually combines persuasion with pure argument alerts you to the likely presence of emotional appeals in this sort of discourse. These appeals to the emotions are accomplished mainly through diction and tone and the studied selection of examples.

So much for the meaning and essential form of the extended argument. We should now look closely at its ingredients, for these will direct our evaluation strategy.

Ingredients

Although there is no universally agreed-on list of ingredients for the extended argument, it's hard to imagine one that does not include the following: (1) a thesis proposition, (2) organization, (3) main points, and (4) developmental devices. Familiarity with these and an ability to use and pick them out are invaluable in constructing and evaluating the extended argument.

The Thesis Proposition.   *The thesis proposition is a statement of the main idea of the argument.* In fiction the main idea is sometimes called the theme, where an underlying idea or "moral" is expressed through the dialogue and action. Since in the extended argument the whole purpose is to compel the listener or reader to a position, the thesis proposition is really a statement of what the argument is all about. Without a thesis, or a main idea, an essay would be a snarl; a collection of incoherent paragraphs and sentences.

As you can imagine, if you're seriously interested in evaluating an extended argument—or constructing one, for that matter—you must determine the thesis, the main idea; you must state the thesis proposition accurately. This is crucial because everything the author offers in support can only be assessed in terms of whether or not it advances the thesis. If you don't know what the thesis is, or if you misrepresent it, you can't intelligently evaluate the argument.

There is no foolproof way of determining the thesis or main idea of an extended argument. Sometimes an author states it directly; in other words, the author actually provides a thesis proposition in the essay. Other times, the thesis proposition is implied, and the reader or listener is left to state it concretely. But even when authors don't actually provide a thesis proposition, you can infer it from an intelligent and close consideration of the argument. *An extended argument always deals with some topic, and its author always has an attitude toward the topic.* When you combine topic and attitude, you come up with the main idea. And when you state the main idea, you have what we're calling the thesis proposition.

Now how do you determine the topic of the argument? The topic is the subject that the argument deals with. To discover the topic, study the paragraphs; scrutinize them. Indeed, paragraph scrutiny is the key to extended argument analysis, as we'll shortly see. Paragraphs are always about somebody or something. And that somebody or something is the topic of the argument. So to find out what the topic of the argument is, discover the common concern of the paragraphs.

Once you've discovered the argument's topic, find out what the author is interested in telling you about it. That will reveal the author's attitude or viewpoint. Having isolated topic and attitude, you'll have the main idea. A statement of this main idea is the thesis proposition.

What we've said so far can be graphically illustrated with a simple tree diagram, to be read from top to bottom. Thus,

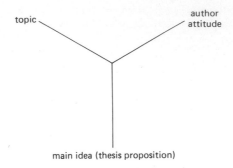

If we are dealing with actual extended arguments, we might get relationships such as these:

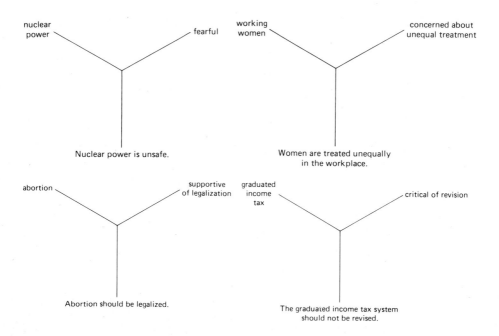

Notice that in the preceding examples the theses are one of two kinds. They are either attempts to convince the reader that something is or is not a fact (for example, "Nuclear energy is safe"; "Women are treated unequally in the workplace") or to compel the reader to do something ("Abortion should be legalized"; "The graduated income-tax system should not be revised"). For purposes of analysis, for determining an argument's thesis, it's helpful to view theses as falling into these categories.

In summary, given an argument's topic and author's attitude, you have its main idea and thus its thesis. You can then formulate a thesis proposition, understanding that the entire essay presumably advances this proposition. From this we can infer that the concept of a thesis shouldn't mystify. After all, every extended argument must be about something and every author must have an attitude toward that something. In other words, every extended argument must have a main idea. Isolate it and you have the thesis; state it and you have the thesis proposition. And it's in the light of this proposition that you can subsequently evaluate every paragraph in the argument.

*EXERCISE 18-1 _____

A good way to practice detecting thesis propositions is by noting the main idea of a paragraph. Remembering that a thesis proposition is a statement of the main idea, write the thesis proposition for each of the following paragraphs:

1. "In our society, food is often connected with recreation. We go out for coffee, invite friends over for drinks, celebrate special occasions with cakes or big meals. We can't think of baseball without thinking of hot dogs and beer, and eating is so often an accompaniment to watching TV that we talk of TV snacks and TV dinners. Just as Pavlov's dogs learned to salivate at the sound of a bell, the activities we associate with food can become signals to eat. Watching TV becomes a signal for potato chips; talking with friends becomes a signal for coffee and doughnuts; nodding over a book tells us its time for pie and milk." (Michael J. Mahoney and Kathryn Mahoney, "Fight Fat with Behavior Control," _Psychology Today,_ May 1976)

2. "Although much of society has changed over the last 20 years, Kulka and Weingarten concluded that reactions to parental divorce have not. They found no differences between people from intact and nonintact families in overall adjustment or depression in adulthood. However, young adults (between 21 and 34 years old) from divorced families were less likely to be 'very happy' and more likely to report symptoms of poor physical health than those from intact families. Throughout life, people of all ages from divorced families remembered their childhood as the most unhappy time of life. They were also more likely to say that as adults, they had been 'on the verge of a nervous breakdown.' Feelings of anxiety were more prevalent among men whose parents were divorced, lending support to Hetherington's notion that the effects of divorce may be more pervasive and long-lasting for men than for women." (Carin Rubinstein, "The Children of Divorce as Adults," _Psychology Today,_ January 1980)

3. "The ultimate survival training area, the continent [Antarctica] provides long periods of cold and isolation that test our ingenuity, technology, and stamina. Its pure, nearly pristine environment is the site of a great deal of basic research. Teams from around the world go to test equipment, the environment, its organisms, and, most of all, themselves. This year the National Science Foundation will spend over $55 million to conduct reserch there, to study such diverse topics as the geological formation of the continent and the effects of temperatures on bacteria. NASA is searching there for ways to relieve the strain on people of long periods of confinement. The long Antarctic winters are ideal for testing the isolation stress that slowly erodes the stability of astronauts during our prolonged manned space missions." (Eric Rosen, "White Continent," _Omni,_ December 1977)

Organization. _Organization refers to how the argument is structured._ Generally speaking, there are two ways that an extended argument is organized, and both involve the thesis proposition.

In the first way, the thesis is stated or implied early in the essay, in the opening paragraphs, which hereafter we'll take to mean the first two or three paragraphs. These are then followed by supporting materials. The movement then is roughly from the general to the specific, much in the form of an inverted pyramid:

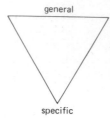

Sometimes, however, writers present their supporting materials first, especially when dealing with controversial topics. It is not until the closing paragraphs—hereafter taken to mean the final two or three paragraphs—that they state or imply their thesis. The movement, then, is roughly from the specific to the general, much in the form of a pyramid:

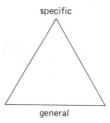

Since a well-constructed argumentative paragraph is really a microcosm of a well-constructed extended argument, we can illustrate these basic organizational patterns with the help of two simple paragraphs, which happen to be adapted from advertisements:

> *Inverted pyramid (general to specific):* Even though our country enjoys one of the highest standards of living and is the largest producer of food products in the world, there are serious gaps in our national diet, most frequently because of poor eating habits. These deficiencies are not limited to low-income groups but cut across all economic and social levels. According to the most recent information, 20 to 50 percent of Americans run some risk of not meeting the U.S. Recommended Daily Allowance for at least one or more of the vitamins C, A, B_1 (thiamine), B_2 (riboflavin), and folic acid. Minerals such as iron and calcium are also likely to be insufficient. If you're dieting or skipping meals, you may be eliminating foods that contain many vitamins, including C, E, and B-complex vitamins.[1]

> *Pyramid (specific to general):* Watch a kangaroo go. At Tidbinbilla they hop to it at better than 30 miles per hour. Buy a boomerang from a man called Mulga Bill and chances are he'll throw in some instruction for free. Add to your rock collection. The local scene produced the Bee Gees, Helen Reddy, Peter Allen, Olivia Newton-John. Go to jail. Stand in the tiny cell where Ned Kelly, the notorious bush-ranger, was incarcerated. Get out to the Outback—to Ayers

[1] A Hoffmann-La Roche advertisement.

Rock, the world's biggest monolith. Around its base are secret caves with painted walls telling of the Aboriginal Dreamtime. Stare at stalactites and stalagmites at Jenolan Caves. Meet a jackeroo or a jilleroo. They're young ranch hands learning the business on a sheep station. Outside Canberra you can see a sheep dog "round 'em up." He takes the shortest route from one side to the other: across the backs of the woolies. Come see the wonders Down Under in Australia. They could well turn your world upside down.[2]

Main Points. *Main points are the principal support assertions offered to advance the thesis.* This is a crucial part of any extended argument, for the argument's thesis proposition stands or falls on the strength of its undergirding. Furthermore, the main points comprise the bulk of an analytical work. Usually, it's not difficult to isolate the main points of an argument, especially when the essay is tightly organized. But even when it isn't, a close reading of the paragraphs and sensitivity to the connections between them should be enough to reveal the main points the author is making to advance the thesis.

Take as an example the following essay, which deals with American education. Even though it's many years old, it's still pertinent. Read it through and try to determine what the main points are. Remember that usually several paragraphs are spent developing a single point, so it's incorrect to assume that every paragraph asserts a separate point that is intended to support the thesis.

Four Things That Threaten Our Schools[3]

FELIX MORLEY

In his disquieting book, *Danger in Washington*, the former superintendent of schools in that city asserts that procedures now in force there are "a threat to free public education." He adds that this is the case "not only in Washington, but throughout the country."

Supporting that gloomy appraisal the education editor of *The New York Times* writes, apropos the protracted teachers' strike in that city: "The distintegration of the school system has become a possibility." He is talking of distintegration not in the racial but in the general sense.

Against this background a staff reporter of *The Wall Street Journal* investigates Russian education policy and finds it "aimed primarily at finding the best students and then urging them on to greater academic achievements" That observer is especially impressed by the current Russian discrimination in favor of demonstrated ability. Yet this sort of favoritism, as Dr. Carl F. Hensen tells his story, was the reason for his ouster last year as head of the public school system in the capital of the United States.

It is not surprising that there is a profound difference between the philosophy of public education here and in Soviet Russia. But it is startling to be told that we deny the value of competition in secondary education, even as the communists scrap Marxist theories of natural intellectual equality.

From our viewpoint the results of this ironical divergence are not happy. All over Russia, it is reported, there is a well-disciplined and well-accepted effort to move ahead in the vital educational process. In many of our big city school

---

[2]A Qantas advertisement.
[3]Reprinted by permission from *Nation's Business,* December 1968. Copyright 1968 by *Nation's Business,* Chamber of Commerce of the United States.

systems, on the other hand, unrest, frustration and professional pessimism are only too apparent.

In four separate areas one may now observe conditions which suppress individual distinction in our public schooling. Each is making a contribution to the present demoralization.

That most strongly emphasized in Dr. Hansen's book is the planned retardation of ability, illustrated both by the automatic promotion of incompetent pupils and by the refusal to give any meaningful reports on individual performance. A big issue, in the case of the Washington superintendent, was his insistence on the "track system." This in general grouped students in accordance with demonstrated ability, though without denial of passage from the "basic" track to one of the three higher divisions. In a court decision, in June, 1967, a federal judge labeled this ability grouping discriminatory and therefore unconstitutional.

Since the local board of education made no appeal, the verdict stands; which makes it seemingly illegal for any public school in the country to classify pupils by ability, at least openly. Of course competent and courageous teachers will continue to give special consideration to able students. Without such stimulative direction the process of education would be unworthy of that name. But this *cause celebre* in the nation's capital has been an encouragement to mediocre performance in every public school. It sanctifies the already strong position of those who think there should be no competition except in athletics.

This helps to emphasize that the teaching profession itself is the second educational field in which initiative is now actively discouraged. Here, too, Dr. Hansen's observations are timely, especially in regard to the unionization of teachers. As he aptly observes, this development inevitably discredits the teacher who puts the training of his or her pupils first. From the union viewpoint featherbedding is preferable to speed-up and any instructor who opposes a strike call is a potential scab.

Moreover, unionization builds a wall between the teaching and the administrative divisions in the public schools, even though close relations between these functions are essential.

Dr. Hansen wrote *Danger in Washington* with special reference to that city and before the protracted teacher strike which paralyzed the New York City schools for a large portion of the current academic year. Otherwise his comments on "the growing unproductiveness of the teacher" might well have been stronger. Regardless of the rights and wrongs in the New York or any other particular issue, it is clearly demoralizing for the pupils when teachers strike. The psychological effect goes far beyond the loss of study time.

When teachers play hooky en masse, why should pupils feel any obligation to take their studies seriously? What arguments can a dropout teacher use to influence a pupil who would like to do the same? And why not have truant officers for defecting teachers as well as for the defecting taught?

Ill-judged intervention by the federal government has in many instances proved itself a third demoralizing factor in public education. Here Dr. Hansen has certainly been close to the source of the difficulty. In the Washington "showcase" he has witnessed the development of an enforcement machinery that "has reached an incomprehensible complexity, and promises to grow in this respect . . . until it becomes unmanageable."

The thesis proposition of this essay could be stated, Present trends in American education pose a serious threat to our public school system. That's what the author is arguing. To advance his thesis, he makes roughly four key points:

1. There is advancement of incompetent students and a deemphasis on ability grouping, which has been encouraged by inadequate integration practices and court rulings against ability grouping. This point is developed in paragraphs six and seven.
2. There is a unionizing of teachers, which blunts the teacher's focus on student well-being and divides teachers and administrators. Paragraphs eight through ten develop this point.
3. There is federal financial aid, which allows government to interfere with school administration—paragraphs eleven through thirteen.
4. There is low morale among students in big-city school systems—paragraphs fourteen and fifteen.

In evaluating the soundness of the author's extended argument, it's necessary to evaluate the soundness of each of these points, or supporting ideas. And that requires a close and critical inspection of the paragraphs in which the points are made. Helpful in this inspection is an awareness of how authors develop their supporting points.

Developmental Patterns. *The term* developmental patterns *refers to the devices used in the extended argument to present the evidence or support for the thesis*. In arguing their cases, writers have a variety of techniques available to help compel readers to their viewpoints. We won't exhaust them here, but we will focus on some common ones of particular relevance in bringing practical logic to bear on the extended argument. As we briefly consider each, we'll mention things to be cautious of in your evaluations or constructions, especially fallacies. The devices we'll consider are (1) facts and opinions, (2) illustrations, (3) analogy, (4) cause and effect, (5) authority, and (6) statistics.

1. *Facts and opinions.* When writers offer evidence to support their theses, the evidence will be fact or opinion or a combination of the two. Providing facts and opinions to support a thesis is perhaps the most common way to develop an extended argument.

In everyday parlance, facts are what is actually the case. They're objective and verifiable. That water boils at 212 degrees Fahrenheit, that Sacramento is not the capital of the United States, that the sun rises in the East—all are facts. Anyone who wants to can confirm these assertions. Relevant facts, of course, are strong support for a thesis.

But be careful. Always make sure the facts are accurate and that they present the *whole* picture. What is untrue is not a fact; what suppresses significant information may be true but may be committing the fallacy of concealed evidence. What's more, facts must be pertinent to the point at issue; otherwise they're red herrings. Another thing: Make sure the author provides *enough* facts to justify the point. If the facts are insufficient, the point made is likely a hasty conclusion, in which event it doesn't at all support the argument's thesis.

In contrast to facts, opinions are what someone believes to be the case. Opinions are subjective. Although we can verify that the author holds the opinion, we can't verify the opinion itself. If we could, it wouldn't be an opinion at all, but a fact. Thus, if a ballistics expert testifies that two particular bullets came from the same gun, that's an opinion, not a fact. But this doesn't mean that opinions don't advance points and, ultimately, the proposition theses of arguments. On the contrary, opinions can be a potent source of evidence, especially where there's consensus of expert opinion. So if every ballistics expert asked, or an overwhelming majority, agreed that the two bullets came from the same gun, that testimony would probably have the weight of fact. It should be clear, then, that authority figures prominently in the credibility of opinions, and so we should be thoroughly familiar with the principles of governing appeals to authority, as outlined in a previous chapter.

EXERCISE 18-2 _____

Indicate whether each of the following propositions is an opinion, fact, or both.

1. *Crocodile Dundee* is among the ten best films ever made.
2. Isaac Newton was a mathematician and physicist.
3. Without sunlight there can be no life.
4. Taking the vitamin selenium reduces your chances of getting cancer.
5. Jimmy Carter was elected President in 1976 and thereby destroyed the myth that only someone "plugged into" the Washington political scene could become President.
6. The professor indicated that any student who earned a B in his class could easily earn an A in a comparable course taught by someone else.
7. What a fortunate thing that in the fire no one was injured.
8. Shortly after the speaker began her lecture, the audience thinned out, which led many to believe that more than a few found her remarks uninteresting.
9. Mohammed Ali is the greatest boxer in history.
10. All of the world's major religions teach the same thing.
11. *ET* is the most popular movie ever made.
12. You're really irresponsible if you drink and drive.
13. I was just thinking about Mom when she called, so I guess we have some sort of psychic connection.
14. Women are superior to men as evidenced by the fact that they live longer, on average.
15. *Practical Logic* is a wonderful text since it combines traditional logical studies with topical, real-life examples.

    2. Illustrations. Illustrations are writers' attempts to make something clear or to show what they're talking about. Ordinarily writers signal illustrations. The most common signals are the phrases *for example* and *for instance.* But frequently a single word in a sentence signals an illustration. Thus, "A *number* of stories are told about President Lincoln"; "*Many* things are inefficient about the postal service"; "To understand why the Equal Rights Amendment should be passed, Americans should be aware of *several* facts.' The italicized words signal illustrations that will help support the point.

    Illustrations may take the form of a single example or a series of them. An example is a specific instance used to make a point clear. Here's an example of an example used to make a point:

> Throughout history, men have tried various ingenious methods for sorting out truth tellers from liars. A medieval "truth by trial" technique called for thrusting a suspect's hand into a fire; if it was not burned, he was judged innocent. An ancient Chinese test required a suspected wrongdoer to chew rice powder while

being questioned. If the powder was dry when he spit it out afterward, the man was condemned—on the theory that the tension of lying had blocked his salivary glands, producing a dry mouth.[4]

Other times, illustrations may take the form of anecdotes, brief clarifying stories:

> Even though they'll rarely admit it, little boys do like little girls and vice versa. A teacher recently observed this courting ritual between second graders during recess break. A little boy, the acknowledged "tough guy" in the class, found a dead snake on the playground. To the accompaniment of cheers and jeers from the other boys, he picked it up and slung it carelessly around his neck. Then he marched purposefully across the playground to where the girls were huddled, shrieking and squealing. Unerringly he sought her out, the loudest squealer of them all, and stopped in front of her. In the silence that followed, the young lover cast his trophy at the feet of his beloved. Secure in the knowledge that he had bestowed a gift of inestimable value, he turned and strode away, while behind him the shrieks and squeals of outraged femininity broke out anew.[5]

There are several things to consider about this illustration, which leads us to some cautions in evaluating and constructing illustrations.

Illustrations don't prove anything, nor are they intended to. The purpose of an illustration is to illuminate; an illustration is a word picture of the writer's point. Nevertheless, when properly selected and within the context of a larger and varied developmental pattern, illustrations can advance the thesis proposition by compelling acceptance of the point being made. The key thing is that the illustration must be a good one, and that means that it must satisfy certain requirements.

Although there are a number of requirements that illustrations should fulfill, two are noteworthy here. One is that the illustration should *accurately* illustrate the generalization or abstraction it's intended to clarify. Notice that in the preceding paragraph about little boys and girls, the anecdote is supposed to illustrate that kids do indeed like members of the opposite gender. But does it? At the very best the anecdote seems to illustrate that little *boys* may like little girls, but it doesn't illustrate that little girls like little boys. So you could say that the illustration is irrelevant to the conclusion. If the writer had qualified the generalization thesis, the illustration at least *might be* relevant.

Notice the "might be" in the last sentence. Even if the anecdote were being used to illustrate that little boys really do like little girls, there's serious question whether it does. The writer is *interpreting* the little boy's behavior as a sort of ritualistic display of affection. But that seems a hasty conclusion. Maybe the boy was being sadistic. After all, he left the girls shrieking and squealing with outrage, didn't he? Why interpret the behavior as ritualistic affection? If we accept the anecdote as actual, as reporting something that actually occurred, surely the writer appears to be serving up a mixture of fact and *opinion*, the opinion part being the interpretation or value judgment.

In any event, the anecdote of itself doesn't really clarify the generalization

[4]Berkeley Rice, "The Truth Machine," *Psychology Today,* June 1978.
[5]Joan C. Roloff and Virginia Brosseit, *Paragraphs* (Encino, Calif.: Glencoe Publishing Co., 1979), pp. 109–10.

thesis. So it doesn't pass a basic test of a good illustration. If we want to talk logic, we can therefore say that the illustration constitutes a red herring for accepting the thesis; that it involves an unsubstantiated opinion that relies on a hasty conclusion.

If you want an illustration of an undoubtedly effective use of an illustration, consider this selection from Studs Terkel's "Here Am I, a Worker." All you need to know to appreciate the series of examples is that Terkel is trying to illustrate that today's workers desire to be thought of as human being and not just workers.

> Steve Hamilton is a professional baseball player. At 37 he has come to the end of his career as a major-league pitcher. "I've never been a big star. I've done about as good as I can with the equipment I have. I played with Mickey Mantle and with Willie Mays. People always recognize them. But for someone to recognize me, it really made me feel good. I think everybody gets a kick out of feeling special."

> Mike Fitzgerald was born the same year as Hamilton. He is a laborer in a steel mill. "I feel like the guys who built the pyramids. Somebody built 'em. Somebody built the Empire State Building, too. There's hard work behind it. I would like to see a building, say the Empire State, with a foot-wide strip from top to bottom and the name of every bricklayer on it, the name of every electrician. So when a guy walked by, he could take his son and say, 'See, that's me over there on the 45th floor. I put that steel beam in.' Picasso can point to a painting. I think I've done harder work than Picasso, and what can I point to? Everybody should have something to point to."

> Sharon Atkins is 24 years old. She's been to college and acidly observes, "The first myth that blew up in my face is that a college education will get you a worthwhile job." For the last two years she's been a receptionist at an advertising agency. "I didn't look at myself as 'just a dumb broad' at the front desk, who took phone calls and messages. I thought I was something else. The office taught me differently."

> Among her contemporaries there is no such rejection; job and status have no meaning. Blue collar or white, teacher or cabbie, her friends judge her and themselves by their beingness. Nora Watson, a young journalist, recounts a party game, Who Are You? Older people respond with their job titles: "I'm a copy writer," "I'm an accountant." The young say, "I'm me, my name is so-and-so."

> Harry Stallings, 27, is a spot welder on the assembly line at an auto plant. "They'll give better care to that machine than they will to you. If it breaks down, there's somebody out there to fix it right away. If I break down, I'm just pushed over to the other side till another man takes my place. The only thing the company has in mind is to keep that line running. A man would be more eager to do a better job if he were given proper respect and the time to do it."[6]

We've presented this selection at length, not just to show an illustration that's appropriate to the generalization or abstraction that the writer wishes to clarify, but also to show a *second* requirement a good illustration must fulfill. The second requirement is that the illustration must offer a *fair* representation of the generalization or abstraction under discussion. Otherwise, the illustration will con-

---

[6]Studs Terkel, "Here Am I, a Worker," in Leonard Silk, ed., *Capitalism: The Moving Target* (New York: Quadrangle, 1974), pp. 68–69.

stitute a biased sample, which of course would not help establish the author's point or, by implication, the thesis proposition. Notice the variety—in age, sex, occupation—that Terkel employs in his illustration. Suppose, in contrast, that he had confined his illustration to males under twenty-five working in automotives. Such a restricted illustration, no matter how many examples were used, would not support the claim about *younger workers as a class*.

So in evaluating the worth of illustrations, make sure (1) that they actually clarify the generalization or abstraction at issue and (2) that they're fairly representative of the generalization or abstraction. By failing to meet these requirements, an illustration can end up being a red herring, a biased sample, or one of a variety of other informal fallacies.

*EXERCISE 18-3

Evaluate the use of illustration in the following paragraphs.

1. "Statistics can be surprising. A friend of mine in his 70s, a very lively fellow and extraordinarily cheerful, likes to while away his senior citizenship—what we used to call old age—by collecting droll statistics from government sources that confute the assumptions on which most Presidents and Congresses appear to run the government. He has come up, for instance, with an item that does not, I imagine, cause George Meany or other labor leaders sleepless nights; namely, that there are more 'hair stylists' in the United States than unionized steelworkers. Another lulu, for which he invites an explanation in mixed company, is that there are more married men in this country than married women. It will come as no surprise to harassed symphony orchestras, though it may to the commissioner of baseball, to learn that more people go to symphony concerts than go to baseball games." (Alistair Cooke, "Focus on the Arts," *The World Book Yearbook,* 1978)

2. "In rooms where students have considerable freedom to move about on their own during seatwork and study periods, the teacher himself often becomes the center of little groups of waiting students. One of the most typical social arrangements in such settings is that in which the teacher is chatting with one student or examining his work while two or three others stand by, books and papers in hand, waiting to have the teacher evaluate their work, give them further direction, answer their questions, or in some other fashion enable them to move along. At such moments it is not unusual for one or two of the seated students also to have their hands raised, propped at the elbow, waiting patiently for the teacher to get around to them." (Philip W. Jackson, *Life in Classrooms*)

3. "When god-like Odysseus returned from the wars in Troy, he hanged, all on one rope, some dozen slave girls whom he suspected of misbehavior during his absence. This hanging involved no question of propriety, much less justice. The disposal of property was then, as now, a matter of expediency, not of right and wrong. Criteria of right and wrong were not lacking from Odysseus' Greece. The ethical structure of that day covered wives, but had not been extended to human chattels." (Aldo Leopold, "The Conservation Ethic," *The Journal of Forestry,* vol. 31, 1933)

4. "Sexual morality is a bottomless pit of problems. A competent employee with ten years of experience in one company happened to be a young woman who dated lots of men, including other workers. Her amours were a favorite subject of office gossip. On two occasions a jilted sweetheart stomped into her office and threatened her. Management got so irritated it told her to leave: she was a loose woman and a danger to morale. Rushing to her defense, the union claimed that her private life was her own business and that it was management's job to keep out intruders, not hers. When the case went to arbitration, the union's argument prevailed over management's and the young woman got her job back." (David W. Ewing, *Freedom Inside the Organization: Bringing Civil Liberties to the Workplace*)

3. *Analogy*. The analogy is another developmental pattern writers often make use of in establishing points in support of a thesis. We needn't detail that device here because we've done it amply in a preceding chapter. Suffice it to say that you should distinguish argumentative and nonargumentative uses of the analogy and be thoroughly familiar with the criteria for a good analogy. Remember that, although the argumentative analogy is a compelling device when used properly, it is more often used incorrectly. So beware the false analogy in an extended argument that reasons analogically to make a point.

4. *Cause and effect*. Like the preceding patterns, cause and effect figures prominently in the extended argument. Again, we've explored this subject in a preceding chapter. Review that material, paying particular attention to the importance of determining what is meant by "cause," to what method is used to establish causation, and to the difference between simple correlation and a causal connection. And of course, make sure you understand and are able to detect the fallacies of questionable causation, post hoc, slippery slope and oversimplification.

An additional point about cause-and-effect patterns of development: Generally, causal analysis takes the form of reasoning from cause to effect or from effect to cause. Here's an example of a cause-to-effect developmental pattern, which has been excerpted from Paul Ehrlich's *The Population Bomb*. Having just established that at present the world's population doubles about every thirty-seven years, Ehrlich writes,

> Let's examine what might happen on the absurd assumption that the population continued to double every thirty-seven years into the indefinite future. If growth continued at that rate for about 900 years, there would be some 60,000,000,000,000,000 people on the face of the earth. Sixty million billion people. This is about 100 persons for each square yard of the Earth's surface land and sea. A British physicist, J. H. Fremlin, guessed that such a multitude might be housed in a continuous 2,000-story building covering our entire planet. The upper 1,000 stories would contain only the apparatus for running this gigantic warren. Ducts, pipes, wires, elevator shafts, etc., would occupy about half of the space in the bottom 1,000 stories. This would leave three or four yards of floor space for each person. I will leave to your imagination the physical details of existence in this ant heap, except to point out that all would not be black. Probably each person would be limited in his travel. Perhaps he could take elevators through all 1,000 residential stories but could travel only within a circle of few hundred yards' radius on any floor. This would permit, however, each person to choose his friends from among some ten million people! And, as Fremlin points out, entertainment on the worldwide TV should be excellent, for at any time "one could expect ten million Shakespeares and rather more Beatles to be alive."[7]

In contrast, here's an example of an effect to cause developmental pattern:

> The National Commission on Diabetes, a panel appointed by Congress to study the problem, reported in 1975 that diabetes and its complications cause more than 300,000 deaths in the United States each year, making it the third leading cause of death, behind heart disease and cancer. The number of diabetics in the

---

[7]Paul Ehrlich, *The Population Bomb* (New York: Ballantine, 1969), pp. 14–15.

United States is doubling every fifteen years. A newborn child now faces a 1-in-5 chance of developing diabetes. Ironically, this increase is a direct result of improvements in the treatment of the disease. Diabetics who once might have died young or during periods of stress, such as giving birth, are now living relatively normal lives. They are bearing children who are more likely to develop diabetes.[8]

5. *Authority*. Frequently, extended arguments rely on appeals to authority in developing points. Again, we have dealt with authority as a source of knowledge elsewhere in our study. So we need say no more about this subject here, except to exhort a review of it and its abuses: false authority, popularity, positioning, traditional wisdom.

6. *Statistics*. Finally, the use of statistics often figures in the development of an extended argument. The Ehrlich selection just cited is an example. In our chapter on statistics we noted that statistics may be part and parcel of any inductive process: generalization, analogy, hypothesis, cause. We also isolated some common fallacies connected with the use of statistics: biased sample, biased question, false dilemma, and concealed evidence. You should review these and the observations we made about properly conducting research and polls.

These six developmental devices used in extended argument, then, occur frequently enough for us to be familiar with them. It's rare that they ever occur alone; writers generally use a mix in developing the extended argument. But being aware of how an essay is developing, together with having an awareness of the thesis proposition, organization, and main points, can settle us down to the job of analysis and evaluation. Specifically, these four ingredients suggest a strategy for evaluating the extended argument, a subject that will occupy the rest of this chapter.

A STRATEGY FOR EXTENDED ARGUMENT EVALUATION

What follows is *one suggested* strategy for evaluating the extended argument. The operative words in the preceding sentence are *one* and *suggested*. There are other ways to evaluate arguments besides the one we'll offer. If you encounter one that better serves your idiosyncratic needs, use it. If you find this strategy incomplete, then by all means add to it. In short, there's nothing sacrosanct about what follows.

The proposed strategy is far from perfect. But then we're not seeking perfection so much as functionality or utility. We want something that will facilitate our intelligent analysis of longer pieces of argument. We want a strategy (1) that is not overly complicated, (2) that can be put to immediate and constructive use, (3) that makes use of the ingredients of an extended argument, and (4) that capitalizes on the rest of this text, which is capsulized in the eight-step method developed in Chapter 17. If we can provide such a strategy, then, to return to the homely Hemingway metaphor of our opening chapter, we'll have developed a useful "crap detector."

---

[8] Thomas H. Maugh II, "The Two Faces of Diabetes," *Science Year, 1978* (Chicago: Field Enterprises Educational Corporation, 1979), p. 58.

To begin, we're going to call our strategy the *paragraph scrutiny approach*, or *PS* for short. (Note: *PS*, not *BS*: PS is designed to detect BS.) Why that? Well, scrutiny means a critical examination. Because our strategy relies so heavily on a critical examination of the paragraphs of an extended argument, it seems appropriate to call it the paragraph scrutiny approach. Incidentally, *critical* here does not mean "finding fault with." We're using *critical* in the sense of judging the merit of an argument. When we're judging merit, we're not just seeking fault; we're seeking strength and justification as well. Thus, our paragraph scrutiny strategy refers to a method of extended argument evaluation that relies on a judgment of the merit of the argument's points as developed in its paragraphs. Let's now get into our PS strategy.

Paragraph Scrutiny

Capitalizing on what we've said in this chapter about the ingredients of an extended argument and what we've said in previous chapters about the rules of correct argument, we can reduce our PS strategy to five steps:

1. Prereading the extended argument for the thesis proposition
2. Reading the argument for main supporting points
3. Indicating the developmental patterns used to present the points
4. Filling in missing premises if necessary and checking the argument for formal and informal fallacies
5. Judging the extended argument as compelling or not compelling

In implementing this method it's a good idea to write down each step. Thus, in step 1, actually write down the thesis statement. In step 2, write out the main points and then indicate, in step 3, the developmental patterns used with them. Although this may seem tedious and unnecessary, it's much easier to analyze and evaluate on paper than in your head. And it's generally more efficient. So in applying these steps to an essay, it's recommended that you follow this schematic format:

Thesis statement: _____

Main points:
   1. _____ (Paragraph number; development pattern)
   2. _____   "   "
   3. _____   "   "
   Etc.

Implementing the PS strategy in this way serves several additional purposes. First, it shows how the essay is organized. Second, it immediately reveals the connections, or lack of them, between thesis and supporting points. Third, and most important, it directs your analysis. Your job, after all, is to focus on the argument's main supporting points, to determine whether they compel adherence to the thesis. Your paragraph reference numbers show you precisely where to go in executing PS's step 4, which is the nucleus of argument evaluation. Fourth, listing the developmental patterns used with each point suggests what fallacies to be alert to. For example, you're going to look especially for red herrings and biased sample in points developed through illustrations, false authority in points developed by appeals to authority, and causation fallacies in points developed by cause-and-effect appeals. Naturally, you'll be inspecting for other fallacies as well, but in this way you have a handle on your task, a constructive reference point. Lacking some kind of concrete direction, you easily can be overwhelmed by an essay; in looking for everything, you may find nothing.

A final point: It's by no means necessary to detect every fallacy an extended argument commits to establish its unsoundness. Nor is an essay that commits an occasional fallacy necessarily unsound. What's critical is that the support offered for the main points actually compels acceptance of the thesis. If that support is fallacious, the points don't compel that acceptance. If the support is basically solid, the main points compel acceptance. Thus, support for a point may be compelling, despite an insignificant fallacy or two within it. On the other hand, support for a point may collapse on the basis of a single key fallacy, despite our overlooking a number of other fallacies present. Now it's time to put our PS strategy to work. Let's apply it to the letter about euthanasia that exercised Roberto and Carmen earlier.

Application

For your convenience the letter is reproduced again. Note that the only change made has been to number the paragraphs. Numbering paragraphs consecutively provides handy references when we do our analysis.

Against Legalizing Euthanasia

1   Your recent series once again has raised the issue of euthanasia. A number of voices have been heard advocating the legalization of voluntary euthanasia. While the agonizing plight of many of our terminally ill makes this proposal understandable, there are good reasons to resist liberalizing our euthanasia laws.

2   First of all, no matter how you look at it, euthanasia is killing and killing is wrong. The Bible is clear on that point, and our society has always forbidden it. The fact that somebody voluntarily requests to be killed doesn't make it right. Anyone who says it does is assuming that we have absolute rights over our bodies. But this just isn't so, and to think it is is simply foolish.

3   But even if terminal patients did have a right to a mercy death on request, there's still a question about whether a terminally ill patient is capable of making such a decision "voluntarily." I guess those who advocate voluntary euthanasia believe that patients should be allowed to die on request when they've developed a tolerance to narcotics. Okay, but exactly when are those patients to decide? When they're drugged? If so, then surely their choice can't be considered voluntary. And if they're to decide after the drugs have been withdrawn, this decision can't be voluntary either. Anyone who's had a simple toothache knows how much pain can distort judgment and leave us almost crazy. Imagine how much more likely to be irrational we'd be if we were suffering from some dreadful terminal disease and suddenly had our ration of morphine discontinued.

4   Even granting that such a decision could be completely voluntary, is it really wise to offer such a choice to the gravely ill? I remember how, before she died of stomach cancer, my mother became obsessed with the idea that she was an emotional and financial burden on her family. Why, she actually kept apologizing to us that she went on living! Had she the option of euthanasia, she might

have taken it—not because she was tired of living, but because she felt guilty about living!

5   I shudder to think of the stress that such a choice would have put on us, her family. Surely, we would have been divided. Some of us would have said, "Yes, let mother die," while others would have resisted out of a sense of love or devotion or gratitude, even guilt.

6   Then there's the whole question of mistaken diagnoses. Doctors aren't infallible. Even the best of them errs. The story is told of the brilliant diagnostician Richard Cabot who, when he was retiring, was given the complete medical histories and results of careful examinations of two patients. The patients had died and only the pathologist who'd seen the descriptions of their post-mortems knew their exact diagnoses. The pathologist asked Cabot for his diagnoses. Guess what—the eminent Dr. Cabot blew both of them! Now if a brilliant diagnostician can make a mistake, what about a less accomplished doctor? Let's face it: There's always the possibility of a wrong diagnosis. But once a person dies, there's obviously no chance of correcting it.

7   But suppose we could be sure of diagnoses. Even so, there's always the chance that some new pain-relieving drug, even a cure, is just around the corner. Many years ago the president of the American Public Health Association made this point forcefully when he said: "No one can say today what will be incurable tomorrow. No one can predict what disease will be fatal or permanently incurable until medicine becomes stationary and sterile."

8   But I think the thing that frightens me the most about legalizing voluntary euthanasia is that it will open the door for the legalization of *involuntary* euthanasia. If we allow people to play God and decide when and how they'll die, it won't be long before society will be deciding when and how defective infants, the old and senile, and the hopelessly insane will die as well.

Step 1: *Preread for the thesis.* After numbering the paragraphs consecutively, we can quickly look at the title and the very first paragraph for the topic and the author's attitude toward it, the main idea or thesis. We could write the thesis statement as follows: "Voluntary euthanasia should not be legalized."

Step 2. *Read the argument for the main supporting points.* The letter offers six points. They can be listed as follows, together with paragraph references.

Thesis statement: Voluntary euthanasia should not be legalized.
Main points:
1. That euthanasia is, by definition, killing and killing is wrong (paragraph 2)
2. That it's impossible to ascertain that consent is voluntary (paragraph 3)
3. That allowing a death decision is unwise (paragraphs 4 and 5)
4. That diagnoses can be mistaken (paragraph 6)
5. That relief or cures can be imminent (paragraph 7)
6. That abuses will follow the legalization (paragraph 8)
(Note: It's conceivable that some would consider paragraphs 4 and 5, that is, point 3, as supporting material for point 2, in which case the letter could be viewed as making just five points.)

Step 3: *Indicate the developmental patterns used to advance the main points.* Perhaps the most efficient way to do this is to characterize each paragraph. It's not necessary to note every pattern used in every paragraph; the key patterns will do. The number before each pattern stands for the number of the point being supported and the number of the paragraph in the argument. That is, 1–

2 means, first point, second paragraph; 3–4 means third point, fourth paragraph. Thus, we can list the developmental patterns in the letter as

Point 1 (paragraph 2)
    1–2: opinion, authority
Point 2 (paragraph 3)
    2–3: fact, analogy
Point 3 (paragraphs 4, 5)
    3–4: illustration
    3–5: fact/opinion, illustration
Point 4 (paragraph 6)
    4–6: illustration
Point 5 (paragraph 7)
    5–7: fact, authority
Point 6 (paragraph 8)
    6–8: cause and effect

Step 4: *Fill in missing premises if necessary and check argument for formal and informal fallacies.* As we can see from our developmental profile, the letter has a mix of patterns, but appeals to authority, fact and opinion, and illustration predominate. So in applying this step we should be especially mindful of illegitimate use of these devices: false authority, irrelevant reason, unsubstantiated opinion, and hasty conclusions.

In applying this step you may wish to note fallacies right on the essay itself. This is all right. But in all fairness, criticism should be justified; and *justification requires a word or two of explanation for calling a claim fallacious.* Sometimes the margins provide enough space for this, but usually they don't. So we'll leave the essay unmarked and transcribe our critical remarks elsewhere. Incidentally, implementing this step in longer argument analysis can really be fun if you approach it from the viewpoint of honing your analytical powers and gaining knowledge of a subject. But the most gratification is derived from establishing a measure of intellectual control over the argumentative messages people send you. With the control comes confidence in your ability to respond intelligently to argumentative discourse, to reject or espouse on rational grounds the opinions served up to you.

The following analysis is not intended to exhaust the euthanasia issue, or even the letter in question. Nor is any claim made for its being an unimpeachable critique. Far from it. Indeed, you're invited to react critically to the analysis: to question and amend it, and above all, to view the analysis as an attempt to provide some logical basis for accepting or rejecting the proposition thesis *as it is advanced by its author.* The italicized clause is very important. It means that for purposes of evaluation, we are to consider only what the author offers— not what our own personal feelings may be or additional supporting material the author failed to include. This means that we must set aside our own opinion about the author's thesis and be as objective as we possibly can be in evaluating his letter.[9] That's no easy task, for as we've seen elsewhere, we all have a tendency toward provincialism, to overlook weaknesses in claims we support, to harp on and exaggerate them in claims we don't support. Our job is simply to judge the merit of the extended argument as it appears. This means that we could assess

[9]Review Rational Reconstruction and Validity in Chapter 15.

an extended argument as unsound, uncompelling, *while at the same time happening to agree with the thesis*.

One other point: The letter isn't filled with technical material. In some essays, including those on euthanasia, the technical material is forest-thick. Nevertheless, most times we don't need an expert's knowledge of a subject to respond intelligently to the messages around us. An abusive *ad hominem*, a *false authority*, or a *bad analogy* are fallacious appeals, whether they appear in articles dealing with familiar subjects or ones whose subject matter mystifies us. Whatever the subject, usually we can raise intelligent questions based on the principles of correct argument when we suspect those principles are being flouted. Now, let's go to our letter.

Point 1 (paragraph 2). Point 1–2 views euthanasia as a form of killing. We can take this as a fact based on definition. But that such "killing is wrong" is an *opinion*, not a fact. It's a value judgment that needs considerable justification, and probably qualification. Clearly, the letter is implying that *all* killing is wrong, from which it would follow that euthanasia, a form of killing, is wrong. But what about killing in self-defense or in capital punishment? If the author considers that either of these or any other form of killing is justifiable, he can't hold that "all killing is wrong." If all killing is not wrong, euthanasia may not be wrong. If, upon questioning, the author admits that not all killing is wrong but that euthanasia is wrong, he must be prepared to demonstrate this belief. In any event, he leaves his value judgment as an *unsupported opinion*. Well, not entirely. He mentions the Bible. But since there's both disagreement about the warranty of the Bible as an infallible source of knowledge and the wrongness of euthanasia, this appeal to authority must be considered a *false* one. Besides, the author's reference to "that point" is *ambiguous*. "That point" can refer to the assertion that "euthanasia is killing" or that "killing is wrong" or both. The reference to "it" in "forbidden it" must refer to euthanasia since society has not always forbidden every form of killing. But that society has always forbidden euthanasia is an appeal to traditional wisdom; although we can take the claim as fact, that fact doesn't demonstrate that society has been *justified* in always condemning euthanasia or that its continued prohibition of it is defensible. Our author does seize on a crucial assumption made by many who support the legalization of voluntary euthanasia: that individuals have absolute rights over their bodies. Unfortunately, rather than refuting the claim, he assails it with an *abusive ad hominem*: "simply foolish."

Conclusions about the support offered for point 1: The point that euthanasia is wrong because it's killing goes unsubstantiated because the supporting material rests on a number of fallacious appeals, including false authority, traditional wisdom, ambiguity, and ad hominem.

Point 2 (paragraph 3). Point 2–3 does report accurately that those who favor the legalization of euthanasia often hypothesize cases in which terminal patients have developed a tolerance to drugs that have been administered over a long period of time. The letter makes fair use of the analogy. But the paragraph sets up a *false dilemma*: Either consent is obtained when patients are drugged or when they're crazed with pain after drugs have been withdrawn. Presumably, either way the choice isn't voluntary. There is, however, another situational possibility: when patients are not yet suffering pain but are faced with imminent death. Of course, the author could reply that the consent of patients in such situations is an uninformed and anticipatory consent, and that patients can't or shouldn't commit themselves to be killed in the future. Still, there may be cases in which patients not under pain indicate a desire for ultimate euthanasia and reaffirm that request when under pain. No matter, the question of what constitutes consent is a tricky one that can't be dismissed in the false dilemma that this letter serves up. This doesn't necessarily mean that the author is incorrect in his assertion, but that he hasn't engaged those cases in which consent seems at least possible. Nor has he attempted to define precisely what he means by "consent."

Conclusions about the support offered for point 2. The point that it's impossible to ascertain that consent is voluntary goes unsubstantiated because the support offered relies exclusively on a false dilemma.

Point 3 (paragraphs 4, 5). Point 3–4 offers the first of two reasons for claiming that legalizing euthanasia is unwise. The first suggests that patients who face a death decision might give consent only to relieve their family's trouble of caring for them. Although in some cases this may be true, we are offered no other support to defend this implied generalization than one personal illustration. And yet, in arguing against legislation, it seems reasonable to ask that the proposed legislation, which is intended to enlarge personal liberty, be shown to jeopardize large numbers of patients in the way the letter suggests. That demonstration lacking, the conclusion that patients will be opting for euthanasia out of guilt seems to be a *hasty conclusion* or *faulty generalization*. A more subtle point relates to the questionable assumption underlying this argument: that deciding to die because of the inordinate hardships one's protracted suffering is causing one's family is somehow an impure motive that discredits the patient and family alike. This is a *value judgment that needs support*.

Point 3–5 presumably attempts to show that legalizing euthanasia is unwise because it will put undue stress on the families of the terminally ill. But again, a single illustration doesn't warrant such a *sweeping generalization,* which is what the letter seems to be implying. Furthermore, the author conceals or ignores the fact that under current law families feel stress that sometimes strains the limits of human endurance. (Curiously, he implies this point in the preceding paragraph when he argues that patients will opt for euthanasia out of concern for their suffering families.) True, faced with a euthanasia decision for a loved one, a family will confront an agonizing decision. But is such a decision any more stressful than what they're currently faced with: standing by helpless as their loved ones suffer a painful death?

Conclusions about the support offered for point 3: The point that allowing a death decision would be unwise for patient and family alike goes unsubstantiated. The support offered seems to *conceal evidence* and lead only to a *hasty conclusion*.

Point 4 (paragraph 6). Point 4–6 uses an illustration to make the point of mistaken diagnoses. But is the illustration typical? Surely the number of correct diagnoses outnumber incorrect ones. To conclude on the basis of this *single example* that diagnoses of terminal diseases are typically mistaken or in large number mistaken appears to be a *hasty conclusion*. It also smacks of an *appeal to fear*. The point may be that even the slightest possibility of miscalculation should discourage the legalization of euthanasia. But by the same token, what about the many medical procedures and operations that are performed daily? There's always present a risk of misdiagnosis, in which case patients can be harmed, sometimes irreparably. Indeed, any operation carries a risk to life; often the risk is grave. The medical profession itself admits that too many operations and medical procedures are unnecessary. What are we to say of all this? That medical procedures shouldn't be allowed? It is true that euthanasia is unique in that its object is not to save or prolong life but to end it. But euthanasia also aims to end pain, and the saving of pain is widely considered to be a legitimate aim of medical practice. The letter's author might object that we don't know for sure that euthanasia, in fact, effects a net saving of pain. But how are we to find out? Apparently by trying euthanasia. To dismiss summarily the possibililty that euthanasia may result in a net saving of pain is to commit the fallacy of invincible ignorance. Finally, it's possible to question the relevancy of this whole point. After all, the issue of mistaken diagnosis is a medical, not a legal, one. Even if there were a high likelihood of mistaken diagnoses of terminal diseases, is that relevant to the question of whether or not individuals should have a legal right to euthanasia?

Conclusions about the support offered for point 4: The point that mistaken diagnoses are possible is obviously true. But the letter has failed to demonstrate precisely why this possibility argues against the legalization of euthanasia. Even if it does, the single example given is not enough to warrant the generalization that *mistaken diagnoses* of terminal diseases are rather commonplace. If the generalization isn't intended, the letter must demonstrate why the atypical mistaken diagnosis should be used to deny euthanasia to what may be large numbers of correctly diagnosed patients who may desire it.

Point 5 (paragraph 7).   Point 5–7 argues that if euthanasia is legalized some patients may end up being killed when relief or cure is "just around the corner." "Just around the corner" is *vague.* Does it mean a day before, a week before, a month before, a year before, or several years before relief or cure is discovered? The phrase isn't only obscure; it effectively *conceals the fact* that when medical discoveries are made, some time passes before the new drugs are available for widespread use. It's not as if one day we haven't a clue about a cure for liver cancer, but the next day we have the cure itself. In the interim between discovery and general availability of drugs, the euthanasia option could be halted for those affected; or at least those affected could be informed. In addition, the author *conceals the fact* that relief or cure would apply only to those in the group to whom the discovery applies. Are we to leave the remainder to suffer in order to preclude risk to these patients? In any event, the letter leaves this point undeveloped. It relies instead on an appeal to authority, which although legitimate, simply reiterates the point, which is a rather obvious one to begin with.

Conclusions about the support offered for point 5: The point that relief or cure may be imminent suffers from vagueness. It also conceals evidence.

Point 6 (paragraph 8).   Point 6–8 uses the "wedge" argument to argue against the legalization of euthanasia. The argument is made that should voluntary euthanasia be legalized, various forms of involuntary euthanasia will necessarily follow. But there's nothing inevitable about this chain of events at all. There's no reason to expect that the other issues can't and won't be taken up individually, if in fact they ever arise. The argument's a *slippery slope*.

Conclusions about the support offered for point 6: The point that legalizing euthanasia will lead to abuses is not substantiated because the support offered relies on a *slippery slope*.

Step 5: *Assess the argument as compelling or not compelling.* If step 4 has been implemented correctly and thoroughly, in most cases this final step should present few problems. Respecting the letter to the editor, if we're correct in our analysis, it's evident that none of its points is supported adequately. Therefore, this essay is not compelling. This in no way implies disagreement with the author's thesis but only that in the view of one analyst, he has failed to justify it.

SUMMARY

This chapter dealt with the extended argument, a longer piece of discourse that combines argument and persuasion to compel the listener or reader to adopt another position, another manner of thinking, or another solution to a problem. Its form generally includes the following elements: (1) an analysis of a problem, (2) a proposed solution developed or supported by factual and logical details and evidence, (3) a refutation of the opposing position, and (4) a concluding restatement of the proposed solution. As for its specific content, the extended argument contains the following ingredients: a thesis proposition, main points, organization, and developmental patterns. Respecting the developmental patterns, we can isolate a half dozen key ones: fact and opinion, illustrations, authority, analogy, cause and effect, and statistics. Finally, we developed a strategy for dealing with the extended argument. We called it the paragraph scrutiny strategy, or PS for short. The PS strategy consists of the following steps: (1) prereading the extended argument for the thesis proposition, (2) reading the argument for main supporting points, (3) indicating the developmental patterns used to present the main points, (4) filling in missing premises if necessary and checking for formal and informal fallacies, and (5) judging the extended argument as compelling or not compelling.

Summary Question
We encounter extended arguments regularly, if not daily. The best way to hone any *skill* is through practice. So a most effective way to retain the practical logic skills we've learned is to apply them to arguments in real life. Watch for extended arguments involving any currently controversial topic. Letters to the editor; opinion and editorial pages of newspapers; public addresses; and magazines such as *Harper's, Atlantic Monthly, New Review, Mother Jones,* and so on are fertile sources. With a little practice, applying the PS strategy can become second nature. Then, not only are we in a better position to avoid being mislead, life gets more interesting, too.

Two essays follow. Evaluate them, using the PS strategy.

Living Happily Against the Odds[10]

FRANK TRIPPETT

Inflation. Recession. Iran. Cuba. Unemployment. Taxes. Et cetera. Et cetera. Given the number, gravity and persistence of their country's problems, Americans obviously need occasional relief from national worries so that they can at least try to enjoy their lives as individuals. Yet is has become harder and harder for people to find anything to do or use that does not come with some built-in anxiety. The trouble is that everywhere they turn these days, one thing or another is posted with the red flag of danger, if not with the skull and crossbones of mortal horror.

Such is the impression created by America's all-purpose early alert system. Day after day the air bleats and print blinks with warnings and alarms. Cancer alerts have become almost as commonplace as weather reports. Strictures on how to avoid heart attacks pop up everywhere. Preventive campaigns stir up a constant din of sermons against careless driving, against starting fires, against getting too fat. It is like the continual murmur of doom's own voice.

The symphony of warnings even has elaborate seasonal variations. Christmas, for instance, is the time to avoid giving little Johnny toys that can maim or pajamas treated with carcinogenic flameproofing. But every season brings fresh cautions against some new menacing gunk found in air, water, food, medicines. This year alerts were raised about stuffs used to treat dandruff, insomnia, alcoholism and high blood pressure.

Clearly, the U.S. is now buffeted by a public atmosphere that has grown chronically and pervasively cautionary. Apprehensive outcries wail forth from broadcasts, newspapers, magazines, posters, labels, environmental journals, medical tracts, Government reports, even books. One of the books is a brand-new broadside by Dr. Charles T. McGee, a clinical ecologist of Alamo, Calif., who is quoted above. His 220-page polemic issues a general alarm about multifarious dangers that lurk in every nook and cranny of contemporary civilization. Even fluorescent lighting, he says, may, in some weird way, weaken the muscles. The book, billed as a "crash course in protecting your health from hidden hazards of modern living," is entitled *How to Survive Modern Technology*. Anybody with a frail heart might not even survive the book.

Admittedly modern times are fraught with real hazards, and no sensible person would sniff at prudent precautions. Still, it is hard not to shudder at the sheer volume of disquieting cautions, at the constancy, variety and intensity of the fearful clamor. Indeed, one may reasonably wonder whether the very climate of alarm itself has not become a hazard to health and serenity.

Everybody's psyche now takes a drubbing day in and out from the concatenations of danger. An American can scarcely make a move nowadays without being pushed into a state of alert. Warning about nutrients left out of the diet are as grave as those about pollutants included. Scotch and beer have joined the list of potables that may contain dangerous chemicals. So has mother's milk, in which PCBs have turned up. Birth defects could be linked to caffeine from coffee or any source, it was reported just last month. Even peanut butter, as an occasional bearer of aflatoxin, has been flagged as a menace. Driving? Fasten the seat belt—unless discouraged by warnings that most of them do not work. On the road, even restroom signs often gratuitously warn against VD. Flying? Remember that some passengers get ozone poisoning in those high-altitude supersonic jets. Sleeping? Doing it too little or too much is associated with shortened life spans. Prettying up? It seems that some hair dyes, among other cosmetics, contains malignant agents. Need exercise? Take heed that middle-aged joggers are constantly falling dead on the side roads. Feeling sickly? Steer clear of surgery-mongering doctors. Taking a pill? Make sure it will not hook you. Worried about cancer? That very worry may cause cancer, some say. Anybody thinking of fleeing might peruse another recent book, this one by Dr. Robert A. Shakman. Its title: *Where You Live May Be Hazardous to Your Health*. Its implicit message: You can't escape.

Enough. A complete list of warnings would fill a shelf of books. Plainly the 20th century has turned into the Age of Admonition. It is also clear that the atmosphere is distributing more than a bit of anxiety. A modern form of morbid gallows humor ("Life is hazardous to your health"; "Everything causes cancer") has now become the respectable coin of small talk.

Only a recluse could fail to know somebody who uses less ingenuity in living than in worrying and guarding against subtle hazards. Perhaps the surest sign that the admonitory mood is taking a toll is the fact that Americans have begun to write advice columnists about the problems that all the cautions cause. Warnings about cholesterol in eggs, nitrate in bacon, caffeine in coffee (and, a while back, risky chemicals in even the decaffeinated variety) have sapped the fun out of eating breakfast for some people, it seems. Wrote one such: "I'd try bread and water, but I'm pretty sure that as soon as I begin to enjoy it, I'll find out it's bad for me."

Such hangdog pathos is enough to provoke wistful dreams of returning to the vanished day when a person was guided only by folk wisdom: an apple a day would keep the doctor away. But there is no going back. Today the apple must be checked for sprayed-on toxins. The alarm system is here to stay. It would be foolhardy as well as foolish to suggest that it be shut down; it is, in truth, indispensable for guiding those who wish guidance. What is needed is a strategy for getting through life passably happy despite all the ominous background chatter.

Though sophisticates have long sneered at him, Norman Vincent Peale, who said that "you do not need to be a victim of worry," was not entirely wrong. Thinkers more serious than Peale have construed a fearful attitude as a danger in itself. Jesus of Nazareth advised against fretting even about tomorrow. Psychologist William James saw life itself as a process of risk taking and thought it was debilitating to take risks too much to heart. He urged people to will themselves to be confident of survival, to pretend confidence if necessary, allowing not even the "sweet" cautions of scientists to undermine them.

Cynics may shrug at doctrines of willful optimism. Still, Americans have a right to be optimistic. After all, they are living longer and longer. Perhaps each new alarm should be coupled with a dire warning that life is likely to go on despite all the danger.

Is It Time To Stop Learning?[11]

DAVID S. SAXON

A strange new term has recently crept into our national vocabulary: overeducation. It is a term that would have confounded most Americans in every generation up to this Bicentennial year. For them, education was a social necessity to be provided, an individual good to be sought and an end to be sacrificed for. The only limits were the abilities and aspirations of students and the resources of the community.

What has happened in society today that gives rise to talk of overeducation? Have we actually reached and even passed the socially useful and individually rewarding limits of learning in America? Or have we somehow mislaid our proper measure of the broader values of education in a democratic society?

Let's examine this curious new term, overeducation. Overeducation for *what?* For a full and satisfying life? For a lifetime of changing careers in a rapidly changing world? For active participation in the affairs of a modern democratic government?

No, the term generally means that a person has received more learning, or other learning, than is required for his or her first major job. It may be a perfectly valid description of a person's education in relation to that particular circumstance. But that circumstance, though important, is not the whole of life. And the tendency to measure the value of education against this single, limited yardstick is disastrously shortsighted for both the individual and society.

Throughout our history, American education has been built to other measures, and the results have had a tremendous influence on the nation's development. One such measure has been the need for leadership based on ability and talent rather than rank. The Pilgrims, after just sixteen years of colonizing the New World wilderness, established Harvard College, declaring that "one of the next things we longed for, and looked after was to advance learning and perpetuate it to posterity; dreading to leave an illiterate ministry to the churches, when our present ministers shall lie in the dust." And Thomas Jefferson called for the education of "youth of talent" without regard for their social or economic status as "the keystone of the arch of our government."

Another measure has been the importance of universal education to a democratic society. Benjamin Franklin wrote that "nothing is of more importance for the public weal, than to firm and train up youth in wisdom and virtue. Wise and good men are, in my opinion, the strength of a state; much more so than riches and arms." A third measure has been the advantage of merging the practical and liberal arts. When Abraham Lincoln signed the land-grant college legislation of 1862, he set America on its course toward a distinctive model of higher education, not for the few but for the many, not as a cloister but as the active partner of agriculture and industry and all the other segments of a developing society.

And when Johns Hopkins University in 1876 joined undergraduate education with the most advanced graduate instruction and research, American education was extending its reach toward the farthest frontiers of scientific and scholarly discovery.

Building to these measures has produced in America an educational system that is in many ways unparalleled in history, and this is a healthy perspective from which to view our present shortcomings and the problems that lie ahead.

Certainly education in the United States is unmatched in its accessibility to the highest levels for the broadest cross section of the citizenry, though we have much farther to go in this respect. Our total educational structure is unequaled in its diversity—public and private institutions, religious and secular, local and statewide—and this rich diversity is our protection against control or conformity in the realm of ideas. And nowhere else has there been a more rapid transfer of scholarly discoveries through basic research to practical application.

But have we now, finally, reached the useful limits of our educational resources for many of our citizens? Can we now say to some of them, "You won't need any more formal learning for *your* role in society"? And to *which* Americans shall we say that their future working careers or their cultural horizons or their prospects for civic or political leadership don't seem to warrant the cost of a broad education beyond their immediate occupational needs?

I am painfully aware that academic leaders have themselves too often resorted to strictly economic appeals for support because these seemed easier to explain and justify than the less tangible purposes of learning. We have too often promised more than we could deliver on investments in research, and so have invited disappointed expectations and some disillusion with what education can offer in exchange for its considerable cost. But neither education nor society in general will benefit from a continuing rebuff for these sins.

To the extent that the level of education and society's ability to put it to use are out of balance, then what a peculiarly negative solution—what a tragic waste of human potential—to limit education and learning. Wouldn't it make far better sense to concentrate on how to use the full capacity of all of our citizens?

We need that capacity now. I think we are more in need of wisdom today than at most earlier stages of our history. A broad liberal education is not the only ingredient of wisdom, but it is an essential one. We need all the knowledge we can muster to meet our technological and scientific problems. We need all the accumulated experience and understanding of humanity we can absorb to meet our social problems. And I believe we can ill afford the risk of foreclosing the maximum cultivation of that knowledge and understanding simply because it seems not to be required for immediate vocational purposes.

America's vision for 200 years has been longer than that. Overeducation is an idea whose time must never come.

Glossary

Logical terms are sometimes used with special meanings by particular authors. The following definitions give the meanings that terms have in this book. The glossary is not intended to exhaust the logician's vocabulary but to give the beginning student a simplified list of foundational terms. Each definition is followed by a chapter reference.

abusive ad hominem (fallacy of)   An argument that attacks the person's character, not the person's argument. (5)

accent (fallacy of)   An argument whose justification depends on a shift in emphasis on a word or phrase. (4)

accident (fallacy of)   An argument that applies a general rule to a particular case where special circumstances make the rule inapplicable. (9)

amphiboly   A statement with more than one meaning because of ambiguous grammatical construction. (4)

analogy   A comparison whereby we indicate in what respects two things are similar. (9)

antecedent   In a hypothetical or conditional statement, the portion between the "if" and the "then." (16)

anxiety   The name for a pervasive, all-consuming, often unfocused sense of fear or panic. (2)

argument   A group of propositions, one of which is said to follow logically from the others. (1)

argument from analogy   An inductive argument in which a known similarity that two things share is used as evidence for concluding that the two things are similar in other respects. (9)

argument from ignorance (fallacy of)   An argument that uses an opponent's inability to disprove a conclusion as proof of the conclusion's correctness. (6)

authority   A source of knowledge that relies on an expert outside the self. (7)

begging the question (fallacy of)   An argument that uses same form of its own conclusion as part of the evidence offered to support that very conclusion. (5)

biased question (fallacy of)   An argument based on the answer to a question that is worded to draw a predetermined reply. (12)

biased sample (fallacy of)   An argument that contains a sample that is not representative of the population being studied. (12)

buzzwords   Vague words and phrases that create an impression of action, dynamism, and vitality without actually denoting anything. (3)

categorical proposition   A statement that relates two classes. (13)

causal argument   An argument that attempts to support a causal statement; in evaluating causal arguments, it's necessary to determine whether a relation between *A* and *B* actually exists and whether the relation is that type of causal relation claimed. (11)

causal statement   A statement that reduces to the claim that *A* causes *B*. (11)

circumstantial ad hominem (fallacy of)   An argument that attacks the circumstances of a person's life, not the person's position. (5)

cliché thinking   Occurs whenever a cliché is used uncritically as a premise in an argument or as a substitute for an argument. (4)

common practice (fallacy of)   An argument that attempts to justify wrongdoing on the basis of some practice that's become accepted; a variation of two wrongs make a right. (5)

complex question (fallacy of)   An argument that in asking a question assumes an answer to an unstated prior question. (5)

composition (fallacy of)   An argument that attributes to a whole characteristics of the parts. (4)

compound proposition   A statement that consists of more than one proposition, such as a disjunction or a hypothetical (conditional) statement. (16)

concealed evidence (fallacy of)   An argument that presents only facts that are favorable to its conclusion while suppressing relevant but nonsupporting facts. (12)

conclusion   In an argument, the proposition that is claimed to be logically entailed by the premise. (1)

connotation   In definition, the collection of properties shared by all and only those objects in a term's extension; also called *intension*. (3)

consequent   In a hypothetical or conditional proposition, the portion that follows the "then." (16)

contributory cause   A factor that helps create the total set of conditions, necessary or sufficient, for an effect. (11)

copula   In a standard-form categorical proposition, any form of the linking verb *to be,* which functions to relate subject (S) to predicate (P). (13)

correlation   A connection between properties that members of a group have; correlations don't necessarily imply causation; as distinguished from causal relations, a correlation is a relationship between properties that exist in some *actual* population and always implies a symmetrical relation, whereas a causal relation is defined in terms of a relation between two *hypothetical* versions of the real population and never implies a symmetrical relation. (11)

correspondence theory of truth   The belief that the truth consists of some form of correspondence between statements and facts. (7)

deduction   A mode of reasoning that refers to an argument whose conclusion is claimed to follow from its premises with logical certainty. (1, 7, 13)

defense mechanism   A strategy designed to support a favored self-concept despite contradictory fact. (2)

definition   An explanation of the meaning of a term. (3)

denotation   In definition, the collection or class of objects to which a term may correctly be applied; also called *extension*. (3)

dilemma   A syllogism that contains a hypothetical (conditional) premise and a disjunctive premise and either a categorical proposition (simple dilemma) or a disjunctive (complex dilemma) for a conclusion. (16)

disanalogy   In an argument from analogy, a significant, weakening difference between the things compared. (9)

disjunction   A compound proposition of the either-or form. (16)

disjunctive syllogism   A syllogism consisting of a disjunction and a categorical proposition as premises and another categorical proposition as a conclusion. (16)

disjuncts The propositions asserted by a disjunction. (16)

dismissal An argument that uses the assumption of superiority to advance a conclusion. (5)

dissimilarities In an argument from analogy, significant, strengthening differences between the things compared. (9)

distraction A psychological form of red herring by which we avoid a difficult or painful task, idea, or feeling by substituting a more palatable activity. (2)

emotional appeal An attempt to persuade without reasons. (2)

empiricism The philosophical view that experience is the primary source of knowledge. (7)

enthymeme A fragmented argument; a first-order enthymeme suppresses its major premise; second order, its minor premise; third order, its conclusion. (15)

equivocation (fallacy of) An argument that confuses the separate meanings of a word or phrase. (4) Equivocation can occur visually. (12)

euphemism A polite way of saying the blunt or offensive. (3)

extended argument A longer piece of discourse that combines argument and persuasion to compel the listener or reader to adopt another position, manner of thinking, or solution to a problem. (18)

fallacies of ambiguity Any argument whose errors arise from careless language usage. (4)

fallacies of assumption Arguments that are logically inadequate because they presume as true key assumptions that must be independently verified to establish their conclusions. (5)

fallacy A type of argument that may seem to be correct but isn't. (4, 5)

false analogy (fallacy of) An argument that makes an erroneous comparison. (9)

false authority (fallacy of) An argument that uses as authority one who is not actually expert in the field, uses expert opinion when there's not a consensus of expert opinion, or uses expert opinion when we can't at least in theory verify the claims for ourselves. (7)

false dilemma (fallacy of) An argument that erroneously reduces the number of possible alternatives or positions on an issue. (12)

fear or force (fallacy of) An argument that uses the threat of harm for the acceptance of a conclusion. (5)

figure The position of the middle term in a standard-form categorical syllogism;
Figure 1: M P Figure 2: P M Figure 3: M P Figure 4: P M
       S M S M M S M S. (13)

form In a standard-form categorical proposition, whether the proposition is A, E, I, or O; in a standard-form categorical syllogism, the argument's mood and figure. (13)

formal fallacies Violations of the rules for correct deductive argument. (5, 13, 14, 16)

fragment argument An enthymeme, that is, an incomplete argument. (15)

generalization A statement that covers many specifics. (9)

guilt by association (fallacy of) An argument in which people are judged guilty solely on the basis of the company they keep or the places they frequent. (9)

hairsplitting (trivial objection) A demand for more precision than is possible or necessary in a given case, either because of the nature of the case or its importance. (4)

hasty conclusion (fallacy of) An argument that draws a conclusion based on insufficient evidence. (9)

humor or ridicule (fallacy of) An argument that appeals strictly to humor or ridicule in attacking a position. (5)

hypothesis An empirical statement that finds justification outside ourselves, in the world (6); any unproved or untested assumption (10); in argument, any tentative conclusion that relates and explains a group of different items of information; a good hypothesis should be relevant, compatible with the accepted body of knowledge, testable, predictive, and simple. (10)

hypothetical (conditional) statement   A compound proposition consisting of the "If . . . then" form. (16)

hypothetical syllogism   A syllogism that contains a hypothetical statement as a premise; in a mixed hypothetical syllogism, the premises consist of a hypothetical statement and a categorical proposition; in a pure hypothetical syllogism, the premises consist of hypothetical statements exclusively. (16)

induction   A mode of reasoning that refers to arguments whose conclusions are claimed to be more or less probable. (1, 7, 9)

inductive generalization   A basic type of inductive argument whose conclusion is a generalization. (9)

informal fallacies   Commonplace errors we fall into because of careless language usage or inattention to subject matter. (4)

introjection   A process in which we internalize the values, beliefs, and experiences of others. (2)

invincible ignorance (fallacy of)   An argument that insists on the legitimacy of an idea or principle despite contradictory facts. (5)

jargon   The technical language of a trade, group, or profession. (3)

justification   The property of a well-constructed inductive argument. (1)

laws of logic   Principles presupposed in all human thought and experience. (6)

loaded epithets   An argument that substitutes questionable labels for reasons to advance a favored conclusion. (5)

logic   The study of the rules of correct argument. (1)

logical analogy   A common way to prove a syllogism invalid; it's constructed of the same form as the original syllogism but with premises known to be true and a conclusion known to be false; inadequate for establishing validity. (13)

magical thinking (fallacy of)   An argument that uncritically attributes causal power to thoughts and words. (11)

major premise   In a standard-form categorical syllogism, the premise that contains the major term. (13)

major term   In a standard-form categorical syllogism, the predicate of the conclusion. (13)

margin of error   In a poll or study, the degree to which a statistical generalization may be inaccurate. (12)

meaningless claim   Any argument or claim that is unverifiable either in theory or in this particular case because it contains a meaningless term or expression. (4)

method of agreement   In establishing probable causation, the method that states that if two or more instances of a phenomenon have only one circumstance in common, that circumstance is probably the cause (or the effect) of the phenomenon. (11)

method of concomitant variation   In establishing probable causation, the method that states that whenever a phenomenon varies in a particular way as another phenomenon varies in a particular way, a causal relationship probably exists between them. (11)

method of difference   In establishing probable causation, the method that states that if an instance when the phenomenon occurs and an instance when it doesn't occur have every circumstance in common except one, and that the circumstance occurs only in the former, that circumstance is probably the cause (or the effect) of the phenomenon. (11)

middle term   In a standard-form categorical syllogism, the term that appears in both premises. (13)

Mill's methods   Procedures for establishing probable causation: agreement, difference, concomitant variation; formalized by nineteenth-century English philosopher John Stuart Mill. (11)

minor premise   In a standard-form categorical syllogism, the premise that contains the minor term. (13)

minor term   In a standard-form categorical syllogism, the subject of the conclusion. (13)

modus ponens   Latin phrase for the valid procedure in hypothetical syllogisms consisting of affirming the antecedent, then affirming the consequent. (16)

modus tollens   Latin phrase for the valid procedure in hypothetical syllogisms consisting of denying the consequent, then denying the antecedent. (16)

mood   The order in which a standard-form categorical syllogism appears when properly arranged, that is, in the order of major premise, minor premise, conclusion. (13)

necessary cause   A condition that must be present if the effect is to occur. (11)

negative correlation   A connection between properties that members of a group have, such that B is negatively correlated with A, if and only if the percentage of B's among the A's is less than the percentage of B's among the non-A's. (11)

"new" sophistry   The deliberate use of fallacies, persuasive language, "powerbabble," manipulative techniques, and personal charisma to sell success, health, salvation, or well-being. (8)

nonnormative argument   An argument that contains only nonnormative statements. (17)

nonnormative statement   A true or false assertion used to express matters of empirical or logical fact. (17)

normative argument   An argument that contains a normative statement as a premise. (17)

normative statement   A statement that asserts a value judgment. (17)

objective claim   A proposition whose truth value is independent of any specific individual's knowledge, beliefs, or experiences. (6)

Occam's razor   The principle of taking the simplest explanation as the most likely one; the principle of parsimony; named after the fourteenth-century English philosopher William of Occam, who warned, "Entities should not be multiplied beyond necessity." (10)

outer senses   The senses of seeing, hearing, feeling, tasting, and touching. (7)

oversimplification (fallacy of)   An argument that treats a situation as if it involves only a few significant factors when in fact it involves a complex of many significant, interrelated facets. (11)

paragraph scrutiny (PS)   A strategy for evaluating an extended argument consisting of the following steps: (1) Preread the argument for thesis proposition; (2) read the argument for main supporting points; (3) indicate developmental patterns used to present main points (fact or opinion, illustrations, authority, analogy, cause and effect, statistics); (4) apply the four-step method of argument evaluation; (5) judge the extended argument as compelling or not compelling. (18)

parsimony   In science, the postulate of simplicity, that is, that one should take the simplest explanation as the most likely, other things being equal; Occam's razor. (10)

persuasive definition   A definition that departs from conventional word meaning to influence attitudes. (3)

pity (fallacy of)   An argument that uses pity to advance a conclusion. (5)

poisoning the well (fallacy of)   Occurs when, prior to deliberation, we place an opponent in a position that excludes an unwanted reply. (5)

popularity (fallacy of)   An argument that tries to justify something strictly by appeal to numbers. (7)

positioning (fallacy of)   An argument that tries to capitalize on the earned reputation of a leader in a given field for the purpose of selling something. (7)

positive correlation   A connection between properties that members of a group have, such that B is positively correlated with A if and only if the percentage of B's among A's is greater than the percentage of B's among the non-A's. (11)

post hoc (fallacy of)   An argument that asserts that one event is the cause of another from the mere fact that the first occurred earlier than the second; full name: *post hoc, ergo propter hoc*. (11)

predicate   In a standard-form categorical proposition, the class term expressed after the copula. (13)

prejudging   Arriving at a conclusion before pertinent experience. (2)

premise   In an argument, a proposition that is claimed to entail or help entail the conclusion. (1)

principle of charity   An element of rational reconstruction; the rule that whenever two possible interpretations of an argument are equally likely, one should choose the one that most strengthens the argument. (15)

projection   The process of attributing to others traits that we find undesirable in ourselves. (2)

proposition   A true or false statement. (1)

provincialism   An argument that views things exclusively in terms of one's own group loyalty or vested interest. (6)

pseudoneed   Any condition used as a substitute for a genuine need. (2)

pseudoscience   A term coined by Martin Gardner to refer to a certain category of theories, systems, and explanations, which though claiming to be "scientific," in fact use only the trappings of genuine science while avoiding the rigors of the checks and balances of the scientific method or the scrutiny of disinterested experts. (8)

psychobabble   The misuse of psychological terms and expressions referring to inner states and feelings. (3)

psychological denial   An attitude that refuses to acknowledge the true existence or nature of some unpleasant circumstance. (2)

psychological guilt   A feeling of discomfort that accompanies a perception of failure to act in accordance with our own values. (2)

psychological rationalization   A pseudojustification in which "reasons" are constructed for the sole purpose of justifying a desired conclusion. (2)

puffery   The use of obscure, technical, or complex words and grammar for the purpose of inflating the content of a claim. (3)

quality   In a standard-form categorical proposition, the negative or affirmative nature of the assertion. (13)

questionable causation (fallacy of)   An argument that asserts that a particular circumstance produces a particular phenomenon when there is, in fact, little or no evidence to support such a claim. (11)

randomness   The designation given to a sample drawn from a population in such a way that each member has an equal chance of being drawn. (9, 12)

random sample   A portion of the population drawn in such a way as to ensure that every population member has an equal chance of being selected. (12)

rationalism   The philosophical view that reason is the primary source of knowledge. (7)

red herring   The deliberate introduction of a logically separate and irrelevant issue into a discussion for purposes of deception. (5)

sample   A selection from the population to be generalized about. (12)

scapegoating   A pseudojustification that singles out an innocent individual or group to blame for some undesired condition. (2)

scientific method   A way of investigating a phenomenon that is based on the collection, analysis, and interpretation of evidence to determine the most probable explanation; it consists of (1) a statement of the problem, (2) collection of facts, (3) formulation of a hypothesis, (4) further inferences, (5) identification of inferences. (10)

self-concept   The impression we have of the kind of person we are. (2)

self-supporting premise   One that the arguer does not state (even indirectly) in the fragmented argument, but one taken for granted as helping to entail the conclusion. (15)

sex (fallacious appeal to)   An argument that uses sexual feelings to advance its conclusion. (5)

singular proposition   A proposition that affirms or denies that a particular individual or entity falls within a class. (15)

slang   The language that a large portion of a group often uses and always understands but doesn't consider good, formal usage. (3)

slippery slope (fallacy of)   An argument that objects to a position on the erroneous belief that the position, if taken, will set off a chain of events that ultimately will lead to undesirable action. (11)

sorites   A string of enthymemes. (15)

soundness   The property of an inductive argument that is justified; the property of a deductive argument that's both valid and true. (1)

standard-form categorical proposition   An assertion that relates two classes in one of the following forms: A, All S is P; E, No S is P; I, Some S is P; O, Some S is not P. (13)

standard-form categorical syllogism   A deductive argument that consists of three standard-form categorical propositions and three terms, each of which appears in exactly two of its propositions and is so arranged that the major premise is followed by the minor premise, which, in turn, is followed by the conclusion. (13)

statistical generalization   A statement that asserts that something is true of a percentage of a class. (9)

stereotyping   A phenomenon that occurs when we overlook an individual's unique qualities by viewing him or her only according to a rigid preconception. (2)

stipulative definition   A definition that attaches unique, or at least unconventional, meaning to a term. (3)

stratified random sample   A sampling technique in which relevant strata within the group are identified and a random sample from each stratum is selected in proportion to the number of members in each stratum. (12)

straw man (fallacy of)   An argument that so alters a position that the result is easier to attack than the original. (5)

stress   A state of tension caused by the body's reaction to both internal and external stimuli. (2)

subject   In a standard-form categorical proposition, the class term that appears between the quantifier (*all, no, some*) and the copula (some form of the verb *to be*); in a standard-form categorical syllogism, the subject of the conclusion. (13)

subjective claim   A proposition whose truth value is dependent on the knowledge, beliefs, and experiences of a specific individual. (6)

sufficient cause   Any condition that of itself will bring about a specific effect. (11)

syllogism   A deductive argument that contains two premises and a conclusion. (13)

thesis proposition   In an extended argument, a statement of the main idea together with the author's attitude toward it. (18)

traditional wisdom (fallacy of)   An argument that uses the past to justify claims about the present. (7)

tu quoque (fallacy of)   A version of the ad hominem fallacy in which an argument charges a person with acting in a manner that's inconsistent with the position the person is advocating. (5)

two wrongs make a right   An argument that attempts to justify what's considered wrong by appealing to other instances of the same action. (5)

universal (strong) generalization   A statement that asserts that something is true of all members of a class. (9)

unknowable fact (fallacy of)   An argument that contains a premise that's unknowable, either in principle or in a particular case. (6)

validity The property of a deductive argument whose premises logically entail its conclusion. (1)

Venn diagrams A graphic method of testing the validity of categorical syllogisms by using interlocking circles. (14)

weak generalization A statement that asserts that something is true of some members of a class. (9)

Answers to Selected Exercises

CHAPTER 1

EXERCISE 1-1

1. Nonargument
2. Argument
   Premise: He was miles away when the crime occurred.
   Conclusion: Jones cannot be the murderer.
3. Nonargument
4. Argument
   Premise: Our existence as an autonomous nation is at stake.
   Conclusion: We must begin to develop alternative energy sources.
5. Argument
   Premise: Most doctors want to set their own fees.
   Conclusion: Doctors are natural opponents of socialized medicine.
6. Argument
   Premise: Nobody will take advice but everybody will take money.
   Conclusion: Money is better than advice.
7. Argument
   Premise: Those who criticize and disrupt a nation are its enemies.
   Conclusion: Political dissenters have no place in our society.
8. Argument
   Premise: Those inside can't get out, and those outside don't want to get in.
   Conclusion: There's no good reason for a fence around a cemetery.
9. Argument
   Premise: I've read enough of what you've written.
   Conclusion: I know you'll understand what I'm going to say.

10. Argument
    Premise: Because of all its breaks and cuts, and the inattention, except for action and spinning the dial to find some action. . . .
    Conclusion: It's possible that television viewing is partly responsible for destruction of the narrative sense.
11. Argument
    Premise: In politics nothing happens by chance.
    Conclusion: If it happens, you can bet it was planned that way.
12. Either nonargument or argument. Nonargument if Erikson is merely explaining the nature of the paradox; argument if he's providing justification for the claim.
    Premise: Each man calls his body a separate body, a self-conscious individuality, a personal awareness of the cosmos, and a certain death; and yet he shares this world as a *reality* also perceived and judged by others and as an actuality within which he must commit himself to ceaseless interaction.
    Conclusion: The Golden Rule obviously concerns itself with one of the very basic paradoxes of human existence.
13. Argument
    Premise: We naturally hate whatever makes us despise ourselves.
    Conclusion: It is no wonder that we as often dislike others for their virtues as for their vices.
14. Argument
    Premise: [The cars are] from New York, New Jersey, and Ohio. . . .

Willy's, a bar-restaurant stuffed into an old converted house . . . sounds like a Sunset Strip joint on Saturday night. . . .
Conclusion: Something is very much out of kilter here.

15. Argument

ADDITIONAL EXERCISES

1. a. Argument
   Premise: We can know only our own experiences of things.
   Conclusion: We can't ever be sure that things really exist.

   b. Argument
   Premise: Statistics indicate that speeders have a greater chance of having accidents than those who don't speed.
   Conclusion: It's unwise to exceed posted speed limits.

   c. Argument
   Premise: History indicates that nations divided against themselves don't last long.
   Conclusion: Whether or not we survive depends on whether we can solve internal problems.

   d. Argument
   Premise: The victim is perceived . . . degraded to a mechanism.
   Conclusion: The coarsest type of humor is the practical joke.

   e. Argument
   Premise: The ultimate . . . impulse to destroy.
   Conclusion: We don't destroy . . . but to destroy.

   f. Nonargument

   g. Nonargument

   h. Argument
   Premise: The third group . . . highest values.
   Conclusion: An apparently . . . realization of values.

   i. Nonargument

   j. Argument
   Premise: Like the American . . . actual living.
   Conclusion: They consequently . . . cognitive experience.

   k. Nonargument

Premise: You simply raise the young in a pond and release them; they range out to sea, using their own energies, grow, and then come back.
Conclusion: The shad, perhaps, or any fish that runs upriver would be ideal for sea ranching.

l. Argument
   Premise: For many men ere now. . . time of it.
   Conclusion: Best take life easily . . . have no fear.

CHAPTER 2

EXERCISE 2-1

Answers will vary.

EXERCISE 2-2

Discussion will vary.
1. physical needs
2. physical, actualizing, and emotional
3. actualizing
4. actualizing
5. actualizing

EXERCISE 2-4

Discussion will vary.
1. projection, introjection
2. projection
3. introjection
4. scapegoating
5. scapegoating
6. introjection

CHAPTER 3

EXERCISE 3-1

1. Will vary. A good source is Rom Harre, Jane Morgan, and Christopher O'Neill, *Nicknames: Their Origins and Social Consequences.* (London: Routledge and Kegan Paul, 1979); also, Rom Harre, "What's in a Nickname?" *Psychology Today*, January 1980, pp. 79–84.

2. "Be good" encourages a moral or ethical outlook; "be wise" stresses the importance of knowledge, learning, and

understanding; "be friendly" suggests the importance of social interaction; "be in line" emphasizes order and regimentation; "That is not the Hopi way" implies a tolerance of others but at the same time a commitment to one's own outlook.

3. a. *Concept:* peace
      Reality: war

   b. *Concept:* a harmless move
      Reality: an uprooting of entire villages, usually by force

   c. *Concept:* an important village
      Reality: a village targeted for bombing

   d. *Concept:* restrained, defensive
      Reality: bombing until the enemy is sufficiently weakened or destroyed

   e. *Concept:* destruction of forest or jungle
      Reality: destruction, usually with napalm, of a jungle and, of course, everything in it

4. The attorney general apparently thinks that language can easily be divorced from action. The consequences of such a belief are many: (1) a kind of "doublespeak" and "doublethink"; (2) an erosion of the public's confidence in their leaders—the so-called "credibility gap"; (3) a sullying of truth-telling on a national and personal level.

5. Some wider ramifications: (1) Important, even crucial, issues are perceived at least subconsciously as a "game"; war is anything but a "game" for those who must fight in it. (2) An obsession with "winning" eclipses concern with justice, equality, liberty, e.g., the Watergate scandal. (3) The substantive is trivialized when viewed as a game. (4) Options and solutions are limited by the parameters of the game comparison.

EXERCISE 3-3 _____

1. persuasive   5. persuasive
2. persuasive   6. stipulative
3. persuasive   7. persuasive
4. persuasive   8. stipulative

(Note: One could argue that some definitions contain elements of both. For example, in the light of Marx and Engels's entire work, their persuasive definition, 7, could also be stipulative.)

EXERCISE 3-5 _____

Answers will vary; possibilities include

1. problem breath
2. sleep with, spend the night
3. pleasingly plump, heavy
4. wiry, thin, slim, lean
5. being well-to-do, wealthy, or "comfortable"
6. the remains, the dearly departed
7. appropriating or "borrowing"
8. "interesting"
9. misspeaking, making a "misstatement," "bending the truth"
10. having an affair

EXERCISE 3-7 _____

Answers will vary; possibilities include

1. cram, hit the books
2. cram
3. snap, piece of cake, Mickey Mouse
4. bitch, bear
5. bonehead
6. sneak a peak, "use notes"
7. flunk
8. ace
9. pop quiz or test
10. turkey, dork, Klutz, goof
11. kiss up, brown nose
12. egghead, brain, booker
13. snow job or simply to pad it
14. jock
15. cut class

EXERCISE 3-9 _____

1. sissy, fruit, queer, flit, limp wrist
2. butch, dyke
3. Most likely the first list is larger, possibly because of greater sexual insecurity among American males than

females or more narrowly defined sex roles for American men than women.

EXERCISE 3-11 _____

Answers will vary. There may also be overlap between slang and popularized use of jargon; possibilities include

1. sock hop, cheek to cheek, LP, sour note
2. heavy, bitchin', blast, Lip Synch, to play "air guitar," into the ozone
3. hip, hep, cool, dude, daddio, chick, jazzy, jazzed up, cat, juke joint, juke box
4. longhair, opera buff
5. c 'n w, countrified, honky tonk, goat roper
6. boogie, boogie woogie (considerable overlap with jazz)
7. chow, chow down, chow hound, scarf up, grub, good eats, greasy spoon, shake, fries, burgers
8. 3-D, TV, phone, dual carbs, turbo charged, energized

CHAPTER 4 _____

EXERCISE 4-1 _____

1. vague
2. ambiguous
3. vague and ambiguous
4. ambiguous (perhaps also meaningless)
5. ambiguous
6. ambiguous
7. ambiguous
8. ambiguous
9. ambiguous
10. vague
11. ambiguous
12. ambiguous
13. ambiguous
14. ambiguous
15. ambiguous (play on *bloc*/*block*)

EXERCISE 4-3 _____

1. amphiboly: cannot be corrected without more context

2. amphiboly: "Accused American spies to be put on trial by Iranian court"
3. amphiboly: Would you be angry with me if I told you that you had a beautiful body?
4. hairsplitting
5. equivocation on "no illness"; "no illness is worse than cancer" is amphibolous
6. equivocation on "every third": change to "One-third of the children born . . ."
7. meaningless claim
8. amphiboly caused by unclear reference of "it"
9. equivocation on "order"
10. Prisoner equivocates on both "anything" and "held against you"

CHAPTER 5 _____

EXERCISE 5-1 _____

1. ad hominem (circumstantial and abusive)
2. sex
3. mob appeal
4. ad hominem (circumstantial), poisoning the well
5. mob appeal, fear or force
6. pity
7. fear or force
8. ad hominem (*tu quoque*)
9. ad hominem (circumstantial)
10. fear or force
11. humor, ridicule
12. mob appeal, possibly fear or force
13. pity

EXERCISE 5-3 _____

1. red herring
2. straw man
3. straw man, ridicule
4. two wrongs
5. common practice
6. interviewer creates a distorted view of playing basketball by characterizing it

as "putting a basketball through a hoop"; this can be treated as humor/ridicule; Slats resorts to common practice

7. two wrongs

8. common practice

CHAPTER 6 _____

EXERCISE 6-1 _____

1. a. No
   b. Yes
   c. Yes
   d. No
   e. No, if "something tells me" is taken to be the equivalent of "I have a feeling" or "I think."
   f. Context is important here. Where one is about "to be sick" in the sense of vomiting, the statement can be viewed as an expression of belief and can be accepted. When "to be sick" is intended strictly as a forecast of a condition in the less than immediate future, more is needed than simply belief.

2. a. Disagree. The truth of a proposition does not depend on anyone's knowing it. Whether or not anyone knows it is irrelevant to whether or not there is life in outer space.
   b. Disagree. A proposition must be viewed in the time in which it's asserted. Any proposition, including the one about the United States, must be understood as implying a time reference. Thus, we really have two propositions: "(In this year of 1950) the United States is composed of forty-eight states," and "(In this year of 1981) the United States is composed of fifty states." Each proposition is true.
   c. Agree.
   d. Disagree. A true proposition is true *for* everyone but certainly may not be true *of* everyone (see preceding question). The statement "Persons under twenty-one not admitted" is true for everyone; that is, it applies to everyone.
   e. Disagree: fallacy of argument from ignorance

ADDITIONAL EXERCISES _____

1. ignorance

2. Susan: provincialism
   Jim: unknowable fact

3. unknowable fact

4. provincialism

5. unknowable fact

6. ignorance and provincialism

7. unknowable fact

8. provincialism

9. provincialism

10. possibly provincialism, but given Sirica's attempts at impartiality, probably not

11. provincialism

12. no fallacy

13. unknowable fact, provincialism ("Mischief making" is from the U.S. viewpoint); also, *Time* relies exclusively on the report of a *Time* reporter

14. unknowable fact

15. unknowable fact

16. ignorance

17. provincialism

18. may or may not be provincialism

19. provincialism

20. just an expression of opinion—it is not yet ignorance

21. unknowable fact

22. provincialism

23. unknowable fact (also circular)

24. provincialism

25. provincialism: each expert ultimately sees the problem only in terms of his or her own bailiwick

CHAPTER 7 _____

EXERCISE 7-1 _____

1. are: inner experience

2. are not: judgment needs to be verified against objective criteria

3. are not: person over there needs to be consulted

4. are: this person is claiming to have a particular experience, and the correctness of such a claim is more than a matter of inner conviction

5. are not: solution must be tested

6. are: basically a report of personal, inner experience

7. are not: high blood pressure is an objective condition

8. are not

9. are not: needs verification in terms of your behavior, if not in terms of your statements

10. are: presumably the speaker is accurately reporting a conviction

EXERCISE 7-3 _____

1. yes

2. no: no consensus; can't verify for self without appealing to additional authorities

3. yes: the statement asserts what many theologians believe and *not* that hell exists

4. yes: the statement asserts what the Bible claims and *not* that hell exists; there's probably consensus of biblical opinion that the Bible asserts this, although the opinion is far from universal

5. yes, if "cause" is taken in a contributory sense; that is, that together with oral bacteria sugar contributes to tooth decay; no, if "cause" is taken in the sense of necessary or

sufficient by itself: that is, decay cannot occur in the absence of sugar, or the presence of sugar is enough to produce tooth decay

6. no: violates all criteria for sound authority

7. yes

8. no: no consensus

9. yes

10. no: no consensus

11. no: no consensus

12. yes, if "result" implies a contributory cause to crisis or a necessary cause; no, if "result" implies the sole cause

13. yes and no, as explained in 5

14. yes

15. no: no consensus

16. no: no consensus

17. yes, if consensus among experts

18. yes

19. yes: but comparing two disparate musical styles; will be difficult to find pool of experts that is not limited or biased in favor of rock or classical music

20. yes

21. yes, once there is a consensus

22. yes

23. yes

24. no: no consensus

25. yes

ADDITIONAL EXERCISES _____

1. a. popularity
b. false authority, popularity
c. legitimate authority
d. false authority
e. traditional wisdom
f. popularity
g. popularity
h. positioning
i. popularity
j. false authority
k. traditional wisdom, popularity
l. popularity
m. traditional wisdom
n. legitimate authority

o. positioning
p. popularity
q. traditional wisdom
r. positioning
s. false authority
t. positioning
u. traditional wisdom
v. popularity
w. false authority
x. false authority
y. false authority, originally; Fonda may have become a legitimate authority through experience and education

2. a. yes
   b. yes
   c. no: no consensus
   d. no: no consensus; in fact, the consensus argues to the contrary
   e. yes
   f. yes

3. a. no
   b. no
   c. no
   d. yes, provided the studying and pondering were exhaustive, there's a basis for formulating this "educated hunch"

4. a. sense
   b. authority
   c. reason
   d. sense, authority
   e. reason
   f. reason
   g. sense, authority
   h. authority, sense
   i. sense
   j. sense, authority
   k. authority, sense
   l. reason
   m. reason
   n. reason

CHAPTER 8 _____

EXERCISE 8-1 _____

1. a. Characteristic 1: Cater seems to have worked in isolation from colleagues as evidenced by amateurish writing style, use of private publisher.
   Characteristic 2: refers to stunning "the layman. . . ."
   Characteristic 3: "one of the original thinkers of the 20th century. . . ."
   Characteristic 4: Cater claims that his revelations will "make a shambles of currently popular, and universally accepted ideas of conventional science. . . ."
   Characteristic 6: "Not since Velikovsky . . ."; says he is not likely to endear himself to the scientific community.
   Characteristic 7: see characteristic 4; "He defiles [sic?] the orthodox scientist for keeping the status quo. . . ." (Do you think "defiles"

was meant to be "defies"? Could this be an example of the infamous "Freudian slip"?)

   b. Isolationism: avoids the scrutiny of disinterested experts; implies that money—not truth—was Simon & Schuster's main interest; Taller's motives are unknown; appeals to public, not to experts, for ultimate validation.

   c. Lacks basic grounding in field; appeals to public rather than experts.

   d. A scientist will not necessarily be adept at "working" an audience; a scientist will be limited by professional standards and restrictions; a pseudoscientist will not be constrained by the scientific method or other strict, independent standards of evidence; the public may mistake the pseudoscientist's dogmatic style and sweeping assertions and guarantees for reliable evidence; the scientist's professionally qualified assertions ("so it seems," "probably," "we need more testing to be sure") will pale beside pseudoscientific bombast.

EXERCISE 8-3 _____

1. Unreasonable guarantees; seems to imply that a strong desire is all that is required; overlooks such pertinent factors as ability and insight.

2. Vague—"exciting"—promises; unreasonable guarantees.

3. Oversimplies complex problem; claim is at odds with scientific consensus; something for no effort.

4. Appeal to language of dynamic action *and* the language of success: We can become "entrepreneurs of the possible" and "change agents" in our professional lives. Tone of the quoted passage implies more certainty than is reasonable: implied guarantee of success for "so many people."

CHAPTER 9 _____

EXERCISE 9-1 _____

1. weak
2. weak
3. strong

4. weak
5. weak
6. weak
7. weak
8. weak
9. weak
10. weak

EXERCISE 9-3 _____

1. nonargumentative
2. argumentative
3. argumentative
4. argumentative
5. argumentative
6. nonargumentative
7. nonargumentative
8. argumentative
9. nonargumentative
10. nonargumentative: "horse and

ADDITIONAL EXERCISES _____

1. a. hasty conclusion (also false authority)
   b. hasty conclusion (also accident if Suzy is the kind of person who can rise above the limitation of the school)
   c. accident (also traditional wisdom)
   d. hasty conclusion
   e. hasty conclusion (sample too small; lacks comprehensiveness; margin of error too small)
   f. hasty conclusion
   g. hasty conclusion
   h. guilt by association
   i. guilt by association, hasty conclusion
   j. accident
   k. accident
   l. hasty conclusion
   m. hasty conclusion (also unknowable fact)
   n. accident
   o. guilt by association (also ad hominem)
   p. accident
   q. hasty conclusion
   r. hasty conclusion (also fear or force, ad hominem, straw man)

buggy"; argumentative: "the nations of Africa and Asia"
11. argumentative
12. argumentative
13. argumentative
14. argumentative
15. argumentative

EXERCISE 9-5 _____

1. accident
2. hasty conclusion
3. composition
4. guilt by association
5. division
6. hasty conclusion
7. accident
8. composition
9. accident
10. hasty conclusion

CHAPTER 10 _____

EXERCISE 10-1 _____

1. *Problem:* How could a failing student suddenly turn in a near-perfect paper?
   Facts: Ronald's location next to Bill; Bill's identical works.
   Hypothesis: Ronald cheated from Bill.
   Further inferences: Ronald shouldn't be able to cheat if he's situated sufficiently apart from Bill and closely monitored.
   Verifying inferences: Rinehart implements her inferences and Ronald fails.
2. *Problem:* How could Mork afford such an expensive necklace?
   Facts: Mork isn't working. He can't even afford a decent dinner. Genuine gold necklaces are very expensive.
   Hypothesis: The necklace isn't gold.
   Further inferences: Mork should be able to afford an imitation; a jeweler should be able to say whether the necklace is an imitation.

Verifying inferences: The jeweler confirms her suspicions.

3. *Problem:* How to account for a 30 percent increase in size in yogurt-fed rats compared with non-yogurt-fed rats?

   Facts: The yogurt-fed rats are larger in weight, size, and bones; they also have more energy and are healthier.

   Hypothesis: The bacteria in the yogurt produce a growth factor.

   Further inferences: If it is the bacteria and not, say, milk and milk solids, yogurt-fed rats should be larger than the other rats.

   Verifying further inferences: Tests show that yogurt-fed rats are larger than milk-fed ones.

4. *Problem:* Was cannibalism ever a universal practice?

   Facts: The key fact is that there exists what is thought to be firsthand accounts of cannibalism, which has led to the widespread belief among sociobiologists and anthropologists that universal cannibalism was practiced.

   Hypothesis: Universal cannibalism was never practiced. (Arens)

   Further inferences: The firsthand accounts must be inaccurate. There must be a better explanation for these reports of universal cannibalism.

   Verifying further inferences: Arens does not verify but offers alternative explanations: explorer misinterpretation of tribal languages and gullibility, national self-interest in promoting the slave trade, the tendency to "run down" neighbors. But these additional hypotheses do not verify Arens's inferences nor his hypothesis. What he must do now is to establish the credibility of these explanations by making further inferences and checking them. His reference to the Tupinamba is a beginning but hardly confirms any of Arens's inferences, and certainly not his hypothesis.

5. *Problem:* Who kidnapped and killed the Lindbergh baby?

   Facts: Particulars a, b, c, d, f, g, h, l could be viewed as facts, because they seem logically to precede the formulation of a hypothesis. However, there could be reasonable debate about whether h is a fact or inference following on the hypothesis.

   Hypothesis: Hauptmann kidnapped and killed the baby.

   Further inferences: The notes must have been by Hauptmann; the ladder used in the kidnapping must be Hauptmann's or easily connected with him; Hauptmann probably would have had an injured leg.

   Verifying further inferences: Particulars e, i, j, and k.

ADDITIONAL EXERCISES

1. a. *Problem:* What accounts for suicide attempts?

      Hypothesis: Suicide attempts can be explained as appeals for sympathy.

      Reliability: Weak—one of its inferences doesn't square with the facts.

   b. *Problem:* What's the cause of Trisomy 21?

      Hypothesis: The age of the mother significantly contributes to Trisomy 21.

      Reliability: Weak, since it's been disproved that the disease is correlated exclusively with maternal age.

      Alternative Hypothesis: A virus infection causes the disease.

      Reliability: No judgments are warranted until further extensive testing is done.

   c. *Problem:* How to account for the extermination of the mammoth?

      Hypothesis: The theory of evolution accounts for it.

      Reliability: Weak, since two of its inferences have been disproved.

   d. *Problem:* What accounts for the

generation of worms in dead bodies and decayed plants?

Hypothesis: Putrefied matter accounts for this phenomenon.

Reliability: Weak, since it fails a legitimate test.

Alternative hypothesis: Insemination accounts for this phenomenon.

Reliability: Strong, based on the test conducted, as well as on satisfying other criteria.

e. *Problem:* What causes paralytic poliomyelitis?

Hypothesis: The absence of early exposure to the infection in infancy as a result of the improvement of hygiene.

Reliability: Strong, especially in compatibility and explanatory criteria.

f. *Problem:* What accounts for the gyrations that animals exhibit while sleeping?

Hypothesis: Animals dream.

Reliability: Strong, in the light of the test.

g. *Problem:* What caused "childbed fever"?

Hypothesis: Poor hygiene among doctors and medical students.

Reliability: Strong in the light of his test; also notice how it accounts for the disparity in incidences between midwife-attended mothers vs. doctor-attended mothers.

h. *Problem:* What accounts for the genetic mutations that leave bacteria resistant to bacteriophages?

Hypothesis: Bacteriophages themselves produce the mutations or the mutations arise spontaneously.

Reliability: In the light of the crucial experiment performed, the hypothesis that the mutations arise spontaneously is strong.

i. *Problem:* How does the human memory work?

Hypothesis: The memory changes and stores certain chemicals in the brain.

Reliability: Strong in the light of experiments.

j. *Problem:* What accounts for Uranus's unpredictable course?

Hypothesis: Either Newton's theory is incorrect or something is interfering with Uranus's orbit.

Reliability: In the light of subsequent observations it was established that something was indeed interfering with Uranus's orbit: the planet Neptune. (Notice how the Neptune hypothesis fit in with Newtonian theory, even how the theory was used to calculate the effect of Neptune on Uranus.)

2. Answers will vary.

3. Answers will vary.

4. A strong hypothesis.

CHAPTER 11 _____

EXERCISE 11-2 _____

1. a. Suppose all the victims only shared the circumstance of eating the same salad dressing (agreement) and non-victims shared every other circumstance with victims except having eaten the salad dressing (difference)

b. Suppose that this is a section set up for nursing students and that every other nursing section shows the same female-male ratio (agreement) but no other section does (difference).

c. Suppose that the only relevant characteristic on each occasion is a weak battery (agreement) and that on the occasions that the car has started the battery has tested out strong (difference).

d. Suppose that the only circumstance that these occasions share is when you're speaking to a member of the opposite sex (agreement) and that you never have this difficulty when speaking to a member of your own sex (difference).

2. Agreement: *ABC—abc*
   ADE—ade
   Difference: *ABC—abc*
   BC—bc

A is the effect or the cause or an essential part of the cause of *a*.

3. a. *Correlation:* There are in fact more cases of suicides in the existing population among those for whom Christmas has meaning than among those for whom it does not.
   Cause: There would be more suicides in the general population were Christmas to have a meaning for everyone than if Christmas had no meaning for anyone.

   b. *Correlation:* There are in fact more instances of violence committed by viewers of violent TV programs than by nonviewers of violent TV programs.
   Cause: There would be more cases of violence committed if everyone watched violent TV programs than if no one watched them.

   c. *Correlation:* There is in fact a greater decline in institutional religion membership among those involved in cults than among those not involved in cults.
   Cause: There would be a greater decline in institutional religion membership if everyone were involved with cults than if no one were.

   d. *Correlation:* There are in fact more working women among women sympathetic to the women's liberation movement than among women not sympathetic.
   Cause: There would be more working women if all women were sympathetic to the women's liberation movement than if no women were.

ADDITIONAL EXERCISES

1. False dilemma
2. Concealed evidence: Far more miles are driven within 5 miles of the driver's home than cross-country. (Thus, also incomplete statistic)
3. False dilemma
4. Biased sample: pollster bias
5. Concealed evidence: Very few new cars ever sell for the sticker price.

EXERCISE 11-3

1. questionable causation
2. post hoc
3. questionable causation
4. questionable causation
5. questionable causation (a correlation, perhaps, but not necessarily a causal connection); or, if a cause, then an oversimplification; also, slippery slope
6. slippery slope
7. post hoc
8. questionable causation
9. questionable causation
10. slippery slope
11. magical thinking and post hoc
12. post hoc
13. questionable causation, oversimplification (the dogmatic nature of this assertion is what makes it problematic; with elaboration and in larger context there may be no causal fallacies—or there may be more)

CHAPTER 12
EXERCISE 12-5

1. false dilemma
2. false dilemma
3. false dilemma
4. false dilemma
5. false dilemma
6. false dilemma—a third choice should be given: "No gender preference."
7. false dilemmas
8. false dilemma

6. "Better" is ambiguous.
7. Concealed evidence: In fact, the high-protein diet has been found very dangerous in many instances.
8. All terms are ambiguous.
9. Concealed evidence: The RDA is not necessarily a "full day's supply." How much of a vitamin a person needs varies greatly from person to

person. RDA and MDR (minimal daily requirement) are essentially quantities needed to stave off diseases associated with vitamin deficiency (e.g., beriberi, rickets). Furthermore, no mention is made of ingredients in TANG, such as sugar, which ultimately may injure the consumer/child.

10. The question itself is ambiguous. It can mean (1) how important the subjects actually are to you now that you're graduated or (2) how important what you learned in these courses is to you now that you're graduated. The possible selections are ambiguous, and since different students obviously take different logic or writing courses, any generalizations found on the basis of the questionnaire are very risky.

11. False dilemma

12. The opening sentence biases the question. Also the statement conceals evidence. Tenure laws also protect teachers from capricious and arbitrary dismissal; they in effect guarantee due process, although it's undoubtedly true that in some cases they have the effect of protecting the incompetent. The question suggests that tenure is a kind of privilege. Some would vigorously argue that it's a right.

13. Concealed evidence: The cereal also contains ingredients potentially harmful, such as sugar. "Fortified" is ambiguous.

14. Concealed evidence

15. Concealed evidence: Abuse of Tylenol can cause liver damage. Also, recent research indicates that aspirin may be effective in reducing the chances of heart attack.

16. The word *know* is ambiguous here. It means "awareness of" or "familiar enough with to use."

17. Rife with concealed evidence. For example, studies conducted by Dr. Jean Mayer, a renowned diet authority, and endorsed by the Federal Trade Commission show that a heavy diet of presugared food, even

when washed down with milk, contributes to tooth decay. The same studies reveal that even when fortified with milk, the total effect is one of inadequate nutrition. What's more, nutritional experts have questioned the methodology and evidence behind Kellogg's claim for the nutritional benefits of sugared foods. Of course, sugar contributes nothing to human nutrition besides calories—no vitamins, no minerals, no proteins. A calorie of sugar contains no more energy than a calorie of anything else. In addition, the claim that there's no more sugar in an ounce of ready-sweetened cereal than in an apple, banana, or glass of orange juice is based on cereal containing 30.8 percent sugar. Many cereals contain far more sugar; worse, the refined sugar in a breakfast food seems more likely to cause cavities than the natural sugar in fruits. Finally, contrary to Kellogg's claims, sugar consumption has risen at least 13 percent since 1960, with the consumption among children probably even higher.

18. False dilemma

19. Biased sample

20. Concealed evidence: You will pay taxes when you withdraw. The figures don't account for inflation that often accompanies withdrawals. False dilemma and penalties: There are more promising investments.

21. The second question is important in determining the degree of misrepresenting their views on the first question. If, for example, an overwhelming majority doesn't think its party will nominate a black, a decided absence of racism in the replies to the first is almost meaningless. We can all be tolerant in the abstract, in reacting to a hypothesis, which in this case, would border on fantasy. In contrast, to really believe not only in the possibility of the hypothesis but also in the likelihood of it (that is, that the party will indeed nominate a black) compels us to face squarely and honestly whether

we would be racists in the polling booth. This aside, respondent bias almost certainly will pollute this study: Very few of us even admit to ourselves we are racists, let alone express it openly in a poll.

22. Possible equivocal effect by saying "150%" rather than $300—the direction of bias (if any) depends on which seems better or worse to the intended audience.

23. Concealed evidence: $7.34/2 oz. = $58.72/lb.! Even granting that 1 oz. of freeze-dried coffee is the equivalent of many ounces of ground coffee, we're still talking about a pretty expensive cup of coffee.

24. Concealed evidence: Experts disagree regarding what—in fact—the recommended daily amounts of various vitamins are; many claim that a healthy diet provides most of us with an ample supply; over a certain amount, our bodies dispose of certain vitamins daily, so "mega-doses" are often wasteful—if not dangerous. There appears to be little measurable effective difference between a wide range of vitamin brands, from inexpensive generic ones to high-priced brand-name ones. Note mob appeal, too.

25. Concealed evidence (equivocal, too); ask a science teacher to let you see and heft exactly what 1/3 of .78 oz. is; how big of a bite is it?

CHAPTER 13 _____

EXERCISE 13-1 _____

1. a. Californians; citizens
   b. baseball players; athletes
   c. those breaking the law; criminals
   d. newspapers that suppress news; inadequate sources of information
   e. commercials that rely solely on persuasive techniques to communicate; vehicles of noninformation
   f. nonvoters; citizens . . . wish
   g. nonparticipants . . . Washington; nonenrollees . . . city

2. a. Police officer; a thief
   b. Police officers; thieves

c. Police officers, thieves
d. Non-police officer; a thief
e. Non-police officer; a nonthief
f. Nonthieves; police officers
g. Non-police officers . . . order; violators of the law
h. Police officer . . . can; a person . . . law

EXERCISE 13-3 _____

1. *I*: neither term
2. *E*: *S* (revolutionary); *P* (believer in the status quo)
3. *A*: *S* (men in combat)
4. *A*: *S* (noncombatants . . . pay)
5. *O*: *P* (members of a union)
6. *I*: neither term
7. *O*: *P* (exercises . . . courage)
8. *A*: *S* (students . . . twenty-one)
9. *O*: *P* (hues . . . else)
10. *I*: neither term

EXERCISE 13-4 _____

1. *Major term:* seekers of offices
   Minor term: Republicans
   Third term: political candidates
   Properly ordered as is.

2. *Major term:* true sportsman
   Minor term: dishonest person
   Third term: cheater
   Properly ordered as is.

3. *Major term:* previous creatures
   Minor term: animals
   Third term: endangered species
   Reverse first two statements.

4. *Major term:* lovers of women
   Minor term: lovers of wine
   Third term: epicureans
   Reverse first two statements.

5. *Major term:* pollutants
   Minor term: cigarettes
   Third term: disease carriers
   Properly ordered as is.

6. *Major term:* persons entitled to due process
   Minor term: men
   Third term: equal citizens
   Reverse first two statements.

7. *Major term:* peace lovers
   Minor term: countries

Third term: belligerents
Reverse first two statements.

8. *Major term:* slow runners
Minor term: sprinters
Third term: members of the track team
Proper order: No slow runners are members of the track team.
   All sprinters are members of the track team.
      No sprinters are slow runners.

9. *Major term:* wastes of time
Minor term: TV programs
Third term: bores
Reverse first two statements.

10. *Major term:* means of transportation
Minor term: airlines
Third term: expensive enterprises
Proper order: Some expensive enterprises are poor means of transportation.
   All airlines are expensive enterprises.
      Some airlines are poor means of transportation.

EXERCISE 13-5 ⎯⎯⎯

a. Some objects of worship are cows.
All cows are animals.
Some animals are objects of worship.
IAI-4

b. No opponents of deficit spending are Keynesians.
Some Republicans are Keynesians.
Some Republicans are not opponents of deficit spending.
EIO-2

c. All biologists who believe in Darwinian evolution are college graduates.
No biologist who believes in Darwinian evolution is a literal interpreter of Genesis
No literal interpreter of Genesis is a college graduate.
AEE-3

d. All toothpastes with fluoride are cavity fighters.
Some peppermint toothpastes are cavity fighters.
Some peppermint toothpastes are toothpastes with fluoride.
AII-2

e. All male chauvinists are persons insecure in their own sex roles.
All males interested in females only for sex are male chauvinists.
Some men interested in females only for sex are persons insecure in their own sex roles.
AAI-1

f. Some officers are nonvoters.
All nonparty members are officers.
Some nonparty members are nonvoters.
IAI-1

g. All married persons are consumers.
Some individuals are not married persons.
Some individuals are not consumers.
AOO-1

h. All believers in suffering for suffering's sake are theists.
No one signing a Living Will is a believer in suffering for suffering's sake.
No one signing a Living Will is a theist.
AEE-1

CHAPTER 14 ⎯⎯⎯

EXERCISE 14-1 ⎯⎯⎯

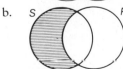

a.

$SP = 0, E$

b.

$S\bar{P} = 0, A$

c.

$SP \neq 0, I$

d.

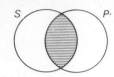

$SP = 0, E$

e.

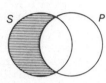

$S\bar{P} = 0, A$

f.

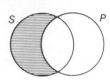

$S\bar{P} = 0, A$

g.

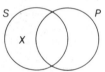

$S\bar{P} \neq 0, 0$

EXERCISE 14-2 ——————

2.a.

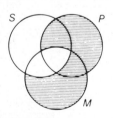

invalid

b.

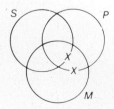

invalid

c.

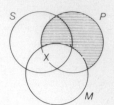

invalid

d.

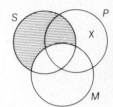

invalid

e.

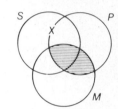

invalid

f.

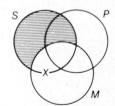

invalid

g.

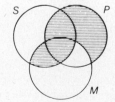

valid

h.

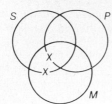

invalid

i.

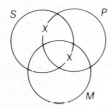

invalid

j.

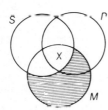

valid

EXERCISE 14-3 _____

1. a. invalid, rule 4, exclusive premises
   b. valid
   c. invalid, rule 3, illicit major
   d. invalid, rule 3, illicit major
   e. invalid, rule 4, exclusive premises
   f. valid
   g. invalid, rule 4, exclusive premises
   h. valid
   i. invalid, rule 6, existential fallacy
   j. invalid, rule 2, undistributed middle term

2. a. invalid, rule 3, illicit major
   b. invalid, rule 6, existential fallacy
   c. invalid, rule 3, illicit minor
   d. invalid, rule 4, exclusive premises; rule 3, illicit major
   e. invalid, rule 3, illicit minor
   f. invalid, rule 3, illicit major
   g. invalid, rule 4, exclusive premises; rule 6, existential fallacy
   h. valid
   i. invalid, rule 6, existential fallacy
   j. valid

CHAPTER 15 _____

EXERCISE 15-2 _____

1. *First order. Major premise:* All books are mysteries. Valid.

2. *First order. Major premise:* All things that are geared to inform are things that warrant scrutiny. Valid.

3. *Second order. Minor premise:* Subjecting people to polygraph tests as a condition of employment threatens privacy. Valid.

4. *Third order. Conclusion:* Education is power. Valid.

5. *First order. Major premise:* All ambitious people are self-serving persons. Valid. (Presumably "people who succeed in politics" is synonymous with "those who run the country.")

6. *First order. Major premise:* All relationships that involve strong elements of both competition and cooperation are complex relationships. Valid.

7. *First order. Major premise:* Anyone who always acts responsibly under pressure and has a long in-depth involvement in government is a person uniquely qualified to be President. Valid.

8. *First order. Major premise:* Any liquor made in America is one you should buy. Valid.

9. *First order. Major premise:* Any action that would risk the safety of every American and Westerner in the Middle East would be the wrong response. Valid.

10. *First order. Major premise:* The unusual is unthinkable. Thus: (The unusual is unthinkable). Putting mobile homes right in the middle of a residential area is unusual. Putting mobile homes right in the middle of a residential area is unthinkable. Valid.

11. *First order. Major premise:* Whatever makes people in government better servants of the people are things that they need. Valid.

12. *First order. Major premise:* Whatever is a source in violation of trust is somewhat untrustworthy. Valid.

13. *First order. Major premise:* Protection against malpractice is something many doctors welcome. Thus: (Protection against malpractice suits is something many doctors welcome.) Informal consent is a protection against malpractice suits. Informal consent is something many doctors welcome. Valid.

14. *First order. Major premise:* Any case of the potential benefits of a medical procedure outweighing any possible danger are cases where people shouldn't be afraid to have it. Valid.

15. *Second and third order. Minor premise:* Jesse Walter's death is by execution. Conclusion: Jesse Walter's death is an instance of making it easier to kill the next time. Valid.

16. *Third order. Conclusion:* Wella Balsam conditioner makes beautiful hair. Valid.

17. *First order. Major premise:* No nation that is ready to give millions of dollars to help starving and dying people is imperialist. Valid.

18. *First order. Major premise:* Any resolution designed to legitimize sex and social relationships other than those that form the basis of divinely ordained marriage, parenthood, and home is moral perversion. Valid.

19. *Second order. Major premise:* Groups that represent consumers, women, blacks, Hispanics, the elderly, and small business are groups in society who share the basic political interests of the building trades. Valid.

20. *First order. Major premise:* Persecuting non-Malays for their religious beliefs is an instance of religious intolerance. Valid.

EXERCISE 15-4 _____

1. (All golfers are persons carrying clubs.)
   Some of these persons are not persons carrying clubs.
   ___
   Some of these persons are not golfers.

2. All cases of past Presidents are cases of males.
   (The case of the next President will likely be a case like that of past Presidents.)
   ___
   The case of the next President will likely be a case of a male.

3. (All girls with great legs are girls I'm not necessarily madly in love with.)
   She is a girl with great legs.
   ___
   She is a girl I'm not necessarily madly in love with.

4. (All cases of a state's paying its counties an incentive for every prisoner they don't send to a county jail is a case that proves economy is not the root of all virtue.)
   California is a case of a state's paying its counties an incentive for every prisoner they don't send to a county jail.
   ___
   California is a case that proves economy is not the root of all virtue.

5. (All cases of a country's refusing to deny economic assistance to nations without a birth control program are cases of contributing to the population explosion.)
   The United States is a case of a country's refusing to deny economic assistance to nations without a birth control program.
   ___
   The United States is a case of contributing to the population explosion.

6. (All cases of a person's not reading the question are cases of not knowing the answer.)
   Mine is a case of a person's not reading the question.
   ___
   Mine is a case of not knowing the answer.

7. (All natives suspicious of outsiders are unfriendly persons.)
   Some natives are natives suspicious of outsiders.

Some natives are unfriendly persons.

8. All those who can be rehabilitated are willing persons.
(Some of these inmates are not willing persons.)

Some of these inmates are not those who can be rehabilitated.

9. All instances of the rate of violent crime increasing after capital punishment has been outlawed are instances that prove capital punishment is a deterrent to crime.
This instance is an instance of the rate . . . deterrent to crime.

This instance is an instance that proves capital punishment is a deterrent to crime.

10. (All bright, loyal, experienced persons who are nonparty members are consultants, but not candidates.)
Jack is a bright, loyal, experienced person who is a nonparty member.

Jack is a consultant, but not a candidate.

EXERCISE 15-5 ───────

1. a. (All ruminants are cud-chewing animals.)
Dogs are not cud-chewing animals.

Dogs are not ruminants.
Sound.

b. (The largest-volume furniture mart in America is the one where you'll necessarily get the best deal on new furniture.)
Jacques Peni is the largest-volume furniture mart in America.

Jacques Peni is the mart where you'll necessarily get the best deal on furniture.
Valid but unsound. Major premise is a faulty generalization and a version of the appeal to popularity.

c. (If a cigarette tastes good like a cigarette should, you should buy it.)
Winston tastes good like a cigarette should.

You should buy Winston.
Valid but unsound. Conditional premise is a hasty conclusion; both premises are ambiguous. Also, concealed evidence: Cigarette smoking contributes to disease.

d. All voters are citizens.
(Some of the people leaving the polling station are not citizens.)

Some of the people leaving the polling station are not voters.
Sound.

e. If Perry Como describes the new Sylvania color set on TV, you should buy it.
(Perry Como has described the new Sylvania color set on TV.)

You should buy it.
Valid but unsound. Conditional premise is a hasty conclusion and false authority. Also, an irrelevant reason, since there's no connection between Como's description and the quality of the TV: red herring.

f. (All people who refuse a polygraph test are people with something to hide.)
The Senator refuses a polygraph test.

The Senator has something to hide.
Valid but unsound. Major premise is untrue, or, more kindly, a faulty generalization and conceals evidence (people often refuse polygraphs on principle).

g. (Whatever helps employment contributes to inflation.)
Government spending helps employment.

Government spending contributes to inflation.

Valid but unsound. Major premise is questionable cause. "Helps" is ambiguous.

h. (All valid arguments are reliable arguments.)
Some persuasive devices are not reliable.

Some persuasive devices are not valid arguments.
Valid but unsound: Untrue major premise.

i. (All liquors that Washington and Lafayette may have planned strategies over are liquors worth buying.)
Martell Brandy is a liquor that Washington and Lafayette may have planned strategies over.

Martell Brandy is a liquor worth buying.
Valid but unsound. Major premise is a false appeal to authority; both premises contain the weasel word "may have."

j. (Whatever meat is labeled "U.S. Certified Grade A" must be very good.)
That meat is labeled "U.S. Certified Grade A."

That meat must be very good.
Valid but unsound. "Very good" is ambiguous. Also concealed evidence; even if "Grade A" in general indicates a high-quality meat, that doesn't mean that this specific package was examined and so judged. What's more, there are all sorts of ways that butchers misrepresent meats and packages. Also concealed is that meat, red meat, isn't necessarily healthful for us to begin with. False authority.

k. (All weight-control aids that help you lose ugly bulges and look more feminine are aids that you should buy.)
Waistlets Gum is a weight-control aid that helps you lose ugly bulges and look more feminine.

Waistlets Gum is an aid you should buy.
Valid but unsound. Major premise is ambiguous ("aids," "more feminine"); faulty generalization; minor premise contains weasel word "helps." Most important, question statistical procedures that presumably led to minor premise because of concealed evidence in almost all popular weight-control claims.

l. (All days the game is postponed are days it's rained.)
Today is a day the game has been postponed.

Today is a day it must have rained.
Sound, providing major premise is true.

m. (All men with lean and hungry looks are ambitious.)
Cassius is a man with a lean and hungry look.

Cassius is ambitious.
Valid but unsound. Major premise is vague (what constitutes a "lean and hungry look") and a faulty generalization (hasty conclusion).

n. (All cigarettes that are natural are cigarettes you should buy.)
Salems are cigarettes that are natural.

Salems are cigarettes you should buy.

Valid but unsound. Major premise is an appeal to popularity, a faulty generalization, and hasty conclusion. "Natural" is equivocal. Concealed evidence: Cigarette smoking contributes to lung disease.

o. (If California has already done more for farm workers than any other state, then I should oppose unemployment compensation for farm workers.)
California has already done

more for farm workers than any other state.

I should oppose unemployment compensation for farm workers.

Valid but unsound. Conditional premise is a hasty conclusion. More important, the statistics on which the minor premise rests conceals evidence: California *has* done more for farm workers than any other state; but other states with farm workers have done next to nothing to improve the lot of farm workers.

p. All people employed here are people listed in the directory.

Maria is not a person listed in the directory.

Maria is not a person employed here.

Sound, provided major premise is true.

q. Some individuals don't benefit from jogging.
(I'm one of those individuals.)

I won't benefit from jogging (from which it follows that I won't start jogging).

Valid but unsound. Minor premise is hasty. Also, "benefit" needs defining; how many are "some"? Is the person in any position to *know* that he or she can't benefit from jogging?

r. (Whenever Pop groans it's tax time.)

This is a time Pop's groaning.

This is tax time.

Sound, providing major premise is true. If Pop groans on other occasions, the assertion is a faulty generalization.

s. (Anyone who never expresses an opinion unless asked to is very wise or empty-headed.)

The president is a person who . . . headed.

The president is very wise or empty-headed.

Valid but unsound. Major premise is a false dilemma and a faulty generalization.

t. (All people are thinkers.)
Poker players are people.

Poker players are thinkers.

Valid but unsound. "Thinkers" is unacceptably ambiguous.

u. (Responsibility is something most people dread.)
Liberty means responsibility.

Liberty is something most people dread.

Valid but unsound. "Most people" is ambiguous. So are "liberty" and "responsibility."

CHAPTER 16 _____

EXERCISE 16-1 ____ __

2, 3, and 4 are negations.

EXERCISE 16-2 _____

1, 4, and 5 are conjunctions.

EXERCISE 16-6 _____

1. G: The Vice-President was guilty of wrongdoing. R: The Vice-President would resign from office.

$$\frac{\sim G \supset \sim R}{R}$$
$$\overline{G}$$

Valid—modus tollens

2. L: There's life in outer space. S: It's probably superior to us. C: It will contact us.

$$\frac{L \supset S}{S \supset C}$$
$$\overline{L \supset C}$$

Valid—if the consequent of the first conditional is taken to mean the same thing as the antecedent of the second; if a stricter approach is taken, the difference between the "probably" in the first premise and its lack in the second leads to an invalidly drawn conclusion.

3. P: A thing precedes itself. C: A thing's its own cause.

$$\frac{P \supset C}{\sim P}$$
$$\overline{\sim C}$$

Invalid—denies the antecedent

4. *B*: This is Brussels. *T*: Today is Tuesday.

$$B \supset T$$
$$\sim T$$
$$\overline{\sim B}$$

Valid—modus tollens

5. *I*: A President is impeached. *N*: No one benefits.

$$I \supset N$$
$$I$$
$$\overline{N}$$

Valid—modus ponens

6. *C*: The witness is the criminal. *A*: The witness is the criminal's accomplice. *L*: The witness will lie.

$$(C \lor A) \supset L$$
$$\sim C \cdot \sim A$$
$$\overline{\sim L}$$

Invalid—denying the antecedent

7. *J*: Joanne knows what she's talking about. *U*: I'm a monkey's uncle.

$$J \supset U$$
$$\sim U$$
$$\overline{\sim J}$$

Valid—modus tollens

8. *T*: Taxes rise. *P*: Consumer purchases decline. *S*: The economy suffers.

$$T \supset P$$
$$P \supset S$$
$$\overline{T \supset S}$$

Valid—pure hypothetical syllogism

9. *K*: The President knows what he's doing with this Star Wars thing. *W*: I'm your wife (and you're my husband).

$$K \supset \sim W$$
$$W$$
$$\overline{\sim K}$$

Valid—modus tollens

10. *H*: Harry goes to town on payday. *B*: Harry comes home broke.

$$H \supset B$$
$$B$$
$$\overline{H}$$

Invalid—affirms consequent

ADDITIONAL EXERCISES

1. *F*: Reagan forgot. *L*: Reagan lied.

$$F \lor L$$
$$\sim L$$
$$\overline{F}$$

Valid

2. *R*: Secular humanism is a religion. *T*: Secular humanism should be taught in public schools.

$$R \supset \sim T$$
$$T$$
$$\overline{\sim R}$$

Valid—modus tollens (if "should" in first premise is overlooked)

3. *S*: I study for my logic final. *L*: I lose my sweetheart. *F*: My life's empty and futile.

$$S \supset L$$
$$L \supset F$$
$$\overline{S \supset F}$$

Valid—pure hypothetical syllogism

4. *M*: I go to the movies. *E*: I enjoy myself. *H*: I stay home. *F*: We have fun together.

$$(M \supset E) \cdot (H \supset F)$$
$$M \lor \sim M \text{ (i.e., } H)$$
$$\overline{E \lor F}$$

Valid—if ~M means the same as H

5. *G*: God exists. *F*: I'm a fool.

$$G \lor F$$
$$G$$
$$\overline{\sim F}$$

Invalid

6. *D*: You think De Niro's a better actor than Stallone. *N*: I'm a nitwit.

$$D \supset N$$
$$\sim N$$
$$\overline{\sim D}$$

Valid—third-order enthymeme (modus tollens)

7. *L*: You love me. *G*: You give me gifts.

$$L \supset G$$
$$G$$
$$\overline{L}$$

Invalid—affirms consequent

8. *L*: I love you. *M*: I want to marry you.

$$L \supset M$$
$$\frac{\sim L}{\sim M}$$

Invalid—denies antecedent

9. *R*: It rains. *C*: The crops die. *S*: The stock dies.

$$(R \supset C) \cdot (\sim R \supset S)$$
$$\frac{R \vee \sim R}{C \vee S}$$

Valid dilemma

10. *Q*: This is question 10. *T*: We're through with this exercise.

$$Q \supset T$$
$$\frac{\sim T}{\sim Q}$$

Valid—modus tollens

CHAPTER 17 ⎯⎯⎯⎯

EXERCISE 17-1 ⎯⎯⎯

1. *unsound:* argument from ignorance
2. *unsound:* guilt by association
3. *unsound:* hasty conclusion
4. *unsound:* unknowable fact
5. *sound,* providing Sarah believes in the doctrine of the Trinity, which is the unexpressed premise.
6. *unsound:* "justice" ambiguous
7. *unsound:* false dilemma
8. *unsound:* equivocation
9. *unsound:* undistributed middle term

   (No pornographic films are made by the Hollywood studios.)

   Some pornographic films are moneymakers.

   Some money making films are not made by the Hollywood studios.

10. *unsound:* hasty conclusion; ambiguous ("turning to"); obscure ("astonishing rate")

EXERCISE 17-3 ⎯⎯⎯

1. *Normative; assumption:* Whatever can promote social justice should be allowed.
2. *Nonnormative; assumption:* Any instance of reverse discrimination in the workplace, indicates that in some instances people are judged on criteria that are not directly job-related.
3. *Normative; assumption:* Whatever saves patients and loved ones from heroic suffering in cases of terminal disease seems advisable.
4. *Normative; assumption:* In cases where a practice is accepted in a country, multinationals should be allowed to engage in it. (Bribery is such a practice.)
5. *Nonnormative; assumption:* Admissions of multimillion dollar bribes and "grease payments" prove that American businesses behave differently overseas from how they behave at home.
6. *Normative; assumption:* When at least 10 percent of the American population is engaged in what is considered psychologically or physically unhealthful behavior, America is a very sick society.
7. *Probably both; assumption:* Whatever's a form of human expression is a statement.
8. *Probably both; assumption:* No one should be forced to pay school taxes unless schools only teach what does not offend the taxpayer.
9. *Normative; assumption:* Nations have similar obligations to those binding on individuals.
10. *Nonnormative; assumption:* Selling weapons to Iran, in effect, protected United States citizens.

EXERCISE 17-4 ⎯⎯⎯

NOTE: In all cases the value words will be interpreted in terms of the three perspectives: personal approval or disapproval, social convention, principle or law. The truth of the statements therefore would be determined on the basis of whether the statements were in accord with these standards.

1. wrong
2. evil
3. ought
4. highest
5. immoral

6. best
7. greatest
8. should not
9. morally justifiable
10. should never
11. political desperation
12. godless
13. threatens
14. justify
15. lousy

CHAPTER 18 _____

EXERCISE 18-1 _____

1. Because of their connection with

food, certain activities can become signals to eat.

2. Divorce can negatively affect the child's sense of well-being in adulthood.

3. Antarctica is an ideal testing ground for our ingenuity, technology, and stamina.

EXERCISE 18-3 _____

1. good use of a series of illustrations
2. good use of a single example
3. good use of single anecdotal example
4. may be good but questionable whether single example warrants such a sweeping generalization

ADDITIONAL EXERCISES: "LIVING HAPPILY AGAINST THE ODDS" _____

Thesis Statement: Americans today need a strategy to help them deal with the anxiety produced by an increasing atmosphere of danger, alert, and warning.

Main Points
1. An atmosphere of gloom and doom pervades the land: paragraphs 1, 2, 3, 4, 6
2. The climate of alarm may itself be a health hazard: paragraphs 6, 7, 8
3. It's impossible to return to a more serene, less cautionary time: paragraphs 6, 9
4. People must learn to cultivate optimism and confidence in the face of the ominous: paragraphs 10, 11

Developmental Patterns
Point 1: paragraphs 1–4, 6
  1–1, 1–2, 1–3, 1–4: illustrations
Point 2: paragraphs 7–8
  2–7: fact/opinion; illustration
  2–8: illustration
Point 3: paragraphs 6, 9
  3–6: authority, illustration
  3–9: fact/opinion
Point 4: paragraphs 10–11
  4–10: authority
  4–11: illustration

Analysis

Point 1: paragraphs 1–4, 1–6

Paragraph 1–1 relies on a series of quick examples to help illustrate the atmosphere of gloom and doom that the author will address. The author may be guilty of some overstatement but the generalization seems warranted.

Paragraph 1–2 contains much emotive language ("bleats," "blinks," "din of sermons," "dooms own voice"). It also relies more obviously on exaggeration and overstatement ("cancer alerts have become almost as commonplace as weather reports"; "strictures on how to avoid heart attacks pop up everywhere").

Paragraph 1–3 effectively uses a series of short examples which seem typical and sufficient to warrant the claim that no season goes by without its own peculiar warnings.

Paragraph 1–4 again uses a series of examples effectively. One might claim that the McGee book, in its appeal to public paranoia, is not typical of the literature in the area, and therefore a biased sample. And certainly, the last sentence is an appeal to humor. On the whole, however, the paragraph seems relevant and compelling.

Paragraph 1–6 completes the litany of examples. For the most part the list is accurate, fair, and quite effective. Whether or not "everybody's psyche now takes a drubbing" is disputable. But the point that the vast majority of Americans are *exposed* to the drubbing is incontestable.

Conclusions about the support offered for point 1: These paragraphs do contain fallacies, but the fallacies don't undermine the essential point that an atmosphere of gloom and doom pervades the land. Indeed, the author makes effective and fair use of illustration to establish the point.

Point 2: paragraphs 2–6, 2–7, 2–8

Paragraph 2–6 claims that worry about cancer may cause cancer. Perhaps so, but the claim goes unsubstantiated; it remains an unknown fact. The reference "some say" is a false appeal to authority. Paragraph 2–7 infers on the basis of some "gallows humor" that the atmosphere is distributing more than a bit of anxiety. This is a hasty conclusion. (Had the author provided sufficient evidence in the next paragraph, this wouldn't much matter; but he doesn't.) What's more, one does not know the degree, if any, of the causal connection between the atmosphere and the anxiety.

Paragraph 2–8 opens with a questionable classification and faulty generalization. It's also ambiguous. To classify letters to advice columnists as "the surest sign" is also questionable. Notice that the letter cited demonstrates only that for some people eating breakfast isn't fun any more. But in the context of the whole paragraph, the example presumably illustrates the generalization that the admonitory mood is taking a toll on Americans. This one sample is far too small, possibly not even typical, to support that generalization.

Conclusions about the support offered for point 2: Fallacies seriously undermine the author's general point that the climate of alarm may itself be a health hazard. The point is not established.

Point 3: paragraphs 3–6, 3–9

Paragraph 3–6's reference to the Shakman book is a false appeal to authority. It's also a straw man. The "implicit message" is one drawn by the author. In fact, safety and danger are relative concepts, as the book in question points out. There has never existed an environment that could be called "perfectly safe." So it's really a phony issue to say that the book implies "You can't escape," since one never could "escape" to begin with. But what one can do is select an environment that's relatively safe, or safer than some other.

Paragraph 3–9 primarily states the author's opinion based on the facts that he's assembled. The opinion that the "alarm system is here to stay" is probably a fair statement. The conclusion about needing a strategy follows logically from this warranted assumption.

Conclusions about the support offered for point 3: Because the point about not being able to return to a former state of serenity is banal, very little support is needed to make it. We can accept the point as a truism.

Point 4: paragraphs 4–10, 4–11

Paragraph 4–10 relies heavily on authority. In fact, a reading of the social scientists, philosophers, and religionists lends considerable authoritative support to the claim. The appeal to authority seems warranted. Paragraph 4–11 speaks exclusively of longevity as the reason that "Americans have a right to be optimistic." But it ignores (conceals) quality of life factors. Who cares if they can live longer if things are miserable? At any rate longevity alone isn't enough to warrant the author's hasty conclusion. The paragraph also conceals the fact that compared to some other societies, Americans are not in fact living "longer and longer."

Conclusions about the support offered for point 4: Despite the logically limp last paragraph, the point that Americans must learn to combat a fearful attitude seems to be established in paragraph 10.

Assessment of the argument as compelling or not compelling: Point 2, which the author doesn't establish, is not vital to his thesis. But the other three points are critical. And he's made them. The argument is a compelling one.

INDEX

TO THE STUDENT

If we are to make *Practical Logic* a better book, we need to have your reactions and suggestions. We want to know what you like about the book and how it could be improved. Please answer the questions below and return this form to Philosophy Editor, c/o Holt, Rinehart and Winston, Inc., 111 Fifth Avenue, New York, NY 10003. THANK YOU!!

Name _____

School _____

Course title _____

Instructor's name _____

Other required texts _____

1. In comparison to other textbooks, the reading level was:

   _____ too difficult _____ just right _____ too easy

2. Did *Practical Logic* succeed in clarifying important principles of logic? Can you give us an example or two?

   _____

   _____

   _____

3. Are there any topics covered in your course not covered in our book? What topics would you like added to *Practical Logic*?

   _____

   _____

   _____

4. Please rate each chapter on a scale of 1 to 6.

	Liked Least				Liked Best		Not Assigned
Argument	1	2	3	4	5	6	_____
The Logical vs. the Psychological	1	2	3	4	5	6	_____
Language and Logic	1	2	3	4	5	6	_____

	Liked Least				Liked Best		Not Assigned
Fallacies of Ambiguity	1	2	3	4	5	6	____
Fallacies of Relevance	1	2	3	4	5	6	____
The Meaning of Knowledge	1	2	3	4	5	6	____
The Sources of Knowledge	1	2	3	4	5	6	____
Bogus Knowledge Claims	1	2	3	4	5	6	____
Inductive Reasoning	1	2	3	4	5	6	____
Scientific Method and Hypotheses	1	2	3	4	5	6	____
Cause	1	2	3	4	5	6	____
Statistics	1	2	3	4	5	6	____
Categorical Syllogisms	1	2	3	4	5	6	____
Testing Categorical Syllogisms for Validity	1	2	3	4	5	6	____
Reconstructing Arguments	1	2	3	4	5	6	____
Symbolic Logic: Disjunctive and Conditional Syllogisms	1	2	3	4	5	6	____
Evaluating Arguments: Normative and Nonnormative	1	2	3	4	5	6	____
The Extended Argument: A Strategy	1	2	3	4	5	6	____

5. Do any chapters need more explanation or examples? Which chapters and why? _____

_____

6. Do any chapters need more (or fewer) exercises? Which chapters and why?

_____

_____

7. Did you use the glossary? How helpful was it? _____

_____

_____

8. Will you keep this book for your library? _____

9. Do you have any additional suggestions, criticisms, or comments about *Practical Logic?* _____